The English Reformation

The English Reformation

Second Edition

A G Dickens

BT Batsford Ltd, London

© A. G. Dickens 1964, 1989

First published 1964
Second edition first published 1989
All rights reserved. No part of this publication
may be reproduced, in any form or by any means,
without permission from the Publisher

Typeset by J&L Composition Ltd, Filey, North Yorkshire
and printed in Great Britain by
Mackays of Chatham plc, Chatham, Kent

Published by B T Batsford Ltd
4 Fitzhardinge Street, London W1H 0AH

A CIP catalogue record for this book is
available from the British Library

ISBN 0 7134 3669 7

Contents

CONTENTS

Preface

An ever-growing Niagara of books and articles on the English Reformation has poured down upon us since 1964, when the first edition of this book was published. The situation is encapsulated in Rosemary O'Day's work *The Debate on the English Reformation* (1986), that impressive historiographical account of the subject from its origins in the sixteenth century. My aim during the last three years has been to sift this huge mass of new information and criticism, an assignment as tough as any I have confronted during more than fifty years of historical writing. Yet even if I were privileged to continue my revising for a further three years, I might still fail to keep pace with the ever-accelerating productivity of my colleagues, both in Britain and in the United States. As usual in such a dilemma, one humbly compromises. Nevertheless these present additions and corrections are already so substantial as to create what is almost a new book, one which furnishes much further information and addresses itself to new problems. To help those hesitant purchasers and busy reviewers who are already familiar with the book in its old form, may I here briefly indicate the main novel features, as distinct from the hundreds of routine adjustments and corrections?

I start with a wholly new chapter, so as to put Tudor England in a much wider temporal and geographical context. Here I ask some fundamental questions about the whole European Reformation and its long-term causes. How can the English Reformation be made dependent upon Henry VIII's divorce and quarrel with Rome, when Protestantism also triumphed in so many other lands outside his control? Did Henry's divorce make it successful in northern and eastern Germany, much of the Netherlands and Switzerland, all Scandinavia including Finland, not to mention its long but temporary occupation of Bohemia and Moravia, or its footholds in Hungary and Poland? And again, what of the temporal context? Were the Reformers justified in arguing that the western Church had already 'gone wrong' during the early centuries of Christianity? To what extent had the Church then sanctioned over-imaginative beliefs and practices, both learned and popular, having little or no warrant in the recorded teachings of Jesus? How far had it retrogressed towards Old Testament legalism, Roman absolutism or Greek philosophy, at the expense of Christian love? On the early Church I write with no independent authority, but seek at least to provoke thinking upon a larger scale and to challenge the all-too-common picture of the Reformation as a mere attack upon late medieval abuses and lapses of discipline. Rather does it need to be reviewed in the context of all Christian history, not merely in that of the later Middle Ages.

The subsequent chapters as far as the death of Henry VIII certainly needed many revisions of detail but, so far as I could see, few fundamental changes. I have however added a new section on Sir Thomas More, that most distinguished, yet nowadays most controversial and 'complicated' opponent of both the Henrician Reformation and the early Protestants. I have also updated Anne Boleyn and Thomas Cromwell, and then described the curious situation during Henry's last years, when minor but influential laymen around the King became sympathetic toward the Reformation. The reign of Edward VI needed some important additions. It saw what was probably the swiftest growth of Protestantism, together with the sectarian origins of English nonconformity, the emigration of foreign Protestants into London and, with the so-called 'commonwealth men', the rise of a Christian economic and social idealism as opposed to a doctrinally-based charity.

Likewise, stirred by the scholarly work of David Loades and others, I looked again at the Marian Reaction and have greatly expanded my former account, while still failing to discover here a potentially creative Catholicism, lacking only time to develop. Whatever the case, Mary's policy certainly furnished Protestantism with an extremely durable weapon: that spectacular series of invaluable martyrdoms! Despite the revisionists, I still take the Marian Reaction as the supreme crisis of the English Reformation.

At this point I started to look back at the story thus far, and so wrote the new, retrospective Chapter 13, which examines three current debates too significant to be omitted, yet too bulky to be handled amid the flow of the preceding narrative. Of these themes the first explores the influence of both Catholic and Protestant anticlericalism upon the Reformation. The second describes the uneven spread of pre-Elizabethan Protestantism across the English landscape and its varied communities. My own special interests have always concerned this grass-roots history of the movement, a subject on which we have learned a great deal since 1964. On both these major issues I try to show why I find myself unable to follow far the revisionist generalizations of Dr. Christopher Haigh. These seem to me unduly influenced by his own admirable researches on highly conservative Lancashire. I believe that anticlericalism was a very important (though not the most important) force of change long before the crisis of the Reformation. I also believe that by 1553 popular Protestantism, however undeveloped in many northern and western areas, had already become strong and ineradicable, not merely in London, Kent and Essex but throughout other politically influential areas of England. In the same Chapter I answer in the affirmative a third potential examination question. Was the English Reformation in some sense a youth movement? Here I am supporting a thesis hitherto ably maintained by Dr. Susan Brigden.

Thereafter in Chapter 14 I re-examine that important stretch of track, now extensively reconstructed by recent work on the Elizabethan Settlement of 1559. Here if anywhere lay the weak point of Sir John Neale's fine achievement on the Elizabethan Parliaments. In Chapter 15 I lightly update my former tabloid account of Puritanism, here transparently inspired by the writings of my friend Patrick Collinson, supplemented by new contributions from certain younger scholars. I also make some references to recent work on the wonderful recovery of English Catholicism and on its social background. The last chapter (16) proceeds along the same general lines as those of the 'old' book, first describing the modest origins of religious toleration, next stressing the highly individual features of the Reformation in England and finally offering some views on those of its effect which have lingered into our own day. Revising my notions of 1964 on reunion of the Churches, I rejoice at their cordial relations in contemporary England, though now without foreseeing or even desiring the wholesale structural integration so widely anticipated a quarter of a century ago. And so in the end each one among us must judge whether the great cataclysm of the sixteenth century has compensated for the damage it inflicted. With occasional misgivings I myself tend to feel that, on balance, it has so done. And even had the Counter Reformation achieved wider successes, would not the intellectual history of the seventeenth and eighteenth centuries have enforced a major contraction of papal influence and traditional Catholic doctrines throughout much of the western world?

In my preface of 1964 I urged that throughout this story the development of Protestant convictions in English society, however varied as between the regions, should be accorded a far more prominent role than hitherto. I also criticised the tendency of earlier historians to allow ordinary men and women 'to fall and disappear through the gaps between the kings, the prelates, the monasteries and the prayer books'. This has sometimes been misinterpreted as a naïve ambition to write the history of the Reformation purely 'from below'. Yet I also wrote then that 'one dare not lose grip of the conventional themes, for governments and leaders remain important; the story will not cohere in their absence'. I still believe that this dual approach must be firmly maintained. To make the Reformation merely sociobiograhical would be as stupid as to make it merely political and constitutional. Whether I have now got this balance right—and meaningful for today— readers must again judge for themselves.

Yet another problem of balance is bound to emerge wherever the Reformation is discussed. In opposition to many of my predecessors, I have long been concerned to moderate that romantic idealisation of medieval life practised so habitually by the Victorians: poets, painters, architects as well as tractarian churchmen. Here the issues are too complex, our own temperaments too varied, to allow the emergence of consensus. Moreover let us frankly admit that this debate will always evoke the contending prejudices of Catholics, Protestants and agnostics.

It was my original intention to acknowledge at this point my debts to specific persons, yet they have become so numerous that any such attempt would be invidious and might even end by provoking irritation among my friends. Many though not all of my debts are indicated by the numerous footnotes, and for the rest I hope to have early opportunities to express gratitude. Much of the latter must go to enthusiastic young scholars, some of them my juniors by half a century, but already accomplished in this field. Of course, I am further than ever from the illusion that such a book can become wholly acceptable or 'definitive'. In the last resort even a historian with long experience and many helpful colleagues can never entirely familiarise himself with every aspect of this immense, hugely documented, but in some respects still obscure story. Where it can be shown that I have ignored or misconceived some of the evidence—and this must all too often have occurred—I trust I shall readily retract and if possible make amends. For every historian who embarks upon so great a theme, humility must become at once the alpha and the omega.

London, October 1988&G.DICKENS

1 The Reformation in a Wider Context

In England as elsewhere, the Protestant Reformation sought first and foremost to establish a gospel-Christianity, to maintain the authority of the New Testament evidence over mere church traditions and human inventions masquerading as universally approved truths and 'unwritten verities'. It belonged to an age with a passion for verification and consequently originated many themes of modern biblical scholarship, though it doubtless failed to grasp their full complexity. This present introductory chapter seeks to demonstrate that the English Reformation formed an integral part of the European movement, and again, that the Reformation did not limit itself to the recent and contemporary problems besetting the Church. Rather did the Reformers seek to cleanse the Church's teaching from those unwarranted additions—made through many centuries—to the recorded gospel of Christ. Borrowing from the humanist classical scholars a long time-scale and a feeling for historical causation, many Protestant controversialists maintained that these accretions had been occurring ever since quite early Christian times. They nevertheless agreed that a 'true Church' had always preserved its thin thread of continuity within the 'Papal Church'.

The first of these contentions would seem little more than a truism. Without question the English Reformation belonged to that far larger breakaway which detached half Europe from the Papacy. In essentials the early English Protestants of the 1520s and 1530s were Lutherans, led by Tyndale, Barnes and Cranmer, by the young Cambridge scholars of the early twenties, by Coverdale and the lesser bible-translators, and by a host of other publicists and pamphleteers with strong continental affinities. Though in regard to the doctrine of the Eucharist some tended to super-impose Zwinglian and then Calvinist definitions, these should not be conceived as fundamental changes of direction. Even Thomas Cromwell, the first great executive of the state-reformation, displayed a cool but unmistakable affinity with the Lutherans. He despised antiquated superstitions and what he regarded as clerical hypocrisy; he boldly printed and distributed the

Bible in English and he strove to link English policy with that of the German Lutheran princes. Eventually his conservative English enemies denounced him not merely on a totally false charge of treason, but also as a heretic, which seems distinctly more appropriate.

True, we must not overlook the native English heresy derived from Wycliffe, yet its permanent importance lies in the fact that, as a kindred but similar biblical faith, it helped to create popular reception-areas for the newly imported Lutheranism. Left to itself, Lollardy lacked the 'modern' weapons needed to break through to the status of a national Church. The influence in England of that other child of Wycliffe, Bohemian Hussitism, can hardly have been a crucial factor. Nevertheless for more than a century before the advent of Luther English critics of the Church could at least observe in Bohemia the spectacle of a people organising its religious reformation on a national scale, liberating itself from Habsburg overlordship and successfully repelling Catholic armies. On the other side, conservative Tudor churchmen, led by Bishop John Fisher, rightly noted those discordant factions among the Hussites which always weakened the Bohemian movement. The Hussite episode should at least have presented a more or less relevant object-lesson, lasting as it did until 1620, when, at the Battle of the White Mountain, Habsburg Catholicism finally smashed the Hussite experiment by force of arms. Meanwhile upon another plane, the so-called Anabaptists, the radical sectarians of Germany and the Netherlands, feared by Catholics and Lutherans alike, had nevertheless started making modest contributions to the Tudor origins of English Nonconformity. It need scarcely be added that the ultimate wave of continental influence came from Calvin, even though his *Institutes of the Christian Religion*, first published in 1536, was for the most part a systematic exposition of Luther's volcanic utterances. By that very fact Calvinism attained a potent influence in England during the later decades of Elizabeth's reign, when it stiffened the Puritan backbone of the Anglican Church at a time when the latter had not yet begun to assimilate the mild but seemly ritualism later associated with Archbishop Laud. Thus at no time did Tudor Protestantism lose touch with its continental progenitors. Neither for that matter did English Catholicism, preserved during its Elizabethan crisis through the heroic invasion of England by the Seminary Priests and Jesuits, young Englishmen trained on the continent for the spiritual reconquest of their native country.

Among the leaders of the Protestant Reformation stood a number of ecclesiastical historians able to examine both the Catholic Church and their own movement in the greater context of Christian history since Apostolic times. By early training these sixteenth-century writers were also classical humanists, students of the Ancient World possessing a sharper sense for dates and documents than that of their medieval predecessors. Yet their attention had also been drawn to long-term history by the Book of Daniel, with its review of the rise and fall of ancient states and empires.[1] In fact a lay humanist, the Strasbourg Protestant Johannes Sleidan, wrote the best textbook on this particular theme, as well as the best 'contemporary history' of the German Reformation.[2] Luther, Melanchthon and the martyrologists

Crespin and Rabus were also among those who reviewed contemporary problems in the light of the whole Bible and of all Christian history. The English Protestant leaders Tyndale, Barnes, Bale and Foxe meanwhile did likewise. The *Acts and Monuments* of John Foxe—the so-called 'Book of Martyrs'—underwent strenuous development, until by the edition of 1570 it had become something like a full-scale history of the Christian Church.[3] By this time the Protestant Reformers' critique of the various historical periods differed from that of their medieval reformist predecessors, such as the historians active amid the Conciliar controversies of the fifteenth century: Dietrich of Niem and Thomas Ebendorfer of Vienna.[4] These latter had been declaring that the Church of their own day had sadly declined from the standards of the early Church, whereas Luther and the sixteenth-century Protestants believed that contemporary evils arose far less from any recent breakdown of discipline than from fundamental errors of doctrine and worship dating back in large measure to the fourth century AD and perhaps earlier still. According to some Protestants the Christian church had started to go astray very soon after Apostolic times. Yet more notably, through the patronage of Emperor Constantine the Great (r. 306–337), it had fallen under the baneful influence of autocratic Roman Imperial ideas. The usefulness of this historical scenario to support ruthless anti-papal propaganda cannot be denied. It formed a powerful prelude to a barrage of Protestant attacks upon the whole record of the Roman Papacy since Constantine. Yet more constructively, it also furthered an appeal for a 'documented' New Testament Christianity, in order to correct a churchly religion which, it was argued, had come to include certain doctrinal and devotional elements over and beyond those taught by Christ and the Apostles. In the light of a growing suspicion toward the ecclesiastical claim to manipulate 'unwritten verities', and of the new respect for early and original sources—and in this case none of substance existed outside the New Testament—there seems indeed to have arisen by this time a powerful case for a change of outlook, though not necessarily for the type of Reformation which happened in the sixteenth century. Yet again, the familiar case for the defence—that the New Testament was the creation and the literary property of the Church, whose official appointees enjoyed a total monopoly of its interpretation—would now seem to contain some very obvious dangers. In real life the gradual distinctions between investigating, developing, diluting and corrupting the message of Christ are extremely subtle. Yet to attack these attitudes from a modern liberal angle is pointless: we are dealing with an anxious age when few people would risk opening 'sacred' matters to the debates of scholars.

Among the many tasks of adjustment besetting Christianity from the fourth century onwards, the most urgent emanated from the Roman Empire itself, arguably more dangerous to Christian ideals in its new friendliness than it had been during its former persecutions. The Emperor Constantine did not make Christianity the 'established religion' of his Empire. His patronage nevertheless enhanced its involvement and its status throughout the whole Graeco-Roman world. At first attracted by the Christian faith as a supposed guarantee of military victories, he was by no means sensitive to its spiritual claims, tending on occasion to confuse it with sun-worship, his previous religion.[5] He nevertheless passed quasi-Christian legislation in favour of the oppressed classes, impelled the faithful to compose their internal differences at the Council of Nicaea (AD 325) and financed a remarkable efflorescence of Christian art and architecture.[6] On their side some devout Christians had long since believed that God had planned a close interweaving of the destinies of Church and Empire.[7] While the city of Rome had been sanctified as their chief goal of pilgrimage by the martyr-doms of both Peter and Paul, the Empire as a whole afforded an easy tolerance to rival cults: the old, sordid Graeco-Roman pantheon, the oriental mystery-religions, the free thinking of Hellenistic philosophers. Throughout Constantine's reign Christianity was far from absorbing its rivals, and according to the historian Orosius, writing about 418, paganism continued to prevail in the country districts.[8] Indeed this luxuriant world of unexacting beliefs remained attractive to simple people during its slow decline. Seeking to ease the transition from paganism, the Christian Church had unwarily permitted its members to develop subsidiary cults resembling those of the old, syncretic polytheism, complete with shrines, holy places and minor miracles. The pagan divinities and heroes were indeed surrender-ing, but only to the quasi-Christian equivalents: guardian angels and useful saints.[9] This metamorphosis considerably minimised—not in official Christian theology but in the daily observances of the people—the monotheistic, christocentric emphasis plainly demanded by the authentic documents of the faith. Here in essence the demotic and superstitious aspects of medieval Christianity had already arrived: here too flourished many of the human 'inventions' due to be denounced as sub-Christian by the Reformers of the sixteenth century. The restoration of the Empire by the Franks and its incorporation of fresh barbarian peoples in the eighth and ninth centuries did not rapidly refine the rulers or the ruled. Despite his later apotheosis, Charlemagne (d. 814) remains one of the Church's rougher diamonds: he was openly polygamous and he also 'converted' the Saxons by offering them the crude alternative of mass-baptism or massacre. In his last years he witnessed with sorrow the invasion of northern France by the heathen Norsemen, and he was not to know that these same intruders, as 'Normans', would soon undergo rapid conversion, prior to becoming the brutal but intelligent and devout imposers of an impressive religious establishment upon others with lengthier Christian traditions, such as the English.

Looking back across that first millennium of Christian history, one is thus struck even more by its embracing tolerance toward non-Christian concepts than by its intolerance toward Christian heresies. For all its resistance to persecution, the Church itself proved strangely hospitable to beliefs and styles of worship which have since come to seem foreign to the spirit of Jesus and the theology of St. Paul alike. From its secular protectors it also tended to inherit some of the Empire's less Christian qualities. The removal of the emperors to Byzantium left the popes, still at Rome, as the dominant figures in Italy. The old, flexible organisation of bishops—which had met earlier crises with no little success—gave way to a centralised autocracy, Roman in spirit. Though frequently hampered by the dissent of secular rulers, the Papacy achieved a formidable dominance over European Christianity by the time of Gregory VII's notable pontificate (1073–85), while the western Church, buttressed by its hierarchy of independent law-courts, developed a juridical character, scarcely rivalled by that legalism of the Pharisees so detested by Jesus. Under this leadership the Church followed in some important respects the Imperial model. After the heroic period of missionary expansion both canon and civil lawyers bulked larger than did preachers and missionaries in the European world of the Middle Ages.

Standing on the summit of this huge pyramid, the medieval popes, however unwillingly, became political rivals of emperors and kings. Thomas Hobbes must admittedly be accounted a hostile witness, yet he did no more than overstate a genuine historical insight when in 1651 he looked back on the Papacy and called it 'the Ghost of the deceased Roman Empire, sitting crowned upon the Grave thereof'.[10] So long as the Church maintained friendly contacts with the Empire and its powerful successor-states, it could normally call upon physical force to crush doctrinal dissenters, and usually, in the authentic Roman style, without permitting any two-way arguments. Everywhere the alliance was also sealed in terms of landed property. Collectively the Church became rich beyond the dreams of avarice because monarchs and magnates invested in salvation. Conversely churches and monasteries became enmeshed in the great feudal mechanisms whereby secular states were then governed. Aided by the quest for social order and by the survival of Old Testament values, the Church helped these states to create a persecuting society.[11] Nevertheless, without question the Church simultaneously implanted the vital seeds of both Graeco-Roman culture and documented Christianity. Literate churchmen educated the progeny of barbarians, advanced the milder arts of civil government, fostered Latin literature and Hellenistic philosophy, thus strengthening the moral sub-structures of medieval civilisation. These shining achievements, symbolised by feats of Romanesque and Gothic architecture, were taken for granted by the narrow logic of the sixteenth-century Reformers, who chiefly recalled that Jesus and Paul had counselled only an outward submission to Caesar, while insisting that the Kingdom of God was not of this world. Providentially though somewhat belatedly, St. Francis of Assisi came to remind medieval society of that higher Kingdom. His message did not die with him in 1226, though it soon lost much of its force. While the Franciscan Order maintained its popularity better than its ideal of poverty, the Dominicans became best known as staffing the Inquisition and acquiring a corporate pride in their role as the watch-dogs (*domini canes*) of orthodoxy. At least by its own definitions of heresy and salvation the Roman Church needed to employ such policemen, since during the later Middle Ages there arose several heresies with varying combinations of perspicacity and obtusity. Despite such complexities, both the main pagan inheritances of the Church, the demotic 'polytheism' and the Roman legalism, survived in great force across the Middle Ages and thence into early modern history. Far from declining in the later Middle Ages, the obsession with saints, shrines and pilgrimages was destined to reach new heights of popularity around 1500. Over much of Europe these cults survived the irony of Erasmus and the denunciations by the Protestants to retain a more regulated but still lively role in modern Catholicism. As for Rome's centralising and organising legacy derived from the Imperial past, it survived to play its part in the impressive recovery of the Roman Church and Papacy from the assaults of Protestantism. The Catholic Reformation of the later sixteenth and seventeenth centuries started to manifest a purer spirituality deriving from authentic Christian sources. Nevertheless this latter recovery had not yet become conspicuous at the time (c.1517-20) when Luther broke out of control. Indeed the Papacy under Alexander VI, Julius II and Leo X, bitterly criticised by its own Italian officialdom, stood at the nadir of its reputation.

Reverting to the medieval period, we should recognise quite another incursion from outside the original Christian message: that of scholasticism. This system had arisen from both classical and Hellenistic thought, ranging from Aristotle to Plotinus: by the twelfth century it had developed to form the foundations of medieval theology and philosophy.[12] Having contributed order and clarity to medieval thinking, this intellectual experiment began to collapse in the fourteenth century as a mainstay of Christian unity and spiritual life. It happened not merely because scholastic thinking could not be assimilated by peasants, craftsmen and barely literate priests, but also because of profound disagreements between the professionals themselves. This process of breakdown within the teaching faculties of the European universities proved slow and uneven, but the resultant theological uncertainties doubtless contributed to the general decline of ecclesiastical authority. Erasmus and Luther were still being antagonised by the embattled armies of Realists and Nominalists, noisily contending for an elusive supremacy. Within most universities, and still more in the new seminaries of the Catholic revival, considerable elements of scholastic teaching were destined to survive the Reformation, yet from the earlier generations of Lorenzo Valla (c.1406-57) and his legatee Erasmus, the biblical and historical thinking of the humanists steadily replaced the systematic, analytical approach which characterised scholasticism. This transfer gained further support from a rise of interest in the writings of St. Augustine, a genuine spiritual descendant of St. Paul and like him a great writer, and a literary rather than a scholastic Father of the Church, whose outlook became highly meaningful for Erasmus, Luther and Calvin alike.

A very different but equally formidable neighbour of medieval and early modern Christianity was that world of ideas we inadequately entitle 'magic'. I refer to the realm of spells, potions, amulets, omens, sorcery, alchemy, astrology, witchcraft, ghosts and fairies—the realm so admirably documented by Keith Thomas for early modern England.[13] In England as elsewhere in early sixteenth-century Europe scarcely anyone, educated or simple, doubted that such a world existed. The people saw it not merely as an abode of mystery and terror but also as a potential source of power, health and riches. Most significantly from our viewpoint, it was the realm manipulated for centuries by 'cunning' men and women, in modern jargon 'white witches'. These were unofficial but sometimes effective practitioners of healing; they also appeared to cure cattle-plagues by spells, or perhaps more genuinely by improving folk-remedies. In addition they recovered lost valuables and even provided love-potions. They resembled the present-day witch-doctors of the Third World, and like them did not rapidly vanish with the arrival of more scientific remedies. They were above all familiar and approachable by peasants. Unfortunately most Christians believed that 'black' witchcraft also existed, and that misguided persons were commonly practising it in league with the Devil. This obsession also failed to evaporate in the early dawn of what we call modern science. Though ridiculed by important Protestant writers like Reginald Scot in his *Discoverie of Witchcraft* (1584), and fundamentally opposed to Puritan belief, the witch-cult revived for a time within certain deluded communities of seventeenth-century England and New England, occasioning gross hysteria and fanaticism.

As a common factor, all acts of magic implied the suspension of the normal laws of nature through the application of appropriate spells of physical objects. Its danger to Christianity arose from a blurring of the frontiers which divided secular from ecclesiastical magic.[14] This occurred on the popular level, rather than among the leaders of the Church. Yet even a theology closely based upon the Scriptures could not accept some entanglement, since miraculous deeds of healing are related in both Testaments of the Bible. Even the most austere theologians were obliged to maintain that suspensions of nature had accompanied the miracles of healing by Jesus and the Apostles. Meanwhile both popular and priestly believers maintained that such events still occurred daily and could be claimed as favours elicited by pious human intercession. Holy water was thought to remedy some diseases, while even the sacred touch of an annointed monarch might heal scrofula. At the lower end of the scale of values, the ringing of consecrated bells averted thunderstorms, while at its upper extremity, the rituals used at the ordination of a priest were believed to endow him with powers of a supernatural order, as displayed by his function in the Mass.

There lay many gradations of significance within both sorts of magic, occult and sanctified. Since Anglo-Saxon times the Church had denounced secular wizardry,[15] and if the clergy had seemed in some measure to compare with the 'cunning' people, this did not ostensibly exalt mere human agencies or derogate from the universal power and responsibility of God. The most apparent competition occurred in fields where the Church seemed most inclined to tolerate legendary superstitions; for example when a particular saint was supposed to confer material benefits comparable with those also supplied by some 'cunning' person. This latter notion became fatuous when based on the popular assumption that certain saints offered specialised services, one curing some particular disease, another recovering lost property. In the first Royal Injunctions (1536) imposed upon the English Church one clause specifically condemns this superstition attending saint-worship, 'as though it were proper or peculiar to that saint to give this commodity or that, seeing all goodness, health and grace ought to be both asked and looked for only of God'.[16] Yet over and above the obvious superstitions, a Church governed by sacramental doctrines involving the instrumentality of physical objects could hardly complain when the popular mind blurred the vital distinctions between secular and ecclesiastical magic. In this field even today's valuations are bound to be diverse. Our ancestors suffered much unassuaged pain, and insofar as these practices brought mental or physical comfort we might be wise to withhold our ridicule. And after all, unexplained cures and alleviations still appear sometimes to emerge from faith-healing activities with a religious background. On the other hand it is hard to follow those amateur social anthropologists who dogmatically extol the good old ways, deplore the very use of the word 'superstition' and attack reformists of the sixteenth century for disturbing the 'comfortable' ignorance of former times. This reactionary attitude reveals a feeble estimate of the progressive forces in early modern medicine and religion alike. To what precise date should this charade have been maintained? After all, one is scarcely furthering any Christian tradition if one praises its more fanciful vagaries as a narcotic, an 'opium of the people'!

Over and above these ambivalent inheritances from the early periods of Christianity, the medieval Church devised some complications of its own. In the eleventh century the masterful Gregory VII did his best to impose celibacy upon secular priests and in that endeavour was followed by his successors. Here was a heroic defiance of human nature, since such priests were compelled to live outside the restraints of the cloister and extend their ministry to women. St. Thomas Aquinas assured the world that clerical celibacy was no law of God but a law of the Church, a distinction clearly necessary to safeguard the repute of the early generations of married clergy, beginning with St. Peter, the first Pope. While the antiquity of clerical marriage did not help offenders against the papal edict, all the refinements of the scholastic world could not infallibly 'expel Nature with a fork': throughout Europe both steady concubinage and casual relationships became by no means rare among the priesthood. Often denounced by critical Catholics, these lapses were inevitably exploited by Protestant propoganda. Following Luther's example, the allowance of clerical marriage became one of the more important social principles of the Reformation.

Other controversial doctrines developed and over-extended by the medieval Church were those relating to purgatory, the place of punishment where people who had died in a state of grace could expiate their venial sins for an appropriate period, pending their admission into Paradise. In substance based upon the ancient and instinctive practice of praying for the dead, purgatory nevertheless rested upon a slender Scriptural basis consisting of dubious inferences.[17] Developed with characteristic grimness by St. Augustine, its true begetter, it was perfected by Aquinas. The latter went so far as to announce that the smallest pain in purgatory was greater than the greatest pain experienced on earth, though he added with remarkable optimism that these intensely suffering souls were nevertheless comforted by the certitude of eventual salvation. They could also, however, be helped by Masses offered on their behalf. In the real world these potentially 'comforting' aspects of purgatory became minimal, as will appear when we cite that terrible passage from Thomas More describing purgatorial sufferings worthy of the Inferno itself. Thence arose far greater complications, when fund-raising popes allowed the unrestricted sale of indulgences by professional 'pardoners' and preaching friars, some of whom in turn assured buyers that by their subscriptions they were shortening the sentences to purgatorial suffering incurred by beloved relatives and friends. The climax came in 1517 when this daring exercise of papal privilege, organised by the banking house of Fugger in Germany, raised the money to build the new St. Peter's in Rome. Hence arose Luther's famous initial protest. And it is fair to add that in 1567 an edict by Pius V imposed restrictions, not on the basic doctrine of Purgatory, but on its more obvious abuses.

Here again it becomes essential to insist upon the international origins of the English religious Reformation. In 1516, the year before Luther broke into open revolt against the mass-sale of Indulgences, Erasmus did something with more fundamental implications. Having demanded since 1503 in his *Enchiridion* a rigorously biblical Christianity, he now published his own Latin translation of the New Testament from Greek texts, thus advancing the claim of humanist scholarship to supersede the revered Latin Vulgate of St. Jerome. Moreover in the preface to this translation Erasmus took a still more radical step when he unequivocally called for the publication of bibles translated accurately from the Greek into the vernacular languages, in order to promote the direct religious re-education of the common people.[18] Luther, still engaged in translating the whole Bible into German, announced in 1524 that God had permitted the Ottoman Turks to conquer Byzantium with the express purpose of driving out Greek scholars so that they might teach the language of the New Testament in western Europe. Whatever the case, half a century before the fall of Byzantium some of the Greeks had already been at work in Italy, supplying this essential basis of an evangelical Christianity.[19] Luther's mode of making this point may seem to modern eyes somewhat curious: like his eminent disciple Melanchthon, he saw human history as a drama written in every detail by God. Nevertheless he was right in perceiving that the superior authenticity of the Greek text over the Vulgate could not be dismissed as a suspect manoeuvre on the part of Valla and Erasmus, but had become a genuine issue in the development of a biblical theology. Though too often simplifying the problems of interpretation, Luther declared war between bible-Christianity and churchly, scholastic Christianity. Within this intellectual context, by 1530 widely apparent, we should also locate the core of the English Reformation. From 1526 onward the translations by Tyndale, Coverdale and others gave the English a vernacular bible with Lutheran commentaries making a resonant impact at all levels of English society, not solely upon the learned.[20] Even in England the evangelical religion was thus started on its gradual course several years before Henry VIII made the political break with Rome, over a decade before Thomas Cromwell persuaded him to allow the placing of English bibles in the churches, and more than two decades before England acquired its first

Protestant government. This real dynamic of the English Reformation has obviously eluded those historians who seek to make this episode a mere act of state, foisted upon a nation which did not want to receive it. This seems to the present writer a simplification by historians rightly aware of English popular conservatism, but all too little aware of the powerful European forces which during the reign of Henry VIII crossed the sea, penetrated that conservatism, and started to loosen its grip, beginning with the accessible south-eastern region of England.

This present introduction has sought to sketch certain important features of the Protestant outlook. It does not however attempt to suggest that the Catholic case for resistance was weak and easily rejected by the nation. The true strength of that case did not depend upon supplying the 'right' answers to the least answerable questions: for example, those concerning transubstantiation, or those asking why the authority conferred by Christ on St. Peter (and on occasion rejected by St. Paul) should have been transferred *ex officio* to every succeeding Bishop of Rome. The clash should not be envisaged as occurring solely on the high theological issues selected by Luther, regarding which many of the clergy, let alone the laity of Europe, had little claim to make intellectual decisions. Yet at all social levels there existed in England prudent people, unlearned on both papal authority and biblical humanism, yet capable of shrewd judgements upon the preservation of Christian faith and morals, upon the unity of England and upon the well-being of their own communities. Whether their varying temperaments led them towards moderate conservatism or moderate reformism, a great many thought it wise to practise co-operation, even with other moderates of contrary inclinations. Leaders such as Luther and Tyndale were in fact similarly anxious to demonstrate their own essential moderation, their determination to retain all the traditional bases of the Christian faith, as defined by its historic creeds. So far from posing as radicals, they tried to demonstrate that it was the papal Church itself which over the centuries had produced the innovators, and that the purpose of their own present Reformation was no more than a restoration of the Christianity which Christ had taught. All the same, as the Lutheran, Zwinglian and sectarian movements advanced, one did not need to be a rigid adherent of papal monarchy in order to fear that the freedom of wild enthusiasts to interpret the Scriptures might well result not only in religious conflict but even in social chaos upon a larger scale. Luther knew that his chances of initiating any reforms of consequence depended upon his ability to dissociate himself from his more radical self-styled followers, and he ended by defining 'the Freedom of a Christian' more cautiously than he had done during the first heady years of his campaign. In 1522 he had in fact been obliged to emerge from his hiding-place on the Wartburg in order to combat those he called 'the mad saints', who were by then threatening to take over his whole enterprise. This left wing soon helped to lead the insurgent German peasants of 1524–5 to disaster and death, while a decade later even the sectarian rebels Karlstadt and Müntzer were surpassed by John of Leyden and those other crazed leaders in the long defence (1535) of the city of Münster against the princes. Amid these events something even more terrifying than a doctrinal division of Christendom seemed to threaten. To peoples already obsessed by images of mortality and by prophecies announcing the imminent end of the world, the news of such excesses rapidly circulated and assumed gigantic proportions. Behind the humble groups of sectarian footsoldiers there rode the Four Horsemen of the Apocalypse. Sectarianism could not be dismissed as trivial or ephemeral, especially in the cases of 'Spiritualist' movements which devalued both Catholicism and biblical humanism by exalting the 'inner light', the divine spark supposedly implanted by God in the minds of select people. Even in 'sensible' England we shall encounter some examples of this particular radical trend, as for example the Family of Love, a relatively durable offshoot of German Anabaptism.

Thus while the radical sects could produce some interesting and almost saintly characters, they had successors who survived to exacerbate the English civil conflicts of the seventeenth century. From the beginning—and not only in England—the sects appeared to be a major obstacle to the advance of mainstream Protestantism. In the event, it is true, catastrophe was avoided, even though the list of European crises intensified by religious partisanship grew considerably from the advent of the Reformation. These conflicts have ranged from the Revolt of the Netherlands and the Thirty Years War to the ever-fluctuating tensions in modern Ireland. In Valois and Bourbon France several decades of chaos gave way to royal absolutism. In Germany and Switzerland the internal cohesion of the cities, in England the loyalty of the nation to the Tudor dynasty did much to avert or postpone revolution. But while Protestants applauded the ideal of a scripturally-educated nation, as already envisaged in 1516 by Erasmus, they should have recalled that he was urging clerics and lay people to learn—and learn in a very short period—the mental discipline needed to live alongside unsolved and insoluble problems, as required by his optimistic vision. Its failure to materialise rapidly did not arise from religious fanaticism alone, or from mere argumentation over the respective roles of biblical and papal authority. In fact the political element was never lacking. Most of these wars could have been avoided by peace-loving rulers, a species rendered rare by greed for territory and by antiquated concepts of honour. In addition there existed deep divisions of custom and temperament between northern and Mediterranean Europe, most of all between the Germanic peoples and Spain. The latter had indeed barely emerged from a religious war of centuries—conducted against Islam on Spanish territory—when it became entangled with the dynastic scheming of the Habsburgs.

If human happiness were the main criterion whereby historical movements should be evaluated, many observers might well deplore the more immediate sequels of the Reformation. Since half Europe would not accept the movement, the religious division, while insufficient to overthrow the social structure, did enhance the already tragic political feuding of the major nations. Again, in neither sector of the continent did the entrenched situations remotely correspond with the hopes of the contestants. In regard to religion for the masses, the Reformation did in the end generate a more accurate, less superstitious understanding of Christianity, sometimes at a heavy cost in joyless mental drudgery. If the Jesuits could be over-zealous, so could the English Puritans and those Lutheran clerics who burdened labouring peasants with endless catechising assemblies.[21]

However we judge these consequences, the course of the Reformation in England still demands to be considered within a long temporal, and a wide geographical context, as well as by reference to its place in English national and local history, its personalities and publications, and its role in the daily life of all the classes, especially those in the middle and lower levels of society. Beyond question, its original motivation and power derived less from politics than from religion, and from the many semi-religious problems besetting the Church. Nevertheless the impacts of the Reformation upon political and social life also attained great importance in England from the middle years of Henry VIII to the revolutions of the seventeenth century and the Settlement of 1688. The fundamental cause of all the national and regional movements were European in scope; they were gradual outgrowths from ancient and medieval Christian situations. Thanks to subsequent emigration, colonisation, missions and literature, the effects of the Reformation eventually became world-wide, though it often remains hard to disentangle them from the accompanying host of secular concomitants. From this point we shall examine the unfolding phenomena in England, making brief excursions to the continent when necessary, and always acknowledging that England could never afford to opt solely for oceanic expansion or solely for membership of Europe. In the short run, so too in the long run. As the former British Empire retreats into its local ghettos and rejects what little the British once believed they had taught its peoples, the continent of Europe now seems to have become Britain's permanent anchorage. So when certain Tudor Englishmen imagined that by a renunciation of the papal allegiance they were liberating themselves from continental influences in order to partner an English Deity, they were sadly deluded!

2 Late Medieval Religion

Conventional Cults and Idioms

There was once a certain knight, whose castle stood upon a highway and who mercilessly robbed passing travellers. Despite his conduct he nevertheless maintained his pious daily prayers to the Blessed Virgin. One day, when it was the turn of a certain holy monk to be stripped by this knight's henchmen, the victim demanded a personal interview with his oppressor, saying he had certain secrets to communicate. Taken inside the castle he asked the knight to assemble his whole household, yet when the knight so obliged him the monk declared that one of its members had absented himself from the assembly. A check revealed that the missing member was a serving man who, when at last located and brought before the monk, proceeded to behave as one insane. Finally he admitted he was no real man but a demon in human guise, who for fourteen years had served the knight by special order of the Devil. The latter had commanded him to watch for the day when his master failed to salute the Virgin in prayer; whenever this fatal moment of neglect should occur, the demon servant would be free to kill the knight and drag his wicked soul to perdition. So far, though ignorant of his precarious situation, the knight had never allowed his devotions to lapse. Now learning the truth he was duly appalled and hurled himself in repentance at the feet of the monk, who commanded the demon to vanish and to trouble the Virgin's devotees no more. With reverence and thanks the knight permitted his saintly deliverer to go free and thenceforth he changed his own life for the better.

This *exemplum*, or story with a moral, was last told not around the year 1200 but by a man who mentions Pope Julius II as still alive. It is one of many such anecdotes in the commonplace book of Thomas Ashby,[1] an Augustinian canon of Bridlington in the days of Henry VII and Henry VIII. This great house had literary traditions dating back to the twelfth century; more important, it rejoiced in its own saint, Canon John of Thwing, who had died in 1379, received canonisation at Rome in 1401 and continued to attract pilgrims from far and wide even in the time of Thomas Ashby. In no small measure the latter's manuscript centres around these two cults of the

Virgin and of St. John of Bridlington. It begins with a long series of items in honour of the former—two rhyming Latin tributes, a group of meditations and prayers centred upon the Virgin and St. Anne, an exposition of the Angelic Salutation, a meditation on the Magnificat. Later on we observe a transcript of the poem *Salve virgo virginum*, and the *exemplum* we have just retold. In St. John and his miracles Ashby's taste for anecdote finds a more extensive scope. We read of the marvellous rescue of the five mariners of Hartlepool, the revival of the dead carpenter, the resurrection of a murdered man who luckily happened to lie unburied because of the coroner's absence. To these miracles, which occur in earlier Bridlington hagiography, Ashby adds another, based on the written testimony of an early fifteenth-century Gascon merchant. This impetuous foreign tourist had failed to wait for the custodian of the shrine and with rash curiosity had presumed to open the capsule containing the head of St. John. In consequence the angry saint had afflicted him with terrible pains in his hand and arm. Journeying south he reached Huntingdon, but his condition worsened and he feared to die. His companions, better instructed in the irascible ways of saints, urged him to return forthwith on an expiatory pilgrimage to Bridlington. Complying he experienced a miraculous cure. The Gascon is then made to end his acknowledgement with an eloquent tribute to St. John, presumably reflecting the exuberant latinity of some Bridlington scribe who drew up the original document.

The local cult is far from exhausted by these items of Thomas Ashby's manuscript. He includes also an office in honour of St. John, records of the canonisation and translation, notes on the foundation of the Priory, and a poem beginning,

> *Brydlyngtonie prior pie*
> *Imitator caste vie,*
> *Representa nos Messye.*

Yet another set of *exempla* illustrates the miracle-working properties of the text 'In the beginning was the Word'. In Aquitaine there were once two beggars, both demoniacs, one of whom noticed that his companion secured more than his fair share of alms. He therefore resolved to get his competitor cured of this all-too-profitable malady and induced a priest to whisper the miraculous text into the successful beggar's ear. Yet the wary priest insisted on repeating it also to the first beggar, who was shocked to find himself cured as well! Again, relates Ashby, we read that a devil once told a holy man there was a certain text quite terrifying to devils, but naturally he refused to divulge it. The holy man then suggested a series of texts but his adversary returned a contemptuous negative to each suggestion. When, however, the enquirer stumbled upon the first words of St. John's Gospel, the infernal creature vanished with a mighty noise. Also, continues our author, a devil appeared to a certain abbot in the form of a beautiful woman, *alliciens eum ad concubitum* as they were alone together in a pleasure-garden—or so I interpret *in viridario*, though this can also mean a plantation. At all events, when the chaste abbot repeated the same text, the devil disappeared in the manner of his kind, *cum magno strepitu*. These improving tales one might well continue, but those already retold will suffice to indicate that at Bridlington a twelfth-century world lingered on while Machiavelli was writing the *Prince*, while the sophisticated talkers at Urbino were giving Castiglione the materials for his *Book of the Courtier*. And if Ashby cannot be placed among the more sophisticated of provincial Englishmen, his case was far from untypical in a generation of priests brought up on the *Golden Legend* and the *Gesta Romanorum*.

The theological and liturgical sections of his book could equally have occurred at any period of the Middle Ages—an exposition of the Fiftieth Psalm, a treatise on the privileges and rites of various festivals, notes on reading in church, on the four necessities for a dying man, on the symbolism of the episcopal mitre and other vestments, a meditation on guardian angels, verses on how to enter a church, an 'objurgation' against the wretched human body, and a scholastic disputation 'On the Day of Judgment, will men be bare or clothed?' Ashby writes almost wholly in Latin, but he has some English verses in a section concerning the sacrament of the altar, his object here being to enjoin implicit belief in transubstantiation and to allay curious questioning:

> The bread is flesh in our credence,
> The wine is blood without doubtance.
> They that believe not this with circumstance,
> But doth themself with curious wit enhance,
> To hell pit shall they wend,
> There to be torment without end.

This section concludes without supporting patristic texts, especially from St. Augustine, to whom the compiler elsewhere often alludes. On the other hand, he ostensibly cites no author later than Jean Beleth, the eminent French theologian of the twelfth century.

I have adduced Thomas Ashby's book, now in Durham University Library, as one of those many unpublished manuscripts we must investigate in order to gain a more authentic and intimate sense of popular religion on the eve of the Reformation. A comparable miscellany is that by his younger contemporary John Gysborn, which may be found among the Sloane manuscripts in the British Museum.[2] This cleric, probably a native of Guisborough in North Yorkshire, joined the Premonstratensian order and at first describes himself as a canon of Coverham. Subsequently he styles himself 'curate' (i.e. parish priest) of Allington in Lincolnshire, but he doubtless served there while still remaining a regular canon, since the benefice of Allington belonged to Newbo, another Premonstratensian house. Gysborn's career unfortunately cannot be dated from the Lincoln diocesan records, but the three or four datable documents in his collection range between the years 1520 and 1531. He begins with liturgical notes on the duties of the deacon and subdeacon at mass in his own order. He then provides detailed English questionnaires for use in the confessional, indicating the methods whereby dutiful pastors discovered the more intimate lapses of their flocks. A rhymed prayer to the Virgin is also in English, though with a Latin refrain, and there follow various prayers to the angels, the patriarchs, the apostles, the martyrs. Then comes an historical account of Confession, a report on a miracle at Exeter, a badge of the Five Wounds drawn in pencil and red ink, a couple of sermons, a further note on sins revealed in the confessional, and two spirited accounts of the pains of hell. Unlike Ashby, Gysborn provides a number of secular items, including a sequence of model letters and three acknowledgements of debt, respectively by a Grantham draper, a yeoman of Donnington and a former rector of Allington. In common Tudor style he also records remedies for stone, colic, strangury, pox and plague; he explains how to make aquavite from herbs, how to engrave upon iron or steel, to grind gold for illuminating and to enamel on gold. Altogether Gysborn stands nearer than Ashby to lay life and there is more than a touch of humour in some of his macaronic poems.

Manuscripts like these two are far from embracing the whole gamut of English devotional life on the eve of the Reformation. They nevertheless exemplify many important elements of the popular and conventional religion[3]—its effort to attain salvation through devout observances, its fantastic emphasis on saints, relics and pilgrimages, its tendency to allow the personality and teaching of Jesus to recede from the focus of the picture. That the connection of such writings with the Christianity of the Gospel is rather tenuous could be demonstrated with almost mathematical precision. The point is reinforced by the testimony of Catholic reformers like Colet, More and Erasmus, for Catholicism as it then existed amongst real men and women was far from homogeneous. People who can sing the same creed together are not necessarily practising the same type of religion. There lay all the difference in the world between Thomas More and the friar whom More found at Coventry superstitiously preaching that a sinner could escape damnation by the simple expedient of saying his rosary every day. It would nevertheless be mistaken to imagine that the religion of saint-cults and observances appealed only to poor and uneducated believers. In 1522 the wealthy pluralist Robert Langton, nephew of a bishop of Salisbury and Winchester, published a book on his interminable pilgrimages on the continent, yet it scarcely mentioned any object of interest other than the shrines of saints.[4] The celebrated shrine of St. Mary of Walsingham attracted the highest-born, and the theological learning of Henry VIII did not prevent him from making the pilgrimage in person. Few can have made it in the sarcastic spirit of Erasmus, who in later years wrote a colloquy ridiculing the commercialisation of the shrine and the ignorance of the canons. And even he did not know that Walsingham Priory had become, amid all its wealth and magnificence, one of the least pure and disciplined religious houses in England. This fact was nevertheless well known to Bishop Nix of Norwich and his officials, who inexorably recorded the details in their visitation-records. But there were fashions in saints and the most famous of all in England had proved a waning financial asset for over a century before this time. At Canterbury the receipts of the shrine and the altars are shown by the official accounts of the fifteenth and sixteenth centuries to have become quite negligible in comparison with the golden shower of the high Middle Ages.[5]

Purgatory; Devotional Reading

Our two 'new' witnesses Ashby and Gysborn scarcely do justice to another debatable feature of late medieval religion—its dogmatic and detailed emphasis upon the horrors of purgatory and the means whereby sinners could mitigate them. Here again we observe no mere cult of the vulgar. In that most terrible—and magnificently written—passage in his *Supplication of Souls*, More himself makes the suffering dead cry out to the living for more prayers and masses:

> If ye pity the blind, there is none so blind as we, which are here in the dark, saving for sights unpleasant, and loathsome, till some comfort come. If ye pity the lame, there is none so lame as we, that neither can creep one foot out of the fire, nor have one hand at liberty to defend our face from the flame. Finally, if ye pity any man in pain, never knew ye pain comparable to ours; whose fire as far passeth in heat all the fires that ever burned upon earth, as the hottest of all those passeth a feigned fire painted on a wall. If ever ye lay sick, and thought the night long and longed sore for day, while every hour seemed longer than five, bethink you then what a long night we silly souls endure, that lie sleepless, restless, burning and broiling in the dark fire one long night of many days, of many weeks, and some of many years together ... You have your physicians with you, that sometime cure and heal you; no physic will help our pain, nor no plaister cool our heat. Your keepers do you great ease, and put you in good comfort; our keepers are such as God keep you from—cruel, damned sprites, odious, envious and hateful, despiteous enemies and despiteful tormentors, and their company more horrible and grievous to us than is the pain itself: and the intolerable torment that they do us, wherewith from top to toe they cease not continually to tear us.[6]

This, it should be recalled, was not hell but merely the long prison-sentence which the average man must anticipate, a sentence liable to be much lengthened because other people were slack about buying masses and indulgences to shorten it. This much must be said because so many idealisers of medieval religion have supposed that the equally inscrutable Deity of the Calvinists represents some sinister novelty, or that fifteenth-century religion had a childlike gaiety and optimism reminiscent of some sweet group of saints by a Sienese master. On the contrary, medieval men were faced by quite terrifying views of punishment in the life to come; it was small wonder that they felt more comfortable with the saints than with God, or that they came to regard the Blessed Virgin as a merciful mediatrix for ever seeking to placate the divine wrath of the Son as Judge. When they discovered the slightness of its scriptural basis, Protestant zealots like Tyndale crudely denounced the doctrine of purgatory and indulgences as a worldwide plot by the priesthood aimed at fleecing poor and rich alike. Yet whatever the credentials of this doctrine, it was sincerely held, and it showed at least an uplifting sense of community with former generations of Christians. Some Englishmen felt profound offence when the government of Edward VI forbade organised intercession for their dead parents and benefactors; they hastened spontaneously to restore the practice when the accession of Queen Mary made it safe. Within this penumbra of Christian doctrine, there lay edification and sincerity as well as superstition.

A vivid impression of the last generation of medieval English Catholics can be gained from the numerous manuscripts of a younger contemporary of John Gysborn—Robert Parkyn, curate of Adwick-le-Street near Doncaster.[7] This man took priest's orders some time before 1541 and soon proved himself an assiduous student and copyist of Richard Rolle and other mystical authors. He subsequently wrote sermons, pious verses and an interesting guide to the contemplative life,[8] which is overwhelmingly medieval by inspiration even if it shows traces of influence by the Jesuit-inspired Dominican, William Peryn. Parkyn also admired More and his fellow-martyr Bishop John Fisher, making copies of their more intimate meditations. Under Queen Mary he wrote a narrative of the Reformation,[9] deploring the English Prayer Books and the Edwardian abrogation of Catholic ritual. All the same, he continued to hold the curacy of Adwick throughout all the ecclesiastical revolutions until his death in 1569. By this time he had begun to make literary contact with the exiled English writers of the Counter Reformation, but there is no sign that he resisted the Elizabethan Settlement or considered relinquishing his office. Robert Parkyn did not live in a private world. His career and beliefs are closely paralleled by those of his neighbouring colleague William Watson, curate of Melton-on-the-Hill, some of whose letters were fortunately preserved among Parkyn's own papers. They show that in November 1555 these two conservatives independently revived the pre-Reformation practice of saying a trental, or series of thirty requiem masses.[10]

It was indeed a harsh and rigid Protestantism which desired to outlaw convictions so deeply grounded. Yet when the old popular religion encountered the Protestant demand for Biblical evidence, it exposed more vulnerable aspects than a belief in the multiplication of intercessory masses. Amongst the manuscript works of this same Robert Parkyn is a versified *Life of Christ*,[11] over 10,000 lines in length and written in seven-line stanzas; he composed it between the years 1548 and 1554, intending it for public readings before his parishioners. With some narrative skill, though in the creaking versification of the period, he combines materials of all four Gospels and then proceeds to cover the first two chapters of *Acts*, ending with Pentecost and the going forth of the apostles to preach. At the outset Parkyn vociferously claims that he will affirm nothing except what can be proved from the scriptural text, and he does in fact often distinguish between the latter and the mere conjectures of patristic and medieval commentators, among whom his favourite is the great Spanish Dominican St. Vincent Ferrer. Despite these good intentions he nevertheless devotes many stanzas to the pretty legends. We are told, for example, that angels informed the Virgin of the temptation in the wilderness, inviting her to send food to the Lord; she did so, but with the request that they should return to her the fragments. Again, Parkyn devotes three equally apocryphal stanzas to the detailed subject-matter of the disputations in the temple. Most reprehensibly of all, since he fails to reveal their lack of scriptural basis, he invents long discussions between the apostles as they await Pentecost, and here he deliberately makes the Virgin appear the dominating figure of the nascent Church. When we reflect that as late as 1550 a virtuous, sincere and by no means uneducated parish priest could so manipulate these passages, we perhaps begin to comprehend, though not necessarily to admire, the impatience of the Reformers. They were dealing with a failure to understand the meaning of evidence, with an invincible addiction to time-honoured fable, with an obstinate denial of the principle which had its origins in humanism—that belief must be based upon a close scrutiny of original sources rather than upon the unsupported authority of medieval doctors or upon writers of pious fiction. Robert Parkyn's intellectual superiors amongst the Catholic clergy may seldom have perpetrated such major lapses, yet they certainly lost influential support through their undue attachment to those 'unwritten verities' which the contemporaries of Erasmus had come to suspect. Here were encounter one of the greatest issues of the Reformation, and it remains an issue upon which modern writers cannot be expected to achieve close agreement. Yet in the present writer's view, the Catholic party lost the struggle in England not simply because they temporised with Henry VIII but also because, in an age when an increasing number of men were reading and thinking for themselves, the intellectual slackness of popular medieval religion played into the hands of Protestant critics.

Our picture of conventional religion arising from these little-known sources finds confirmation in the analysis of printed books made over half a century ago by Dr. Pierre Janelle.[12] Behind these books we sense a considerable body of pious readers and, if we know almost nothing about the number of copies printed, the many editions of certain works testify to their popularity. Of the seventy-four books edited by Caxton from 1470 to 1490, at least twenty-nine are works of edification. In the next decade his chief successor, Wynkyn de Worde, published thirty such religious works in a total list of fifty-four, and this high proportion continues throughout English publishing at least until the decade 1530–40. Between 1490 and 1530 at least twenty-eight editions of the *Hours of the Blessed Virgin* were printed in England. Myrc's *Festial*, the chief English collection of pious legends and miracles, achieved nineteen editions from 1483 to 1532. The delightful but still heavily fabulous *Golden Legend* by Jacob of Voragine was published in 1483 by Caxton who, so far from pruning its luxuriance, added seventy new lives of saints. Its well-maintained popularity is attested by further editions in 1485, 1493, 1498, 1503, 1512 and 1527. During this period books centring around the saints immensely outnumbered any other type of religious book.

Myrc and Voragine had several rivals in this field. Wynkyn de Worde published John of Tynemouth's *Sanctilogium Angliae* in 1516, while the Bridgettine monk Richard Whitford compiled the last of the great English hagiographical collections, the *Martiloge*, and saw it published in 1526. Over and above this steady native output, a large number of similar books came to England from the presses of France and the Netherlands. Guides to appropriate preaching on the various festivals comprise a smaller but still considerable group of publications; of these, *Manipulus Curatorum*, *Pupilla Oculi*, *Exornatorium Curatorum* and others often find mention in the wills of Tudor clergymen. The mystics are represented by several works of Rolle and Hilton, but these writers provided a more *recherché* approach which we shall examine separately. Compared with the public avidity for saints and marvels, both these and the intellectual treatises by scholastic theologians and philosophers account for a tiny part of the labours of English printers. Needless to add, the Bible occupies a negligible place, and the English Bible no place at all. This latter fact was based on the prohibition in 1408 of any translation unless sanctioned by the bishops; it was peculiar to England rather than to Catholic Christendom. Ironically enough, the nation about to be most dominated by the Bible stood as yet among the least directly influenced in the Christian world. In Germany twenty complete translations appeared, together with innumerable partial editions, between 1466 and 1522. In France the first printed translation dates from 1477, while ten years later that of Guiart Desmoulins (1291) was published by Canon Jean de Rély; it was reprinted seven times from 1487 to 1521.

Such works had no printed parallel in England until 1526 when Tyndale published his Protestant New Testament. Here the vernacular Scriptures had been so long associated with the Lollard heresy that our English ecclesiastical establishment would take no chances with either official or private translations. This insular conservatism received an uneasy support from Sir Thomas More who was satisfied to place the whole blame upon Wycliffe.[13] However surprising it may seem today, his attitude was widely shared by responsible people, but by the time Tyndale broke the deadlock there were obviously great numbers of laymen who thought that such reasoning unduly simplified one of the most vital issues of the Christian life. Here we are confronted by one of the great formative factors in the origins of the Reformation. The gradual yet portentous growth of a literate laity, already discernible in the fifteenth-century sources,[14] was far from being limited to the gentry and the richer merchant classes. In the long run it was bound to involve not merely critical attitudes toward the Church but also more constructive intellectual and religious ambitions which could not be excluded from the sphere of religion.

Since we seek to explain the progress of the Reformation, we have chiefly concentrated upon what we suppose to have been the vulnerable aspects of the conventional religion. On the other hand, no reasonable observer would seek to deny that the latter had both inspiring and mitigating features. Above all, it could still inspire lively art and craftsmanship. Despite the decline of glass-painting and the proliferation of mass-produced sculpture by ecclesiastical contractors, the great gothic tradition survived well into the reign of Henry VIII. During the half-century preceding the Reformation numerous splendid churches were still being built or extended in the distinctively English perpendicular style. Parish guilds continued to flourish, funds were raised by church sales and other entertainments, devotional and secular life interpenetrated each other and in a world which afforded the average man little indoor space and privacy, the churches were in a real sense the homes of the people.

Amongst all these lively aspects of medieval church life, at least one has been unduly neglected by most historians of the Reformation. Not long ago Professor Scarisbrick conclusively demonstrated that lay fraternities (or 'religious guilds') played a unique and attractive role in late medieval and early Tudor piety.[15] Their primary function was to provide their members with a dignified funeral, followed by intercessionary masses. As a sideline, even the craft guilds occasionally provided such services, but lay fraternities were specifically religious and social in character, and were not distinguished by their members' secular occupations. They formed collective chantries, in one or more of which almost everyone could find a place, even though some guilds excluded the poor by high entry fees and annual subscriptions. These wealthy guilds commonly maintained schools and almshouses, possessed valuable properties and built magnificent guildhalls. Such were St. Anne's at Lincoln, St. George's at Norwich, St. Mary's at Boston. The Holy Trinity Guild at Coventry employed no less than thirteen full-time priests and owned the fine church of St. John, Bablake. In York there were three such major fraternities: St. Anthony's, Saints Christopher and George, and the Corpus Christi Guild, which supervised those famous Mystery Plays eventually banished by Elizabethan puritanism but restored in recent times. Such splendid foundations do not typify the whole system, since there existed hundreds of modest guilds in small towns and villages. Northamptonshire and Cambridgeshire each boasted over a hundred, but it remains unlikely that we shall ever attain an accurate national total, since the surveys made at the dissolution are defective for some counties, while many such institutions probably never kept extensive archives. Those they did keep must have had inferior chances of survival after the dissolution.

Perhaps the unique feature of the lay fraternities was the fact that their office-holders, with almost negligible exceptions, were lay people elected by lay people. More remarkably still, women could be granted membership in their own right; occasionally they held office, a thing which should remind us that real as opposed to idealised women, even managerial women, had been growing in number and importance since the time of Chaucer's Wife of Bath, and were to gain new opportunities of influence amid the social and religious developments of the Reformation. Of course, the fraternities are unlikely to have included many non-respectable people such as the vagabonds or even the village groups said to have roistered in the alehouses even during the Sunday service-times. Certainly members could be, and sometimes were, expelled for adultery and other moral offences. The important business of a fraternity was transacted at an annual general meeting held on the appropriate saint's day, when the rules were read, subscriptions recorded and lists of membership revised. Within a fraternity charitable practices varied, but some helped their members not merely in sickness but in the event of business losses and failures. As for the basic intercessory functions, these were imaginatively conceived, even deceased persons being admitted to membership, and thus during their time in purgatory presumed to share in the spiritual benefits. Since the very existence of purgatory, let alone the efficiency of earthly prayers therein, was not known to have been taught by Jesus or the Apostles, Protestant theology was soon to condemn both saint-worship and purgatory as both superstitious and exploited for gain. Here, let us acknowledge, 'cold' theology can say one thing, while a warm concern for dead relatives and friends may say another. At all events within a fraternity people made friendships which they confidently expected to continue beyond the grave. That the fraternities helped to hold communities together and brought comfort into the hard and brief lives of our ancestors cannot be doubted: perhaps indeed they diminished the priestly domination of medieval life which, as we shall observe, quite certainly helped to occasion anticlericalism. A fraternity on the contrary met its priests as employees, not merely as confessors and mentors endowed with powers of supernatural origin. Fraternities had thus a dual and controversial character. On the one hand they expressed and promoted Christian love and hope; on the other hand they assumed collective, institutional and even somewhat commercial-ised prayer, both to God and to the saints, as efficacious in the world to come. At all events these Christian societies were part of that purgatorial system exposed to attack by any sort of biblical theology. Whether purgatory existed or not, it had certainly become big business in earthly life! To these themes we shall revert with more specific detail when we come to describe the abolition of the fraternities, along with the chantries and other foundations regarded as superstitious, by the Protestant government of Edward VI.

Since Pugin idealised medieval art and life in contrast with the commercial ugliness and the cold charity of Victorian times, it has not been easy for Englishmen to attain a just view of the changes which swept across their religious culture during the sixteenth century. A more exact knowledge of the social background of medieval art and architecture has struck some heavy blows at Puginesque sentiment. Were not these attractive creations often commissioned by wealthy magnates anxious to buy their way into heaven, or by superstitious worldlings who subscribed to building funds by buying indulgences? Do not the works themselves show that superstition and legend constantly stood at the elbows of designers and carvers? Where lay communities genuinely supplied the means, did they not pay more regard to pretty fictions about the saints than to the searching demands of Pauline theology? When actually Christocentric, did not popular art and literature concentrate unduly upon such favourite themes as the Passion and the Nativity, to the neglect of a fuller and more balanced presentation of Christ's life and teaching? Such questions have been asked by scholars in their zeal to deflate that absurd Victorian romanticism which threw the age of the Reformation into a false perspective. A converse danger has now arisen, at least for those whose religious beliefs occasion no vested interest in the credit of the Middle Ages. After all, scholarship equally respectable can support the existence of a genuine fervour alongside the admitted mundane and mechanical aspects of late medieval patronage. Such fervour may occasionally appear even in the most workaday sources. As it happens, we still have the accounts for the building of the superb steeple of Louth, which in its three hundred feet of soaring grace still bears witness to the devotion and pride of a little town standing somewhat apart from the mainstreams of Tudor England. This marvellous structure was begun in 1501, and over a period of fourteen years it cost over £305. At last, on the eve of Holy Rood Day 1515 the weathercock was erected, 'there being Will Ayleby, parish priest, with many of his brother-priests there present, hallowing the said weathercock and the stone that it stands upon, and so conveyed upon the said broach; and then the said priests singing *Te Deum laudamus* with organs; and then the kirkwardens garte [made] ring all the bells, and caused all the people there being to have bread and ale, and all to the loving of God, Our Lady and All Saints.'[16] It was surely no calculating heart which dictated these words.

The pre-Reformation decades also retained literary forms at once popular and religious, forms which nevertheless vanished without obvious successors amid the multifarious changes of the sixteenth century. We should enter no controversial ground in expressing an aesthetic preference for the delightful macaronic poems and carols of the fifteenth century as compared with the jog-trot of the metrical psalms inflicted by Sternhold and Hopkins upon the mid-Tudor and later generations of Englishmen. Again, the York, Coventry and Chester mystery plays, though already becoming archaic, survived the first onset of Protestant belief through their genuine popularity among the common townspeople. Ultimately, however, these plays foundered upon the hostility of Elizabethan Puritanism.[17]

Cultural forms die; new ones are born. During the century which followed Elizabeth's accession Protestantism itself was to create a great religious literature. The virility of medieval religious art and drama had lain in their power to present Christian belief in pictorial forms. A dual change occurred during the sixteenth century. On the one hand the attention of both artists and writers was increasingly captured by secular themes and patrons—this not only in Protestant countries. On the other hand, emphasis in religion shifted steadily from the image to the printed word, from pictures to literary ideas. The old idioms hence became progressively isolated from the culture of that expanding group, the literate laity. Such changes of emphasis had no doubt begun to take effect by the early years of the century but as yet they do not appear to have diminished the esteem enjoyed by that supreme dramatic and pictorial cycle, the Catholic liturgy itself. On the eve of the Reformation this liturgy had, as it seems to us, its stronger and its weaker aspects. The Christian year, and in particular Holy Week, had been furnished with a sequence of spectacular services often of moving beauty and pertinence. On the fringes lay many half-secular ceremonies, devoid of genuine antiquity, inessential to Catholic belief and in some cases weakened by obscure symbolism or by over-boisterous congregational support. But apart from persons affected by the Lollard heresy there are few evidences of active demand for liturgical reform until, during the last years of Henry VIII, specifically Protestant ideas began to grip large sections of the nation. Thenceforward clear divisions of opinion became manifest at all social levels. The priest-led western rebels of 1549 dismissed the new English Prayer Book as 'a Christmas game'. Yet under Queen Mary, when the old liturgy was revived, the same phrase (in northern dialect, 'a Yule lark') was used against it by some parishioners of Rothwell in the West Riding, while a man of Brampton in Lincolnshire, seeing his vicar ceremonially opening the church doors with the staff of the cross exclaimed, 'What a sport have we towards! Will our vicar run at the quintine (i.e. tilt at the target) with God Almighty?'[18] This proletarian irreverence and popular scepticism of which mid-Tudor records afford numerous examples, undoubtedly precedes Protestantism and stems at least in part from Lollard influences.

Popular Religious Knowledge

If the growing intellectual ambitions of laymen and the extension of literacy imposed on the English hierarchy challenges which it failed to meet, one should not assume that the Church left parishioners ignorant of the creeds or of the significance of the mass. It is generally agreed that parasitic beliefs had attached themselves to the latter, but there agreement ends. Were these dubious notions fully rejected by the responsible theologians? How far did enthusiastic preachers and fund-raisers stimulate them? To what degree was the difficult doctrine of transubstantiation misunderstood by men untrained in scholastic philosophy? The factual research demanded by these interesting questions remains incomplete and the emotional partisanship they have always aroused contributes nothing to their elucidation. That certain vulgar errors were widespread is not in dispute, yet we are not entitled to assume that they vitiated the spiritual life surrounding the mass or that they justified the bitterness of Protestant indignation. Popular theology suggested that those who looked on the host would prosper and avoid blindness or sudden death all that day.[19] Special results were expected from a 'trental' or series of thirty intercessory masses. King Henry VII ordered ten thousand masses for his own soul at the rate of sixpence apiece, at least half as much again as the standard fee.[20] Such beliefs clearly threatened the rite with commercialisation and might well cause it to be regarded in terms of merit mechanically acquired by wealthy investors in the future life. The miracle of transubstantiation itself was sometimes misunderstood in gross materialist senses, but in our present state of knowledge it would seem presumptuous to assert that this was generally the case. Earlier generations of the faithful had, it is true, been much regaled upon stories of consecrated hosts exuding blood and upon other miraculous indications of the corporal presence in the elements, yet too much of the Tudor evidence for such materialism seems to derive from prejudiced Protestant witnesses like John Foxe.

The place of books in the religious instruction of the people forms a better-investigated topic, but it also presents uncertainties. The *Lay Folk's Mass Book*, translated from an early medieval French original, had long circulated in a variety of regional dialects. Primers containing the Hours of Our Lady, the Penitential Psalms and collections of prayers often occur in lay wills over the century preceding the Reformation. We might in fact be tempted to argue too much from these latter books. While over a hundred editions of the Sarum Primer were printed before 1534, their texts are in Latin, though some of them contain in addition certain English devotions. English primers can only have made their serious impact after the onset of the Reformation, since between 1534 and 1547 twenty-eight editions were printed wholly in English, alongside eighteen more in Latin.[21] The nervous attitude toward vernacular books which marked pre-Reformation ecclesiastics in England seems here far less intelligible than in the case of the Bible. Did this fear prompt the authorities to 'play down' doctrinal instruction by means of English books or is their paucity just an index of small demand? When James Gairdner wrote that 'no person of any rank or station in society above mere labouring men seems to have been wholly illiterate' he did not, even if his view be accepted, help with this particular problem, for literacy remains a highly imprecise term. And so far as it goes, the bibliographical evidence certainly does not prove that any considerable proportion of the laity followed or studied the mass in books. On the other hand, visiting London churches in 1500, a Venetian ambassador was impressed by the manner in which pairs of pious lay-people recited antiphonally from their primers the Offices of Our Lady and of the Dead, together with the Penitential and other Psalms, the Litany of the Saints and other collects and prayers.[22]

Despite the limited role of English books and the relative infrequency of sermons outside the larger towns, we need not believe that lay people of average intelligence and devotion lacked reasonable opportunities to learn the elements of Catholic doctrine. Ideas were still chiefly communicated by speech, memories still unimpaired by oceans of print. When illiterate Lollards memorised long sections of the Bible, the dissemination of orthodox fundamentals can scarcely have depended upon vernacular books or even upon licensed sermons. Robert Aske, the pious and intelligent leader of the Pilgrimage of Grace, said that his northern men were 'rude of conditions and not well taught the law of God'. Yet even the North cannot so be dismissed in a phrase, for vast differences of opportunity existed between the shepherds of the remote Pennine dales and the citizens of York with their forty parish churches. And especially in relation to the religion of provincial townsmen, modern writers have too little to say of the friars, whose influence was not in fact killed by Chaucer's irony and who remained both active preachers and frequent legatees in wills during the early years of the sixteenth century.

In these vital matters of religious instruction, it seems risky to generalise concerning perhaps three million people whose material and educational backgrounds varied so widely. It may, however, be suggested that the vast majority of Tudor Englishmen were far less interested in theology than most modern books concerning the Reformation would suggest. On the other hand, atheism and agnosticism (as distinct from sporadic doubts about particular doctrines) scarcely existed. The conventional religion may have distorted or neglected some important Christian truths but England never-theless remained a Christian country. Easily enough we may illustrate the fact that religious belief could not subdue a rampant greed and gangsterism which, having regard to that small population, seem in the legal records to dwarf even the social maladies of our own day. Yet without conventional and institutional Christianity the forces working for refinement and gentle-ness of spirit would have remained far less effective. If the medieval Church had made slow progress in conditioning this turbulent society, the medieval State had, by the fifteenth century, almost come to a dead stop.

Alongside the Protestant Reformation, the Tudor dynasty undertook another sort of reformation—the conditioning of society to the rule of law. Subsequent historians of this phenomenon have too often adopted a complacent version of the doctrine of progress, whereby God inevitably looked after his Englishmen. Ecclesiastical historians in particular have tended unduly to concentrate upon the battles between Church and State, forgetting that the two were always fighting the moral and social battle side by side. Dante's *De Monarchia* became a somewhat academic book even in its own day, yet its apotheosis of peace and law as necessities for man's spiritual development, its vision of the complementary nature of the functions of Church and State, might have furnished many a valuable lesson to those who have ventured to write of the Reformation without under-standing the primary needs of society and the role of the State in ministering to those needs. The Tudor rehabilitation of law and government has enormous importance not merely for church-history but also for the religious history of Englishmen.

Mysticism and the 'New Devotion'

Our reflections upon the orthodox religion have omitted at least one ingredient of much significance and interest—that deepening of the spiritual life in the later Middle Ages usually known as the *devotio moderna*. Though throughout Europe this movement tended to assume the form of a quiet pietism among lay people and secular clergymen, it derived from, and existed alongside, the more austere and exalted mysticism still prevalent within a small élite of the monastic orders. Its chief problem concerned the adaptation of these claustral techniques to life as lived in the rough world. Granting that the higher states of prayer remained difficult of attainment, even for cloistered contemplatives, the writers in the *devotio* tradition claimed that at least the lower steps of the spiritual ladder might, by the use of well-tried exercises, be ascended by men and women obliged to continue in the active life. At all its levels the new devotion aimed at a direct and personal sense of the presence of God. In general, such states of prayer were recognised to involve fleeting contacts with the Divine, though a few specially favoured practitioners might achieve long periods of union, sometimes expressed by the term 'mystic marriage'. Broadly speaking—and simplifying some far from uniform schemes of thought—three major phases of this spiritual journey were envisaged: the purgative way, pursued by means of self-mortification and good works; the illuminative way, a progressive series of 'experiences', often interrupted by periods of dryness and desolation; and the unitive way, begun by advanced contemplatives in this life, yet even by them completed only in the world to come.[23]

From this viewpoint of the Church, the claims of mysticism have always presented problems. Many of its phenomena are not confined to Christians, since analogous techniques and states appear in the literature of Platonism, Buddhism, Taoism, Hinduism and Islam. Moreover in many instances, some of them Christian, a dangerous trend toward pantheism can be detected. This was especially true of Neo-Platonist mysticism, to which the Christian school nevertheless owed profound debts. The notion that God is the whole of Being, that all things have their existence in God, naturally attracted some mystics since it expressed their awareness of absorption into the Divine Being. To cite an extremist, the seventeenth-century Quietist Miguel Molinos thought that the soul should progress through devotion to the Church, then through devotion to Jesus, then into a superior devotion to God alone, so aspiring to a nirvanic union with the Deity. Such tendencies often compelled institutional Christianity, both medieval and modern, to view the contemplative approach with caution. The timid saying, that mysticism begins with mist and ends in schism, enshrines a measure of ecclesiastical wisdom. Yet the Catholic Church always allowed this approach as one of the legitimate ways toward God, provided that it eschewed pantheist extensions and clearly admitted a transcendent God, above, beyond, and infinitely greater than his creation.

Transmitted from Augustine, Gregory and Dionysius the Areopagite across some six centuries to Bernard, Richard of St. Victor, Aquinas and Bonaventura, the tradition assumed an important yet balanced rôle in the versatile religious culture of the high Middle Ages. Then in the fourteenth century it developed one of its most subtle, diverse and influential phases, it refined its techniques and terminology and it began to express itself in a literature capable of emerging from the confines of the cloister. This was the age of the great German Dominicans, Eckhart (died 1327), Tauler (died 1361) and Suso (died 1366); it was the age of the Fleming Ruysbroeck (died 1381), called not without reason the true founder of the *devotio moderna*. In England,[24] the second half of the century saw two great contemplative masters in the anonymous author of *The Cloud of Unknowing* and in Walter Hilton (died 1396), who as an Augustinian canon of Thurgarton in

Nottinghamshire belonged to one of the least mystical orders of the Church. More widely circulated were the voluminous writings of the ardent Yorkshire recluse Richard Rolle (died 1349), a delightful prose-poet of religion but hardly an advanced mystic. These English writers did not confine their message to members of religious orders and Hilton's *Treatise written to a Devout Man* is specifically directed to laymen and secular clergy living 'a mixed life', both active and contemplative. Likewise on the continent, the concepts of mysticism were made social and subdued to pietism through the Brethren of the Common Life, whose schools and charities won such renown, and again through that classic of the new devotion, *The Imitation of Christ*, which soon crossed the narrow seas to rival our native mystics among the devout readers of Yorkist and early Tudor England. On the eve of the Reformation a variety of works inspired by the *devotio* were finding their way into the English printing-presses—not only several editions of *The Imitation* and of works by Rolle and Hilton, but contemporary manuals such as those by the two Bridgettine monks of Syon, William Bonde and Richard Whitford. The latter, among the most prolific devotional authors of the century, was not interrupted by the Henrician dissolution of his house from continuing a succession of books, some of them explicitly designed to help the middle-class laity.

Meanwhile a more heroic asceticism, more ambitious attempts to scale the peaks of contemplation, had characterised members of the Carthusian order, which in England had remained selective and small. The records of their London and Sheen houses display abundant evidence of such activities; even more illuminating are those recently discovered for Mountgrace Priory in Yorkshire. Here, even as late as 1523, worthy recruits continued to compete for each cell as it became vacant.[25] Genuine holiness had even proved a successful business proposition. Since its late foundation in 1396, Mountgrace had built up an annual income of more than £300, and it continued to receive substantial gifts from Lord Clifford and other benefactors almost until the dissolution. Today, as the only well-preserved Carthusian ruin in England, it rewards a visit just as richly as its Cistercian compeers Fountains and Rievaulx. Within sight of the desolate Cleveland moors, set under a steep hill with hanging oakwoods, the greater cloister evokes the solitary life of the Carthusian. Throughout the daily round of prayer each monk remained secluded in his private cell with its tiny garden; he received his frugal meals through a hatch placed at right angles in the thickness of the wall, so as to spare him a distracting glimpse of the attendant lay-brother. Between the great and small courts rises the gaunt, undecorated church, the sole daily meeting-place of the brothers. Of all the monastic sites in England this one reminds us the most forcibly that the desert of late monasticism still had its fountains of living water. No wonder that even as late as the reign of James I, Mountgrace remained the object of secret midnight pilgrimages by 'diverse and sundry superstitious and popishly affected persons'. For once the folk-memory did not greatly err.

During the last half-century of monastic life, spiritual adventure at Mountgrace centred on two personalities. Richard Methley, born in 1452 and dying apparently in 1528, wrote in Latin at least five mystical treatises, three of which have survived.[26] In addition he translated into Latin *The Cloud of Unknowing* and *The Mirror of Simple Souls*, a French contemplative work of the thirteenth century.[27] The only one of his writings as yet printed is a spiritual epistle addressed to Hugh the Hermit, probably the recluse who dwelt in the hermitage still to be seen on the hill above the Priory. It is in English, for the recipient was not learned, and it instructs him how to order his day between work and prayer, how to avoid becoming immersed in rural society and how to sublimate his sexual impulses. 'In the beginning', concludes Methley, 'thou shalt feel some penance or pain, but ever after thou shalt live like a throstle-cock or a nightingale for joy, and thank God, and pray for me.'[28]

In his three extant mystical works this Carthusian describes some of the spiritual experiences which, beginning about 1485, befell him from time to time. On 1 August 1485, for example, he had just celebrated mass and was engaged in prayer when,

> God visited me with great force, for I languished in such love that I almost expired ... Love, and the longing for the beloved, raised me spiritually into heaven, so that, apart from death itself, nothing was lacking to me concerning the glory of God, who sits upon the throne ... As men in peril of fire are only able to ejaculate the single word 'Fire', so, as the languor of love grew stronger, I could scarce think at all, but merely formed in my spirit the words 'love, love, love'; and at last, ceasing even from this, I wondered how I might wholly breathe out my soul, singing in spirit through joy.

These passages have a fairly close parallel in Richard Rolle's *Incendium Amoris* and describe the sensory experiences concerning which readers are cautioned by *The Cloud* and by Walter Hilton. In passages perhaps aimed against Rolle's emphasis, these greater masters dismiss such experiences as gifts made to weaker spirits and not to be confused with the higher contemplation.

Almost contemporary with Methley was John Norton, who entered the order about 1482, became prior of Mountgrace in 1509–10 and died in 1521 or 1522. This monk is also remembered by three surviving mystical treatises[29] and he too refers to ecstasies occurring as early as 1485. If Methley's experiences do not penetrate far beyond the foothills of contemplation, those of Norton seem to lie still more remote from the peaks of that arduous country. He provides graciously-phrased but rather trite dialogues between his own soul and God, and between his soul and his good angel. These, he says explicitly, took place in the spirit, a phrase which seems to exclude any claim to quasi-physical auditions or visions. Certainly he supposed them to have been divinely inspired. He also believed himself to have been granted visions of Our Lady, likewise *in spiritu*. On one of these occasions, surrounded by an assembly of the heavenly host, she revealed to Norton the salvation attained by a recently deceased Carthusian monk. The details are vividly described and may represent hallucinations or dreams provoked by extreme austerities and by concentration upon Christian imagery. Elsewhere we find clear evidence that Norton fell into trances, and we might well recognise him as at once a saintly religious and a psychopath. While his visions may have kinship with those described by Dame Julian of Norwich, they give rise to reflections far less subtle and interesting than hers. Yet if Norton hardly belongs to the cool and bracing world of Walter Hilton, it would be presumptuous to comprehend him wholly within the terms of psychiatric medicine, which has not advanced far in its analysis of such cases. Alongside Prior Norton's autobiographical passages one might place Maurice Chauncy's description of the rigours, visions and the occasional cases of desperate hysteria amongst the last generation of Carthusians in the London house of the Salutation.[30]

As in London, so at Mountgrace, the tradition survived until the Dissolution. The monk Robert Fletcher, who edited Norton's treatises and was also reported to have enjoyed visions, appears in 1539 on the final pension-list of the house. And four years earlier, when the noble London Carthusians were suffering martyrdom, some of their Mountgrace colleagues also fell under suspicion of treason. They were thought to have inspired George Lazenby, a simple Cistercian of Jervaulx, who conversed with Our Lady and had strange dreams, yet who heroically suffered death rather than accept the Royal Supremacy.[31] And one cannot mention these men without recalling the case of that other victim of Henry VIII, the Maid of Kent, who despite her trances and visions was almost certainly an epileptic, and far more clearly a psychopath, than any of the persons we have hitherto named. Yet all of them are related in some degree to that unfortunate tendency of late medieval mysticism—the tendency to attract emotional and idiosyncratic characters and to expect violent psychophysical phenomena as signs of divine favour. Such characteristics became especially obtrusive among saintly nuns like Angela of Foligno, Bridget of Sweden and Dorothea of Prussia; while on a lower level they appear in our own Margery Kempe of Lynn. These were devotees who fell into foaming trances, interviewed angels, enjoyed charming if rather vapid *causeries* with Our Lady, or were helped to roll out altar clothes by the Christ child in person. None of the acknowledged masters regarded such events as essential accompaniments of the contemplative life, while even the most sympathetic of modern authorities tend to see them as contaminations of the pure stream, as aberrations impeding progress toward the higher mystical states. Certainly if the reader turns from these sensationalists to Walter Hilton, he will at once feel himself in a very different world and in contact with an obvious spiritual aristocrat—lucid, sane, exquisitely discriminating, the exponent of an utter selflessness, a soul truly directed toward God and rejecting not only self-advertisement but that last infirmity of noble minds, the temptation to luxuriate in the memory of 'experiences'.

Mysticism and the Reformation

The hysterical tendencies of the new devotion proved by no means its only weakness when it sought to diffuse religion throughout society, and one may feel a deep attraction to this movement without believing that it entertained any solid chances of averting the Protestant Reformation or of capturing the forces and aspirations which made the latter possible. Like Lutheranism, the *devotio* offered a personal, heartfelt and fundamentally non-scholastic religion. During the first two or three decades of the sixteenth century it remained, though within restricted circles, a lively influence. This much we know from the activities of its publicists and from certain well-documented biographies—for example, that of Sir Thomas More, who associated for some years with the London Carthusians and in whose household the graces both of humanism and of the *devotio* can so clearly be discerned. Nevertheless, the demands of contemplation remained too exacting and too technical for ordinary men. If one were to make encouraging progress, one needed somewhat exceptional powers of prolonged concentration, not to mention a measure of asceticism, detachment, self-criticism and charity beyond the resources of moderately devout men amid the bustle and lack of privacy outside the cloister. Despite the optimism of its devotees concerning a 'mixed' life, mysticism could hardly form the basis for a popular religious idiom; such a basis was more likely to be found in the saint-cults and observances or in Lutheranism, which (in theory at least) left everything to God and did not rely upon a 'method' or psychological expertise. One could not graduate to contemplation through the cults; they had to be thoroughly exorcised and unlearned, for they involved a clutter of imagery and creatures. 'Do that in thee is', says *The Cloud*, 'to forget all the creatures that ever God made and the works of them ... Yea, in this work [i.e. contemplation] it profiteth little or nought to think on the kindness or the worthiness of God, nor on our Lady, nor on the Saints or Angel in heaven, nor yet on the joys of heaven.'

Again, the *devotio* did not prove well equipped to inspire a Catholic resistance movement against the claims of Henry VIII. In lay society at least, it tended to create quietist individuals rather than schools of thought or propaganda. In England it gave birth to no organisations, no official leaders. It was not adapted to the militant principles of the Counter Reformation; it avoided rancorous disputation and its orthodoxy was not much concerned with credal asseverations or with such principles of church-government as the Papal Supremacy. To the age's expanding intellectual curiosity it remained hostile, and its manifestoes united to condemn learning as vanity, to dismiss rationalism, scriptural research and scientific knowledge as broken reeds in the world of the spirit. In the words of *The Imitation*:

> For though thou didst know the whole Bible by heart and the sayings of all the philosophers, what doth it profit thee without the love of God and without his grace? ... Surely an humble husbandman that serveth God is better than a proud philospher that, neglecting himself, laboureth to understand the course of the heavens.

These were not the accents of men likely to steer the course of the sixteenth and seventeenth centuries, whether in Catholic or in Protestant countries. Amid the growing spiritual conflict and chaos, the *devotio* supplied no fighting creed. That small section of the English opponents of Henry VIII who were its beneficiaries—More, for example, and the London Carthusians—did not base their resistance upon its principles but upon a series of historical and rational assertions centring around the ideal of a Christendom united under papal leadership. Elsewhere, despite its intrinsic orthodoxy, the diffused pietism of the *devotio* is at least likely to have prepared ordinary minds to receive Protestantism as to receive reformed Catholicism, since it had diverted interest from cult-observances, from the hierarchical chain of command, from the legal mechanisms and the organisation-men of the Church. Yet in the last resort a movement so retiring cannot be thought to have supplied decisive reinforcement to either Reformation or Counter Reformation. The genius of the new devotion has sometimes been compared with that of Quakerism. From our English viewpoint the story of the nation would have been poorer without either of these movements, yet neither of them noticeably deflected the march of our history.

Protestant England lacked niches for the mystical life and for the types of piety which were its derivatives. Despite his admiration for Tauler and for the Brethren of the Common Life, Luther propounded a basically different solution for the dilemma of mankind. Still more remote was Calvinism, and as the later Reformation developed under this second influence, English Protestants were unlikely to take even an academic interest in mystical contemplation. On the other hand, amongst Catholic Englishmen the old arts did not abruptly perish. In the reign of Mary, Richard Whitford was still publishing, and the Yorkshire priest Robert Parkyn still writing, devotional essays with affinities to Rolle, Hilton and *The Imitation*. During the same years the Dominican William Peryn also retained lively impressions from his medieval guides. Yet Peryn, a more characteristic figure of the mid-century than either Whitford or Parkyn, closely based his spiritual exercises upon the work of the Fleming Nicholas van Ess, whom he had met when in exile at Louvain.[32] Here he stood at the parting of the ways, since van Ess had introduced him to a devotion far more 'modern': that of St. Ignatius Loyola, whose ordered thematic meditations and vivid use of mental imagery stand so sharply distinguished from the methods and values of medieval contemplation.

The most remarkable of the English Catholic *émigrés* to continue in the older tradition was the Capuchin Benet Canfield (died 1611), an original mystic who instructed Père Joseph, the 'Grey Eminence' of Richelieu and many other notable Frenchmen, but exercised little influence in England.[33] Not long afterwards Father Augustine Baker (died 1641)[34] was still introducing his English nuns at Cambrai to Richard Rolle and Walter Hilton, yet he was remarking that by now a Latin translation would help them to understand Hilton's antiquated English! Baker himself wrote a famous guide to the spiritual life; toward the earlier mystics it often shows insight as well as scholarship. Yet his original experience and personal achievement were exaggerated by his Benedictine biographer Serenus Cressy, the chaplain of Lady Falkland and after the Restoration a servant to Queen Catherine of Braganza. Cressy (died 1674) may be claimed as the last enthusiastic student of the old tradition before the long period of neglect. By his generation we are dealing with antiquaries rather than practitioners; indeed, in this field of mysticism the whole seventeenth century has an air of revival rather than one of survival. Inexorably the delicate flowers of medieval spirituality had been uprooted by the river in spate and borne away to remote crannies in a backwater of our national life.

3 The Wycliffite Prelude

The Rise of Lollardy

That John Wycliffe and his followers anticipated many of the key-doctrines of Protestantism has never been in dispute. The man himself remains in some respects a mystery; we know so much of his thought, so little of his thoughts, so little of the inner sources of his radicalism. An obstinate North-Country mind endowed with the subtleties of the Oxford schools; a combination of disappointed careerist, temperamental rebel, sincere reformer of immense moral courage; all these and yet further complexities seem to dwell side by side.[1] During his last six years (1378–1384) Wycliffe was no longer a mere academic radical or a mere revivalist. By all the standards of his time he had become a manifest revolutionary and heresiarch. He accepted the Bible as the one sure basis of belief and demanded that it should freely be placed in lay hands. Improving upon the predestinarian doctrines of Archbishop Bradwardine (died 1349), he restricted the true Church to those persons whom God had predestined to salvation. He rejected the doctrine of transubstantiation as a historical novelty and as philosophically unsound, urging that the body and blood of Christ were present in the eucharist not corporally but *sacramentaliter, spiritualiter et virtualiter*. In some passages he seems even to approach receptionism—the doctrine that the efficacy of the consecrated elements depends upon the spiritual state of the communicant. He shared most of the bold anticlerical and Erastian doctrines for which, very shortly before his birth, Marsiglio of Padua had been excommunicated. Upon the Papal Supremacy Wycliffe had long cast doubts; he had likewise advocated clerical marriage, denounced monasticism and placed fanatical emphasis upon the need to disendow a rich and mundane clergy. Anticipating the Lutheran glorification of the godly prince, he elevated temporal rulers above human laws and invested them and other lay magnates with the sacred duty of reforming the Church. Perhaps the only major doctrine of the sixteenth-century Reformers which Wycliffe cannot be said to have anticipated was that of Justification by Faith Alone.

Upon the Reformation abroad he exerted appreciable if indirect influences. John Huss, though affected also by continental predecessors, clearly acknowledged his own teaching to have been inspired by that of Wycliffe; in any case his extensive and often verbal borrowings from the Englishman prove this fact to the hilt.[2] The Hussite Reformation in Bohemia appealed vividly to Luther's generation, which saw in it the sole example of a kingdom which had not only overturned the age-old structures of Church and State but had continued in defiance for a century. Appalled by the anticlericalism of the English Reformation Parliament, Bishop Fisher was quick to recall this warning precedent. On the other hand, the direct influence of Wycliffe's works upon the German and Swiss Reformers cannot be regarded as crucial, even though his name was not forgotten by them, and though in 1525 his *Trialogus* was printed at Basel.

Meanwhile in England Wycliffe's teaching underwent strange modifications and vicissitudes. Despite its complex and scholastic exposition in his Latin works, it soon found vulgarisers and translators who wrote *The Wycket* and other English pamphlets falsely ascribed to Wycliffe's own pen. Within a very few years of his death these doctrines developed a widespread appeal among townsmen, merchants, gentry and even among some of the lower clergy. There were limits to their appeal. The economic restiveness of the peasantry did not in general disturb their doctrinal conservatism, while the revolutionary character of the Wycliffite manifestoes, together with the attack on transubstantiation, alienated the great majority of the ruling and propertied classes. John of Gaunt, who had formerly utilised Wycliffe in a political campaign against the bishops, seems to have protected him while he wrote the last works in his rectory at Lutterworth, yet neither John nor the other magnates were now prepared to back the heresiarch, as in earlier years they had backed the anticlerical reformer. Thus, despite the enthusiasm of a group of knights at court, the Lollards lost any real chance of laying their hands upon the levers of the State. Not in fact until the death of Henry VIII was any Protestant group destined to gain full control of this mechanism.

The earliest Wycliffite cell consisted of the Oxford clerks headed by Nicholas Hereford, who is thought to have made the first Lollard translation of the Scriptures, a deliberately literal and therefore rather unreadable version. In November 1382 these men were forced into submission by Wycliffe's old enemy Archbishop Courtenay, who drove Hereford into exile. There harsh experiences broke his spirit, and when in later years he returned, it was only to recant. At the moment of Courtenay's triumph in Oxford, the term 'Lollard' was applied to the sect in a sermon by the Irish Cistercian Henry Crump; a Middle Dutch word meaning 'mumbler' or 'mutterer' of prayers, it had long been applied to the Beghards and other Netherlandish pietists whose orthodoxy was suspect. In the same year a new and predominantly lay group developed around Leicester, where the message had been brought by Hereford's friend Philip Repingdon, an Augustinian canon of St. Mary's in the Fields near that town. Though Repingdon himself soon conformed and ultimately became a persecuting Bishop of Lincoln, the heresy continued to spread in the Midlands and the Home Counties. Wycliffe's own secretary John Purvey furthered its progress by compiling a much more approachable translation of the Bible, the

basis of the Lollard versions which were to continue circulating in manuscript until the middle years of Henry VIII.

In the last decade of the fourteenth century there emerged in the House
of Commons a vocal group of Lollard partisans counting among its backers
several of the household knights of the young King Richard II. It was this
parliamentary group which in 1395 formulated the 'Twelve Conclusions',
the first manifesto of what had now become far more than an academic
heresy. The document, significantly drawn up in English, deserves attention
as a statement of those Lollard teachings which were to linger so tenaciously
into the period of the Protestant Reformation. It condemns the subordina-
tion of the English Church to Rome, together with transubstantiation,
clerical celibacy and its untoward moral consequences, the consecration of
physical objects (as akin to necromancy), prayers for the dead, pilgrimages,
images and the excessive preoccupation of the Church with the arts and
crafts. In addition it denounces the work of prelates as temporal rulers and
judges, declares all forms of warfare contrary to the teaching of the New
Testament and denies that confession to a priest is necessary for salvation.[3]

The 'Twelve Conclusions' are a list of reform-demands and hence fail to
stress the two chief positive teachings now axiomatic to Lollard partisans—
that the clergy should emphasise preaching rather than the sacraments and
that the vernacular Bible should be freely placed in the hands of the laity,
learned and unlearned alike. These numerous denials and assertions cover
the large majority of charges which we find brought against Lollard heretics
in the records of the ecclesiastical courts. The summaries attempted by later
anti-Lollard writers like Thomas Netter and Bishop Reginald Pecock also
correspond, allowing for their inevitable hostility, with the 'Twelve Conclusions'. It should not, however, be supposed that every Lollard defendant
was charged with a wide selection from these beliefs or that all the Lollard
groups and individuals showed uniform emphases. Persecution forced
Lollardy to become a surreptitious congregational sect, lacking effective
national leaders and hence precise formularies. Moreover, like most religions
which inclined to Biblical fundamentalism and encouraged judgment upon
the Scriptures by unqualified persons, it inevitably developed a fringe of
cranks. Here, however, we reach a difficult subject, for in some court-cases
the articles of accusation were doubtless based upon the testimony of foolish
or malevolent witnesses. Both ecclesiastical and lay courts often showed
gross unfairness toward defendants of any sort. Another difficulty arises
when we attempt to distinguish between the genuine Lollards and the
sceptics who may have been encouraged by Lollardy yet were motivated by
incredulity rather than by religious idealism. Altogether, the weak features
of the movement become apparent enough, though a certain strength shines
alongside its weakness. It zealously sought to recover from the Scriptures an
authentic sense of the person and spirit of Jesus. It argued with force that the
materialism, the pride, the elaborate ritual and coercive jurisdiction of the
Church found no justification in the lives of Christ and his disciples as
recorded in the New Testament. It made a special appeal to the underdogs of
feudal and ecclesiastical society by permitting them a far more active rôle in

the management of their religious lives. In short, it had many of the lively features which characterised the English sects of the Stuart period.

This proletarian character of Lollardy developed rapidly during the earlier decades of the fifteenth century, when the movement was stripped of its political aspirations. From their advent the Lancastrian kings backed the bishops in a fresh campaign against heresy. In 1401 Purvey was forced to recant, William Sawtre burned and the Statute *De Heretico Comburendo* passed through Parliament. These steps failed, however, to crush the Lollard parliamentarians, who produced bills nine years later to soften the laws against heresy and to distribute the surplus wealth of the Church between the King, a newly-created nobility and such useful institutions as hospitals. Then, in the early days of 1414, catastrophe intervened when Sir John Oldcastle, a leading convert imprisoned for heresy, escaped and planned a Lollard march upon London from all parts of the kingdom. Easily overthrown by Henry V at St. Giles' Fields, this rash gathering resulted in numerous arrests of leaders and suspects. Deprived of influential backing the cause was obliged to move underground. Though a Lollard political plot came to official notice as late as 1431, the devotees of the fifteenth century had in general abandoned their hopes of winning over the dominant classes of the realm. Lollardy became a pertinacious rather than a heroic faith, occupying quiet groups of tradesmen and artisans, but here and there attracting a few priests, merchants and professional men. From the mid-century the record of prosecutions becomes less frequent, and we are left wondering whether the number of adherents had declined or whether in that troubled period Church and State lacked the opportunity and the zeal to persecute it. If, however, a real decline occurred, there must certainly have followed a marked revival in the last decade of the century. From about the year 1490 we hear with ever-increasing frequency of Lollard heretics and of official attempts to obliterate the sect. This fact has an obvious interest for historians of the English Reformation.[4]

Lollard Survival

The former tendency to overlook the evidence for early Tudor heresy was in some measure due to the distaste of once-fashionable historians for the most informative of our sources, the *Acts and Monuments* of John Foxe. The martyrologist, who was a large-scale compiler rather than a fastidious historian, showed immense industry in amassing documentary information even if his standards of accuracy are not those of modern scholarship. When all due reservations have been made, it cannot sanely be maintained that Foxe fabricated this mass of detailed and circumstantial information about early Tudor Lollardy. To have done so would have necessitated diabolical inventive powers and erudition, including a study of the parish registers of Buckinghamshire, in which a large proportion of the surnames and several of the actual persons occur. Such wholesale forgery would also have been highly foolish at a date (Foxe was collecting these materials from about 1552 onwards) when so many of the people and the events remained well within living memory. Again, no forger would have given, as Foxe gives, a host of precise references to episcopal records. In some cases he received detailed support from surviving documents; in others his sources have clearly been lost.[5] That this view involves no guesswork can be illustrated from the situation in regard to the York archiepiscopal records. In this diocese we have details of well over seventy cases brought against heretics during the reigns of Henry VIII and Mary, but of these only some half-dozen come from the archbishop's formal registers. The rest are mainly derived from certain surviving act books of the court of audience.[6] Yet in the most dioceses the equivalents of these York act books are today completely or almost wholly missing. At Lincoln, for example, there are no longer act books covering those periods of persecution by Bishops Smyth and Longland which Foxe describes; hence Fox cannot for a moment be charged with fabrication simply because the surviving Lincoln records do not provide close corroboration.

Bishops' registers are indeed most selective compilations and usually preserve only a few 'model' cases. Nevertheless we should expect, if Lollardy were indeed common, to find in them at least a number of scattered cases. This in fact we do find. The present writer is acquainted with seventeen or eighteen episcopal registers of the period 1490 to 1530, and every one shows at least some Lollard cases.[7] Fresh examples are continually coming to light in hitherto unknown registers and court books, while other sequences of information occur in the London chronicles, in the significations of excommunication at the Public Record Office, in the State papers and many other secular sources. Even if Foxe had never written, we should still know a great deal concerning Tudor Lollardy, some of it unknown to Foxe himself. Our complaint against Foxe should not be one of exaggeration but one of incompleteness, a charge which might incidentally be supported by the fact that at least eighteen known Lollard martyrs do not appear in his pages.

We now stand in a position to attempt a summary sketch of the distribution and nature of heresy in early Tudor England. That its inspiration was overwhelmingly Wycliffe, at least until about 1530, would not for a moment be disputed by anyone who read the original texts and who had even an elementary acquaintance with earlier Lollard processes.

In the early decades of the sixteenth century the most striking group of Lollard communities was to be found in the Chiltern area of Buckinghamshire, then near the southern extremity of the great diocese of Lincoln.[8] Amersham, a prominent centre in 1414, 1425 and 1461, had again developed into a considerable focus of Lollardy by 1495. In 1506 or 1507 Bishop Smyth dealt with over sixty heretics here and over twenty at Buckingham. All these recanted and did penance, except two who were ultimately burned. There were further abjurations in 1508, while some of the Buckinghamshire heretics are known to have attended Colet's sermons at St. Paul's and expressed warm approval for his reforming views. In 1521 Bishop Longland attacked them on a larger scale. Nearly 350 persons were accused before him in the long and complex proceedings preserved in such detail by Foxe. We do not know how many of these people were convicted, but the martyrologist records six as executed (four of whom appear also in the significations) and about fifty abjurations. Perhaps the real severity of the blow arose from the demoralised recriminations amongst the accused. By far the greater number of the accusers were themselves reported as heretics; wives and husbands informed against each other; parents accused their offspring and vice versa; several people gave evidence against their instructors in Lollard doctrine. It says something for the substantial integrity of Foxe that he did not 'edit' this material, for it furnished a Protestant hagiographer with singularly feeble propaganda. The heretical doctrines he mentions had all been familiar since the earliest days of Lollardy—disbelief in transubstantiation, reading the English Scriptures, using rude expressions about church bells, saints' images, pilgrimage, purgatory and the claim that the Pope could release souls from the latter on the payment of money. Dissent was sometimes expressed in coarse, home-made terminology. One heretic called the image on the rood 'Block-almighty'; another, referring to transubstantiation, said that he threshed God Almighty out of straw; a third, hearing the bell in a country steeple, said 'Lo, yonder is a fair bell, an it were to hang about any cow's neck in this town'.

Further important heretical cells existed in the diocese of London, both in the city itself and in the county of Essex.[9] The London chroniclers report a steady succession of offenders going to the stake or doing public penance throughout the reign of Henry VII. Bishop Fitzjames prosecuted at least forty offenders in 1510 and another thirty-seven in 1517, on each of these occasions two relapsed heretics being burned. Of these four victims, three abjured, were reconciled to the Church and then consumed by fire amid the consolations of the faith. Meanwhile in 1514 the affair of Richard Hunne, the heretical merchant who was found hanged in the episcopal prison at St. Paul's, convulsed the city and provoked a crisis between Church and State which we must reserve for another context. This scandal does, however, throw some light upon the position of the Lollards. We cannot doubt that formal heretics as yet constituted a tiny part of the city population, yet the immense uproar which followed the murder shows that the citizens abhorred Bishop Fitzjames and his officials infinitely more than they abhorred a strong suspicion of heresy brought against an otherwise respectable neighbour. And when his chancellor was arrested for the murder, Fitzjames besought Wolsey to help him, 'For assured I am [that] if my chancellor be tried by any twelve men in London, they be so maliciously set in favour of heretical pravity that they will cast and condemn my clerk though he were as innocent as Abel'. And that the bishop did not say this in momentary anger appears from the fact that he repeated it some weeks later in the House of Lords, adding with gross exaggeration that if the obstinate jurymen went unpunished, 'I dare not keep my house for heretics'.

In the years succeeding the death of Richard Hunne a leading figure amongst the activist Lollards in London and Essex was John Hacker, known as 'old father Hacker', a water-bearer of Coleman Street and a convert of some years' standing. About 1520 this man was distributing heretical books at Burford and in 1521, being then also involved with the Buckinghamshire Lollards, was compelled to abjure by the authorities of the diocese of Lincoln. Associated with him, and more prominent in the subsequent years, were John Stacey, also of Coleman Street, and Lawrence Maxwell, of Aldermanbury parish close by. These two were prominent members of the Tilers' and Bricklayers' Company and had wide contacts both inside and outside London. Stacey kept a man in his house 'to write the Apocalypse in English', the costs being met by John Sercot, a grocer. From this Lollard background Stacey and Maxwell graduated in later years to Lutheranism and took a prominent part in distributing imported Lutheran books. Coleman Street itself, though within a few years of Guildhall, was in fact destined to become for many years the centre of various heretical sects. Hacker's group had close connections with the Lollards of Colchester and of Buckinghamshire but its ultimate importance lay in the fact that it provided a ready-made organisation to promote the Lutheran book-trade of the late twenties. Another of Hacker's disciples was the leather-merchant John Tewkesbury, whom Bishop Tunstall persuaded to recant Lollard opinions but who went on to encounter actual Lutheran propaganda in Tyndale's book *The Wicked Mammon*, copies of which he proceeded to sell to others. Robert Necton, another Londoner who sold imported books in and around London, also had previous connections with the Lollards accused before Bishop Longland of Lincoln in 1521. By the mid-twenties the situation in the London diocese had become so notorious that Tunstall and his successor Stokesley were forced to attempt an extensive purge. Between 1527 and 1532 more than 200 heretics are alleged by Foxe (who gives the names and particulars) to have abjured after conviction in the diocesan courts. Of these people about half came from the city and half from Colchester, Steeple Bumpstead, Birdbrook and other places in Essex. By this time substantial foreign influences had begun to merge with Lollardy, yet the evidence strongly suggests that the old English heresy remained for years afterwards the basic, perhaps the predominant, element. Such few commendations of Lutheranism as we find in these circles prove no more than that Lollards had recognised kindred teachings in the German heresiarch and that they derived courage from the news that orthodox beliefs and ceremonies were being abolished overseas.

In Kent, especially around Tenterden, Cranbrook and Benenden, several Lollard communities were denounced to Archbishop Warham, who in 1511–12 received nearly fifty abjurations and delivered five offenders to the secular arm for burning. Here Foxe receives detailed support from the unusually informative register kept by the Archbishop.[10]

One of the less specific stories of Foxe concerns a 'glorious and sweet society of faithful favourers' in Berkshire. This had existed for some fifteen years when, soon after 1500, six or seven score of its members were forced to abjure at Newbury and three or four burned. Foxe obviously knew very little about this community but the diocesan registers of Salisbury show various penances done by Berkshire Lollards in 1499, eight cases being recorded for Reading, six in and around Faringdon, five in Wantage and one at Hungerford.[11] In the west Midlands, Coventry maintained its former pre-eminence. Foxe, who had lived there, gives a very precise account of seven 'godly martyrs', including a widow, who in 1519 suffered burning.[12] One of the fugitives from this group was captured on his return and so went to the stake alone. Concerning this and other west Midland groups, the discovery at Lichfield of a court book of Bishop Geoffrey Blythe has added substantial information.[13] In 1511–12 about seventy-four heretics (a third of them women) appeared before the diocesan court and their names include some given by Foxe. A few also came from Birmingham where the congregation may have been an offshoot of the larger one at Coventry. One of the Birmingham offenders is said to have associated with many heretics in Bristol, and some scattered references to heresy in this latter city occur elsewhere. To the late efflorescence of the Lollard heresy in the towns and cloth-making districts of Yorkshire and Nottinghamshire we shall shortly return.

Our sources afford much information on the social status of the Lollards. All save a few belonged to the common people—weavers, wheelwrights, smiths, carpenters, shoemakers, tailors and other tradesmen, 'of whom', writes Foxe, 'few or none were learned, being simple labourers and artificers, but as it pleased the Lord to work in them knowledge and understanding by reading a few English books, such as they could get in corners'. Craftsmen and town-workers bulk larger than mere husbandmen; as a class they were more mobile and enjoyed more contacts inside and outside their various trades. A small handful of secular priests, an odd friar and a schoolmaster also appear, while in London some merchants and middle-class men became involved. Of the four London heretics who resorted to a conference at Amersham, one was a goldsmith and one, Thomas Grove, a well-off butcher, able to give no less than £20 to Dr. Wilcocks, vicar general of the diocese of London, to avoid doing open penance. In general, however, the social background bore much resemblance to that of the seventeenth-century congregational dissent to which late Lollardy had such marked religious affinities. Of these people many must have been unable to read, yet illiteracy was then quite compatible with a measure of doctrinal and scriptural knowledge. Some of the Buckinghamshire heretics knew the *Epistle of St. James* by heart; this practical, down-to-earth book was a general favourite amongst Lollards, though the *Apocalypse* certainly nourished their visionary moods. Not a few were specifically charged with possessing, reading and hearing the vernacular Scriptures. Of other suspect works we hear most of *The Wycket*, though all English books, even the more innocent-seeming *Prick of Conscience* and the *Shepherd's Calendar*, tended to bring suspicion upon proletarian owners.

Without question, the influence of Lollardy extended beyond those areas where organised Lollard congregations existed. As already suggested, the diocesan records at York have recently yielded numerous hitherto unknown trials for heresy under Henry VIII and Mary. This enormous diocese comprised Yorkshire, Nottinghamshire and, until 1541, parts of Westmorland, Cumberland and Lancashire. In general, it can be described as conservative in religion and social outlook; certainly it contained none of the major centres of heresy. Between 1500 and 1528 records of only three cases of Lollard heresy have been discovered, though this low figure is doubtless due in part to the absence of diocesan act books during this period. Here, however, such cases may still have remained rare in that the Lollard 'revival', so apparent in many other parts of England, may not have spread to the North during the first two decades of the century. Whatever be the case, from 1528 the recorded situation alters and by the end of the reign about thirty cases of heresy appear, some in the registers proper but most in the act books of the court of audience, which effectively survive from 1534. Only in three cases amongst all these does the least sign of Lutheran or Zwinglian belief occur, and of these two concern priests. The rest, all of them involving proletarian offenders, continue to exhibit conventional Lollard beliefs and in no detail would the groups of charges seem out of place in a record dating from the year 1510, or indeed from 1410. By this second half of the reign of Henry VIII everyone had heard of Luther, yet this did not make every heretic a Lutheran, let alone an informed Lutheran.

The northern heretics during the later years of Henry VIII afford a spectacle of surprising complexity. Old Wycliffite tenets are beginning to merge with the new continental beliefs; meanwhile the crude radicalism, to which we have already alluded, repeatedly asserts itself, but almost always as an obvious derivative from well-known Lollard teachings. One man, objecting to saints' days, made ill-mannered aspersions on the moral character of St. Mary Magdalen but was so unwise as to broadcast them under the parson's window by the church of All Saints, North Street, York. Another case is that of William Bull, a young clothworker from Dewsbury, who went off to ply his craft in Suffolk and returned in 1543 with violent if now old-established views on holy water, extreme unction and the confessional. 'The font', he remarked, 'is but a stinking tarn, and he had rather be christened in the running river than in the said tarn, standing stinking by half a year, for when God made the world, he hallowed both water and land.' And why, he continued in substance, should I confess to the priest when I have 'japed' a fair woman? If he got the chance, the knavish priest would always be ready to use her the same way. But if I recite the creed and confess directly to God, calling to God with a sorry heart for my offence, God will forgive me. This is not only the authentic proletarian accent; if a trifle coarsely illustrated, it is also a true expression of Lollardy. Such authenticity did not, however, amuse the judges of the court of audience at York. The plain-spoken young man suffered a spell in the unsavoury archiepiscopal prison and after his recantation was doubtless glad to keep his pungent views to himself.

John Foxe tended overmuch to see Lollardy through prim Elizabethan eyes and to see it as a local phenomenon involving organised and informed groups with clear-cut beliefs. In certain areas such groups admittedly existed, yet outside them heretical ideas circulated freely about the country-side, in the cities and ports, in the little weaving-towns. These ideas were widely held, sometimes by people without special claims to piety, often by those who lacked pretensions to any heretical system of belief. Their importance may well have lain in their ability to sharpen in many minds the vaguer but widely diffused anticlericalism of the age, for whatever Lollardy involved it always involved anticlericalism. Such an atmosphere was described in the court at York by Richard Flynte, parish clerk of Topcliffe in the North Riding, who had refused to confess to his priest from 1540 to 1542. Charged with this offence, he admitted 'he was not confessed by the said time, saying the cause moving him to the same was that there was a saying in the country, that a man might lift up his heart and confess himself to God Almighty, and needed not to be confessed at a priest'. When the judges, anxious to trace the disseminators of this old saying, asked from whom he had heard it, Flynte replied 'that as he shall make answer to God, he knoweth not, nor yet in what place'. Likewise in Bishop Fisher's register, the Rochester joiner John Dissenger is found to remark, 'I have heard say in the city of London that we should not worship saints, but God only ... also I have heard say that a man should not show his confessor all his sins that he had done.[14] It seems of real significance that such opinions were circulating even in the slow-moving areas, while Henry VIII continued staunchly to uphold the confessional. Certainly it would be an exaggeration to call such men as Flynte and Dissenger Lollards, or to suppose them converts to Lutheran novelties. Such old heresies had been floating in solution, now here, now there, for generations; they had been attracting people because of the desire of many laymen (and indeed of some priests) to be free of hierarchical control and canon law, to become resonsible for their own souls before God. As for Lollardy, the prime mover of this shifting world, it boasted its congregations, its preachers, even its heroes, yet in general it was an evasive, unheroic and underground affair. It lay far too low in society to achieve a Reformation unaided, yet through this very fact it could avoid obliteration by the judicial machinery of Church and State.

We have suggested that late Lollardy suffered grave disadvantages by its lack of national organisation. On the other hand, the inference should not be made that the scattered Lollard areas lacked means of inter-communication. Lollardy had its missionaries, one of whom we have already encountered in the person of John Hacker. A still better example is that of Thomas Man, who in March 1518 suffered burning at Smithfield as a relapsed heretic.[15] As early as 1511 he had been imprisoned by Bishop Smyth of Lincoln for denying transubstantiation, auricular confession, extreme unction and image-worship. Man was also alleged to have claimed that the holy men of his own sect were priests, that pulpits were lying-stools and that the popish Church was not the Church of God but a synagogue. After a long term in the episcopal prison he recanted and underwent further confinement for penance in Osney Abbey. Contriving in due course to escape from the diocese of Lincoln he lived among the Lollards of Suffolk and Essex, but this area seems to have formed merely a base for his missionary sorties. At the time of his second trial and conviction a witness testified that Man had 'been in divers places and countries in England, and had instructed very many, as at Amersham, at London, at Billericay, at Chelmsford, at Stratford-Langthorne, at Uxbridge, at Burnham, at Henley-on-Thames, in Suffolk and Norfolk, at Newbury and divers places more'. Man himself confessed that at Windsor he had discovered a Lollard group formed by fugitives from the persecutions at Amersham, 'a godly and great company, which had continued in that doctrine and teaching twenty-three years'. From this and other clues we can deduce that certain periods at least saw a flow of information and ideas between the communities of Buckinghamshire, of East Anglia, of London and the Thames Valley. Tudor provincial society contained large mobile elements and the part played by wandering cloth-workers in the dissemination of heresy has already been observed. The case of the young Yorkshireman William Bull suggests how the counties of Suffolk, Essex and Kent (where both native and continental heresies flourished in the reign of Henry VIII) were `enabled to stir up sympathy in remoter and more conservative parts of England. Actual contagion as well as similarity of background seems to account for the fact that in Yorkshire late Lollardy and early Protestantism both became prominent in the clothing-areas of the West Riding and especially in Halifax and Leeds.

Connections between Lollardy and Lutheranism

What evidence can be found of contact between the Lollard groups and early Lutheranism? How often did the Lutheran book-agents, who were active in England from the late twenties, find backers in people with established Lollard affinities? Considering the secret character of these transactions, it is surprising how many instances of them can be produced. We have already found substantial examples of transition from Lollardy to Lutheranism in the Coleman Street group centred around the persons of Hacker, Stacey and Maxwell. Many others can be added. The chief vehicle of early Lutheranism was Tyndale's New Testament of 1526 which, printed in Antwerp, was soon finding eager buyers among the native dissenters. In 1527 an Essex Lollard, John Tyball of Steeple Bumpstead, related in court how he and a friend had visited that leading colporteur, the Augustinian friar Robert Barnes, in order to acquire a copy. In Barnes' chamber at the Austin Friars in London they found several callers including a merchant reading a book. They hastened to establish their bona fides with Barnes and related how they had begun to win over the curate of Steeple Bumpstead to their views. They even produced a copy of their old Lollard manuscript-Bible:

> ... certain old books that they had: as of four Evangelists, and certain epistles of Peter and Paul in English. Which books the said friar did little regard, and made a twit of it, and said, 'A point for them, for that they be not to be regarded toward [i.e. compared with] the new printed Testament in English, for it is of more cleaner English.'

Barnes proved himself a competent salesman, and he ended by inducing them to buy a copy of Tyndale's version for 3s. 2d. (about a week's wage for a skilled craftsman) 'and desired them that they would keep it close'.[16]

From what he calls a 'register' of Bishop Longland dated 1530 Foxe collected a story indicating a different aspect of the contact between Lollards and Lutheranism. In the house of John Taylor of Hughenden a group of eleven men, mainly from West Wycombe and Chesham, had met to hear one Nicholas Field of London who had recently been in Germany and had returned with fascinating reports. He first 'read a parcel of Scripture in English unto them', and then

> expounded to them many things; as that they that went on pilgrimage were accursed: that it booted not to pray to images, for they were but stocks made of wood, and could not help a man: that God Almighty biddeth us work as well one day as another, saving the Sunday; for six days he wrought, and the seventh day he rested: that they needed not to fast so many fasting days, except the ember days; for he was beyond the sea in Almany, and there they used not so to fast, nor to make such holy days.

Field also asserted that monetary offerings to the Church did no good and were not needed by their recipients. When one of his audience objected that offerings maintained God's service, he replied, 'Nay, they maintain great houses, as abbeys and others.' He then went on to declare that men should say the Paternoster, the Ave Maria and the Creed in English, and again that 'the sacrament of the altar was not, as it was pretended, the flesh, blood and bone of Christ; but a sacrament, that is, a typical signification of his holy body.'[17] With the single exception of this last expression (which suggests Zwingli, perhaps *via* Tyndale), there is very little in Field's discourse which a Lollard audience can have found novel. We are left wondering how much Lutheran theology an agent like Field had in fact absorbed. Was he a Lollard who had merely acquired a superficial smattering of the continental ideas or did he in fact expound the central Lutheran doctrine of Justification by Faith, only to have it forgotten by these country Lollards who remembered the more familiar elements of his teaching? In his case, we shall presumably remain ignorant of the precise situation, but that some men of heretical leanings did establish direct yet wholly superficial contacts with Lutheranism can be illustrated from other anecdotes.

The diocesan records of Lincoln contain an interesting narrative concerning a group of Hull seamen, which helps to illustrate these mental complexities of the transition.[18] After returning in 1527 from a long visit to Netherlandish and German ports, these men talked too much and fell under suspicion of heresy, yet their examinations show that they had only skimmed the surfaces of continental heresy. In the words of one, they tarried five weeks in Bremen and found that 'The people did follow Luther's works, and no masses were said there, but on the Sunday the priest would revest himself and go to the altar, and proceeded till nigh the sacring time, and then the priest and all that were in the church, old and young, would sing after their mother tongue, and there was no sacring.' Asked whether he had visited Germany to learn Luther's opinions, this man answered: 'Nay, and they were not nigh Luther, not by fifty Dutch miles.' There are hints indeed that some of these seamen had already acquired an interest in unorthodox ideas before their visit to Germany, yet once there they had seemingly learned little about Lutheran doctrine. This type of contact is precisely what one would expect to find on the popular level. Yet one of them had acquired a copy of Tyndale's recently published New Testament and it seems probable that such a man would begin to understand continental Protestantism from the prefaces which Tyndale attached to the scriptural text.

As our examples have indicated, the old heresy and the new began to merge together from about the time Tyndale's Testament came into English hands. From this stage onward the turmoil of anti-Catholic teachings prevalent in Germany began to be paralleled in England, and if we seek to tabulate and classify individual heretics by means of neat textbook-labels we are clearly parting from realities. One cannot tabulate the waves of the sea. Nevertheless, for decades after the coming of Lutheranism, numerous prosecutions took place in the ecclesiastical courts, during which the accused exhibited a whole group of very characteristic Lollard beliefs and showed no sign whatsoever of the justificatory and sacramental teachings peculiar to Luther or Zwingli. In 1541 the English merchant Richard Hilles told the Swiss Reformer Bullinger that a young man supposedly burned for Lutheran heresies had in fact held the opinions of 'our Wycliffe'.[19] In the exceptionally well-documented diocese of York the prevalence of this neo-Lollardy remains marked not only throughout the later years of Henry VIII but even in the reign of Mary. One of the Marian offenders is even charged with the *crimen Lollardiae*, which in this official context probably represents something more precise than the vulgar equation of 'loller' with 'heretic'. Though this situation may be especially characteristic of heresy in the remoter and more conservative provinces, where Anglican and other modern Protestant forces were slow to infiltrate, the late survival of Lollardy even in London and south-eastern England has been spontaneously noticed by more than one local historian. Though Amersham gave a warm welcome to John Knox when he visited the place in the reign of Edward VI, the former Lollard areas of Buckinghamshire tended to resist both Anglicanism and Calvinism during the days of Elizabeth; instead they proceeded to evolve a congregational dissent bearing the suggestion of local continuity from the medieval past. In various parts of East Anglia and south-eastern England, even in the North at Halifax, a strongly Puritan or dissenting tradition seems to show continuity of growth from local mid-Tudor radicalism based mainly on Lollardy.

Though the survival of Wycliffite elements can thus be traced in the annals of English dissent into and beyond the reign of Mary, their latest manifestations lack any great significance in our national history. By 1530 they had already accomplished their two main services to the Reformation. In the first place fifteenth-century Lollardy helped to exclude the possibility of Catholic reforms by hardening the minds of the English bishops and their officials into a sterile, negative and rigid attitude toward all criticism and toward the English Scriptures. The predicament of Bishop Fitzjames amongst his unaffectionate flock of Londoners forms no more than an extreme example of a widespread situation. If their fear of heretics impelled them to refuse even the legitimate aspirations of a new age, the bishops would become more dependent than ever upon the King, and he more than ever enabled to bend them to his will. The second and more important function of the Lollards in English history lay in the fact that they provided a spring-board of critical dissent from which the Protestant Reformation could overleap the walls of orthodoxy. The Lollards were the allies and in some measure the begetters of the anticlerical forces which made possible the Henrician revolution, yet they were something more, and the successes of Protestantism seem not wholly intelligible without reference to this earlier ground-swell of popular dissent. The Lollards demonstrably provided reception-areas for Lutheranism. They preserved, though often in crude and mutilated forms, the image of a personal, scriptural, non-sacramental, non-hierarchic and lay-dominated religion. For good or ill, these emphases were prophetic. On the other hand, such a sect almost inevitably fell victim to its own qualities. Its hostility to institutions led many of its adherents or potential adherents into negativism, unbelief and incoherence. Moreover its apparent threat to social and ecclesiastical stability deprived it of power to capture the ruling classes. A Bible-religion, it lacked access to the printing presses until after 1530. So limited and debarred, it could become no more than an abortive Reformation. It created an underground and there awaited the appearance of liberators. When liberation finally came, it was compelled, like any underground resistance, to yield the leadership to regular armies with heavier and more modern equipment.

That Lollardy thus survived and contributed in some significant degree toward the Protestant Reformation is a fact based upon incontrovertible evidence. This was, moreover, the impression of informed contemporaries. At the moment when the gradual transition to Protestantism was beginning, no one knew more of these matters than Bishop Tunstall. When in 1528 he licensed Sir Thomas More to read heretical books, Tunstall coupled the two heresies together: 'There have been found certain children of iniquity who are endeavouring to bring into our land the old and accursed Wycliffite heresy, and along with it the Lutheran heresy, foster-daughter of Wycliffe's.'[20] But five years earlier he had put the matter more directly and accurately in a letter to Erasmus: 'It is no question of pernicious novelty; it is only that new arms are being added to the great crowd of Wycliffite heresies.'[21] And that the clergy in general were still concerned with the old heresies as late as 1536 may easily be ascertained by a perusal of the *mala dogmata* then alleged by Convocation 'to be commonly preached, taught and spoken ... to the slander of this noble realm, disquietness of the people, damage of Christian souls, not without fear of many other inconveniences and perils.'[22] This long list of evil doctrines proves on examination little more than a splendid anthology of old-established Lollard opinions, mostly given in the crude terms of uneducated heretics. By no stretch of the imagination can the list of *mala dogmata* be thought an anti-Lutheran or anti-Zwinglian document. To the recent advent of Anabaptist doctrines, then limited to foreign immigrants, it may refer under two or three heads, but this element also remains subordinate. Altogether, if the English clergy were perturbed in 1536 by any doctrines save those of neo-Lollardy, they made extremely little of the fact. Conversely, by this time Protestant intellectuals had begun to see Lollard writings as serviceable additions to their arsenal of Reformation-propaganda.[23] Between 1530 and the death of Henry VIII, at last nine Wycliffite treatises are known to have been set forth in print by Gough, Redman, Bale and other publicists, who preceded Foxe in realising the usefulness of a religious pedigree, especially one of an all-English character.

4 Scenes from Clerical Life

Wolsey and Rome

When Henry VIII quarrelled with Pope Clement VII over his proposed divorce, the Church of England lay like a broad, rich and somewhat defenceless province between the contending hosts of Crown and Papacy. But long before the first shots of this campaign had been fired, the members of the English Church itself had also become locked in a series of tensions ostensibly related little to the main struggle but in the end exercising no small influence upon its result. Of such internal maladjustments the most spectacular and the most recent were those occasioned by the truly fabulous career of Thomas Wolsey, for whom the mass of Englishmen, clerical as well as lay, had developed an intense dislike. His tactlessness and financial demands in Parliament, his repression of the nobility, his development of Chancery jurisdiction at the expense of the influential common lawyers, his costly and ineffective foreign policy, his failure to execute radical reforms in the Church, his voracious appetite for other clergymen's privileges, the Roman basis of his authority as Legate, each of these features attracted powerful enemies. Above all, his personal arrogance, his enormous wealth and splendid ostentation were resented and freely contrasted with his origin as the butcher's son from East Anglia. To an increasing extent Wolsey's policy became based upon his legatine office; in England the justification for his unique powers would disappear the moment he ceased being able to manipulate papal jurisdiction. Hence he strove to keep Rome out of hostile hands, or at least to stand well with whichever European power might threaten to dominate the Papacy. And when at last in 1527–8 his King demanded of him the supreme act of manipulation, his fatal moment had arrived, for it so happened that another hand was now inexorably closing upon the controls—the hand of the Queen's nephew, the Emperor Charles V. Though the enormous concentration of secular and ecclesiastical powers in the hands of the Lord Chancellor and Cardinal Legate came to offend the whole nation, the unprecedented extent of his legatine privileges gave rise to a special hatred amongst churchmen. The intensity of this feeling is but thinly disguised by their servile respect. He was not even Archbishop of Canterbury, but as *legatus a latere*, a special envoy of the Holy See, he had elevated a vast range of emergency powers into a permanent system centred upon his own person and offices. He could reform all clergy however eminent, reduce them to honest living, correct, chastise and punish them by himself or by deputy; he could grant degrees in theology, arts and medicine, dispense with canonical impediments to holy orders, appoint to benefices, legitimise bastards, absolve people from excommunication and other ecclesiastical sentences and penalties: all this notwithstanding any former restrictions placed upon legatine authority. Never had such a tyranny been seen in the English Church. It was small wonder that the University of Oxford addressed Wolsey as *majestas*; small wonder again that the chronicler of Butley Priory, one of the last of our monastic annalists, wrote of *gaudium humanum*, when at last he heard that the upstart from nearby Ipswich had died in disgrace.[1] And while in fact ecclesiastics were the main sufferers under Wolsey's system, it provided also a lurid theme for anticlerical demagogues, who did not stop to reflect that the King must bear chief responsibility for this portentous phenomenon. Of course, though here we must criticise Wolsey as a churchman, we ought never to forget that he was also a great servant of the state. The value of his personal achievement in developing the Star Chamber is now generally acknowledged.[2] In Wolsey's favour it should also be noted that he lacked persecuting zeal; again that he was undeniably intelligent and thus probably well aware of his own moral shortcomings.

Whatever its ultimate causes, the misuse of ecclesiastical wealth and privilege provided a heavy bludgeon to beat churchmen. Here Wolsey had not behaved with conspicuous tact. His natural son Thomas Wynter while still a schoolboy was dean of Wells, provost of Beverley, archdeacon of York, archdeacon of Richmond, chancellor of Salisbury, prebendary of Wells, York, Salisbury, Lincoln and Southwell, rector of Rudby in Yorkshire and of St. Matthew's, Ipswich. And to make the youth a trifle more secure as he grew up, he was handed further preferments until his annual revenues amounted to about £2,700, then over 250 times the income of a poor country parson.[3] It is true that his father prudently retained much of this fantastic income in his own hands leaving Thomas to live upon an allowance of £200, yet even this represented the income of a well-off landowner.

Wolsey's career exerted a dramatic influence upon that of Archbishop William Warham and hence upon the initial crisis of the English Reformation. A typical civil service prelate, Warham had in 1504 been promoted to Canterbury over the head of the more distinguished Richard Fox. This move to secure a subservient primate had distant repercussions which would have surprised its author Henry VII, since Warham's respectable mediocrity is among the important negative factors of our story. Flattered as an intellectual leader by the adroit Erasmus, he patronised humanists without participating in their scholarship. A considerable nepotist in his own right, he displayed no sense of urgency over Church-reform at a stage when reform need not have entailed revolution. From 1515 the jurisdiction of

Canterbury was in large part superseded by Wolsey's legatine powers, and during the next 15 years Warham seemed even in his own eyes the mere shadow of an archbishop. As a long-standing devotee of Thomas Becket, he conceived on Wolsey's fall an ambition to tread the perilous path of his martyred predecessor, yet his resolution proved fleeting. At the moment of its confrontation by the naked force of the temporal power, the English Church had at its head no Becket to fight for its ancient privileges, but an old and broken man bred in the service of the King and long inured to personal impotence.[4]

As the manager of Roman authority in England, Wolsey undoubtedly stimulated the dislike of his fellow Englishmen for Roman jurisdiction. When Wolsey was hated, inevitably some measure of that hatred became directed against Rome. 'All his grandeur', wrote Wolsey's colleague Cardinal Campeggio, 'is connected with the authority of the Holy See.' Accordingly the outbursts of a hostile but still Catholic nobility were directed against Roman legates and cardinals in general. When on his fall he wailed to the Duke of Norfolk, 'My authority and dignity legatine is gone, wherein consisted all my high honour', the Duke was swift to answer, 'A straw for your legacy! I never esteemed your honour the more or higher for that.' Lord Darcy, though ardent in his attachment to the old faith, proposed a statute that no further legate should ever be admitted to the country. The Duke of Suffolk was mutton-headed enough to express the viewpoint of less exalted people: 'It was never merry in England while we had cardinals among us!'[5]

This attitude cannot be attributed solely to the malign influence of Wolsey. In English eyes the decline of papal prestige since the Avignon Captivity and the Great Schism had not been repaired by the triumph of the Popes over the Conciliar Movement. Even Sir Thomas More doubted in earlier life the arguments for the Papal Supremacy over the Church, and he claimed to have been reconverted by the King himself in that famous royal book against Luther. Though there is no evidence that ordinary Englishmen spent their time grieving over the sins of the Borgias, there were those who, like Wolsey's own secretary Richard Pace, saw Rome at first hand and were duly shocked. Cuthbert Tunstall, one of the most doctrinally conservative of Henry VIII's bishops, resented papal taxation and remembered witnessing the overweening pride of Julius II: 'I saw myself, being then present thirty-four years ago, when Julius, then being bishop of Rome, stood on his feet and one of his chamberlains held up his skirt, because it stood not as he thought with his dignity that he should do it himself, that his shoe might appear, while a nobleman of great age prostrated himself upon the ground and kissed his shoe.'[6]

While the love-hate complex of educated Englishmen toward Italy may perhaps already have been operating at the expense of the Papacy, we should attach far more significance to that ingrained chauvinism of the common people, which had blazed up so often in medieval London and which again so savagely displayed itself in the 'Evil May-day' riots of 1517. This indiscriminate emotion could readily turn, or be turned, against any foreign power. When Rome fell in 1527, alleges Hall, 'the King was sorry and so were many prelates: but the commonalty little mourned for it, and said the Pope was a ruffian, and was not meet for the room: wherefore they said that he began the mischief, and so he was well served'.[7] Such a mentality did not represent serious thinking about the Papal supremacy, yet it must have provided fertile ground for the later suggestions of the London anticlerical pamphleteer Simon Fish, that the realm had for centuries 'stood tributary unto a cruel devilish bloodsupper' at Rome.

Whatever may have been the case in the remote reign of Henry III, this financial charge was quite untrue in the time of Wolsey. Peter's Pence, the only papal tax paid by the laity, amounted to less than £200 annually for the whole of England. The clergy paid larger, yet still far from astronomical, taxes. About twenty religious corporations yielded a regular *census* in return for privileges granted by Rome, while some 500 bodies, including cathedral chapters and religious houses, paid very small sums as 'procurations' or wages to the papal collectors. Much more important was the fluctuating income accruing to Rome from clergy who received papal provisions to benefices. In the cases of the bishops and great abbots a whole series of payments and fees became due under this head, the chief being annates or first-fruits. Between 1485 and 1533 the average annual total of all these, and some other minor taxes, stood at about £4,800. The hypocrisy, conscious or otherwise, of the Acts which abolished these 'intolerable and importable' payments, became manifest when Henry VIII, the new head of the English Church, proceeded vastly to increase its financial burdens. Whereas on the eve of the Henrician changes King and Pope together collected about £17,300 annually from the national Church, the King between 1535 and 1547 probably amassed an annual sum in the region of £47,000.[8] That the clergy were not in fact ruined, that a large part of this money came from richly beneficed clerics and that the real value of these payments had fallen rapidly with the inflation, these facts must also be conceded. All the same, it remains impossible to regard the early Tudor Church as a milch-cow of the Papacy or to deny that its 'liberation' from Rome resulted in a new and heavier financial bondage.

The Bishops and Higher Clergy

Somewhat outside the intoxicating world of Wolsey and his favourites stood the bishops, many of whom were, or had been, important civil servants, ambassadors and royal councillors. They had commonly spent their best years working for the King—somewhat uneasily, it is true, for several tried to make amends by spending their last years in their dioceses. After Richard Fox had been supplanted at court by Wolsey he passed the last twelve years of his life at Winchester. He wrote to Wolsey in 1517 that he had utterly renounced 'meddling with worldly matters, specially concerning the war or anything to it appertaining: whereof of the many intolerable enormities that I have seen ensue by the said war in time past, I have no little remorse in my conscience, thinking that if I did continual penance for it all the days of my life, though I should live twenty years longer than I may do, I could not yet make sufficient recompense therefor'. Yet how difficult Fox sometimes found this renunciation of the great world! Within a few days he confesses to Wolsey that he is forever thinking of state affairs, as if 'I were daily attending upon you in the King's Council'.[9] Even so, despite the conspicuous exception of Wolsey, 'Caesarian' bishops and deans tended to become less numerous after the accession of Henry VIII, while recent research has discovered in at least three dioceses—Chichester, Ely and Lincoln—a spirit of zeal and reform largely but by no means solely directed toward the technicalities of administration. It remains true that only one of the many bishops appointed on the eve of the Reformation emerges as a major religious character. This was John Fisher, who detested Wolsey and adorned the poorest see in England, that of Rochester, from 1504 until his martyr's death in 1535. Far more typical of the abler Henrician bishops is John Longland, an upright, zealous prelate of markedly conservative views, who strove with dedication against clerical indiscipline and Lollardy, dying in 1547 still very much master of his huge diocese.[10] Faced by their grand households, which had given offence to medieval moralists, we should be aware that the facts of geography compelled a zealous bishop with a large diocese to maintain numerous houses, while all diocesans were expected to dispense traditional hospitality and patronage as peers of the realm. Their political and economic independence was menaced by kings, magnates and even mobs during the civil strife of the fifteenth century, while in time of peace the conventionally pious Henry VII had not hesitated to burden several bishoprics by imposing legalistic financial forfeitures. Under Henry VIII the bishops and other senior clergy remained appointees of the Crown and proved habitually responsive to its pressures.[11] Apart from Fisher, they gave the King no trouble when in the 1530s he staged his Royal Supremacy. In addition the continuance of Lollardy froze the bishops in their magisterial postures, most especially in regard to the growing demand for easier access to the Scriptures. As we shall observe, when William Tyndale begged Bishop Tunstall to subvent his translation of the Bible into English, he received a refusal. Thus compelled to execute the task abroad, Tyndale could present intelligent lay people with a formidable challenge, when he argued (in print) that the bishops were still excluding the laity from what they were now beginning to see as the most authentic record of the Christianity of Christ.

Modern historians of the Middle Ages, who often take medieval religion as the Christian norm, sometimes seek to justify the late medieval and early Tudor bishops by pointing to their creditable administrative performance. Yet amid the flow of ideas from 1520 onwards this criterion became ever less relevant. A hierarchy which excelled in diocesan administration but took little direct part in Christian teaching was no longer responding to the expectations of the younger scholars, the educated urban classes and a growing body of more or less literate craftsmen. The world was moving on.

To Lutherans, Erasmians and Lollards alike, mere disciplinary and administrative reforms now seemed insignificant in comparison with preaching and with nourishment at the biblical fountainhead of the Faith. The secular tasks of the bishops did not, however, represent one of the more overt ecclesiastical tensions; neither does the occupation of English sees by foreign absentees. That of Worcester, it is true, was held successively by four Italians from 1497 to 1534; but this situation cannot be paralleled elsewhere during the same period. Apart from the small Lollard minority, who rejected episcopal authority outright, the mass of Englishmen were ostensibly hardened to the absentee system by centuries of usage. Their absences and their grandeur doubtless offended moralists like Gascoigne and Colet, yet there appears little evidence that such factors occasioned public resentment between the accession of Henry VII and the rise of Protestantism half a century later. It seems likely enough that the early Tudor bishops, freed from the ugly partisanship which had marked the Wars of the Roses, enjoyed more esteem than their predecessors.

While the bishops spent so much time on secular business, their dioceses did not in fact go untended. They delegated their spiritual functions to suffragan bishops, who in the early Tudor years were numerous; in almost every see they are found confirming, consecrating and ordaining. These were relatively humble figures, often friars and graduates in theology. The bishop's chancellor, a graduate in civil or canon law, was his chief legal adviser and by this time normally held in addition the office of official principal, presiding as such over the consistory court of the diocese. The sequestrator-general or commissary-general was the collector of the bishop's spiritual income, an important part of which arose from sequestrated benefices—those which fell into the bishop's hand during vacancies or when legal coercion was being applied to their refractory holders. Many dioceses had a sequestrator in each archdeaconry. The bishop's temporal revenues, forming a more substantial part of his income, needed their own hierarchy of stewards, bailiffs and receivers. Outside this very self-sufficient secretariat, the galaxy of episcopal, archidiaconal and peculiar courts ground through their ancient routines, keeping the morals of all men under observation; their notaries scribbled down the sins and quarrels of society in spidery hands across those countless thousands of pages with which modern historians are gradually becoming more familiar. The system was hard, mechanical and institutional. It held every temptation to avarice and careerism, and the lavish rewards, whether in the King's service or in that of a bishop, went to clerics who were primarily lawyers by training and never concerned themselves in any real sense with the cure of souls. It would not necessarily have been humanised by the more frequent presence of the bishops, since they stood far less close to their clergy and people than do their modern counterparts. Despite their heavy expenditure in the royal service most diocesan bishops were wealthy lords, each with several residences, a host of underlings and a long rent-roll. The curtailment of episcopal revenues under the Tudors was no doubt carried to excessive lengths, yet it probably benefited the spiritual health of the Church. And had the surplus revenues, together with the monastic lands, been more constructively employed by the Crown, England could have been made a charitable and educational Elysium.

The behaviour of the English bishops during the Henrician schism seems in no small degree to have been conditioned by their academic backgrounds, and most had undergone legal training. Of the lawyers, a small minority were canonists and by far the greater part had taken degrees in the civil law. Here lay perhaps the gravest weakness in the spiritual leadership of the English Church and one of the reasons why its whole thinking became pervaded with legalism and denuded of missionary spirit. This civilian emphasis harmonised admirably with the bureaucratic and diplomatic employment of the bishops; more important, it helps to explain why, almost to a man, they followed King Henry when he severed relations with the Papacy. They were already well attuned to the claims of the sovereign State. That the dispute over the Supremacy did not seem to them primarily one of doctrinal import may be seen in the active adherence to the royal cause of conservatives like Gardiner and Bonner, who followed Henry with alacrity but went to prison rather than accept Protestant doctrine under Edward VI. The claims of Caesar failed to alarm men nourished upon Justinian, and even a Royal Supremacy as sweeping as that envisaged by the tendentious theologian on the throne did not lie outside their intellectual orbits. Such academic influences seem to have continued in operation throughout the subsequent years. With the fall of the monasteries the episcopal bench obtained several new recruits in the form of distinguished ex-monks, most of them university-trained theologians. Like the few other theologically-educated bishops these men tended to become Reforming Henricians, while their colleagues trained in the law generally adopted the standpoint of Catholic Henricians. Yet the significant fact remains that both groups marched behind the King.[12]

Just below the bishops, yet towering above the rank and file of the parish clergy, stood a group of civil service pluralists—deans, prebendaries and archdeacons, who dominated the two Convocations and whose unflagging royalism contributed so much to the triumph of the Henrician Reformation. Of these we may take as an example Thomas Magnus, a striking figure in northern administration and diplomacy throughout the half-century preceding his death in 1550 at the age of 87. Born of middle-class parents at Newark, Magnus rose as a protégé of Archbishop Savage and took a doctorate at some foreign university. He held the archdeaconry of the East Riding from 1504 to 1550, a canonry at Windsor from 1520 to 1547 and another at Lincoln from 1521 to 1548. By the mid-thirties he was also master of St. Leonard's Hospital at York, master of the wealthy college of St. Sepulchre's near York Minster, master of Sibthorpe College, Nottinghamshire, vicar of Kendal, rector of Bedale, Kirkby-in-Cleveland and Sessay. At this time his eight benefices in the York diocese alone yielded him the enormous income of £814 per annum. Yet these great emoluments had not been bestowed upon Magnus in vain, for he ranks among the most devoted servants of the dynasty. For a time he served on the Privy Council; he worked as treasurer with the northern armies and participated in at least five diplomatic missions to Scotland, achieving close personal relationships with James V and Queen Margaret.

When in 1525 Henry VIII sent his natural son the Duke of Richmond to be titular head of the Council in the North, Magnus served as that Council's surveyor and receiver-general, rescuing its accounts from the confusion into which lay incapacity had plunged them. He was also the agent who in 1531 impelled the restive northern clergy to pay the King a large fine in order to avoid charges under the Statute of Praemunire. In 1533, now assisted by Bishop Rowland Lee, that indefatigable champion of law and order in Wales and the Marches, Magnus induced the northern Convocation to accept the unpopular royal divorce. Already at this time he wrote that his 'old body is now so oft clogged with infirmity and unwieldiness' and he had already begun to make his peace with a higher Sovereign by founding a grammar school and a song school at Newark. His last years were nevertheless to be spent in the less congenial reign of Edward VI. Despite his untiring devotion to the Crown he can have had little sympathy with Protestantism since, when his will came to be proved, it provided that a chantry should be founded to pray for the souls of his father, mother and sisters. But this clause had now been rendered void by the recent dissolution of all chantries. His executors also failed to gratify his wish to be buried in York Minster beside the superb tomb of his long-dead patron Archbishop Savage. Instead he sleeps beneath a fine portrait brass in the chancel of the parish church of Sessay. Should one wish to sense in one life the inwardness of the Henrician revolution, one should study Thomas Magnus rather than Thomas More.[13]

The Parish Clergy

Turning to those lesser animals within the great ark of the Church, the parish clergy, we observe a body so heterogeneous as to defy generalisation. If they tended to lack spiritual and intellectual distinction, this fact, as both Dean Colet and More forcibly stated, was to some extent the fault of the bishops. 'All who offer themselves', wrote the former, 'are forthwith admitted without hindrance. Hence proceed and emanate those hosts of both unlearned and wicked priests which are in the Church.' 'I wot well', comments More, 'there be therein many very lewd and naught [i.e. wicked]. And surely wheresoever there is a multitude it is not without miracle possible to be otherwise. But now if the bishops would once take into priesthood better laymen and fewer (for of us be they made) all the matter were more than half amended.'[14]

The growing concern felt by the founders of Cambridge colleges for the professional education of the secular clergy has been stressed by Janelle, who also notices the anxiety of many humbler testators to ensure that their pious instructions should be executed only by priests of good moral repute.[15] And by no means all senior ecclesiastics were complacent over the situation. Apart from Colet one of its critics was William Melton, who had been John Fisher's tutor at Michaelhouse, Cambridge, and who served from 1496 until his death in 1528 as chancellor of York Minster. About the year 1510 this learned dignitary published a *Sermo Exhortatorius* on the vexed subject of clerical education and it was accompanied by an *imprimatur* from Colet himself. Melton here stresses the extreme responsibility and dignity of the priest's office, which in these days has been degraded by crowds of rude and stupid clerics. At ordination every aspirant should have a moderate grasp of Latin and be in a position to make further progress merely by private study. Otherwise, experience has shown that he will continue in notorious ignorance to his dying day. Here, declares Melton, lies the reason why so many country clerics take to dicing, drinking, hunting and wenching; if they begin in ignorance, how can they ever profit or delight in sacred studies?[16] This thesis cannot be dismissed as the prejudice of a former don, since Latin was in every respect the gateway to that mental life without which any rural clergyman was more than likely to run to seed. Melton's argument forms a strong indictment of the system whereby the direct study of the Scriptures had been sealed from non-Latinists, while nevertheless numbers of very poor Latinists were permitted to enter holy orders. Despite such strictures, some contemporary diocesan records show bishops ordaining several hundreds of men a year in circumstances apparently excluding the possibility of thorough examination and without due thought to their subsequent employment. Melton writes as if examination were a serious business, but in his own diocese of York the annual total of ordinations rose from 75 in 1453 to 363 in 1508, and continued to rise. In the three years 1515/16/17 there were ordained 546 priests and 644 acolytes, together with 123 regular clergy. Even allowing for short life-expectancy, these seem large figures for a diocese containing less than 900 parishes and chapelries, together with over 400 chantries. The case of York diocese does not however seem to be exceptional. In the diocese of Lincoln 2,609 men were ordained to the secular priesthood from February 1496 to December 1520, and while on paper 2,706 parishes became vacant during that period, a very large number of these were held in plurality, so that nothing approaching that figure became available for the new ordinands.[17] The pressure of benefice-hunters remained high. It should, however, be stressed that on what might be regarded as an average occasion, less than 30 clerics presented themselves before the bishop and serious questioning could well have occurred. The names of the rejected were not registered, but occasionally we hear of a candidate being told to study for a year or so before reappearing. On such issues fragmentary evidence proves little, yet Peter Heath has shown that the cumulative evidence pointing to inadequate selection procedures is much too formidable to be ignored.[18] Nevertheless the educational standards of the parish clergy, though by any reasonable criteria lower than those toward the end of the sixteenth century, did vary to a very considerable extent. The university graduates who sought benefices early in that century were obviously favoured by patrons and had far better chances of promotion in the Church.

While many prominent clergy showed increasing concern for these matters from the early years of the century, Convocation began to propose effective measures only in 1529, when lay interference already loomed large.

While the Church could boast too little by way of vocational selection, many ordinands tended to be thrust into a clerical underworld, since they were ordained without adequate 'title', or spiritual function carrying a financial competence. Again, some clerics lingered permanently in minor orders, lacking the status and most of the functions we now associate with the term clergy, yet still apt to bring discredit on the whole profession. And amongst so large a body of celibates there were inevitably enough sexual lapses to give some substance to the meaner types of anticlerical propaganda. The lurid contrast between the exalted functions of the priesthood and the behaviour of a mundane (and often lightly punished) minority gave genuine offence to the pious as well as dangerous ammunition to the malevolent and the hypocritical.

For many a country parson life on six days of the week was not markedly different from that of a substantial yeoman. He farmed his glebe of forty or sixty acres in the common fields. He ploughed and reaped with his neighbours, and when he drafted his will it was as full of sheep and pigs and wains and sacks of malt as that of any layman. A vicar was paid in kind by the small tithes; he shared with his parishioners in the yield of the land and he suffered its asperity in time of dearth. Both before and after the Reformation tithes nevertheless produced a considerable number of lawsuits and in the aggregate they must have made a marked contribution to popular anticlericalism. A classic exemplar, doubtless unusual in its violence and prolongation, may be found in the quarrel of 1530 between the parishioners of Hayes, Middlesex, and their vicar Henry Gold. For various reasons, Gold also had his backers inside and outside the parish. The matter soon proceeded to large-scale riots and, with the parishioners coming armed to church, the Star Chamber took cognizance of the dispute as a threat to public order. The detail occupies over forty fascinating pages of Sir Geoffrey Elton's *Star Chamber Stories*.[19] Tithes had long lost their personal and quasi-sacred character; even before the Reformation, they were commonly farmed out to laymen and regarded as a mere rent. All things considered, the economic situation of the country priest was by no means richly privileged. While on the one hand he owed no services to the lord of the manor, on the other local custom might expect him to keep a bull and a boar for the use of the parish. His income might be burdened by the pension of a predecessor, which he had agreed to pay before presentation to the living. If his tithes were substantial, he often found them difficult to collect in full and he paid higher taxes than laymen of similar means. In a farming economy his lack of a family may have proved on balance an economic disadvantage.

By no means all the parochial clergy fitted into this pattern. The system of appropriations, once well-intentioned but now so harmful in its results, produced one sort of exception. A religious house to which a benefice was appropriated usually ordained a vicarage, endowing the vicar either with a stipend or with the small tithes and other minor revenues, while itself retaining the greater tithes. It might, especially if it were one of the numerous houses of regular canons, appoint one of its own members to act as vicar. On the other hand, it might appoint a mere unbeneficed chaplain or curate, paying him a small annual salary and thus making him dismissable at the will of the house. Both these latter two procedures seemed to outsiders, especially to critical laymen, modes of exploiting to the last penny the ancient endowments which should have gone to find educated and efficient ministers. In Lincolnshire 311 out of the 628 parochial benefices were appropriated on the eve of the Reformation, while Yorkshire then had about 622 parish churches of which 392 were appropriated. In the latter county the position was probably worse than in any part of England, since of the 392 more than 100 were served by these poor, removable priests in place of vicars.[20]

The monasteries were the most flagrant but by no means the sole converters of parish endowments to new purposes. The Church was little touched by egalitarian concepts and in not a few cases the lucky recipient of several livings had nothing to recommend him save high connections. And while pluralities and non-residence sometimes provided the means whereby young men were enabled to undertake a prolonged university education, such grants were too often unlimited by considerations of need. Notable beneficiaries of the system, such as John Colet and Reginald Pole, came of wealthy families which could easily have provided for their maintenance. The royal physician Thomas Linacre likewise received several rich benefices years before he was even ordained priest.[21] Such cases were nevertheless exceptional. Though in certain episcopal visitation-records the absentees comprise anything between a tenth and a quarter of the total beneficed clergy, the great majority of them were licensed to be absent for what early Tudor opinion considered adequate reasons. Most were bishop's chaplains, diocesan administrators and ecclesiastical lawyers. Others were chaplains to noblemen, clerics afflicted by physical incapacity or licensed to go on a pilgrimage. We naturally hear most of those cases (no doubt a small minority) where parish affairs went badly astray under a neglectful *locum tenens*. And in general we should certainly blame the system rather than the rapacity of individual clerics. It says little for the mental flexibility and the pastoral sense of kings, bishops, founders and patrons that they could evolve no better method for the support of monasteries, clerical officials and students than one liable to injure the spiritual life of the common people. Yet by the same token the failure of their post-Reformation successors to achieve anything more than a slow and piecemeal improvement forms an equally depressing spectacle.

In addition to the poorer vicars and chaplains, the unprivileged section of the late medieval church contained several thousand chantry priests and—especially in the sparsely-populated uplands of the North—priests who served in small chapelries dependent upon a mother church. A chantry was normally a private endowment in real property to ensure masses for the soul of the founder and his kin, but often it had other functions which we propose to discuss at some length in a later chapter. The great majority of these thousands of stipendiary curates, chantry and chapel-priests worked for very small salaries ranging between £4 and £7 per annum: these already represented proletarian incomes and were destined soon to fall swiftly in purchasing power under the stress of inflation. Many rectors and vicars had little more; there was no economic difference between the unbeneficed and the poorest of the beneficed. Of course, some are known to have owned landed property: others had moveable goods in such quantities as to suggest substantial private sources of income. An analysis has been made by Mr. Heath of the annual values attached to parochial livings by the great survey of 1535. In the fairly typical diocese of Coventry and Lichfield there appear 210 rectories and 187 vicarages. Of these 397 livings, 87 per cent were worth less than £20 per annum; 79 per cent less than £15; 60 per cent less than £10 and 10 per cent less than £5. Half the rectories and 72 per cent of the vicarages fell below the £10 level: the level at which, said Latimer a few years later, a parson 'is not able to buy him books, nor give his neighbour drink'.[22]

Observers of the period did not differ concerning the low intellectual quality of an underpaid parish clergy. Archbishop Edward Lee of York wrote to Thomas Cromwell in 1535 that many of his priests were so uneducated that they simply could not understand, let alone accept, the arguments advanced in favour of the Royal Supremacy. 'Doubtless many of our curates can scant perceive it. Many benefices be so exile, of £4, £5, £6, that no learned man will take them, and therefore we be fain to take such as be presented, so they be honest of conversation and can competently understand that they read, and minister sacraments and sacramentals, observing the due form and right.... And in all my diocese I do not know secular priests that can preach, any number necessary for such a diocese, truly not xii, and they that have the best benefices be not here resident.'[23]

Except in London and some neighbouring areas the resident parish clergy contained a minute percentage of graduates; armed with a modest grammar school latinity the average priest learned his job by the empirical methods of apprenticeship. Yet the very varied educational standards of the parish clergy did not necessarily correspond with the values of their benefices. Of this we may cite mid-Tudor examples amongst Archbishop Lee's own clergy. Marmaduke Atkinson, rector of Bainton (a very good living worth £35 per annum) was accused of incompetence in the Archbishop's Court of Audience by his own curate Edmund Pepper. The curate had seen Atkinson lingering at the altar unable to find the gospel for the day. When Pepper at last sent up the parish clerk to show him the place, 'he would not of long time believe it was the gospel for that day, and said unto the clerk that he thought that it had been longer.' Pepper had also heard him read out *nobis* for *vobis* and 'sound the accusative case for the ablative case and one case for another'.[24] At the other extreme in the same diocese there stood the relatively learned Robert Parkyn, whose curacy at Adwick-le-Street afforded him a stipend of less than £6 a year, since it had been appropriated to Hampole Priory. It is fair to remark that this assiduous student and writer inherited some family lands and that his brother, a fellow of Trinity College, Cambridge, sometimes sent him parcels of books by the carrier.[25]

When the time came to propound new schemes of church-government, these lower clergy confronted the government with an important but problematic class. From the viewpoint of Henry VIII they were not as 'safe' as the bishops. The unlearned had the conservatism of immobility, while even the educated, especially outside London and the south-eastern counties, were by no means familiar with books and theories (Erastian, Protestant, humanist, or civilian) conducive to change or even to open-mindedness. And despite their limitations, despite the rancour which often existed between clergy and laity, the former continued to be a key-class upon which at least rural laymen relied in large part for the transmission of ideas. So long as the doctrine of transubstantiation found general acceptance, the humblest or most sinful priest, by whose hands the actual body of God was ministered to the faithful, preserved a certain distinction which set him apart from the common run of men. In the event of his treason this distinction did not, it is true, preserve him from the common hangman's rope and knife, yet the weapon of terror needed to be used but sparingly during the process of the Reformation, since the problem of seditious priests was rendered by various factors less formidable than might have been expected. Not a few of the clergy became involved in treasonable speeches or helped to lead the Pilgrimage of Grace, the Western Rising of 1549 and other rebellious movements. Yet these men constituted a tiny proportion of the whole body. We cannot doubt that a far larger group detested theological and liturgical innovation but nevertheless obeyed governmental orders. Robert Parkyn's narrative of the Reformation shows that he promptly executed commands which he regarded as heretical under Edward VI, while he died in office after a further decade of obedience to the commands of Elizabeth. Tudor government was not primarily concerned to open windows into men's souls and the parish clergy were in general modest and timid men, blessed at least in the sense that they were poor in spirit. Well aware of the limitations of their learning they remained content to follow in the wake of their bishops and archdeacons. They varied widely in their devotion to principles and in their degree of detachment from merely secular calculations. The changes of the age broke upon them but gradually, and during the whole reign of Henry VIII they had to swallow—apart from the overthrow of the Papal Supremacy—no doctrinal changes of substance. As for that Supremacy, the numerous other factors we have already mentioned and the lapse of time since its effective exercise in England continued to weaken its appeal. What little we know of the private thoughts of conservative priests suggest that changes in ritual and in sacramental doctrine, together with the abolition of requiem masses, troubled them far more than the severance of the Roman bond.

Above all, unless they were led by their superiors, the parish clergy had no mechanisms for making protests or planning resistance. In the two Convocations the archdeacons and other *ex-officio* members outnumbered the proctors of the parish clergy, but these proctors also tended in fact to be safe and senior men. The custom-ridden conservatives to whom the sharp-tongued John Bale gave the collective title of Doctor Dodypoll[26] were not potential martyrs for a Catholic ideal. And the upper reaches of the Christian Church have at most periods of its history been well populated by Dodypolls.

The Religious Houses

If until recent years the secular clergy received too little notice from historians of the Reformation, the regulars perhaps received too much. It is indeed easy to overestimate the scale of English monasticism towards the end of the middle ages, since the shell had become too big for the oyster. The huge and romantic piles of masonry left on such sites as those of Fountains and Rievaulx, or such immense converted buildings as those at Gloucester, Durham or Peterborough can prove highly misleading. Indeed, the tendency of English monks to overbuild in a manner quite disproportionate to their numbers had long ago presented them with one of their major economic problems. The total number of English and Welsh religious persons, which fell from about 12,000 in 1500 to 11,000 or less in 1534, was quite insignificant compared with, say, the immense and ever-growing armies in Spain. The nuns in particular represent a startlingly small group; they numbered over 2,000 in 1500, falling to about 1,600 at the time of the Dissolution, and living in about communities. An exhaustive survey for England and Wales shows at the Dissolution about 825 religious houses of all types.[27] Consequently a house of average size numbered about twelve actual religious persons, but even this figure gives little notion of the difficulties attaching to excessively small establishments, where discipline so often proved hard to maintain. A calculation by Dr. G. W. O. Woodward deals with 205 of the 'lesser' monasteries dissolved in 1536, for which we happen to possess actual or approximate totals. In these houses the total of religious persons lies between a maximum of 1,651 and a minimum of 1,557. This suggests a national average for the lesser houses of between 7 and 8.[28] A good many places fell below this figure and certain of those which Wolsey suppressed in favour of his own new colleges boasted only one or two monks.

Needless to say, all these figures take no account of the lay officials and personal servants or of the corrodians—lay people who had bought the right to live as pensioners in monasteries. At the larger and wealthier houses the number of servants had tended to become by any standards excessive. At Rievaulx there were 122 for only twenty-two monks; at Gloucester eighty-six for twenty-six monks. The detailed household-list of 1538 for Butley Priory shows what a smaller but well-endowed house could do; it had only twelve canons but two chaplains, eleven domestic servants, a master of the children, seven children 'kept on alms to learning', three cooks, a slaughterman, a sacristan, a cooper, three bakers and brewers, two horse-keepers, two maltsters, a porter, six laundresses, two bedemen and some thirty-four workers of all sorts on the home farm and gardens. The whole community at Butley thus numbered eighty-four persons.[29] Despite such figures, it now appears that in the past we have tended to exaggerate this feature of late monastic life. Many of these dependents, especially the husbandmen, obviously cannot in a self-sufficient rural community be accounted as evidence of luxurious living. Moreover, there exist numerous establishment-lists of the lesser monasteries made at the time of their dissolution in 1536 and these show a far more modest picture. In these poorer houses the household servants scarcely outnumber the monks and canons, whilst in the case of the smaller nunneries they number less than half the total of actual nuns. It would therefore seem erroneous to suppose that the rank and file of religious persons were lavishly attended or that the financial difficulties of the monasteries sprang primarily from the burden of swollen staffs. When, however, their reform or dissolution came under discussion, scandal tended to matter more than statistics. The term 'abbey-lubbers' had come into general circulation to denote the supposed hordes of idle and vicious servants surrounding the monasteries. And like all medieval servants, those of the great monasteries had a strong *esprit de corps* which could lead them into long-standing feuds with neighbouring townsmen and others.

At the suppression the annual revenue of all houses of men and women was returned at £136,362, a sum which probably covered about half the total wealth of the English Church and seems all the more impressive since for over a century the monasteries had received extremely few major bene-factions. Yet, as usual, the gross figure conveys a false impression of the average actualities. The whole of the nunneries account for only £15,000, while the 'lesser' houses, constituting nearly half the total number, enjoyed less than one-ninth of this total income.[30] In their dimensions as in their discipline and social importance, the individual religous houses display extreme variations. St. Mary's of York with its superb buildings, its far-flung estates and its gross revenue of more than £2,000 a year lay only a few miles distant from Nunburnholme, with a tiny group of nuns living on an annual income of £10.[31] In material attributes and worldly influence the two resembled each other as little as a London department-store resembles a village shop. Again, the friars, who still mattered in the devotional life of society, were 'non-possessioner religious' and lacked landed estates or notable wealth of any kind. Not surprisingly, a number of radical thinkers and Protestant Reformers arose from their ranks.

Despite the controversies which have always surrounded the problems and the fate of the monasteries, they may nevertheless be regarded as the least mysterious and best-documented section of the Church. We know all about them we could reasonably expect to know, and reputable historians are nowadays not seriously divided about the facts. Our knowledge of the disciplinary conditions depends in no sense upon the reports of government hirelings; it depends upon a variety of more trustworthy documents and principally upon the frequent episcopal visitations to which most of the orders were subject. At least three large printed collections of visitation records cover the decades immediately preceding the Dissolution. They refer respectively to the dioceses of Lincoln[32] and Norwich,[33] and to the Premonstratensian houses,[34] which had their own visitors. In addition, numerous visitations of individual houses and of smaller groups have been published.

These materials need careful handling, for it is their business to record sins and faults. The hasty reader has every temptation to gloss over the many enquiries which reveal no shortcomings of importance and to bestow his attentions upon episodes more lurid and picturesque. Moreover, these are confidential enquiries unintended for the delectation of inquisitive outsiders like ourselves. The bishop usually saw each monk privately, and each lay under an obligation to reveal the shortcomings, great and small, of his fellows. Neither laymen nor secular priests have ever been so remorselessly dissected, and in their position any other group might have looked worse. The great majority of houses bore little resemblance to those sinks of iniquity which Protestant propagandists once believed them to be. In most visitations faults relatively venial come to light; there was, for example, a widespread tendency for monks and nuns to own articles of private property and to assume lay dress. Amongst the monks of Norwich, for example, we encounter some with exquisite purses and one with red silk bows on his shoes. The latter did not, says the record, blush to lift his frock before the prior and the junior monks so as to display his elegant footwear, while some of the novices appeared in top boots and hats with satin rosettes. Even the abbot of St. Mary's, York, was charged with sartorial magnificence, while the canons of Warter Priory were reproved by the Archbishop for wearing 'silken girdles ornamented with gold and silver, and gold and silver rings'.[35] Abbots and priors commonly maintained expensive separate households and luxurious tables; they often failed to present accounts or to consult the brethren on important transactions; sometimes they assigned leases and offices to lay relatives, who might exercise undue authority or even prey upon the monastic revenues. Chronic disharmony between heads of houses and their subordinates proved by no means rare, though here we must beware of deducting a serious feud whenever a monk dutifully exposed the faults of his brethren to the bishop. Again, it would be unjust to assess late medieval monasticism from its voluminous documentation after the year 1530. During these final stages the threat of catastrophe hung in the air, morale ran low and many of the heads themselves were government nominees selected for their pliancy rather than for their monastic vitues.

When all these many qualifying factors have been taken into account, one is still tempted to think that no major section of the early Tudor Church stood more grievously in need of reform and fresh inspiration than did the regular clergy. That even the better houses had their few chronic misfits cannot occasion surprise when so many immature persons were accepted without serious tests of vocation and when no machinery functioned adequately to discard the failures. The pressure of episcopal authority proved unequal and spasmodic; a grossly inefficient or secular-minded monk could easily continue to hold important offices even after his failings had become notoriously apparent. A small house which happened to acquire a corrupt head could easily degenerate into violence and vice, yet the number which might thus be described was small and one might well marvel that it was not greater.[36] The difficulties did not arise solely from poor selective and disciplinary routines. The religious orders had never solved a more basic problem—how to find suitable and constructive employment for their members outside the hours of prayer and praise. Monks did not personally construct buildings or till the land; extremely few had ever illuminated manuscripts or created works of art; the Tudor successors of the great monastic chroniclers were both rare and professionally degenerate. The minority of monks fitted to undertake university courses (357, including friars, appear in the Oxford registers from 1505 to 1538[37]) tended to huddle for long years in the houses of study supported at Oxford and Cambridge by the more important monastic orders. When they at last returned, they found little scope for their academic talents.

Outside the universities monks played an almost negligible rôle in early Tudor education. As for the schools in certain of the greater houses, these comprised a small fraction of the national school-population and in any case usually employed secular priests as teachers. Spiritual ministration to the laity was likewise not the function of the majority of religious orders, though an important exception was formed by the preaching friars and by those regular canons who served the parish churches pertaining to their houses. For the ordinary monk or canon life had become in many respects more comfortable than the laborious, often squalid lives of labourers, artisans and small merchants; for the heads of the large houses life had become by any standard lordly and luxurious. Perhaps the most subtly disturbing of all Tudor monastic documents is the journal of William More, prior of Worcester from 1518 to 1536.[38] Hence there emerges no vicious character but a gracious, easy-going country gentleman, generous to his relatives and a popular figure in the county society. Avoiding the life of the cloister he moves between his several manor-houses, immersed in secular business, always extremely attentive to his own health and comfort. William More was indeed no monk in the sense demanded either by St. Bernard or by the religious orders of our own day, yet for many years he guided without notoriety the fortunes of one of the renowned cathedral priories of England.

Then as now, it was too easy for outsiders to speak in censorious tones, and the blame for all these shortcomings should not be attributed solely to the monks and to their ecclesiastical superiors. On all sides the enforcement of discipline was hampered by selfish and interfering laymen who contended for monastic stewardships and leases, built up their factions within the cloister or the abbot's household and engaged in drinking-parties and sports with the denizens of poorly-ruled communities. The religious houses were accepted as long-standing members of local society; people sponged upon them, quarrelled with them in endless lawsuits, hobnobbed with them and distracted them from the life of religion. Until their very last years there are no signs that the laity desired or anticipated a general dissolution and a scramble to buy monastic lands. On the other hand, the evidence does not suggest that most monasteries were conspicuously beloved by their surrounding populations. Even during the ostensibly pro-monastic Pilgrimage of Grace there occurred, according to the extant records, almost as many local instances of ill-will as of good-will on the part of the rebels toward the northern houses.

With certain exceptions, there seems no strong reason why the monks should have commanded the unmixed affections of their neighbours. To the latter they appeared in everyday life as landlords, receivers of rents and tithes, rival traders, unsatisfactory proprietors of churches, which they seemed to regard as investments, to the neglect of the fabric and the parishioners. In relation to their tenants they were not noticeably more generous than lay lords and, as Wolsey's enquiries of 1517 showed,[39] some had already joined in the tendency to enclose lands and expel tenants. When Sir Thomas More protested against harsh enclosures, he placed among the worst offenders 'certain abbots, holy men no doubt'.[40] One of the bitterest passages in Jerome Barlow's anticlerical *Burial of the Mass* (c. 1527–8) is directed against rent-raising by abbeys.[41] In 1517 the Abbot of Peterborough became involved in fierce and unscrupulous legal contests with the local townsmen on account of his forcible enclosures of parts of the fens,[42] whilst in 1526 the men of Orford rioted against enclosures made by Butley Priory on what they claimed to be common land.[43] What with repairs to overelaborate buildings, royal taxation and other heavy overheads, most houses stood in debt and simply could not afford to practise quixotic landlordism. In any case, their agrarian policies must often have been framed by the laymen who acted as their stewards and understewards.

In the more thinly-populated areas of England monastic hospitality benefited travellers of all types; it was dispensed to everyone from dukes to beggars and not based upon fine calculations of social need or moral desert. At the time of the Dissolution royal commissioners and other laymen praised the beneficence of certan individual houses,[44] and their passing must have had its effect upon the amenities of their districts. At the same time middle-class disdain for indiscriminate charity had begun to pervade the atmosphere and to blame religious houses for fostering rogues and vagabonds. In the *Valor Ecclesiasticus,* the great survey of ecclesiastical incomes made in 1535, the monasteries appear to bestow less than three per cent of their income in alms,[45] but charges of ungenerosity based upon such percentages are to be deprecated, since the royal commissioners for the *Valor* allowed the houses to submit only those alms which they were legally obliged to disburse by the provision of benefactors. How much the monks gave casually out of general income or in the form of food and broken meats, we shall never be able to compute, but their spontaneous giving can hardly have made a major impact upon the national problem of pauperism. Needless to add, English monasticism had failed to initiate charitable, teaching, nursing and missionary orders and organisations such as those which were beginning to appear in Germany and Italy and were soon to figure among the chief glories of the Catholic Counter-Reformation.

To this spectacle of an uninspired and lukewarm establishment contemporaries rightly acknowledged three notable exceptions—the Franciscan Observants, the Carthusians and the Bridgettines, all numerically small orders, maintaining close relations with each other, holding a strong allegiance to the Holy See and a consequent disposition, when the Henrician crisis arrived, to reject the King's new claims. With very few exceptions, the genuine monastic martyrs came from these restricted circles. The Observants, who alone among the orders in England represented a recent reform-movement, had only seven houses here, and of these the royal foundation at Greenwich had become the most important. Not only did it enjoy the King's direct patronage but it also supplied confessors to Queen Katherine and her daughter Mary. More aristocratic, intellectual and wealthy was the single English Bridgettine house of Syon, near Isleworth.[46] This was in effect a double house, with some sixty nuns and twenty-five brethren, the latter acting as chaplains and directors to the former. Among them were many Cambridge graduates and after 1500 at least six former fellows of colleges in that University. Syon boasted a reputation for strict observance, a remarkable library, a strong interest in the English mystics and important contemporary devotional writers in William Bonde and Richard Whitford.

Even more exacting in its vocational demands was the Carthusian order. Its nine houses in England (seven of them founded between 1340 and 1414) all maintained to the Dissolution an unblemished name for devotion together with a magnificent corporate spirit which sometimes verged upon spiritual pride. Alongside its saints it also found room for a number of tormented and restless characters whose devotional capacities fell short of their romantic aspirations. In this regard the famous London house of the Salutation was unfortunate to leave as its historian the superstitous Maurice Chauncy, who seems so unable to distinguish genuine spirituality from hysteria.[47] Yet even through the eyes of this inept hagiographer we receive a vivid impression of the balanced sanity, the sweet rigour of Prior Houghton, the gallant faith and selflessness of that part of his community which in 1535 followed him to the gibbet or died in chains. If they did not, as Froude oddly imagined, die for religious freedom, they died for a conviction as sincerely felt as the love of God which had first led them along the hard and high paths of the Carthusian life. The Tudor age bred no nobler Englishmen than these, and the inhumanity of their punishment must remain among the fouler blots upon the record of Henry VIII. Of Mountgrace, the Charterhouse second in importance to that of London, we have already said more than a little and said it perhaps in too captious and critical a spirit. In expressing reserve concerning the spiritual penetration of monks like Richard Methley and John Norton, we were inevitably placing them alongside great contemplatives like Ruysbroeck and Hilton. With these exalted standards they cannot for a moment pretend to compare, yet they, and no doubt most of their brethren, exhibited a standard of devotion far above that of the mass of contemporary English monks. Owing to its lonely situation Mountgrace could not radiate an influence comparable with that of the London house, yet it did not fail to command wide veneration throughout the North. Had the average rural religious house displayed half its virtue, the attitude of Tudor Englishmen toward monasticism would have been vastly different from that which prevailed at the meeting of the Reformation Parliament.

The Situation of the Church

Such, then, in bald outline was the situation of the English clergy during the early decades of the sixteenth century. Their power and influence in society was more apparent than real. They were beginning to lose their once effortless intellectual ascendancy. They stood in no favourable posture to wage any conflict against the growing pretensions of the laity and of the State. Their leaders lacked inspiration, unity and loyalty to the supranational concept of Christendom. While the Papacy as yet needed to reform itself before it could inaugurate reform within the national churches, our English Church remained too full of conflicting interests, too complacent in its conservative and legalist routines to reform itself. During the reign of Wolsey its internal chasms widened. One of these lay between the Cardinal Legate and the bishops, another between the upper and lower clergy, a third between the seculars and the regulars. Of the chasm which was steadily growing between clergy and laity we have already said something and shall shortly be bound to say more. Whereas the secular clergy tended to encounter resentment as an unduly privileged caste within the national society, the monks now found themselves seated upon an even more precarious limb of the tree of commonwealth. Nevertheless, when we reflect upon the causes of the Reformation, it is easily possible to exaggerate the importance of particular tensions and personal failings. Had Wolsey experienced a fiercer urge to reform, even his immense legal powers could scarcely have accomplished more than gradual and superficial changes. But the hour was later than most men supposed and reforms on this scale would not have availed to prevent either the state-revolution of Henry VIII or the subsequent conquests of Protestantism.

Writers who feel no personal attraction toward Protestant concepts have often tried to explain the advance of Protestantism too purely in terms of these tensions and weaknesses we have just described, sometimes merely in terms of fainthearted and confused bishops faced by a grasping and turbulent laity. However great weight may be attached to these negative factors, it should never be forgotten that Protestant beliefs came to exercise positive claims upon certain types of mind, that they have steadily continued to exercise such claims and that most of their holders cannot be dismissed as rebellious neurotics, politicians, or self-deluded profiteers. Some men were drawn to Protestantism by its adherence to the recorded teaching of Jesus and the Apostles; some by hatreds and heady enthusiasms; some by the belief that it was an escape-route from the broad road to damnation. But the magnetic process was real enough and it came to operate quite extensively throughout English society. Whatever our various confessional allegiances, we can scarcely begin to understand the Reformation without some sober and sympathetic effort to examine Protestantism from the inside. Any other approach is in danger of ignoring some of the plainest realities in our national history. Like the old Lollardy before it, the new Lutheranism floated upon a tide of negative criticisms, yet its positive affirmations were well trimmed to catch the winds blowing through the sixteenth century. These affirmations now demand our notice.

5 Lutherans and Humanists

Justification by Faith: Luther and Zwingli

Warmly as we may reject the notion that all the essential ingredients of the English Reformation were made in Germany and Switzerland, we are bound to recognise that from the third decade of the century our religious history became closely interlocked with the great turmoil on the continent. The personal story of Martin Luther, necessary as it is to explain some aspects of his theology, cannot here concern us in detail. By any criterion, he is a mountainous phenomenon in the history of religion and his flanks are littered with the corpses of incautious climbers who thought to scale him with a few pieces of simple equipment—Anglican, Catholic, Freudian, Marxist—or for that matter Lutheran![1] By focusing too narrowly upon his emotional experiences many observers have failed to grasp that he became expert in the critical methods of textual study introduced by Valla, Erasmus and Reuchlin. Luther saw in the flight of Byzantine scholars to western Europe a divine plan to expand Greek scholarship, the essential key to Christ's and St. Paul's teaching. He demanded an expert application of linguistic humanism (*die Sprachen*) as the foundation of a scriptural Christianity, distinct from both scholasticism and the popular cults. This renewed religion should be related not solely to salvation but also to Christian service on the lower plane of the commonwealth. Without these rational and humanist approaches, Luther could not have attracted so many scholars and statesmen to his cause.

Between 1517, when he denounced indulgences in his ninety-five theses, and 1520, when he published his three revolutionary manifestoes, Luther formulated both his doctrinal and his practical programmes. He summoned the German princes to undertake the reform of the Church, to abolish papal taxation, to dissolve the religious orders, to abrogate pilgrimages, clerical celibacy and masses for the dead. He also denied the doctrine of transubstantiation, though he proceeded to replace it by a far from simple or radical alternative. He limited the sacraments to the scriptural two, baptism and the eucharist, while to the laity he assigned communion in both kinds. But the keystone of his doctrine, one unparalleled in Wycliffism, was the doctrine of Justification by Faith Alone, or solifidianism. This he based in the main upon the teaching of St. Paul, though he found for it a considerable measure of support in the anti-Pelagian writings of St. Augustine and in his favourite fourteenth-century German mystics, Johann Tauler and the anonymous author of the *Theologia Germanica*. Moreover, he stated this doctrine with all the fervour of a liberated soul, for it had proved his own way of escape from an intolerable predicament of the spirit. Whatever its merits, we gravely underestimate this doctrine if we think of it as yet one more theological proposition added to the multitude. Once understood it developed an intimate power to alter both the inner lives and the religious habits of the millions who came to accept its message. Justification by Faith can best be understood by re-reading that early masterpiece of Christian theology the *Epistle to the Romans*, followed by Tyndale's *Prologue to Romans*, which is a translation from one of Luther's own commentaries. This *Prologue* acquires all the more interest when recognised as the actual vehicle which brought Luther's salient doctrine to the first generation of English Protestants.

The antithesis between God and man presented by Luther, and indeed by the Apostle himself, is stark in the extreme.[2] On the one hand stands the Deity in his unutterable majesty and justice; on the other languishes man in his corrupt self-centredness; his wretched nature being curved inward upon itself, he remains unable even to approach the divine standards by his own pitiful observances and good works. But if God's righteousness is terrifying, his loving purpose toward man is boundless. In the Son he had furnished man with the sole means of transcending this awful inadequacy. God will justify men—put them in a right relationship with himself—only if they abandon all reliance upon personal merit and place their whole trust in the merits of Christ. Truly, good works are an inevitable outcome of this faith, yet in themselves they contribute nothing to justification and salvation; they can form a dangerous stumbling-block to misguided men, who take pride in them as a title to redemption. To this sequence of thought St. Paul repeatedly returns, and Luther took it as the very heart of early Christian theology.

> For (again from Scripture) 'no human being can be justified in the sight of God' for having kept the law: law brings only the consciousness of sin.... Therefore, now that we have been justified through faith, let us continue at peace with God through our Lord Jesus Christ, through whom we have been allowed to enter the sphere of God's grace, where we now stand.... Israel made great efforts after a law of righteousness, but never attained to it. Why was this? Because their efforts were not based on faith, but (as they supposed) on deeds.... For they ignore God's way of righteousness, and try to set up their own, and therefore they have not submitted themselves to God's righteousness. For Christ ends the law and brings righteousness for everyone who has faith.

These are not Luther's words, but those of *Romans* (iii, 20; v, 1–2; ix, 31–2; x, 2–4). The Apostle pursues a similar course in *Galatians* (ii, 16; iii, 11–12)

83

and nowhere does he (or his follower) make the point more concisely than in the second chapter of *Ephesians*. Having dwelt on the redemption of the flock from the death of sin by the quickening power of Christ, the writer concludes: 'For it is by his grace that you are saved, through trusting him; it is not your own doing. It is God's gift, not a reward for work done. There is nothing for anyone to boast of. For we are God's handwork, created in Christ Jesus to devote ourselves to the good deeds for which God has designed us'.

Reiterated with force by St. Augustine, the doctrine of Justification by Faith had not, of course, been ignored by medieval theologians, yet they had shown, rightly or wrongly, a marked indisposition to accept it without reserves. On the one hand, elements of human merit had been implicitly and explicitly introduced in the scheme; on the other, it had been too lightly assumed that the Apostle referred to grace as conveyed by the sacraments. Again, the Pauline conception of faith had come to be identified with intellectual assent to credal propositions. Interpreting St. Paul, Luther is especially insistent upon the distinction between *assensus* and *fiducia*; it is the latter we need, the infinitely humble, yet infinitely confident trust of the sinner in God's redeeming mercy. The hesitations and qualifications of Luther's predecessors and opponents are, of course, intelligible enough. There were other passages suggesting modificatory trends in New Testament thought, notably the *Epistle of St. James*, with its stress upon good works, which Luther dismissed as 'an epistle of straw'. More important, the doctrine seemed above all others hard to accept in its fullness, for it shattered every man-made notion of justice and morality. The response of the conventional moralist could only be that of the Good Brother in the parable of the Prodigal Son: 'You know how I have slaved for you all these years; I never once disobeyed your orders; and you never gave me so much as a kid, for a feast with my friends. But now that this son of yours turns up, after running through your money with his women, you kill the fatted calf for him.' But now all this moral accountancy was thrust aside by Luther. God is no longer seen as weighing up a man's life; no longer does God stand like an inn-keeper, chalking up the items and the prices to be paid for them. His grace is in no sense a prize for the pupil with the highest terminal total of marks. And all this is only the first unpalatable draught to be swallowed by the naturally law-abiding, by the people who have that insidious gift, a 'good conscience'. So whole-hearted an emphasis upon the unaided rôle of God in justifying and saving certain undeserving men (but not others!) obviously entails a doctrine of predestination. Well aware of this necessity St. Paul proceeds in *Romans* to sketch a predestinatory system, and he is none too happy in his attempts to reconcile it with human free will (*Romans*, viii, ix). Once again this element, elaborated by St. Augustine, received full acceptance from Luther and in due time was to achieve a rich yet debatable development at the hands of Calvin.

There may well be other acceptable definitions of Justification by Faith, yet the present writer finds it difficult, in view of so many corroborative passages in the New Testament, to see why Luther's version should so swiftly have been dismissed as heretical. Indeed, while some non-Lutheran authorities have in recent times accorded this version more sympathy, others still continue to dismiss it as conducive to gross immorality. These critics believe that Luther regarded human nature with a total pessimism and deprived man of free will and moral responsibility. Yet does not this view amputate an important limb of Luther's theology? His total reliance upon Christ's sacrifice applies only to the high plane of salvation, not to the lower plane of human relationships in this terrestrial life. Regarding the latter, Luther remains insistent on obedience to Christian moral laws. So far from despising man, he exalts human reason and free will *on this level*, even though they do not contribute to eternal salvation.[3] Yet he reiterates Matthew, vii,18, to the effect that only a good tree can bear good fruit, so that persistent breaches of the moral law are signs that a man has not been justified or chosen by God. All in all, Luther's version might well seem more 'optimistic' and merciful than, for example, the terrifying passage by Thomas More on purgatory, which we cited when discussing that belief. As an ordinary Christian facing death, which version would one supplicate? Would it be Luther's fatherly God, kind and generous toward repentant believers, or alternatively More's God, the stern Judge, the menacing gaoler, who forces all save the saints into purgatorial sentences of awful suffering? Moreoever if Luther's doctrine really produced immorality, should the fact not register in actual societies? Were the subjects of Lutheran princes, or the Swiss Reformed communities, less moral (and moralistic) than their contemporaries, the Italians of the High Renaissance? This question seems by no means difficult to answer!

In the early sixteenth century a heavy emphasis upon Justification by Faith was bound to play havoc with the cults of the popular religion. It struck at the foundations of saint-worship, pilgrimages, formal penances, pardons, indulgences, intercessory masses, chantries and a host of other institutions, since not merely the abuses and superstitions associated with them, but even the beliefs underlying them became suspect; they seemed to be futile attempts to build up human 'merit' and distractions from the creation of the new relationship between God and man. To Luther the main purpose of the mass itself was to strengthen the faith of the individual communicant. He could see in the Scriptures no reason for regarding it as a 'good work' from which other persons might benefit. To regard it as in any sense a sacrifice merely derogated from the all-sufficiency of Christ's unique sacrifice on the Cross. Everything in scholastic theology which lacked a direct basis in the Scriptures now fell under suspicion. Aristotle, the high priest of medieval rationalism, suffered dethronement as a pagan influence; the old truth, as docketed in Aristotelian pigeon-holes, was cancelled in favour of a new truth both personal and subjective. Here, in short, was a prototype of modern existentialism and if it proved destructive of many medieval concepts it was destined to stand at least equally opposed to the comfortable sub-Protestant liberalism of the eighteenth and nineteenth centuries.

Hard upon the heels of Luther's teaching came news of the independent

Reformation carried out by Huldrych Zwingli at Zürich and imitated at Bern, Basel and elsewhere. Switzerland's lack of effective central government and episcopal control, its central position and multilateral culture, made it an ideal focus for religious experimentation. Between his call to the Great Minster at Zürich in 1518 and his heroic death fighting against the Catholic cantons in 1531, Zwingli with the aid of the council abolished the old worship with a thoroughness greater than that advocated by Luther. He was at once a humanist teacher deeply indebted to Erasmus and the most radical of the century's major reformers. More tolerant than either Luther or Calvin, he believed that salvation lay in believing the essentials of the Gospels, rather than in assent to precise formulae devised by any Church.[4] He allowed great personal freedom to interpret the Bible, yet he was careful to guide such interpretation by a hitherto unparalleled torrent of instruction from the pulpit. In the appeal to European radicalism he had certain advantages over Luther through his clear-headed simplicity; if he did not speak so grandly of salvation, he enunciated a sacramental doctrine more comprehensible than that of Luther and one more in line with popular heterodoxy like that of the Lollards. Luther while rejecting transubstantiation at his Marburg Colloquy with Zwingli in 1529, had illustrated his concept of the real presence in the elements by the famous analogy of the fire and the iron. When the two are combined, the fire communicates heat and light to the iron, yet neither loses its original identity. 'While both bread and wine continue there, it can be said with truth, This is My body; this wine is My blood, and conversely.' On the other hand, Zwingli dismissed all notions of a change in the elements at consecration and taught that 'a sacrament is a sign of a sacred thing, that is of grace which has been given.' While he took very seriously the communicant's preparation to receive the sacrament, he believed the latter 'nothing else than a commemoration'. In other words, 'This is my body', he interpreted the word 'is' as 'signifies'. To disprove both Catholic transubstantiation and Lutheran 'real presence' he used the argument that, since the Ascension, Christ's body had been in heaven. At Marburg this problem of the eucharist divided the Lutherans from the Zwinglians, but on the other doctrinal issues they attained substantial agreement.

At the outset, we may add that the influence of Zwingli upon the earliest English Reformers still needs disentanglement. Men like William Tyndale and John Frith were attracted by his doctrines, while the present writer recently encountered his sacramental teaching in the case of an obscure Yorkshire parish priest charged with heresy in 1535. At the same time, before we proceed to study English Protestants, we must again be on our guard against attaching tidy 'Lutheran', 'Zwinglian', 'Calvanist' and other labels to these very eclectic Englishmen; we must beware of compartmentalising the torrent of doctrines which by 1530 was flowing into England.

Within the teaching of both Luther and Zwingli lay an outspoken emphasis upon the claims of the individual Christian conscience, an emphasis which contained at least the elements of religious liberty and toleration.

Hardly, however, had such notions been formulated when enormous claims to a direct spiritual inspiration were made by idealists like Carlstadt and Müntzer; they horrified Luther and henceforth impelled the 'moderate' Reformers to fight with decreasing tolerance on two fronts. This new and more radical drive for Reformation assumed most formidable power in the varied groups broadly known as Anabaptists, which owed something to late medieval pietistic traditions but which are usually regarded as coming to birth in 1523 at Zürich under the shadow of Zwinglianism. During the subsequent two decades Anabaptism spread throughout Europe and, as we shall observe, achieved by about 1550 a certain significance in regard to the English Reformation. Yet the initial impulses underlying the new Protestanism in England sprang predominantly from Luther, to a far lesser extent from Zwingli and as yet scarcely at all from the radical sectarians on the continent.

Christian Humanism

Despite its inherent attractions, the first successes of Lutheranism in England are not self-explanatory. The ground had been prepared for its reception not merely by Lollard doctrines but by various forces more subtle and intellectual. We have already seen that the *devotio moderna* had tended to deflect interest from the cults and ecclesiastical institutions in favour of an interior and personal religion. In addition, Luther's replacement of scholastic theology by biblical theology had been preceded by the slow discrediting of the whole structure of scholasticism. To the process of attrition the nominalist philosophy of William of Occam had contributed a powerful solvent. This companion of Marsiglio had argued impressively enough that man depended purely upon revelation for his knowledge of theological truths. Even the existence and attributes of God were not discoverable by reason but must be accepted by blind faith. The Occamists denied the whole scholastic assumption that reason must harmonise with faith, philosophy with theology, Aristotle with Christ. Thanks to them and to other internal influences, the scholastic world stood in no position to defend orthodoxy when Luther made his challenge. He in fact received his training from Occamist teachers; though he finally parted from them, they helped to inspire his tendency to treat faith and reason as antitheses and his demand that the 'blind pagan teacher' Aristotle should be banished from the universities.[5]

The rôle of nominalism among the English Reformers deserves more investigation than scholars have yet provided. Nevertheless, we are unlikely ever to regard its influence as comparable with that other longstanding solvent of scholasticism—the humanist approach to the problems of literature, history, religion and the art of living. Why, by the third decade of the sixteenth century, were so many educated Englishmen prepared to abandon their class-prejudices against heresy and listen to Lutheranism, or even to more radical emphases? Certainly, if the Lutheran comet had appeared above the English horizon twenty years earlier, the watchers would have raised very different cries. This preparatory change of atmosphere is often loosely called the New Learning and in its origins owes much to the influence of the Italian humanists, who even before Petrarch's day had abandoned scholastic philosophy and theology in favour of literary, historical and philological studies. Thanks largely to Lorenzo Valla, by the time of Erasmus and Colet this approach had been fully transferred to the study of the Scriptures. In English theological life the shift of standpoint and method showed itself clearly in 1496-7 when Colet returned from Italy and delivered his famous Oxford lectures on Paul's *Epistle to the Romans*. It may be granted that the future dean of St. Paul's did not deduce nearly as much as Luther deduced from this same book. Yet in comparison with its medieval predecessors his commentary cannot but impress by its freshness, its common sense, its breadth of outlook, its relative modernity.[6]

Colet brushes aside the old treatment of the Bible as a verbally-inspired arsenal of texts; he will have nothing of the schoolmen's neglect of the literal sense in favour of allegorical, tropological and anagogical interpretations. He looks at the book anew, and his lectures are anything but the usual *catenae* of subservient references to patristic and medieval exegetes. He applies the humanist critique to the Bible as fearlessly as to a text of Cicero or Virgil. He is interested in the book as a whole; he is plainly fascinated by the life and mind of Paul; he realises he is dealing with a real man in a real historical setting and he reaches down his Suetonius in order to discuss the social background of Paul's Roman congregation. Humanists were seldom profuse in acknowledging the help they derived from others and it would be mistaken to suppose Colet was unaided by any trends in medieval exegesis. During the late Middle Ages there stood among the most widely read of Biblical commentators that famous doctor of the Parish schools, Nicholas of Lyra (c. 1270-1340), whose work reappeared in many editions from the early days of printing. Nicholas had made outspoken attacks upon those who had multiplied the mystical senses of Scripture so as to choke the plain, literal sense; his radicalism in this regard caused him at last to become notorious as an alleged inspirer of Luther: 'If Lyra had not lyred, Luther would not have danced.' Unjust as this saying may have been, Lyra's influence upon the early Tudor period is no mere surmise; his books appear quite frequently in the wills and inventories of English clergymen between 1500 and 1550. To many of these men they must have been more familiar than the sermons of Colet and they perhaps contributed materially toward the triumph of the humanist approach as the new century advanced.

Certain of Colet's emphases are admittedly akin to those subsequently forthcoming from Luther. Nowhere does he speak with more warmth than when urging, with St. Paul, that 'rites and ceremonies neither purify the spirit nor justify the man'. Again, he turns aside from discussing Paul's collections for famine-relief and contrasts their voluntary character with the 'money extorted by bitter exactions under the names of tithes and oblations'. Not without intrepidity Colet contrasts the covetous tithe-seekers of his day with the example of Paul, who chose to 'get his living by labouring with his hands at the trade of tentmaking, so as to avoid even suspicion of avarice or scandal to the Gospel'. Nevertheless, Colet's exposition of *Romans* cannot be regarded as more than a half-way house toward that of Luther. He paid little attention to Paul's determinism; unlike Luther, he specifically upheld the free agency of man, whose will was 'secretly accompanied' but not forcibly coerced by God's providence. Man's guilt and not God's will supplied the cause of his condemnation. The strongest influences upon Colet were the Neoplatonists Ficino and Pico della Mirandola, whose thinking did not lead in Luther's direction. The corruptions of the Church and of society strike Colet not so much as universal and inherent in the fallen nature of man but rather as disorders from a more perfect norm. Again, unlike Luther, he will not oppose violent perversions by counter-violence; if, as is possible, he began in his last days to consider Luther's criticisms and remedies, he must surely have felt misgivings as well as some measure of approval. Yet if Colet lacked the demonic force of Luther, he was more sternly independent and forthright than Erasmus. He apparently believed in transubstantiation, held the mass to be a propitiatory sacrifice, accepted all seven sacraments and accompanied his denunciation of papal scandals by an acknowledgement of the Papal Supremacy. Nevertheless, one cannot be surprised that he was admired by the Lollards and accused of heresy by Bishop Fitzjames. He is a Catholic with a special place in the history of Protestantism. The latter was above all a Biblical religion, and Colet's chief distinction lies in the fact that he stressed, well before Luther and Tyndale, the extreme relevance to contemporary religious problems of the Scriptures, historically, humanly and literally considered. He stands both among the causes and the symptoms of that climatic change which swept across English intellectual life during the early decades of the century.

In this same process the writings of Erasmus can also claim a formative rôle; despite immense differences of temperament, of teaching, of fundamental aims, there remain some elements of truth in the cliché: 'Erasmus laid the egg that Luther hatched.' Erasmus had been demanding a scriptural Christianity since 1503 and vernacular bibles for the people since 1516: the young Luther was fully aware of his works. Conversely, around 1520 Erasmus, while deploring Luther's violent language, regarded him as an honest critic of their common enemies, the obscurantist monks and schoolmen: he even urged the Elector of Saxony to protect Luther against the Pope. The influence of Erasmus, and of his counterparts among the German humanists, extended beyond their ridicule of ecclesiastical corruption and superstition, beyond the application of humanist methods to the Scriptures. From them there also emanated a modishness which for a time attracted even natural conservatives like Thomas More. As a result of their propaganda one had to accept humanist values or risk becoming a figure of fun as an obscurantist. Convinced or not, one had to be very old, very obtuse or very courageous to avoid turning one's back on the past and joining the movement. Its compulsion lay not merely in the intrinsic worth of the new approaches but in the mounting conviction that a golden age of enlightenment had at last arrived. Here was a new era because it so firmly believed itself to be a new era. This mood of confidence did not last long, but it accomplished wonders while it lasted, and Lutheranism entered into its heritage. Whatever the power of his shoulder Luther had not to shift the dead weight of what we now call 'medieval tradition'. While we cannot doubt that the European impact of Erasmus accomplished no small part of this primary task, the narrower problem concerning his influence upon the earlier stages of the English Reformation still admits of argument and might repay further investigation. The earliest known society of English Lutherans originated about 1520 in Cambridge, where in 1511–14 Erasmus had worked upon the Greek text of his New Testament and revised the Latin version formerly inspired by Colet. Yet none of the known personal associates of Erasmus in Cambridge was destined to prominence among the Reformers. On the other hand William Tyndale's first literary work was a translation into English of the *Enchiridion* of Erasmus, whose Latin New Testament, based directly on the Greek text, exerted a powerful influence upon the Lutheran cell in Cambridge and upon its offspring at Oxford. To cite one of several known cases, Thomas Bilney confessed that he sought eagerly for a copy, allured in the first place by the Latin rather than by a desire to attain Christian truth. And we shall shortly encounter another case in Anthony Dalaber, who turned to Erasmus's Latin Testament in his hour of peril.

The Erasmian climate pervaded in varying degrees the minds of many European intellectuals throughout the suceeding decades. It became a natural tendency in a classically-educated age to co-ordinate the teaching of the great pagan moralists with that of the New Testament, to see in Christianity a mode of this life rather than a way of salvation for the next, even to envisage a cool, reasonable religion, a Christianity without tears. But the present writer finds himself unable to join the distinguished Dutch historian who takes Christian humanism to be the 'major Reformation' as opposed to the 'minor Reformation' of the Protestants.[7] To regard the former as an integrated movement in the same sense as the latter would be to ignore the great complexity and the rather impalpable character of humanist trends after the death of Erasmus. To call these thought-tendencies a Reformation only creates semantic confusion. They did not create churches or closely shape the religious lives of ordinary men. Even upon statesmen their influence is hard to define and establish. Henry VIII did not dissolve the monasteries because Erasmus ridiculed monks. By any reckoning and by comparison with any movement, there was nothing 'minor' about the Protestant Reformation. One should not inflate the historic claims of Christian humanism by exaggerating its modernity, by supposing it to be more in accord than Protestantism with our own world, by falsely investing it with the paternity of modern scepticism, liberalism, agnosticism, or scientific materialism. Millions of people are still Lutherans, Calvinists and Anglicans but few are Erasmians or Christian humanists in the Renaissance meaning of this now ambiguous term. The ideas of Galileo and Harvey, of Shakespeare and Milton, of Descartes, Newton and Voltaire were no mere developments from the ideas of Erasmus. We shall later have occasion to observe the increasing range, versatility and secularism apparent in the Elizabethan outlook. Yet this process cannot properly be labelled Christian humanism; it sprang from many causes and it cannot be fitted into conceptual moulds fashioned from the cultural history of the Netherlands.

Early Lutheran Circles

If modern admirers of early English Protestantism desired to establish a national shrine, they could select none better than the little Cambridge church of St. Edward, King and Martyr. It still contains the small pulpit, made about 1510, from which Barnes, Bilney and Latimer preached. It was the church of Trinity Hall and Clare, the colleges of the two latter Reformers, and its parish contained (on the site now appropriately occupied by the Cavendish Laboratory) the Augustinian Friary whence Robert Barnes went forth on the travels which ultimately led him to the feet of Martin Luther. In a later age the first Cambridge edition of the Authorised Version was printed in this parish by Thomas Buck, whose memorial survives there along with those of two of the translators. Most notably of all, St. Edward's parish also included the White Horse, sardonically called 'Little Germany', where Cambridge scholars first gathered to discuss the new German doctrines.

Of these meetings we know very little save the meagre traditions recorded by John Foxe, who does not attempt to date the origins.[8] They could have begun before the year 1520, since the first holocaust of Lutheran books in Cambridge seems to have taken place at the end of that year or early in the next. On 12 May 1521 a far more magnificent burning took place at St. Paul's in London, where, before an enormous crowd, Wolsey took the chair under a canopy of cloth of gold, attended by a brilliant throng of peers, bishops and foreign ambassadors. Yet these events are by no means the earliest evidence of Lutheran studies in this country. In February 1519 two of Luther's correspondents separately told him that his books were being exported to England, while later in the same year Erasmus informed him that certain very great people in England were admiring his writings. The identity of these mysterious *maximi* can only be a matter for conjecture. A more solid fact appears in the daily ledger of the Oxford bookseller, John Dorne, who sold some dozen books by Luther between 29 January and late December 1520. It was nevertheless in the other university that the first and most influential group of Lutheran intellectuals developed.

The great majority of the men who led the first generation of English Protestants were in residence at Cambridge during the years when the White Horse meetings were in progress. This is true of Tyndale, Joye, Roy, Barnes, Coverdale, Bilney, Latimer, Cranmer, Frith, Lambert, Ridley, Rowland Taylor, Thomas Arthur, Matthew Parker and many others who preached, wrote, accepted high office or embraced martyrdom in the cause. One cannot doubt that in this informal setting many of them first encountered and discussed Lutheran doctrines. The usual chairman was Robert Barnes, then prior of the Augustinians. Bishop Stephen Gardiner, who in his youth probably attended some of the meetings, later described Barnes as 'a trim minion friar Augustine, one of a merry scoffing wit, friar-like and as a good fellow in company well beloved of many.'[9] On the strength of this tart testimonial from a bitter opponent, certain modern historians have depicted a public-house wrangle presided over by the loudest voice. There is no real basis for this image. Whatever his indiscretions Barnes was a very serious and dedicated Reformer who dared everything for his religion and died at the stake. He had already studied at Louvain and was a respected teacher of the classics; he was soon to lecture on the New Testament of Erasmus and to become involved in serious trouble for denouncing the pomp and splendour of Wolsey.[10]

Not for long was English Lutheranism the preserve of Cambridge intellectuals. That groups of London businessmen should soon interest themselves was only to be expected. We have already observed the continuity from Lollardy to Lutheranism in these circles and we shall shortly contemplate the London anticlericalism which centred around the murder of Richard Hunne, that scandal which stank continuously in the nostrils of Londoners until the Reformation Parliament. In addition, the large community of foreign traders in the capital contributed to the spread of the new heresy. Early in 1526 several of the Hanse merchants of the Stilyard were prosecuted for holding Lutheran heresies and importing Lutheran books when they returned from their periodic visits to their own country. About a year later two of them abjured and did penance at St. Paul's along with Robert Barnes.[11]

From this time onwards English merchants in both London and Antwerp began to play a crucial part in the drama. The share of the trading communities in other ports received clear acknowledgement in 1530 from Bishop Nix of Norwich who wrote, 'I am "accombred" with such as keepeth and readeth these erroneous books in English and believe and give credence to the same ... the gentlemen and the "commenty" [commonalty] be not greatly infect[ed], but merchants and such that hath their abiding not far from the sea.'[12] Reformation history cannot be converted into a mere shadow of economic and social history, for the same religious ideas embraced countries where the economic and social structures differed markedly from their English counterparts. Nevertheless, the spread of Protestant doctrines was greatly facilitated by the international connections, the anticlerical outlook, the mobility and relative political immunity of the merchant classes throughout Europe. Ideas, not in themselves economic, advanced naturally along the lines laid down by economic men; trade often built the circuits, if it did not supply the generators and the current. Alongside the heretical ex-friars and other university men we have always to reckon with resolute and moneyed groups in the larger trading-centres. Compared with the contribution of these two groups to the Reformation, that of the squirearchy has often been overestimated, and nowhere more than in England where ownership of land has been commonly regarded as conferring intellectual influence.

William Tyndale

Unquestionably the most remarkable figure among the first generation of English Protestants was William Tyndale.[13] Born in Gloucestershire about 1495, he took his M.A. from Magdalen Hall, Oxford, in 1515. Thereafter he also studied briefly at Cambridge, yet there is no certainty that he joined the group at the White Horse. His whole career shows a stark independence of groups, fashions and hero-worship. Mentally as well as physically he was an austere man, devoted to an idea and infinitely laborious in acquiring the technical equipment needed for its realisation. Buschius, one of the humanists who contributed to the *Epistolae Obscurorum Virorum*, referred to him as 'an Englishmen ... who is so skilful in seven tongues, Hebrew, Greek, Latin, Italian, Spanish, English, French, that whichever he speaks, you would think it his native tongue.'

While serving as tutor in the household of Sir John Walsh at Little Sodbury, Tyndale preached on College Green in Bristol and fell foul of the local priests whose ignorance he despised, and of the archdeacon of Gloucester. At this time he had resolved at all costs to translate the New Testament, in his own words, 'because I had perceived by experience how that it was impossible to establish the lay people in any truth except the Scripture were plainly laid before their eyes in their mother tongue, that they might see the process, order and meaning of the text'. This work he offered to do in the household of Cuthbert Tunstall, Bishop of London, but the prelate replied that his household was full and advised him to seek patronage in the city. This proved in the event the most fateful of many miscalculations by the English bishops in the matter of biblical translation. Tyndale resentfully took Tunstall's advice and went to labour day and night for six months in the house of a very different patron, the rich cloth merchant Humphrey Monmouth. Here he entered the obscure world of the 'Christian Brethren'. Soon afterwards this term was used of the secret society of London merchants engaged in subventing and importing books by English Protestants on the continent; it was also loosely applied to Lollards and we have already observed this older tradition among the merchants. On the one hand, Humphrey Monmouth and his associates belonged to the international world of Lutheranism; on the other, they were certainly linked with men of Lollard background in the distribution of these forbidden books from abroad. When in 1524 Tyndale went on to Wittenberg and met Luther, Monmouth was transferring money to Hamburg for his use, and Tyndale's subsequent publishing work can scarcely be explained except upon a basis of large-scale subsidisation by English merchants. The connection became overt in later years when Tyndale resided mostly in the English house of the

Merchant Adventurers at Antwerp. He was only the first of a series of Protestant scholars and translators to operate under this patronage, and Europe's greatest commercial city became in a very real sense the cradle of the English Reformation.

Along with his amanuensis, the ex-Observant Friar William Roy, Tyndale began in 1525 printing his New Testament at Cologne. Though forced to flee by the local magistrates, he completed it at Worms, a Protestant city, before the end of the year. Copies began streaming into England by March 1526: the efforts of Warham, Tunstall and More to check their spread proved almost uniformly fruitless. The successive editions of the work (revised 1526, 1534, 1535, and having a number of so-called pirate editions published in the Netherlands) provided a text at once splendid and homely in character, a text which has dominated all successive translations until our own day, for nine-tenths of the Authorised Version itself derived from Tyndale. Both here and in his original writings Tyndale showed himself a prophet of our language; he divined the genius of a predominantly teutonic tongue and so remained more readable and less 'dated' than most other writers for the next two over-latinised centuries. His translation owed most to the Greek Testament of Erasmus: it was philologically sound and careful, yet we cannot blame the authorities of that period for finding it tendentious. Admittedly, he was right in translating μετανοειτε by 'repent' instead of by the official 'do penance' (pœnitentiam agite). On the other hand, when he gave 'congregation' for ἐκκλησία, and 'senior' (later 'elder') for πρεσβύτερος, he was making no secret of his subversive intentions towards the visible Church and the priesthood. He firmly believed that the Bible came first and should invariably determine the doctrines, institutions and ceremonies of a Church which had come to bear little or no relation to that of the New Testament. In such cases as these he therefore studiously chose terms which were philologically accurate, yet could not be used to bolster up current ecclesiastical usages. It had been exciting for learned men when Erasmus had similarly utilised such basic terms; it was now revolutionary to hand laymen a Bible which seemed not even to mention priests or the Church. Yet the charge of intellectual dishonesty should never have been made against Tyndale; he was brutally honest—and even more radical than his orthodox critics have supposed! Tyndale's greatness as linguist and writer of English prose was by no means matched by his treatment of church history. Overlooking the genuine saints and scholars of the Middle Ages, he regarded the medieval priesthood as guilty of a gigantic plot to control both worlds, the spiritual and the secular. He believed the most dubious anticlerical stories: that Archbishop Arundel overthrew Richard II and that 'the good Duke' Humphrey of Gloucester had been murdered by clergymen in revenge for his opposition to their deceptions and sorceries. To such views he was doubtless led by resentment against the apparent failure of the medieval clergy to understand the centrality of the Bible and to supply biblical education. In the famous octavo of 1526 his prefaces were based on Luther's but he avoided marginal notes, and his work might well have been more effectively done had he continued this policy. To later editions, while improving his text, he added an array of marginal notes crudely attacking the Pope, the hierarchy and the priesthood. Likewise his translation of the Pentateuch (1530), though in itself an almost equally remarkable contribution to English Protestant scholarship, was disfigured by similar glosses, making Scripture a vehicle for a partisan position rather than allowing it to speak for itself.

Whatever the effect of such garnishings, the New Testament made a triumphant entry into the field. There is every reason to believe that many readers of moderate or even conservative views studied it with eagerness over the next decade. Perusing contemporary records one encounters it in the most unlikely places. Robert Plumpton, scion of a Lincolnshire and Yorkshire family later distinguished for its loyalty to Catholicism, wrote in 1536 from the Inner Temple to his mother: 'If it will please you to read the Introducement, ye shall see marvellous things hid in it. And as for the understanding of it, doubt not, for God will give knowledge to whom he will give knowledge of the Scriptures, as soon to a shepherd as a priest, if he ask knowledge of God faithfully.' Plumpton even cites the preface which Tyndale added to his 1534 edition and makes specific references to the famous *Prologue* to *Romans*. Besides the copy he sent his mother, it appears that his father already had another at home in larger print. In a second letter, Robert continues: 'Dearly beloved Mother in the Lord, I write not this to bring you into any heresy, but to teach you the clear light of God's doctrine ... Mother, you have much to thank God that it would please him to give you licence to live until this time, for the gospel of Christ was never so truly preached as it is now. Wherefore I pray to God that he will give you grace to have knowledge of his Scriptures.[15] It was in the next year 1537 that Edward Fox, Bishop of Hereford, addressed the assembled episcopate: 'Make not yourselves the laughing-stock of the world; light is sprung up, and is scattering all the clouds. The lay people know the Scriptures better than many of us'.[16]

Our own age can only by an effort of imagination grasp the full impact of the vernacular Bible upon a generation more ardent and narrow in its Christianity than our own, yet from which the private study of the Scriptures had been so rigorously withheld. It is hard indeed to recapture that blissful sense of release and new awakening. But it was a dawn made doubly poignant by tempest and sudden death. In May 1535 Tyndale himself was tempted by the squalid betrayer Henry Phillips (who posed as one of his converts) to pass outside the immunity of the English House in Antwerp. At once he was seized by agents of the Council at Brussels and imprisoned in the Castle of Vilvorde. After long disputations he was condemned in August 1536 for obstinate heresy and in the following October strangled, his body being consigned to the flames. Biased contemporaries like the chronicler Edward Hall blamed the machinations of English bishops, yet much as the news may have pleased these sorely-tried officials, their actual participation cannot be proved or fairly presumed.

Despite his courage and integrity, his selfless devotion and fine linguistic sense, William Tyndale lacked those endearing qualities which are fostered by human affections. Like many another dedicated Protestant he grievously underestimated the more reputable of his opponents and the religious achievement of the centuries preceding his own. He supposed that the greater part of medieval institutional Christianity was a priestly confidence-trick based upon avarice. For his conservative adversaries he had little better to say than that they were 'dreamers and natural beasts, without the seal of the Spirit of God; but sealed with the mark of the beast and with cankered consciences'.[17] To most men who met him privately Tyndale seemed a gentle creature, but in public life he was an able, angular and bigoted controversialist who gave and expected no quarter. He had suffered and seen his friends suffer. The combat had become mortal and, in an age of abusiveness and overstatement, he received few examples of temperance from the other side. While it would be pointless to look for modern liberalism in the pamphlet-war between Tyndale and Thomas More, this dreary verbosity, this infrequency of true intellectual and spiritual penetration shows neither disputant at his best. On both sides there looms not only a closed mind, a refusal to admit any legitimate differences of doctrinal viewpoint, but a personal uncharity so bitter that it seems to blunt the weapons of controversy themselves. The clash of these two good men stands among the most depressing spectacles of the English Reformation because it involved the imposition of that century's least Christian habits upon its most devoted minds.

Nevertheless it has been recently demonstrated that a detailed examination of these particular exchanges can reveal the standpoints of these two highly sincere authors, who were soon to die heroically in defence of their respective faiths.[18] In fact they display resemblances as well as contrasts. Their social and political views had much in common. Both apotheosised the family as the all-important unit within a Christian society. Alike, they wanted to bring religion to the masses and remained fully aware of the influences exerted by the rulers and other political agencies of their time. Both were Christian humanists in the linguistic-grammatical tradition initiated by Valla and Erasmus in strong condemnation of the dialecticians in the universities. In this particular respect they owe obvious debts to Erasmus, who in his *Paraclesis* of 1516 had so outrageously made a sharp distinction between 'Aristotelians' and 'Christians'. In opposition to some reactionaries of the day, both More and Tyndale upheld Greek studies as the basic tool of New Testament studies: they accepted from Erasmus the case for translating the Greek text into the vernacular languages. Yet here, while More's acceptance proved hesitant, Tyndale had gone ahead and with total dedication had completed the job. Beyond these issues the significant clashes appear. While Tyndale held the Scriptures to be self-authenticating, More insisted that they had always been authenticated, and must also be interpreted, by the living Church, and in accordance with its ancient traditions. He thus placed heavy shackles upon all independent biblical scholarship. Among their other disagreements, perhaps the most basic lay in and near the sacramental field. Obedient to tradition, More believed in ritual consecration, hallowing, cleansing, healing: he saw the priests—whose personal imperfections he recognised—as *ex-officio* connected up with supernatural forces. In contrast, and resembling not the Lutherans but the Zwinglians, Tyndale rejected these quasi-automatic sources of spirituality. He doubted the possibility of modern miracles and discounted not only transubstantiation and other 'real presence' doctrines of the mass, but also religious mysteries and allegories of all kinds. As a writer he seems intent to reduce Christian doctrine to a series of plain verbal definitions. In our modern, secular jargon, nobody of that period, except perhaps his follower John Frith, was less 'superstitious'. Concerning the implications of Thomas More's conservative standpoint we shall presently comment at greater length.

Until 1530 Tyndale followed Luther's theology, but from the time of his work upon the Pentateuch he laid increasing stress upon law, alongside Luther's stress upon gospel. The sinner is indeed justified by faith before God, but he then justifies himself before men by obedience to the moral law, while God covenants himself to show mercy toward the law-abiding. This bi-focal scheme doubtless qualifies for a place among the many progenitors of that complex phenomenon: English Puritan theology. Tyndale's political thought represents a link between Lutheran theory and the English Schism as effected by Henry VIII. The German Lutherans mounted the chariot of the godly prince not merely because they recognised his shining countenance alongside those of the prophets in the Old Testament history but also because they had no other strong political allies. Where political necessity enjoined a course of action, one could always discover the relevant scriptural texts. And where the godly prince did not exist, it was clearly necessary to invent him, or at least to collaborate with one less transparently inspired, and hope he would make a tolerable substitute. What practical alternative existed? Lutheranism could expect little support from the prelates; it dare not ally itself with the popular visionaries, with the hopeless economic agony of peasant-rebellions or with the predatory kites and crows among the doomed neo-feudal classes. Its natural and actual allies, the urban traders, could not rule great regions and—despite the very independent policy of certain great Imperial cities—also had ample incentives to collaborate with the princes. Yet when one stops to reflect, almost all these phrases, these basic elements of the German picture, could apply also to the England of Henry VIII.

It seems therefore natural enough that Tyndale's political deductions, even when framed with England in mind, should assume a close conformity with those of Luther. His *Obedience of a Christian Man* (1528) is an unflinching exposition of the divine right of kings, who should hasten to shake off their thraldom to the Church and whose subjects are bound to obey them as a matter of religious duty. 'He that judgeth the King, judgeth God and damneth God's law and ordinance ... the King is, in this world, without law; and may at his lust do right or wrong, and shall give accounts to God alone.' Here Tyndale preached with immense conviction, yet he preached more than he practised. When the royal divorce-suit developed, he soon began to condemn the King's proceedings. Subsequently he repelled the blandishments of Thomas Cromwell, refusing to become a royalist literary champion until Henry VIII should introduce Lutheran principles into England. It was safer to argue with the godly prince when one lived outside his dominions! In this inconsistence Tyndale did but prophesy future changes of attitude among non-Lutheran Protestants in many parts of Europe, including England: prince-worship was not in fact to be their permanent habit. But for the time being the apotheosis of monarchy had become general: it seems almost as prominent among doctrinal conservatives as among Lutherans. In England itself the distinguished anti-Lutheran Stephen Gardiner was about to embrace royal autocracy in terms as eloquent and whole-hearted as those of Tyndale. An age sick of anarchy and near-anarchy was quoting amid general approbation the adage, *The Wrath of the Prince is Death*. For most men life was short and hard even in times of political peace and order, and it would ill befit a twentieth-century critic to begrudge them their limited version of social security.

With his assistants Tyndale had some curious experiences. Friar Roy, born of Jewish stock in Calais, had joined the Observants at Greenwich and ultimately fled to matriculate at Wittenberg. He gave Tyndale useful mechanical help during the crucial months of 1525 but was too open-mouthed and could only be disciplined when he had no money. Dismissed for his indiscretions he somehow obtained funds, translated a Protestant tract and employed another fugitive friar from Greenwich, Jerome Barlow, to write the *Burial of the Mass*, a scurrilous attack in verse upon the ecclesiastical establishment in general and upon the public and private life of Wolsey in particular.[19] Tyndale's grave dislike for these frothy characters and methods was amply justified by the outcome. On Wolsey's fall Barlow begged the King's permission to return home and did atonement by assaulting his former friends in a *Dialogue against the Lutheran Factions*. Meanwhile William Roy disappeared from the Netherlands and from history, though it was later rumoured that he managed to get himself burned for heresy in Portugal about the year 1531. A more substantial figure in Tyndale's entourage was the former fellow of Peterhouse, George Joye,[20] who assisted the master in the controversy with More, and may have written *The Supper of the Lord*, usually attributed to Tyndale himself. Joye produced his own translation of the Psalms (1530) and certain other books of the Old Testament but these inferior productions derived merely from the Latin of Zwingli and others, since Joye, unlike Tyndale, had little knowledge of Hebrew. The friendship between them finally collapsed when in 1534 Joye pirated an edition of Tyndale's New Testament with some impudent emendations of his own. He had still a long career before him as a minor publicist but he never began to compare in importance with Miles Coverdale, the chief legatee and successor of Tyndale. This former Augustinian friar, once a follower of Barnes at Cambridge, went out in 1529 to meet Tyndale by appointment at Hamburg and there worked under him on the Pentateuch. Coverdale then seems to have followed his chief back to Antwerp, where in 1534 they were certainly in company and associating with John Rogers, another important future translator of the Scriptures. Hence, on the eve of his betrayal, Tyndale had found disciples capable of carrying his labours to full fruition. It was a sure instinct which prompted him to cry out at the stake 'Lord, open the King of England's eyes.' The remaining tasks were indeed as much political as literary, and they called for men with more tact and instinct than Tyndale.

Garret, Frith and Bilney

During Tyndale's activities at Antwerp, such English Lutherans as Robert Barnes and Thomas Garret were selling his New Testament wherever they could elude the vigilance of the bishops. They were helped by a most heterogeneous set of allies. Amongst those prosecuted in 1528 for distributing Tyndale's Testament and certain Lutheran writings were Jeffery Lome, a former porter of St. Anthony's School, Sygar Nicholson, a Stationer of Cambridge, and John Raimund, a 'Dutchman' who had brought 500 copies of the Testament into England. But the story of Garret and his friends at Oxford remains the most intimate and appealing of those preserved.[21] This young cleric pursued a successful academic career both at Oxford, where he proceeded M.A. in 1524, and at Cambridge, where he later achieved his doctorate. Long before this last stage he had entered the Protestant book-trade. In December 1525 Erasmus mentions him among the booksellers to whom he sends greetings, and the following year, supplied by the London book-seller Gough, he was back at Oxford selling both Latin texts and Tyndale's New Testament. In 1527 he also visited Reading Abbey, corrupting the prior (as conservatives alleged) by selling him over sixty books. At this time he was also curate of the London church of All Hallows, Honey Lane, but his parochial duties do not appear to have prevented him from taking the Thames Valley as his parish. In 1527 Dr. John London, then Warden of New College, wrote to the Bishop of Lincoln that 'this unhappy Mr. Garret was in Oxford at Easter and after that ... he sought out all such that were given to Greek, Hebrew and the polite Latin tongue, and pretended he would learn Hebrew and Greek, and bought books of new things to allure them: after that he procured a great number of corrupt books and secretly did distribute them among his acquaintance in sundry colleges and halls.' Under this stimulus the Oxford Protestant cell had swiftly developed. Dr. London went on to relate how Garret's young friend Anthony Dalaber had confessed to borrowing a number of Lutheran books from John Clark, an associate of Garret and one of the Cambridge men recently transferred by Wolsey to his new Cardinal College in Oxford. To London, a deep-dyed Oxonian, the true reason for these dark developments had now become only too obvious. 'Would God my Lord's Grace had never been motioned to call him [Clark] nor any other Cambridge man unto his most towardly College!' Meanwhile Dr. Cottisford, commissary of the Bishop of Lincoln, set about the task of destroying this nest of heretics.

In later years Anthony Dalaber wrote an affecting account of his encounter with Garret when the latter, now a hunted fugitive, sought refuge in Dalaber's rooms at Gloucester College. Both were understandably agitated, since Garret had already been captured once and had just escaped from a locked room, while the commissary was at evensong.

But now, with deep sighs and plenty of tears, he prayed me to help him to convey him away; and so he cast off his hood and his gown, wherein he came unto me, and desired me to give him a coat with sleeves, if I had any; and told me that he would go into Wales, and thence convey himself into Germany, if he might. Then I put on him a sleeved coat of mine, of fine cloth in grain, which my mother had given me. He would have another manner of cap of me, but I had none but priestlike, such as his own was. Then kneeled we both down together upon our knees, and lifting up our hearts and hands to God, our heavenly Father, desired him, with plenty of tears, so to conduct and prosper him in his journey, that he might well escape the danger of all his enemies.... And then we embraced, and kissed the one the other, the tears so abundantly flowing out from both our eyes, that we all be-wet both our faces, and scarcely for sorrow could we speak one to another.... When he was gone down the stairs from my chamber, I straightways did shut my chamber-door, and went into my study, shutting the door unto me, and took the New Testament of Erasmus translation into my hands, kneeled down on my knees, and with many a deep sigh and salt tear, I did with much deliberation read over the tenth chapter of St. Matthew's Gospel; and when I had so done, with fervent prayer I did commit unto God ... our dearly beloved brother Garret.

The commissary, pale with anxiety over the escape of his prisoner, was soon seen consulting with the Dean of Cardinal College and with Dr. London. He had Dalaber's room searched, thoroughly cross-questioned the young accomplice and finally set him in the stocks, where his fellow-Protestant Clark encouraged him to bear the persecution with thankfulness. These steps did not, however, locate the fugitive Garret. London himself relates how the commissary, 'being in extreme pensiveness, knew no other remedy but this extraordinary [one]; and caused a figure to be made by one expert in astronomy; and his judgement doth continually persist upon this: that [Garret] fled in a tawny coat south-eastward, and is in the middle of London and will shortly to the seaside'. This divination was shrewd but as it happened wrong, for Garret had started off westward and was soon captured by the proctors in the neighbouring village of Hinksey. He saved himself for a future martyrdom by abjuring and carrying a penitential faggot in open procession along with Dalaber down the High Street. Afterwards they were imprisoned for a time at Osney until Wolsey magnanimously gave Garret work—the innocuous task of copying documents. But Clark and several others of the Oxford group had less reason to feel gratitude. The prison of Cardinal College into which they were thrown was also the storehouse for the salt fish and, what with its stench and a constant diet of fish from February to August, Clark, Sumner and Bailey died of some infection. Perhaps Wolsey, amid the pressure of affairs, merely forgot to have them released; perhaps he felt no urgency, since these men had gravely marred the beginnings of his beautiful new college.

Another of these much-abused Cambridge intruders into Oxford managed during the débâcle to arrange a speedy withdrawal to the continent. He was John Frith, seemingly among the most interesting personalities to emerge from the records of early English Protestantism.[22] Escaping to Marburg, he first helped Tyndale, and then in 1529 published a tract called *Antithesis, wherein are compared together Christ's acts and our holy father the pope's*, an antithesis not unexpectedly made to the marked disadvantage of the latter. Subsequently in *A Disputation of Purgatory* he answered with cool precision, but without vituperation, More's *Supplication of Souls*. Frith's return to England in 1532 led, after various adventures, to his imprisonment and the betrayal to More of a discourse on the sacrament, written for a friend but not for publication. More reported that this work 'teacheth in a few leaves shortly all the poison that Wyclif, Oecolampadius, Huss, Tyndale and Zwinglius have taught in all their books before.' Everything we know of Frith's writings and reputation suggests a mind of high ability and independence; had he survived, his must have become one of the great names of the age.

That More had good reason to place this antagonist well to the left of Luther can be proved by reference to Frith's writings, by his discipleship to Oecolampadius (who held Zwinglian views on the eucharist) and by records of the examination which led in 1533 to Frith's martyrdom at the stake. He was examined upon two articles, purgatory and transubstantiation, yet in his own submission he did not die for any rigid denial of these two doctrines but for the principle that a particular doctrine on either point was not a necessary part of a Christian's faith. 'The cause of my death is this', wrote Frith, 'because I cannot in conscience abjure and swear that our prelates' opinion of the sacrament (that is, that the substance of bread and wine is verily changed into the flesh and blood of our Saviour Jesus Christ) is an undoubted article of the faith, necessary to be believed under pain of damnation.' To a greater extent than any other of our early Protestants, Frith thus upheld a certain degree of religious freedom. To make all dogmas equally binding, to abolish the distinction between an article of faith and a thing indifferent, had indeed become ever more characteristic of medieval orthodoxy, especially where the findings of Thomist Aristotelianism had been accorded a special reverence. The attack on excessive dogmatism was not original to Frith; it had already become a tenet of the more liberal Lutherans and was soon to become a leading concept of the intellectuals surrounding Thomas Cromwell.

In their reaction against what they considered the arrogance of the schoolmen, Luther made and Melanchthon developed the important distinction between necessary and immutable things, and *adiaphora*, things indifferent.[23] The concept was one of genuine antiquity, since it could be based upon several texts in St. Paul (e.g., *Colossians*, ii, 16–20; *I Timothy*, iv,

1–5;*Galatians*, ii, 3–5:v, 13–15). It also claimed support from Augustine's letter to Januarius and from the most liberal opinion of the fifteenth century, including that of Gerson, John of Wesel and Wessel Gansfort. However attractive we modern observers with a similar cast of mind may find adiaphorism, we should also acknowledge the limited nature of its effectiveness under sixteenth-century conditons. Certainly it provided no easy track towards reunion. When men had agreed to place such obvious things as holidays, fasts, and vestments under the heading *adiaphora*, how much more could be included? How many would go so far as Frith and include purgatory or even transubstantiation? The challenges presented by the concept to the charity and scholarship of Christians remain permanent, but during the early years of the Reformation it remained a forlorn hope of a world little prepared to accept its broader implications.

In the gallery of early English Protestants Thomas Bilney should be placed somewhat apart from the rest.[24] He was an independent reformer whose spiritual struggles had much in common with those of Luther, but his heresy, if such it can be called, involved little more than a denial of intercession to saints and of the current purgatorial doctrines. A Norfolk man, born about 1495, he received ordination from Bishop West of Ely in 1519 and at some later date took his LL.B. from Trinity Hall, Cambridge, being elected a fellow there. Using the New Testament of Erasmus at first for its Latin, he went on to reflect more deeply on its substance and to experience a personal conversion. 'Immediately, I seemed unto myself inwardly to feel a marvellous comfort and quietness, insomuch as my bruised bones leaped for joy.' This feeling arose from his acceptance of the Pauline doctrine of Justification by Faith, from which, again like Luther, he deduced the vanity of a religion based on external observances. To his dying day he remained orthodox on the Papal Supremacy, the authority of the Church, the doctrines of transubstantiation and confession. With regret Foxe himself admits Bilney's substantial orthodoxy. When people with more decidedly Protestant leanings like Robert Barnes and John Lambert were 'converted' by Bilney, this may mean little more than the fact that he first brought home to them the full meaning of a personal religion. Nevertheless, when he converted Hugh Latimer in 1524, this did in fact make Latimer cease attacking the Lutherans. Bilney at this time entertained puritanical scruples against strong language and even against music. On the other hand, he distributed his goods to the poor and the prisoners, often visiting the lazar houses and the equally foul prisons of Cambridge. In Latimer's words he was 'meek and charitable, a simple good soul, not fit for this world'.

In July 1525 Bilney was licensed to preach throughout the diocese of Ely, but he did so elsewhere, disputing with a friar at Ipswich concerning the veneration of images and being twice hauled out of the pulpit at Norwich by people who thought his views heretical. About 1526 Wolsey summoned him for denouncing saint-worship and caused him to take an oath that he did not hold, and would not disseminate, Luther's doctrine. In November 1527 he came again before Wolsey, from whom Tunstall of London took over the case. During this trial he freely admitted that Luther was 'a wicked and detestable heretic' and claimed that he himself had not wittingly taught Luther's doctrine. On the evidence of hostile witnesses Tunstall declared him convicted of heresy and then refused to reopen the case and hear favourable testimony. The bishop nevertheless twice postponed judgement to allow the accused an opportunity of recanting. This Bilney finally did under pressure from his friends, though he appears to have made it clear that he doubted his own guilt. Having being imprisoned in the Tower for a year he reaffirmed his recantation and was allowed by Wolsey to return to Cambridge. His melancholy temperament had been deeply affected by these experiences, and his companions were afraid to leave him alone. For two years he tried to live with the conviction that he had betrayed his principles. Then he announced that he was going 'up to Jerusalem', meaning that he intended to court martyrdom. This he did effectively enough by field-preaching in Norfolk and by giving the anchoress at Norwich a copy of Tyndale's New Testament. Approached by Bishop Nix's officers he was soon condemned, degraded and handed over to the secular arm by Dr. Pellys, the diocesan chancellor. Before going to the Lollard's Pit at St. Leonard's Hill in August 1531, he heard mass, received the eucharist, accepted confession and absolution. The future primate Matthew Parker, who was an eye-witness, denied the official story that he made a recantation at the stake, but the dispute over this point remains academic, for he had little of substance to recant.

While Latimer and Dr. Edward Crome, also examined about this time, could be saved by influential favour, the case of a relapsed heretic like Bilney remained hopeless. As in the secular courts, the position of an unpopular defendant in the hands of the Church was always perilous. The charge of heresy could too easily be brought against any critic of ancient practices and privileges; it had even been made by some enthusiasts against that stout Catholic Dr. Standish, when in 1515 he had championed the King's claims in a merely juridical dispute. The case of poor Bilney shows the rigid, merciless legalism of the system at its worst, yet in a sense he also fell victim to his own impatient scrupulosity. Had he waited a very few years, he would have been given nearly all he wanted by the conservative King and bishops. By his martyrdom he perhaps accomplished less than he might have done by continuing the simple call to faith and repentance, the mission to individuals he had already shown himself so well equipped to conduct. Bilney's memory and example worked fruitfully in the minds of a few friends, but among the people the affair occasioned no great scandal, since his earlier recantation had given him the repute of a relapsed heretic. The critics of the Church did not exploit his case as they had exploited that of Hunne; they needed broader targets and were already finding plenty elsewhere.

Frith and Bilney were by no means the only educated Reformers who failed to adapt themselves neatly to Luther's patterns. Amongst the most influential figures in Cambridge during the later twenties was George Stafford, a young Fellow of Pembroke Hall, who refused to base his New Testament lectures on the time-honoured *Sentences* of Peter Lombard, or to waste time upon figurative and anagogical interpretations.[25] A hearer of his expositions of St. Paul recalled that 'he seemed of a dead man to make him alive again and ... to set him forth in his native colours'. This method lay well within the tradition of Colet; both Stafford and his friend William Warner (later actually called the Cambridge Colet) could probably have joined Bilney and Latimer in disclaiming the influence of Luther. This did not save Stafford from being reported for heterodoxy to the Cardinal, but before encountering trouble from that quarter he died of the plague—which he happened to contract through his zealous efforts to extricate another Cambridge scholar from the toils of black magic!

So far from simplifying the pattern of the conflict, the advent of continental Protestantism soon made it more involved. Observing the thirties we cannot profitably think in simple terms of a Protestant-versus-Catholic struggle, since both sides, and especially the former, show profound divisions. The welter of beliefs and emphases had now become almost as confusing as in central Europe itself. This new decade, which in England saw the decisive political and confiscatory measures, remained, doctrinally speaking, an indecisive period of argument and uncertainty. Meanwhile a political, legal and expropriating Reformation went ahead without tarrying for theological agreement. The fixed point in a shifting world was the essential harmony between King and Parliament. But on the eve of these momentous changes it seemed perfectly possible that the King himself might inaugurate a sudden religious move to the left. When, late in 1528, Cardinal Campeggio returned to England in order to hear the royal divorce-suit, he was appalled to find Lutheran books freely circulating at court and to hear talk of a negotiation between the King and the Lutherans. At this time the Defender of the Faith was not above hinting that, in the event of his divorce being refused, he might embrace such radical notions. And as late as December 1529 he told the Imperial ambassador Chapuys that if Luther had limited himself to inveighing against the vices, abuses and errors of the clergy, instead of attacking the sacraments of the Church and other divine institutions, everybody would have followed him and written in his favour. 'Nevertheless', continued Henry, 'though the said Luther had evidently mixed up a good deal of heresy in his books, that was not a sufficient reason for reproving and rejecting the many truths he had brought to light.'[26] As we now know, the King was interested in putting pressure upon Rome and never seriously intended marching alongside the Lutherans. Quite apart from his Catholic doctrinal convictions, he always meant to be master in his own house rather than the junior partner and paymaster of some international theocracy. Nevertheless, his mood in December 1529 presaged ill for the Church, and his loyal lay subjects, at this time assembled in Parliament, were only too eager to help in paring down the voluminous privileges of the clergy. Before, however, we survey this first climax of the revolution, we have one last expanse of background to scan—the earlier story of tension between Church and State, the story which attained its climax in this so-called Reformation Parliament of 1529 to 1536. In a later chapter (ch. 13) we shall return in order to survey a related but even more complex phenomenon; that of anticlericalism in English social and literary life from the time of Wycliffe to that of Henry VIII. Meanwhile the political clash with the Papacy and the English Church, the clash which dominated the last twenty years of Henry's reign, will now demand our immediate attention.

6 State versus Church

The Growth of Erastianism

The English Protestant Reformation arose and grew largely in opposition to the will of Henry VIII. Yet for his own reasons the King soon initiated another Reformation, which was bound ere long to affect the course and character of the first. During the thirties he consummated a dual revolution, severing the English Church from the Papacy and subjugating it to the control of the Crown in Parliament. This act of state was made possible by the many influences we have already described, in particular by the weak hold of the Church upon political opinion. Once executed, the royal revolution became in itself a causal influence and did not fail to exert marked effects upon the religious, intellectual and social history of the nation. Had Henry patched up his quarrel with the Papacy in 1533, the spread of English Protestantism would probably have been retarded; some sort of concordat with Rome, however insecure, might for a time have been maintained. Powerful forces were nevertheless at work to promote drastic action at Government level, and only exceptional forbearance on both sides could have avoided a desperate crisis. The conflict between Church and State did not centre solely around the problem of the royal divorce; it was a conflict with its own involved history, its own compulsions. This being the case, the revolutionary measures of the Reformation Parliament cannot be understood without reference to certain earlier crises, which had lacked neither bitterness nor memorable qualities and which had already imposed some conspicuous statutory limitations upon the English Church. And alongside the more dramatic episodes we must not fail to observe something more fundamental—the gradual, exacerbating growth of anti-papal and Erastian[1] opinion in English political circles. Such opinion had, in addition, an academic background. When the powerful states of Renaissance Europe sought various forms of control over the churches within their power, they could find in medieval theory a plenitude of justificatory arguments. In Dante, in the publicists who espoused the cause of Philip IV of France against the popes, in Marsiglio of Padua and in Wycliffe, there abounded Erastian notions drawn from biblical, theological, philosophical and historical sources. Wycliffe was neither the greatest nor the most original of the medieval Erastians; moreover, it can clearly be shown that he was not the one who provided the main fund of these ideas to the defenders of Henrician Reformation in England. All these distinctions may be claimed with some confidence for Marsiglio, the most portentous of medieval rebels.[2] Both medical doctor and theologian, he won renown in those schools at Paris and Padua which also gave birth to the chief medieval forbears of modern natural science. In 1326, two years after the anonymous publication of his notorious work *Defensor Pacis*, his authorship became known and he fled to the service of the excommunicated Emperor Louis of Bavaria, with whose cause he remained closely involved until his death in 1342. Marsiglio's own excommunication at the hands of Pope John XXII can have surprised few contemporaries, since the *Defensor* was the most able, audacious and elaborate attack ever made upon the pretensions of the medieval Church. Arising from a reconsideration of Aristotelian doctrines it ended as a prophetic forerunner of the Protestant Erastianism of the sixteenth century, the democratic theory of the nineteenth and the State-worship of the twentieth. Briefly, it saw the secular State as the only cohesive force which could create a civilised life for man on earth, and it strove to exclude the Church from all worldly power and jurisdiction. The State is omnipotent, self-sufficient and entirely responsible for supplying the needs of its people for this present life. It derives its authority from the whole people, who retain the ultimate right to decide upon its institutional forms. The Church, on the other hand, is clearly bidden to centre its thought and action upon the next world. Here on earth it can claim no rights, no property, no jurisdiction save those which the State sees fit to lend it.

Marsiglio explicitly compares the functions of the clergy to those of physicians. They must celebrate religious rites, admonish the wicked, instruct men how to achieve everlasting life and to avoid damnation. But Christ's teaching gave them no authority to impose temporal punishment for sin or even to assign penances. Heresy, if punished at all in this world, should only be punished as a civil offence. The clergy should be subject, equally with laymen, to all the provisions of State-law; they can claim no prescriptive rights to tithes or tax-exemptions unless the State thinks it expedient to grant them such privileges. Moreover, all church-officials from popes and bishops downward receive their offices from civil rulers; so long as they obtain their emoluments, they can legitimately be compelled by these rulers to perform their religious duties, and if found unsatisfactory can be deposed by civil action. The Church consists of the whole people; it is simply the citizen-body organised (and organised as simply as possible) for other-worldly purposes. Marsiglio at least begins to approach the Lutheran notion of the priesthood of all believers when he says that laymen are also churchmen, *viri ecclesiastici*. While Christ instituted the priesthood, such offices as those of pope and bishop remain of human institution and their holders have no spiritual qualities or rights beyond those of simple priests. The Pope can claim no authority as the successor of St. Peter; even Peter himself enjoyed no pre-eminence over the other apostles; he is not called a bishop, and indeed there exists no adequate historical proof that he was ever in Rome. The ecclesiastical primacy of Rome obviously arose, argues Marsiglio, from the fact that the city was the capital of the Empire. This being so, papal decretals and canon law in general have no binding force except in so far as the State may sanction them. Christian doctrine and conduct have only one sure basis—the New Testament.

Marsiglio was the boldest thinker of an age when many thinkers had been provoked to Erastianism by the excessive claims of Boniface VIII and by the succeeding Avignonese Captivity, which, incidentally, had a parellel in the Habsburg captivity of the sixteenth century. Some of his views had been anticipated by Dubois and John of Paris; many were shared by his associate in the imperial service, William of Occam, or were to be elaborated in the next generation by Wycliffe. They did not suffer oblivion amid the more moderate and statesmanlike efforts of the Conciliar Movement, and in some directions they were reinforced by the irreverent humanist scholarship of the fifteenth century. Even Marsiglio had believed in the Donation of Constantine, the forged document whereby the Papacy imagined itself to have derived a vast jurisdiction from the Emperor. His unquiet spirit might have rejoiced almost a century after his death when Lorenzo Valla, later on to become himself a great papal official, conclusively proved the spurious character of the Donation.

It would be easy to exaggerate and to misunderstand the impact of fourteenth- and fifteenth-century theorists upon the Reformation at home and abroad. Early Tudor Englishmen did not in general develop Erastian and anticlerical views through reading authors like Marsiglio and Wycliffe. Such views arose in the main through practical abuses, quarrels, scandals and conflicts of interest. Theory tended to remain in the storehouse until the political situation demanded its production and its use as propaganda. This, as we shall observe, was particularly the case with Marsiglio of Padua, who enjoyed his heyday in England only when the propagandists supporting the actions of Henry VIII found in the *Defensor* a valuable armoury of weapons. Until the King of England actually found himself in a situation analogous to that of the Emperor Louis, the views of Marsiglio played little part in the formulation of English opinion or in the conduct of Anglo-Papal relations.

Tensions between Church and State

With marked success over long periods, medieval Europe had maintained a compromise between the notion of a Universal Church, governed at the centre by its own popes and councils, yet at the many points where it touched and comprehended secular life yielding large areas of jurisdiction and influence to the various states. This division of authority did not lie along the lines which modern minds would regard as dividing the spiritual from the temporal. In England as elsewhere the church courts dealt, as one would anticipate, with heresy, blasphemy, contempt of clerical authority, absence from church services, dereliction of duty by the clergy. Yet they also dealt with perjury, slander, drunkenness, sorcery, incontinence, adultery, matrimonial disputes and the probate of wills. On the other side, the King's courts had resolutely maintained their jurisdiction over all matters involving the real estate of the Church, including the important sphere of advowsons. The State never relaxed its view that all benefices and ecclesiastical corporations owed their physical existence to royal and noble benefaction, while the King never forgot that he was lord of all the land in England. Again, after those lurid scenes in which the figure of Thomas Becket bulked so large, a relatively stable compromise had been achieved concerning jurisdiction over criminal clergy. Other compromises had been forced upon kings and popes by plain common sense. Whether or not, for example, a diocesan bishop was a royal minister, he always retained extensive secular duties and feudal obligations. It was hence highly desirable (and usually the case after Edward II's reign) that chapters should consult the King, and the King the Pope, concerning the choice of persons to occupy episcopal sees.

Nationalism within the English Church grew in strength throughout the medieval centuries; one could list many prominent clergy whose actions proclaim that in all practical matters they considered themselves primarily Englishmen rather than subjects of the Roman Pontiff. All the same, the common medieval term *Ecclesia Anglicana* never meant 'Church of England' in the post-Reformation sense of an independent national Church claiming parity with that of Rome. Whatever its material reservations, the medieval English Church acknowledged the spiritual overlordship and jurisdiction of the Papacy. It administered in its courts a body of law based upon papal decrees and upon the canons of international church councils. Only on its fringes—for example, on matters concerning tithes and testamentary jurisdiction—had this law been modified by English national custom.

So far as the persons and property of the clergy were concerned, the balance of real power had fluctuated along with the political exigencies of the realm and of the Papacy. At the end of John's reign and under Henry III the measure of papal control stood high. Under Edward III and Richard II, when the prestige of a reputedly pro-French or divided papacy sank to its nadir, the actual powers of the Crown rose in marked degree and the English bishops looked increasingly to the King as their master. This was the period distinguished in England by the statutes of Provisors and *Praemunire*.[3] The former statutes, of which four were made from 1351 to 1389, were framed to curb papal 'provisions', or appointments to vacant English benefices over the heads of ordinary patrons. Disregarded even by Edward III himself, they did little to diminish the frequency of such provisions, which continued numerous until the Reformation. The three *Praemunire* statutes (1353, 1365, 1393) were designed to check papal encroachments against the rights of the Crown; they were likewise the outcome of temporary situations and speedily disregarded. They culminated in the so-called Great Statute (1393) and, since this was the law to be used by Henry VIII with such paralysing effect against the English clergy, we should note here its original intentions.

The Great Statute involved in substance a protest against two hostile manœuvres by Pope Boniface IX. He had threated to excommunicate English bishops who enforced decisions of the King's courts regarding advowsons; he had also criticised the acceptance of secular offices by certain bishops and had threatened to shift them from see to see, thus shaking a government heavily dependent upon clerical ministers. The Great Statute was a political manifesto meant to impress the Pope with the determination and unity of the kingdom. It did not prohibit the entry of all papal bulls or otherwise threaten the wholesale exclusion of papal jurisdiction from England; it merely threatened with forfeiture of land and goods all persons who should introduce papal bulls in order to execute these two specific threats against the bishops. The particular quarrel was soon healed, and for many years relations were resumed as if the Great Statute had never been enacted. So loosely, however, had its text been drafted that in subsequent times lay lawyers began to envisage its use as a multi-purpose weapon against ecclesiastical jurisdiction. Humphrey Duke of Gloucester attempted to employ it in order to weaken his rival Cardinal Beaufort, while later in the fifteenth century Crown lawyers invoked certain of its passages to suggest that the Church courts were of dubious legality, as representing a 'foreign' jurisdiction. While no responsible statesmen then anticipated either a severance from Roman jurisdiction or a drastic interference with the age-old operations of the canon law, the two-handed engine continued to stand without, still capable of smiting, even were its mechanism rusted and its original purposes largely forgotten.

This period of royal ascendancy continued under the Lancastrian kings, who banished or even executed rebellious bishops and who thrice compelled prelates to refuse cardinalates, even though duly nominated in Rome. Meanwhile on a lower level, fifteenth-century common lawyers did all they could to encroach upon the jurisdiction of the church courts. But the advent of the Tudor dynasty formed no landmark; the reign of Henry VII was far from presaging major crises in Anglo-Papal or Church-State relations. On both fronts, it appears in retrospect one of the more harmonious chapters in the long story. The King and the Pope behaved as wily managing directors combining to dominate the supine body of shareholders known as *Ecclesia Anglicana*. To the English bishops and senior clergy the reign cannot indeed have seemed a honeymoon between the temporal power and the clergy. The royal policy seems riddled with minor anticlerical actions, mostly financial in character; in particular, the recognizances exacted from the bishops during Henry's later years left them owing enormous debts to the Crown. Even in relations with the popes, the balance of tangible advantage had now tipped decisively to the side of the King, who extracted many privileges from Rome but suffered little hard cash to leave England for the papal coffers. No pope disputed his nominations to English preferments, which were always made with strict regard to the interests of the Crown. Seldom if ever before had the episcopal bench and the more sumptuous benefices been more solidly packed with royal administrators and diplomats. On the other hand, like his Lancastrian forbears, the King ostentatiously displayed his abhorrence for heresy, and on one occasion he even troubled to convert a Lollard at the stake before burning him, *pour encourager les autres*.

The two Church-State tensions which then assumed prominence would have attracted little subsequent notice but for their sequels under Henry VIII. Their appearance under both kings was nevertheless more than accidental, because both related to that most basic task of the dynasty—the imposition of law and order upon a turbulent people recently torn by civil strife. The two problems were those of sanctuary and benefit of clergy. Exemption from the harsher punishments of secular justice had in former times been extended not only to clerics in major and minor orders but even to such laymen as were supposedly capable of receiving ordination through their ability to read Latin. The requirement commonly involved stumbling through a so-called 'neck-verse', after which modest feat the criminal, delivered to the bishop, might succeed in purging himself by oath-helpers or in escaping with a relatively mild penance. Perpetrators of treason and of certain felonies had already been debarred from claiming benefit, and the innovations under Henry VII merely resulted in a slight enlargement of these excluded categories. The statute of 1489 provided that any felon claiming clerical privilege should be branded on the thumb and that, if he claimed it a second time, his plea should be refused unless he could prove himself actually in holy orders. A second statute (1497) deprived a layman of the claim if he had committed petty treason by murdering his lord or master. So far as concerned the right of santuary,[4] the severest problems arose in connection with great chartered sanctuaries like those of Durham and Beverley. By taking refuge here many serious criminals escaped justice, since—unlike those who sought sanctuary in an ordinary church—they were not required to abjure the realm after forty days but might linger there unpunished for life provided they took oaths of obedience to the lord of the jurisdiction. Once subject to him they could not be made answerable for further crimes, even those committed outside the sanctuary-area. In 1487 the judges held in the case of Humphrey Stafford (who had tried to start a rising against Henry VII) that sanctuary did not avail in cases of high treason, a development later supported by a papal bull. When, however, these various measures are taken together, they constitute a very modest advance of the State into the domains of the Church. The claims of the first Tudor might have been made by any late medieval King; they can hardly be regarded as a prelude to the work of the Reformation Parliament.

During the later years of the reign, it is true, certain royal officials developed radical views. One of these was the King's unjustly notorious agent Edmund Dudley, destined along with his colleague Sir Richard Empson to be thrown to the wolves by Henry VIII. The modern interest in Dudley's book *The Tree of Commonwealth*[5] may seem antiquarian in character; while written in 1509–10 during its author's imprisonment in the Tower, it lay unprinted until a century ago, and hence cannot rank in the sequence of Erastian books which helped to form Tudor opinion. It nevertheless throws light upon those trends of thought among early Tudor lawyers and officials which foreshadowed some aspects of the coming Royal

Supremacy. Long before men had heard of Luther and his godly princes, Dudley argued that church-reform was an urgent task which must be pursued under royal guidance. The King was by right not merely the protector but the overseer of the Church, for he appointed the bishops and was responsible for making them conscientious in the punishment of wrongdoers. Moreover, he should foster concord within the realm by adjudging disputes between the clergy and the laity. 'And no man', concludes Dudley, 'can do it but the Prince.' At the time these words were written, the new King was but nineteen years of age, his mind filled by antique notions of military glory on the fields of France. If then, or for several years to come, he ever heard his servants talking along Dudley's lines, he is unlikely to have reflected upon their full implications. In Sir Thomas More's pregnant phrase, the lion did not yet know his strength.

The Hunne Affair and its Sequels

To a modern reader, the eccelesiastic history of Henry VIII's first year does not lack some prophetic notes. When Archbishop Warham called a provincial council for January 1510 the text of his summons dwelt upon the hostile attitude of the laity toward the clergy and the rights of the Church. And if one did not know their date, one would attribute his lurid phrases to the period of the Reformation Parliament twenty years later. Dean Colet, chosen to preach the inaugural sermon, placed the blame for this lay malevolence upon the 'evil life' of the clergy themselves. 'Ye will have the Church's liberty, and not be drawn before secular judges, and that also is right ... but if ye desire this liberty, first unloose yourself from the worldly bondage.' With puritanical severity, Colet then thundered against their moral laxity, greed, immersion in secular business, and he called for a series of specific reforms—stricter examination of candidates for orders, the gift of benefices to worthy men, rehabilitation of the religious orders, more frequent provincial councils, strictly canonical elections to bishoprics, injunctions against simony, non-residence, dissolute clerics, the wasteful use of episcopal revenues and the 'filths and uncleanliness' of ecclesiastical courts. After this rousing start the gathering proceeded to an anticlimax. Its reform-committee included strong personalities like Colet himself, Bishop Fisher and Bishop Nix of Norwich, but it managed to produce only three constitutions directed against unruly stipendiary priests, simoniacs and improper clerical costume. No real programme of reform emerged, and the provincial council soon fell back into wearisome jurisdictional disputes of the sort which had bedevilled the careers of bishops and their officials throughout the Middle Ages.[6]

Early in the new reign serious discussion still centred on benefit of clergy, and in 1512 its scope was again somewhat circumscribed by an Act of Parliament which removed benefit from persons not in orders, if they committed murder or felony in churches, were guilty of murder or robbery on the highway, or robbery accompanied by murder or violence in private houses. Even this moderate reform still lay *sub judice*, since the Act was couched as a temporary one, to operate only under the next Parliament. In May 1514 a further complication arose when the Pope promulgated a declaration that no layman had authority over a cleric by any law, human or divine—a position which seemed to threaten the compromises attained in England centuries ago. Yet before this matter could be revived in Parliament, it became merged in the graver series of disputes which arose from the murder of Richard Hunne. To this astonishing story, concerning which some important discoveries were published as recently as 1961, we have hitherto made only passing allusions. Since it forms a landmark in the development of Erastian and anticlerical opinion, it now demands a steadier glance.[7]

Richard Hunne was a merchant tailor and freeman of the city of London with a hitherto good personal reputation. As we now know, his troubles began not a few months but three years before his death. In March 1511 his infant son died in the parish of St. Mary Matfelon, Whitechapel, and the rector Thomas Dryffeld demanded the bearing sheet by way of mortuary dues. Hunne refused, on the ground that the sheet belonged to him and not to the baby. In April 1512, rather sordidly, the rector instituted proceedings at Lambeth and there on 13 May Cuthbert Tunstall (then Warham's chancellor) decided the case against Hunne. In January 1513 Hunne brought a charge of slander against the rector's assistant priest, Henry Marshall, alleging that in the previous month Marshall had refused to conduct evensong in his presence, since he was 'accursed'. This slur, it was claimed, had injured Hunne's credit with his business associates. The slander-case was never settled but went through a series of adjournments until Hunne's death. Meanwhile, in Hilary Term 1513 Hunne instituted another suit, also in the King's Bench, against the rector Thomas Dryffeld and others, the charge being that they had offended against the *Praemunire* Statutes. He was not the first litigant to attempt such a counterstroke against the church courts, but there may have been a measure of truth in More's characterisation of Hunne as 'a man high minded and set on the glory of a victory'. It is now apparent that this *Praemunire* suit was also never in fact settled; it was repeatedly adjourned on a point of law, the last adjournment being from Michaelmas 1514 to Hilary 1515, by which latter date Hunne was dead.

In view of the hostility of the secular courts, Hunne's use of this weapon was naturally regarded as provocative by the clergy, and at this stage the Bishop of London, Richard Fitzjames, took a hand. He was an elderly but venturesome prelate, ready to go to any lengths in the defence of ecclesiastical interests. Sir Thomas More's later references to him are surprisingly polite, considering that he had persecuted Colet and that Erasmus thought him the worst type of superstitious reactionary. In this affair he lived well up to his reputation and augmented his already marked unpopularity in London.

On the bishop's order Hunne was arrested, and a search of his house yielded some heretical books, including a Wycliffite Bible. Pending his trial he was confined in the Lollards' Tower at the south-west corner of Old St. Paul's. On Saturday 2 December 1514 he was taken to Fulham for examination by Fitzjames. Brought back to the prison he was discovered the following morning hanging in his cell. A coroner's jury refused to return a verdict of suicide, since the body and the state of the cell showed signs that Hunne had been strangled before his neck had been broken. After a long examination of those able to trace the movements of the persons involved, the jury found a verdict of wilful murder against the Bishop's chancellor, Dr. Horsey, and against two of Horsey's henchmen. One of these was the gaoler Charles Joseph who had been one of the defendants in Hunne's *Praemunire* suit. Joseph subsequently confessed that he and others had strangled Hunne; the usual story that he made this admission under duress depends merely upon the assertion of Fitzjames, an unsupported assertion which involves various improbabilities.

The three were duly indicted, but the ecclesiastical authorities managed to prevent their being brought to trial, an outcome which convinced London lay opinion that they had indeed perpetrated a murder of revenge and intimidation. When a court presided over by Fitzjames pronounced Hunne a contumacious heretic and handed over the body to be burned at Smithfield, the atmosphere became still further poisoned, since this judgment literally reduced his family to pauperism, entailing as it did the forfeiture of his property to the Crown. From the legal viewpoint this was rightly thought a strange judgment, for Hunne had not been convicted in his lifetime and no just inference of his final contumacy could be made. The London diarist Wriothesley summed up the impression of the man in the street when he wrote that Hunne 'was made a heretic for suing a *Praemunire*'. Here we may leave the personal aspects of Hunne's case, though not without a word of warning against most of the literature which has accumulated around it. The conflicting accounts by More, Hall and Foxe, written long afterwards by highly-prejudiced propagandists ignorant of the documents, remain all but worthless. Of Gairdner's equally prejudiced attempt to exculpate the churchmen,[8] the less said the better.

The grave disturbances raised in London by the scandal of Hunne's death represent no sudden and isolated upsurge of anticlerical feeling on the part of his fellow-citizens. We have commented elsewhere on the importance of tithe-disputes as a background against which ill-feeling between clergy and laity should be viewed. Especially is this true of the Londoners.[9] For at least two centuries they had engaged in periodic but often bitter conflicts with their parish priests over the assessment of their tithes, and the city records show that this struggle had again reached one of its more chronic phases. Quarrels, law-suits, negotiations and short-lived awards dragged on until 1534, when Thomas Cromwell and other high officials arbitrated on the dispute and had their awards confirmed by Act of Parliament. In addition, other prominent cases concerning mortuary dues and offerings occurred in London both before and after the case of Hunne. The city remained small enough to allow the personalities of the contestants to become widely known, yet it was large enough to develop a formidable volume of mass resentment, whether against foreign traders, exacting clergymen or any other group whose interests were distinguishable from those of the citizen-body.

For our purposes, the political sequels of the Hunne affair are far more important than its resemblances to detective-fiction. When in February 1515 the Commons met under its shadow, they staged a passionate counter-attack upon benefit of clergy and soon attempted to renew the temporary statute of 1512. At this juncture Richard Kidderminster, the distinguished and scholarly Abbot of Winchcombe, preached at Paul's Cross that such a measure contravened the law of God and the liberties of the Church. Whatever the force of his arguments they were at least in harmony with the recent papal declaration. The temporal Lords and some of the Commons retorted with an appeal to the King, who, never averse to take part in a display of learning, arranged a disputation on this issue. Here the Church was represented by Abbot Kidderminster, the King by Dr. Henry Standish, warden of the Greyfriars and a favourite court-preacher. The latter denied that a papal decree upholding the immunity of clerics in minor orders could apply to England. When the Abbot quoted the text 'Touch not mine anointed', Standish tried in the manner of the humanist generation to put the Psalm into its historical context. Parliament adjourned in April, but the dispute died down only to revive on its reassembly in November. It was then that Standish received a summons to appear before Convocation and, foreseeing an imminent charge of heresy, appealed for protection to the King. In the wrangles which followed, the temporal Lords, the Commons, the justices and the common lawyers all viewed the immunities of the clergy against the emotional background of the Hunne case. Some of their opponents, equally uncompromising, went so far as to deny long-established English law by asserting that a cleric could not even be brought to answer, let alone be tried, in a secular court. Dr. Standish and his supporter Dr. Veysey, dean of the King's chapel, replied that this claim manifestly defied ancient practice. In a subsequent dispute at the Blackfriars, the judges widened the scope of the debate by accusing Convocation of a breach of *Praemunire* and by asserting that the King could hold a Parliament without the Lords spiritual, who had the right to appear merely by reason of their temporal possessions. The judges made clear their view that Parliament was not only the highest court of the realm but derived its authority from lay sources alone.

The final meeting of the series was held at Baynard's Castle, and here Wolsey (whose dual position commands some sympathy) presented an apology for the churchmen, urging that they had not thought of diminishing the royal prerogative. On the other hand, he petitioned that the dispute over benefit of clergy might be referred to Rome; he and everyone else well knew which way judgement would there be given. When the King told the bishops that Dr. Standish had answered their points, Richard Fox, then on the point of resignation from political life, exploded in fury, 'Sir, I warrant you Dr. Standish will not abide by his opinion at his peril.' This was an open threat which allowed Standish to gain sympathy by another dramatic appeal for royal protection. 'What should one poor friar do alone', he cried, 'against all the bishops and clergy of England?' While the King had no intention of handing over his champion to the mercy of the bishops, he was still young, conventional and dependent on a great ecclesiastic as his chief minister. Having reasserted the freedom of English kings from any earthly superior, he assumed the rôle of peacemaker and allowed the struggle to end with honour even. Horsey appeared in the King's Bench, pleaded not guilty and obtained his discharge, while Standish was likewise dismissed by Convocation. Henry caused his parliamentary agents to drop the bill which stripped benefit from minor clerics; he also allowed the attack on mortuary dues to languish. But with equal significance, he refused to remit the matter to Rome and in 1518–19 he made both Standish and Veysey bishops.

The precise importance of this crisis of 1514–15 remains far from easy to assess. To regard it as a dress-rehearsal of the Henrician Reformation would be misleading, but it did to some extent foreshadow the initial stages of the Reformation Parliament in 1529–32, when reforms were being pressed upon the Church yet without schismatic designs against Rome. In 1515 the rival armies of Church and State had been drawn up in full battle order; they had exchanged loud shouts of defiance and even a few blows. Nevertheless, their generals had no intention of allowing serious bloodshed, pitched battles or extensive conquests. Wolsey, the most influential amongst them, was a *condottiere* engaged for high fees by both sides. Yet this mustering of the forces did not lack significance, and the King was left to meditate at leisure upon the spectacle. Should Church-State relations threaten in future to become strained, he would know in advance the muster-rolls both of his followers and of his opponents.

Apart from a strong Erastian faction amongst the knights and burgesses of the Commons, the whole legal fraternity from the judges downwards had now shown itself more than willing to assault the ranks of clerical privilege. From this same profession there soon arose the earlier anticlerical and royalist pamphleteers, while the Inns of Court, always a great formative force in Tudor life, were also to contain in the late twenties something regarded by the King with far less favourable eyes—a strong Protestant cell. Even so, the crisis we have described lacked any immediate sequel. Apart from that of the year 1523 there were no Parliaments for the remainder of Wolsey's ministry and so fewer chances of another frontal clash. The King was anything but a natural revolutionary, and for many years to come he had no personal motives to exercise his strength against the Church. In 1521 he published his book *Assertio Septem Sacramentorum*, denouncing the heresies of Luther; it sold well in numerous Latin, English and German versions and, dedicated to Leo X, earned for its author and his successors the title *Defender of the Faith*. Yet while the events of 1514–15 remained so vividly alive in the minds of Londoners until the Reformation Parliament, Henry himself can scarcely have forgotten their lessons. The historian Polydore Vergil, then London agent of the papal collector, had written that the people were 'raging against the clergy, or would be if the King's Majesty were not curbing their fury'.[10] What an enviable position for a King, and how unenviable for the Church and the Papacy, should the latter become unable to give an increasingly egotistical King what he most wanted in the world!

While the Cardinal's ministry attracted hatred against Wolsey in person, it also increased the violence of indiscriminate anticlericalism, which began to develop into general attacks upon the Church even before Wolsey vanished from the scene. 'Nearly all the people here hate the priests', wrote Chapuys a month after the assembly of the Reformation Parliament in November 1529. Both the lay grievances of the twenties and the clerical reaction are clearly recorded by the chronicler Edward Hall in his account of its first session.[11] Here Sir Henry Guildford declared that he had paid the enormous sum of 1,000 marks to the Lord Cardinal and the Archbishop of Canterbury for probate of the will of Sir William Compton. With heavy sarcasm other members claimed that the clergy, such was their charity, would take a dead man's only cow from his beggared children rather than forgo their mortuary dues. Ecclesiastics, they alleged, were also exacting landlords, grinding the faces of poor husbandmen; abbots kept tanneries and traded in wool like temporal merchants; beneficed clergy resided at court and in the households of lords; they took everything from their parishioners, leaving them without preaching and instruction, to the peril of their souls; unlearned priests held ten or twelve benefices, while learned scholars at the universities lacked the means to study. When the unfortunate clergy heard this parliamentary chorus, it seemed to them as if the whole lay world had been suddenly inspired by the Devil to turn and rend them. 'My lords', exclaimed Bishop Fisher in the Upper House, 'you see daily what bills come hither from the Commons House, and all to the destruction of the Church. For God's sake, see what a realm the kingdom of Bohemia was, and when the Church went down, then fell the glory of the kingdom: now with the Commons is nothing but down with the Church: and all this, me seemeth, is for lack of faith only.'

These jeremiads, reported to the Commons, only served to enhance their rage and make them exclaim that they were slandered as heretics in the presence of the Lords. Their Speaker set off with thirty members to the King's presence. 'Are we infidels, are we Saracens, are we pagans and heathens, that the laws which we establish should be thought not worthy to be kept by Christian men? I beseech your Highness to call that bishop before you, and bid him speak more discretely of such a number as be in the Commons House.' The King, careful as ever not to cross them, soon brought about a superficial reconciliation, and Fisher had to explain away his irate words. During these exchanges the faults of both sides appear with painful clarity. The Commons generalised unjustly from the darkest aspects of canon law and church-administration. The ecclesiastical hierarchy thought nothing so important as the maintenance of every privilege and source of income which churchmen had gained in very different times. Meanwhile, some of their more incautious officials managed to keep alive the bitter memories of Hunne's case. The best-known of these follies arose in relation to the will of a Gloucestershire gentleman, William Tracy of Toddington. When this document came in 1531 to be proved in the Prerogative Court of

Canterbury, Tracy was found to have used the form which later became common in Protestant wills; he had written that he trusted to be saved only by the merits of Christ and did not rely upon the works of men, or upon saints or masses.[12] After Archbishop Warham had consulted Convocation as to the will's orthodoxy, Tracy was pronounced a heretic and orders were sent to Dr. Parker, chancellor of the Worcester diocese, to exhume the corpse from consecrated ground. Not only did Parker comply, but he also burned it, a childish blunder, for it was agreed that only the King's officers could burn a heretic, dead or alive. Informed of this offensive zeal the King sent for Parker, who pleaded the Archbishop's orders. But Warham was now dead; the plea availed nothing and the offender was compelled to forfeit the very large sum of £300 to gain his pardon.

St. German and Simon Fish

These hostile exchanges meanwhile had their analogies in the literary field. Here we encounter one of the founders of Henrician legal and political theory in Christopher St. German, who unlike his luckless contemporary Edmund Dudley, survived not only to utilise the press but also to participate in the actual crisis of the struggle.[13] Born about 1460, the son of a Warwickshire knight, educated at Oxford and the Inner Temple, St. German was already an old man when he came to prominence in the controversies surrounding the Henrician revolution. As a jurist he took little interest in religious dogma, to which his approach was conservative. This made him the greater menace to the clergy, who found themselves unable to pin him down by a colourable charge of heresy; it allowed him free rein to indulge his grand passion, for he was the very embodiment of the old hatred felt by the common lawyers for ecclesiastical jurisdiction. After 1532 he was to become a thoroughgoing defender of each new position occupied by the King, but his earlier works antedate the revolutionary years and may claim a conspicuous place among those which prepared public opinion for drastic change.

St. German's first book, published in 1532, was called *Dialogus de fundamentis legum et de conscientia*, being an academic discussion in Latin between a doctor and a student concerning theories of law and equity and their relation to the law of England. In 1530 St. German published a second dialogue, this time in the vernacular; then in the following year came a free translation of the first dialogue and an appendix of thirteen 'Additions' containing some important views on the powers of Parliament in relation to the Church. The English version and its extensions, together known as *Doctor and Student*, not only enunciated anticlerical doctrine but also exerted a prolonged influence on English thought, since they formed a guide for law-students up to the time of Blackstone. Also among St. German's formative works stands his *Division between the Spirituality and Temporality*, published in 1532 and often regarded as part of a royal propaganda-campaign then in its initial stages. In fact, no documentary proof indicates a connection at this date between the author and the government. The *Division* attracted the attentions of Sir Thomas More, who devoted much of his *Apology* to an attack upon it. When in 1533 St. German replied with his *Dialogue betwixt Salem and Bizance*, More again intervened and closed the controversy with his *Debellacyon of Salem and Bizance*. This sharp conflict did not, however, exhaust the energies of the formidable septuagenarian, who then produced three more controversial pamphlets, keeping well abreast of the governmental advance and seeing with exceptional clarity and prescience the full implications of the newly-enunciated Royal Supremacy.

From the first, St. German had much to say about abuses of ecclesiastical jurisdiction; he always entertained an exalted conception of the rights of the State and came near to equating the English common law with the Law of Reason itself. Nevertheless, the modernity of his earlier views could easily be exaggerated. Repeatedly he refers to Gerson (who had died a century earlier) to prove that canon law is far from being identical with divine law and, again, that jurisdiction over all temporal things belongs to the secular State. If he does not mention Marsiglio of Padua by name, his debt to that patriarch of radical Erastianism becomes clear when, for example, he says that the clergy 'undoubtedly make not the Church, for the whole congregation of Christian people maketh the Church'. Again, St. German's theory of English law is closely based upon Sir John Fortescue's *jus politicum et regale*—the notion that a King of England must obtain the consent of his subjects in order to legislate. With this traditional background he can never think in terms of a royal autocracy, and in *Doctor and Student* he stresses the necessity of parliamentary consent to English law-making. It is in this emphasis upon parliamentary sovereignty and statute law that the earlier works of St. German most obviously foreshadow the changes about to be executed by the Reformation Parliament. From 1530–32 St. German was claiming for Parliament cognizance of all matters affecting property, goods and money; it may justly, he argued, legislate upon mortuary-dues, prevent the further transference of lands into mortmain or prohibit bishops from charging visitation fees upon religious foundations. One startling passage of the *Division between the Spirituality and Temporality* even assigns to Parliament an absolute power to redistribute all temporal things between subjects, whether laymen or clergy. On the other side, St. German will not allow to the church courts the right to decree the forfeiture of the goods of a heretic. Likewise, if a man be excommunicated in a church court for debt or trespass, he may forthwith sue for a writ of *Praemunire facias* against his ecclesiastical opponents. In *Doctor and Student* the author would leave the Church with jurisdiction only in the narrow category of 'mere spiritual things'. Though he puts his case with more precision and verve than his predecessors, he is nevertheless in his earlier works carrying old ideas to extremities rather than inventing new ones. The *Division* does not go far beyond the dialogues, and together they cannot be said to constitute a wholly revolutionary theory of Church and State. They assert that the

Church has often exceeded its legal authority in relation to English statutes and customs and in relation to the divine law. They glorify the common law and assert the omnicompetence, even the infallibility, of Parliament in all causes concerned with property and temporal things. On the other hand, they as yet present neither an attack upon the Papacy nor the suggestion that ecclesiastical jurisdiction in England derives from the Crown. These later and more advanced phases of St. German's thought proceeded *pari passu* with the actual statutes of the Reformation Parliament.

Sir Thomas More ridiculed St. German's grave and judicial pose as a 'pacifier' of these disputes, and his trick of avoiding specific charges against the clergy by prefacing his anticlerical stories with the phrase, 'Some say'. 'All his some says', retorts More, 'be of his own saying.' The first criticism seems to have substantial justice, for the tears of St. German over clerical misdeeds are indeed those of the crocodile. The second has less justice, since in those times a man could not, without fear of plague-ridden dungeons, make specific charges against bishops and ecclesiastical courts. And however slight the sincerity behind his professed solicitude for the Church, St. German's polemical methods seem urbane in comparison with those of the London rabble-rousers to whom we now turn. Into this Grub Street category Simon Fish must fall, though he was also a lawyer with the same professional prejudices as St. German. His *Supplication of Beggars* can scarcely be claimed as a serious Protestant pamphlet; it exemplifies anti-clericalism in its most virulent, unprincipled and eloquent form. Driven into exile through a quarrel with Wolsey, Fish subsequently helped to distribute copies of Tyndale's New Testament; he was also circulating his *Supplication* in London as early as 1529. According to a picturesque story in Foxe, Anne Boleyn introduced it to the King, who 'kept the book in his bosom for three or four days'. Henry then made contact with Mrs. Fish and persuaded her to produce her husband, who lay in hiding only a mile from the court. If we may believe an anecdote almost too good to be true, the King then 'embraced him with loving countenance', took him hunting for several hours and gave him his own signet to protect him against the hostility of the Chancellor, Sir Thomas More. Whatever the accuracy of these stories, the contents of the book were calculated to please Henry, who no doubt saw in Fish a potentially valuable henchman should the threatened struggle develop. Unfortunately for such a design, the pamphleteer died of the plague in the following year, 1531. His wife must also have felt strong religious convictions, since she then married the son of a Gloucestershire knight, James Bainham, one of the Protestants allegedly whipped by order of Sir Thomas More in his garden. Whatever the reliability of this other story, Bainham was certainly burned at the stake in 1532.

In the *Supplication* Fish makes none of St. German's pretensions to judicial calm and conciliation.[14] Every punch is as hard as the author can make it and not a few are directed below the belt. We must attempt to summarise Fish's argument in something like his own manner, since a polite synopsis of full-flooded Tudor propaganda would miss the point. This argument is couched in the form of a supplication coming from the outcasts of society and directed to the King. The lepers, the sick, the needy, the impotent, complain to the King that they die of hunger, because of these holy beggars and vagabonds—bishops, abbots, priests, monks, friars, pardoners and summoners, who have taken into their hands a third of the kingdom. Even the poor tithe-paying housewife must account for every tenth egg or be taken as a heretic. And what money they pull in by probates, mortuaries, pardons and fines! Above all (and here the figures rise well into the realms of fantasy) a vast income of over £40,000 goes to the begging friars. Is it any marvel that secular taxes can be levied only with great difficulty? The Turk himself would never be gaining ground in Christendom if he had to cope with such a horde of locusts within his realm. What are the holy thieves doing with these annual exactions from the people? Nothing, except translating all rule, power, lordship, authority, obedience and dignity from your Grace to themselves. 'Since the days when King John was made tributary to Rome, your most noble realm (alas for shame!) has stood tributary, not unto any kind of temporal prince, but unto a cruel devilish blood-supper, drunken with the blood of the saints and martyrs of Christ ever since.' And what do they more? Truly, nothing but apply themselves, by all the sleights they may, to corrupt every man's wife, daughter and maid, that licentiousness should reign over all your subjects, that no man should know his own child, that their bastards should inherit every man's possessions to the disinheritance of the right-begotten children. Lured by their superfluous riches into unclean lust, they carry disease about the realm; some even boast among their fellows that they have meddled with a hundred women. Some have run off with men's wives and goods as well, reducing whole families to beggary.

Where is your sword, the poor people ask the King, where is your power that should punish such felonies committed by this generation? How many more people would there be in the realm if these celibates had married? What woman will work for threepence a day, if she can have at least twenty pence for gratifying a monk or friar? What honest person dare take into his service any man or woman who has been at school with a spiritual man? Who can get justice against the clergy, when all the learned men of the realm are paid fees by them? If poor Richard Hunne had not sued a priest, he would have yet been alive. Did not your noble predecessors provide statutes against mortmain? Yet notwithstanding, have not the clergy gotten into their hands more land than ever? What law can be made against them? In return for all these riches, they can only claim to deliver our souls out of purgatory by their prayers. Yet, as learned men now declare, there is no purgatory; it was a thing invented by the covetous spirituality. In any event, they will pray for nobody unless they are given money. People who protest against the system are called heretics, forced to do penance or burned at the stake. Christ submitted himself to temporal government, gave Caesar his due, and taught that the higher powers must always be obeyed. To conceal these teachings, the clergy will not allow the New Testament to go abroad in the mother tongue. And did not Dr. Allen, the Cardinal's chancellor, seek to deprive your Grace of such pleas as belong to your high courts and to withdraw them to the church courts? Did not Dr. Horsey murder Richard Hunne when he sued for your writ of *Praemunire*? And your own Lord Chancellor, hitherto always a cleric, will take care to maintain his own ecclesiastical kingdom, even though all temporal kingdoms in the world should be destroyed. What remedy is there for us, the poor and the sick? Should men found more hospitals? No, the more the worse, for always the fat of the whole foundation hangs on the priests' beards. If your Grace will build us a sure hospital, take from these oppressors all their ill-gotten gains. Set these sturdy lubbers to work, to get them wives of their own, to earn their livings by the sweat of their faces! Tie these holy thieves to the cart's tail, to be whipped naked about every market town till they fall to labour and cease to take the bread from our mouths! Then shall the profligates decrease; then shall these exactions end; then shall your own power no longer be filched from you; then shall idle people be set to work, matrimony be better kept, population and wealth increase; then shall the gospel be preached and we shall duly pray to God for your most noble estate long to endure.

These were cruel, unjust and wildly exaggerated attacks, yet since clerical avarice and immorality were far from totally fictitious, the *Supplication* retained just that substratum of truth which made it dangerous. Tavern-talk had now found open and eloquent expression. No lay politician with half an eye could fail to see the uses of such invective, should the worst come to the worst. If the King in fact carried the pamphlet about in his pocket, this was not because he believed it to be an impartial report on the state of his realm.

When such prime examples of anticlericalism have been fully described, many sides of a complex phenomenon continue to elude our grasp. When Bishop Fisher exclaimed 'All this, me seemeth, is for lack of faith only', he may have been using inaccurate terminology, yet he was sensing a real change of spirit. The younger generation, the one which had become adult during the reign of Henry VIII, was not yet deeply pervaded by formal heresy. Even if it had sickened of those clerics who raised the cry of heresy whenever laymen pressed for church-reforms, it had not yet committed itself to Protestant doctrines. Nevertheless, it had lost interest in numerous attitudes and observances which had meant much to Fisher's generation. These mid-Tudor people differed as much from their fathers and grand-fathers as we differ from the Victorians. The growth of anticlericalism was but one symptom of a shift in values. Another was that large-scale secularisation of chantries and other minor foundations which in all parts of England marked the thirties and forties. Many Englishmen felt no more compunction in diverting chantry-funds to practical uses, both public and private, than we should feel in demolishing the once-mighty Bethesda Chapel in some depopulated area of an industrial city. The subjects of Henry VIII tended to be unsentimental and mundane, both in their charities and in their greed. This change of spirit was not initiated by Henry VIII or Thomas Cromwell, let alone by continental heresiarchs. At no time in Christian history has the world stood as still as elderly churchmen have wished: even when they are saints they cannot stop it moving and, if they seek a measure of influence upon public life, they must attempt to understand its ambivalent values. The year 1530 was not an opportune moment for prophecy. Some of the men of destiny were already presenting their claims, yet some had not yet shown their faces. At this moment John Calvin had not finally broken with Rome, and Ignatius Loyola had not yet founded the Society of Jesus. Had Fisher been able to see ahead thirty or forty years, he would have witnessed, alongside the immense growth of secular interests, a world which had by no means lost its interest in the Christian faith, a world which still held fiercely on theological matters, yet a world in which all the protagonists, even those who revered his memory, had at least agreed to discard his own fifteenth-century patterns of thought.

First Stages of the Reformation Parliament

When Parliament at last met on 3 November 1529 the reform of ecclesiastical abuses, including the removal of Wolsey, was obviously anticipated by the government, the members and the public alike.[15] But not even the most sanguine anticlerical can have foreseen the magnitude of the revolution to be consummated during the following six years. At the outset no one cause inspired the calling of this Parliament. Though the new Lord Chancellor Sir Thomas More began the session with a bitter attack on Wolsey, Parliament was not called especially to deal with the latter by attainder, since when the writs went out the normal processes of law had scarcely been initiated against him. It was not summoned for urgent legislation on the royal divorce, which it did not even discuss until 1533. And since it made no grant of supply until 1534, it seems not to have been assembled to solve a financial crisis. Yet more than six years had elapsed since the last session. Ecclesiastical problems apart, many secular ones demanded legislation; how many can be seen from the enormous list of statutes passed by this Parliament. Despite occasional interference with by-elections by ministers and magnates, the Reformation Parliament was not 'packed' to any significant extent: it did not need to be, since all Tudor parliaments contained a solid phalanx of office-holders and other members wholly reliable in the eyes of the government. If anything, this Parliament was remarkable for the number of occasions on which it displayed a spirit of independence, even for the extent to which it was flattered and cajoled by the King and his ministers. Nevertheless, to assert that the Commons accurately represented the will of any classes other than the gentry and the merchant-oligarchies would be a rash assertion; this would also be rash if made concerning any parliament before 1832!

We may scarcely doubt that at this moment the problem of the divorce lay uppermost in Henry's own mind. He was already considering indirect methods by which Parliament could be made to strengthen his hand. During the previous year the King's agents, Stephen Gardiner and Edward Fox, had already been threatening Pope Clement VII with the possibilities of an English schism and a General Council of the Church. In 1528, however, Henry had still maintained optimism regarding his divorce; however anxious to spur on the Pope he had no real desire to proceed to extremes. As yet he had not finally parted company with Wolsey, the resplendent symbol of papalism. Now, however, the nemesis of a persistent failure to control Rome had overtaken the Cardinal, and a few days before Parliament met, a bill of indictment under *Praemunire* was preferred against him in the King's Bench. It accused Wolsey of specific offences under the common law—for example, presenting to the livings of other patrons, annexing the testamentary jurisdiction of other bishops and using his legatine authority to extract pensions from abbots. The resultant spectacle—the most powerful legate in English history humbly acknowledging the right of the King's court to try him for illegal exercise of his papal powers—shook the edifice of clerical privilege to its foundations.[16] The time had also come to put much heavier pressures upon Clement by giving parliamentary anticlericalism its head. Over the next three years there followed a sequence of statutes which, though still carefully avoiding schism, involved the most serious curtailment of ecclesiastical privilege since the fourteenth century. Mortuary dues and probate fees were closely regulated by scales of charges according to the means of the payer. Pluralities were limited, beneficed priests forbidden to accept chantries and clerics forbidden to indulge in trading. Those below the order of sub-deacon now forfeited benefit of clergy, should they be charged with murder, treason, arson, burglary or highway-robbery. Of this legislation by far the most interesting and prophetic item is that clause of the Pluralities Act (21 Henry VIII cap. 13) which invalidates any present or future papal licence 'contrary to the present Act'. A ready assumption of the power of statute to debar the operation of papal jurisdiction in England thus appeared in the very first session of the Reformation Parliament.[17]

In 1530 the King also allowed his legal advisers to put the Statute of *Praemunire* to a test even greater than that involved in the prosecution of Wolsey. There resulted a somewhat complex operation, the nature of which has been investigated by Professor Scarisbrick.[18] In the summer of 1530 writs of *Praemunire facias* were issued against eight bishops and seven other prominent divines, the charge being that they had aided Wolsey in his offences by assigning to him a part of their incomes. Though the fact was notoriously true, the suggestion of guilt remained absurd. Almost all churchmen from archdeacons upward had been in the habit of making these peace-offerings, not to enhance the power of Wolsey but simply to prevent him from infringing their privileges by means of his omnicompetent papal powers. But before this suit against the fifteen defendants had reached any conclusion, the plan of attack was broadened into a crude and sweeping accusation against the whole of the English clergy. Edward Hall and other contemporaries say that they were charged with accepting Wolsey's legatine powers, but the subsequent Act of Pardon alleges that they had exercised ecclesiastical jurisdiction 'contrary to the form of the Statutes of Provisors, Provisions and *Praemunire*'. As we now know, however, Bishop Stokesley reported that certain councillors had altered the text of the pardon, a fact which might possibly account for this discrepancy. Whatever the case, when the Convocations met in January 1531, they accepted this preposterous situation by resolving to bribe off the Crown. In return for their pardons, the clergy of the Province of Canterbury offered £100,000 and those of York £18,840. The King graciously allowed them to pay by instalments spread over five years but, when invited to define the future scope of *Praemunire*, he refused. The most hardened of his lawyers might indeed have felt some embarrassment if asked to explain this legal fairyland. 'But we will provide', said Lord Chancellor Audley to Gardiner, 'that the *Praemunire* shall ever hand over your heads and so we laymen shall be sure to enjoy our inheritance by the Common Laws and Acts of Parliament.'[19] From Henry's viewpoint the beauty of the weapon lay in its vagueness; he was not likely to debar himself from further arbitrary aggressions by telling his clergy just what they could and could not do. Flushed with his success he urged them in the following month to acknowledge his sole right to the title 'Protector and Supreme Head of the English Church and Clergy'. Not yet entirely subservient, they insisted on adding the clause 'so far as the law of Christ allows', thus making an acknowledgment considerably more limited than the one they came to accept two years later.

As for the King, he can have attached little weight to such pathetic reservations and safeguards. At his coronation two decades earlier, he had refused to take a general oath to maintain the rights of the 'holy church', and he had sworn more concretely to maintain those of 'the Holy Church of England', moreover adding the proviso that such rights must not be 'prejudicial to his jurisdiction and dignity royal'. Amid the transactions of 1530–31, the submission and Pardon of the Clergy, did Henry see himself giving more substance to this old concept of his powers? Or, apart from clearing the Papacy from the path to his divorce, did he seek in the main to relieve the English Church of a very large sum of money? These alternatives have lately been disputed with much erudition by Doctors John Guy and George Bernard.[20] The present writer is almost disposed to believe that the monarch, his ministers, friends and critics were busily juggling with *all* these ideas. In sum the Pardon of the Clergy can well be taken as one of the significant steps along the approach toward the Royal Supremacy enunciated a couple of years later, toward the subjugation of the English Church and the final expulsion of papal jurisdiction throughout the kingdom.

The Divorce

These advances against the English Church had appreciably augmented Henry's power but, when he paused to think of his own original purpose, he must have felt bitter disappointment. Bullying his English clergy had failed to produce from Rome the divorce he had been seeking for the last four years. Concerning this theme, we need not here follow the interminable analyses of diplomacy and litigation compiled by historians; for our present purpose the upshot has much significance, the day-to-day exchanges very little.[21] Detestable as were the King's monumental egotism, his moralising self-deception, his inhuman treatment of Katherine, one finds it hard to avoid the impression that the ecclesiastical historians have accorded him rather less than justice. Not for long can his case be intelligently discussed as that of a private man anxious to rid himself of a stale and ageing spouse. He could have lived as licentiously as Charles V or Francis I without troubling about divorce and remarriage. Even the phrase 'reason of state' seems rather inadequate to convey his motive, for nothing less than the fate of the nation lay in the balance.

The work of the dynasty remained fragile; neo-feudal reaction and the old spirit of lawlessness were by no means broken. The King had a sickly daughter, but the last female sovereign had been Matilda, whose experiences afforded no great comfort to historically-minded Englishmen. Desperately, indeed, any kingdom of that period needed a strong and mature male heir, for the worst fate which could befall it would spring from irresolute rule, from a minority, from a disputed succession. Moreover, even before Anne Boleyn was born, there had existed genuine doubts among the canon lawyers of Europe concerning the validity of the unusual dispensation by which Julius II had permitted the child-marriage of Henry and Katherine. On far less plausible grounds rulers and magnates had gained decrees of nullity. Louis XII had arranged one in order to marry the heiress of Brittany. In 1527 a divorce had been granted at Rome on the flimsiest of grounds to Henry's immoral sister, Queen Margaret of Scotland; the following year Clement VII confirmed the earlier divorce (obtained under highly dubious circumstances) of his brother-in-law the Duke of Suffolk. Had Henry's plea been indecently weak in law, had his wish to remarry rested purely on private grounds, had not Rome over many years alternately encouraged and repelled him, he would have had little cause for bitterness and less claim for sympathy.

By the time of the Church-State crisis the divorce presented no novel issue. The role of Katherine as a permanent, active and in fact formally accredited ambassador of Spain had long since occasioned tension between the royal pair, and in 1514, when her father Ferdinand had betrayed English interests, people believed that Henry intended forthwith to repudiate the Queen. Yet the crucial factor in the collapse of the marriage was that extraordinary succession of miscarriages, stillbirths and infant deaths which accounted for all their offspring apart from the Princess Mary. Katherine's last failure occurred in 1518, and the following year her desperate but still hopeful husband vowed to lead a crusade against the Turk if he could be granted a male heir. No English King had lost so many children, and an age which saw the hand of God in far less remarkable coincidences was not slow to remember the curse of childlessness pronounced by *Leviticus* against a man who should marry his brother's wife. That Henry himself came to believe this we have no reason to doubt. By 1525 he had given up hope, though he was still only 34; he began to study the theology and canon law of divorce, concerning which, wrote the Papal Legate Campeggio, he soon knew more than any divine. He and his Council even considered entailing the succession upon the little Duke of Richmond, the natural son who had been so styled with deliberate reference to the title of Henry VII before Bosworth. In March 1527 the King began serious legal proceedings. It is not known whether he already planned a marriage with Anne Boleyn; certainly he was doing so by the following autumn, when he sent Dr. William Knight to procure a dispensation to that end. His famous love-letters date from about this time; the unwonted depth of his affection added not a little to his rancour as move succeeded hopeless move and stalemate gradually confronted him.

The key to Henry's problem lay not in the merits of his legal case but in the military control of Rome by the Emperor Charles V, and this control had been intermittently but steadily tightening ever since 1527, when the imperial armies had subjected the papal city to such appalling sack and slaughter. Clement VII, despite his own conciliatory character, had no freedom to grant Henry a divorce against the will of his political master, who had no special affection for his aunt but had to placate the intense pride of his Spanish subjects in their national monarchy and their royal family. In England itself the position had become all too clear by 1529, when Campeggio left England, the now useless Wolsey was cashiered and Henry understood that the verdict would go against him if he allowed the case to be transferred to Rome. Wolsey had now been replaced by an inferior triumvirate. The Duke of Norfolk was a competent soldier and negotiator, unprincipled except in his loyalty to the King but without originality as statesman or administrator. Henry's brother-in-law and boon-companion the upstart Duke of Suffolk was a less competent soldier but a good sportsman and a fine figure on ceremonial occasions. The Earl of Wiltshire was Anne Boleyn's father and so grandfather of our greatest Queen; even so, he remained a nonentity. Though as early as January 1531 Norfolk told Chapuys that papal jurisdiction was invalid in England,[22] he and his colleagues lacked the legal and political expertise to take the revolutionary steps indicated by the failure of their pressure upon Rome. The years of their ascendancy saw the frenzied search for favourable patristic texts and papal decrees, the consultation and bribery of universities throughout Europe, the bombastic citation of legend to prove the self-sufficiency of English jurisdiction. As a richly characteristic scene, we can picture Edward Carne and William Bennet, Henry's agents in Rome, frequenting the Vatican Library on a plea of disinterested research, but in fact ransacking the papal registers in their master's cause, while the suspicious librarians followed them from volume to volume in an attempt to discover exactly what they were about.[23]

Like the rest of the King's researchers these agents found singularly little comfort to their master, whose attitude toward Rome became deeply and permanently poisoned; all the more deeply since he entertained an inflated notion of his former services to the Holy See. Sick of trying to conduct the game according to the ancient rules, he resolved at last upon more heroic remedies, and he called in a new type of minister, one ready to work out a merely national solution of the problem, one ready to pass far beyond the divorce into new concepts of political organisation, one who possessed a fully professional knowledge of legal instruments and the apparatus of propaganda. This virtuoso of statecraft was Thomas Cromwell.

The place of the royal divorce in the history of the Reformation will always remain a subject for argument. Protestant writers have tended to dismiss it as a mere 'occasion' rather than a genuine cause; Catholics have sometimes regarded the divorce as the chief cause of the cataclysm and supposed that, had it not been pressed, England might well have remained a Catholic nation. To the present writer neither of these views seems wholly acceptable. The Protestants have too readily assumed the inevitability of a Reformation similar in timing and in character to the one which actually occurred. The divorce was something more than a mere 'occasion'; without it the schism would not have been consummated by 1533-4. Had Henry either abandoned or obtained his divorce he would most likely have tried, and with success, to hold his realm in some sort of spiritual allegiance to Rome, though it seems inconceivable that he or his people would tamely have reverted to any earlier situation. We may well agree with Pollard that the Pope's refusal of the divorce 'alienated the only power which might have kept in check the anti-papal and anti-sacerdotal tendencies then growing up in England'.

On the other side, we must avoid the temptation to equate the Henrician Schism with the Protestant Reformation. The divorce-suit did not create either Protestantism or those anti-papal and anti-sacerdotal forces which smoothed its path. That such forces were diverse in origin and deep-laid in society we have endeavoured to indicate in our earlier chapters. That by the thirties they had begun to put down roots throughout the dominant classes and regions of England cannot be doubted. And so far as the new beliefs are concerned, it must be acknowledged that, irrespective of his relations with Rome, Henry VIII could not have frozen the English in their religious posture of the year 1530. Even during the last seven years of his reign, when he was attempting to check Protestantism, it was spreading more rapidly than ever before, and it captured the government immediately upon his death. When we are tempted to underestimate its expansive capacities, we should recall that in the Netherlands, in Scotland and elsewhere, it soon played havoc with the plans of kings and governments. At the death of Henry VIII Calvinism still lay, so far as England was concerned, in the womb of the future; but its new challenge, politically more formidable than that of Lutheranism, was bound to be made some day, whatever the complexion of future English governments. Moreoever, the special attractions of Protestantism for the ruling classes rapidly manifested themselves; Henry VIII was not immortal and a strong chance remained that future rulers of England would be captured by Protestant beliefs. The most knowledgeable among us cannot speculate with much profit regarding the probable courses of history, had the divorce-problem been solved in Rome or had it never presented itself. Yet was the divorce anything more than one of the many dangerous reefs which English Catholicism had to circumnavigate? And English Catholicism, despite its gilded decorations, was an old, unseaworthy and ill-commanded galleon, scarcely able to continue its voyage without the new seamen and shipwrights produced (but produced far too late in the day) by the Counter-Reformation.

Over and above these considerations, the divorce and its attendant schism gradually merged into a developing European pattern destined to persist for another century—a pattern which continually set English nationalism at loggerheads with English Catholicism and which at any stage was liable to plunge the latter into disaster. At all events by the mid-century, this pattern clearly consisted of a powerful Spain, seeking not only to curb the Atlantine enterprises of the north-European peoples but to control the Mediterranean, the Italian peninsula and with them a reluctant but often rather powerless Papacy. In that age political and religious controls could not be kept apart, and one finds it impossible to imagine a people as tough, as active and as independent as the Tudor English acquiescing for any length of time in a Christendom organised along these Habsburg lines. In some sense, national schisms like that of England became more possible from 1503, when Spain overran the kingdom of Naples and began to establish its long dominance over central Italy. Even if Henry VIII had remained a model of matrimonial respectability, even if the ministers of Edward VI had been converted by a stray Jesuit, even if Queen Mary had survived for another decade, it still requires a vivid imagination to envisage the English as dutiful children of the Holy See at the end of the century. And amongst the many forbidding obstacles, Philip II and Calvin are the two which first catch the eye.

7 Statutes and Bibles: The Henrician Revolution

Two Strange Evangelicals

Thomas Cromwell, who laid the legal foundations of the national Church, was in every sense one of the 'new men' brought to the fore by the increasingly flexible outlook of the sixteenth century.[1] That his character showed a certain hardness can only be expected of one who received his training in hard schools, of a *parvenu* who rose to precarious eminence amid a court-society riddled with intrigue and snobbish pretensions. He was born about 1485, the son of a turbulent person who combined the businesses of brewer, fuller and blacksmith at Putney. His sisters married well, and the elder gave birth to that Sir Richard Williams who took the name of Cromwell and is remembered as great-grandfather of the Protector. In his late teens Thomas adventurously sought his fortune abroad and is said to have served in 1503 with the French army at the disastrous battle of the Garigliano. Drawing the obvious conclusion he then entered the service of the banking family of Frescobaldi and worked in northern Italy for two years or more. Armed with this experience he accompanied some English traders to the Netherlands and there became a business-consultant, making reports to London merchants on the all-important state of the Antwerp market. Cromwell's early backgrounds were hence as intensely urban, lay and non-feudal as any in Europe; he enjoyed every opportunity to free himself from the blue-blooded and ecclesiastical prejudices of a moribund yet far from dead medieval world. He was no boor; he had the sense not only to brush up his Latin but to acquire a grasp of Italian literature and ideas which educated contemporaries acknowledged to be far more than superficial. His most familiar portrait is very far from conveying the whole of his personality. He could talk amusingly and he showed good taste in furniture, books, pictures, food and wine; having made his fortune he lived with discretion and elegance, avoiding the grandiose style which had attracted such hatred against Wolsey.

In Antwerp, the greatest commercial and financial capital since ancient times, Cromwell perfected the knowledge of commerce and finance which he displayed to such advantage during his years of power. From Italy he seems to have derived even more fundamental lessons. Unlike the great majority of his fellow countrymen, he learned to think in terms of function and efficiency, to disregard hidebound traditions and all-embracing philosophical systems, to discard that canting rationalisation of self-interest in terms of religious duty which became an embarrassing feature of the outlook of Henry VIII and many mid-Tudor Englishmen. On the other hand, he was no agnostic and, in so far as his cool temperament allowed, he appears to have been genuinely attracted to the ideas which stemmed from Luther. There are numerous improbabilities in Reginald Pole's story that, as early as 1528, four years before the publication of *The Prince*, Cromwell was propounding cynical doctrines based upon that work. If we seek for a fundamental book on Church and State which helped to inspire Cromwell's revolutionary ideas, we are more likely to find this in the *Defensor Pacis* of Marsiglio.

We have already summarised the conclusions of a work too profoundly rebellious to be accepted by its own century, yet destined to exercise widespread influence upon the age of Renaissance and Reformation. Its adoption by Cromwell and his circle remains no matter of guesswork. In the years 1533–5 Richard Sampson, Edward Fox and Thomas Starkey[2] explicitly used Marsilian doctrines to justify the overthrow of papal jurisdiction in England, and the last-named was under direct Cromwellian patronage. More important, in 1535 Cromwell personally supplied the money to another henchman, William Marshall, in order to finance the first English translation of the *Defensor Pacis*.[3] Two years earlier Cromwell had already summarised its doctrine in a few masterly phrases of his Act of Appeals.[4] 'This realm of England is an Empire ... governed by one Supreme Head and King having the dignity and royal estate of the imperial Crown of the same, unto whom a body politic, compact of all sorts and degrees of people divided in terms and by names of spiritualty and temporalty, be bounden and owe to bear, next to God, a natural and humble obedience.'

On the other hand, though he is said once to have quoted in council the old civilian adage, 'What pleases the Prince, has the force of law', there is no real evidence that Cromwell based his measures upon the authoritarian principles of the civil law. By training and outlook he and his followers were common lawyers. And at every stage his public career was concerned with the House of Commons, through which he consistently worked. Hard as he strove to make the Crown rich and powerful, his supposed intention to make Henry VIII an irresponsible despot may be regarded as a myth, for no statesman ever sought with more zeal to express sovereignty in terms of laws and institutions. When all has been said of Italy and Antwerp, another vital development of Cromwell's education came after his return to England.

This event occurred about the year 1512, when he married a woman of gentle background and settled in London. During the obscure years which followed, he must have embarked upon an intensive study of the common law, since by the period 1520–24 he had already become a solicitor entrusted with important business by Wolsey and other personages. He sat in the

Parliament of 1523, from which year dates a long parliamentary speech on foreign policy written in the hand of one of his clerks. We cannot prove that he delivered this oration, but it shows that Cromwell was already thinking for himself on the leading issues of national policy. It is as much of an opposition-speech as any made at that time in the Commons. While criticising Wolsey's expensive and hazardous plans for a campaign in France, it gives priority to the task of uniting England and Scotland.

Despite such views, within a year or two Cromwell became one of the leading members of Wolsey's enormous household and he was soon employed upon the Cardinal's most enlightened project—the suppression of some twenty-nine monasteries in order to found colleges at Oxford and Ipswich. This was in itself a task of no small magnitude, since while none of these houses boasted more than ten members, two of them (Daventry and St. Frideswide's, Oxford) had annual incomes exceeding £200 and three others incomes between £189 and £125. Here the newcomer displayed that infinite capacity for taking pains which in later years impressed all observers. The opportunity to change some aspect of an outworn system always brought forth his single-minded attention to detail, and in a world of amateur administrators he began to shine forth as superbly professional. Though he later claimed to have received few material rewards from Wolsey, he cannot have neglected his numerous opportunities for receiving fees and presents. The will which he drafted in 1529, a few weeks before Wolsey's fall, shows that he possessed very considerable resources and proposed to make a number of lavish benefactions to London charities. Likewise when he came to power, Cromwell showed himself both grasping and generous. If, like any other Tudor minister, he disdained no gift in return for his favours, he also fed two hundred paupers daily at his gate, spent his means in the service of the Crown, gambled like a gentleman and was always ready to oblige an old friend or to win a new one.

On the dismissal of Wolsey he stood in obvious danger as the known lieutenant of that unpopular minister, but after a moment of weakness, even of tears, he resolutely rode off from Esher to London, gained the favour of the King and through the good offices of Sir William Paulet entered the first session of the Reformation Parliament as member for Taunton.[5] Here he defended Wolsey's remaining interests with a conspicuous if finely-calculated loyalty, which gained him far more credit from contemporaries than from his ungenerous modern biographers. By January 1531 he was sworn of the King's Council and within two years held the appointments of master of the King's Jewels, clerk of the Hanaper and chancellor of the Exchequer. None of these could then be called an important office but together they enabled him to begin the rehabilitation of Crown finance and to attract the attention of the King. In 1534 he became principal secretary, an office which he was allowed to extend into a ministry of all affairs, and from this point his surviving state papers leave an impression of laborious omnicompetence hardly rivalled by any other minister in English history.

Our present concern is with Cromwell's ecclesiastical policy, yet it should be recognised that this policy becomes intelligible only in a general setting of administrative reform. The problems of Church, State and society at large were then closely intertwined. The eight years of Cromwell's ministry form a truly notable episode in the history of the English State. In that of the English Church they are equally revolutionary years, in part destructive, in part as highly constructive. And it cannot reasonably be questioned that Cromwell supplied their chief guiding force. Like Wolsey before him, he received from the King enough independence to be able to set his personal seal upon the period of his ministry. By contrast, outside these eight years, the reign of Henry VIII has scarcely a single creative or revolutionary achievement to its credit. The King's will-power, his courage, his decisiveness, his immense capacity to inspire adulation, these preserved the integrity of the kingdom and paved the way for the long Elizabethan peace which Englishmen were to enjoy amid a chaotic Europe. But otherwise his personal touch proved sterile; he was too egotistical, too emotional, too interested in kingly pleasures, too conservative to initiate new techniques of government, new paths of progress for English society. Yet between the years 1532 and 1540 all is different. Creation, destruction and change are visible on all sides; something like a planned revolution issues from the mind of a minister who is known to have reflected not merely upon practical administrative reform but upon the theory and ultimate purposes of government. Cromwell had his own clear vision of the sovereign State as transcending the turmoil and division inherited from both the defects and the death-struggles of feudal society. While he was subjugating the Church to the Crown in Parliament, he was also curtailing feudal liberties and sanctuaries, bringing a new order to crime-troubled Wales and a conciliar justice to the North, where a Percy still counted for more than a Tudor. Again, he was overthrowing the Geraldines in Ireland, striving to build up co-operation with the Scots, initiating the Tudor poor laws, attracting the cloth-trade from the Netherlands to England, checking the export of coin and reforming the whole complex of the financial courts. By the time it was dissolved in 1536 the Reformation Parliament had passed about seventy social and economic statutes, besides another thirty-seven concerning the reform of the law, both criminal and civil. Above all Cromwell proved himself a great manager of Parliament and a great drafter of statutes, the common lawyer who dominated a period of legislation far more intensive and more complex than that of any earlier Parliament or ministry.

Never before had the estates of England been called upon to execute so prolonged, so integrated, so radical a programme, or one more likely to affect the lives of common Englishmen. Beginning with the restricted problem of the divorce, Cromwell ended by reshaping the multilateral relationships of Crown and Parliament with the clergy, the gentry and the common people. Through and with Parliament he resolved the mounting tensions of earlier Tudor society into a new equilibrium which survived the stresses placed upon it by bigotry and incompetence and which in its essentials outlasted the dynasty.

Since Thomas Cromwell played so prominent a part in the early stages of the Henrician Reformation, it would seem reasonable to glance at his own religious opinions.[6] As befitted a businessman and a servant of the Crown, he did not parade such thoughts, and his earlier background can hardly have stimulated them. During these adventurous years he obviously learned to think in cool, functional terms about the worlds of politics, economics and even religion. As a layman in Wolsey's ecclesiastical world he doubtless continued to judge theology by its public effects and clergymen by their practical conduct. As chief minister he joined in the suppression of the monasteries in order to endow the Crown, yet like Erasmus, Luther and many other people of that day, he despised monasticism itself and needed no financial arguments to make him act with conviction.

Often misjudged by Victorian clerical writers as an agnostic and a ruthless intriguer, Cromwell deserved this reputation no more than did the great majority of the King's servants—indeed less when we take into account his vulnerability in the face of the jealous aristocratic and clerical establishments. His will of 1529 gives no hint of Lutheran sympathies. If by any chance he had begun to entertain them, he nevertheless still presented himself in this document as a conventional uncritical Catholic, invoking the saints and making the usual pious bequests. Thus his move toward a distinctively Protestant position may well have been incomplete until the decade of his ministerial career. While Cromwell's earlier reading in Italian secular literature impressed insular Englishmen, the martyrologist Foxe—who came to revere him as a 'valiant soldier and captain of Christ'— reports that on a journey to Rome he memorised the whole of Erasmus's Latin translation of the New Testament.[7] If this story be true, it does not necessarily mean that Cromwell was craftily brushing up his meagre Latin with a view to undertaking a legal career. In later years he obviously grasped and energetically furthered the Lutheran concept of a Scripturally-based religion. As will appear, his most momentous achievement—and one arising from his very personal exertions—was the bold organisation of the printing and national distribution (1538-9) of the English Bible, and essentially the Bible as translated by Tyndale and Coverdale. As Vicegerent of the English Church, Cromwell worked well with Archbishop Cranmer and had friendly relationships with notorious Protestants like Latimer, Coverdale and Barnes, even with the convicted sacramentarian John Lambert.[8] The Injunctions of 1536 and 1538, which went out in his name, are by no means the only documents which attest his mature dislike of the abuses relating to images, relics, pilgrimages and the invocation of saints, even though he never tried to enforce the entire abolition. Insofar as he reflected on Christian doctrine he avoided, though rather narrowly, a total acceptance of Luther's teachings. He seems, for example, to have thought good works—as well as faith—to be necessary for salvation.[9] The northern rebels of 1536 were taught by their leaders to see him as a sinister, hard-line radical, while his aristocratic enemies, led by the third Duke of Norfolk, not only resented his upstart origins but added sacramentarian heresy to treason in the list of fabricated charges which in 1540 sent him to the scaffold. No minister in English history was ever overthrown by tactics more cynically conspiratorial. Appropriately, the man who swore to the specific untruths was the same who had betrayed Thomas More: Sir Richard Riche, Chancellor of the Augmentations, who owed his career to the patronage of both.

When he achieved power, Cromwell's thinking on both religious and secular problems was influenced by the group of scholars whom he employed to create the publicity required by the growth of printing, the most notable being Thomas Starkey, a reforming humanist but not a Lutheran.[10] From these cosmopolitan circles Cromwell acquired the most fruitful principle of his career: that of the *via media*, that middle road in affairs of Church and State which rejected both stiff reaction and presumptuous innovation. This he proclaimed on 12 April 1540 in his last speech to Parliament,[11] which six years later was to be echoed in the same place by King Henry himself.[12] Faithfully revived by Sir Nicholas Bacon and Bishop John Jewel, the *via media* was to be canonised in the England of Elizabeth and William Cecil.[13] For mere politicians its beauty lay in its adaptability to most situations. Yet in the case of Cromwell and his successors it also foreshadowed important aspects of the English Church, amongst the founders of which he must assuredly be numbered. The weakness of Cromwell's link with the Reformation lay in the fact that his virtually Lutheran aims always threatened to outrun the King's theological conservatism. They eventually did so in 1539-40, and the fatal charges against him were to include heresy as well as treason. His close association with Cranmer, especially in the struggle for the English Bible, will shortly attract our attention.

Another controversial advocate of the Reformation at court was none other than Anne Boleyn, whose tragic 'thousand days' has been so widely popularised. The present writer must confess to a certain unsteadiness regarding her role and personality. For some years he has felt, along with Dr. Ives, the best of all her biographers, that she should probably be regarded as innocent of the charges of adultery made against her in April 1536, having been 'framed' by a hostile faction at court. It now seems difficult to survey the voluminous evidence—as lately set forth by Dr. Bernard—without being driven toward the reverse probability of her guilt.[14] This would not greatly matter, did it not affect the nature of her championship of the Reformation. From the very specific evidence of her ladies it emerges rather firmly that her behaviour both toward them, and toward her several intimate male friends in the royal household, must have been provocative and imprudent in the extreme. One of her supposed lovers, the unfortunate young musician Mark Smeaton, showed himself as naïve, genuinely devoted and desperately jealous of his rivals. Having confessed to three occasions of adultery with the Queen, and having been condemned to death, would not Mark at last have withdrawn a false confession in order to save her? Instead he went to his execution merely acknowledging that he deserved death for his offence. Above all, it seems quite certain that the King, having examined the evidence in detail, became entirely convinced of Anne's guilt. There remains no convincing evidence that he was manipulated by a confederacy of her enemies: he was ever suspicious and intelligent, unlikely to be fooled in such a matter. Wayward and independent, Anne had told other people that she no longer loved Henry, who had obviously become ever less lovable, except perhaps by some intensely conscientious zealot like his last wife Katherine Parr. It has been suggested that Anne believed him infertile, and sought to conceive the much-needed male heir to the throne by associating with other men. Not so long ago, this idea was romantically adumbrated by a distinguished British historian, but it must surely remain in the realm of conjecture.

On the other hand the evidence for the Queen's attraction towards the evangelical cause, probably first developed at the court of France, cannot be dismissed as nugatory.[15] Her constant patronage of Protestant clergymen, refugees and booksellers, together with her enthusiasm for translations of the Bible into both French and English are indicated by numerous anecdotes. The picture of the keen, evangelical devotee depends partly but by no means solely upon evidence collected by John Foxe and William Latimer after the accession of her daughter Elizabeth, when it had indeed become important to rehabilitate her reputation as a Protestant. The most facile solution of this engima would be to demote Anne to the status of a mere *politique*, a Lutheran not by piety but by policy and self-interest, a role she had excellent reasons for playing in order to increase her influence. This was presumably the view of her enemies, for example the Imperial ambassador Chapuys, who stresses her political importance as a Lutheran and a prime supporter of the break with Rome.[16] All the same, this frigid estimate may also represent a simplification. Does she not become more credible as one of those many self-destructive personalities insecurely poised between resolution and impulse, the spirit and the flesh? Why should her lapses have precluded a measure of sincerity? Jealous, untameable and passionate, resenting her thraldom to an ageing monarch no longer her devoted suitor, did she not also overplay her hand and take appalling risks? This scenario seems at least preferable to the alternative versions: it fits the evidence far better than the image of the simple pietist or that of the cold schemer. Like many stormy, divided and inconsistent people, Anne probably experienced depressions and had her unsteady moods of repentance. We are told that she made munificent gifts to poor people who had nothing whatever to bestow in return. George Bernard has cited evidence suggesting that, whatever her general inclination to Lutheran doctrine, she believed at the approach of death that her good deeds might after all help to save her. Here it might be wise to leave the matter, perhaps with a half-sincere apology for treading terribly close to that iron curtain which is thought to separate history from fiction! Since however we linked her name with that of Thomas Cromwell, we might end the topic by casting doubt upon the suggestion that he finally turned against her and took an active part in her destruction. While the idea looks improbable, the evidence adduced in its favour would seem remarkably weak. One thing appears certain: that Cromwell could not possibly have saved her from the wrath of the King.

The Henrician Statutes

The first year of Cromwell's ministry saw the destruction of the legislative independence of the English Church, a process which had effectively commenced with the drafting of the Supplication of the Commons against the Ordinaries. The origins, gradual development and ultimate purposes of this document are still debated;[17] it survives in several versions, the dating of which presents some intricate puzzles. The earliest apparently belongs to the year 1529, when Thomas Cromwell as an ordinary member is thought to have drafted it on behalf of the House of Commons. Do the revisions of 1532 indicate a spontaneous resurgence of anticlerical zeal in the Commons, or should the Supplication be regarded from this point as the instrument of a government-sponsored attack upon the Church? This question has been closely argued, but the evidence may never allow of a precise answer. In any case its broader significance should not be exaggerated. By 1532 Cromwell and other ministers were using the document, yet it remains equally clear that the rank and file of the Commons had lost none of their hostile spirit of 1529 and that they responded swiftly to the lead from above. The actual text of the Supplication[18] represents a fusion of their multiple grievances with the narrower designs of the Crown. As redrafted in 1532, it cleverly links together two main themes which in everyday life were not very intimately connected—the legislative action of the Church, which the King wanted to control, and the practices of the ecclesiastical courts, from which the laity desired to liberate themselves. It begins by blaming discord and heresy upon the uncharitable activities of ecclesiastical officials, and it then descends to 'particular griefs', though without citing names, dates and events. The first is the power of Convocation to make ecclesiastical laws without the consent of the laity, and at their expense, particularly since those laws are not set forth in English and may so be infringed out of mere ignorance. The Supplication then enlarges upon the inordinate delays, prosecutions over trivialities and high fees current in the church courts, the vexatious examinations and imprisonments of offenders, the subtle traps set for people unlucky enough to be charged with heresy. For good measure, some miscellaneous accusations are thrown in: payments are extorted by some priests for administering the sacraments; nepotism still results in the presentations of minors to benefices; the excessive number of holy days conduces to 'execrable vices' and 'wanton sports'.

On 18 March 1532 the Speaker, Thomas Audley, presented the Supplication to the King, who after a curious delay sent it on 12 April to Archbishop Warham, requesting a speedy answer. This challenge came at a moment when the ecclesiastics were showing a real disposition to resist and even to inaugurate reforms on their own account. The previous February Warham had made a formal protest against all acts of the present Parliament derogatory to the Roman Pontiff, to ecclesiastical power or to the privileges of the See of Canterbury.[19] In March he had excommunicated Hugh Latimer, then in favour at court, on charges of heresy, and in reply the government had trumped up a charge under *Praemunire* against Warham, on the technical ground that he had consecrated Dr. Henry Standish before the latter had done homage to the King. Meanwhile in January and February Convocation itself had at long last begun to develop an impressive programme of reforms. Though its new canons centred around the theme of heresy, they also included measures to ensure closer examination of the credentials and education of ordinands to compel beneficed clergy to reside, to increase the penalties imposed on clerics who committed fornication or indulged in scandalous field-sports and even to impose a weekly minimum of six hours' scriptural study upon incumbents.[20] This development cannot have seemed welcome to the more bitter opponents of the clergy. It is hard to avoid the suspicion that there were now many laymen who no longer sincerely wished to see the Church set its own house in order and who were correspondingly eager to press on with the reduction of its powers before it could recover prestige.

On receiving the Supplication, Warham transmitted it to the Lower House of Convocation, whence there soon emerged a lengthy Answer of the Ordinaries,[21] inspired in large part by Bishop Gardiner. This defence naturally pointed to the unspecific nature of the charges made in the Supplication and to the injustice of blaming a long-accepted system for the faults of isolated individuals. So far did lay malice extend, that divers of the clergy were even being subjected to physical violence, 'so injured in their own persons, thrown down in the kennel in the open street at mid-day, even here within your own city and elsewhere'. The Answer concluded with a moving appeal to the King as protector of the English Church, but the clergy were soon to discover that they had to buy his protection with something more tangible than fair words. On 30 April Henry handed their reply to the Speaker along with a heavy hint. 'We think their answer will smally please you, for it seemeth to us very slender. You be a great sort of wise men; I doubt not but you will look circumspectly on the matter, and we will be indifferent between you.' Having thus encouraged the Commons to maintain their attack he proceeded on 10 May to deliver his own, and confronted Convocation with these demands—that it should pass no new legislation unless he licensed it to do so, and that existent canons should be referred for approval or disapproval to a royal commission of thirty-two members, half of them laymen. The next day he again summoned and addressed the Speaker and a deputation of the House: 'Well-beloved subjects, we thought that the clergy of our realm had been our subjects wholly, but now we have well perceived that they be but half our subjects; yea, and scarce our subjects; for all the prelates at their consecration make an oath to the Pope, clean contrary to the oath that they make to us, so that they seem to be his subjects, and not ours.' So saying, he handed them copies of these two customary oaths, which the Speaker later caused to be read in the House itself.[22]

The matter as well as the manner of this oblique menace to the clergy is worthy of note. The demand for a single sovereignty and an undivided allegiance savours strongly of the known convictions of Thomas Cromwell; moreover, the whole design to fetter clerical legislation stems from the first section of the Supplication of the Commons, also attributable to that minister. The King was already being guided into a territory unfamiliar to his predecessors on the throne of England, into far-reaching and fundamental doctrines which passed well beyond his immediate and personal aims. From this stage we cannot understand Crown policy if we continue to envisage Thomas Cromwell as merely a smart lawyer who made his fortune by solving the King's matrimonial problem. For good or ill, he is a figure of far greater significance in our history.

Whatever doctrines underlay the royal tactics, they proved immediately effective. At this point the clerical front suddenly crumbled, and on 15 May Convocation acceded to all the royal demands by the document known as the Submission of the Clergy. Only seven bishops, it is true, actually attended the crucial session; of these, three consented only with reservations, while one (Clerk of Bath and Wells) refused his support. Yet Warham himself stood among the submissive, and we can give no clear explanation for the sudden collapse of his resistance. Here was a tragic anticlimax, for the Primate can hardly have come overnight to believe in this degree of surrender; he had little to lose and could have made matters very difficult for the King. His death the following August came somewhat as a happy release from a situation even more intolerable than his former place under the shadow of Wolsey. By Sir Thomas More the Submission seems to have been accepted as a landmark; at all events, his resignation of the Chancellorship the following day is not thought to have been purely due to his ill-health, the proffered excuse. In due course he was succeeded in office by Thomas Audley, a prominent agent in the same transactions. For the clergy in general, the Submission represented a further appeal to the King against the Commons. By giving him control over their law-giving functions they avoided the hazard of a far worse fate—the wholesale destruction of their courts and their legal privileges at the hands of Parliament. The King proved less anticlerical than his subjects, and in the last resort he honoured his promise to stand between the laity and the clergy. Having used the Commons as a bugbear to frighten Convocation into handing him its legislative power, he then showed no enthusiasm concerning the rest of the lay demands and refrained from that radical overhaul or abolition of ecclesiastical jurisdiction to which the Commons aspired. Henry VIII was in fact the manipulator, not the creator, of anticlerical sentiment. Neither he nor his successors would follow it to the point of destroying the legal functions of the Church in society, and his situation in 1532 dimly foreshadows that of Elizabeth, standing half a century later between her puritanical Commons and her sorely-pressed Church.

While the Submission of the Clergy applied only indirectly to the divorce-suit, the year 1532 did not pass without some intensification of the direct pressure upon Rome. Annates were not conditionally withheld, pending negotiations for their abolition, and the Act effecting this also stated that should the Pope delay or deny bulls of consecration, bishops might be consecrated by English authority alone. Should he respond by excommunication or interdict, the King and his subjects might 'without any scruple of conscience' continue to enjoy the sacraments and services of the Church, any papal censures notwithstanding. Early in 1533 this threat extorted from Rome the necessary instruments for the consecration of the King's strange candidate for the See of Canterbury, Thomas Cranmer.

Also in 1533 Cromwell produced his most critical piece of legislation— the Act in Restraint of Appeals, containing that famous preamble we have already observed. By here calling England an 'Empire', Cromwell designated it a sovereign state, with a King who owed no submission to any other human ruler and who was invested with plenary power to give his people justice in all causes. In the sense of full temporal sovereignty, the claim to Empire had been repeatedly made by medieval kings and, long before quarrelling with the Pope or the Emperor, Henry had attributed to himself an imperial title. Throughout Europe humanists had been applying the word *imperium* to the rule of kings, but in England its use was more than semantic. Here men seriously believed the legends whereby their kings descended from Arthur, who in turn descended from the Emperor Constantine and his allegedly British mother, Helena. In addition to divorce-precedents, Carne and Bennet had been ordered to seek in the papal archives any acknowledgment of an imperial authority held by Henry's predecessors. In his conversation of January 1531 with Chapuys, the Duke of Norfolk also alluded to 'these venerable British traditions' in remarks which passed well above the head of his ill-informed hearer. About a year after the passing of the Appeals Act, Polydore Vergil, the Italian archdeacon of Wells, published his famous *Anglica Historia*, asserting that an imperial crown had descended on modern English kings in an unbroken line from Constantine. Henceforward the claim was to be made in a steady succession of Tudor statutes, while before the end of the century the term Empire began also to be applied to the overseas expension of the English State. Its importance in relation to the Reformation should not, however, be overstated. It is true that during the drafting of the Act of Appeals, the King for a time suggested that he should claim to derive his spiritual jurisdiction from this imperial authority, but he found that the claim could not be substantiated by reference to the Holy Roman Empire or to other precedents. He thus ultimately refrained from pressing this emotive but historically circumscribed term, and instead he based his spiritual jurisdiction upon a special claim to a Royal Supremacy over the English Church.[23]

In the text of the Act of Appeals the assertion of Empire is vaguely based upon 'divers sundry old authentic histories and chronicles' and accompanied by the Marsilian definition of spirituality and temporality. The claim to sovereignty once made, the rest of the Act proceeds in a lower key to practical considerations. That part of the body politic called the spirituality or the English Church, it continues, have always had sufficient 'knowledge, integrity and sufficiency of number' to settle spiritual causes without appeals to Rome. Such appeals, despite the laws of former English kings, continued to cause the present King and his subjects cost, vexation and delay. Henceforth all cases concerning matrimony, testaments and tithes shall be finally settled in England. In ecclesiastical suits, appeal shall be from the archdeacon to the bishop's court and from the latter to the archiepiscopal court. But in matters concerning the King and his successors, an appeal shall go to the Upper House of Convocation, without traversing the lower courts. In some parliamentary circles this government measure proved unpopular, though its known critics were disturbed not by its doctrinal corollaries but by the fear that the Pope might organise a European trade-embargo against England. Such misgivings were ably handled by Cromwell, and shortly after the passage of the act in March 1533 he received open acknowledgment as the King's chief minister.

Far-reaching as were the consequences of this decisive measure, its immediate purpose was to grasp the nettle of the divorce and to make way for the King's speedy re-marriage. This had become urgent, since Anne Boleyn was already known to be pregnant; she actually gave birth to the Princess Elizabeth the following September. By May, after some careful lobbying, Cromwell secured large majorities in both Convocations for two propositions. The first stated that the Pope had possessed no legitimate power to permit the marriage of Henry to Katherine of Aragon, after she had consummated her former marriage with his brother Arthur. The second alleged (despite Katherine's own denial) that such consummation had been adequately proved. On this basis the new Archbishop, long a whole-hearted adherent of Henry's cause, could complete the work. He was licensed to hear the suit, and before the end of the month had declared Katherine's marriage to Henry null and void from its inception. Katherine refused to appear before him, yet under the recent Act her counsel were checkmated and could now appeal no further.

Having thus cut through the tangled skein of the divorce Cromwell was left free to elaborate a new legal relationship between Church and State. With remarkable expedition he produced a series of statutes to this end, and passed them through Parliament during the two crowded sessions of the year 1534. The so-called Act in Restraint of Annates had a far wider significance than its title would suggest. It not only withdrew annates from Rome but also forbade Englishmen to procure papal bulls for the consecration of bishops. Moreover, it instituted the process whereby at each vacancy a cathedral chapter was obliged to elect as bishop the person nominated by the King in his letters missive, accompanying the royal *congé d'élire* or licence to elect. Failure to do so, or failure on the part of the Archbishop or bishops to consecrate the person elected, would expose the offending parties to the dreaded penalties of *Praemunire*. Revived by Queen Elizabeth, the procedure continues to this day, and the durable character of the Henrician legislation is illustrated by the fact that this very situation is still causing disquiet in the Anglican Church, which now might well be credited with enough maturity to select its own bishops. These misgivings seem the more intelligible since that odd legatee of Henry VIII, the prime minister of the day, who could be an atheist, selects bishops for the Sovereign's nomination. Another feature of our day which would have seemed even stranger to Henry is the role played in the selection by the patronage secretary of the prime minister.

The Dispensations Act finally stopped all payments to Rome and then stipulated that dispensations (licences to allow departures from the canon law) should be issued by the Archbishop of Canterbury. Characteristically enough, Cromwell also forestalled by lay controls the possibility that extortionate fees or unreasonable refusals would be occasioned by the Archbishop's officials. Fixed fees for every sort of dispensation would not be agreed and made public, and all grants daily recorded by the clerk of the Chancery. Should a dispensation not emerge upon a reasonable claim, then the Lord Chancellor might issue a writ enjoining the Archbishop under penalty either to grant it or to explain his refusal in Chancery.

The Act for Submission of the Clergy put the existing submission into statutory form by forbidding Convocation to legislate except by the licence of the Crown; it permitted the King to appoint a committee to allow or disallow canons passed by that body. Another cause prohibited all appeals whatsoever to Rome and allowed appeals from the archiepiscopal courts to the Court of Chancery. The first Succession Act vested succession to the Crown in the heirs of Henry and Anne, making it treason to slander the marriage and enjoining that every subject of full age should take an oath to uphold this Act. The latter clause Henry soon showed himself ready to use against eminent opponents of the divorce. When Bishop Fisher and Sir Thomas More refused to take this oath, they were sent to the Tower. They did not dispute the right of Parliament to settle the succession, but they rejected the Royal Supremacy and the assertion that the King's first marriage had been unlawful.

During the late session of this same year 1534, the revolution was substantially completed by the passage of three more statutes. The Act of Supremacy recognised the royal headship as already in existence, and specifically assigned to the Crown the power to conduct visitation of the clergy. This was a clear sign from the King that, although he did not claim to consecrate bishops or to administer the sacraments in person, he had no intention of remaining a mere secular protector of the national Church. He meant to exercise certain spiritual functions hitherto pertaining to the Papacy and the bishops; he annexed the power to correct the opinions of preachers, to supervise the formulation of doctrine, to reform the canon law, to visit and discipline both regular and secular clergy, and even (as happened in the case of John Lambert, which we shall describe) to try heretics in person. Henry's theological knowledge and self-righteousness gave his Supremacy a dangerously personal character, and it was well for the future health of the national Church that his immediate successors were a minor and two women, all less inclined or less able to undertake the personal exercise of caesaro-papalism.

There followed a striking manifestation of 'imperial' power when Henry proceeded to appoint Thomas Cromwell as his deputy. It has recently been pointed out that Cromwell's rise to power over the Church occurred in two stages.[24] In January 1535 he received a vicegerency devised merely to convey general powers of visitation over the Church and intended to apply in the main to the monasteries. Eighteen months later (July 1536) came the omnicompetent vicegerency in a grandiloquent commission modelled on those formerly granted by the papacy to Wolsey. Thenceforth until his fall in 1540, as sole vicegerent, vicar general and special commissary, the blacksmith's son held unlimited ecclesiastical jurisdiction in England, subject only to the King's pleasure. Invested with such powers as no lay subject has held before or since, Cromwell proceeded not only to reorganise ecclesiastical taxation and conduct a visitation of the monasteries, but also to take official precedence over the whole episcopate. Early in 1537, for example, he presided over an important doctrinal debate between the bishops, and displayed patent sympathy with the progressives against John Stokesley, Bishop of London, who staunchly upheld Catholic views of the sacraments and of the 'unwritten verities' of Christian belief. We fortunately possess a detailed account of this episode from the pen of the Scottish Reformer Alexander Alesius, whom Cromwell happened to encounter in the street and took along to the meeting.[25] The debate having begun, he did not hesitate to introduce Alesius to the assembled episcopate as 'the King's scholar' and allow him to speak in violent contravention of Stokesley's arguments. Such an event must indeed have brought home to the bishops the revolutionary character of the Royal Supremacy to which they had become subject.

The respective rôles of Parliament and Convocation as partners in the exercise of this royal supremacy cannot be defined in any simple formula by reference to Henrician legislation and practice. Dr. Woodward has rightly suggested[26] that these statutes and their sequels indicate two divergent tendencies. The famous preamble of the Appeals Act seems to envisage Parliament and Convocation as two concurrent powers, each operating within its own sphere. Similarly, the Act for the Submission of the Clergy places Convocation in a direct relation with the King, a relation parallel to that enjoyed by Parliament. In fact, the King issued articles of faith and (in 1536) curtailed the list of saints' days by the advice and assent of Convocation alone. Through his vicegerent he conducted monastic visitations and issued royal injunctions to the clergy without reference to Parliament. Yet alongside this theory of concurrent powers there ran also a marked tendency to regard Parliament as the superior power and statute law as superior to cannon law. The submission accepted by Convocation had to be regularised by Parliament; Convocation's acknowledgment of the supreme headship had ultimately to be restated in statutory form. From 1540 onwards even the clerical subsidies, granted for centuries by Convocation, were steadily confirmed by Parliament. The Annates Acts, invading the spiritual sphere without reference to Convocation, had already decided that the consecration of bishops without papal approval would be valid. Still more strikingly, the Six Articles Act of 1539 imposed doctrine by the sole authority of the King in Parliament. The vicegerent and eight bishops who drafted the Act sat as a committee of the House of Lords, Convocation not being consulted, while a layman, the Duke of Norfolk, introduced this important religious measure into Parliament. Altogether, while the 'concurrent' theory in the Appeals Act may well have been seriously intended, it often receded into the background. The superior function of Parliament, though irregularly exercised, was from the first so often allowed that Henry's successors had little chance of guarding the English Church as a sacred preserve of monarchy and clergy.[27] Henry, confident in his personal ascendancy and religious learning, is unlikely to have foreseen these future implications. Thomas Cromwell, the parliamentarian, the common lawyer, the institutionalising statesman, may well have foreseen them with equanimity.

The Act for First Fruits and Tenths, judged at least by its intentions, looks the most heavy-handed of all Parliamentary measures imposed upon churchmen. If after perusing it they shared that overwhelming gratitude to the King expressed in its magniloquent preamble, they must have been singularly patriotic Englishmen. It not only annexed the first fruits of bishoprics to the Crown, but extended this exaction to all spiritual benefices, high and low alike. Moreover, it demanded a tenth of their net incomes as a fixed annual tax, beginning at Christmas 1535.

This statute immediately involved one of Cromwell's most remarkable administrative exploits—the compilation of the *Valor Ecclesiasticus*, a detailed assessment of all clerical incomes from those of bishoprics down to those of vicarages and chapels. The compilers first took each taxpayer's gross income, then deducted certain allowances to arrive at his net income, then divided the latter by ten. But the allowances were rigorously limited to the following: fees of stewards and other monastic officials; regular rents and pensions; regular alms distributed under the wills of donors; regular diocesan payments. Though now incomplete for some dioceses, this magnificent survey (since printed in six large folio volumes)[28] is by far the most informative single source on the economic history of the Tudor Church, and is worthy in its fashion to be placed alongside Domesday Book. Likewise impressive is the correspondence by which Cromwell guided the army of amateur administrators charged with the great task. Though many under-assessments of income appear to have remained, the sum of well over £40,000 per annum formed a vast addition to the royal revenue. Before 1542 the Crown had never derived so much as this from its landed estates.[29] Fortunately for the clergy, the inflation soon increased the nominal values of rectories and vicarages, whereas Cromwell's successors contented themselves with levying taxation on the assessments of his *Valor*. From Elizabeth's reign as the burden of clerical subsidies grew, that of first fruits and tenths continued to diminish, until by the time of Queen Anne they had become almost negligible.

Cromwell's first Treason Act made it treasonable to desire, even in words, any bodily harm to the King, Queen or heir apparent, to deprive them of their dignities and titles, to declare the King a heretic, tyrant or usurper, or to detain his ships or weapons. The oft-repeated notion that this legislation first made high treason of seditious words has been proved untrue,[30] yet understandably it remained the only one of these measures to arouse real disquiet amongst the gentry and in Parliament itself. Events soon conspired to remove this tension. Within two years the threats of foreign powers and the rise of treason and rebellion at home brought the vast majority of the nation to the royal standpoint. Little objection arose to the

Treason Act of 1536, which imposed the penalties of treason upon any clerical or lay official who refused an oath renouncing the jurisdiction of Rome, or to that of 1539, which threatened all persons seeking to go abroad in order to avoid penalties arising from religious disobedience. Even by Tudor standards, extensions to the treason laws looked oppressive in 1534, but they looked far less so by 1536, when the public peril had become genuine enough. Cromwell did not need to browbeat the courts trying persons accused of plots or papalist sympathies. Unasked, jurors now condemned suspects even on flimsy evidence, and a dismayed people made itself his accomplice in defending the Royal Supremacy by every means in its power.

Resistances

This chain of events has the inexorable character of tragedy. Once Henry chose the methods proposed by Cromwell, he was bound to encounter a certain measure of resistance from various minority-groups, ranging from noble idealists to backward-looking feudalists. In a state which lacked police forces and a standing army, this opposition inevitably attracted its unpleasant rewards—harsh and capacious treason laws, counter-espionage, violent prosecutors and juries over-anxious to demonstrate their loyalty. From the secular viewpoint, there was no logical alternative to forcible repression, however unsatisfactory the mechanism available. English history of the fifteenth century and continental history during the sixteenth combined to instil one obvious lesson—that civil war ranked as the worst disaster which could befall a people in this world. To Cromwell, his mind perhaps mainly on the Wars of the Roses, the lessons of history left no room for hesitation, and the reader curious to follow his thinking need only turn to the preamble of the first Succession Act with its insistence upon the 'great effusion and destruction of man's blood', which would spring from the 'sinister appetite and affection' of overmighty subjects arrogating to themselves the right to determine the succession. The majority of the Tudor English abhorred the fanaticism which would plunge a nation into blood upon an issue of religious dogma or canon law. If they clumsily executed too many in-nocents, blunderers and idealists along with the political traitors, at least they did not, with Alva, burn hosts of heretics, or with Charles V and the German princes, slaughter deluded peasants in their tens of thousands. By comparison with these events, or with many episodes in the so-called Wars of Religion, even the tragic crisis of Henry's reign represents mercy itself in terms of the actual volume of human suffering inflicted. The King was far from compassionate by temperament, and he bears the moral guilt for not a few avoidable executions, including those of his two greatest servants, Thomas More and Thomas Cromwell. Yet in the last resort he fully understood the psychological risks of mass-killing in an English landscape.

And only the uninformed critics of Thomas Cromwell have imagined that the minister was a Robespierre. There is no evidence to show that he enjoined severity upon the King and, if a readiness to shed blood had really been a part of his impassive nature, very much more would have been shed during his years of power.

The opposition was not a party. It displayed all the tints of the spectrum without their co-ordination. At its bright end was Sir Thomas More, who as a former minister grasped the civilising duties and achievements of the dynasty, yet on the highest principles found himself obliged to put first the unity of Christendom under papal headship. More was never other than a Catholic, but within that broad definition he showed distinct changes of emphasis. He had his monastic Middle Ages with the London Carthusians, his critical Renaissance with Erasmus, his Counter-Reformation when (on his own showing) he was converted to papalism and actively persecuted the heretics. More's character and ideas now seem complex and controversial to a far greater extent than biographers were willing to concede only a few decades ago. The theme demands so much space that we propose to discuss it separately at the end of this chapter.[31] Alongside him were the Carthusian and Observant victims, understanding far less of the political perils of the day, but beyond criticism in the purity of motive which led them to the gibbet or the dungeon. Somewhat less close than often imagined stood John Fisher, whose saintly personal character should not obscure the extreme unwisdom of his treasonable conversations with the Imperial ambassador Chapuys, that devoted friend of Queen Katherine and equally devoted organiser of opposition.[32] Here was no sudden impulse, since Fisher had long been obsessed by the royal divorce and had written at least seven 'books' supporting the Queen's case with considerable ability and learning.

The reactionary elements of the nobility are ranged in various positions toward the dark end of the spectrum. These magnates formed a menace to the security of the nation, since they could not understand that Tudor England had outgrown the mad bloodshed and faction, the king-making and king-breaking of the fifteenth century. They included active neo-feudalists like Lord Abergavenny, Sir James Griffith ap Howell, Lord Edmund Bray and Lord Darcy; they included also some more mildly disloyal and irresolute groups like that of the Courtenays and the Poles, broken up in 1538 by the discovery of the so-called Exeter Conspiracy.[33] Few of all these men can command much sympathy, because they were destructive anachronists rather than religious objectors. Amid the ruling classes there developed in fact no split along doctrinal lines. Those magnates who did most to preserve Henry's throne amid sedition and rebellion—the Duke of Norfolk and the Earl of Shrewsbury—nevertheless held Catholic beliefs, detesting Cromwell and all those of Reforming outlook. Amongst the higher clergy the impressive feature is the virtual unanimity with which they followed the lead of the King. Only one, John Fisher, accepted martyrdom over the Supremacy. Only one divine of eminence, Reginald Pole, chose exile on account of his beliefs. Those heads of monasteries accused of treason or complicity in rebellion may, with one or two exceptions like Abbot Cooke of Reading, be classed as unlucky victims rather than as deliberate martyrs. The parish clergy, as we have already observed, were in general modest men who quietly accepted the decisions of authority, yet a number of them certainly helped to stir up the group of risings known as the Pilgrimage of Grace. It is also through this latter, one of the best-documented episodes of Tudor history, that we learn most concerning the nature of opposition amongst the laity.

Exactly how far was this most formidable of all the challenges to Henry VIII an anti-Reformation rebellion?[34] It remains hard to answer the question with brevity and precision. The voluminous sources point in many directions, and their problems are complicated by the fact that there were four different risings. The Lincolnshire rebellion of 1–12 October 1536 had virtually collapsed before the northern men rose. The main Pilgrimage under Robert Aske affected Yorkshire, Lancashire and the north-eastern counties. It lasted from 9 October to 5 December 1536. As lately re-investigated by S. M. Harrison, the accompanying revolt in Cumberland and Westmorland (which flared up for a second time in the January of 1537) is no longer regarded as a mainly social-revolutionary event. While here economic discontents existed, so did genuine elements of religious reaction. Democratic leadership coincided also with strong social and political conservatism, while in Cumberland these restraints were strengthened by the necessity of maintaining the military structure of the West March against Scotland. The second Yorkshire rising occurred under the leadership of Sir Francis Bigod, no Catholic but a violent Protestant and critic of the monasteries. In January 1537 he brought out his tenants and neighbours, not to oppose the Reformation but to rearm the North against the royal retribution which he saw must needs follow upon the main rising. Our present interest thus centres upon Aske's rebellion and, to a lesser extent, upon the trouble in Lincolnshire. The latter was a chaotic, ignominious and rather sordid affair which can scarcely be dignified as the protest of a Catholic society against the Reformation. Its leaders, headed by 'Captain Cobbler', were simple men. The local gentry joined only when pressed by the commons, and at the first chance they strove to allay the trouble. The general hatred was directed chiefly against an unpopular bishop and his officials and against the collectors of a royal subsidy. While the Lincolnshire insurgents feared the material consequences of the dissolution of the smaller monasteries, they were motivated still more powerfully by wild rumours that the King intended to suppress many parish churches and to confiscate church plate. As for the Royal Supremacy, it receives mention but once in the Lincolnshire records,[35] and this only in order to be accepted by the rebels.

The main Pilgrimage shows a more exhilarating but even more complex list of motives. Led by an attractive religious idealist, it was joined—though often involuntarily—by most of the leading gentle families in the North. Despite some disorder and looting (even at the expense of the monasteries) a large army was assembled in orderly fashion on the banks of the Don, an army more powerful and inured to warfare than the royalist levies sent to oppose it. The conservative North was more dangerous than the conservative West Country, since it was kept in good military training by the Scots and since so many of its gentry were attached in clientage to the feudal houses of Percy, Neville and Dacre, which had traditions of rebellion. Many of the leaders of the Pilgrimage were paid servants of the Percys and felt as a notable grievance the disinheritance of Sir Thomas Percy by his brother, the childless sixth Earl of Northumberland, who had willed the great Percy estates to the King. Another quasi-feudal figure was the aged Lord Darcy, a deeply-trusted servant of the Crown who had long plotted with the imperial ambassador Chapuys and who, at the outset of the revolt, surrendered the key-fortress of Pontefract and joined the rebels. The Pilgrimage was not a White Rose movement, though it might have developed this character had Reginald Pole, a member of the House of York, succeeded in returning to lead it. The northern gentry, like those of Lincolnshire, hated the recent Statute of Uses, which forbade them to settle portions on their younger sons and, by making mortgages illegal, greatly decreased their ability to borrow cash. Many of them held lucrative monastic stewardships and hence had a vested interest in the preservation of the religious houses. They all disliked the recent treason-laws and detested Cromwell for trying the grand jury of Yorkshire in the Star Chamber, on the ground that it had wrongfully acquitted a murderer.

While under Aske's leadership conservative religious feeling briefly helped to hold the actual rebellion together, during the preparatory period of restiveness we hear of little save the heavy economic grievances of the masses. Such material issues continued to bulk very large in the main set of articles drawn up by the leaders at Pontefract on 2–4 December at the climax of the Yorkshire revolt. In a time of bad harvests and cattle-plagues the smaller men suffered additional irritations from hard landlords like the Earl of Cumberland, whose enclosures and entry-fines had provoked an extensive riot the previous year amongst his tenants in the Yorkshire dales. The northerners also suffered from a lack of coin and, seeing the smaller monasteries in process of dissolution, they feared a further drain of currency to non-resident southern landlords, who might succeed the monks. As we shall see, this did not happen on any great scale, but the fear was intelligible enough. According to the clear statement of Robert Aske, this was the main reason why the mass of his followers disliked the Dissolution of the monasteries.[36]

At this moment only some fifteen small houses had in fact been suppressed in Yorshire. Though in a few cases monks were restored by rebel sympathisers, some mobs showed hostility to their local houses, while the great majority of the monks kept aloof from the movement. As elsewhere in England, the royal divorce was unpopular in the north, but many simpletons went on to imagine that innocent, bluff King Hal was being misled by the parvenu Cromwell and a knot of heretical bishops. Though the northern gentry and clergy were not wholly untouched by Protestantism, conservative religious and social views still predominated at all levels. The common people, as Aske remarked, were 'rude of conditions and not well taught the law of God'. Their conservatism was neither theologically informed nor incompatible with a certain amount of anticlericalism, yet they were sufficiently taught by their priests to dislike the idea of heresy. One cannot doubt that most of them heartily approved that clause in the rebel articles which criticised heretical books and doctrines. On the other hand, there is little evidence that the problem of the Supremacy interested the laity, while the senior clergy, ordered to discuss this matter by the leaders of the Pilgrimage, were equally divided over the claims of King and Pope until Aske broke into their meeting and urged them to support the latter. They finally agreed that the King might retain the title 'Head of the Church' but that he could not exercise spiritual powers, even that of visitation.[37]

Rationalising historians have too often neglected the irrational elements observable in popular rebellions, and the Pilgrimage of Grace is in this respect no exception. It was riddled with rumour, fable, folklore and prophecy, particularly by those prophecies concerning the rise and fall of kings which are traceable to the writings of Geoffrey Monmouth and which had appeared on former occasions, for example in the days of Hotspur and Henry IV. Even educated men took those superstitions seriously. Wilfrid Holme, the Protestant squire of Huntington near York, wrote a long poem on the Pilgrimage of Grace within a few months of its occurrence, his main object being not so much to deride the phrophecies as to prove that they could not refer to the reign of Henry VIII.[38] Richard Morison, one of Cromwell's most gifted humanist writers, attacked the 'Welsh' prophecies and then proceeded to develop counter-prophecies in favour of Henry, basing them upon the *Book of Esdras*.[39] Even, however, if its picturesque vagaries be disregarded, one may scarcely maintain that the Pilgrimage of Grace had practical or moral claims to form an alternative government. The ability to formulate a list of grievances did not give it genuine coherence. The gentry, themselves divided by bitter factions, had complaints essentially different from those of the commons. Reluctant to join the movement, they were only too glad to believe the promises made on the King's behalf by the Duke of Norfolk and to go home and discourage any further tendencies to revolt.

Paradoxically, the Pilgrimage could not succeed until it failed, since only the legal Tudor government could mitigate any of its grievances and since legal government could not function until rebellion had been patently repressed. A monarchy based on prestige and little else could not usefully have continued as a puppet of rebellion. Henry VIII, who understood Tudor rule better than his modern critics, could not sleep soundly in his bed until some routine of punishment had been applied to at least a few of the ring-leaders. Having induced the great host to disperse by vicarious promises, he stood in the dilemma of Machiavelli's prince—he could hardly ensure stable government without infringing the principles of private morality. Yet even if, like any other contemporary ruler, he believed that promises made under duress to rebels had no binding force, he could do little to restore his wounded prestige unless his opponents played into his hands. This they proceeded to do. In January 1537 Sir Francis Bigod renewed the revolt and the gentry, full of terrified second thoughts, vied with each other to suppress him. Soon afterwards, renewed risings in Cumberland also disposed opinion in favour of the government and produced an atmosphere in which not only the recent rebels but many of the original leaders could be brought to trial on slender charges. This spectacle remains unsavoury, yet the facile moralising in which romantic admirers of the Pilgrimage have indulged will not bear serious examination. Most of the subjects of Henry VIII believed that rebellion itself was a sin, and they had excellent reasons—not all of them pragmatic—for taking this view. The fabric of civilised life remained tenuous in the extreme; once shattered, it could not be pieced together so easily as by our modern techniques and by our modern minds, so conditioned to law-seeking. Rebellion aimed at changing the government was emphatically not the Tudor equivalent of a general election; it was a desperate gamble with the very life of a people.

That the events of 1536–7 formed the major crisis of the dynasty and that they bear relevance to the history of the Reformation cannot be denied. Nevertheless, the military success of the Pilgrimage would not necessarily have strangled the new religious movements in their childhood. Its failure did not inevitably entail their triumph. Its complex shapes have too often been trimmed to match modern doctrines and too neatly dovetailed into the story of English religion. Aske himself strove to unite its manifold and conflicting grievances into a sense of religious purpose, and for a few days at least he seems to have been partially successful. Yet viewed as a whole, the Pilgrimage cannot for a moment be fairly summarised as a devout crusade to save the rights of Holy Church, to re-edify the monasteries, to overthrow low-born heretics, to restore England to a papalist Christendom. Even the abilities of Robert Aske could not subdue the jarring discords of northern England into this beautiful symphony. The roots of the movement were decidedly economic, its demands predominantly secular, its interest in Rome almost negligible, its leading repressors not Protestant merchants but the highest nobility in the land, who shared its own hostile views towards heresy. In short, the English remained incapable of staging genuine Wars of Religion. Conversely, readers of Sir Geoffrey Elton's *Policy and Police* will need no reminder that a mingling of social, economic, political and religious discontents was far from being limited during these years to the northern counties. Thanks to the massive survival of Thomas Cromwell's correspondence, they are well documented for most parts of the realm.

Parish Registers

The remarkable body of statutes whereby the government and taxation of the English Church were transferred from Rome to England formed only one part of Cromwell's work as vicegerent. The Dissolution of the monasteries, which one should not allow to bulk too large in his career, poses questions of such complexity that we propose to reserve the whole matter to our next chapter. Another episode, the introduction of parish registers by his injunctions of 1538, must at least briefly claim our attention, since nothing illustrates more clearly that Reformation, as understood by Cromwell, did mean reform as well as confiscation.[40] Several years before this national institution of registers, some few humble but sensible parish priests had independently begun to record baptisms, marriages and deaths. In the absence of other records, and amid the small communities of that period, the possibility of marriage within the prohibited degrees presented a constant hazard. No aspect of ecclesiastical law during the Middle Ages lay in so confused a state as that relating to matrimony. Numerous divorces disguised as decrees of nullity were sought and given on grounds of pre-contracts made in infancy or substantiated only by flimsy evidence. Other marriages fell under dispute on grounds of distant blood-relationship, while a further gratuitous series of complexities arose through the arrogance of canonists who invented rules of spiritual affinity between a baptised person and his kin on the one hand, and his sponsors and their kin on the other. This meant that a man could be prosecuted for incest because he had married as his second wife the god-daughter of his first wife. A Church which adopted these irresponsible fantasies and yet failed to organise baptismal and matrimonial records was indeed inviting forcible reform at the hands of the State. Cromwell did not clean up the whole of this Augean stable but at least he made an important contribution to the task.

Early English Bibles

Far more profound in its effects than the introduction of parish registers, more profound even than the Dissolution of the monasteries, was Cromwell's patronage of the English Bible.[41] However persistently ecclesiastical historians may have overlooked the evidence, there can be no doubts about his early interest in the matter or about his zeal and effectiveness when it came to setting forth translations of the Scriptures. We can believe or disbelieve John Foxe's story that Cromwell memorised the whole of the Latin New Testament of Erasmus while journeying between England and Rome. This task he may have undertaken primarily in order to improve his Latin, yet if so, a close knowledge of the text, enjoyed by extremely few laymen at that date, could scarcely have remained without some deeper influences upon his mind. In 1527, or earlier, Miles Coverdale, as yet an Augustinian friar, wrote to Cromwell with enthusiasm about his study of the Scriptures, dropping a heavy hint about his lack of the necessary books and mentioning the 'godly communication' between the two of them 'in Master Moorys house upon Easter eve'[42] This passage refers in all likelihood to a discussion at the house of Sir Thomas More, whom Cromwell knew well and deeply respected up to the time of his martyrdom. Coverdale, soon a figure second only to Tyndale in the early history of the English Bible, does not in fact claim to have been actually engaged in translation as early as 1527, but it is not without interest that he was discussing his preparatory studies with his patron Cromwell five years before the latter's ministry began.

By 1534 the King's former distaste for biblical translators and translations, previously stimulated by Tyndale's defiance, had notably diminished. Under the influence of Cranmer and Cromwell, the Convocation of Canterbury now thought it safe to petition the King 'that the holy Scripture shall be translated into the vulgar tongue by certain upright and learned men, to be meted out and delivered to the people for their instructions'. While Tyndale could not openly be used, another instrument was coming to hand. Without awaiting a change of heart in England Coverdale had been hard at work in exile and in 1535, probably at Zürich, published his Bible with an unauthorised dedication to the King.

This was the first complete Bible to be printed in English, for Tyndale had printed, in addition to his New Testament, only translations of the Pentateuch and the *Book of Jonah*. Coverdale was less well qualified to complete the Old Testament, since he knew little or no Hebrew. Hence he incurred a heavy debt to the literal translation from that language into Latin published in 1528 by the Italian Dominican, Santes Pagninus. On the other hand, he had a complete command of German—it sometimes registers adversely upon his English—and made extensive use of Luther's translation and of another German version (largely independent of Luther) published at Zürich in 1531. Nevertheless, his chief obligation was still to Tyndale, long passages of whose New Testament he reproduced with but minor alterations. For all that, he did rather more than merely complete Tyndale's Old Testament. No translator had a better ear for the well-turned phrase and for the ring of a sentence. His independent talent appears to best advantage in that occasionally inaccurate yet lovely version of the Psalms which can still be read in the Anglican Prayer Book. The Church of England, fortunate at least in its literary instincts, continued to prefer Coverdale's Psalms even after the appearance of the Authorised Version of the Bible; they are accordingly still sung at matins and evensong, and for this particular purpose could not be bettered. Even in their obscure moments they have the mellow beauty of some ancient, familiar window with slightly jumbled glass; one would scarcely have the imperfections set right.

In Coverdale the government had found a collaborator far more amenable than Tyndale. 'I am but a private man', he wrote 'and am obedient under the higher powers.' Though a former disciple of Barnes at Cambridge, and now forced into exile through his bold preaching against images and the confessional, he did not offend Catholic susceptibilities by loading his margins with abuse, and he even altered his original title-page and prologue so as to lessen the impression of his dependence on the German theologians. An eventful career still lay before this mild-mannered but consistent Reformer. Having been allowed to return to England under Cromwell he spent Henry's last reactionary years abroad, but returned under Edward VI. As Lord Russell's chaplain during the troubled summer of 1549 he preached through the West Country in order to pacify the rebellion. Having been rewarded with the bishopric of Exeter, Coverdale stood in peril at Mary's accession, and he may well have owned his life to a fortunate family relationship. During the thirties he took as wife a Scottish gentlewoman, whose sister married the Protestant scholar John Macalpine. The latter, also exiled, had risen to influence with the King of Denmark and now prevailed upon that monarch to intercede with Mary for Coverdale's release. The translator hence gained permission to retire to Denmark, whence he moved on to Germany and Switzerland, returning in time to help in the consecration of Elizabeth's archbishop, Matthew Parker. Having refused his former see he then held a London living, revered as a patriarch by all Protestants. Two years before his death in 1568, he also resigned even this benefice as incompatible with his leadership of the nascent Puritan school of thought. We shall shortly refer to Coverdale's main task for Cromwell—the compilation of the Great Bible, which forms the chief memorial of a major and too often neglected figure of the English Reformation.

Meanwhile in August 1535 the Southwark printer James Nicholson (a Netherlander by origin) begged Cromwell's support for the publication of Coverdale's Bible in England. The minister then presumably urged the King to overcome the resistance of the bishops and, according to an anecdote related in Elizabethan times,[43] Henry asked the demurring prelates whether they could find any heresies in the work. When they replied in the negative, he said, 'If there by no heresies, then in God's name let it go abroad among our people.' Some reason exists for believing that Anne Boleyn helped to win his tolerance toward a work by one of his exiled Lutheran subjects. Not long afterwards, in July 1536, Cromwell prepared a set of ecclesiastical injunctions which contained an order to every parson to provide volumes of the whole Bible, both in Latin and in English, and to place them in the choir of his church 'for every man that will to look and read thereon'. The laity must be encouraged to read the English Bible 'as the very word of God and the spiritual food of man's soul', but also charitably exhorted not to engage in contention over its meaning. Three copies of the 1536 injunctions have survived containing this bold article, yet about the time of Anne Boleyn's fall Cromwell for the moment erased it from his articles. The enterprising Nicholson was nevertheless permitted to print Coverdale, and so successful did the book prove that in 1537 he issued two revised editions.

At this point a competitor entered the market in the shape of a translation by John Rogers, chaplain to the house of English merchants at Antwerp, who used the pseudonym Thomas Matthew. This so-called 'Matthew Bible' first attracted the attention of Cranmer, who in August 1537 brought it to Cromwell. The latter then prevailed upon the King to allow its sale throughout the Kingdom—another testimony to the remarkable influence of the minister and his liberal policy, since everyone knew that Rogers had worked intimately with both Tyndale and Coverdale and that he was closely involved with the German Lutherans. This translator possessed a sound knowledge of both Greek and Hebrew, but wherever possible he made his New Testament follow Tyndale's. For the Old Testament he drew much inspiration not only from Coverdale but from Lefèvre of Etaples and from

Olivetan of Noyon, the relative and mentor of the young Calvin. In one respect, Rogers stood at the end of a tradition, for this was the last of the English Bibles with prefaces and glosses owing a large debt to those of Luther himself. His text is also provided with more than 2,100 notes, drawing heavily upon those by Lefèvre, Olivetan, Bucer, Tyndale and other well-known commentators but superior to those of Tyndale in point of moderation and charity. Nearly two decades later Rogers won distinction as protomartyr of the Marian persecution. He was burnt at Smithfield in February 1555 in the presence of his Flemish wife, a baby at her breast, and of their ten children. If we may follow Fox's account his interrogation by Stephen Gardiner expresses the point at issue in this matter of biblical translation. Gardiner stressed the intermediary rôle of the living Church: 'No, thou canst prove nothing by Scripture, the Scripture is dead, it must have a lively expositor.' Rogers replied, 'No, the Scripture is alive.[44]

The publisher of the Matthew Bible was Richard Grafton, a grocer of London and a merchant adventurer of Antwerp, whose letters to Cromwell display a rather naïve mixture of piety and business acumen. The great difficulties then attendant upon biblical publishing should not, however, be overlooked. Men like Grafton invested large sums but had no comforting foreknowledge that the Bible would ever become a best-seller. On the one hand, they feared that at any moment Gardiner might overthrow Cromwell and procure a reversal of the royal policy. On the other, they were beset by trade rivals unrestrained by modern laws of copyright. These facts should be remembered as we read Grafton's godly phrases and see him sell Cromwell six copies, beseeching him to grant a copyright for three years and to compel every parish priest to buy a copy and every abbey to buy six. In the event, Cromwell licensed both the cheap Coverdale Bible published by Nicholson and the dearer Matthew Bible of Grafton. Though as yet he did not force either upon the clergy, he urged the bishops to do so, and thus promoted the sales of both publications. A circular letter sent to the bishops early in 1538 urges them to exhort the laity to read the Bible and to fix a date by which every parson must lay forth an English Bible for public reading in his church. The evidence indicates that even the conservative bishops followed this directive. On the other hand, if a report on the diocese of Lincoln in September 1539[45] provides a representative picture, a good many parishes must have been slow to comply, a feature more likely to have been occasioned by administrative slackness or by a shortage of copies or money rather than by any resistance on doctrinal grounds.

The Great Bible

If one understands Cromwell's neat mind aright, this semi-organised situation would never have appealed to him as other than temporary. For some time he had been planning a new and authoritative English Bible. Early in 1538 he entrusted the revision to Coverdale, the printing to Richard Grafton and his partner Whitchurch. The sequel suggests that he would have been wise to envisage an all-English production, but his thoughts inevitably turned to Paris, since he wanted to complete a work of high technical quality in the minimum time. 'Printing is finer there than elsewhere', he told the French ambassador, 'and with the great number of printers and abundance of paper, books are there dispatched sooner than in any other country.'[46] So Grafton and Whitchurch set off for Paris and by June 1538 were at work with their French printer Regnault. Ironically enough, our ambassador at the French Court was Gardiner, who left in the October to be succeeded by Edmund Bonner, his future colleague in the Marian persecution. In mid-December with dramatic suddenness the Inquisitor-General of France stopped the work and summoned Regnault to appear before him, while Grafton and Whitchurch wisely fled to England. Cromwell then delivered a strong protest to the French government, arguing that the proposed Bible could not spread heresy in France, being a mere literal translation to help Englishman who knew no Latin. He also revealed that he had sunk £400 of his own money in the enterprise.

In relating the sequel Foxe tells his usual good story. 'The Englishmen posted away as fast as they could to save themselves, leaving behind them all their bibles ... and [would never have] recovered them, saving that the lieutenant criminal, having them delivered unto him in a place of Paris (like Smithfield) called Maulbert Place, was somewhat moved with covetousness and sold four great dry vats of them to a haberdasher to lap in caps, and these were bought again, but the rest were burned.' And he goes on to relate how Grafton and Whitchurch ultimately returned to Paris and obtained permission to bring Regnault's presses, type and workmen to England.[47] The bibliographical evidence in fact suggests that the printing took place in two stages and that the type-setting, apart from that of the *Apocrypha*, had been largely executed in Paris. Considering all these obstacles, the completion of the work in London by April 1539 illustrates the assiduity of these early printers and the driving force with which Cromwell accomplished a task. Foxe's final story seems, however, more debatable. He blames the interference of the French Inquisitor upon 'the hatred of the bishops, namely Stephen Gardiner and his fellows, who mightily did stomach and malign the printing thereof'. This is the type of charge not to be believed on the sole authority of Foxe. Yet Gardiner showed himself a consistent adversary of the open Bible; he was in Paris long enough to set opposition in motion and his warmest admirers would not deny his title to be considered an accomplished political intriguer. On first arriving in Paris Grafton and Whitchurch had written to Cromwell offering to reveal the names of certain persons already complaining against them to the University of Paris, 'and most chiefly of our own countrymen'.[48] Even so, it cannot be proved to the hilt that these objectors were Gardiner's secret agents. As for Bonner, he was at this time a dutiful Cromwellian and gave his chief every support in the matter of the English bible.

Despite these vicissitudes the Great Bible, as it came to be called, duly appeared in April 1539. A year later it achieved a second edition with a famous preface by Cranmer, and by the end of 1541 it had run through no less than five further editions. A letter written by Cranmer to Cromwell in November 1539[49] indicates the continued personal supervision maintained by the minister. Whitchurch, accompanied by the King's printer Thomas Berthelet, had just called on the Archbishop, and Berthelet had urged Cranmer to have the selling price fixed at 13s. 4d. Whitchurch had nevertheless reminded them that Cromwell preferred a price of ten shillings. If, reports Cranmer, Cromwell would grant the firm a monopoly of the Great Bible, Whitchurch would with reluctance accept the lower figure. In response Cromwell obtained a patent forbidding any printer to print an English Bible without his permission. Under this arrangement he could give Grafton and Whitchurch reasonable protection, but in fact he did not accord them a complete monopoly. In the same year he permitted Berthelet to publish a new translation by Richard Taverner, another of his close adherents[50] and a keen student of the Lutheran commentators. Taverner's Old Testament has little interest, in that he knew no Hebrew but followed Coverdale and Pagninus. On the other hand, his knowledge of Greek was excellent; his rendering of the New Testament is closer to the Greek than those of his predecessors, sometimes anticipating both the Rheims New Testament of 1582 and the Authorised Version itself. His notes and accessories are mainly drawn from the Matthew Bible. Finally, in April 1540 Cromwell also allowed Berthelet to print a cheap edition of the Great Bible for purposes of private reading.

The success of the Great Bible proved no more than its just desert, for it turned out to be Coverdale's masterpiece. Beginning with the Matthew Bible (itself owing a good deal to Coverdale's own earlier work) he improved this with the aid of the New Testament of Erasmus and, more important, with that of Sebastian Münster's able Latin translation of the Old Testament published in 1535 alongside a Hebrew text. The politic hand of Cromwell appears in a gesture made to placate the affection of Catholics for the Vulgate. When the Vulgate added anything to the Hebrew or Greek text, Coverdale agreed to insert the addition in small type and in brackets. He also toned down a few offensive expressions, yet without essentially altering the Protestant terminology deriving from Tyndale. In general this proved a sober, tasteful and workmanlike production. If it sacrifices some of Tyndale's freshness and force, if its accuracy does not achieve modern standards, it may nevertheless be claimed as more consistent and more exact than its predecessors. Cranmer's preface to the second edition has been rightly praised both for its style and its sentiments, but the use of the term 'Cranmer's Bible' has been among the more absurd of popular misnomers. That the Archbishop took a warm interest in the Great Bible is not in dispute, but literary responsibility for this (and all other early translations) belongs to the English Lutherans in the Tyndale tradition. The political initiative, the planning of publication, the finance, the pressure to impose the Great Bible upon the English Church, these came from the vicegerent Thomas Cromwell.

Effects of the English Bible

The outdated opinion that Cromwell's attitude to religion was purely worldly, negative and sinister was based not on a serious study of Cromwell's character and designs but on an obsession with the monastic dissolution to the neglect of the innumerable proofs that Cromwell had creative and positive views on ecclesiastical reform. As luck will have it, we can trace his lively interest in the Bible to a point much earlier than his rise to political eminence, while his obvious (and ultimately fatal) leanings toward Lutheranism must have involved an understanding of the principles central to that school of thought. One who reads without prejudice his letters, his injunctions, his final parliamentary speech of 12 April 1540, cannot doubt his positive desire to establish a religion based upon the Bible, a religion eschewing on the one hand blind trust in ecclesiastical tradition and on the other the brawling of self-appointed expositors. But in the mind of such a man this desire was far from remaining unworldly; Cromwell did not think about the vernacular Bible in exactly the same terms as Tyndale. His political task bade him to consider the Bible in its social setting, and here no clear division existed between the spiritual and the temporal. One cannot study his injunctions without sensing his zeal to create a scripturally-educated laity as the backbone of an orderly Christian commonwealth. He had his own statesmanlike reasons for hoping, as Erasmus had hoped twenty years earlier, that the gospels might be read by travellers on their journeys and 'that the husbandman may sing parts of them as his plough, that the weaver may hum them at his shuttle'.

The Reformers, the Erasmians, the Cromwellians who entertained such ambitions would not have been dissatisfied could they have looked forward for a couple of centuries into English history. Concerning the immense influence of the vernacular Bible upon both the religious and the secular history of the English people and their colonial offspring, one cannot write save in the danger of perpetrating cant and cliché. Upon the Bible stood both Anglicanism and Nonconformity. Especially during our golden seventeenth century the Bible worked as a midwife to bring forth a whole great literature. It enabled a tinker of Bedford to write *The Pilgrim's Progress*. In an age when Milton could believe that God had chosen his Englishmen to perform his special tasks, it was the Bible which nerved the arm of Oliver Cromwell and fortified the spirit of the pioneers in New England. Without it we can scarcely imagine English constitutionalism or English imperial expansion. It was a capacious literature which, especially under conditions of unscientific exegesis, could be applied to any human situation and made to yield a quasi-supernatural sanction to many courses of conduct. In short, it provoked and it rationalised the theory and the action of those three great centuries during which Britain placed her stamp upon world history. For the mass of her people, this was the true Renaissance, the creative revival of Antiquity.

The English Lutherans, organised by a lay-minister and applauded by a half-Protestant Archbishop, first provided vernacular Bibles at a time when many of the English hierarchy still opposed so radical departure from medieval principles. Only a few staunch ecclesiasts have believed that the Henrician bishops would have taken the initiative to provide a tolerable version, or for that matter any version, of the Scriptures. But it remains too easy to be wise after the event and to castigate conservatives like More for their zeal to suppress the Lutheran translations and for their timorous refusal of an alternative. They were merely maintaining an established English policy in a period of crisis which threatened to engulf an ecclesiastical and social order they felt committed to preserve. With more reason we may permit ourselves a smile at the expense of Gardiner, who faced by the failure of total prohibition demanded that many debatable words (and indeed many non-debatable ones) should be wrapped up in Latin neologisms: 'Behold the ancille of the Lord' ... 'This is my dilect son in whom complacui.'[51]

The governors of the Tudor commonwealth stood in a position not wholly unlike that of modern liberal governments seeking to extend full democracy to unripe peoples. Over-confident in their little knowledge and their adolescent pride, the learners rush in, to the peril of themselves and of others. Yet the stage has arrived when they can learn only from their own errors, when they can be restrained only by a repression more harmful than the abuse of freedom itself. Their state must become worse before it can become better. That in 1538 there were a good many Englishmen prepared to abuse the liberty of the Gospel became at once clear, yet further attempts to restrict access proved half-hearted and ineffective. Of the several canyons across which Thomas Cromwell led the English nation, this was perhaps the widest and the deepest. If the Cromwellian statutes crippled papalism, the English Bible was destined to cripple caesaro-papalism. It even involved in substance the great debate of eighteenth-century Europe; It involved faith in the capacity of human nature for self-improvement. The demand from below was bound to become progressive; men rapidly sensed that after so many centuries of hierarchical and autocratic Christianity they were only demanding a liberty which early Christians had assumed as a matter of course. A Christian country could not educate its laity and then prohibit their access to the written sources of Christian belief. Tudor laymen had to be treated like adults because they believed themselves to be such. Though the art of state-propaganda was now advancing, Tudor governments could neither suppress the appetite for the Bible, once they had whetted it, nor could they successfully prescribe the conclusions to be drawn from biblical study.

These remoter effects were by no means fully discernible in the year 1538, when the English Bible became an established feature of the national life. Its more immediate effects were of a simpler character. It clinched the victory of the régime over papal authority and over the saint-cults. As it happened, the latter had just received further discredit when John Hilsey, the former Dominican who had succeeded Fisher as Bishop of Rochester, exposed the Blood of Hailes, the Rood of Boxley and other time-honoured frauds. As now expounded, the Scriptures constituted a more fundamental if less sensational attack upon this aspect of medieval religion. It was not merely that the New Testament provided so slight a foundation for these cults, but rather that St. Paul laid such emphasis upon salvation through the merits of Christ. If Bible-reading tended to overstress the Old Testament, it also popularised Pauline theology, that intellectual element of the faith which could not have been spread abroad by the theatrical modes of presentation used by the medieval Church upon a less literate public. And whatever happened in later years, the initial perusal of the Scriptures tended to enhance rather than undermine monarchical power. In the Old Testament one read much concerning godly Kings, while the New Testament at least gave Caesar his due. In both Testaments one might frequently encounter prophets announcing the good tidings, but one could sense singularly little of the medieval or Renaissance papacy. Alongside the much-debated Petrine texts one could even read the prolonged rebuke administered by Paul in *Galatians*, ii, 11–12: 'But when Peter was come to Antioch, I withstood him openly, because he was worthy to be blamed ... '[52] Yet in the last resort the most potent effects of Bible-reading are unlikely to have been in this text-hunting, beloved as it was by Tudor theologians. They are perhaps to be found in the general atmosphere of Gospel Christianity. The unaffected simplicity which marked the lives of Jesus Christ and the Apostles stood in bizarre contrast with the immense legal and coercive apparatus, the great wealth and splendid architectural exploits of the later medieval and Renaissance Church. Though this contrast had been expressed by Savonarola and other Catholic reformers, its full force could only be experienced by a man who had read the Gospels for himself.

In the Bible, in the notion of a return to the original spirit of Christianity, in the rebirth of a fragment of the ancient world so infinitely more precious to Christians than the glories of Greece and the grandeurs of Rome, here lay the true strength of the Reformation. One who has never felt this nostalgia, this desire to sweep away the accretions, to cross the centuries to the homeland, can understand little of the compulsive attraction of the New Testament, even less of the limited but real successes achieved by Protestant-ism, successes which cannot, any more than those of the Counter-Reformation, be explained away by reference to ambitious kings and greedy nobles.

Nevertheless, along this path of biblical study lay some yawning pits into which hapless Christians did not fail to stumble. Too many readers, both educated and uneducated, would not be satisfied to present their conclusions as reasonable hypotheses or as starting-points for fresh thought and investigation. Instead, the old demon of the medieval schools reappeared in more insidious guise—the spiritual pride which, even when faced by the obscurer problems of theology, worked through cocksure ratiocination to precise verbal definition, through counter-dogma to counter-persecution. Offered a vision of the free, the enquiring, the charitable, the tentative and modest mind, they turned their backs upon it and entered a prison cell not very dissimilar to the one they had just left. It began to appear that the Spirit of Truth had denied infallibility to the successors of St. Peter, to Aristotle, to the metaphysicians of Paris, only to bestow this wondrous gift upon the theologians of Zürich, Geneva, or Cambridge. Revolutions seldom make large immediate contributions to the liberty of man. If the Reformation in the end augmented our spiritual liberty, it did so slowly and by devious ways which many of its original champions could neither have anticipated nor desired.

Thomas More: Controversial Saint

The most distinguished but most controversial adversary of the English Reformation now demands a substantial digression. Should that Erasmian phrase 'a man for all seasons' be taken to describe a flawless saint, serenely in command of all worldly situations, it would nowadays appear misguided. Thomas More's canonisation in 1935 was followed two years later by the elegant yet simplifying biography by R. W. Chambers.[53] This and many other selective accounts have derived essentially from the *Life* by More's son-in-law William Roper, no chronological biography but a series of intimate, moving, but wholly uncritical recollections set down in 1557.[54] The same canonising spirit breathes through every page of Roper's ardent successors, Harpsfield[55] and Stapleton.[56] In later times Froude's Protestant bigotry resulted in passages of gross reversal. Until recent years few if any modern biographers achieved anything resembling a balanced portrait of this august but complex figure. That throughout his whole life Thomas More never abandoned sincere and strenuous purposes as a man of religion, that during his final months as prisoner and steadfast martyr he attained sanctity in the discharge of his conscience, these facts would not be seriously disputed by any fair and informed biographer. Yet even this glorious withdrawal from the world should not remove the hero's earlier life from all criticism and controversy, always provided that we cannot reasonably expect him to be a modern, irenical Christian. Endowed with many virtues and graces, More nevertheless suffered lifelong distractions and inner tensions. Until the last phase he sought indefatigably for position and profit, first amid the contentious routines of the Bar and then in a succession of secular offices and perquisites. He knew well, and pursued with zeal, the arts of the courtier, devious as they had to be in so perilous a time. His days were lightened by a spontaneous wit, by family affections, by assiduous reading and imaginative thought. By contrast his life was also marked by obsolete forms of self-mortification and shadowed by polemical writing which, however sincere, seems too often laden with hatreds almost as crude as those expressed by his Protestant contemporary John Bale. Taking his life as a whole, the icon and the iconoclasm have been equally misplaced. Readers hitherto nourished by R. W. Chambers should at least take into account a number of realistic modifications: two pioneering essays (1972, 1980) by Sir Geoffrey Elton,[57] the expert analysis of More's official career by John Guy,[58] the capacious and fair-minded biography by Richard Marius[59] and the penetrating survey of his thought and writings by Alistair Fox.[60]

Against these revisionists Dr. Brendan Bradshaw has published a brilliant counter-revision, staunchly defending Thomas More on all counts.[61] This essay has become obligatory reading, though it raises too many complex issues to be adequately discussed in this present crowded book. Bradshaw supplements some of Fox's themes by a justified emphasis upon More's Platonism. In masterly analyses of More's *Dialogue concerning Heresies* (1529) and of his *Apology* (1533) he answers those critics who have characterised the polemical writings as shapeless and badly organised. Bradshaw also shows that More did not primarily centre his loyalties around the Papacy or the General Councils of the Church, but rather around the 'common corps of Christendom'. This is surely true; yet worried by the nebulous character of this body, one is compelled to recall that the threatened obliteration of papal authority in England did after all become the occasion of More's deliberate martyrdom. Bradshaw wisely urges caution when seeking to explain More's ideas by reference to his supposed psychological pressures. Discretion is here indeed necessary, though some of the data are striking enough to invite at least a tentative hypothesis of this sort. Not a few readers will conclude that Dr. Bradshaw has somewhat magnified the historical role and the intellectual breadth of Thomas More. In particular, toward the end of his essay he seeks to tie More very closely to Erasmus, both being advocates of an 'alternative' Reformation, based upon humanist ideals, upon the dignity of human free will, as mankind struggles to contribute in some small degree to its own salvation. In contrast, the present writer has totally failed to regard the two men as meaningfully conjoined in any such practical enterprise. Throughout by far the greater part of the story these fellow-humanists, however deep their early mutual admiration, displayed such fundamental divergences that one must doubt whether they ever came face to face in a serious discussion concerning the problems of the Church. More's few criticisms of the priesthood are as mild as he could credibly make them. On the other hand, was not Erasmus the prime anticlerical, the most persistent and wounding satirist of the contemporary Church, the habitual castigator of scholastic reactionaries, of blue-blooded canons, of warlike popes and even of superstitious laymen? With some justice it has been said that Erasmus did more harm to monasticism than did Luther himself. In fact from the 1520s, led by the papal legate, Aleander, the enemies of Erasmus did not scruple to charge him with heresy. Both the Papacy and the Council of Trent recognised this situation, when they came to ban the works of Erasmus.[62] Again, having urged the return to a Scriptural Christianity in his *Enchiridion* (written 1501, published 1503–4), Erasmus went on to a demand vernacular bibles for working-class people in his *Paraclesis* (1516). Here was the great evangelical enterprise from which Erasmus never withdrew. By contrast More at first defended the principle of translation, yet he later shrank from its implications. Again, despite his criticisms of Luther's harsh language, did not Erasmus in his *Axiomata* of 1520 urge the Elector of Saxony to protect Luther against his ultra-Catholic enemies, since Luther was so much more disinterested and honest than they, more sincere even than the denunciatory Bull issued by Pope Leo X himself?[63] And whereas More never envisaged the slightest compromise with the Lutherans, Erasmus as late as 1524 sketched a basis for reconciliation in his optimistic colloquy *De Fide*.[64] He also corresponded amicably with his warm admirer Philip Melanchthon,[65] who happened also to be Luther's famous second-in-command. From the other side Luther's painter Cranach went so far as to include Erasmus in his famous group of Protestant leaders.[66] Even among the Zwinglians and the sectarian writers, hated by Luther and More alike, the liberal ideas of Erasmus reappear in countless places.[67] Erasmus surely deserves his place among the fathers of religious toleration, despite the fact that, under very heavy orthodox pressures, he staged a literary tournament with Luther over the Freedom of the Will, a topic which had hitherto not very deeply interested him.[68] So, most emphatically, More and Erasmus cannot be presented in any realistic sense as the heavenly twins of a reformist Catholicism! In broad terms it might be said that Erasmus was always a liberator, while More, with ever-increasing emphasis, joined forces with the most cautious, conservative prelates.

How should we regard More's inward disharmonies, or rather spiritual discomforts? Even on the selective witness of Roper, one can hardly doubt the violence of the clash between More's early monastic aspirations and the confrontation with his own sexuality which made him choose marriage. Though the decision was wise, the ensuing complications became serious, because he seems never to have banished that celibate ideal imprinted upon him during the years he spent alongside the London Carthusians.[69] The agony of this spiritual 'defeat' may perhaps help to explain his continual self-whipping and his penitential wearing of a hair-shirt, bizarre forms of piety by that period and possibly unique among Tudor laymen. There remain numerous indications, direct and indirect, that throughout his two marriages More persisted in regarding sexuality, even in wedlock, as tainted by sin.[70] He even pointed out that it was easier for a celibate to remain 'chaste' than for a married man! Doubtless this propensity continued to be fostered by his favourite authors. Paul, Augustine, Pico della Mirandola and the Platonists all emphasised the sharp division between spirit and flesh, an emphasis illustrated in parallel by the *Enchiridion* of Erasmus, who nevertheless in real life neither sought marriage nor needed lugubrious penances to keep his instincts under control. Meanwhile, Thomas More doubtless became well aware of the dramatic inhibitions and remedies which both the early Fathers and some medieval saints recommended to the faithful. His hair-shirt forcibly reminds one of that worn by that other native of London and Chancellor, Thomas Becket, whose conflict with Henry II would soon be regarded as prefiguring the crisis of the Henrician Reformation. Of course, amid those austerities in middle life, More can hardly have foreseen that he himself would re-enact the story of a king's trusted servant and friend, who had to die for transferring his allegiance to the Church. No doubt all these experiences and literary influences worked upon a mind predisposed to pessimism, nurtured in the law, and versed in the penitential aspects of medieval religion. As already observed, he wrote most terrifying accounts of the physical anguish experienced by sinners, both in the hour of death and throughout the long ages of suffering in Purgatory. Similar judicial emphases and fears are common among his contemporaries: they inflicted suffering upon Luther himself until he 'discovered' the loving kindness of a redeeming God and so could reject monasticism, together with that mural painting of Christ the Judge, sitting upon a rainbow to judge the dead, the image which had so disturbed him as a child.

While sixteenth-century minds seldom lend themselves to catch-phrases drawn from a textbook of psychology, we may with some degree of probability suppose that contending forces, psychological, literary, doctrinal, all contributed to More's well-documented sense of human depravity, and hence to his violent detestation of heresy and of any revisions which seemed to oppose the ancient teachings of the Church. Though by no means unique in so doing, he exploded with marked ferocity against the marriages of the Protestant clergy, especially against the union of Luther with an ex-nun, a special offence given the label of 'incest' by him and other conservative writers. For More, Luther is 'a fond friar, an apostate, an open incestuous lecher, a plain limb of the Devil, and a manifest messenger from hell'.[71]

Whatever its genesis, More's pronounced horror against the sins of the flesh probably intensified and gave shape to that general apprehension and world-weariness still widespread, though seldom so vociferously expressed, among both Catholic and Protestant intellectuals of the sixteenth century in transalpine Europe. The current social-religious unrest, supposedly a portent of the coming day of doom, oppressed many anxious minds. Dürer's *Four Horsemen of the Apocalypse* provides the dominant image of the period. Yet in the case of Thomas More the fear of anarchy aroused practical as well as emotional convictions. He came to see the powers of the ancient Roman Church as the great dam which was holding back the flood of disorder and had so far sufficed to conserve the moral and political structures of Europe. Sceptical in early life concerning the authority of Rome, he had then studied the history of the Papacy and had concluded that an institution so long preserved must surely be sanctioned and upheld by God.[72] Already familiar with the Lollard menace, he soon took cognizance of Luther as a satanic agent, far more capable than the earlier heretics of overwhelming the Church's protective barrier. Convinced that chaos could only be averted if Church and State joined in the ruthless extirpation of heresy, he also waged a bitter war of words with the English heresiarch William Tyndale, 'that beast and hell-hound of the Devil's kennel'.[73] More's appointment as Lord Chancellor on 26 October 1529 enabled him to organise a campaign against a number of known heretics still alive in England.

That More did in fact persecute heretics, and did so by his own elaborate definitions of 'heresy' and 'persecution', was fully demonstrated by Leland Miles in 1965.[74] It cannot be denied that More insisted with total clarity that heretics convicted in the ecclesiastical courts must be duly burned by the State, the chief executive officer of which he had now become. In the last chapter of his *Dialogue concerning heresies* (1528) More is indeed a hardliner on the burning of heretics, making strange attempts to show that the

Apostles agreed with his view, and upbraiding the clergy for their lack of severity. This duty is 'lawful, necessary and well done', since heretics do not respond to gentle tactics and must therefore be killed to prevent them from infecting others.[75] He clearly believed that heresy threatened the secular commonwealth, besides constituting a crime against God and the Church. For him heresy cancelled out all the personal virtues of its practitioners. Every heretic was totally wrong and insincere in every belief and on every occasion. More even accused Tyndale of fostering sedition and rebellion, whereas in fact Tyndale—along with most Lutherans—stood consistent at the opposite extreme, inculcating the religious duty of non-resistance even when facing the most tyrannical ruler.[76] Having successfully prayed that his own son-in-law Roper might be delivered from an attraction to heresy, More then pitilessly denounced other young men (who had gone to the stake) as totally deserving their punishment.[77] He so refers to the main victims burned during his brief Chancellorship: Tewkesbury, Bayfield, Bilney and Hytton, the last being recalled as 'the Devil's stinking martyr'. More once claimed in all good faith that he hated only the vices of heretics, not their persons, though his savage words make us wonder how far he really achieved this delicate distinction in the heat of his battle to preserve Church and State. As Lord Chancellor he did not merely acquiesce in the procedures: he played an active personal role in the arrest, interrogation and imprisonment of several suspects.[78] Certainly he could perceive no trace of sincerity in such persons, whose offences sprang only from the 'malicious folly' of a 'poisoned, proud, obstinate heart'. In fact the struggle was still in its small, early stages, and during the two-and-a-half years of his Chancellorship only four, or possibly six, of the many heretics arrested actually went to the stake. No doubt he would have extended the list, had not the more notorious ringleaders already fled to the continent. All the same the other evidence obliges us to exonerate him from the stain of personal cruelty: the very violence of his language suggests that he was struggling to conceal the pain to which his office and his conscience had exposed him. In the years 1529–32 a considerable proportion of serious-minded and normally humane Englishmen no doubt approved his actions and would have contrasted them with the slack enforcement of the heresy laws by his predecessor Wolsey. Today our strictures should be restrained, but we can say that More failed to join that growing minority of people such as Erasmus, who aided by a touch of cynicism as well as by a natural delicacy of spirit, had begun to move away from these ferocious medieval values. And we might add that in nearly all other Catholic saints we are accustomed to see a more expansive compassion and a lesser belief in the efficacy of punitive laws. Like many others before and since, More continued to believe that the exalted end justified the terrorising means. On the other hand he would have been shocked or amused by the misconceptions of those modern devotees who have wanted to make him a freedom-fighter against a tyrannical State!

Thomas More's intense preoccupation with the maintenance of order, mental and physical, would seem only natural and consistent in the son of a judge who laboured as a barrister, became an undersheriff of the City of London, then a royal councillor and finally the chief law-officer of the Crown. His championship of legal authority was far from being limited to the sphere of religion, and it does not conflict with the concepts of his *Utopia*, which is no mere futurist fantasy but a rationalisation of strong government.[79] The Utopians nowadays seem to inhabit a rather heavy-handed collectivist state, resting on practical reason as distinct from Christian revelation. On this basis each citizen may follow his own religious concepts and even gently recommend them to others, though contentious proselytizing will be punished by exile and bondage. Moreover in Utopia a priesthood, smaller in number but better selected than that of Europe, enjoys high prestige and power.

In the real world, it is true, More admitted the existence of some ignorant and incapable clergymen,[80] but he blamed the problems mainly on the laity, never showing the persistently anticlerical spirit of Erasmus. In later life he could be most stubborn, for example in defending the ecclesiastical gaolers by insisting on the suicide of Richard Hunne against all the strong evidence for his murder.[81] Even so, qualifications are demanded. As we observed in comparing him with Tyndale, More was also a Christian humanist: he cannot be grouped with those scholastic reactionaries who detested the critical approach hitherto developed by Valla, Colet and Erasmus, and applied by them to the original Greek texts of the New Testament. He warmly upheld the right of Erasmus to translate the Greek into modern Latin, in possible rivalry with the revered Vulgate text.[82] Nevertheless while Erasmus went on to demand vernacular bibles for the use of ploughmen, weavers, travellers and 'even the lowliest women',[83] More developed some powerful reservations. Like the early Tudor bishops he was reluctant to place the English Scriptures in the hands of uneducated people; and while in principle he accepted proposals for an official translation, he nevertheless felt that the bishops should keep control of its circulation by licensing suitable people to read it.[84] Indeed he firmly believed that by her traditional methods the Church could adequately teach the Gospel, while Christians could achieve salvation under her guidance, without pursuing Scriptural studies in person. In his considered view, the laws and the Church, not the confused heretics and the greedy printer-publishers, should regulate this new situation.

In observing More's highly successful career, there seems little need to defend him against cross charges of sordid materialism. His case cannot, it is true, be assessed by reference to the paragons of Catholic sanctity. He neglected few opportunities to earn money, and at the Bar made at least £400 a year, forty or more times the income of an English parish priest of that day. He also bought wardships, accepted lucrative offices and valuable grants of land from the Crown. He built a sumptuous mansion at Chelsea, where he often transacted his duties as Chancellor. In politics he could on occasion be ruthless. Having for years adroitly flattered the poweful Wolsey, he eventually showed his real opinion by savaging the fallen minister in Parliament. However unsaintly, all these activities represent normal practice among Tudor lawyers, officials and courtiers. A conventional saint could not have supported a large family and have risen to the office of Lord Chancellor, a pinnacle hitherto usually occupied by bishops with fat incomes which did not have to be earned by hard personal labour. This first lay Chancellor had little use for the trappings of wealth and not the slightest propensity toward self-indulgence. In most respects he was a better Puritan than the classical Puritans of a later day. Within the family circle he extolled the virtues of hard work and self-improvement, placing idleness and time-wasting among the worst of sins.[85] Dr. Marius suggests that his violent outbursts of polemic represent the safety-valve of one who constantly lived under extreme pressure of business and who is even known to have suffered sinister chest-pains![86] Certainly during his later years his already profound sense of insecurity was deepened by the notorious hazards of the Henrician court, where ambitious climbers rose and fell, not a few withdrawn from competition by the executioner's axe. When the King visited him at Chelsea and walked in conversation with his arm around More's neck, the Chancellor entertained no illusions. 'If my head should win him a castle in France ... it should not fail to go'.[87] That touch of grim but endearing humour had every justification, though in the event the King was soon to claim his head over an issue far more fundamental. Thus with a heroism greater even than that of Samson, he ended by pulling down this worldly temple of his own patient construction. In his truly devout and spiritual writings in the Tower of London we see Thomas More resolutely renouncing worldly ambitions and preparing himself to die for a still attractive yet already clouded ideal: that at all costs the English nation should retain membership of an ordered Christendom under the Papacy and the consensus of fifteen centuries. The authentic odour of sanctity has at last become perceptible!

8 The Great Transfer

Motives for the Dissolution

'This year many dreadful gales, much rain, lightning and thunder especially in summertime, and at odd times throughout the year; also divers sudden mortal fevers, and the charity of many people grows cold; no love, not the least devotion remains in the people, but rather many false opinions and schisms against the sacraments of the Church.' With these words of doom the Augustinian canon of Butley Priory in Suffolk continued his chronicle in the year 1534.[1] To his troubled spirit even the elements seemed to unite in proclaiming the end of an era.

In this same year Thomas Cromwell and his colleagues discussed a certain scheme for the financial nationalisation of the English Church which would have justified the darkest forebodings of this depressed ecclesiastic. These memoranda, still among the State papers,[2] envisage the dissolution of all monasteries with less than thirteen inmates, the transfer of episcopal lands to the Crown and a staff of salaried bishops. In addition, the King would receive annates and half the incomes of cathedrals and collegiate churches. How seriously Cromwell took this radical scheme we do not know, but in the event it was discarded. Perhaps it seemed to involve too much risk of alienating and uniting the whole clerical order. The Crown was remarkably unprejudiced in its readiness to take money from any possible source, ecclesiastical or lay, yet on mature reflection the monasteries must have seemed by far the safest victims. They had broad lands, compliant heads, hostile critics in the parliamentary classes and among the secular clergy. They did not enjoy anything like that measure of popular esteem which modern romantics have thought to observe. Certainly they were not dissolved because of any dangerous devotion to the Papacy; anyone who believed this of any save an exiguous minority of English monks must have been highly prejudiced or foolish. What of the notion that the purchase of ex-monastic lands would bind a wavering nobility and squirearchy to the Crown? As will appear, some contemporaries did entertain this thought, yet it seems to play a far larger part in modern analyses than in the actual records of the Dissolution-years. While Cromwell was prepared to make some discreet alienations of land to certain key figures, his main aim was to endow the Crown in perpetuity, not to make it a mere channel for the enrichment of others. We should view the Dissolution alongside the remark he made to the King on the eve of his execution: 'If it had been or were in my power to make you so rich as ye might enrich all men, God help me as I would do it.'[3]

Following the unhappy experiences of Wolsey with Parliament, there had arisen financial needs which dwarfed those of the Cardinal himself. The enrichment of the Crown had again become the first and most obvious duty of its servants. In general the nation appreciated the internal order bestowed by the monarchy, while yet lacking all eagerness to pay for this blessing. The great inflation occasioned by American silver had by no means reached its acute stage, yet the expenses of government, especially the cost of ships and cannon, were fast multiplying. The monarchies of Europe staggered under mounting debts and soaring rates of interest; even the great Emperor Charles V on at least one occasion owed the preservation of his throne to the prompt financial support of the House of Fugger.[4] In addition to world trends Henry VIII had his own peculiar problems during the crisis of his Reformation. From 1534 the risk of invasion (a risk admittedly increased by the divorce and the schism) demanded great military expenditure. The defence of the northern marches, the Geraldine rebellion and the Pilgrimage of Grace all cost very large sums, while the Reformation Parliament proved far more lavish in protestations of loyalty than in offers of hard cash. Thomas Cromwell, an experienced member of the Commons, no doubt suspected that parliamentary enthusiasm for the King's causes would flourish in inverse proportion with the lay subsidies demanded by the Crown. Under these circumstances national defence and stable government could scarcely be preserved save by some large-scale exploitation of the resources of the Church. Otherwise, only by the most quiescent of policies, by the utmost good fortune in foreign relations, by a rigorous retrenchment of expenditure, could Henry VIII have avoided a dangerous crisis during the last decade of his reign. The exigencies of his situation have often been concealed from historians by two facts—that he had to hand a minister of exceptional foresight and that he could pillage many rich but defenceless ecclesiastical corporations. In a very real sense, the whole nation was the partner of King and minister in the ruthless enterprise of dissolution.

The enterprise itself had been too well described by Professors Knowles, G.W.O. Woodward and Joyce Youings to demand further general narratives.[5] Indeed, if we adhered rigorously to our main theme, we might almost avoid this topic, since the fate of the monasteries had only indirect connections with the rise of Protestantism. Even so, if a dissolution motivated by finance had not occurred in the thirties, a dissolution motivated in some measure by religion must have occurred as soon as Protestant teachings were professed by the governing class. Celibate communities which fostered the cult of the saints would have placed an impossible burden upon the meagre fund of Protestant tolerance.

The attitude of Thomas Cromwell toward the monasteries demands a rather more careful appreciation than most writers have accorded it. As an efficient layman he had plumbed the depths of monastic inefficiency, while men of his background had never been imbued with any sense of the historic achievements of monasticism. He evidently regarded the religious orders as beyond reform and without claims to a place in the new society he was planning. In addition, there seems every reason to think of him as more powerfully swayed than most Henrician officials by Lutheran influences, which can only have deepened his prejudices. He may consciously have taken his cue from the policy of dissolution already exemplified by the Lutheran rulers of Germany and Scandinavia. Familiar as were his relations with many individual monks, and little as his impassive temperament allowed of strong hatreds, he set about the destruction of the English religious houses with something resembling alacrity. In the conservative atmosphere of the King's service he was in no position to avow the religious ideas behind his dislike of monasticism; he could scarcely declare that the King desperately needed its wealth. There remained only one basis upon which a general dissolution could publicly be recommended—that of bad discipline and general inefficiency. These features were far from wholly imaginary, yet an objective report upon the monasteries might not have carried conviction in Parliament, and Cromwell never left anything to chance. Under these circumstances the final visitation lacked scruple, and the minister, who has been unjustly blamed for so many alleged offences, must in this case be allotted much of the responsibility. The best one can say is that sixteenth-century politicians and administrators lacked the impartiality which (in Britain at all events) we expect today even from the least sensitive of their successors.

The Process of Dissolution

The exploits of Cromwell's visitors, the 'satrapic' Legh, the garrulous Layton, the pliable Dr. London and their colleagues have often been recounted in terms of an intelligible distaste. With but few exceptions like the laymen John Tregonwell and John ap Rice, they were careerist secular clergy imbued with a full share of the age-old dislike of seculars for regulars. Their attitude was far from uniformly harsh. They spoke well of some religious houses and often proved mindful of the personal interests of particular monks. Certain of their charges of misbehaviour can be corroborated in those few cases where a recent episcopal visitation can be produced or when some other less tainted source happens to survive. Indeed, the deliberate fabrication of monastic shortcomings and vices does not seem to have been their normal habit. They found little need for pure fiction. As a matter of visitation-routine, monks were accustomed to informing against one another, but by this date the morale upon which this system depended had reached a low ebb. Moreover, by a novel perversion of the traditional procedure, evidence was now also taken from witnesses outside the cloister, many of whom may have been inspired by personal grudges, by rumours and modish tendencies to anticlericalism. Self-appointed experts on monasticism could be found at every corner, and they received no little encouragement from the too intimate social relations subsisting between many religious persons and their lay neighbours. If an official visitor believed, or affected to believe, half the scandal he heard under these circumstances, he would certainly need no imagination in order to compile an unfavourable report on monasticism. And the speed with which these men perambulated the monasteries was often even greater than that of a hasty medieval bishop, and hence even less likely to have permitted any real sifting of complaints and accusations. The main objective of the Cromwellian team was to complete an unfavourable report in readiness for the Parliament of 1536.

The precise effect of this report has not been adequately recorded. In subsequent years Latimer said in the course of a sermon, 'For when their enormities were first read in the parliament house, they were so great and abominable that there was nothing but "down with them".'[6] This late recollection by a prejudiced witness need not necessarily be accepted as the universal verdict of Parliament, and even less attention need be paid to the contrary tradition (which first appears in Spelman[7]) that Henry secured the passage of the Act by openly threatening to decapitate reluctant members of the Commons. Some debate did occur and certain amendments protected the many interests of the laity, who had no assurance as yet that they would benefit directly or indirectly from the Dissolution. The various phases of the latter from 1535 to 1540 may appear to us smooth and premeditated, yet we cannot be certain that, when drafting the Act of 1536 the government itself anticipated the dissolution of the 'greater' monasteries in any immediate future. If it did so, one may well wonder why it was so incautious as to allow the preamble of this first Act to praise the discipline still maintained in the 'greater' houses. Nevertheless, some parliamentarians seem to have perceived the second stage to be implicit in the first. 'Even at that time', reports Edward Hall, 'one said in the parliament house that these [i.e. the 'lesser' monasteries] were as thorns, but the great abbots were putrified old oaks, and they must needs follow.'[8]

The Act had a smaller immediate impact than its text might suggest. Though in appearance it dissolved all houses with incomes of less than £200, a considerable number of these (about 67 of the 304 covered by the Act) obtained exemptions. To cite an extreme example, in the Yorkshire district of the Court of Augmentations, no less than thirty-three of the fifty houses had incomes below the limit, yet of these only fifteen actually underwent suppression in 1536. The rest were not spared momentarily to placate the northern malcontents, because in fact they were not dissolved until 1539. And though the Crown gained fees (and the Augmentations officials *douceurs*) for such favours, the chief reason for this delay was not financial. It seems to have been an accommodation problem. At this stage religious persons could either take a dispensation to leave religion altogether or else be transferred to another house, and in Yorkshire an embarrassingly large number appear to have made the second choice.[9] Another interesting recent discovery has, however, emphasised the great number of those elsewhere who voluntarily withdrew. A register at Lambeth shows that at least 975 monks and canons took this course, mainly in 1536–7, and were willing to depart without awaiting pensions. Of these men with weak vocations a mere handful seem to have received benefices as secular clergy, and at present we have no information regarding the future of the rest. It would appear that many must have merged without regret into lay life.[10]

The Pilgrimage cannot be regarded as a predominantly pro-monastic rising, yet its failure speeded the overthrow of the greater English monasteries. By a strained interpretation of the law, houses were declared forfeit to Crown when their heads were attainted of treason. Jervaulx, Whalley, Barlings, Kirkstead, Holm Cultram and Bridlington fell under this rule, as if they have been private estates. From this stage there ensued throughout England a steady stream of surrenders by the heads of surviving houses, about 188 of whom took this course between 1537 and 1540. Some succumbed reluctantly to pressure from government agents. Others showed themselves eager to earn their pensions by staging an efficient transfer and obliging Cromwell, who in so many cases had originally chosen them for office. When in 1539 the final Act of Dissolution came to be passed, little remained of the once noble edifice of English monasticism. This Act was framed not so much to dissolve houses as to recognise the surrenders already made and to remove any legal queries concerning the King's title to the monastic lands. On 23 March 1540 the last survivor, Waltham Abbey, made its surrender, and by that date the minister himself had scarcely four months to live.

From the Dissolution sprang an administrative experiment of great interest. In April 1536 Cromwell set up the Court of Augmentations to manage ex-monastic lands and administer their revenues, its organisation being originally based upon that of the Duchy of Lancaster. With its many regional receivers and other officials it soon attained the stature of a national treasury and by 1544 its annual revenues had reached the enormous figure of £253,292, more than doubling the combined incomes of the Courts of General Surveyors, First Fruits and Wards. For a time it seemed to have no powerful rivals. The Chamber, revived by Henry VII to deal with the great increases of Crown revenue, had now fallen into decline, while no one could yet have foreseen the ultimate revival of the long-decadent Exchequer. Beginning with practical problems set by the Dissolution, Cromwell thus appeared to have created an institution which might permanently control the Crown lands and dominate the financial structure of the State. Nevertheless, after the death of its creator in 1540, the discipline, integrity and effectiveness of the Court of Augmentations began to show patent signs of decline. Though reformed in 1547, when it absorbed the Court of General Surveyors, the Augmentations never fully recovered its authority. In 1553–4 it fell victim to a new movement of financial reform backed by William Paulet, Marquis of Winchester, and by one of its former officials Sir Walter Mildmay, who envisaged its incorporation (together with Wards, First Fruits and the Duchy of Lancaster) into a reorganised national Exchequer.[11]

Almost all the leading officials of the Augmentations were prominent Henrician Catholics: Lord Chancellor Audley, the brothers Southwell, Sir John Gostwick and Sir Thomas Pope. Even the unprincipled Sir Richard Rich, Chancellor of the Court, was at least a conscientious persecutor of Protestants. In the destruction, division and purchase of the monastic lands the lead was emphatically not taken by men of the new faith but by men who hated Luther and Cranmer, men who in time became pillars of the Catholic reaction under Queen Mary.

The Ex-Religious

The provision made for the ex-religious remained thoroughly in character with the mundane, insensitive but by no means grossly inhumane spirit of mid-Tudor England. Drama, heroism and martyrdom were not the lot of the dispossessed, and it has been claimed with some justice that they received gentler treatment than the victims of later dissolutions on the Continent. Heads of houses were pensioned on a scale far more lavish than their subordinates, and in many cases they soon rose to bishoprics, deaneries and substantial livings.[12] The average pension of an ordinary monk or regular canon stood at the not unreasonable figure of five or six pounds per annum, which in the years 1540–50 represents the wage of an unskilled workman or the stipend of a poor priest with a single chantry. Here, however, generosity reached its limit. The nuns, whose estates seldom proved extensive, received very small pensions and could not, of course, seek to augment them by any other form of ecclesiastical employment. The King, so scrupulous in these matters, debarred by law the marriage of ex-religious persons and, by the time the government of Edward VI reversed this decision, most ex-nuns must have missed their chances of matrimony.

Here and there among the multitudinous wills of the period we encounter nuns of gentle family settling down comfortably amid their nephews and nieces. Perhaps they were wiser than the few who took advantage of the Edwardian Act permitting marriage, only to be divorced a few years later by Queen Mary. In the Marian court books at York we can trace the stories of a few such victims of governmental inconsistency. In 1554–5 Margaret Basforth of Thornaby[13] was accused of solemnising and consummating marriage with Roger Newstead, gresman of Thornaby. She admitted having professed in the nunnery of Moxby at the age of fourteen and she had been only twenty at its dissolution. The couple were now, nearly twenty years later, ordered by the Archbishop's court to desist from cohabitation, never to meet save in church or market, never to talk save in the presence of three or four persons. Margaret was also ordered to resume monastic apparel at her own expense, but kindly licensed to live outside the nunnery of Moxby, though it had been disused since 1536 and showed no signs of being resuscitated. By chance we happen to know that this particular story had a fortunate ending. Long years afterwards in 1586 Margaret gave evidence at York in a tithe-cause involving the lands of her former house, and in her evidence she described how she and the 'other younge nunns' of Moxby had helped there with the haymaking over half a century ago. But she now appears once again as wife to Roger Newstead, gresman of Thornaby!

A less attractive tale is that of Jane Fairfax,[14] a former nun of Sinningthwaite who had first retired to her ancestral home at Nun Appleton, made famous under later Fairfaxes by Andrew Marvell. Then in recent years she had gone to live with her relative Guy Fairfax near Gilling. Perhaps through difficulties arising from their kinship, they had failed to marry, yet now in 1555 they had a three-year-old child. Separated and ordered to do penance the unhappy pair reappeared in court not long afterwards on a charge of renewed cohabitation, but the further outcome remains unknown. Other former nuns, whose lives ran in quieter courses, continue to occur in the official pension-lists of the mid-Elizabethan years. Their pensions were not only small but subject, like rich benefices and higher pensions, to a flat-rate tax of ten per cent. We have, for example, a list of 1573 showing several aged Yorkshire nuns paying four shillings per annum on their pensions of £2 6s. 8d.[15] Under Elizabeth the wheels of Tudor bureaucracy ground no less small than under her father.

The other considerable group without any reason to laud governmental generosity was that of the friars, over 1,000 in number, who were turned out unpensioned. Despite their old reputation for preaching smoothly and winning silver they possessed little property and hence by the standards of the age did not qualify to enter the pension-lists. Their training fitted them for parochial functions though it is by no means certain that they found places more rapidly than the monks and canons. When the Dominicans of Gloucester were dissolved, they numbered only a prior and six friars. The records of episcopal visitations held two years later, and again eight years later, show all these seven men serving as stipendiary priests in parishes within and around Gloucester. At least two of them subsequently secured actual benefices in the area. There are nevertheless reasons for believing that this group enjoyed more than average good fortune.[16]

Like most operations of Tudor officialdom the payment of pensions to the dispossessed involved occasional irregularities and delays but the only known general crisis arose late in the reign of Edward VI. A major enquiry conducted in 1552–3[17] surveyed payments not only to ex-religious but to former stewards, corrodians, chantry-priests and others now on the pension-lists of the Court of Augmentations. The returns extant today cover fourteen counties and possibly about half the total number of such grantees then on the books. Speculation, fraud and sales of patents were all found negligible in extent. On the other hand, formidable arrears of payment had accumulated by the autumn of 1552. Of the 800 ex-religious represented in these lists 406 stood in some sort of arrears. About two-thirds of the unlucky claimants had remained unpaid for one year, one-tenth for eighteen months or longer. It seems fair to add that by this time the government's financial position had become appalling and that the clerical pensioners do not appear to have been singled out for special neglect. Again, in view of the standards of sixteenth-century officialdom and the low tone of politics during the last years of Edward VI, it says something for the relative probity of the English tradition that so elaborate and exhaustive an enquiry should at this moment have been undertaken.

On these official lists the rank-and-file of the laymen who had formerly served the monasteries do not appear, and it has sometimes been supposed that their plight at the Dissolution must have constituted an important part of the social problem set by that event. This claim cannot be substantiated. The majority of such employees were husbandmen and other outdoor workers on the home-farms and such other estates as had not been leased. These people must have been needed by the new owners, and stood in no worse condition than other husbandmen in their localities. Many of the indoor servants, it is true, would have to seek employment elsewhere, but the scattered clues certainly do not suggest that they were set adrift penniless. Certain cases are known where they were paid off with rewards amounting to a year's wages, a settlement ultra-generous by the standards of any society. All in all, though we have still much to learn concerning the transactions of the dispersal and the later history of the dispersed, it seems unlikely that many of the latter, clerical or lay, underwent grievous privations. Where hardship existed, it is more likely to have been psychological, and we should probably reserve most of our sympathies for those of the actual religious who did not feel that secular legislation absolved them from their vows or whose minds were otherwise irrevocably geared to a communal life. These elements may be seen in the alacrity with which a few small groups reassembled during Mary's brief attempt to revive monasticism. We may also detect them in two or three authenticated examples of parties who continued living together after the Dissolution. In July 1558, for example, a little band of the former monks of Monk Bretton, headed by their prior William Brown, still dwelt together at Worsborough, not far from their old home.[18] In their rooms they preserved the large library of their house, which they had bought with their own money and which they now proceeded to catalogue in their disused cartulary. The result forms one of our most valuable late monastic book-lists, yet one would gladly exchange it for a diary describing their lives in retirement, their reflections on the new world, their relations with each other and such fragments of the old life in community they were able to maintain. By way of contrast we should observe that a good many former monks and friars did not 'live in the past': a surprisingly large number are known to have embraced Protestant doctrines and made their way in a new world.[19]

Results of the Dissolution

The *Valor Ecclesiasticus* probably tends to underestimate monastic incomes and it omits few of the poorer houses. The gross income of all those included amounts to £161,853; their net income after the deduction of allowances to £136,361.[20] The latter figure represents considerably more than three times the income of all the Crown estates on the eve of the Dissolution. About a quarter of the gross income arose from tithes, glebes and other proceeds of benefices appropriated to the monasteries; the rest was ordinary temporal income, chiefly from rural estates. These figures do not include the incomes of colleges, chantries and minor foundations dissolved during the last years of Henry VIII or under Edward VI. In addition to this immense income the Crown acquired a very large lump sum from the sale of bullion, plate and other valuables. The immense loss of patronage sustained by the Church included the innumerable stewardships and other monastic offices which had given ecclesiastics so close a hold over important laymen. The monasteries also possessed the right of presentation to about two-fifths of the parochial benefices in England and most of these advowsons remained with the Crown or were soon transferred elsewhere. In the House of Lords the disappearance of the mitred abbots meant that the clerical vote declined from an absolute majority to a minority.

In terms of material splendour, of pageantry, of iconography, of the type of devotion stimulated by these instruments, the Church now fell into an immense decline. Even though the English cathedrals and parish churches were to be spared that extreme degree of vandalism perpetrated in some continental Protestant countries, every lover of the past and of the arts must regret that more was not saved from the treasures of the monasteries. Perhaps the most irreparable of all this damage was occasioned by the melting-down of reliquaries, images and other splendid examples of medieval metal-work and jewellery. That Protestant Reformers should have welcomed an abatement of the emphasis hitherto placed on the plastic arts, one may find intelligible, and there were Catholic reformers who shared their misgivings. Yet it remains a sad thing that these changes came at a moment when the need of the government for cash had become so insatiable, when public museums did not exist, when disinterested connoisseurship and antiquarianism had not passed their raw infancy in England. The injury to scholarship occasioned by the dispersal of monastic libraries was also extensive, though it has sometimes been overstated. Contemporary scholars and collectors were by no means oblivious to the problems of preservation. Henry VIII, aided by John Leland, made a systematic and apparently personal attempt to acquire the choice items for his own collection; out of the 400 of his books now in the Royal collection in the British Museum, about 250 can be traced back to fifty-five medieval libraries, mainly monastic. The King failed, however, to set up the great national repository of which Leland dreamed, and the immediate work of preservation which has left us several thousands of former monastic books was in the main accomplished by many small local collectors throughout the country. A considerable proportion must nevertheless have been lost, for while we know of 500 manuscripts from Durham, 300 from Christ Church, Canterbury, about 250 from Bury and 250 from St. Augustine's, Canterbury, there remain at the other extreme some 400 medieval libraries, mostly smaller monastic ones, each of which is represented by only ten or less extant books. The destruction appears to have been most complete in the small houses, certain of which can be shown by late medieval catalogues to have had libraries, now entirely or almost entirely perished.[21] Our loss does not lie so much in the total disappearance of important works as in the decreased bulk of evidence available to modern paleographers, whose ability to recreate the cultural relationships of the Middle Ages depends upon the comparative study of actual manuscripts on the largest possible scale.

More obvious but perhaps somewhat less grievous was the loss of fine architecture, since not a few of the greatest examples have survived in the monastic cathedrals and elsewhere.[22] Our gothic cities nevertheless lost much of their beauty and no square mile of England changed with the Dissolution in so spectacular a manner as did London. It contained twenty-three religious houses of importance, the precincts of which presented a forlorn spectacle during the decades of reconstruction. Occupying so much of the city's area, they provided welcome space for that gigantic growth of population and housing which overtook the Tudor capital, but the spate of building in Elizabethan and Jacobean London had a wholly secular character. If Shakespeare's city contained a far more diversified and exciting society than those of the past it had lost many of its attractive landmarks and refreshing spaces. It had gained little in terms of public order, since most of the lawless immunities were suffered to survive. But while Whitefriars, the haven of debtors, became Walter Scott's 'Alsatia', the franchise formerly belonging to the Blackfriars made possible the establishment of theatres, in the second of which Shakespeare himself became a lessee.[23] He did not need to leave London to find

Bare ruin'd choirs where late the sweet birds sang.

The planned effects of the suppression proved far from negligible, though they did not correspond with the magnitude of the King's initial designs. At this time he genuinely aspired to increase the number of bishops and bishoprics, and already in 1534 he had begun a scheme for appointing more suffragans. At the Dissolution he sketched in his own hand a plan for the erection of thirteen new sees, based upon former monastic buildings and lands.[24] In the event only six emerged—those of Peterborough, Gloucester, Oxford, Chester, Bristol and Westminster, the last-named to be dissolved in 1550. Meanwhile the monastic chapters of Coventry, Rochester, Winchester, Ely, Durham, Carlisle and Norwich were abolished and replaced by deans and secular canons, these being in many cases the former abbots, priors and monks. While the secular cathedral at Lichfield was preserved, the monastic cathedral at Coventry was disbanded and demolished, with untoward effects upon the already declining economy of the city. The reorganised cathedral churches received new statutes, and, together with those of the wholly new dioceses, they became known as Cathedrals of the New Foundation.[25] This was a less drastic reorganisation than the circumstances demanded, yet it was a far more fundamental reform than the Church had been able to accomplish for itself in recent centuries. Likewise the common charge that Henry failed to use his new wealth in the cause of education was long ago shown by Mr. Leach to be untrue: 'He did it on a scale which entitles him to the praise of being, in a sense, the greatest of school founders.'[26] At Canterbury, Carlisle, Ely, Norwich, Rochester and Worcester the cathedral grammar schools were amply re-endowed and placed under the patronage of the deans and chapters. At Bristol, Chester, Gloucester, Peterborough and Westminster new cathedral schools replaced old grammar schools of various origin and government; they were also much increased in wealth and henceforth managed by the new secular chapters of those cathedrals. At Oxford Henry carried to completion Wolsey's great scheme of Christ Church; at Cambridge he founded Trinity College, which soon outdistanced all its rivals in either university. At Cambridge in 1540 and at Oxford in 1546 he established the Regius professorships in theology, medicine, civil law, Hebrew and Greek—five in each university, and each one endowed with the handsome annual salary of £40. In addition, it would be easy to draw up a considerable list of private beneficiaries from the Dissolution who later became prominent as founders of schools and colleges. Far more indeed should have been made of this unique opportunity, but the share which went to education cannot justly be called insignificant.

Judged by Thomas Cromwell's main purpose the Dissolution can be dubbed a failure, since it tided the Crown over one period of crisis but failed to endow it with a huge and permanent non-parliamentary income. The pointless irony of Cromwell's overthrow in 1540 was followed by a greater irony—the rapid alienation of a major part of the monastic lands. The Crown did not, it is true, forfeit all benefit from these lands, since the many estates which were sold subject to knight service continued to yield reliefs, profits of wardship and other feudal dues. Yet these sums, however considerable, were small compared with those which would have accrued had the same estates remained in the King's hands. Amid the insecurities of his time, when the monarchy towered like a beacon about the turbulent waters of English society, Cromwell's financial plan made good political sense. Nevertheless, had the monarchy somehow succeeded in retaining these new resources for another hundred years, the rise of English liberty would have been more painful and slow. If the King held unprecedented power at Cromwell's death, this was not due to the recent Statute of Proclamations, which merely regularised a long-existent situation. It was due to the possession of enormous rent-rolls, the true sinews of executive power. Yet within seven years these sinews had withered beyond all chance of recovery. The actual effects of the Dissolution upon our history seem as nothing compared with its potential importance at the moment when it was first consummated.

A more complex and equally significant question remains—what place should we assign to the Dissolution in the social and economic history of England? Until very recent years, almost every attempt to treat this matter was blatantly invalidated by the religious or other doctrinaire convictions which the enquirer allowed to dictate his factual selection and hence his answers. Today it would be difficult even for a prejudiced writer to produce verdicts so crude. We now possess far more evidence and, if much of it proves complex and even contradictory, it is real evidence. We no longer generalise about economic developments on the mere basis of contemporary pamphleteering or pulpit-literature, much less upon that formed by the conjectures of Spelman, Fuller, and William Cobbett. The present incomplete state of research still leaves little room for dogmatism, but it has long since destroyed the simple black-and-white pictures still being painted sixty years ago, when some reputable writers had not yet ceased propounding the 'catastrophic' view of the Dissolution. They told of monks and nuns reduced to beggary, up to 80,000 monastic dependents deprived of their daily bread, the 'proverbially liberal' abbots replaced by lay landlords, who rack-rented their poor tenants, enclosed for pasture, drove men off the land and destroyed villages and rights of common. One well-known author even attributed to the Dissolution both the economic troubles of the Tudor towns and the general rise in commodity prices. While the present writer is very far from idealising the subsequent squirearchic period of English social and economic history—it was inevitable rather than equitable—he remains wholly convinced that this tragic view attached to the fall of monastic ownership was based upon no valid contemporary evidence, that it is today held by no competent economic historians and that it will never re-establish itself in the field of serious scholarship.

The mid-Tudor preachers and pamphleteers who denounced enclosers and rent-raisers were in general not economists but moralists. Even the genuine analysts of the known economic data did not understand all the factors causing poverty in England and they were certainly at loss to explain the true causes of the European price-rise. This antedated the fall of the monasteries, which cannot be taken even as one of its minor causal factors. As we now know, two enormous causes were at work: the pressure of Europe's rising population upon her relatively static production and subsequently the inrush of silver, especially that from Peru in the forties and afterwards. Compared with these factors, even Henry VIII's debasement of the English coinage probably takes a minor place in the story. Yet even so, the moralists make very little of the monasteries. With the partial exception of Brinklow[27] (who merely hated the new landlords even more than he hated the old monks) this English literature is remarkable for the lack of emphasis which, in seeking to analyse the causes of poverty, it places upon the Dissolution. The Doctor in the *Discourse of the Common Weal*[28] specifically denies that the Dissolution was a major cause of high prices, while even Latimer's famous denunciations of covetousness are far from being solely directed against landlords.[29]

The Dissolution occurred at a time when the demand for wool was still high, but this fell off from 1550, with the result that the urge to convert arable to pasture diminished. Yet even earlier, much enclosure had been directed to other purposes; it often resulted in great increases of productivity and it did not necessarily involve the substitution of sheep for men. Sometimes it was actually carried out by yeomen and other peasant-farmers. Though Tudor enclosures affected a small proportion of the land, they admittedly continued to have their place among the causes of agrarian discontent, at all events in the Midlands. But their lack of connection with the suppression of the monasteries appears chiefly in the now certain fact that the chief damage had been done long before this suppression. Professor Beresford has shown that the real spate of rural depopulation by enclosure lay between about 1440 and 1520.[30] This was already an old grievance when Henry VII and Wolsey tried to check its progress by legislation and special commissions. We have seen that monastic landlords, who were not in fact 'proverbially liberal', had taken part in it. Certainly there seems no reason to suppose that the retention of religious houses would have checked its continuance.

If the Dissolution did not ruin England by releasing a rush of ruinous enclosures, it cannot be shown to have produced an orgy of rack-renting. Rent cannot be discussed in isolation from its actual purchasing power, from prices. Now prices began to rise throughout Europe as early as 1510; between 1540 and 1560 they roughly doubled and they continued to rise thereafter. Hence a landlord who failed to raise his rents and entry-fines would have been a fool or a saint. Rent-raising is hence far from equivalent to predatory landlordism. The controversy over rent does not much concern lords who ground the faces of the poor. It does not much concern the genuine poor at all; it concerns the relations of landlords with tenant-farmers, who were prospering through the exceptional boom in the prices of farm produce and who naturally wanted the best of both worlds—the new high prices they received, together with their old low rents. But the rising number of these tenants who saw large profits in extended farms meant ruthless competition between them to gain leases and hence an opportunity for landowners to raise rents and so keep themselves abreast of the price-rise. Under these circumstances then, it would seem reasonable to begin talk of rack-renting when we see landlords enhancing rents at a faster rate than that of the rise in food prices, which latter determined the ability of their tenant-farmers to pay their rents. Again, ethical verdicts against the owners might perhaps be justified could it convincingly be shown that their excessive demands, duly passed on by farmers to the consumer, were a main originating factor of the price rise. Though during recent decades we have obtained a fair amount of evidence regarding the movement of rent and prices during the sixteenth and earlier seventeenth centuries, neither of these charges can be substantiated.

Until recently most authorities supposed the contrary: that rents lagged behind prices, to the impoverishment of many landlords. The Knight, another of the speakers in the *Discourse of the Common Weal*, makes this claim on behalf of his own class.[31] Lord Dacre and others have shown that our preoccupation with the 'rise of the gentry' in the period 1540–1640 should not blind us to the converse fact that many gentry-families fell in the economic scale. They ran this danger, it is claimed, especially if they were 'mere' landlords, unable to supplement normal agrarian incomes by professional, official, or mercantile earnings or by exploiting mineral resources.[32] Many landlords were indeed hampered in their efforts to keep abreast of the inflation by something more than a traditional and unbusinesslike outlook; they were hampered by the inelasticity of tenures, by the fact that some of their tenants enjoyed long leases or were copyholders safeguarded by law against increases of rent. Modern research into the movement of rent has, however, tended to take a more optimistic view of the position of Tudor and early Stuart landlords. It has been indicated that no simple formula applies and that, while some landlords adopted a commercial attitude, others were more interested in the social patronage and power arising from land.[33] Rents and fines (which latter play an ever-increasing part) rose very unevenly as between different places and different types of land, but the prosperity of the tenant did not necessarily advance at the expense of the lord.

Mr. Kerridge found some unusually reliable evidence on Wiltshire rents, which for the most part rose quite impressively; the Herberts, the main family here involved, kept pace with the rise of food prices. Here and elsewhere, however, this rise of rents does not begin with the period of Dissolution, currency debasement and early influx of silver. During the twenty years *before* the Dissolution the Herberts had already more than doubled their rents per acre for new leases, and the process continued, though more slowly, during the succeeding century. Miss Finch's interesting study of five Northamptonshire families[34] also shows that land could prove a very sound long-term investment, yet that it failed to yield the spectacular profits so often arising from trade, finance and public office—profits which commonly formed the original means of acquiring landed estates. Here there existed a substantial identity of interest between landlords and tenants; enclosures did not in general develop amid struggle and hardship. The single oppressive landlord, Sir Thomas Tresham, must be regarded as untypical, since recusancy-fines had made his financial situation desperate. A subsequent contributor, Dr. Alan Simpson,[35] based his rent-researches on certain East Anglian estates; he concluded that 'mere' landlordism could with care be made to pay here, that in the great majority of manors inflexible tenures did not gravely prejudice the owner's position, that farmers were able to take rising rents in their stride, that alongside the spectacular successes and failures most landed families maintained a solid if moderate prosperity. Pending still more studies, confident generalising should perhaps be avoided, but it seems already clear that in this cooler and more scientific atmosphere the rack-renting ogre and the starving tenant have evaporated into the same limbo as the 'proverbially liberal' abbot; as we shall shortly see, they are not the only figments of the former doctrinaire approach to be threatened with that fate.

The theory that the suppression of the monasteries was a major cause of urban poverty has nothing to commend it. All urban historians would agree that the severe strain besetting the old corporate towns had both general and local causes, most of them operative and the subjects of loud complaint well over half a century before the Dissolution. If, for example, we look at the case of York, one of our best documented municipalites, we find 'decay' on the lips of the citizens by the first years of Henry VIII, or earlier. When mid-Tudor and Elizabethan mayors of York, give detailed analyses of industrial decline,[36] they do not even mention the fall of the religious houses, though there had been many in the city. From York to Bodmin townsmen had often looked with hostile eyes upon their local houses and had been indisposed to idealise them at any stage. But the lands and economic interests of the monasteries were overwhelmingly rural, and with rare exceptions it is outside the sphere of town life that the main effects of the Dissolution must be sought.

The Successors of the Monks

Who received the monastic lands and on what terms? The original grantees in the patent rolls can easily be listed, numbered and, after a fashion, classified, Dr. Savine's account of the original grants is well known.[37] It shows that Henry VIII refrained from making many quixotic gifts of land to his favourites. Of the 1,593 original grants made in his reign, only forty-one were gifts, while another twenty-eight were combinations of gifts with sale or exchange. The lucky few were great magnates like Norfolk, Suffolk and Shrewsbury, who had just preserved the throne, or leading officials like Cromwell, Audley, Rich and Pope, who had rendered notable services to the Crown. By no means all the grants to these few were gifts; some on closer examination prove to be exchanges and purchases. The great majority of the grantees paid good money.[38] In December 1539 a commission to sell lands to the clear yearly value of £6,000 was issued to Cromwell and Sir Richard Rich; this lays down a minimum purchase price of twenty times the annual rent, which was in fact the normal price asked and received in the great majority of transactions under Henry VIII. It also appears that a few buyers fared better than this during the last years of the reign, when a buyer's market existed and the King needed money more urgently than aspiring purchasers demanded land. Certainly the Crown profited less than would have been the case had it been able to sell more gradually and so avail itself of the steady rise in land values.

We know when and why the monastic lands were sold by the Crown. Despite the commission of December 1539 little of the land was alienated before Cromwell's fall. The rush to sell began with the new commission of May 1543 and according to Savine's calculation about two-thirds of the whole had been alienated by 1547. Broadly speaking, these lands went to pay for the war of 1542–6 against Scotland and France. This is estimated to have cost over £2,000,000, and in addition to these ex-monastic properties other valuable Crown lands were sold off during its course. This was the period when small men joined together in purchasing-sydicates. In October 1544, for example, seventy-seven Londoners (including seventeen brewers, ten cloth-workers, five tallow-chandlers, five bowyers, six innholders and a varied assortment of leather-sellers, girdlers, dyers, stationers, cutlers and doctors) bought monastic lands for £843.[39] Even more, it was the period of obscure individual buyers like Richard Andrews of Woodstock, who bought and sold, sometimes alone, sometimes with one or more of a variety of partners, monastic estates worth many thousands of pounds. These groups and individuals, who re-sold almost immediately, were in some cases mere speculators, yet the notion of an orgy of speculation has been challenged with force by Sir John Habakkuk. The fact that values stood so steadily at twenty years' purchase is indeed difficult to reconcile with such a supposition. Again, resale no doubt often occurred merely because purchasers found they had bought more than their resources warranted or because they discovered more profitable investments elsewhere. There appear strong reasons for supposing that many of these obscure buyers, who so swiftly reconveyed their purchases to better-known men, were really mere proxies acting for the latter and not the true purchasers. Since the sales were conducted in London, it was doubtless useful to be represented by agents who knew the procedure and were given discretionary powers to acquire temporarily under their own names. Exactly the same phenomenon occurred a century later, when buyers of confiscated lands under the Commonwealth made extensive use of agents and trustees.

Whatever the extent of speculative buying, a large proportion of the original grantees possess little interest for the social and economic historian. They were here today and gone tomorrow; they were not the owners who stayed on the land and governed the lives of the yeomanry and peasantry. Savine's well-known classification of the grantees under Henry VIII hence tells us little of the more settled pattern of ownership which emerged from these years of greatest flux. For what they are worth, his figures run somewhat as follows. Spiritual corporations—deans and chapters—seem to occupy a prominent rôle with grants worth £20,000 out of a total of £90,000. Since, however, nearly all these transactions involved mere exchanges of land with the Crown, this particular figure has little significance. Some thirty-eight peers account for £16,000 annual value; courtiers, £7,000; royal officials £14,000; lawyers, £1,500; 'industrials' (?industrialists), £6,000. Of a total of £90,000 annual value, some £23,500 is reckoned as going to people of uncertain status, mainly gentry. Needless to remark, these categories remain arbitrary, since a large proportion of the grantees could be placed at will under two or more classes. Most courtiers and the more prominent Crown officials were also country gentry. From these not very meaningful figures we must turn to questions more weighty but more difficult to answer with precision.

Into what type of ownership did the monastic lands settle within twenty years of the Dissolution? From what social groups were these longer-term owners drawn? Though we cannot answer these questions with complete confidence, we have at least learned to regard with scepticism the uninformed generalisations of our predecessors. Only by undertaking many patient regional and local studies can we hope to achieve more accurate knowledge. For example, Dr. R. B. Smith's detailed survey of economics and society in the West Riding in the decade 1535–46[40] has shown within that area no less than five major regions with differing agrarian conditions, social structures and monastic elements. Likewise the relatively democratic Fenland farming described by Dr. Joan Thirsk[41] and the 'peasant aristocracies' in Professor Hoskins' Midland villages[42] do not fit into the conventional squire-dominated picture of post-Dissolution landlordism. Neither the monastic economy nor its successors can rightly be covered by any crisp formula applicable to all the districts and regions of England.

In addition to that of Dr. Smith certain other regional surveys are also pertinent to our enquiries, notably that made by Mr. Hodgett for the Lincolnshire ex-monastic lands[43] and that by Professor Youings for those of Devon.[44] In Lincolnshire three great noblemen, Suffolk, Rutland and Clinton, all prominent for their services to the King, initially gained substantial grants, but these were in part exchanges. Moreover, they did not seek to consolidate their holdings in that county, and all three afterwards parted with substantial portions of their grants. In addition to the local gentry the early buyers included certain prominent Augmentations officials and royal servants. But several of these enterprising functionaries, such as Sir Thomas Henneage and Robert Tyrwhitt, also belonged to the Lincolnshire gentry and might with equal sense be placed in either class. Typical of the more permanent elements among the purchasers were three Henneage brothers, whose ancestors had held manors in Lincolnshire since 1435. Both before and after the Dissolution they and their descendants figure on all the commissions of the peace, for sewers and for gaol delivery. A fourth brother was dean of Lincoln. A Henneage was high sheriff of the county in 1576, 1585, 1598 and 1629. In these later times members of the family adhered, like the Tyrwhitts, to the old religion; they suffered for their recusancy even though their fortunes had been enhanced by the Reformation. Here, it may be added, is a pattern by no means uncommon also amongst the gentry of Yorkshire and Lancashire. Local gentlemen with well-known names but lesser opportunities—many owned only one or two manors—also bulk large among the Lincolnshire purchasers. Other early grantees were obscurer men, whose surnames and small parcels of land strongly indicate that they belonged to the more substantial of the local yeomanry. But relatively few of the direct grants from the Crown went to yeomen. Many more of this class purchased at second and third hand; not infrequently they bought parcels which they already held as leaseholders. Very few corporate bodies acquired Lincolnshire monastic land, a minor exception being the corporation of Boston, which acquired property inside the town belonging to several local houses. An exceptionally interesting group is formed by the few big operators. In Lincolnshire by far the largest of these were John Bellow (who narrowly escaped murder in the Lincolnshire rising which inaugurated the Pilgrimage of Grace) and his associate John Broxholme. These men, though usually accounted London businessmen, came of Lincolnshire families and obviously possessed valuable local knowledge. By some means unknown they were able to raise capital on a very large scale. Between July 1545 and November 1546 Bellow and Broxholme paid the Crown £7,800, but, judging from the number of licences to alienate afterwards granted to them, they were speculating or acting as agents for others rather than seeking to found great estates in their native country. In Lincolnshire as elsewhere there appear very few indications that a new type of landowner was settling upon the land. The story is that of a transfer into the hands of a large body of men already well established in the county, men varied in means and status—richer gentry, small gentry, younger sons and yeomen, but almost all of them settled members of an agrarian society and conversant with its opportunities, customs and obligations.

In the case of Devon Professor Youings edited and analysed the group of records which promises most to modern questioners—the Particulars for Grants in the Augmentations records, which can be made to yield a picture of development over the decades succeeding the Dissolution. In Devon the great majority of grants consisted of property valued at under £20, most of it sold at the rate of twenty years purchase, or more. Gifts were few in number, much the most important being the donation to the Russell family which the King deliberately made great in Devon in order that it should replace the fallen Courtenays and provide a reliable leadership in a potentially troublesome area. Some heads of the older families managed to raise capital; often, it would appear, with great effort. Larger purchasers were Devon-born lawyers and royal officials, several of whom had been monastic stewards and already possessed an intimate knowledge of the lands they bought. A very small proportion was acquired by merchants, though those of Totnes bought some rural land and those of Exeter some urban property. London merchants proved a negligible factor amongst the Devon purchasers. In this county, resales, whether for speculative or other purposes, assumed far less prominence than in Lincolnshire and other more accessible areas.

By 1558 a pattern is observable in Devon. The Russells and the canons of Windsor owned between them nearly a quarter of the property so far alienated by the Crown. Less than a tenth was held by people who had come in from outside Devon. The ostensibly 'new men' were not in fact strangers; they were of Devon gentry-stock, younger sons or heads of junior branches of well-known families, men who had earned money by active careers, often in the royal service. Monastic lands in Devon did not go to a handful of very rich men; they increased the number of moderate-sized estates. They neither made the rich much richer nor did they create a new species of landowner. By 1558 these lands had been distributed, mostly in small parcels, amongst a very considerable number of persons, though even now no large proportion was owned by yeomen or tradesmen. At every stage of the story we hear little or nothing of that figure beloved by doctrinaire historians—the absentee landlord emancipated from the need to keep face in the county and armed with a merchant's greedy ideas on profit. The merchant-turned-landlord cannot be dismissed as a myth but, so far as the present writer's observations in various other areas extend, he was an exceptional figure, and there seems every likelihood that his outlook and practices were speedily assimilated to those of the established class. The same presumably applies to the clothiers who bought monastic lands, for they were substantial men and landowners already. A few among this interesting group are incidentally known to have converted monastic buildings to industrial use. An Oxfordshire clothier applied for properties of Abingdon Abbey on the ground that he already employed 500 workmen and could employ more, given suitable premises. William Stumpe, another big industrialist, actually established a rudimentary factory in buildings of Malmesbury Abbey.[45]

In the West Riding Dr. Smith traced the stories of the twenty-one purchasers or families who held sixty per cent of the ex-monastic land in 1546 and who include all the larger grantees.[46] Of these twenty-one no fewer than ten were the heads of established landed houses, even though at this moment the northern gentry, who lacked ready cash, were not pressing forward in large numbers. The ten included four peers, Cumberland, Shrewsbury, Wharton and Latimer, together with Sir Gervase Clifton of Nottinghamshire, Guy Fairfax of Steeton, Thomas Malleverer and Arthur Kay of Woodsome. Of the other eleven, younger sons of established northern families numbered four, or rather seven, if we include younger sons who had risen on the basis of legal and official careers. In this group we might place the tough lawyer Sir Leonard Beckwith, whose Yorkshire interests before the Dissolution had been but small, but who, after triumphing over charges of fraud, died in 1557 with estates worth £360 per annum. His position as county Augmentations receiver was not unconnected with his ascent. Yet by no means all these younger sons founded branches of lasting importance in the area. One purchaser, Richard Paver, was a yeoman-farmer who achieved a considerable measure of success in his efforts to rise into the gentry. The remaining three grantees might indeed be called townsmen. One was a Londoner, presumably an agent or speculator, who disappears shortly afterwards, while another, Richard Pymond of Wakefield, had no children and also failed to found a landed family. The third was the financier Sir Richard Gresham, a Lord Mayor of London, preserver of the London hospitals and father of the even more famous Sir Thomas Gresham. Parts of his purchases still remained with the family in the Elizabethan period. Altogether, this seems a most undramatic picture and exceedingly discouraging for the theory that the Dissolution introduced a new type of landlord to the countryside. We need more such regional surveys, and when they are forthcoming some may show divergences from these three. It will nevertheless be surprising if they radically change the broad pattern we have just observed.

At this stage it also seems appropriate to stress the irrelevance of this transfer of land to the controversy between Protestants and Catholics. While retaining many choice estates, Henry VIII granted or sold off the the greater part of the monastic lands between 1539 and his death in 1547.[47] During the whole of this period most forms of Protestantism remain proscribed. So far as I have observed, not the slightest evidence exists that conservative doctrinal beliefs caused men to desist from buying monastic lands or that a leaning to Protestant beliefs increased their eagerness to purchase. Some of the greatest recipients, for example the Duke of Norfolk and the Earl of Shrewsbury, stood among the leaders of religious reaction. And we have already observed examples of families with consistent Catholic traditions, families soon due to suffer for their faith, which nevertheless made extensive purchases of abbey-lands. This absence of doctrinaire control is everywhere characteristic of the whole process of the transfer. 'It is indeed worthy of comment that of the leading figures concerned in the Dissolution in Cornwall, not one was a Protestant: Sir Thomas Arundell no more than Sir John Tregonwell, neither Prideaux nor Prior Mundy. The sympathies of each were unmistakably Catholic.' So concludes Dr. A. L. Rowse after examining the chief Cornish purchasers.[48] Encouraged by this spectacle Protestant controversialists might well urge that the chief denouncers of property-speculation and greedy landlordism were Protestant utopians and moralists like John Hales and Hugh Latimer. Even so, they would be unwise to press these claims too far, since selfish and socially reactionary politicians were soon to cash in upon the Protestant movement, tarnishing its reputation for economic and social idealism. From first to last, the acquisition of monastic lands suggested itself to men of all opinions in terms of strict business. The compunction, the sentiment, the nice scruples, the superstition that an evil destiny awaited the buyers, these were invented by later and more poetic generations. In general, it would seem reasonable to envisage the commonest and most typical successors of the monks as gentry of established local families, conservative-minded churchmen but loyal servants of the monarchy, not necessarily rich but always anxious to maintain or to build up a good reputation with all classes in the shire. We know the minds of these people fairly well. Their ambitions and their place in society seem unlikely to have allowed them to resemble the rack-renting absentee landlords of nineteenth-century Ireland.

Some 'New Monastics'

Thanks to the standard collection of Tudor economic documents, generations of students have taken as typical of the 'new monastics' Sir John York,[49] who in 1553 attempted to raise the rents of twenty-seven tenancies in the liberty of Whitby Strand from the old monastic total of £28 to a new figure of £64 per annum. By this stage of the inflation the old rents must have become absurdly low, and the tenants were doubtless now receiving nearly double the old prices for their produce. Even so, this landlord had tried to progress faster than most and presumably deserved to be taken to court. The story is one of a notoriously ambitious owner of unusual background. Though the grandson of a mayor of York, Sir John was a financial agent of the Crown, a leading merchant, an absentee in London and a politician; he was in fact in the Tower for complicity with Northumberland's plot when his Whitby tenants brought their case. More important, the matter ended happily for the tenants, since he immediately promised to abandon his claims to higher rents during their leases. The case thus illustrates little more than the fact that some tenants could get redress in the courts; if the transition to lay landlordism is to be given a dramatic air, many cases more disturbing than this will need to be discovered! But there is no reason whatever to make Sir John York a typical image—we have in fact others which might serve better.

In order to be sure of these situations, we need more than the one-sided evidence of a landlord's opponents in a single law-suit, but as yet the more intimate and balanced pictures emerge in relatively few cases. One of these is the case of Sir William Petre,[50] who accomplished the remarkable feat of remaining Secretary of State from 1544 to 1557. During this period he built up two great estates—in Devon, his native county, and in Essex, where his wife had brought him the nucleus of the Ingatestone estate. It is certain that his growing prosperity was not financed by rent-raising. His accounts show that by 1556 his assured return on his outlay in Essex amounted to only five per cent per annum, to which another one or two per cent could be added for 'casualties', e.g. income from manor courts and the sale of timber. Not until his last years (he died in 1572) were rents giving him a return of seven per cent on his original capital—a low rate of interest by Tudor standards, and lower still when we take into account the immensity of the inflation during the thirty years covered by Petre's investments in land.

When working thirty years ago in Washington, the present writer happened to find amongst the Loseley papers in the Folger Library a memorandum on estate and household management by Sir John Gostwick, treasurer of First Fruits and Tenths and a close associate of Thomas Cromwell.[51] In all his obvious attributes this man seems to form a shining textbook-exemplar of the Crown official who entered into the heritage of the monks. Of old but hitherto undistinguished county stock the diligent Gostwick had risen to high administrative office and to important territorial status in his native county of Bedford. A buyer of monastic lands, he was at the same time largely Catholic in doctrinal belief. He protested to Cromwell against anti-ecclesiastical propaganda, and in later years he incurred the wrath of the King for speaking against Cranmer's heresies in Parliament. About 1540 Gostwick wrote for his heir these careful instructions concerning his chief manor at Willington. Here he actually urges his successor not to levy fines on the entry of new tenants at a greater rate than the customary minimum of one year's rent. He again adjures him never to increase the rents of his tenant-farmers unless he sees the latter imposing increases upon their own subtenants—a humane and stabilising principle and a further salutary reminder that a landlord's policy affected in the first place substantial tenants now making hitherto unparalleled profits. Gostwick then urges that a certain tenant, who had contracted to supply wheat and peas, should not be released from his bargain: 'He may bear it very well, for he hath a goodly farm of you.' Sir John is indeed quite hard-headed; he demands efficient service from his miller (who must not be a married man) and from his farm-hands. He sternly refuses to allow leases of more than twenty years. On the other hand, he is a fair employer and he knows that it pays to be fair.

If he be a good herdsman, let him have good wages, for he may soon save his wages; and let him have livery such as you give carters. Let Sottill never go from you ... for ye shall never have a better herdsman.... And let Henry Wild have the keeping of the pastures with certain milch kine, which will help him, his wife and his children, for God knoweth, he can make but little shift for himself.

Behind all this lies Gostwick's desire to gain credit among the neighbours as well as to remain in good odour with God and the King.

Item, I charge you of my blessing to get the good will and favour of all your neighbours, as well in Willington as in the whole shire, and to do for them and help them in all other causes according to your power. And in your so doing you shall please God and also have the love of them.

And as if in order to become the quintessential example of his type, Gostwick ends with the political creed which the Tudors and their great ministers sought to implant.

And be true to God, the King and your friend. And if your friend do open his mind and secret counsel to you, I charge you if it be to keep counsel ... open it not, for if you do, you are not to be trusted with no man:— unless your friend should open to you felony or treason. Then I charge you not to keep his counsel, but open it to two or three of the next justices of peace which dwelleth next unto you, or else to one or two of the King's most honourable Council, if you may get unto them. But in any wise, utter it as soon as is possible, for the longer you keep it, the worse it is for you, and the more danger toward God and the King's Majesty.

Here, it would seem, is the so-called 'new man', the leader of society brought increasingly to the fore by a multitude of changes. He is no ogre, no economic abstraction; his is no impersonal management; to him workmen and tenants are real people; though far from oblivious to the main chance he still lives in a custom-governed rural society. For such a climber, in a world still affected by aristocratic ideals, excessive avarice and grasping innovations would prove merely self-defeating. Altogether, Sir John Gostwick has obvious limitations, but he looks to me an improvement upon the leaders of the former bastard-feudal society. Pending fuller knowledge, why should we not view this rising class in terms of known facts and probabilities rather than in terms of ideology and melodrama? And if we must indulge in this dubious mental pastime of building images or types, there seems good reasons to accept the rather benevolent Sir John Gostwick as more typical than the over-thrustful though not very horrific Sir John York.

The Rise of the Gentry

While the Dissolution did not ruin the humble or dramatically alter the character of English landlordism, it clearly helped to change the balance of social groups within the nation. The decline of clerical wealth and territorial influence, the corresponding rise of large elements among the gentry, as acquirers of land, tithes and advowsons, these are far-reaching developments which certainly owed much to the Dissolution. The causes and implications of this shift, political, social and economic, have for many years been the subject of heated debate, a debate which can never be resolved to universal satisfaction. The broad thesis of change was expounded as early as the mid-seventeenth century by James Harrington. Power, he urged, gravitates towards the groups which hold a preponderance of land. The division of great monastic and baronial estates amongst the gentry and yeomanry enriched and enlarged this group.[52] Indirectly it thus created the demand of the House of Commons for political and constitutional change which, though fended off for a while by the romantic appeal of Queen Elizabeth, ultimately led to the Civil War. However great Harrington's simplifications and the inaccuracies of his modern misinterpreters, the broad sense of this hypothesis continues to command respect. Yet should we not think at least as much of the numerical expansion of the landed gentry as of their individual enrichment? Unless many heralds' visitations are uniformly misleading, the century which followed the secularising of church lands saw in every shire a remarkable multiplication of gentle families and of the more substantial yeomen-farmers from whose ranks new gentry were constantly being recruited.

Around the year 1600 Yorkshire had a total population of about 300,000 but it contained nearly 600 gentle families, each of which (since the gentry married young and bred rapidly) might have dozens or scores of living representatives.[53] Camden's visitation of Warwickshire in 1619[54] produced over 230 gentle pedigrees; the visitations of Surrey from 1530 to 1623[55] show about 240 and those of Lincolnshire between 1560 and 1660[56] nearly 1,000. In the two latter cases not all these families existed simultaneously, yet on the other hand the lists are incomplete, and they naturally omit all yeoman-families, even though some of these were more ancient and wealthy than many gentle families. The editor of the Lincolnshire pedigrees comments on the enormous rise in their number between 1562 and 1634. The pedigrees in the Essex heralds' visitations increase from 144 in 1558 to 336 in 1634.[57] The same impression is given by the vast number of applications for the grant or confirmation of arms during the Elizabethan period and the seventeenth century.[58] In general, these multitudinous successors of the monks inhabited superior farmhouses, not stately dukeries. Nothing can be more misleading to students of Tudor and Stuart England than a visit to Burghley House, to Montacute, to Audley End, to Hardwick Hall. These superb piles did not belong to gentlemen of anything resembling average resources. For obvious reasons the growth in numbers hastened the decline of clientage to great noble families; it extended the relations of the gentry not upwards, but downwards and outwards into the professional, the farming, the trading classes. The disruptive force of clientage, still dangerous under Edward VI, was gradually exchanged for something far more creative, yet equally difficult for governments to handle—a huge gentry and near-gentry, law-abiding, yet capable of absorbing puritanical and legal theories opposed to a powerful monarchy.

On the local level the effects of these changes also appear impressive. While collectively the gentry began to gravitate toward a more active function in the State, the squire extended his rôle as leader of village life—this not merely as justice of the peace, as chief landowner, as uncle of the vicar, but also in many cases as the recipient of tithes and advowsons formerly in monastic hands. As for advowsons, though they gave many a family a closer hold over its village church and clergy, they did not come every squire's way, since the Crown granted so many to the bishops and kept so many others in its own hands. The increased devolution of the greater tithes to the gentry constitutes a result of profounder importance. The so-called 'spiritual' income of the former abbeys had comprised about a quarter of their total receipts, and tithes formed by far its major part. Tithes thus represented a large field of investment for laymen. The transfer of the greater tithes into their hands was eased by the fact that the monks themselves had normally entrusted their collection not to vicars, who had no personal interest in exacting them, but to lay bailiffs or special receivers. In many cases the monks had actually leased them for long periods of years to laymen. In the popular mind tithe was hence already assimilated to temporal revenue and no outcry of sacrilege arose when it was bought by the 'new monastics' of the squirearchy.

The social and cultural effects of this transformation of a feudal and ecclesiastical society to one dominated by gentry, yeomanry and traders are obviously complex and far-reaching, and here again the pressures exerted by the Dissolution merge inextricably with a bewildering range of forces, many of them international and totally unconnected with the ecclesiastical policy of the Crown. Yet about this same time the English ceased being a nation of church-builders, or even of castle-builders; they poured their material resources into manor-houses, farm-houses and town-houses; also, let it be recognised, into education and other practical charities. They abandoned the last shreds of their former veneration for the celibate devotee and produced a large narcissistic literature, both religious and secular, devoted to the needs and praises of lay family-men of the middle and gentle classes. During these decades too, the same classes tended increasingly to abandon the image for the printed word; they continued to narrow the gap in matters of literacy which had separated them from the clergy. Amid this profound and many-sided change in the spirit of the age we feel tempted to place the Dissolution of the monasteries in the category of effects as well as in that of causes.

What pressures did the Dissolution exert upon subsequent religious settlements and opinions in England? However freely religious conservatives bought monastic lands, did not the reception of abbey lands induce many families to desire, in the longer run, a 'forward policy' in religion? That such a tendency developed seems possible enough, but the notion must nevertheless be stated with cautious reserves, since the known anecdotes hardly warrant generalisation. Here at least is one of them. Writing to Thomas Cromwell during the actual Dissolution from his home in Cornwall,

Sir Richard Grenville, high marshal of Calais, sued for the purchase or gift of some monastic land. Otherwise, he said, he would stand in a different position from that of most men of worship in the realm. He was glad to see overthrown 'these orgulous persons and devourers of God's word and takers away of the glory of Christ'. The monks had been also 'takers away of the wealth of the realm and sprys to the devilish bishop of Rome'. In order that his heirs may be of the same mind for their profit, Grenville would gladly buy some of the suppressed lands in these parts, even if this meant selling part of his inheritance.[59] We see here an important family becoming not only bound more closely to the Crown but committed to suspect any reversal of ecclesiastical policy which might betoken the revival of monasticism and the restoration of its former estate. This naïve admixture of cupidity and genuine conviction cannot have been uncommon in the minds of the first generation which purchased dissolution properties. On the other hand, this fact did not tie every future government to a Protestant doctrinal policy. Henry's persecution under the Six Articles was still to come; later on Queen Mary's more ambitious Catholicism had its turn; but neither ruler was dissuaded from doctrinal reaction by any resistance from apprehensive land-grantees. Nevertheless, at least the worldly scope of future Catholic reactions remained very limited. Certainly Henry and Mary might maintain or restore Catholic liturgies, but they could not rebuild the material fabric of the medieval church. Given another decade of life and a much more liberal supply of English commonsense, the Spanish Tudor might just conceivably have preserved the soul of English Catholicism, yet from the beginning she had no chance whatever of re-endowing it with its former body. And many a landowner, even among the Catholic-minded, must have breathed a sigh of relief when Mary passed, sorrowing but unlamented, from a scene well and truly set by her own father.

9 A Balance of Forces

The Henrician Parties

During the revolutionary years 1532-40 two pressure-groups contended for the ear of the King. The radical group, headed by Cromwell and Cranmer, stood for the policy of the open Bible and for the further diminution of ecclesiastical wealth and privilege. Increasingly it felt the attraction of Lutheran teachings and envisaged an alliance with the German princes of that faith. It enlisted some of the ablest writers in the kingdom, but only a handful of its adherents ascended to the bishops' bench—Nicholas Shaxton to Salisbury, Hugh Latimer to Worcester and Edward Fox to Hereford. During Cromwell's vicegerency the new Archbishop took a very modest part in the formulation of policy, and no one can have foreseen the great influence he was destined to exercise upon the history of English religion.[1] The second son of the squire of Aslockton in Nottinghamshire, Thomas Cranmer had spent a quarter of a century in residence at Cambridge without attaining any fame beyond his fellowship at Jesus College. About 1515-16 he had married obscurely but had lost his wife in childbed very shortly afterwards. By 1520 he had been ordained priest; six years later he became a doctor of Divinity and as a university examiner was demanding from ordinands a high standard of scriptural knowledge. Already he stood amongst those theologians who, in the tradition of Colet, exalted the authority of the Bible above that of the medieval schoolmen. Nevertheless, we lack evidence that he either attended the White Horse meetings or entertained especially hostile views concerning the Papacy. He must during his Cambridge days have been laying the foundations of that admirable knowledge of Christian liturgies from which was to spring the main achievement of his life.

In 1529 Cranmer had engaged the King's personal interest by his suggestion that the divorce was a problem to be settled by theologians and not by canon lawyers in the courts. Entering the royal service, he accompanied the Earl of Wiltshire to Italy and took part in eliciting the opinions of the Italian universities. After his return to England in 1530 he continued in intimate association with the Boleyn family; probably living in their household and serving as chaplain to Anne. Sent in 1532 on an embassy to the Emperor, he quietly married a niece of the prominent Lutheran divine Andreas Osiander, but this idyll was soon disturbed when Henry recalled him—no doubt at the instigation of the Boleyns—and made him Archbishop of Canterbury in succession to Warham. Later on he was tacitly allowed to bring over his wife, but had to keep her so far in the background as to give rise to the fable that he carried her about in a chest.[2]

From this point, leaving the most arduous public tasks to Cromwell, Cranmer set about a more intimate enterprise which enabled him to survive the minister and hence to preside over the second stage of the English Reformation. Armed with modesty, sound scholarship and pleasant manners he gained a unique place in the trust and affections of the King. 'You were born in a happy hour', Cromwell told him, 'for do or say what you will, the King will always well take it at your hand.' From the first he was ready to purchase this privileged relationship by his subservience to Henry's demands. Without awkward questions he managed the successive annulments of the King's ill-fated marriages. That of Anne Boleyn herself he appears to have annulled on the delicate grounds of Henry's own earlier association with her sister Mary.

Cranmer took only a minor part in the condemnation of two sacramentarian heretics, having tried hard to convert them. He showed extreme mildness toward conservative opponents, whom he thought to win over by gradualism and persuasion. His approaches were not only merciful but tentative and he has therefore attracted contempt from observers who cannot admit the possibility of legitimate doubts concerning eucharistic doctrine. It should nevertheless be observed that during the thirties Cranmer did not even approach the eucharistic heresies of men like John Lambert; his opinions shifted but slowly, and his acceptance of Henry's doctrinal conservatism cannot reasonably be diagnosed as that of a plotter biding his opportunity until the King's death. Again, his apparent subservience cannot be attributed to mere cowardice. On the contrary, he took many risks on humanitarian grounds; he alone interceded for Fisher and More, for Anne Boleyn and the Princess Mary, for Thomas Cromwell and for Bishop Tunstall. In later life his courage rose in fits and starts, yet he gave more evidence of that virtue than did the majority of men in high office. The integrating principle of Cranmer's career has rightly been found in his belief that a divine sanction underlay the royal authority. Like his adversary Gardiner—and most responsible Englishmen—he saw in the strong hand of monarchy the nation's one hope of vanquishing false doctrine, aristocratic faction, popular rebellion and foreign invasion. With his eyes wide open he accepted for the English Church the possibility of a new bondage in place of the old bondage to Rome. Along with most of the senior clergy—but by virtue of his position more conspicuously than any—he appeared ready to accept any command of the Sovereign which did not involve gross and manifest sin.

Cranmer excepted, the more prominent of Cromwell's partisans tended to prove embarrassing in prosperity or unreliable in adversity. Amongst the laymen Cromwell was bound to attract climbers like Audley and Rich, both of whom betrayed him the moment treachery promised a certain reward. Again, Protestants as indiscreet as Latimer and Shaxton made matters difficult for a government attempting to hold the bishops together and to coax conservatives like John Stokesley of London into moderate reforms. In particular, Cromwell's surviving correspondence with Shaxton exemplifies the shortcomings of an academic Reformer who failed to realise that even ecclesiastical politics represent the art of the possible. This former Cambridge theologian and *habitué* of the White Horse attained the See of Salisbury through the patronage of Anne Boleyn, to whom he owed £200 at the time of her execution. Once in his bishopric, Shaxton justified Cromwell's taunt that he had 'a stomach more meet for an emperor than for a bishop'. He tried hard to revive the former supremacy of the prelates of Salisbury over the local mayor and aldermen, who appealed to Cromwell against his claims. In 1538 a more serious difference arose when Shaxton attempted to expel a Catholic reader from Reading Abbey and to replace him by a Reformer. As vicegerent, Cromwell took this contentious matter into his own hands, and in the course of an unusually frank correspondence plain words came from both sides. A modern reader with the conventional view of Thomas Cromwell would hardly recognise as his that strangely heartfelt, even emotional letter sent to Shaxton in March 1538.[3] In the calling of a statesman the minister claims to be doing God's work as well as any priest. 'I do not cease to give thanks that it hath pleased his goodness to use me as an instrument and to work somewhat by me.... My prayer is that God give me no longer life than I shall be glad to use mine office in edification and not in destruction.'

Somewhat apart, yet also among the clients of Thomas Cromwell, stood the ex-Carmelite John Bale, one of the stranger human creations of early academic Protestantism.[4] Having a large family and small means his parents had consigned him at the tender age of twelve to the Norwich Carmelites, who seem to have taken good care of his education. In 1529 he took his B.D. at Cambridge and about this time was converted to Protestantism by Thomas, first Lord Wentworth, a soldier and later a privy councillor to Edward VI, who must have been among the earliest English laymen to disseminate the new doctrines. Bale soon became immersed in varied literary activities and the list of his works includes some ninety separate items, including those lost or as yet unprinted.[5] He laid the foundations of English literary biography,[6] made extensive collections of Carmelite antiquities[7] and set a pattern for his younger friend Foxe by writing biographies of Protestant heroes like Sir John Oldcastle, Anne Askew[8] and Martin Luther. His plays occupy a striking position between the old 'morality' and the Elizabethan drama. Writing under the patronage of Cromwell he did much to initiate the strong blast of Protestant propaganda which came from our nascent national theatre. His best-known drama *King John* (the first version of which seems to have been performed in Cranmer's household at Christmas 1538[9]) featured that monarch as England's heroic defender against the tyranny of Rome.[10] Even in an age of bitter pamphleteering, Bale's controversial works grossly outshone the rest, though they are sometimes relieved by a real literary flair and by touches of biographical interest. His life has all the ingredients for a novel. His two periods of continental exile were separated under Edward VI by a short (and sensationally-terminated) career as Bishop of Ossory in Ireland. When at last the accession of Elizabeth brought him into calmer waters, Bale wisely refrained from rejoining his Irish friends and enemies, but finished his days in a Canterbury prebend. Through all these adventures he had the solace of his faithful wife Dorothy and, if his private demeanour was half so rancorous as his public one, she must be placed among the unsung heroines of the English Reformation.

Among the more effective elements in the Cromwellian group were other publicists and printers, who within six years emitted nearly fifty books defending the new settlement. Perhaps for the first time in history a government monopolised the presses in order to commend its policies to a people by something approaching mass propaganda. Of Cromwell's writers the most thoughtful was Thomas Starkey, the most prolific Richard Morison. Both these men were Italianate humanists who had enjoyed the patronage of Reginald Pole in Italy; they wielded their pens in Cromwell's service from 1535 and were patriotic Henricians rather than Protestants. Both were far more than mere topical pamphleteers. While thundering against the sin of rebellion they did not hesitate to criticise the existent social structure, understanding well that the roots of popular unrest were economic rather than religious. Another member of the group was the printer and translator William Marshall, who, aided by a £20 loan from Cromwell, published in 1535 the first English version of Marsiglio's *Defensor Pacis*. Yet another was Richard Taverner, a convinced Lutheran who is mentioned as Cromwell's client in 1533 and who translated not only the Bible but Melanchthon and other Protestant authors.[11] These men wrote in English for the people, not in Latin for the rulers and scholars of Europe. They were by origin poor scholars, not great officials in Church or State. Like Cranmer they believed in a greater measure of educational opportunity, and they thought that the peace of the commonwealth depended upon a progressive improvement in the harsh lot of the poor. Alongside its insensitivity to suffering the sixteenth century displayed a passionate interest in the problems of social amelioration; as a true child of the age, the English Reformation could scarcely help translating some of this idealism into religious terms.

The difficult situation of the Cromwell-Cranmer group can be illustrated by reference to its part in the tragic story of the heretic John Lambert.[12] This former fellow of Queens' College, Cambridge, had been one of Bilney's converts; he later became a chaplain at the notorious English House of the Merchant Adventurers in Antwerp and an associate of Tyndale and Frith. On Sir Thomas More's insistence he had been sent back to England and confronted by Warham with forty-five charges of heresy, to which he composed able and learned answers. Kept in protective custody at the Archbishop's manor-house at Otford, Lambert obtained his release on

Warham's death and thereafter ran a school in London. In 1536 the Duke of Norfolk and other noble traditionalists complained about attacks made by him upon the worship of the saints. He thus appeared before Cranmer, Shaxton and Latimer, who, while personally in agreement with the accused, were desperately anxious to avoid a frontal clash with his influential accusers. Deeply embarrassed, they offered to release him if he would state that prayers to saints were unnecessary yet not sinful. This compromise the scrupulous Lambert rejected and he further exasperated the prelates by declining to accept even a secret release from confinement. They hence remitted him to Lord Chancellor Audley, who kept him in prison for a time.

In the autumn of 1538, now again at liberty, Lambert decided to tread much more dangerous ground. He attended a sermon on the eucharist by John Taylor, himself a sympathiser with Lutheran doctrine and in later days deprived by Queen Mary of the bishopric of Lincoln. After the sermon Lambert sought out the preacher for disputation, but Dr. Taylor unwisely told him to set down his opinions on paper. Having received these opinions, Taylor consulted Robert Barnes, who had now become a member of a commission to extirpate Anabaptist sectaries. Seeing himself as guardian of a Lutheran orthodoxy, Barnes advised Taylor to forward Lambert's paper to the Archbishop. The last and most curious link of this upward chain was then forged by Cranmer himself.

It so happened that at this moment the King, disappointed in the Lutheran princes, desired not merely to placate Catholic opinion but to gain the friendship of the great Catholic powers. Cranmer can hardly have been unaware of his master's eagerness to impress Europe with a spectacle of orthodoxy when he now allowed and even advised Lambert to appeal to the King in person. It does not follow that Cranmer consciously offered the heretic as a sacrifice to Henry's diplomatic needs.

Lambert's doctrinal position appears in a *Treatise upon the Sacrament* addressed at this stage to the King. It was based upon the far from novel contention that since Christ had bodily ascended into heaven, he could not in a corporeal sense be in the sacrament. 'Thus, O most gracious and godly prince, do I confess and acknowledge that the bread of the sacrament is truly Christ's body, and the wine to be truly his blood, according to the words of the institution of the same sacrement; but in a certain wise, that is to wit, figuratively, sacramentally or significantly.' And in support of a non-corporeal presence he cites Tertullian, Augustine and Jerome. It may be inaccurate to dismiss Lambert as a straightforward sacramentarian; some of his phraseology does not differ markedly from that which we shall see Cranmer himself adopting under Ridley's influence some eight years later.

John Foxe describes the trial scene with his usual vividness and not without evident touches of malice. It was splendidly staged for the benefit of its Europe-wide audience. Symbolising an awful doctrinal purity, the King appeared clad in white from head to foot. With the accused he soon showed himself in his most brutal and peremptory mood. Cranmer tried in contrast to reason quietly with 'brother Lambert', but being no great disputant made little headway against the able opponent. The other bishops intervened in relay; the King bullied, the audience was violent in its hostility toward Lambert, who nevertheless acquitted himself well until exhausted by five hours of continuous bombardment. As torches were brought in at five o'clock that winter afternoon, the voice of the defendant died into a stupefied silence; he submitted himself to the King's mercy, and the King, unmoved, ordered the hitherto silent Cromwell to read out the sentence. On the morning of the execution, if Foxe is to be believed, Cromwell held an interview with the doomed man in his private room, after which Lambert was allowed to breakfast with the gentlemen in Cromwell's hall. This much the minister may indeed have ventured, but the rumour that he asked Lambert's forgiveness sounds like the wishful thinking of Protestants. What we know for certain is that Cromwell sent off a report of the trial to Sir Thomas Wyatt in Paris, lauding in Byzantine phrases the King's inestimable gravity, wisdom and benignity. 'I wished the princes and potentates of Christendom to have had a meet place for them there to have seen it.' Behind the minister's sardonic sense of humour and Italianate sophistication there doubtless lurked a certain conviction of duty done. He was no doubt more sorry for Lambert than for most of the King's victims, but he had to disseminate the propaganda. Like his friend the Archbishop, he held an uncomfortable and insecure position, but he had no intention of risking it over a pertinacious enthusiast who had gone so busily about the world in search of trouble.

The conservative group of courtiers and officials which stood in opposition to Cromwell and Cranmer was led by the Duke of Norfolk and by his son's former tutor, Stephen Gardiner, Bishop of Winchester. On its fringes stood the majority of the bishops, headed by the virtuous Catholic humanist Cuthbert Tunstall of Durham. It lacked ideas on religion or on government, but it had a priceless asset in the King's deep suspicion of doctrinal change, and its leaders did not lack talents appropriate to their opportunities. We have already remarked upon the Duke's blind loyalty, his lack of scruple and his talent for court-intrigue. In this field Gardiner proved himself an even subtler schemer; the memory of his humble origins certainly failed to soften a proud and ambitious spirit. Unlike Cranmer he was every inch a man of affairs—a committee-leader and negotiator who never achieved the rank of a creative statesman. His fine legal training and diplomatic experience were accompanied by little political originality, his sincere hatred of heresy by no marked spiritual endowments. Yet he and his associates were as good Henricians as their opponents, and intellectually they stood even closer to the king's conventional mind. In the practical matters of the divorce, the Papacy, the Royal Supremacy, they took (but with some misgivings in Tunstall's case) a diametrically opposite line from that of Fisher and More.

Gardiner's famous book *De Vera Obedientia* (1535) leans as strongly toward the uncompromising doctrines of Marsiglio as any of the works arising from the circle of Thomas Cromwell.[13] The true Christian, it argues, must obey those whom God has appointed his representatives on earth; their authority resembles that of masters over servants, fathers over children. Set above all such god-given rulers, the Princes stand at the very apex of human society. When Parliament recently proposed that King Henry should proclaim himself Head of the Church, it was guiltless of innovation; it was disburdening the nation of the privileges falsely assumed by the bishop of Rome. To Gardiner as to Marsiglio the individuals who composed the kingdom were the same as those who composed the Church within the kingdom, and the ruler who was head of the former must logically be head of the latter. 'Is John', he asks, 'the King's subject only as an inhabitant of England, and the same John not the King's subject as a Christian?' The Church in England is not, of course, the whole Church, but it is another aspect of the kingdom of England. There can be only one sovereign power in a kingdom. To the *imperium* of a King Scripture sets no limit, and it is sinful to prescribe any limits to the obedience due from a subject. Illustrating the legitimacy of Henry's claims Gardiner cites a series of precedents from the Old Testament down to Justinian, who legislated not only upon the clergy but upon Christian doctrine itself. Despite some acknowledgements wrung from them under duress, Christian princes have never really believed the bishop of Rome to be rightful head of the Church. Had they believed this, how could they so frequently have defied popes? Had the popes really believed their own claims, how could they have consented to such legislation as the English statutes of Provisors and *Praemunire*? And how could Our Lord have given an authority to the popes which he declined to exercise himself? Of the primacy as defined by Rome no trace appears in the pages of Scripture, and such headship as that historically conceded to the popes had arisen merely from human tradition. They can claim no rightful jurisdiction over churches other than that of Rome and, if they attempt to exceed their rights, they must suffer the consequences. They should seek to manifest a primacy in virtue, not in political power. And in his conclusion Gardiner reveals a nationalism as blunt as that of any popular writer. The English government has now agreed that its people shall have no further dealings with Rome; hence it remains the plain duty of every English subject to obey without question.

In Queen Mary's time Gardiner alleged he had written *De Vera Obedientia* out of fear, lest he should suffer the same death as Fisher and More. This excuse he may by then have persuaded himself to accept but it fails to carry conviction. Unjust as were some of the punishments meted out during the crisis, the King could scarcely have procured the execution of a bishop merely on account of his failure to compose a really outstanding and powerful defence of the Royal Supremacy. The modern apologists who have accepted his pleas should surely reflect that in 1535 the credit of the Papacy had not yet begun to rise from its nadir, even among such doctrinally conservative bishops. Not satisfied with enunciating erastian theory Gardiner even wrote a tract to justify the execution of Fisher. This Janelle seeks to explain by the phrase, 'he was quite simply abject'. But it remains far easier to suppose that in 1535 Gardiner accepted the whole royalist position and really believed what he wrote. His later career revealed that he, like Cranmer, was no mere coward, but if Cranmer's biography and opinions cannot be made wholly consistent, neither can Gardiner's. Amid the enormous psychological pressures of the period who save men of heroic simplicity could occupy high office and yet emerge with a record of consistent belief and profession?

The Fall of Cromwell

Despite the responsible spirit in which Cromwell exercised the functions of vicegerent, his overthrow by Norfolk and Gardiner resulted from an unwonted act of imprudence as well as from a measure of ill-luck. He failed to check a dangerous trend which involved the English Reformation in the unpredictable turmoil of continental Europe. More perilously still, he had assumed responsibility for one of Henry's matrimonial adventures. Though in most English minds France remained the traditional foe, the King's schismatic policy and his humiliation of Katherine had now alienated the other 'great power' of Europe in the person of the Emperor. From the English viewpoint Charles V was first and foremost ruler of the Netherlands, with which brilliant and prosperous region so much of our trade and our civilisation had long been intimately related. To Cromwell, as to any man who had worked for years in Antwerp, a war with Charles V seemed a heavy penalty to pay for the divorce and the Royal Supremacy.[14] Yet a bleak threat now appeared that King Francis would bury his feud with Charles, uniting both great powers in a crusade against England. Given that a *rapprochement* with Charles could not immediately be achieved, it seemed prudent at least to keep him occupied in Germany by supporting the Lutheran princes who, led by the Elector of Saxony and the Landgrave of Hesse, had formed the Schmalkaldic League. After long preliminary investigations Cromwell sent Edward Fox in 1535 to ask under what conditions these princes would accept Henry as a member of their League. They demanded not merely financial backing but an acceptance of the Confession of Augsburg as the basis for a Lutheran Reformation in England. This price Henry found too high. He replied that he had every intention of setting forth true doctrine according to the Scriptures, that he was reckoned 'somewhat learned' and that, with the assistance of other learned men in his realm, he could manage the sacred task without foreign help. Thenceforward he maintained this posture during years of negotiations with the Lutherans. It was an attitude based upon something more than religious conservatism, upon more than a natural desire to manage his own Reformation. England had not at this date the resources to become—as she became in the prosperous Hanoverian age—the paymaster of German princes. Moreover, Henry never felt himself in extreme danger. He stood prepared to gamble on the unlikelihood of an offensive alliance between Francis and Charles. Even if the worst should happen, he trusted in his strengthened navy to cripple any attempt at invasion.

Armed with this assessment of the facts Henry felt no strong impulse to toe the Lutheran party-line. The Ten Articles which he caused Convocation to adopt in 1536 have often been taken as a conciliatory approach toward the recent Wittenberg Articles, but they might rather be used to exemplify our English talent for concocting ambiguous and flexible documents. They mention, it is true, only three sacraments (baptism, penance and the eucharist), but they define these in an orthodox sense and do not deny the validity of the other four accepted by Catholics. Their phraseology concerning the eucharist could be interpreted in a Lutheran sense, yet it likewise admits of transubstantiation, in which doctrine the King maintained a steadfast personal belief. They contradict the Lutherans by retaining auricular confession and penance. They also defend prayers for the dead, while yet avoiding a definition of purgatory and acknowledging that Scripture does not tell us exactly where the dead are, the name of that place or the pains there imposed. On the vital topic of Justification a definition by Melanchthon is cited, but then the solifidian position is carefully avoided by the phrase 'sinners attain this justification by contrition and faith joined with charity'.[15]

Whatever his personal beliefs and diplomatic ambitions, Cromwell cannot seriously have hoped to coerce the King in doctrinal matters and his continuance in office by no means guaranteed that further favours would be shown to the Protestants. In actual fact the next year saw a fresh compromise between the two parties along lines even more conservative than those of the Ten Articles. This was embodied in the *Institution of a Christian Man*, usually called *The Bishop's Book*, which took the form of an elaborate exposition of the Creed, the Seven Sacraments, the Ten Commandments, the Lord's Prayer and the Ave Maria[16]. After much consultation, argument and answering of questionnaires, it was completed in July 1537 by a large committee of bishops and divines. It gratified the conservatives by restoring the four sacraments (matrimony, confirmation, holy orders and extreme unction) omitted from the Ten Articles. Taken as a whole it looked a Catholic rather than a Lutheran document. Yet it refrained from imposing transubstantiation, acknowledged the lower status of these non-scriptural sacraments and placed emphasis on scriptural authority and on current problems like that of Justification. It constituted more than a mere reiteration of medieval doctrine. Perhaps the most remarkable passage is that in the exposition of the Creed which sets forth the theory of a Church Universal, composed of free and equal national churches. In almost every detail this passage might still be accepted as a classic statement of the Anglican position. Both groups of bishops—including Gardiner, who was in France— signed the Book. Yet the King carefully refrained from giving it his authority and used it instead to test the theological appetite of the nation. Early in 1538 he suggested many revisions with a view to another edition, and these were criticised with great frankness by Cranmer, who even went so far as to correct the royal grammar. The King at no time sent the book to Parliament or to Convocation; he merely commended it for study by clerics having the cure of souls. Knowing the parish clergy, one may doubt whether *The Bishop's Book* made much impact upon them; its length, expense and sophistication must likewise have placed it above the heads of most literate laymen.

While the desultory exchanges with the Lutheran princes dragged through the year 1538 and into the spring of 1539, the plans of Cromwell began to diverge ominously from those of the King. While the former strove to keep open the channels and even to widen them by a marriage-alliance with the ducal house of Cleves, the King—no doubt encouraged by the Duke of Norfolk and the conservative bishops—resolved upon 'a devise for the unity in religion' couched in conservative, not to say reactionary terms. The new Parliament assembled on 28 April and at Henry's request a committee was set up in the Lords consisting of Cromwell as vicegerent and of four Reformers (Cranmer, Latimer, Goodrich of Ely and Salcot *alias* Capon of Bangor) and four Catholics (Lee of York, Tunstall, Clerk of Bath and Wells and Aldrich of Carlisle). When, as the king doubtless anticipated, holy deadlock ensued, he took personal command and authorised Norfolk on 16 May to offer six articles to Parliament for discussion. These were politely framed as questions, but Henry already knew the right answers; he in fact revised with his own hand the earliest extant draft of the Six Articles Act. Its enactment was virtually decided in the predominantly Catholic House of Lords and through the intervention of the King, who came down in person to the debate and, in the words of one approving peer, 'confounded them all with God's learning'. It is certain that Cranmer opposed some of the Act's provisions in the Lords and that, even after the King's pronounce-ment, he spoke against it in Convocation. It is not thought that he ventured to oppose transubstantiation, but it seems probable enough that he defended the marriage of priests, opposed the necessity of the confessional and advocated the communion of the laity in both kinds. Ceasing this resistance only just short of the danger-point he then surrendered responsibility to the King and agreed, though with reluctance, to join in enforcing the Act during the rest of the reign. It proposed a persecution more ferocious than that of the church courts and marked a mood of determination on the King's part to stamp out nonconformity in his realm. It upheld transubstantiation, the sufficiency for laymen of communion in one kind, clerical celibacy, the obligation to keep vows of chastity, the orthodoxy of private masses and of auricular confession. Should a man deny transubstantiation, he would incur death by burning and total forfeiture of property—even abjuration would not save him. Obstinate denial of any other of the articles rendered an offender liable to the same penalties, except that in the event of abjuration he would merely suffer imprisonment at the King's pleasure, while sentence of death would only be passed on a man twice convicted of such felony. Even to Henry and the Lords the Act seemed on second thoughts a trifle heavy-handed; by an amendment of 1540 priests and women twice convicted of concubinage were exempted from the death-penalty. In the event, the persecution proved intermittent and the total number of victims small. From the first, however, the Protestant minority among the clergy saw the Act as a disastrous defeat at the hands of Gardiner and Norfolk. Shaxton and Latimer resigned their sees, while Cranmer himself was compelled to return his wife to her people in Germany. Thomas Cromwell, momentarily shaken, strove to regain his hold upon the King, and for a few months it seemed as if his pertinacity would be rewarded.

At this moment threatening continental developments seemed to be aiding his endeavours. In the summer of 1538 the Emperor Charles had met King Francis at Aigues-Mortes, and in January 1539 they came together again at Toledo, where they agreed to make no alliance with Henry except by mutual consent. While these overtures did not presage any immediate anti-English crusade, they added some weight to Cromwell's demand for alliances, and Henry agreed to allow further negotiations with the Lutheran princes. This time Cromwell resolved to abandon theological debates and to concentrate upon marriage-alliances. Two of these were proposed, one between the Princess Mary and the young Duke William of Cleves, the other between Henry himself and Anne, the elder of Duke William's unmarried sisters. The Cleves dukedom, though modest in extent and resources, lay at a focal point between Emperor Charles in the Netherlands, and the lands of the rebellious Lutherans. Again, the ducal family had recently inherited Gelderland, a province also claimed by Charles. While not yet formal Protestants themselves, William and Anne had a sister married to the Lutheran Elector of Saxony, who thereby became their chief protector against the Emperor.

The outcome of the Cleves negotiation displayed Henry in his most petulant and irresponsible mood. With ill grace he married the unattractive Anne in January 1540. Finding himself unable to consummate the match, rendered increasingly irascible by the decline of his health, irritated by the continual pressure of the Lutherans for a doctrinal agreement, he soon afterwards listened to the criticisms directed against his minister by Gardiner and Norfolk. Cromwell was destroyed without trial by an Act of Attainder based upon fabricated charges of heresy and treason. Of the judicial murders sanctioned by Henry this was perhaps the least intelligible, and in later years he certainly realised the pointlessness of killing the most loyal and industrious minister ever to serve a King of England. Cromwell did not die gloriously for a cause, as did his one-time friend Thomas More, but Protestant propagandists made what capital they could of the event. At least he made an edifying speech on the scaffold and this, duly written up by Grafton, was later on embellished in the accepted tradition of Renaissance historiography by John Foxe, who paraded the deceased minister as a 'valiant soldier and captain of Christ'.

Two days after his execution Smithfield saw a more spectacular and fundamentally more meaningful event—the hanging of three Catholic traitors and the burning of three Protestant heretics.[17] The latter were the more eminent of their species, for they included those pillars of early English Lutheranism, Thomas Garret and Robert Barnes. Despite their theology both these men had become staunch Henricians, and Barnes had for a time controlled his naturally impulsive disposition and made a praiseworthy ambassador to the Lutherans. But the significance of this *auto-da-fé* lay not in its individual victims but in its studied impartiality, in the perceptiveness with which the monarch fostered his new and unique creation. Under the stern eye of their own godly prince Englishmen already found themselves marching along a *via media*.

The Origins of Anglicanism

We have already observed that Cromwell's leanings toward Lutheranism should be taken quite seriously; they were not invented by Foxe. Throughout his ministry he stood deeply involved with the radical group, which was Protestant or turning Protestant as fast as it dared. His efforts to establish the English Bible reflect not merely a long-standing personal interest but a characteristic determination to imprint something indelibly on the English mind. The content of the years 1532–40 proves on examination religious as much as legal; it also involves a process passing beyond the mere absorption of Lutheran theology. At a time when so many modern ideas were coming to birth, there arose the concept of an independent national Church, the basis of which was stated in prophetically Anglican terms in *The Bishops' Book*. In exploring Cromwell's religious standpoint we alluded to his concept of *via media*: that the English nation should pursue a middle path between 'Romish' superstition and 'licentious' heresy. Cromwell himself made the point clearly in his speech at the opening of Parliament on 12 April 1540.[18] Yet five years earlier it had been stated with equal fluency and greater elaboration by his publicist Thomas Starkey in *An Exhortation to the People*.[19] This not unworthy forerunner of Hooker points with true English complacency to the dreadful disorder in Germany, which has arisen concerning 'things in no point necessary to man's salvation, but about ceremonies and traditions'. Both in Germany and in England, the right path, argues Starkey, lies somewhere between those who 'stiffly stick in the old ceremonies and rites of the church, wherein they have been of youth brought up', and, on the other side, the arrogance of those who indiscriminately deny all pious customs, and will accept nothing but Scripture—and Scripture interpreted after their own fancy. 'For those men, under the pretence of liberty, covertly purpose to destroy all Christian policy, and so in conclusion bring all to manifest ruin and utter confusion.' This attitude of disapproval combined with the ingrained xenophobia of Henrician Englishmen to demand a highly cautious approach to the continental Reformation, a less than semi-detached relationship with foreign churches and a periodic resort to ambiguities and doctrinal compromises worked out in committee.

The nascent Church did not, however, lack a positive basis, even though this could be stated only in broad terms. In the view of Cranmer and Cromwell 'a pure and sincere doctrine of the Christian faith' should be formulated closely upon Scriptural authority, should be set forth by a Christian King in Parliament and accepted by the people without opinionated haggling over details. Such a notion appealed more readily to laymen than to the clergy, whose professional training made them more conscious of impending intellectual difficulties and whose traditions tended to fetter them to the notion of an orthodoxy based on precise scholastic definition. On the other hand, the very concept of a Scriptural religion encouraged, and almost entailed, a neglect of Aquinas and Scotus in favour of the humanist and educational ideals of the new age. Against an Erasmian background it stressed a sound learning in the sacred text and in the early Fathers of the Church. Its ideal human type was no longer the disputant of the schools, but the patristic scholar in the deanery or the Bible-reading priest in the vicarage. These latter figures the Anglican Church has never ceased to produce, yet as we shall later observe, impending cultural changes were about to create many interesting mutations and variants.

Whatever their political limitations, the Reformers comprised many of the best scholars then living in England. Men like Tyndale, Cranmer, Ridley, Coverdale, Cheke, Parker and Jewel were proving, or were soon to prove, more than a match for the English conservatives of their generation. The latter, so often trained in the law and occupied by official duties, lacked both the time and the intellectual background to become worthy exponents or regenerators of Catholic theology. As for the liberal elements in later Anglican thought, these too had their Henrician forerunners, not merely in Frith but in Starkey himself, for it was he who introduced Melanchthon's doctrine of *adiaphora*, or 'things indifferent', to a permanent place in the Anglican scheme. The whole plan of the Ten Articles is also adiaphorist. In Latimer the Henricians had their Evangelical, in Gardiner their High Churchman, whose uneasily maintained place in Queen Mary's establishment has often been allowed to obscure this more accurate image. From the first, the coherence of Anglicanism depended upon the State. Confronted by this motley scene of the thirties one must detest the King's fitful acts of terror, yet one cannot avoid admiring that strength of character which combined into one organism men and opinions so exceedingly diverse.

If this curious situation tended to inhibit constructive theology, it did not prevent the promulgation of a series of commonsense, practical reforms. The first and clearest examples of Anglican reform may be seen in the two sets of ecclesiastical injunctions imposed by Cromwell in 1536 and in 1538.[20] Of the former series those with educational aspects may perhaps be accorded most significance. The clergy are ordered to teach the Paternoster, the Articles of Faith and the Ten Commandments both to their congregations and to the young. They must urge parents to educate their children or apprentice them to honest occupations, since crime and social disorder will result from their failure. Rich clerics must support scholars at the universities and grammar schools; if non-resident, they must distribute a fortieth part of their incomes to the poor and a fifth to repairing the chancels of their churches. The injunctions of 1538 are those which we have already observed as providing for parish registers. They demand in addition the examination of parishioners in the articles of the faith, quarterly sermons by licensed preachers based upon Scriptural religion, the removal of such images as are abused and the provision by non-resident incumbents of curates able to do their work.

The immediate effectiveness of many of these rules may be doubted, yet at least they began that unduly slow process whereby a good many of the hoary anomalies of the late medieval church were mitigated and ecclesiastical practice brought nearer toward the rising expectations of the period. Such modest and mundane reforms sprang naturally from our Tudor age, with its deep aspirations to good order in Church, commonwealth and society at large. And though parallel reforms were ere long to spring from the continental Counter-Reformation, these of the thirties are typically English in spirit as well as earlier in date. Both before and after the Reformation the religious life of England was not outstandingly productive of saints, mystics and ascetics, of those extraordinary beings who are best fostered and best kept in order by the Church of Rome. As a people we have scarcely grasped the deepest implications of either Catholicism or Protestantism; we have tended to avoid the peaks and the abysses of both, and our greatest men have seldom found it easy to operate within the framework of either. If we have in any respect excelled, it has been in the provision of conditions enabling average Christians to practise a devotion heartfelt enough, yet not so deeply committed as to demand a severance from secular activities and values. If such sober aims and methods are deemed especially characteristic of the Anglican Church, then the thirties can boast one more claim to have laid the foundations of that Church.

Nevertheless, at this primitive stage certain features prominent in later Anglicanism lay as yet undeveloped. Though Cranmer and others were privately questioning transubstantiation, this doctrine was still enforced by the courts and presumably held by the majority of those clerics and laymen who reflected on matters of doctrine. Though Calvinism was coming to birth in Geneva, no one could yet have predicted its immense influence over the next generation of Anglicans. Again, at the time of Cromwell's fall only the first tentative steps had been taken toward a vernacular liturgy. By 1538 Cranmer was devising the first of his schemes for an English Prayer Book.[21] He is unlikely to have embarked upon such plans, however tentatively, without the sanction of the King, who was at this moment still seeking an accord with the Lutheran princes. While the preface to his scheme derived from the revised Breviary produced in 1535 by the Spanish Franciscan Cardinal Quignon, his drafts for matins and evensong were inspired by the work of Luther's intimate friend, Johann Bugenhagen, a copy of which had just been presented to the King. Again, various unofficial and semi-official primers, printed in English during the thirties, were now habituating the laity to the notion of vernacular prayers and offices.[22] Of these publications the best known are by William Marshall, whose blunt attacks on the veneration of saints soon caused his primer to be banned, and by the talented ex-Dominican John Hilsey, Bishop of Rochester. The latter naturally dedicated his work to his patron Cromwell, who published a second edition in 1539 after the author's death. The primer forms another characteristic manifesto of the Henrician *via media*, denouncing various superstitions, yet condemning Zwinglian disbelief in real and corporeal presence. Altogether, movement had at least begun on the liturgical front, and even the reaction of 1539–40 by no means brought it to a standstill.

Thomas Cromwell's eight-year ministry is now widely recognised as a period when the formation of the modern English State underwent a marked acceleration. In the history of religion we have traditionally regarded it as a period of clearance, as the period when the government swept away the papal connection and the monasteries, while legally subordinating the national Church to the control of the Crown in Parliament. The foregoing paragraphs are intended to suggest that this traditional view is an incomplete view, that the inner significance of this astonishing fourth decade of the sixteenth century should be seen in relation to the Anglican future as much as to the medieval past. Already the government and the intellectuals were groping their way toward a Reformation of compromise and detachment, partly because these attitudes come naturally to the English temperament, partly in consequence of a patriotic distrust for foreign models, partly since both Catholic and Lutheran powers failed to comprehend our situation, most of all because the divisions between Englishmen made it safer to attempt a settlement based on balance and comprehension rather than upon a narrow orthodoxy. However one measures these forces, it remains imperceptive to date the genesis of Anglicanism from the accession of Elizabeth, or even from the publication of Cranmer's First Prayer Book.

Cranmer's Position during Henry's Last Years

If in 1539–40 the King tilted the balance, he never unhinged it. From the fall of Wolsey to the time of his death his situation resembled that of his daughter Elizabeth, in that he took constant pains to avoid becoming the instrument of any group or any one idea. Tudor monarchs were essentially lonely figures; they knew that the courtly pomp of their entourage masked self-seeking and faction, as well as a fund of genuine devotion. It was their ceaseless and highly personal task to disentangle these warring elements, a task which over the years might have made the gentlest character moody and suspicious. Yet even as the King's health and temper declined, only for short periods did his intellect lose control of his emotions. He soon showed he had every intention of maintaining a two-party system in his executive and in the Church, so long as he could be sure both parties were wholeheartedly Henrician. Events soon conspired to restore a better equilibrium. A little over a year after Cromwell's fall the misconduct of Katherine Howard abased the prestige of her uncle Norfolk, who had contrived that Henry should marry her on the rebound from Anne of Cleves. From July 1543, when the King married Katherine Parr, Protestant opinions once more began to make progress at Court. They were cautiously favoured by the Queen and several noble ladies, again by Sir William Butts, the King's personal physician and a friend of Cranmer. Increasingly identified with the cause of further moderate Reform were the two ablest of the younger men of action, the men destined successively to dominate the reign of Edward VI— Edward Seymour, Earl of Hertford, and John Dudley, Lord Lisle. Despite the efforts of its advocates, the Six Articles persecution was never allowed to reach these high quarters. Yet at the time of the Parr marriage four humble men about the Court at Windsor were condemned, two of them being singers of the Chapel Royal. John Marbeck, interestingly enough, had made extracts from the writings of Calvin, but he had powerful friends, received a pardon and so lived to become one of the fathers of English music. The others, who went with constancy to the flames, included Marbeck's colleague Robert Testwood, who with more ingenuity than taste had altered the wording of an anthem so as to protest against the worship of the Virgin Mary.[23] After this trial accusations were directed against some of the King's gentlemen, but their imprudences were hushed up by a whole series of royal pardons, while the condemnation of the obnoxious Dr. London for perjury also helped to enjoin prudence upon the heresy-hunters.

The King's steady reluctance to allow his personal favourites to be brought within the net does much to account for the survival of his chaplain Cranmer during these difficult years. Admittedly, the Archbishop's situation remained uncomfortable. In Convocation his enemy Gardiner commanded an easy majority, while the resignations of Latimer and Shaxton limited his episcopal backers to Goodrich of Ely and Barlow of St. David's, neither of them being a figure of weight. The true source of strength for the Reformers lay in the maintenance of Cranmer's personal bond with the King, who not only defended him against several concerted attacks but allowed him to continue planning advanced liturgical reforms. When a group of malevolent Canterbury canons, perhaps backed by Gardiner, make charges of heresy against their Archbishop, Henry called at Lambeth, took Cranmer for an outing on his barge and menacingly remarked, 'Ah, my chaplain, I have news for you. I know now who is the greatest heretic in Kent.' But he ended by placing Cranmer in charge of the enquiry against himself.[24] On another occasion, when Sir John Gostwick raised the question of Cranmer's orthodoxy in the House of Commons, Henry sent a messenger to warn him off. 'Tell that varlet Gostwick that if he do not acknowledge his fault unto my lord of Canterbury ... I will sure both make him a poor Gostwick, and otherwise punish him, to the example of others.' Even after these rebuffs Norfolk and other members of the Council attempted to procure Cranmer's overthrow, only to be snubbed by the royal command, 'I pray you, use not my friends so.'

The Bishops' Book

Meanwhile the conservative bishops were having by far the better of the argument when it came to the long-anticipated revision of *The Bishops' Book*. After a long period of gestation, this was first presented to Convocation early in 1543 under the title *The Necessary Doctrine and Erudition of a Christian Man*.[25] The modifications appear to have been negotiated and written chiefly by Cranmer and three other bishops: Thomas Thirlby of Westminster, Nicholas Heath of Rochester and John Salcot of Salisbury. Yet had Stephen Gardiner written the whole work himself it could scarcely have been more to his taste. The Book clearly upheld transubstantiation, made no distinction between the scriptural and the non-scriptural sacraments and frankly described the lay demand for communion in both kinds as 'pestiferous and devilish'. While sanctioning prayers and masses for the dead, it nevertheless acknowledged that every mass was offered for the whole congregation of Christian people and that its benefits could not be limited to private persons or purposes. In general terms it also denounced the financial abuses of purgatory, blaming them upon the Papacy. By implication correcting Tyndale, it said that the 'word *ecclesia* is in English called *Church*', but it naturally distinguished between the Church Universal and its components the national churches, with their diversity of traditions and ceremonies. Again, Scripture itself commits ministration to bishops and priests, whereas the grouping of dioceses under patriarchs, primates, arch-bishops or metropolitans springs merely from man-made law. In particular, the Bishop of Rome's claim to sovereignty over the rest cannot be maintained by reference to the Scriptures, to the ancient General Councils or even to the general consent of the Catholic Church. The unity of the latter is not conserved by his authority and the Church of Rome has no unique claim to be called Catholic. The only universal governor of the whole Christian Church is Jesus Christ, whom all Christians are bound to obey. But next to him they must obey Christian kings and princes, 'which be the heads governing under him of the particular churches'.

The 'new' developments in *The Necessary Doctrine* are few, but important. Luther's solifidianism is more clearly rejected than hitherto. Men are not justified by faith alone and the righteousness of Christ is not 'imputed' to them, as Luther supposed. They win justification by faith coupled together with hope, charity, fear of God and repentance. Justification means 'the making of us righteous afore God' and is based on life-long effort; at any time a man may lose it by sin and no man is entitled to any comfortable 'assurance' of his own salvation. Again in opposition to Luther, the freedom of the human will is asserted; the will remains free to choose good by the assistance of divine grace, free to choose evil by rejecting that assistance. In this scheme of justification and salvation good works have a necessary rôle. But by good works we mean, say the authors, neither the superstitious observances of monks and nuns, nor works done to earn human respect, nor merely corporal works, but rather 'all inward and spiritual works ... as the love and fear of God, joy in God, godly meditations and thoughts, patience, humility and such like'. On a lower level the penitence of the converted sinner and the penances he performs may also be admitted as good works.

It remains impossible to do justice in a few sentences to this outstanding example of committee-theology which happens also to be a neglected masterpiece of Tudor prose, combining the grand writing of its predecessor *The Bishops' Book* with a greater conciseness and an improved arrangement. Fully authorised by the king and furnished with a preface by him, it inevitably became known as *The King's Book*. The title still seems most appropriate, for the work forms the handsomest monument of Henry's experiment in Anglo-Catholicism. And after standing for little more than three years it collapsed for ever at the moment of the monarch's death. Though no doubt owing some of its literary merit to Thomas Cranmer, it might also be described as a monument to the defeat of the Archbishop in committee. In later years he was to accuse Gardiner of 'seducing' Henry into accepting the book, but his rival was able to retort with justice that it had also been accepted by Parliament and that Cranmer himself had made no complaint while the King lived but had sanctioned its use in his diocese. From every logical viewpoint save that of extreme erastianism Cranmer stood in an unenviable position during the King's declining years. Any Archbishop of Canterbury was a great servant of the State; he could neither live a retired life nor avoid direct participation in the actions of his Sovereign. Cranmer was compelled to sit on the Privy Council and there suffer himself to be pushed along by Gardiner, for in that setting the decisive official had every advantage over the tentative scholar. A man fully aware of the pros and cons of every doctrine, a man wholly prepared in his open-mindedness to allow his studies to lead him to fresh conclusions, such a man could scarcely be at home in the ruthless ecclesiastical politics of that intolerant century.

Cranmer's Eucharistic Beliefs and Liturgical Plans

Cranmer's private beliefs concerning the central problem of the eucharist developed but slowly and were much influenced by a mind with a keener cutting edge—that of his former chaplain Nicholas Ridley, trained in the schools of Cambridge, Louvain and Paris. The evidence for Cranmer's own doctrinal development contains exasperating difficulties and seeming contradictions. Since eminent scholars have always differed on some issues,[26] it would ill befit a non-specialist to declare for any one hypothesis. A letter of Cranmer to Cromwell concerning the sacramentarian Adam Damplip strongly suggests that the Archbishop had already in 1538 abandoned his belief in transubstantiation, yet that he continued to attach importance to a real presence in the sacrament, possibly in general consonance with the Lutheran doctrine. In that same year he was doubtless sincere enough in expressing disagreement with John Lambert. At his trial in 1555 Cranmer told his judges he had been converted to his later view of the eucharist by Nicholas Ridley and that this change had taken place shortly before 1548. A preface to one of his works, published at Emden in 1557 and attributed to his close friend Sir John Cheke, gives the exact date as 1546. We also have Ridley's own assurance that in 1545 he, Ridley, had been convinced by a 'new' doctrine through reading the work *De Corpore et Sanguine Domini* of the ninth-century Benedictine Ratramnus of Corbie.

At this date the revival of Ratramnus did not represent any very profound research, for the book had been printed at Cologne in 1531 and at Geneva in 1541 and its author's name—often in the form 'Bertram'—was often bandied between Tudor controversialists. The doctrine itself involved a dual and simultaneous operation. On the one hand, the recipient's body received and fed upon the symbolic bread and wine; on the other, his soul received and fed upon the body and blood of Christ, their presence being spiritual only and not corporeal. Ridley was to enunciate this doctrine in his disputation with Queen Mary's Catholic theologians in April 1554, while Cranmer himself maintained it during a similar disputation in April 1555. 'The soul', he claimed, 'is fed with the body of Christ, the body with the sacrament ... so one thing is done outwardly, another inwardly: like as in baptism, the external element, whereby the body is washed, is one; so the internal element, whereby the soul is cleansed, is another ... Outwardly we eat the sacrament: inwardly we eat the body of Christ.'

These ostensibly simple phrases concealed a multitude of metaphysical and historical problems: some modern theologians think them not far from Zwinglian symbolism while others regard them as closely related to pre-medieval Catholic tradition and as presenting a genuine *via media*, quite distinct from transubstantiation or consubstantiation or the radical teaching of Zwingli and the other Swiss Reformers. Cranmer's own indecisions of the year 1548 provide further complications. He then published a translation of the catechism by the Lutheran Justus Jonas, which taught the real presence in a manner wholly unacceptable to the Zwinglians and which Cranmer toned down but did not completely revise. On the other hand, in December 1548 Cranmer's speech in the House of Lords debate on the eucharist suggests that his view had now been strongly affected by his recent discussions with the Zwinglian immigrant John à Lasco. It has, however, been forcibly argued that this last phase was brief and that Cranmer thereafter maintained the Ratramnian compromise until his trial. He then claimed that he had held only two briefs, presumably regarding his 'real presence' belief of c.1538–46 as still Catholic and meaning by his second position the Ratramnian view to which Ridley had converted him.

This was a simplification but it need not be taken as disingenuous. Two points seem now generally agreed. Both Ridley and Cranmer were revolted by the crudely irreverent attacks made against the sacrament of the altar by the proletarian extremists of the reign of Edward VI. Again, neither of them can be regarded as at any stage a mere shadow of any continental theologian. Those Marian judges (and modern critics) who depicted Cranmer as first orthodox, then a Lutheran, then a Zwinglian, did not merely simplify his development; they also ignored the massive evidence concerning his independent study of the early Fathers and of later theologians. In particular, his acceptance of Ridley's viewpoint occurred three years before the arrival in England of the eminent Martin Bucer, who had come by a different route to a similar doctrine of the eucharist but whose influence upon Cranmer lay in other directions. Everyone who has studied the growth of Cranmer's convictions must sometimes have shared the feeling of Cardinal Gasquet, who found it 'difficult to determine with precision, at any given time, the exact phase of a mind so shifting'. Yet if we go on to imply that a man was a fool or a knave to move from one position to another, especially in relation to this particular doctrine, we misunderstand the enquiring spirit of these years, the doctrinal maelstrom which caused even the unimaginative Gardiner to show uncertainties and Tunstall, the most conservative of Henry's bishops, to regret Innocent III's rigid definition of transubstantiation, while accepting it as a loyal son of the Church.

It is nowadays widely admitted that Cranmer's late interest in Swiss eucharistic doctrine by no means makes him a slavish disciple of Zwingli but rather the main English exponent of the 'true presence' belief agreed between Calvin and Bullinger at the Zürich Agreement (*Consensus Tigurinus*) of 1549. That the Archbishop was as eager as any Continental divine to bridge the divide between the Lutherans and the Swiss may be readily deduced from his repeated plea for a 'godly synod' to unite the Protestant cause. Increasing stress is laid upon his Patristic studies, though here he was much influenced by the writings of Oecolampadius, the humanist Reformer of Basle. At an early and formative stage of his career Cranmer urged upon his correspondent Vadianus that 'the writings of every man must be read with discrimination'. Modern research, as exemplified by Peter N. Brooks, is not content to make him a confused rebel in a Catholic English context. Rather should he be observed amid the complex debate among those European theologians who could no longer accept either the fiat of Innocent III or the Aristotelian metaphysics of Aquinas. Thus the simplistic image of 'doubting Thomas' must give way to that of a Cranmer with a scholarly, investigative mind.

Meanwhile, during the years 1540–47 Cranmer busied himself far less with speculations on the mass than with projects for an English Prayer Book. He was not alone in his desire to simplify and to rationalise the divine offices, which as collected in the Breviary had reached an elaboration and a complexity quite out of touch with the needs of secular clerics and laymen. This demand had already been recognised by reforming Catholics. It was under commission from Clement VII and with the final approval of Paul III that Quignon had revised the Breviary; and this revision continued to form a basis for Cranmer's studies during the forties and for his Prayer Book of 1549. He did not enjoy a complete monopoly of the liturgical field. In 1543 a committee of bishops produced a *Rationale of Ceremonial* which proved to be a competent but most conservative anthology of medieval usages.[27] Cranmer, who doubtless bore not a little of the responsibility for its quiet suppression, soon hastened to produce a first instalment of his own work. This was the English Litany, printed in May 1544 and thereafter used by Royal command in the churches. Here he displayed not only a splendid gift of English phrase but a marked flair for selecting ideas from different sources—the Sarum and York Uses, Quignon, Luther and others—and fusing them into a devotional unity able to commend itself to successive generations of English churchmen. Its quality may still be assessed in the Prayer Book version, though the invocations to the Virgin and the saints, retained in 1549, were omitted altogether in 1552 and subsequently. To make a point of detail, Cranmer's skill in this *genre* may be seen in his grouping of the petitions. The Latin litany had the frequent congregational responses: 'Ab omni malo: *libera nos Domine*. Ab insidiis diaboli: *libera nos Domine*. A ventura ira: *libera nos Domine*', and so forth. But Cranmer's version has 'From all evil and mischief; from sin, from all crafts and assaults of the devil; from thy wrath, and from everlasting damnation, *Good Lord, deliver us*'.[28]

Henry did not envisage doctrinal change when he permitted Cranmer to plan a modification of the mass by the insertion of devotional passages in English. This project nevertheless went far beyond mere translation. It entailed a radical change of purpose, whereby the infrequent lay communion and the many private masses of medieval custom would be replaced by a regular congregational service. Though this *Order of Communion* was not published until almost a year after Henry's death, the work had been almost completed during his reign: being again in a forward state of mind, he would probably have sanctioned its use had he lived a little longer. This was not the only one of Cranmer's schemes which bore fruit in the subsequent reign. To deal with the problem of disaffected, extravagant and illiterate preaching, he had taken the initiative in compiling a *Book of Homilies*, twelve in number, four or five of which he wrote personally, while assigning two others to the conservatives Harpsfield and Bonner.[29] In 1543 he laid these sermons before Convocation, but for reasons now obscure no immediate progress ensued. A more successful enterprise was the so-called King's Primer, published in 1545 with a royal preface ordaining that all schoolmasters must use it to instruct their pupils 'next after their A.B.C.' and that no other primer should henceforth be read, printed or sold. The literary and liturgical superiority of this work to its predecessors has been taken to show the hand of the Archbishop, though the King's marked complacency over its merits suggests that he may also have taken a personal share in its revision.

The Bible and Public Opinion

During these years many preparations for a future Protestant advance were taking place behind the façade of reaction. Amongst Cranmer's partial successes we may count his ability to contain the violent attacks made by his adversaries against the English Bible. From the outset the Gardiner faction found it easy to prey upon Henry's fears concerning the policy of the open Bible; the more easy since even the Great Bible could scarcely be regarded as other than a Protestant document. Cranmer must have been acting under pressure when in the Convocation of 1542 he asked the bishops whether the English Bible could be retained without 'scandal, error and open offence to Christ's faithful people'. The majority of the bishops replied that it could not, unless it were first corrected by the Vulgate. Upon this, the New Testament was divided into fifteen portions and assigned to as many bishops for summary examination, while the Lower House of Convocation was encouraged to produce a list of errors from the Old Testament.

Committees of bishops were then appointed to accomplish the actual revision, and at this point Gardiner produced his exotic list of Latinisms from the Vulgate, which he desired to embody in a revised version. On 10 March 1542, however, the Archbishop suddenly reported that the King had decided to have the Bible examined by the two universities. This, as he doubtless foresaw, procured a useful delay, but the conservatives were not slow to follow another line of attack. In the spring of 1543 they induced the King to let them bring into Parliament an 'Act for the Advancement of True Religion'. It condemned 'crafty false and untrue' translations, including that of Tyndale, while limiting the reading of the licensed Bibles on a class-basis not unlike that of the medieval sumptuary laws. Noblemen and gentlemen might read to their families at home, substantial merchants and gentlewomen were trusted to read by themselves, while the common people must not read the Scriptures at all.[30]

Amongst our somewhat meagre evidence concerning popular Bible reading at this stage is the vivid narrative by William Malden,[31] describing his experiences as a youth at Chelmsford. When Henry VIII set forth the Scriptures to be read in churches, he recalls, 'Immediately after, divers poor men in the town of Chelmsford in the county of Essex, where my father dwelled and I [was] born and with him brought up, the said poor men brought the New Testament of Jesus Christ, and on Sundays did sit reading in [the] lower end of the church, and many would flock about them to hear their reading.' Finding his son among this study-group, Malden senior pulled him out and made him say the Latin matins. 'Then I saw I could not be in rest. Then, thought I, I will learn to read English, and then I will have the New Testament and read thereon myself; and then had I learned of an English prymer as far as *Patris sapientia*, and then on Sundays I plied my English prymer. The May-tide following, I and my father's prentice Thomas Jeffrey laid our money together and bought the New Testament in English, and hid it in our bed straw and so exercised it at convenient times.' Soon afterwards young Malden was sent to keep a shop some distance away, thus gaining a better chance to pursue his forbidden studies. One day he remonstrated with his mother for worshipping the crucifix: 'Then I went and hid Frith's book on the Sacrament, and then I went to bed.' In response to these actions his distraught father beat him, put a halter round his neck and might have strangled him but for his mother's intervention. No doubt the Reformation occasioned many such emotional clashes between the generations, each well-intentioned by its own lights. And as for the elder Malden, he may perhaps have thought some calculated violence at this stage preferable to seeing his son involved in dangerous charges of heresy.

The text of the prohibitory Act of 1543 suggests how widespread Bible-reading had now become by listing amongst the unprivileged classes 'women, artificers, apprentices, journeymen, servingmen under the degree of yeomen, husbandmen and labourers'. The King perhaps exaggerated the situation when in his famous last speech to Parliament (24 December 1545) he complained that the 'most precious jewel, the Word of God, is disputed, rhymed, sung and jangled in every alehouse and tavern'. Naturally, the more literate members of the working classes read aloud to the illiterate, and inability to read did not exclude a man from Biblical study and from the convictions it entailed. In the pages of Foxe we encounter offenders with little or no knowledge of reading and writing, who yet argued over texts with their prosecutors and disputed the more familiar points of doctrinal controversy. That the prohibition of 1543 caused distress among such people is suggested by the chance survival of a copy of Thomas Langley's *Abridgement of Polydore Vergil* (published in April 1546) containing a bucolic inscription by a Gloucestershire shepherd named Robert Williams. This man apparently kept the flock of William Latimer, the humanist parson of Saintbury and Weston-sub-Edge, who had in fact died the previous year. 'At Oxforde, the yere 1546, browt down to Seynbury by John Darbye, pryse 14d, when I kepe Mr. Letymer's shype. I bout thys boke when the Testament was obberagatyd [abrogated], that shepeherdys myght not red hit. I prey God amende that blyndnes. Wryt by Robert Wyllyams keppynge shepe uppon Seynbury Hill, 1546.[32]

This quiet and dignified protest forms a contrast with more sensational acts of defiance like that of the young London tailor John Porter.[33] At St. Paul's Bishop Bonner had set up six public Bibles, foridding readers to gather crowds, to expound the Scriptures or to disturb the services. Foxe admits that Porter gathered a multitude and read in a 'very audible' voice. He was also charged with expounding the text and thrown into prison where, alleges the martyrologist, he was loaded with chains and found dead by the morning. In all likelihood, Porter's death in prison (perhaps from starvation) took place two years later in 1542, when the bishop's chancellor kept him there on an unconfirmed charge of sacramentarian heresy. Whatever the precise details, we can believe that cruel punishments were sometimes imposed; yet Porter may well have been one of those brave but impatient enthusiasts who brought trouble upon themselves without substantially advancing the cause. As the story of the Reformation unfolds, it suggests with increasing emphasis that by no means all the arrogance lay on the side of the bishops.

Eagerly as we sift the scattered evidence concerning the early impact of the English Bible upon the common people, we should not assume that at every stage this development was the most vital factor in the progress of the Reformation. At this moment the future of the movement did not lie so much with Gloucestershire shepherds and London tailors as with their economic and social superiors. The fact that the gentry and the middle classes continued to read the Bible mattered far more than the fact that poor men suffered a temporary restraint. At the moment of his greatest power Henry VIII dared not attempt to wrest the Bible from the hands of the political classes, and amongst them a New Learning, compounded of biblicism, Erasmian reformism and Protestant beliefs, seems to have continued steadily developing throughout the Cromwellian years and the years of ostensible reaction which followed. With a view to discerning trends of religious opinion the present writer made a study of the religious phraseology of wills—mainly those of gentry, substantial yeomen and clergy—in Yorkshire and Nottinghamshire throughout the middle decades of the century.[34] The traditional Catholic form involved bequeathing one's soul not only to Christ, or to Almighty God, but also to the Blessed Virgin and the glorious company of the saints. Though in individual cases testamentary forms may have been influenced by some person other that the testator, anything like a mass movement to omit mention of the Virgin and the saints must reflect a decline of these cults. This seems especially probable in the later years of Henry VIII, when no legal or social pressures induced testators to abandon the traditional forms. And even in these conservative and slow-moving parts of England such a trend begins in the late thirties, becoming steadily more marked in the reign of Edward VI. The following table should be viewed with less reverence than we accord to modern statistics, yet it does not fail to tell a story.

Years	Traditional Wills	Non-traditional Wills
1538–40	70	9
1541–44	82	33
1545–46	99	32
1547	24	15
1548	24	19
1549	23	24
1550	18	31
1551	21	35
1552–3	29	29

Moreover, from 1537–8 small but steadily growing minorities of these testators do not merely omit the saints, but also use positively Protestant terms, stressing salvation through the merits of Christ alone. Such, for example, were William Holmes and Robert Thomson of Halifax, a great parish comprising many weaving communities with an early (and thereafter continuous) Protestant tradition. These men in 1538 specifically reject the intercession of the saints, commending their souls 'unto Christ Jesu, my maker and redeemer, in whom, and by the merits of whose blessed passion, is all my whole trust of clean remission of all my sins'.[35]

In this same year Robert Ferrar, prior of Nostell yet a fervent Protestant, graphically described to Cromwell the ardent desire of men in the clothing towns of the West Riding to hear the Gospel preached; he even suggested a plan to turn his own priory into a school and a centre for evangelism.[36] Similar hints occur in other sources. Wilfrid Holme of Huntington near York, who wrote in 1537 his long denunciation of the Pilgrimage of Grace, gives us a deeper insight into the minds of these provincial squires who were at once hero-worshippers of Henry VIII, believers in Justification by Faith, enemies of saint-worship and exponents of critical attitudes which can be traced back to Reuchlin and Erasmus.[37] In Holme's view a Golden Age was already at hand. Scholastic philosophy, ungodly medieval science, the mumbo-jumbo of saints, relics and pilgrimages, the lusts of hypocritical monks and nuns would all be swept away, and the godly monarch would lead forth the nation in the light of the Gospel. Some of these are modern phrases, but that they summarise Holme's attitude with entire fairness will, I think, be admitted by any reader who can stomach his high-flown diction. Even in these remoter provinces a fair proportion of the gentry had been educated at the Inns of Court; very many leaders of local opinion were frequent visitors to London, where they had every opportunity to encounter new religious opinions. Amongst the substantial classes, and even amongst the populace of London, the Home Counties and East Anglia, these opinions were making still more rapid progress during the last decade of Henry VIII. On the passage of the Six Articles Act more than 500 Londoners were immediately indicted (and many arrested) as notorious disbelievers in its provisions,[38] and no doubt this number, though hitherto unknown in such a context, could have been multiplied, given more official energy and more commodious gaols. In the same year the heretical preaching of the Scots Reformer George Wishart gained many converts among the citizens of Bristol, where feeling between the rival parties apparently ran as high as it had done six years earlier under the stimulus of Latimer's preaching.[39] If under the threat of the Six Articles most Protestants used discretion, their numbers continued to grow.

Opinion in Tudor England was not created by Acts of Parliament, and its development cannot be gauged by reading the Statute Book. Whatever the King might say, most Protestants do not seem to have believed that at any stage he had wholly abandoned Reformation principles. Religious opinion never became stabilised. Protestantism was emphatically never limited to the clerical group which acknowledged the leadership of Cranmer or to the knot of 'advanced' courtiers under Edward Seymour, Earl of Hertford, who in January 1547 awaited the impending death of their master with a strange mixture of grief and impatience. Yet these latter were the men upon whom the next phase of the Reformation depended, and by some remarkable strokes of fortune the key to the new reign had just been pressed into their hands.

The Last Henrician Phase

From the middle 1530s educated English people—courtiers, humanists, dons, publishers and readers of serious treatises—were increasingly confronted by Erasmus as well as by Luther and the Swiss Reformers. Several of his works were becoming available in English translation during the later years of Henry VIII.[40] Though a harsh critic of the clergy, Erasmus offered a middle path between 'medieval' rigour and 'heretical' innovation. While he convinced many moderates of the need for reforms based upon the unique authority of the New Testament, he demonstrated that such reforms did not entail the acceptance of Luther's every doctrinal deduction and controversial expletive. Alongside Erasmian attitudes, educated English men and women also acquired awareness of the humanist evangelicals in French upper-class and court circles. This change of atmosphere, however restrained, gradually affected the personal relationship of Henry VIII with the Reformation. Even as he shook off the crypto-protestant Cromwell and renewed persecution under the Six Articles, the King and many of his entourage fell under the subtle influence of men who quietly and in varying degrees accepted the main tenets of Luther, and who enlisted Henry's help in order to resist the overbearing Bishop Gardiner and other clerical conservatives.

During the last two or three years of his reign the King's health markedly deteriorated, while his control of business, though never negligible, became looser and more fitful.[41] Increasingly devoted to pious literature, he allowed the leading officials of his Privy Chamber to seal his documents and to control the access of suitors for his favours. Insofar as he had close personal friends, they were now the gentlemen of the Chamber, especially his man-of-all-work Sir Anthony Denny (who in 1544 was knighted and became chief gentleman) and Sir William Butts, his chief physician.[42] The oddity of this situation lay in the fact that both these men, so close to the 'Catholic' monarch, were among the most zealous evangelicals in the kingdom. They led charmed lives within the very crater of the slowly subsiding but still dangerous volcano. Unfortunately we lack transcripts of the daily discourse between the King and these devoted companions who made his physical decline tolerable. We might conjecture that they avoided such delicate themes as transubstantiation and Martin Luther's lack of respect for the ruler whom he had called 'Squire Henry', yet doubtless many matters in the field of religious policy could still be discussed. After all Cromwell and Cranmer had left the king and his servants inextricably bound together in some 'godly' tasks, such as the maintenance of a biblical Christianity. John Foxe the martyrologist looked back at this Henrician *dénouement* as a significant stage of divine guidance.

> So long as Queen Anne [Boleyn], Thomas Cromwell, Archbishop Cranmer, Master Denny, Dr. Butts and such like were about him and could prevail with him, what organ of Christ's glory did more good in the Church than he?[43]

With the King himself as its chosen weapon, the Chamber proved well able to protect its own, and when the heresy-hunters ventured to attack his intimates therein, Henry soon warned them off in brusque terms, as offending against his own royal dignity.[44] Within and around the Chamber there extended a close evangelical network, both male and female. With his huge salary and grants, Butts appears to have been a most influential member. He was or had been physician to Wolsey, Norfolk, Anne Boleyn, Jane Seymour, Henry Fitzroy, Duke of Richmond, and the Princess Mary—to mention but a few of his distinguished patients. His wife was gentlewoman to the Princess Mary, toward whom Butts was fiercely protective, despite his strong personal attachment to the Gospel and his friendships with Cranmer, Latimer and Sir John Cheke.[45] Sir William Herbert, also active in the Chamber and later Earl of Pembroke, was brother-in-law to Queen Katherine Parr, herself an obvious evangelical. Denny's handsome wife Jane, also suspected of heresy, ventured to send eight shillings to the martyr Anne Askew, then in the Tower. Meanwhile Lady Denny's mother Lady Katherine Champernoun and her sister Katherine Ashley were both governesses to the Princess Elizabeth.[46] By an appropriate symbolism Herbert and Denny, faithful to the last, were to ride in triumph on the King's funeral hearse alongside the coffin, prior to joining his former secretary Paget in the manipulation of his last will and testament.

Meanwhile during the last weeks this courtly group fell into line with the Seymour faction, led by Prince Edward's uncle the Earl of Hertford, the future Protector Somerset. On the other side stood the now elderly Duke of Norfolk and his son, the poet Henry Earl of Surrey, later famous for nativising the sonnet in English literature. The complexity of influences there and the ubiquity of the new doctrines are also illustrated by the case of the latter. Some of his biographers, unduly impressed by his father's conservatism and by his own lethal feud with Hertford and the Seymours, have regarded Surrey as a Catholic.[47] This simplification appears somewhat naïve when one studies his verse-paraphrases of Ecclesiastes and Psalms, obviously much affected by the evangelical religion.[48] As with his cousin Anne Boleyn, he had perhaps encountered this influence during his prolonged visits to France, though his English background supplies other obvious motivations. Certainly his older friend and fellow-poet Sir Thomas Wyatt (d.1542), an unambiguous Protestant, influenced Surrey's work, having also published similar biblical paraphrases, commended appropriately by one of Surrey's own sonnets. Again, Surrey shows familiarity with Coverdale's translation of the Bible, and had associated closely with other Protestant humanists including Sir Anthony Denny.

It need scarcely be added that these preliminary manoeuvres involved the upbringing and education of the young heir to the throne. Despite the sentimental fables of Victorian biographers, the three children of Henry VIII were not educated by his last Queen, for Katherine Parr, however literate in English, was no expert in the ancient classics, the staple material of any courtly education.[49] Indeed one or two anecdotes have occasioned some distinct exaggerations of her influence upon the King himself. In fact Edward's precocious learning, together with that resolute Protestantism displayed not long after his accession to the throne, are attributable to his actual teachers, who belonged to the Cambridge set closely associated with Denny and others of the Privy Chamber.

From the age of six Prince Edward had been taught by Dr. Richard Cox, whose subsequent dramatic part in the furtherance of the Reformation we shall have ample opportunity to witness.[50] In July 1544 Sir John Cheke, the greatest English classicist of his day, was summoned from Cambridge 'as a supplement to Mr. Cox', and soon became one of the very few to gain the affections of the reserved boy. Cheke was already in trouble with Gardiner, who even forced him to desist from teaching the revised pronunciation of

Greek, and he ultimately fell victim to the Marian persecution. The third among Edward's tutors was the celebrated Sir Anthony Cooke, who had qualified for the post by making his own daughters the most learned women in England. His religious opinions matched those of Cox and Cheke, and in 1559 he was to become one of the two leaders of that party in the House of Commons which forced through the Elizabethan settlement. Like the leading members of the Privy Chamber, these men held distinctly Protestant opinions and it is hardly possible to believe that the King had no inkling of their proclivities. Though we have no right to presume that he had divined the future to the extent of training his successor for a course of action which he himself hesitated to adopt, few of his earlier decisions proved more momentous in regard to the English Reformation than his selection of his son's tutors. Edward's precocity and strongly Protestant views are well attested from the time of his accession; they played a real part in subsequent events, since he was called upon to take a quasi-adult part in public events and would not have been easy to manipulate by any save Protestant politicians.

During the summer months of the year 1546 the outcome of the party-struggle was far from being a foregone conclusion. At this time the Catholic party remained energetic in the Privy Council and still in good hopes of stamping out heresy. The well-known London preacher Dr. Crome had been forced into public recantation, Latimer closely examined, Shaxton driven into preaching against his former friends. An energetic drive against notorious heretics in London found its main victims in Anne Askew and John Lascells, who on 16 July were burned with two others for refusing transubstantiation.[51] Only a year later, attracted by Anne's extraordinary fortitude, John Bale published in her honour the remarkably vivid collection of original materials subsequently utilised by Foxe.[52] If the documents present anything like an accurate picture, this daughter of a Lincolnshire knight proved herself an educated, pert and formidable disputant, quite unabashed by Gardiner and Bonner, who both attempted to re-convert and save her. The villains of the story are not churchmen, but Lord Chancellor Wriothesley and Sir Richard Rich, who racked Anne in the Tower with their own hands in an unsuccessful attempt to make her implicate her alleged patrons, Queen Katherine Parr, the Duchess of Suffolk and the Countesses of Sussex and Hertford. Her friend John Lascells, though a somewhat obscure figure, was in all likelihood the real intellectual leader of the group. He was a gentleman of good Nottinghamshire family, a member of Furnivall's Inn, a sewer of the King's Chamber, and almost certainly that same John Lascells who in 1541 had given important evidence concerning the misconduct of Katherine Howard. From this last point he may well have become a target for revenge. On examination he left no doubts regarding his defiance of the Six Articles, and the polemical letter which he wrote in prison was recognised in later years by the Jesuit Robert Parsons as a most persuasive document. In the course of an elaborate attack upon its sacramental teaching Parsons asserted that Lascells had passed beyond Luther, Zwingli and Calvin, and claimed that his doctrine derived from Andreas

Carlstadt, the extremist who had been denounced by Luther himself
Equally well, Lascells and his friends might be regarded as disciples of John
Frith. These two martyrs and their plebeian fellow-sufferers also appear
to exemplify the democratic tendencies inevitable within a persecuted
minority. In London there had developed heretical groups compounded of
people with varied social and educational backgrounds and it became
increasingly easy for working-class Protestants to gain indoctrination from
educated leaders.

By the time of these martyrdoms the Seymours had become predominant
at Court, while during a banquet given in August to Admiral d'Annebaul
the King himself suggested that England and France should act in concert to
extirpate popery and establish a communion service in place of the mass
Cranmer, who related this story to his secretary and biographer Morice, also
claimed that the King had ordered him to prepare such a plan for submission
to the French court. On 26 December the failing ruler nominated a Council
of Regency for his son. Virtually all its sixteen members belonged to the
'new' families, and its strong personalities leaned toward Protestantism
Noting the omission of Bishop Gardiner's name, Henry's close friend Sir
Anthony Browne knelt at the royal bedside and asked whether it might be
due to negligence. 'Hold your peace', growled the King, 'I remembered him
well enough, and of good purpose have left him out. ... I could myself use
him, and rule him to all manner of purposes, as seemed good unto me, but so
will you never do.'

It now remained for the Seymour faction to overthrow that last political
bulwark of Catholicism, the Howard family. Thanks to its internal quarrels
and to the recklessness of Norfolk's brilliant son the Earl of Surrey, the task
proved unexpectedly simple.[53] This 'foolish proud boy' had begun seriously
to overplay his hand, for he could boast no services to match Hertford's two
ably-managed expeditions into Scotland. Indeed, not long before, Surrey's
defeat at the hands of the French near Boulogne had been retrieved by
Hertford in person. He was now loudly demanding the future regency for
his father and announcing his intentions of settling faithfully with friend and
foe when the Howards should come into their own. Within a few months
Surrey threw away all the advantages built up by his father's long years of
subservience, and his conduct ensured that the Catholic party would enter
the new reign without its traditional lay leadership. Yet he was not a
Catholic martyr and could not be presented as such; he could not even build
up a party, for the new nobility and the King's servants had no intention of
quarrelling and dividing along religious lines at the behest of an arrogant
young man who overstressed the claims of ancient ancestry. Sir Richard
Southwell, who denounced Surrey for treasonably using the arms of Edward
the Confessor, was a pious Catholic and in later years a pillar of Queen
Mary's government. Wriothesley, who took a large part in investigating the
charges against Surrey, had achieved notoriety as a persecutor of Protestants
The accusations themselves sprang in part from internal family quarrels and
particularly from the fratricidal hatred of Surrey's own sister, the Duchess of
Richmond. They were flimsy enough, but the jury, apparently encouraged

by Henry's minister Paget, found the accused guilty. He went to the block on 19 January 1547, while the old Duke was being condemned by the more deliberate process of attainder for concealing these offences. Norfolk would in fact have followed his son on 28 January, had he not at the last moment been reprieved by the death of the sovereign whom he had served both fairly and foully throughout a long and momentous reign. About two o'clock on the morning of that same day Henry died, assured and rational to the end. And speech having at last failed him, he had firmly gripped Cranmer's hand when urged so to display his confidence in the mercy of the Lord. In that confidence had ever lain his greatness and his peril.

10 The Reformation under Somerset

Calvin and Calvinism

Before Henry's death there began a gradual infiltration into England of Protestant concepts more advanced than those of Luther. Having at first engaged the interest of university theologians, they presently extended to a new generation of Bible-reading lay people. Deriving mainly from Zürich, Strassburg and Geneva these ideas became increasingly dominated by the intellect of John Calvin.[1] Amid the Protestant refugees from Mary's persecution, and subsequently among the more religious of Elizabeth's subjects, Calvinism became the weightiest of the many foreign influences brought to bear upon the English Reformation. At this moment of its first incursion we must therefore pause to reflect, however inadequately, upon its origins and character.

When Henry died, Calvin had already held sway in Geneva for nearly six years. As a religious and social leader he possessed immense qualifications: a natural intensity of moral feeling; an acute and systematic mind, nourished by a long humanist, legal and theological training under the best teachers of France; a splendid lucidity of expression both in Latin and in French; a temperament which could combine tireless concentration upon essentials with an ability to compromise over details. Though he had no use for traditional mysticism, Calvin experienced toward the end of 1533 a conversion which left him, as he supposed, utterly subdued to the power of God and no more (but no less) than an instrument of the divine purpose. Henceforth he stood in the most parlous of all spiritual situations, for he never doubted his own special mission to reform the Church or the peculiar validity of the theological system revealed by God to his intellect as the basis for that great Reform. Religious history supplies other examples of such terrifying convictions, but seldom if ever have they been allied with gifts more capable of devising and implementing a practical programme. He spoke as one having authority and, when men had heard him, they tended to feel that his rivals were scribes and pharisees.

For nearly three years after his conversion Calvin wandered about

France, talking, writing, narrowly skirting the nets of persecution and ripening his mind in contact with the many Protestants and reforming humanists who still contrived to flourish under Francis I. In March 1536 he published anonymously, and dedicated to that King, the first edition of his *Christianae Religionis Institutio*, which underwent so many expansions and rearrangements before reaching its definitive form in 1559. Without doubt the ablest of all Protestant essays in systematic theology, its basis is biblical and its resemblance to a *Summa Theologica* no more than superficial.

In this same year, while avoiding the forces of Francis and Charles on a journey from Italy to Paris, he made a fortuitous visit to Geneva. There he found himself detained by the appeal of the local Protestant firebrand Guillaume Farel, who two months earlier had gained a precarious local ascendancy. Their first attempts to establish a new order ran into powerful opposition on the city council and led to their expulsion. Withdrawing in 1538 to Strasburg, Calvin ministered to the French colony in that great city of refuge, married Idelette de Bure and wrote a fine French translation of his own book. He also gained a wider vision of international religious politics, concerning which he learned most from Martin Bucer, the Strasburg reformer then attempting to mediate between the Lutherans and the Zwinglians. From Bucer and from Melanchthon—he became friendly with the latter at the Diet of Ratisbon—Calvin accepted only what they could contribute toward his own system. Meanwhile in faction-ridden Geneva his party had regained the upper hand, and from the time of his recall in 1541 he trampled down one opponent after another in his steady march toward the triumphant theocracy of his later years.

By the mid-century the growing success of the Genevan experiment had already brought him a special authority throughout the Protestant world. When Englishmen first came under his spell, he was already becoming a Hildebrand among the Reformed, one seated in a state better ordered—or so it seemed to many who looked beyond the plastic arts—than the rival establishment which bestrode Renaissance Italy. If a man enjoyed theological instruction, could live a moral life and avoid criticising the government, Geneva offered him unequalled advantage in public order, social justice and educational opportunity. If he fully accepted this interpretation of Christianity, Geneva became, in the words of John Knox, 'the maist perfyt schoole of Chryst that ever was in the erth since the dayis of the Apostillis'. By an unsurpassed feat of committee-government, psychological tyranny and social engineering Calvin and his successors turned this confused and demoralised town into one of the proud centres of European culture.

Then, and for long afterwards, such a regeneration could only be accomplished on the basis of theological concepts, yet any attempt to summarise those of Calvin runs in danger of caricaturing some deep and subtle passages of thought. His predestinarian doctrine was the culmination of a long revival operative at least since the fourteenth century. He did not pursue it so far as some of his successors, and alongside it he composed some noble reflections on the loving kindness of God and the work of Christ the Redeemer. Nevertheless his development of this doctrine has always been taken as Calvin's chief legacy. He took over Luther's basic doctrines of the total sovereignty of God, the total corruption of man, Justification by Faith Alone, together with their corollary of each man's predestination to bliss or damnation by the sovereign will of God. This last teaching Calvin drove to that conclusion which St. Paul himself had hesitated to elaborate. By any standards he must be ranked among the greatest of biblical theologians, yet here he made some bold deductions falling well outside any direct statement in the Scriptures. Before the universe began, God had by his terrible purpose (*decretum horribile*) chosen some men for eternal salvation and others for eternal reprobation. In both cases God made the choice quite irrespective of their personal merits and demerits, which he could perfectly foresee. How satisfactorily Calvin reconciled this crushing omnipotence of God with the total responsibility of man for evil may be left to professional theologians to assess. He himself faces the task and frankly admits it cannot be accomplished by mere human intelligence. Yet once a devotee had learned to live with this baffling central antinomy, the rest of the system might well seem more intelligible, more consistent and more adult than those offered by timid thinkers unwilling (as most Christians are) to face the disturbing implications of divine omnipotence. Here was a coherent system which seemed to fill the aching void left when men abandoned the Catholic Church, a system which assuaged that dread of chaos ever besetting our sixteenth-century ancestors. Alongside it the Anglicanism of Cranmer tended to appear as little more than a *moyen de vivre*, that of Elizabeth at best a staging-post on the way to the City of God once and for all exemplified in Geneva. And if some lightly built minds despaired to find themselves caught up in God's machine, robuster ones developed an invincible certainty that they would pass perfected through its wheels.

So far from inducing fatalism, Calvinist doctrine instilled a burning desire to prove to oneself and others that one's name stood upon the roll of the elect. And how otherwise than by an alacrity to fight the good fight? Calvin did not personally advocate revolt, resistance and tyrannicide. His mission was not only to restore a spiritual dynamic to the Reformation but also to bring order into a world where Luther's message seemed in process of degenerating into subjectivism, individualism and licence. But ere long the chief danger was seen to come not from the Anabaptist sectaries but from the original enemy. The Roman Church had already begun to recover its inspiration and its influence. Protestants soon needed doctrines of resistance against political Catholicism and, whatever Calvin had said, they were swiftly guided to the necessary biblical texts. The time was not far distant when an equally political Calvinism would strengthen the arms of French Huguenots, Dutch Sea-beggars, Scots Covenanters and English Puritans. This muscular Calvinism saved the Reformation. In a sense it even served the cause of liberty, since so often it promoted national or regional self-determination. And much of its effectiveness sprang from something Geneva had given it—an essentially cellular organisation under which large numbers of men could retain a substantial unity of belief, while yet being trained to worship and fight in the small group. This in turn sprang from the success of the Genevan model in integrating a body of highly-trained pastors, teachers and deacons with committees of lay elders nominated by the city magistrates and exercising moral supervision over congregations. However intolerable to modern eyes, this control was based chiefly upon persuasion; excommunication and other forcible sanctions were used only as last resorts. The operative word in John Knox's description was 'school'. The system was less narrowly juridical, more personal, more pedagogic, than that of medieval discipline. It also allowed far greater scope for lay initiative. True, many of Calvin's adherents found themselves confronted by a harsh struggle, when later in the century they sought for example to convert the huge conservative areas of France, or even the most resistant districts of northern England. Nevertheless in more sophisticated communities and especially in the cities, Calvinism solved the ancient problem of anticlericalism, and not simply by demanding more of its clergy. At last the essence of the social revolution behind the Reformation was understood and a place found for the solid, pious, educated layman, who demanded a share in matters hitherto monopolised by bishops and kings. Whatever his doctrinal arrogance, Calvin showed himself more perceptive than Elizabeth and her successors in thus canalising and controlling that aspect of the Reformation which might be called the lay demand. In Elizabeth's England the retention of an old-style clerical hierarchy tended to limit the legal expression of this demand to the House of Commons and, by neglecting it at the lower levels, to produce a series of tensions which later almost destroyed the monarchy and the Anglican Church themselves.

Our glance at Calvinism has taken us far beyond the year 1547, and we are already in danger of antedating its importance. It is true that in the reign we are about to describe Calvin's influence already became manifest in England. He sent advice several times to Edward VI and to Protector Somerset, who both held him in high esteem. Sir John Cheke and Edward's French tutor Jean Bellemain were also among Calvin's correspondents, as were many of the foreign Protestant visitors, from the eminent Martin Bucer downward. The M.P. Bartholomew Traheron, keeper of Edward VI's library and tutor to the Duke of Suffolk, had been with Calvin in Geneva in 1546 and accepted his system. Again, in the writings of several leading English divines ample evidence of Calvinist doctrinal emphases can be observed, for example in those of the two future martyrs, John Bradford, chaplain to the King and canon of St Paul's, and John Philpot, archdeacon of Winchester.[2] Yet for many years to come most Englishmen saw Calvin merely as one of the greater stars among the Protestant galaxy. English divines still paid much regard to Johann Brenz, who had established Lutheranism in Württemberg, to Bucer of Strassburg, who was soon to end his days in England, and to Heinrich Bullinger, Zwingli's successor as chief pastor at Zürich, who in 1549 concluded with Calvin a treaty on the eucharist called the Zürich Agreement (*Consensus Tigurinus*). In so far as they depended on foreign inspiration, the popular pamphlets attacking the mass—and these became legion in 1547–49—mostly adopted a Zwinglian standpoint. But at least the new English trends were non-Lutheran and increasingly directed toward Switzerland, where after due inspection connoisseurs of religious landscapes tended to find that of Geneva especially fascinating. Yet Geneva was a city-state and England a national monarchy. It needed no genius to perceive that, for Englishmen, Calvinist ideas on church government and church-state relations would afford difficulties far greater than those attaching to predestinarian theology. Calvin had abolished the Lutheran pattern of erastianism and had related his church with his little state by links impossible to reproduce in the kingdom of England, impossible even when the Crown lay in the hands of a Protector or a clique of noblemen.

Protector Somerset

The subsequent phase of the English Reformation depended in large part upon the outcome of Hertford's plot to take charge of the nine-years-old King and to establish himself as Protector. The will of Henry VIII had given the Council no presiding officer and had intended its decision to be made by a majority vote of equals. The speed and audacity of the action whereby Hertford seized regal powers stands in strange contrast with his fumbling approach to the later crises of his career. All was made possible through the compliance of the two men who had been standing at Henry's elbow—Sir William Paget, since 1543 one of the Secretaries of State, and Sir Anthony Browne, Master of the Horse. The former was the son of a sergeant-at-mace of the City of London; later on he not only discovered blue blood in his veins but obtained a patent of nobility. He also discovered, when it became safe so to do, that he had been a keen Protestant in the early days at Cambridge. Yet his religion seems never to have been very fervent; rather may he be regarded as *par excellence* the lay civil servant and ambassador. On the other hand, Sir Anthony Browne favoured the old religion, even though he soon showed himself ready to subordinate its claims to those of the State. As recipient of Battle Abbey he stood prominent among the 'new monastics', and as an intimate friend of the King he had recently been appointed guardian to Edward and Mary. To him or to Denny—the story is told of both—had just fallen the unenviable task of breaking the news to his master that the hour of death was at hand.

Immediately before the end, and again an hour after it, Hertford and Paget paced the gallery outside the King's room in the Palace of Westminster. Their conversations ended with Paget's agreement to support the ambitions of the Earl, to keep the King's death secret for a few days and to publish only so much of the will as favoured their aims. Hertford then hastened to get possession of the young King at Hatfield. During his return journey on 30 January he met Browne at Enfield and persuaded him to back the plan of a Protectorate as most likely to ensure stable government. On the same day Hertford adopted the style 'we'; on 31 January he arrived with Edward at the Tower, published the news of Henry's death and assembled the Council. When Paget proposed that Hertford should be made Protector, the rest of the members seemed evenly divided on the essential matter of future religious policy. Cranmer, Hertford and Lisle backed Reformation; Tunstall, Wriothesley and Browne were Henrician Catholics. But with Gardiner excluded, Browne adhering to Hertford, Tunstall an elderly and never very forceful servant of the Crown, the only strong opposition came from Wriothesley. It was easily overborne, and by 5 March the Chancellor found himself removed from the Council. Throughout the month of February offices were showered upon the Earl, while on 12 March his patent as Protector gave him an authority only just short of royal. The official form of prayer spoke of him as 'caused by Providence to rule', and he soon ventured to address the King of France as 'brother'.[3]

This sudden restoration of quasi-monarchical government in the person of a mature, able and opinionated nobleman undoubtedly hastened the advance of the Reformation in England. Hertford was the first Protestant to enjoy independent control of the State. If he was not, as some historians have alleged, a 'rank Calvinist' at his accession, he soon established cordial contact with Calvin, who urged him to undertake forthwith a Reformation along Genevan lines. Yet he intended no Calvinist theocracy, and in accepting his leadership Archbishop Cranmer found himself manipulated by an erastianism at least as thoroughgoing as that which had dominated the previous reign. This situation became plain in the first of Hertford's ecclesiastical measures—the issue of fresh commissions to the bishops, making their offices tenable only at the pleasure of the Crown, and subject to their good conduct. When on 20 February Cranmer addressed Edward at the coronation, he too was not backward in asserting the divine right of kings or in denying theories of popular election and papal claims to deprive monarchs.[4] During the summer a visitation of the Church by royal commissioners temporarily inhibited the powers of the bishops; Thomas Cromwell's injunctions were reissued and enforced by the commissioners, who placed in the churches copies of Nicholas Udall's edition of the *Paraphrases* of Erasmus, and of the *Book of Homilies*, at last issued from the press.[5] While the latter taught Justification by Faith in terms much nearer to those of Luther than Anglican commentators have been willing to acknowledge, the former also advanced the cause of the Reformation, since Erasmus had made the gospel-story a vehicle for countless pointed allusions to the pride, pomp and contentiousness of the early sixteenth-century Church. The availability of the *Paraphrases* in the churches continued to be enforced under Elizabeth, and over the years its impact upon humble readers must have become significant. Alongside these official actions a certain amount of lawless image-breaking occurred in various towns, while a spate of unofficial publications, including irreverent attacks upon the mass, showed that Protestant extremism had fully realised the opportunities offered by the change of government. Gardiner and Bonner resisted the royal visitation, the former on the grounds that the injunctions lacked parliamentary sanction and that the King should not be heavily committed during his minority.

Both bishops were sent to the Fleet prison, where Bonner made a rapid submission but Gardiner maintained his defiance until released under a general pardon in January 1548. Meanwhile in the late August of 1547 Hertford, now Duke of Somerset, went north for his Scottish campaign, an episode made notable not merely by his victory at Pinkie but by his attempt to convert the Lowlands through the distribution of cartloads of Bibles. Ironically enough, this spectacular success contributed much to his ultimate failure, since it induced him to put the conquest of Scotland at the very top of his agenda: its huge cost and impracticability were soon to become manifest. He returned in October amid a blaze of glory, and in the following two months he passed an important group of government measures through the first Parliament of the reign.

Of these measures the most striking was the Act removing Henry's harsh additions to the old treason laws of Edward III, together with the Statute *De Haeretico Comburendo*, the Six Articles Act, all restrictions on printing, reading, teaching or expounding the Scriptures, and even the Act giving royal proclamations the force of law. Some attempt was made to placate Catholic and moderate Protestant opinion by a measure threatening irreverent speakers against the sacrament of the altar with fines and imprisonment, but the same Act ordered that communion should henceforth be administered to the laity under both kinds and should be denied to no one without lawful cause. The elaborate Henrician procedure of *congé d'élire* and letters missive for the election of bishops was swept away. Henceforth they were to be appointed by mere letters patent, their courts held in the King's name, and by implication their character as State officials displayed beyond all argument. This change, though destined to be short-lived, represented a resounding triumph for Marsilian and Cromwellian theory. The important Act confiscating chantries and other religious endowments also dates from the same revolutionary session of Parliament, and we shall shortly examine its effects.

This spate of legislation has not undeservedly been called a self-denying orgy on the part of Somerset's government.[6] It tended not merely to move faster than public opinion, but to ignore the hard facts of sixteenth-century political life. As events were to prove, the government was not yet strong enough to deprive itself of so many powers. The merits of liberalism are relative to a nation's social and political maturity, and Englishmen remained as yet incapable of the self-discipline demanded by so rapid a withdrawal of the late King's heavy hand. Yet at this stage Parliament, Convocation and public opinion made themselves Somerset's accomplices; everywhere an unmistakable mood of relaxation became apparent and the Duke proceeded to further enterprises in a spirit of overweening confidence.

The new ruler of England could boast many qualifications for his office.[7] Amongst his fellow noblemen he could claim the closest blood-relationship with King Edward. As a soldier he had succeeded in every operation to which he had been called. His presence was handsome, his moral reputation good, his adherence to Reformation principles sincere. He desired to win friends and to govern by consent; he was credited with a genuine sympathy for the hardships of the lower orders, and amongst them he enjoyed to the end a tenacious popularity. On the other hand he aroused little affection among his peers: to them he gave an impression of aloofness and arrogance which doubtless hastened his loss of influence and his catastrophic fall. Dr. Bush, more critical than Pollard and other previous biographers, has shown how deeply Somerset aspired to the final conquest of Scotland, an enterprise incompatible with any active endeavour to benefit the poor. He also doubled the use of proclamations and imposed severe punishments for relatively trivial offences. Nevertheless he disliked religious persecution, and the period of his rule saw less of it than any part of the Tudor age, possibly less than any comparable period before the Revolution of 1688. Yet in the event, he soon came to display an equally impressive array of handicaps, shortcomings and misconceptions. While he could claim political incentives to build up a private fortune, he grasped at money and spent it with unnecessary ostentation. Having inherited estates worth £2,400 a year, he had acquired since 1540 an additional income of over £2,000, while under Edward VI he was soon to achieve the splendid total of £7,400 in landed income, besides other official emoluments. Soon after his accession he began to build Somerset House, removing various episcopal buildings to clear the site and gathering his materials not merely from the former Clerkenwell Priory but also by demolishing the cloister of St. Paul's Cathedral and other ecclesiastical fabrics. He took a warm personal interest in the work, and John Knox lamented the fact that he preferred watching his masons to hearing sermons. This episode perhaps did as much as any to tarnish the image of the Reformation; for the first time, the scale of the operation and the prominence of its author enabled men to say that the greed of Protestant magnates exceeded even that of their conservative compeers.

Along with Somerset many noblemen and gentry more acquisitive and less idealistic had also mounted the chariot of the Reformation, and of these men two would have brought great hazards to a statesman far wiser than Somerset. One was that resolute intriguer John Dudley, formerly Lord Lisle and now become Earl of Warwick. The other was Somerset's own brother Thomas Seymour, whose harsh but not undeserved condemnation in March 1549 looked like a case of fratricide to those ignorant of his treacherous folly. To this quarrel a major contribution had already been made by Somerset's wife Anne Stanhope, who disputed with furious pride the precedence allowed to Thomas Seymour's wife, the former Queen Katherine Parr. Yet even had he been spared these family trials, Somerset could scarcely have survived, for he lacked the instinct, the wariness, the patience, the sense of timing which marks the true politician. There yawned a fatal gap between his admirable theories and their implementation in a difficult world. His own adherent Paget warned him concerning the folly of 'having so many irons in the fire'. Against a background of falling revenue he faced two major problems—agrarian unrest and the divergence of Scotland—either of which would have tested the resources of any statesman. But during the years 1547–9 he attempted not only to solve them together and in haste but to accompany the feat by new programmes of secularisation and liturgical reform. Even then he might have managed to survive, had he not in the summer of 1549 allowed Dudley control of the military forces to put down Kett's Revolt in Norfolk. This elementary blunder serves to illustrate the true weaknesses of his position and his equipment. In a society where overmighty subjects and their 'affinities' of lesser men were still threatening to restore the chaos of the fifteenth century, Somerset lacked that healing magic which lay only in the touch of a crowned king. He should have faced the fact squarely and picked up some cruder weapon. Might this not have been an enlarged version of that force of foreign mercenaries which fought so effectively against the rebels? Had such a force been kept under his personal command, it might have compensated for the want of an inherited authority; it could at least have enabled the Duke to overawe his rivals on the Council, for they in their turn could boast no securer hold upon the loyalties of the nation at large. At all events, faced by the instructive story of Protector Somerset, no historian can avoid the temptation to be wise after the event.

The Edwardian Dissolutions

So far as ordinary Englishmen were concerned, the most important measure of Edward's first Parliament was the one which assigned to the Crown all chantries, free chapels, colleges, hospitals, fraternities, guilds and similar institutions throughout England and Wales.[8] This return to the policy of secularisation can have surprised no one, since by an Act of 1545 Parliament had already allowed King Henry to appropriate these foundations during his lifetime.[9] This earlier Chantries Act had not denounced them on doctrinal grounds but had boldly stated that the money forthcoming from their dissolution was needed for the war against France and Scotland. The old King had already caused his commissioners to make a survey of the extensive properties involved and had actually seized a number of them.[10]

The new Chantries Act was legally necessitated by Henry's death, yet it also adopted a different and openly Protestant standpoint. According to its preamble, superstitious errors and ignorance of salvation through the death of Christ had been caused 'by devising and phantasying vain opinions of purgatory and masses satisfactory, to be done for them which be departed'. These false beliefs had been chiefly maintained by the abuse of chantries, but now these superstitious institutions could be put to good and godly uses 'as in erecting of grammar schools to the education of youth in virtue and godliness, the further augmenting of the universities, and better provision for the poor and needy'. The Act ostensibly gives the King not only religious institutions, but *all* guilds and fraternities, since the government was well aware that many of the more secular ones supported observances of a 'superstitious' nature. It may well be that some of the civilian lawyers actually envisaged a wholesale attack on corporations, which they detested as impugning the sovereignty of the State. But the government dared not touch the general funds of secular guilds and it merely levied a charge on such guilds, covering the funds they had hitherto devoted to 'superstitious' usages. Until its spokesmen explained this limited aim, severe opposition threatened to develop in the House of Commons. In pursuance of the Act new surveys were completed by the summer of 1548; they supplemented the Henrician surveys in that they paid less attention to the lands and properties but more to the characters of the incumbents and to the degree of usefulness claimed for the various foundations.

In the August of the same year Somerset appointed two special commissioners, Robert Kelway and Sir Walter Mildmay, to assign pensions to the dispossessed priests and to sanction the continuance of certain 'necessary' institutions. Mainly speaking, these last were the grammar schools attached to chantries and collegiate churches, and the endowments of chaplains in the outlying chapels of large parishes, which could not be dissolved without grave local inconvenience. Though many of the Henrician Surveys have been lost, most of the Edwardian documentation can still be studied at the Public Record Office. Considerable selections from this mass of documents have already been published,[11] and their voluminous character can be gathered from the fact that the Henrician and Edwardian Surveys for Yorkshire alone occupy over 550 pages of print.[12] The evaluation of all this material in terms of social and religious history represents a complex and often tedious task, which in many areas has been neglected or considered merely from the viewpoint of the local antiquarian.

The traditional figures concerning the various foundations have not yet been fully checked by modern research. Camden and other early historians reckoned 2,374 chantries and chapels, 90 colleges and 110 hospitals, but these estimates are based upon the *Valor Ecclesiasticus* of 1535, which, though valuable for the monasteries, omits numerous chantries and other minor institutions subsequently recorded in the Henrician and Edwardian Chantry Surveys.[13] Since even these latter are incomplete, accurate totals may prove impossible to achieve, but whatever the case Camden's figure for chantries will require a considerable increase. Dr. Kreider's valuable sampling of counties suggests that they were very unevenly distributed. While in wealthy London some 100 parishes contained more than 300 such minor foundations, about half the English rural parishes did not have any at all. On the other hand in the West Riding of Yorkshire they considerably outnumber the parishes, and the impression remains that in the conservative North the enthusiasm to found and to maintain had been greater than in many other areas.[14]

As will appear, the Edwardian government is no longer thought to have hastily and improvidently sold off the chantry lands at bargain prices. In any event the social effects of the Edwardian dissolution cannot be adequately measured in terms of the land-market and the revenues of the State. Chantries, endowed chapels, religious guilds and stipendiary priests bore a far closer relation to parish life and to the laity than did the monasteries. Unlike the latter they had in most cases been founded during the fourteenth and fifteenth centuries by merchants and gentry, whose descendants often took an active interest in their management. Despite the decline of the impulse to found chantries, a few had originated quite recently. Whereas the monastic estates had been overwhelmingly rural, a large part of the chantry properties lay in the towns. The multiplication of chantries may be regarded as an aspect of 'the rise of a middle class'; here the hard-headed, unsentimental businessmen of the later Middle Ages had given impressive witness to the Faith as understood in that period.

A chantry was essentially an endowment—usually in real estate—to provide masses for the souls of the founder and of others nominated by him. The incumbent who drew the stipend commonly said these masses at a particular altar in a cathedral, collegiate or parish church, but a separate chapel or other physical structure did not necessarily form part of the foundation. In regard to the underlying doctrines, we cannot accurately guess the extent to which Englishmen in the year 1547 continued to believe in purgatory, in 'satisfactory' masses and in other beliefs criticised by the Edwardian Act. If a man really believed that the ministrations of a chantry priest shortened the bitter years of purgatory for himself and his dearest departed relatives, then the Dissolution gave him great spiritual offence and became a matter for his passionate concern. That such ardent believers existed we can prove; that by this time they were very numerous, except probably among older people in the more conservative areas, we may well doubt. The evidence suggests that a marked decline of interest, a more secular and sceptical attitude, was beginning to manifest itself even before the rise of Protestant beliefs. A widespread decline in the number of intercessory foundations becomes evident after 1530. We shall see this decline exemplified in some routine transactions, yet it could also occur in unlikely places. In 1535 there were in Lincoln Cathedral 53 priests serving 36 foundations of this sort, yet in 1548, before the official dissolution had been accomplished, there remained only 17 priests serving 11 foundations.[15] However brutal its intrusion, the Edwardian government discovered here a world already in decay, a world sadly in need of control, reform and revitalising influences.

The Surveys prove beyond all doubt that the conversion of endowments to secular purposes, their 'resumption' by patrons, their outright embezzlement or forcible seizure, had become exceedingly common during the previous two decades. Yet it is fair to add that, throughout these years, rumours of impending confiscation by the government had encouraged such actions. One may even sympathise with the emotions of a squire who felt he had a better title than any government to the lands his grandfather had devoted to the support of a chantry. In the Suffolk Surveys,[16] for example, one Richard Sawyer had encroached on land belonging to a chantry at Mildenhall; the free chapels of Palgrave, Cowlinge, Lindsey and Ufford all had lay 'incumbents', who left the chaplaincies vacant and drew the stipends themselves; the Duchess of Norfolk's officials had removed the bell belonging to the free chapel in Long Melford parish, while the Duke had ten years ago seized certain copyhold lands hitherto devoted to maintaining a guild priest at Framlingham. Likewise in the Somerset Surveys[17] we read that at Ailston Sutton the chapel was utterly decayed; in Babcary parish, Foddington Chapel had fallen down and (not unnaturally) was noted to be 'clearly decayed'; at Congresbury, St. Michael's Chapel served for storing lime and the parishioners were offering to buy it; at Wiveliscombe the chapel was also used as a store, no mass having been said there for eight years. At Winford the chapel had actually been purchased by the parishioners nine years earlier, while at Yatton the people wanted to buy the old chapel 'to make therewith a sluice against the rage of the sea'. At Aller, Ashbrittle, Long Ashton, North Cadbury, Long Road, Pawlett, North Petherton and Wraxall, the rents of chantries, chapels and other foundations had been withheld from their true purposes upon one pretext or another. A free chapel in Clevedon parish had lacked any incumbent since about 1535; at Charlton Adam the chantry priest had drawn his stipend regularly but had said no masses for twenty or thirty years. And the foregoing Somerset instances of decay and expropriation are by no means all those revealed by the commissioners in this moderate-sized county. The supposed conservatism and simple piety of the Henrician North Country had imposed little more restraint, for the Yorkshire commissioners gave a formidable list of 're-sumptions' and embezzlements both by laymen and by clerics, a list too long to be recited here.[18]

Apart from personal greed, and from a desire to forestall the government, the prevalent spirit of utilitarianism also played its part. At Henbury, the Gloucestershire village lying between Bristol and the Severn, the rents and profits which had formerly supported a priest had been for some years devoted to repairing the riveside embankments, and the parishioners explained that sixty years earlier the river had here broken its banks, flooding the marsh and drowning no less than 220 of their predecessors.[19] When the Edwardian Chantries Act was being debated, a stern opposition arose—but on economic grounds—from the burgesses of Coventry and of Lynn, who were finally placated by Somerset's promises to restore the lands of their religious guilds. But the representatives of Lynn demonstrated that the income had already long been used to maintain the pier and sea-banks and to prevent inundation of the neighbouring countryside.[20] For a variety of economic reasons trade and manufacture had declined in several old cities like York and Coventry, which strove to secure the gift or cheap purchase of the extensive chantry properties within their walls. As early as 1536, over ten years before the Edwardian dissolution, the city council of York had staged a little dissolution of its own by special Act of Parliament empowering it to abolish nine chantries and various lesser endowments and so to relieve its embarrassed municipal finances.[21] Nevertheless, deliberate acts of secularisation had probably wrought less havoc than the common tendency of urban property to lose its value. In the two neighbouring Oxford parishes of St. Mary Magdalen and St. Michael's the chantry priests had been maintained by the rents of two breweries, one of which, said the commissioners, was *in magna ruina pro defectu reparacionis*, while the other had 'fallen in far decay', yielding only £2 6s. 8d. instead of its former £6 per annum.[22] Some minor endowments were even more insecurely based. At Nettlebed in Oxfordshire a widow named Ann Eaton had given a cow worth ten shillings to maintain a lamp before the altar, but when the Reformers abolished such lamps the old lady—no doubt in high dudgeon—withdrew the cow and died shortly afterwards. The unsympathetic commissioners nevertheless debited the parishioners of Nettlebed with the sum of ten shillings![23]

Quite apart from such minor anecdotes, we should flatter our medieval ancestors if we supposed that they had carefully and lovingly maintained all their religious and charitable institutions until these fell into greedy hands at the Reformation. The situation was in fact less simple. In Yorkshire at least ninety-four hospitals or almshouses are known to have existed at some time or other during the Middle Ages. But of these no less than fifty-five had vanished altogether before the year 1500, while a further seventeen had become in effect the property of a master or chaplain and no longer maintained any paupers. Of the remainder four had their surviving inmates pensioned off by the Edwardian commissioners, three disappeared about this time, possibly by actual dissolution, while fifteen continued intact, in some cases being strengthened by private re-endowment soon afterwards.[24]

In relation to the popular religion the functions of all these numerous and disparate foundations varied so greatly as to defy any simple generalisation. While chantry priests did not officially have cure of souls, they were often more than singers of masses for the dead. They had commonly been placed by their founders under the direction of the parish incumbent, and helped him with some of the parochial duties. At Doncaster, for example, there were no less than seven chantry priests, and together, so the commissioners were told, they could scarcely hear the confessions of the 2,000 communicants during Lent and then administer the sacraments in Holy Week, together with all the other business of the parish church.[25] Even so, the same number of parishioners at Sheffield had the services of only three stipendiary priests,[26] while in Crosthwaite parish, Cumberland, also with about 2,000 communicants, only one such priest had been provided.[27] Some at least of the masses said by chantry priests were attended by congregations. At Wakefield, Doncaster and Newark they were combined with the *missa pro itinerantibus*—the mass at four or five o'clock, frequented for example in these three places by the early-rising wool-traders on their way to Boston from the sheep-farms of Yorkshire. The chantry of St. Agnes in the parish of St. Denis, York, had been founded in 1424 by an alderman to provide a mass between eleven o'clock and noon, but subsequently the parishioners had brought it forward by seven hours, both for their own convenience and for that of travellers, who heard mass here on their way out of the city.[28] Needless to say, the spectacle often proves less inspiring. A considerable proportion of chantry priests belonged to the cathedrals; they swelled the already enormous contingent of cathedral clergy, had too little to do and had usually been organised in colleges in order to curb their former indiscipline. Often enough the uneven incidence of private charity had endowed small parishes while neglecting large ones. At Oxford, for example, the parish of St. Giles with only eighty communicants had an assistant priest; St.

Michael's another for 200, St. Ebbe's none for 363, while not many miles away the town of Thame had only one for 1,200.[29]

In terms of mid-Tudor prices most chantries were wretchedly endowed; their very existence helped to perpetuate and enlarge the self-selected, ill-educated lower strata of the clerical profession. Yet we need scarcely observe that such imperfections supplied arguments for reorganising and not for confiscating these useful or potentially useful endowments. The ministers of Edward VI committed at least two offences against the principles of logic and integrity. In their Chantries Act they spoke of converting the endowments to the needs of education and of the poor, yet they failed to found genuinely new grammar-schools and almshouses. Moreover, even if it be granted that a Protestant religion needed a far smaller clerical body, a large parish still demanded proper provision for one or more assistant priests. In some pressing cases such provision was made; in others it was not. The best that can be said of this unedifying transaction is that the government lay in desperate financial straits and that the merchants and gentry (whose reluctance to pay taxation had done much to produce the crisis) did in course of time accept their responsibilities, did found new schools and almshouses, did endow curacies in the parishes. In view of these complex circumstances, how far can we safely generalise concerning the religious and social results of the Edwardian dissolutions? While remembering that many individual institutions were hybrids, we need to take a careful glance at each basic type in turn.

The disappearance of the chantries must chiefly be viewed alongside the changes imposed by official religious policy. In so far as people ceased to believe in the doctrine of intercessory masses for souls in purgatory, chantries lost their main reason for existence. In so far as a minority persisted in this belief, the dissolution occasioned spiritual offence, yet there is not much evidence for any resistance movement in the form of private masses. The chantry priests themselves suffered no great hardship; in accordance with the Act of 1547 they were awarded pensions payable like those of ex-monks by the Court of Augmentations. Certain chantry foundations had also comprised grammar schools, and the dissolution hence takes a place in the history of English education. Teaching was not indeed the normal duty of a chantry priest; in Shropshire about six out of fifty such priests conducted schools, in Yorkshire about thirty out of 400.[30] With extremely few exceptions the chantry grammar schools were refounded as Edward VI grammar schools, and their masters were assigned salaries at the current rate and paid by the Augmentations. The real problem concerns the longer-term effects of this arrangement, since these salaries, tied to fixed amounts, declined in real value during an age of steady inflation. It has been argued that the pre-Reformation endowment in real property would, amid the general rise in rents, have provided a steadier basis. This contention would nevertheless seem arguable, since one has only to examine the Chantry Surveys themselves to see how often an endowment in urban rents could slump disastrously. When critics of the Edwardian dissolutions go beyond this point to speak of the whole Reformation period as one of decline for English schools, their mistake can be indicated with some precision.[31] In any area it is sufficient to compile a careful census of schools with their dates of foundation or first appearance in records. This has recently been done in the case of Yorkshire, then not an exceptionally rich or progressive area. In that county about forty-six grammar schools existed during the first half of the sixteenth century. Scarcely any of these collapsed as a result of the Chantries Act, and no fewer than sixty-eight new schools appear for the first time between 1545 and 1603.[32] Even so, Dr. Jo Ann Moran has in recent years greatly extended the documentary evidence arising from the whole diocese of York, which included Nottinghamshire and Yorkshire minus Richmondshire.[33] She also counted both grammar and elementary schools existing there *before* 1548, thus working from a much larger number of schools. From this material Dr. Moran deduced that the conventional picture of an educational expansion under the twin auspices of humanism and Protestantism must represent a distinct simplification. In the diocese of York the surge appears to have begun as early as 1500. More controversially, Dr. Moran attributes it mainly to the demand for more clergy. Yet there existed other and possibly stronger motives. Amid the rising mercantile and industrial development of such an area, we hear from still earlier dates of merchants writing 'bills in their own hands', sending letters and keeping accounts. Already before 1500 this world may well have constituted a prior claim in the eyes of many northern laymen who probably founded schools and sent their own sons there with business careers in mind.

Tudor Englishmen, Catholics and Protestants alike, were highly aware of the importance of education. Even the odious Sir Richard Rich ended in 1564 by founding Felsted School near his splendid Essex mansion. The educational idealism and practical beneficence of Reformers like Cranmer, Latimer, Archbishop Holgate, Thomas Lever, Walter Mildmay and Thomas Becon cannot be questioned. The last of these, though among the more tasteless Protestant bigots, was nevertheless the first Englishman to campaign for the establishment of girls' schools. 'It is expedient', he wrote, 'that by public authority schools for women children be erected and set up in every Christian commonwealth, and honest, safe, wise, discreet, sober, grave and learned matrons made rulers and mistresses of the same, and that honest and liberal stipends be appointed for the said schoolmistresses, which shall travail in the bringing up of young maids.'[34] These particular proposals went ahead of public opinion, yet no Protestant, no Elizabethan Anglican could claim to be logical if he failed to support the idea of universal education. This spate of new foundations and re-foundations came from men whose religion demanded at least an ability to read the Scriptures and the Prayer Book. The hapless ministers of Edward VI may well have done more harm than good to English schools, but the short period of their rule formed only a parenthesis in a very different story.

Of the other foundations threatened by the Chantries Acts the most essential to public worship were those chapels of ease and free chapels which did service for outlying portions of large parishes. They were especially important in the hill-country running from Derbyshire up to Cumberland.

Here there were parishes ten or twenty miles across, and each containing a dozen or more villages and hamlets. An extreme case was that of the huge parish of Whalley, 180 square miles in area, with some thirty townships and a population reckoned at ten thousand. It contained and needed fifteen chapels. In Lancashire as a whole about two-thirds of the churches were in law only chapels of mother-churches.[35] In many parts of England seasonal flooding separated communities from their main parish church. Of Wombwell chapel in Darfield parish the commissioners wrote, 'The necessity is that there is a water between the said church and the chapel, that the inhabitants there can by no means come to the said church at divers times.'[36] Again, some chapelries were held to their inferior status by legal anomalies, even though in all physical respects they resembled important parishes. Woodstock in Oxfordshire, a mere chapelry of Bladon, had some 360 communicants, over half the population of the parish, and enjoyed the services of three priests.[37] In a very different setting the port of Hull boasted in its church of the Holy Trinity the largest parish church in all England, yet this still remained a chapel of the rural parish of Hessle, some five miles outside the walls of the town. Thanks to stupid drafting the Chantries Act imperilled all endowed chapels, but even the ministers of Edward VI did not expect parishioners to swim torrents in order to escape excommunication, or the people of a leading port to manage without a church. Though the records of the commissioners for continuance are scattered and incomplete, they appear to have preserved nearly all the more essential chapels. In Oxfordshire, however, some undesirable dissolutions sprang from the surprising discretion allowed to the over-zealous deputy surveyor, John Maynard.[38] In East Yorkshire the surveyor John Bellow, probably guilty of peculation, was waging a venomous feud at this time with the local magnate Sir John Constable.[39] In Lancashire also the proceedings of the commissioners suggest corruption and involved gross inconsistency. No less than 25 chapels there were considered not to be exempt from the Act, and were sold off. In most cases they were nevertheless sold back to the parishioners for small sums and so continued in service.[40] Here and there affronts to local pride as well as to convenience may have aroused anger against the emissaries of the government. In the summer of 1549, while Kett's Revolt and the Western Rising were in full swing, a much smaller rising occurred around Ayton near Scarborough, during which the prominent chantry commissioner Matthew White and some of his associates were killed. These rebels seem to have had several grievances, yet it is noticeable that Ayton chapel had been dissolved in the previous year and the lead removed from its roof. Moreover, after the trouble had died down, the villagers combined to thatch the building and were still maintaining it by a self-imposed rate in the early seventeenth century.[41]

With regard to the hospitals or almshouses we have already seen that many medieval foundations had vanished long before the Reformation owing to neglect, declining revenues or perversion of the founders' intentions. The great majority of those still active in 1547 survived the Chantries Act, but often through the action of municipalities which, having bought or begged them from the Crown, thenceforward administered them on a municipal basis. Once again, the total was in due course augmented by a large number of Elizabethan and later almshouses. On the other hand, it can only have damaged the reputation of Protestantism whenever a Protestant government allowed any functioning almshouse to disappear, or to survive merely through local initiative, because it was in no sense a controversial institution. Concerning the parish fraternities, which we have already observed in their prosperous days, the chantry certificates tend to depict their final stage of decline, though some appear to have remained lively to the end. Here however the Edwardian government felt no sympathy since so many of them encouraged saint-worship, for example by maintaining candles at the altars of cathedrals and parish churches in honour of specified saints. Perhaps about half of them still helped their members in time of undeserved poverty, paid burial expenses or afforded some other rudimentary form of social insurance. In exceptional cases they had become centres of local factions. Their masters held positions of great social distinction, but did not always conduct their affairs in an atmosphere of old-world piety. About 1533 numerous witnesses testifed in the Star Chamber that two prominent aldermen of York, the former masters of the united guilds of St. Christopher and St. George, had not only been unconstitutionally elected but had embezzled substantial amounts of the funds. Amid further charges and counter-charges the quarrel was dragged into Chancery, into the Council in the North and even into the ecclesiastical court. An astonishing amount of foul linen was washed in public and the honour of another alderman's wife besmirched during a consequential suit for slander.[42] Such prominent guilds were often closely involved with municipal corporations. These York guilds had in fact helped to rebuild the magnificent Guildhall of York and possessed a share in its use. And when their end came in 1548–9, the city council, after protracted negotiations, managed to purchase their properties.[43]

The incidental activities of these associations were most varied. The remarkable York guild of Corpus Christi managed the famous Mystery Plays and also supervised a hospital. At Banbury that of Our Lady kept four priests who were regarded as necessary to minister to the 1,400 communicants. Among the non-controversial functions of certain guilds was the maintenance of schools, and here again the outcome of the dissolution proved on the whole reasonable.[44] At Ludlow the wealthy Palmers' guild, with a net annual income of £87, maintained a school; so did the Trinity guild at Chipping Norton, that of Our Lady at Burford, the three North Riding guilds at Pickering, Middleton and Northallerton.[45] Such schools survived under conditions similar to those of the chantry-schools. Perhaps the best-known of all our former guild-schools is that of Stratford-on-Avon, conducted until the dissolution by the guild of the Holy Cross, but in 1552 repurchased from the Crown and managed by the corporation. This recovery took place in good time—some dozen years before the birth of its most famous pupil.

Of the colleges and collegiate churches at least eighteen had already surrendered their properties to Henry VIII between 1541 and 1547, in the manner of the monasteries before them.[46] The wealth, organisation and social importance of such foundations varied immensely.[47] At one end of the scale were modest parish churches, administered by a corporate body of four or five priests; at the other end were the superb minsters of Ripon, Beverley and Southwell, having the prestige and some of the functions of regional sub-cathedrals in the immense diocese of York. In general, however, two types predominated. The first consisted of old foundations, many of them royal, each with a dean and a number of prebends financed from specified estates. Such, for example, were the churches of Westbury-on-Trym near Bristol, St. Mary's-in-the-Fields at Norwich, St. Mary's at Shrewsbury, St. Martin's-le-Grand in London, Wimborne Minster in Dorset and St. Mary Magdalene at Bridgnorth. Their prebends were very commonly regarded as the perquisites of successful administrators. All the prebends at St. Martin's-le-Grand and Bridgnorth were at the disposal of the Crown and went almost entirely to the King's clerks, especially to those of the Wardrobe. The other main type comprised the colleges of chantry priests founded by wealthy clerics and magnates during the fourteenth and fifteenth centuries. In many cases, like Cotterstock in Northamptonshire and Sibthorpe in Nottinghamshire, ordinary parish churches had been elevated to this status, with a master or provost and a body of chaplains exercising the parochial functions. Elsewhere, as at Wappenham, Northamptonshire, a collegiate chantry of several chaplains might be founded in a parish church, yet without legally appropriating the church itself to the new body. There were also colleges for cathedral chantry priests, as at York and Wells, and yet others in which educational purposes bulked large. Of the latter class a good example appears at Rotherham, where in 1480 Archbishop Thomas Rotherham had included in his establishment three schoolmasters—one for grammar, one for writing and a third for music. But of such foundations by far the most magnificent were the colleges of Eton and of St. Mary at Winchester, where the fame of the schools soon overshadowed that of the colleges themselves. In general, it may be said that the Edwardian changes did not interfere castastrophically with the educational and parochial work of these institutions. In such instances where the colleges suffered dissolution, the commissioners for continuance took action to secure the survival of the attached grammar schools. Likewise collegiate churches with pastoral functions did not cease to operate but merely reverted to the status (and the reduced staffing) of ordinary parish churches.

What effect did the Edwardian dissolutions exert upon the course of the English Reformation? Recent investigations have cast doubt upon W. K. Jordan's view that the Edwardian politicians wastefully sold off the vast majority of these acquisitions. In fact the Crown retained much of the property, and even when it did sell, the prices were generally realistic. Examining the fate of the Yorkshire and Nottinghamshire chantry lands, Dr. Kitching has estimated that no less than three-quarters of the income of 1548 was still being accounted for in the Augmentations at Michaelmas 1553.[48] If the fall of the monasteries may be thought to have occupied too much space in our Tudor histories, this second phase of destruction has certainly been permitted too little, for it impinged far more obviously and directly upon the spiritual and social life of the English people. The fall of religious houses hurt few people outside their walls, but now the ministers of Edward VI were operating upon a more sensitive area of the nation's anatomy. That some loss of social amenities did in fact occur may be proved from the cases of the more beneficent guilds, or from those relatively few instances where functioning schools and hospitals disappeared in the rush or were refounded after delays and difficulties. Thanks, however, to the policy of continuance and to energetic local action, such grievous cases of loss were far from numerous, while the claim that appreciable damage was done, even temporarily, to education seems dubious. Yet while the institutional and material losses should not be over-dramatised, they do not constitute the whole of the adverse balance. We have nowadays begun to take more interest in the psychological and religious aspects of Tudor social history, and with some confidence we may maintain that this revival of secularisation tended to lower the cohesion and morale of the nation. From the outset of the new reign gloomy prophets had quoted the text 'Woe be to thee, O land, whose King is a boy'. Now there had duly appeared factions among the rulers, inflation, plague, war and widespread agrarian unrest. Against this ominous background the sordid competition of all classes for a share in ecclesiastical spoils impugned the credit both of the government and of the religious principles which that government was claiming to promote by destroying 'superstitious' institutions.

Within two years of its apparent triumph the Reformation had begun to pay a heavy price for its involvement with coarse-grained and bankrupt politicians. It had indeed much to lose at this moment. We ignore much evidence if we suppose that in 1549 the nation was divided into two parties, one of ardent Catholics, another of ardent Protestants. On the contrary, there existed a large uncommitted element, cautious, waiting for a lead, but all too ready to be offended and disillusioned by the errors of profiteers and extremists. Tudor opinion was quick to detect the upstart and the self-seeker. Protestants who laid claim to a spiritual religion were vulnerable from many sides; they had perhaps less to fear from frontal attacks by their Catholic opponents than from the undermining influences of distaste and cynicism. Michael Sherbrook, who was rector of Wickersley near Rotherham throughout almost the whole of Elizabeth's reign, has left us certain memories from his youth which preserve something of this atmosphere.[49] His father had bought some properties of Roche Abbey and in later days told Michael he saw no reason to entertain grudges against the monks themselves. Yet the old man had added significantly, 'Might I not, as well as others, have some profit of the spoil of the Abbey? For I did see all would away; and therefore I did as others did.' Turning to the Edwardian dissolutions Sherbrook himself recalls seeing churchwardens selling off church goods at bargain prices, while a clandestine trade developed in old brasses and gravestones. The story even circulated that Thomas Bosvill, a Duchy of Lancaster official, had stolen the great bell from the steeple of

Laughton and carried it away in the night. Sherbrook also comments in scandalised terms on the dissolution of the College of Rotherham.

> The foundation whereof was not to make a malt-house, as it is now used: but it was to this end and purpose, that the master thereof should be a preacher, and to have three fellows within it; of the which fellows, one should freely teach a grammar school within the town for all that came to it: the second should teach freely a writing school, and the third a song school ... but so soon as the said house was dissolved, neither preacher nor schoolmaster was provided, but the town hired the schoolmaster for the school many years after, until they made unto the Queen's Majesty, and obtained £10 yearly toward the finding of the schoolmaster for the grammar school; which cost the town not a little before they could get it.[50]

These complaints Sherbrook accompanies by sarcastic comment on the insatiable demands of the politicians; and as an example of poetic justice he points to the impoverishment of the State at the very time when it was behaving most rapaciously toward the Church.

These comments, it is true, were made long after the event, and made by a stubborn believer in a mythical golden age before the Reformation, yet they help to recover the atmosphere of disillusion which beset the later years of Edward VI. Meanwhile people who persisted in Catholic doctrine reflected upon the work of destruction in more strictly religious terms. In the reign of Mary a petition was addressed to Cardinal Pole pleading for the restoration of the Trinity Hospital at Pontefract. The petitioner was John Hamerton, sub-controller of the Household to Henry VIII and Queen Mary, and a member of a West Riding family notable over a long period for its Catholic sympathies.

> My Lord [he pleads] we had in that town one abbey, two colleges, a house of friars preachers, one ancress, one hermit, four chantry priests, one guild priest. Of all these, the inhabitants of the town of Pomfret are neither relieved bodily nor ghostly. We have there left an unlearned vicar, which hireth two priests, for indeed he is not able to discharge the cure other ways, and I dare say the vicar's living is under forty marks. ... My suit to your noble Grace at this present is, most humbly to desire your Grace that you will have compassion of the great misery that this said town of Pomfret is fallen into, both bodily and ghostly since the godly foundations aforesaid hath been so amiss ordered and misused, and the holy sanctuaries of God so pitifully defiled and spoiled.[51]

Queen Elizabeth subsequently revived the almshouse, and an analysis of the situation at Pontefract might well suggest that Hamerton's petition gives the blackest view, at the most cheerless moment, of an unusually unfortunate town. Nevertheless, such a document doubtless represents the viewpoint of the large conservative element in English society during the years before people made physical and mental readjustments to the new order. To Catholic opinion the problem set by these legal confiscations did not seem primarily social and economic. Alongside the destruction of chantries, guilds and chapels, they witnessed the disappearance of a large clerical society from their midst, the silencing of masses, the rupture of both visible and spiritual ties, which over so many centuries had linked rude provincial men with the great world of the Faith. In taking an essentially religious view of these events, these Englishmen seem to the present writer to have had every justification. Whatever its interest for the social historian, the Edwardian dissolution exerted its profounder effects in the field of religion. In large part it proved destructive, for while it helped to debar a revival of Catholic devotion it clearly contained elements which injured the reputation of Protestantism. Nevertheless, it was in no small degree bound up with the constructive doctrinal and liturgical changes which we must now describe.

The First Prayer Book and the Rebellions

The triumph of Somerset freed Cranmer from conservative shackles, but the Archbishop, as cautious in his relative freedom as he had been compliant under Henry's tutelage, refrained from sponsoring any swift doctrinal and liturgical revolution. About January 1548 he circulated a questionnaire to the bishops, inviting their views on the nature of the mass and on the desirability of celebrating it in the English language. Concerning the latter problem the episcopate displayed a number of divergent opinions. Holgate of York showed himself strongly in favour of a vernacular service, while at the other extreme Bonner and Tunstall would allow of no more than a few English prayers 'for the instruction and stirring of the devotion of the people'[52] The immediate sequel to this enquiry was the *Order of Communion*, a brief pamphlet issued by royal proclamation on 8 March 1548 and appointed for use from the subsequent Easter. It paved the way toward an English prayer book by inserting into the Latin mass English prayers of preparation for communion. While continuing communion in both kinds of the laity, it said nothing clearly repugnant to Catholic sacramental doctrine.[53] It nevertheless encountered opposition among the clergy, who soon discovered that more radical experiments were following upon its heels. By May 1548 mass, matins and evensong, wholly in English, were being allowed in St. Paul's and in certain London churches. Here too, masses at which the priest alone communicated no longer appeared in the daily routine. Meanwhile, during the early months of the year, the Privy Council abolished the ceremonies of candles at Candlemas, ashes on Ash Wednesday, palms on Palm Sunday, creeping to the cross on Good Friday and the use of holy bread and water. The Council also decreed the abolition not merely of 'abused' images but of 'all the images remaining in any church or chapel.'

During the month of September a number of bishops and other divines of both parties assembled at Chertsey and at Windsor to decide upon 'a uniform order of prayer'.[54] Though mystery still surrounds their deliberations, they were evidently confronted with a draft of Cranmer's First Prayer Book and accorded it some sort of general assent. The Book was probably never submitted to a formal session of Convocation, though later official statements attempted to suggest the contrary.[55] When at last in mid-December it came to be openly debated in Parliament, the deep divisions among the bishops became manifest. The doctrine of the eucharist remained the central issue. Tunstall of Durham, Rugg of Norwich, Bonner of London, Heath of Worcester, Day of Chichester, Skip of Hereford and Thirlby of Westminster all continued to uphold transubstantiation, while Ridley of Rochester, Holbeach of Lincoln and Goodrich of Ely maintained in substance the teaching to which Ridley had recently converted Cranmer. The Primate's early interventions in the debate seem to have been marked by some confused thinking. Though he continued to agree substantially with Ridley's group, he was anxious to avoid a final breach with the conservatives. In addition, his views had been complicated for the moment by the arguments of the foreign theologians recently arrived in England.[56] Despite these polemics the new liturgy had passed through both houses of Parliament by 21 January 1549; it received the royal assent on 14 March and came into operation as the sole legal form of worship by Whit Sunday 9 June.

Though wholly in the English language, this Prayer Book remained a masterpiece of compromise, even of studied ambiguity. While it did not specifically deny Catholic doctrine, its ambiguous phrases were understood by its author in a Protestant sense and intended to enable Protestants to use it with a good conscience. In essentials it was a revision of the old Sarum Use, chiefly influenced by Quignon's Breviary, by the Lutheran Church Orders and by the *Consultatio* of Hermann von Wied, Archbishop of Cologne, the last work being itself a conservative attempt to combine medieval and Lutheran usages. For the first time in England all the rites required by clergy and people were now comprehended in one volume, while no formula was left in Latin, so that the people could understand the whole of the priest's rôle as well as their own. To a large extent the order of the Latin mass was retained, but with some changes carefully designed to remove the notions that each mass was a sacrifice supplementing the sacrifice of the Cross and that any change in the substance of the bread and wine took place at consecration. Cranmer and his associates made direct and independent reference to patristic opinions and were no longer reverent disciples of Wittenberg; they had apparently rejected the basic Lutheran concepts of a real presence and the ubiquity of Christ's glorified body. Again, apart from the words of Christ's institution, the Lutheran rite abolished the Canon— the long prayer containing the consecration of the bread and wine. In the Prayer Book, however, the Canon was kept in modified form, substituting for the idea of a placatory sacrifice what the Reformers considered the older emphasis upon a thanksgiving and a memorial-service. Here only one sacrifice is pleaded—that of Christ on the Cross, 'who made there (by his oblation once offered) a full, perfect, and sufficient sacrifice, oblation and satisfaction, for the sins of the whole world'. The moderate character of the

Book had one outcome most annoying to its author. From his apartment in the Tower Bishop Gardiner announced himself prepared to use it and claimed that its phraseology implied, if it did not specifically affirm, the doctrine of transubstantiation. This degree of latitude had certainly never been intended by the Primate.

To the common man the use of the English language must have seemed by far the strongest element of novelty. Taken merely as a spectacle the mass underwent little significant alteration; even the medieval vestments, alb and cope, survived. There also lingered various old-fashioned pieties frowned upon by all Protestants save the most conservative. The Canon still included a prayer for the dead, a commemoration of the Virgin Mary and other saints. Auricular confession was still sanctioned, though its use became a matter for the individual conscience. Anointing was omitted at confirmation but retained at baptism, while extreme unction could still be found in the service for the visitation of the sick. There is no evidence that contemporaries were over-awed by the literary excellence of the First Prayer Book. Yet as we now see it, Cranmer here attains a mature mastery of language, selection and arrangement. Whatever further changes the future might bring, the new Church was henceforth furnished with a devotional asset ranking second after the English Bible. One Anglican at least is prepared to admit that for him the Prayer Book sometimes seems a shade over-felicitous. Intoxicated by verbal beauty, the feeble spirit can find a barrier—or invent a sub-Christian cult—as readily as when confronted by images and incense. Idolatry is a term with wider connotations than the early Reformers supposed!

The concluding item of the Prayer Book has an independent historical interest and it survived into the 1662 book still widely used in the Church of England. It is entitled *Of ceremonies, why some should be abolished and some retained*. Here church ceremonies are seen as human inventions. Some, we are told, were devised with godly intent, but at length turned to vanity and superstition. Others arose directly from indiscreet devotion, from a 'zeal without knowledge'. Long tolerated, these developed into abuses, blinded the people and obscured the glory of God. They should be 'cut away and clean rejected'. Yet other ceremonies, though also of human origin, the Church of England intends to preserve, because they 'make for a decent order' and 'pertain to edification'. Considered in itself, the retention or omission of a ceremony is a small thing, yet the contemptuous breaking with 'a common order and discipline' must offend God. St. Paul wrote, 'Let all things be done among you in a seemly and due order'. Unauthorised individuals must therefore not presume to disrupt this order. Yet the minds of men are diverse. Some are so addicted to old customs, that the least departure becomes a crisis of conscience, while at the other extreme we see 'new fangled' people, who despise everything except recent innovations. In his day St. Augustine protested against the sheer number of ceremonies; but what would he have said had he witnessed their subsequent multiplication, which has confounded and darkened Christ's blessings? Unlike the law of Moses, Christ's gospel is not a ceremonial law 'to serve God in bondage to a shadow'. On the contrary, it is meant to be followed 'in freedom of spirit.' The message concludes with the argument that each nation should refrain from condemning the practices of other nations. Yet each should use such ceremonies as it thinks best to set forth God's glory and to bring its people to godly living without error, superstition or abuse. Written far better than this foregoing abbreviation, here is a thoughtful, reasoning, sensible document. It grasps the need for an ecclesiastical order based on compromise between extremes, and so admirably illustrates the ideals of the more conservative English Reformers. Obviously it forms a touching memorial to Thomas Cranmer and to those many Tudor Englishmen who understood the need of their nation for a *via media*. Yet does it not also convey a universal message, which a very large part of the human race in our own time has still to assimilate?

The first Edwardian Act of Uniformity, with its interestingly graduated penalties, was to form the model for its better-known Elizabethan successor. It begins with the plea that the variations between the medieval uses had caused offence and confusion—a mistaken or even disingenuous plea, since they had done so to a distinctly less extent than had the recent Protestant experiments. For refusal to use the new Prayer Book, for using other forms of worship or for 'depraving' it, a cleric became liable to lose the profit of one of his benefices for a year and to suffer six months' imprisonment. For a second such offence he would permanently lose all benefices and go to prison for a year. For a third offence life imprisonment would follow. Again, any person openly attacking the Book or procuring a cleric to use other forms of service would incur fines—£10 for the first offence, £20 for the second and loss of all goods for the third. On the other hand, no penal clause was directed against laymen absenting themselves from church, cognizance of this offence being still left to the church courts.

Though this Act was less harsh than that of the Six Articles, it proved in general severe enough to ensure compliance by the clergy, and the Prayer Book was utilised even by those priests who (like Robert Parkyn in Yorkshire) are known to have disliked its innovations. By far the most striking exception arose in the so-called Prayer Book Rebellion which raged in Devon and Cornwall from June to August 1549.[57] Secular motives, personal enmities, economic grievances all played a large part in this affair, yet one cannot doubt the presence of an authentic if indiscriminate religious conservatism, which was sedulously fostered by the numerous parish priests among the leadership. Richard Carew, the famous Elizabethan antiquary of Cornwall, relates how even the boys of Bodmin School divided themselves into two fighting factions, the Old Religion and the New, each under its captain. Their exploits (which included killing a calf by gunpowder) were ended by a general thrashing at the hands of the schoolmaster. Some of their elders were not noticeably more adult. In particular, the leaders of the revolt produced one of the least discriminating documents of the period. They demanded the restoration of the Six Articles; the Latin mass with communion in merely one kind for the laity, and this only at Easter; a ban on the English Bible, for otherwise the clergy could not confound the heretics;

the restoration of ashes and psalms; the use every Sunday of holy bread and water. The sacrament should be reserved and worshipped as before; those refusing should die as heretics. The rebels described the new Prayer Book as 'but like a Christmas game ... and so we Cornish men (whereof certain of us understand no English) utterly refuse this new English'. In his reply Cranmer could not resist the temptation to ask whether any more of them understood Latin. The issue concerning the papal Supremacy proved insignificant and the rebels merely sought a return to the days of King Henry 'of blessed memory'.

This manifesto has too often been accepted as typifying the attitude of simple Englishmen toward the Edwardian Reformation. Public opinion, even among the peasantry, proved in fact far from homogeneous throughout the several risings in the summer of 1549. Kett's revolt in Norfolk,[58] significantly from the first in the hands of laymen, produced a strongly anticlerical manifesto and, though essentially a revolt against enclosures, had a Protestant flavour in so far as it took notice of religious issues. The manifesto urges that priests should not be permitted to buy any more lands and that their present properties should be let to laymen; that priests unable to preach should be replaced; that all incumbents should reside in their benefices and not be gentlemen's chaplains; that all clergy with benefices worth ten pounds a year or more should teach poor children the catechism and primer; that tithes should be commuted for cash. Taking their cue from the quasi-Lutheran article of the German peasant-rebels of 1524–5, the Norfolk leaders propounded their famous demand, 'We pray that all bondmen may be made free, for God made all free with his precious blood-shedding.' Moreover, a Norwich incumbent daily used the new Prayer Book in the great public services held by the rebels on Mousehold Heath, while Matthew Parker, the local man with a distinguished future, preached to large congregations under the 'Oak of Reformation'. In short, this was not a revolt against the Protestant government, the policies of which it approved, but against the Norfolk gentry. It did not march on London but concentrated upon rectifying the regional situation.

Peasant opinion was usually malleable on non-agrarian issues. At this same time in Oxfordshire the local clergy were angered by the opinions enunciated at Oxford by the foreign Reformer Peter Martyr. They managed to call out a force of insurgents and several of them ended their lives dangling on ropes from their church-steeples at Deddington, Chipping Norton, Bloxham and other places. Even, however, within the conservative areas other groups diverged from the priest-peasant alliance. In Devon and Cornwall the seafaring population supported the new religion and a group of sailors saved Sir Walter Raleigh's father from the countrymen. The people of the towns also strongly tended to oppose the latter, Exeter independently withstanding a pertinacious seige of six weeks. The Yorkshire rioters of 1549, though encouraged by foolish prophecies, certainly opposed the Edwardian Reformation. Yet by far the most significant feature of this northern tumult was its utter inability to spread beyond a very small area along the boundaries of the North and East Ridings.[59] After the Pilgrimage of Grace prudential considerations outweighed doctrinal misgivings in the North Country.

Protestant Propaganda

The staunch but unreasoning conservatism of the Cornish peasantry was no more and no less typical of England than its direct antithesis—the torrent of Protestant writings which marked the rule of Somerset and in particular the year 1548. John Bale, who had fled to the Netherlands on the fall of his patron Cromwell, returned and wrote with undiminished vigour. Not a few of the humbler controversialists did their best to match him in bitterness of spirit and in the pungency with which they attacked the mass. A characteristic example appears in the verse-dialogue on the sacrament of the altar between the ploughman John Bon and a parson,[60] the former a sarcastic rationalist, the latter a reactionary clerical with a perverted idea of transubstantiation,

> And after that we consecrate very God and man,
> And turn the bread to flesh with five words we can.

Though operating for the most part through the London presses, the Reforming publicists were active in some other towns, notably in Ipswich.[61] The founder of this local group may have been the schoolmaster and physician Richard Argentine, an enthusiastic Reformer under Edward VI, a strong Catholic under Mary and a remorseful Anglican under Elizabeth. The printers connected with him were Anthony Scoloker, whose seven or eight Ipswich books include three translations made by Argentine from continental Protestant writings, and John Oswen, who produced at Ipswich in 1548 no fewer than ten books by Calvin, Oecolampadius, Melanchthon and other Reformers. Oswen then moved on to Worcester and there continued his propaganda. Two other Ipswich writers, Peter Moone and John Ramsey, composed for Oswen coarse attacks upon the Catholic clergy and upon transubstantiation. Ramsey's *Plaster for a Galled Horse* does not scruple to conjure up the picture of a 'godmaker' (his term for a priest) intimately fondling a whore before going to the altar to celebrate mass. Peter Moone headed a local company of players and like Bale represents that interesting connection between the infant national theatre and the Reformation. His rhymed *Treatise of Certain Things Abused* recalls the old proletarian anticlericalism as much as the more constructive emphases of the new theology:[62]

> This mass, as they [the priesthood] supposed, was alone sufficient
> To pacify God's wrath for our wretched misery.
> Free forgiveness of sins, being never so unpenitent,
> Might be received at the mass: this was their doctrine daily.

No small time were we blinded with such popish peltry,
Making us pay for the holy consecration.
Like thieves that were insatiate, they robbed soul and body,
Without the fear of God's Word, the light of our salvation.

. . . . .

Let us forsake all ceremonies that to Scripture be not consonant,
Traditions of forefathers wherein we have been led,
And with the lively Word of God let us now be conversant,
For therein shall we see with what baggage we were fed,
Wandering in the Pope's laws, forsaking Christ our head,
Heaping upon ourselves the more greater damnation.
Thus were traditions and ceremonies maintained in the stead
Of God's true and sincere Word, the light of our salvation.

That these raucous proto-puritans had their more persuasive aspects can scarcely be questioned. John Ramsey's other publication, *A Corosive*, is an earnest little evangelical tract which resists the temptation to turn aside and abuse the Catholics. In fact, by no means all the propaganda of these years consists of crude invective and intolerant satire. In this year, for example, Richard Tracy (son of the William Tracy associated with Tyndale and Frith) published two treatises soberly opposing transubstantiation by reference to pre-medieval traditions and taking a position nearer to Frith than to Luther.[63] Again, during the last years of Henry VIII and throughout the reign of Edward VI, Henry Brinklow, William Turner, dean of Wells, and several other Protestant publicists deplored the whole concept of juridical persecution; some of these men were liberal adiaphorists, while others took the view that spiritual error should be opposed only by spiritual weapons.[64]

The pamphleteers do not, of course, adequately represent the whole range of Protestant literature during the reign of Edward VI. In 1547 there appeared a first edition of nineteen metrical Psalms by Thomas Sternhold, a gentleman of the royal household who in 1543 had been under suspicion for Protestant views. In 1549, the year of Sternhold's death, the Suffolk clergyman John Hopkins published a larger selection of Psalms by Sternhold, along with some of his own versions. A third edition containing some forty-four Psalms appeared in 1557, by which time the English exiles in Geneva were publishing in their metrical Psalter some of these versions, supplemented by others of their own. The long-continued popularity of such trite and heavy verses has been attributed to the fact that Sternhold largely used the popular ballad-metre of *Chevy Chase*. At least for scrupulous bibliolaters, the metrical Psalms solved the problem of finding something easy to sing, which—unlike the *Te Deum* and Luther's hymns—could also pass as fully scriptural.[65]

Though the state of English poetry afforded a poor weapon to the Reformers, it was quite otherwise with English prose. Apart from Cranmer's work a host of Edwardian writings illustrates this important advantage. Nowhere may it be observed more clearly than in Hugh Latimer's famous

Sermon of the Plough, preached at St. Paul's on 18 January 1548. Medieval sermons, even those of John Fisher in the previous generation, cannot show anything to match this fusion of flexible language with deep feeling, both religious and humane. As we re-read these warm-hearted paragraphs, the early Tudor clerical tradition seems suddenly remote from us; we seem to have crossed a watershed into a new territory of the spirit. Latimer has little importance as a theologian, and if his message was primarily religious it concerned itself scarcely less with social morality. In his mind and in that of his friend and fellow-martyr John Bradford the notion of the Commonwealth has a deep religious connotation; it almost involves a species of Christian socialism. From the prison to which Queen Mary's advent consigned him Bradford cried, 'O this is a sin, dear Father, that I always have been a private man more than a commonwealth man; always I seek for mine own commodity, contemning that which maketh to the commodity of others.'

The reign of Edward VI forms the period within which Protestant intellectuals evaluated those problems of poverty and social tension so noticeable in England throughout the central decades of the sixteenth century. These problems sprang from many causes: the international inflation resulting from the influx of American silver, the debasement of English coinage, the steeply mounting costs of warfare, the trade-cycles and the widespread urban decline, the enclosures for sheep-farming, and the process of adjustment to the dissolution of monasteries and other foundations. The Edwardian preachers, administrators and writers who tried to analyse and amend this situation became known as 'commonwealth-men'. They represent more than a fashionable theme of discussion yet distinctly less than an integrated political party.[66] They were mostly liberal Protestants yet cautious social thinkers unaffected by the revolutionary spirit current among the continental sectarians. They circulated no agreed programme and their emphases differed. The most familiar names are those of moralists rather than economists, while many published too late to claim recognition as inspirers of the commission against enclosures appointed in the summer of 1548 by Protector Somerset. Before and after the rebellions of 1549 the two famous preachers, Hugh Latimer and Thomas Lever, championed the cause of the unprivileged while sternly condemning rebellion in all its forms. They attacked the graziers, enclosers and rent-raisers, regarding them not so much as oppressors of the destitute but rather as the predators who stopped honest yeomen from sending their abler sons to the universities and from marrying off their daughters. Lever in particular registered the obvious Protestant complaint: that most English people, though rescued from the 'darkness' of popery, had so far conspicuously failed to derive moral or social benefits from the Reformation. The need to expand literacy—and education in general—often occupied their minds. Lever in particular demanded more and better schools, which should be financed from the revenues of former church lands and from the profits amassed by the undeserving beneficiaries of the price-rise.

An intellectual protestant clergyman who must now be placed in this loose-knit group is William Turner, better known as 'the father of English botany' than as the author of persistent and savage attacks upon Bishop Gardiner. His Henrician and Marian periods of enforced continental exile were divided by the prosperous Edwardian years, when he served as physician to Protector Somerset and as Dean of Wells. As recently shown by Dr Whitney Jones, Turner's voluminous works demonstrate a clear sympathy with the political and social ideals of the 'commonwealth-men'.[67]

A less eminent figure but a more effective social propagandist was Robert Crowley,[68] the Oxford graduate who edited and printed that venerable document of English social democracy, The Vision of Piers Plowman. In 1551, when ordained deacon by Bishop Ridley, he was also described as a stationer of London. Crowley published his own views intensively for about three years before going into exile under Mary and eventually emerging as a strong Puritan partisan in the reign of Elizabeth. As a social critic he stood somewhat to the left of Latimer and Lever, maintaining that all men had equal rights to the fruits of the earth gained by their toil, working people being the 'natural' heirs to wealth. Yet as things stood, by means of rack-renting and inflationary valuations of property, covetous landlords had prevented poorer people from entering the land-market. While deprecating the use of force to recover popular manorial rights, Crowley agreed with the preachers concerning the undue expense of university education: he also joined in the time-honoured attacks upon idle clergymen, who appeared to contribute so little to the creation of a more equitable and prosperous society.

The commonwealth-man most closely associated with Somerset's anti-enclosure policy was John Hales, M.P. for Preston, a largely self-taught scholar who in 1548 converted St. John's Hospital at Coventry into a free school. Already in the summer of that year Hales played an energetic role as a commissioner for enclosures, while vainly attempting to push various acts through the Commons, mainly in order to improve supplies of meat and dairy-products. As Dr. Bush has maintained,[69] Somerset's support for Hales proved less than solid, since the Protector seemingly wanted to gain popular acclaim from such policies, but only so long as they did not impede the flow of money to the Scottish war. The Protestant convictions of Hales are transparent enough. On Mary's accession his property was confiscated and he remained abroad throughout the rest of the reign, participating in the internal controversies of the exiles.

Closely associated with William Cecil as secretary to Somerset, and later to the young King, Sir Thomas Smith certainly belongs to this company, if only as the real author of the Discourse of the Commonweal (c.1549), formerly attributed to Hales.[70] Smith was also a Protestant and by no means devoid of idealism, yet he shows a sharper awareness of economic processes and hard realities than the rest of the Edwardians. He refused to believe that human covetousness could be eradicated, or that any particular pressure-group held a monopoly of practical wisdom. He acknowledged that the government could give some modest encouragement to social reform, but doubted whether it could remove the material and moral obstacles by any elaborate code of propaganda and legislation. Smith did however consider that the restoration of the coinage would in itself bring favourable economic forces into play. After Elizabeth's accession his close friend Cecil worked along similarly prosaic lines, and with some measure of success.

Such figures as these—together with Sir Walter Mildmay, Sir John Cheke and the ecclesiastics Cranmer, Ridley, Hooper, Bradford, Parker and Scory—represent the more humane aspects of the Edwardian years.[71] And while they owed something to earlier denouncers of enclosures like Simon Fish and Henry Brinkelow, and indeed to the social criticism of Erasmus and More, they can as appropriately be related to Thomas Cromwell and to his publicists Clement Armstrong, William Marshall, Sir Richard Morison and Thomas Starkey, who not many years earlier had also sought to build a new social, educational and administrative system upon the ruins of the medieval Church and the old aristocracy. Cromwell himself used the terms 'commonwealth' and 'public weal' in the same sense as did his Edwardian successors, besides vividly displaying similar secular ideals in his Injunctions to the Clergy of 1536.[72] In short, alongside the grasping opportunists, the capacious Protestant bandwagon also contained some champions of social morality and common sense, who thought in terms of the nation's total structure, and who to this day help in some degree to exonerate the English Reformation from the charge of being governed by a mixture of religious naïveté and material greed. Above all, a state working toward a just, ordered and prosperous society begin to acquire a Christian role of its own, by no means dependant upon the Church. Here was a dim foreshadowing of nineteenth-century Christian socialism.

Perhaps the most characteristic of all Edwardian religious writers was Thomas Becon,[73] who while yet a boy had learned his Protestant zeal at Cambridge from Latimer and George Stafford. His writings reflect not a little of the former's engaging vitality. It was indeed the fortune of Protestantism during the years following More's death to recruit not only the hacks but most of the real literary talent in the religious field. Between 1541 and his death in 1567, Becon published some seventy devotional and controversial works, certain of which ran into so many editions as to claim places among the Tudor best-sellers. Deliberately he strained every nerve to reach the common man or at least the swiftly-growing class of *bourgeois* readers. 'In all my sermons and writings', he remarks, 'I have not attempted matters of high knowledge and far removed from the common sense and capacity of the people. ... To teach the people to know themselves and their salvation in the blood of Christ through faith, and to walk worthy of the kindness of God, leading a life agreeable to the same, hath only been the stop and work where-unto I have directed all my studies and travails both in preaching and in writing.' Yet Becon has in fair measure the weakness as well as the strength of his tribe. 'I have sought', he continues, 'in all my doings to offend none but to please the godly. And therefore have I ever used a temperate, moderate and quiet kind, both of preaching and of writing.' Here at least he deceived himself, for alongside the sweetness and the light are at least a few passages of invective which Bale himself might have envied. It exceeded the bounds of Christian quietness to call the Marian clergy who put away their wives 'filthy dogs', to construct elaborate parallels between Queen Mary and Jezebel, to compare Catholic priests with those of Baal, or to call Gardiner—

> that great wolf, whose face is like unto the face of a she-bear that is robbed of her young ones, whose eyes continually burn with the unquenchable flames of the deadly cockatrice, whose teeth are like to the venomous toshes of the ramping lion, whose mouth is full of cursed speaking and bitterness, whose tongue speaketh extreme blasphemies against thee and thy holy Anointed, whose lips are full of deadly poison, whose throat is an open sepulchre, whose breath foameth and bloweth out threatening and slaughter against the disciples of the Lord, whose heart without ceasing imagineth wickedness, whose hands have a delight to be imbrued with the blood of the saints, whose feet are swift to shed blood, whose whole man, both body and soul, go always up and down musing of mischief.

And if such diatribes may be explained by the cruelty of the Marian persecution, the same plea will not cover those crudely offensive, almost obscene, passages in *The Displaying of the Popish Mass*, which Becon wrote in exile toward the end of Mary's reign. In the spirit as in the flesh, 'total' war can lead good men into ugly courses.

It could scarcely have been expected that Somerset's optimistic liberalism would impose charity upon the controversialists. Even less did it avail to prevent private acts of iconoclasm and truculent outbursts by wandering preachers. In London people referred to the reserved sacrament as 'Jack in the Box', 'Round Robin' or in other opprobrious terms.[74] Under the year 1548 Robert Parkyn relates how on Rogation Day 'no procession was made about the fields, but cruel tyrants did cast down all crosses standing in open ways despitefully ... yea, and also the pixes hanging over the altars (wherein was remaining Christ's blessed body under form of bread) was despitefully cast away as things most abominable; and [heretics] did not pass of the blessed hosts therein contained, but vilainously despised them, uttering such words as it did abhor true Christian ears for to hear: but only that Christ's mercy is so much, it was marvel that the earth did not open and swallow up such vilainous persons, as it did Dathan and Abiron.'

Showing equal sincerity in the opposite cause, one of the gospellers has left us a vivid account of his exploits during the reign of Edward VI.[75] His incidental information on the religious factions in various towns of southern England is perhaps of greater interest than his personal biography. Thomas Hancock graduated B.A. at Oxford in 1532 and subsequently became curate of Amport in Hampshire. In 1546 he was suspended from sacerdotal functions for casting doubt on the sacrificial character of the mass, and in the following year preached at Christchurch, his native place, citing *John*, xvi, to prove that the host elevated by the priest could not be God, because God was invisible. 'Then you that do kneel unto it, pray to it, and honour it as God, do make an idol of it, and yourselves do commit most horrible idolatry.' The vicar, who was sitting opposite the pulpit, then interposed, 'Mr. Hancock, you have done well until now, and now have you played an ill cow's part, which, when she hath given a good mess of milk, overthroweth all with her foot, and so all is lost.' Having said this the vicar, though approving some of Hancock's views, stumped out of church in a rage. Hancock afterwards went on to Salisbury and, in a sermon before the diocesan chancellors of Winchester and Salisbury, not only inveighed against superstitious ceremonies but also 'against the idol of the altar, proving it to be an idol and no God by the first of St. John's Gospel' (i.e. *John*, i, 18: 'No man hath seen God at any time'). The mayor, Thomas Chafyn, with the recent legislation in mind, charged him with giving a nickname to the sacrament and would have jailed him instantly had not six honest men offered to stand surety for his appearance at the forthcoming assizes. Hancock obviously enjoyed much support from the substantial men of Salisbury. At the assizes a woollen-draper named Harry Dymoke assured the Lord Chief Justice 'that a hundred of them would be bound in an hundred pound for me; another said that a thousand of them would be bound in 1,000 pound for me'. At this the Lord Chief Justice taxed Hancock with causing an uproar and compelled him to find ten sureties of £10 each and also to sign a recognizance of £90 for his future conformity to the law. Undefeated, he rode immediately to interview the Protector himself at Syon, obtained an order to cancel the sureties, tracked the Lord Chief Justice to Southampton and flourished a letter to this effect. The Lord Chief Justice remarked that Southampton 'was a haven town, and that if I should teach such doctrine as I taught at Salisbury, the town would be divided, and so should it be a way or a gap for the enemy to enter in'. When Hancock nevertheless pressed for permission to enter the pulpit, the mayor of Southampton persuaded him to allow another preacher, one Griffith, to take his place. But this substitute, much to Hancock's joy, improved upon his original by openly reproaching the Lord Chief Justice for suffering images to remain in churches and the 'idol' to hang above the altars.

In the same year Hancock was called to minister at Poole in Dorset, at that time a wealthy town in favour with the government and ready to embrace God's Word: 'They were the first that in that part of England were called Protestants.' Nevertheless a Catholic faction remained, being led by Thomas White, a very rich and elderly merchant who had repeatedly served as mayor. When on All Saints Day Hancock refused to say the *dirige*, White and two other former mayors of Poole threatened to disembowel him in the church itself. Again he went up to interview Somerset and his secretary William Cecil, returning with 'another letter for my quietness in preaching of God's Word in the town of Poole.' Under this powerful protection he continued to minister there, until the advent of Mary forced him to flee the country with his wife and children. In Geneva they awaited better days. 'In the which city, I praise God, I did see my Lord God most purely and truly honoured, and sin most straitly punished: so it may be well called a holy city, a City of God.' In such minds was English Puritanism coming to birth.

The Fall of Somerset

This atmosphere of political, social and religious confusion did much to discredit Somerset and to bring about his fall in the autumn of 1549. By this stage he could number few friends among the governing classes. Every convinced Protestant was demanding a liturgy more radical than that of the First Prayer Book. The Catholics resented a continuing series of affronts. In September they saw Bishop Bonner tried and deprived by means of a commission erected by the Council and headed by Cranmer and Ridley. The charge followed upon Bonner's refusal to proclaim in a sermon the unfettered authority of an infant King, the implications being obvious enough. Yet the bishop skilfully strove to make it appear that his offence lay in his championship of transubstantiation.[76] Meanwhile, irrespective of their religious views, the gentry and the wealthier citizens of London detested Somerset's sympathy with the unprivileged orders of society and with such social liberals as Latimer and Hales. Landlords found concrete reasons for their distaste when they surveyed the damage inflicted upon their property during the revolts of the summer. Nevertheless, to achieve political change these malcontents needed a highly-placed leader, and in the last resort the fall of Somerset sprang in large part from the personal ambitions of the magnate to whom the Protector had with such consummate folly entrusted a large part of the armed forces. John Dudley, Earl of Warwick, permitted himself no sentimental loyalties, and by October every circumstance conspired to favour his intrigues with the other lords of the Council.

The crucial moment arrived when the Catholic politicians (the former Chancellor, Thomas Wriothesley, Earl of Southampton, the Earl of Arundel and Sir Richard Southwell) proved gullible enough to believe that Warwick would co-operate with them to reverse Somerset's Protestant policy. Even more surprisingly, Cranmer in effect took part with the plotters by first persuading the Protector to surrender and then by presiding at the Council meeting (14 October) which sent him to the Tower. These questionable steps cannot be justified by the plea that Cranmer foresaw Warwick's future championship of the Reformation, since people were at this moment anticipating the contrary. One must suppose that Cranmer took the obvious way to preserve political unity by backing the stronger group; perhaps he took it with real conviction when Somerset unwisely attempted to raise the common people.[77] An indulgent observer of his conduct might add that he had no means of preventing the coup, that he and Somerset could not have waged a successful civil war and that he did all in his power to obtain kindly treatment for the fallen Protector. At all events, for the time being Cranmer's luck held. At the end of the month it became evident that Warwick had decided to continue the Reformation and to oust his conservative backers. By February 1550 Wriothesley had been expelled from the Council, Southwell imprisoned in the Fleet and Arundel placed under house-arrest, while Gardiner and Bonner remained in the Tower. Somerset himself was liberated on 6 February. Having resumed his office of Lord Admiral, Warwick became President of the Council and proceeded to distribute the spoils to his adherents. Lord Russell obtained the earldom of Bedford, William Paulet, Lord St. John, that of Wiltshire, and Paget a barony. Meanwhile the Protestants in their joyous relief were proving themselves even poorer judges of character than Warwick's Catholic dupes.[78] The political theorist John Ponet, later Bishop of Rochester and of Winchester, compared the Earl with Alcibiades. More conventionally, Bale selected Moses for that honour. John Hooper, soon to receive the See of Gloucester, hailed the new ruler as a 'faithful and intrepid soldier of Christ', 'a most holy and fearless instrument of the word of God'. The succeeding years were indeed to be marked by a strange alliance between Hooper, 'the father of English Nonconformity', and one of the less attractive political supporters of the English Reformation.

11 The Reformation under Northumberland

Northumberland's Position

During the uneasy years of his power Warwick (who made himself Duke of Northumberland in October 1551) faced a series of interlocking problems which could not be solved by mere ruthlessness.[1] Financial embarrassment has been a common fate of English governments but few if any have experienced it more acutely than his. He could reject continental ambitions, allowing the prestige of England to reach an abysmal level. He could not, however, avoid making handsome grants to his greedy supporters or expensively underpinning his rule by what amounted to a standing army under the newly-invented lords lieutenants. Any recourse to heavier direct taxation threatened special difficulties, since the less legitimate and popular a governor, the less dare he face Parliament with demands for subsidies. In 1551 the Duke resorted to a further debasement of the coinage and followed this by a device of remarkable crudity. Having met some of its liabilities with the debased shillings the government then depreciated their value to ninepence, later to sixpence, demanding payment from its own unfortunate debtors in the deflated currency.

Upon a problem of this magnitude such church property as could still be seized made little impression. Even the hitherto buoyant Court of Augmentations defaulted for a time on its payments; many monks and chantry priests faced arrears of six to eighteen months on their pensions. The chantry lands continued to be sold off, and Cranmer offended Northumberland by suggesting that the remainder should henceforth be kept until the King's coming of age. From the viewpoint of the politicians this idealism was no more helpful than Latimer's magnificent denunciations of human covetousness, or the conviction amongst Catholics that death and plague sprang from divine wrath against an apostate nation.

Not long after Somerset's release from the Tower it became evident that he might recover a big following in Parliament. His agent Richard Whalley busily canvassed support for a plan to denounce the inefficiency of the government during the next session and therefore to restore Somerset to his protectorate. These activities formed the basis for the charges of treason levelled against the former Protector during the autumn of 1551 and, though Somerset had not advanced his ambitions with any ardour, his fate was sealed by the demonstrations of popularity accompanying his trial in the December. He was pronounced guilty of felony (though not of treason) and Northumberland needed to act quickly in order to dispose of him before the meeting of Parliament called for 23 January 1552. The method employed was effective rather than subtle. By altering the phraseology of an instruction by the young King to the Council, Northumberland converted an order for the trial of Somerset's confederates into an order for Somerset's execution. When this event was staged the very day before Parliament met, the fallen statesman behaved with great resignation and dignity. By now he had wearied of the long contention. It so happened that a panic beset the crowd, but he disdained to take what witnesses thought an easy chance of escape.

Like Northumberland's later attempt to confer the crown upon his own daughter-in-law Jane, the judicial murder of Somerset reveals the desperate streak in the policy and character of King Edward's second overseer. His problems should nevertheless entail a certain small measure of sympathy, and not solely in regard to the financial crisis caused by Somerset's enterprises. Northumberland could not seek to govern without the Council, since he had to retain the loyalty of his fellow-magnates. Again, his Protestantism may possibly indicate some personal conviction, but it was anyhow necessitated in order to manipulate the sincerely Protestant King. Should that manipulation fail, Northumberland was doomed. On the other hand his widespread unpopularity at Edward's death was destined to contribute much to the alienation of those Protestants who could foresee Mary's Catholic reaction, and yet transferred their allegiance to her as the legitimate heir.[2]

Foreign Influences and Sectarian Groups

In this atmosphere, darkening still further as the sweating-sickness succeeded the plague, the advances of the Reformation were bound to prove insecure and ambivalent, yet the self-centred intrigues of Northumberland did not exclude certain positive developments. Among the more interesting of these was the rising influence of foreign theologians and continental religious movements. For some time Archbishop Cranmer had been attempting to link England with international Protestantism by consulting with governments and scholars abroad.[3] His friendship with Osiander, his marriage, his many contacts with foreign Reformers, all disposed him to this end. The men he befriended display in their life-stories almost the whole range of European religious politics, yet amongst them one grievous omission remained. Cranmer failed to persuade Melanchthon or any other representative leader of the Lutherans to visit England. Though henceforth foreign influences upon the English Reformation steadily increased, they came not from Wittenberg but from Strassburg, Zürich and Geneva. The Saxon Reformers, having gained their local objectives, left the leadership of international Protestantism to others, and their renunciation has an especial importance in the history of English religion.

Even before the end of 1547 the two Italians Pietro Martire Vermigli (Peter Martyr) and Bernardino Ochino had come to England after spending a period in Strassburg, now a major focus of Reformation thought. Having first received a government pension Martyr became in 1548 Regius Professor at Oxford, where a Protestant party soon developed but where people could still be startled when he took his wife, a former nun, to live with him in Christ Church. Ochino, once a Capuchin and a favourite preacher of Charles V, had been led into the new beliefs by Martyr and had ministered to the Italian protestants in Augsburg. For him Cranmer secured a prebend at Canterbury, where he wrote busily against Rome and even against Calvin. Meanwhile the Emperor had begun more actively to encourage an exodus from those territories where his writ ran. Following up his victory at Mühlberg he imposed from May 1548 the Interim of Augsburg, an alleged compromise which could not in fact be accepted by any convinced Protestant since, while it granted clerical marriage and communion for the laity in both kinds, it retained transubstantiation, saint-worship, the seven sacraments and Catholic ceremonial in general. Over 400 Protestant clergy are said to have left southern Germany at this time. Yet the more eminent of the newcomers were not passive refugees; they soon showed themselves curious to observe and eager to influence the situation in this hitherto little-known island. In 1548 Cranmer also received Francisco de Encinas (Dryander), a Spanish nobleman who had for some time occupied a position to the left of centre among the Lutherans. In the autumn of the same year there appeared John à Lasco, the son of a Polish squire, an old friend of Erasmus, a former archdeacon of Warsaw and latterly living at Emden as superintendent of the Reformed churches of Friesland. This divine held advanced Zwinglian and Calvinist views; he had contacted Cranmer and influenced Hooper even before his first brief visit to England in 1548. Returning in 1550 he was named as superintendent over the four other ministers in the charter which granted the foreign Protestants in London the use of the Austin Friars,[4] on which site their successors of the 'Dutch Church' still worship.

By far the most distinguished of the newcomers was Martin Bucer,[5] who already stood among the acknowledged patriarchs of the continental Reformation. Beginning his career as a Dominican and an admirer of Erasmus he had in 1518 been won over by Luther, had secured a papal dispensation from his monastic vows, had married in 1522, and the following year had come to Strassburg. Here Matthew Zell and Wolfgang Capito had already initiated a Reformation, but ere long they accepted the newcomer as their leader. Under his guidance Strassburg became not only an eminent school of biblical studies but the great haven of the needy, the oppressed and the religious refugees from Calvin downwards. In sacramental and other doctrines Bucer developed independently of Luther, yet he was among the least arrogant of Reformers, believing that outside the primary beliefs there were many points on which differences of view remained inevitable and perfectly tolerable. It was he who wrote those rare and refreshing words: 'Flee formulae, bear with the weak. While all faith is placed in Christ, the thing is safe. It is not given for all to see the same thing at the same time.'[6] He was also a bold, but a thoughtful and creative liturgist.

After Zwingli's death Bucer became pre-eminent among the leaders of the Reformed churches in Switzerland and south Germany, placing Strassburg alongside Wittenberg and Geneva as the third centre of the international movement. During the three years of Calvin's exclusion from Geneva, he had used his opportunities to form a close friendship with the great Frenchman, and his influence became noticeable in the 1539 edition of Calvin's *Institutes*. When Charles V imposed his Interim upon Strassburg, it was time for Bucer to go; despite his failing health he adventurously accepted the most arduous of many invitations and accompanied by his friend the Hebraist Paul Fagius he slowly made his way toward England. This was the man whom Cranmer received with great honour at Lambeth in April 1549 and who by the end of the year occupied the Regius chair at Cambridge. There he completed his treatise *De Regno Christi*, at once a retrospect and a forerunner of Puritan idealism. Though his conservatism disappointed the most radical Reformers at Cambridge, his presence sealed the triumph of Protestantism in that important focus of theological ideas. Cranmer, finding his view of the eucharist especially congenial, consulted him often and allowed him an important share in drafting the Ordinal of March 1550. As will appear, Bucer's part in the framing of the Second Edwardian Prayer Book also proved appreciable, and but for his death in February 1551 this verbose, earnest but singularly charitable German divine might well have prompted a more effective *rapprochement* toward the continental schools. In the very last months of his life Bucer was apparently brought by Peter Martyr to the Zwinglian standpoint on the eucharist, yet his influence upon Cranmer did not belong to this phase. Interred with every mark of honour in Great St. Mary's his body lay there for six years until the Marian authorities exhumed and burned it—along with that of Fagius and a cart-load of books—upon Market Hill. But in 1560 the university restored the pair to honour in a solemn ceremony, the public orator remarking that 'whereas in every singular place was executed a singular kind of cruelty, ... this was proper or peculiar to Cambridge, to exercise the cruelty upon the dead, which in other places was extended but to the quick'.

Paul Fagius, a former professor of Hebrew at Strassburg and Heidelberg, had died soon after his arrival and appointment as reader in that subject at Cambridge. There he was succeeded in office by John Immanuel Tremellius, by birth a Jew of Lucca but converted by Reginald Pole. Already a protégé of Cranmer at Lambeth in 1547, he was styled 'King's reader of Hebrew' in 1549; he also derived emoluments from a Carlisle prebend before the accession of Mary brought about his return to the continent. As a Calvinist he was to fall foul more than once of Lutheran rulers, but he managed to revisit England early in Elizabeth's reign. The Calvinist element among the refugees was also represented by Valérand Poullain, who had followed Calvin as minister to the French congregation at Strassburg. After a brief visit Poullain returned to superintend a colony of Flemish weavers planted by Protector Somerset amid the ruins of Glastonbury Abbey, and in Mary's reign he became closely involved in the affairs of English Protestant refugees at Frankfurt. Another foreigner of some importance between 1548 and 1553 was the Fleming John Utenhove, who took a prominent part in the Glastonbury colony, co-operated with à Lasco in organising the congregations of foreign refugees and became 'first elder' of the Foreigners' Church at the Austin Friars.[7]

Within the category of immigrant divines we may also place John Knox[8], since both in Edwardian England and amongst the exiles from Mary's persecution he influenced the course of the English Reformation years before he began to dominate its Scottish counterpart. The circumstances which preceded his appearance have a melodramatic character. Though he had studied at either St. Andrews or Glasgow and had accepted orders, Knox does not appear to have exercised clerical functions or to have begun his intensive study of the Scriptures until about the time of his association with his forerunner George Wishart. The latter is often classed as a Lutheran, but he imported into his country some of the advanced ideas of the Swiss Reformers and translated the *First Helvetic Confession* into Scots. He also preceded Knox in setting the tenor of uncompromising zeal and measureless invective which came to mark the Scottish Reformers. Pursued as a heretic by Cardinal Beaton, Wishart received shelter in 1545 from certain Lothian gentlemen who were then employing Knox as tutor to their sons. Shortly before Wishart's arrest Knox had accompanied him on a preaching visit to Haddington, bearing a 'twa-handed sweard, which commonly was caryed with the said Maister George'. The burning of Wishart on 1 March 1546 was followed on 29 May by the murder of Beaton at the hands of Wishart's admirers, who took refuge in the castle of St. Andrews. Knox's patrons induced him to join the besieged party, now headed by the ex-Dominican John Rough, the deprived Secretary of State Henry Balnaves and the poet Sir David Lyndsay. These leaders soon perceived the magnetic character of Knox's preaching and formally urged him to assume the ministry. Demurring at first, he succumbed to an emotional appeal made by John Rough in a sermon. The congregation expressed its approval and for the first time in Scotland asserted the claim of a congregation to select its own spiritual leader. This was the significant pattern deriving from the Reformed religion of democratic Switzerland, not from its Evangelical rival in prince-ridden Germany.

At the end of July 1547 the French Queen Regent of Scotland captured St. Andrews with the aid of a fleet of French galleys. In breach of the surrender terms the defenders were not only transported to France but indefinitely detained. Knox himself remained on his galley, which presently returned to Scotland, but he did not recover his liberty until early in 1549, when the English government interceded on his behalf and gained his services. In April the Privy Council started paying him a regular salary as preacher at Berwick, where he lived for nearly two years and attracted large congregations. Cited by Bishop Tunstall before the Council in the North for his attacks on the mass, Knox replied in the form of a syllogism: 'All service invented by the brain of man in the religion of God, without his express command, is idolatry. The mass is invented by the brain of man without the command of God; therefore it is idolatry.' Tunstall soon became powerless and no further steps were taken to silence the Scot. At the end of 1550 he removed to Newcastle to serve as preacher at the church of St. Nicholas. Though with his usual boldness he denounced the execution of Somerset, Northumberland saw his value and retained his services.

John Knox was not in fact the only Scottish Reformer to transfer his activities to England. At these same northern places he had been preceded by his friend John Rough, who had earlier been receiving a large annual pension from Henry VIII for promoting English interests in Scotland. While escaping Knox's harsh experiences, Rough had been constrained to take refuge in England soon after the battle of Pinkie. After an interview Somerset had continued his pension and sent him to preach at Carlisle, Berwick and Newcastle. In due course Rough met Archbishop Holgate, who found him a stipend at Hull, where he seems to have founded the strongly Protestant tradition which later marked that port. The popular success of these preachers in northern England, where Scotsmen in general remained so unpopular, gives a striking example of the hunger for religious instruction which existed in that sermon-starved society. Late in Edward's reign the future martyrs John Bradford and George Marsh were preaching with success in the populous towns of south Lancashire. Robert Ferrar had found this hunger in earlier years, while the careers of Bernard Gilpin and Edmund Bunney, the northern apostles of the subsequent decades, were to prove its continued intensity. In 1551 the government planned to exploit this fluid situation in the conservative provinces by appointing six itinerant ministers to tour in rotation Lancashire, Yorkshire, the Borders, Wales, Devon and Hampshire. Yet this scheme had little time to bear fruit, while the Elizabethan government was to revive it belatedly and half-heartedly.[9]

The lesser foreign immigrants were mainly poor fugitives from persecution in France and the Netherlands. With their advent arose the longstanding and honourable tradition whereby England, to her great mental enrichment, has admitted so many refugees from foreign oppression. At this time over 5,000 of them are said to have settled in London alone. To their congregations Cranmer assigned a high degree of autonomy, despite the less liberal views of Ridley, who doubted the wisdom of licensing wholesale contraventions of the Act of Uniformity. It was also Cranmer who planned to call an international congress of Protestants and in March 1552 sounded Calvin, Bullinger and Melanchthon. More dogmatic than the English Primate, these eminent leaders sensed the depth of Protestant differences, especially on the important matter of the eucharist, and they soon displayed a lack of enthusiasm fatal to the project.

A less attractive side of Cranmer's outlook may be observed in his asperity toward a very different movement of foreign origin—that of the Anabaptist sects,[10] which during the last three decades had spread so portentously through Switzerland, central and eastern Europe and the Netherlands. Today many aspects of this movement are receiving far more sympathetic treatment than in the past. The Anabaptists may be placed among the pioneers of the liberalising process in western history, while the abominable severity with which thousands of their harmless members were hounded to death forms one of the darker chapters in the history of continental persecution. On the other hand, it might with equal reason be contended that the early excesses of Anabaptism retarded the growth of religious liberty. The most infuriating aspect of the movement lay in its inclusion of so many disparate and inconsistent groups, incapable of formulating any common policy. So-called Anabaptists can be found to represent Arianism, Socinianism, Pelagianism, Manichaeism, Docetism, Millenarianism, mysticism and communism. Their varied programmes embrace almost every imaginable reform from pacifism to polygamy. Undoubtedly a few of them entertained the antinomian perversion of the text 'To the pure all things are pure'. They almost all rejected the baptism of infants, believing that the rite should be administered only on profession of faith. Even more offensively to contemporaries, some of them denied the Incarnation on the ground that if Christ had derived flesh from the Virgin he would have shared the sinfulness of human nature. Neither the prophetic demand for spiritual liberty made by the continental Anabaptist 'prophets' and writers, nor the heartfelt piety discoverable among their followers should blind us to the fearsome problems which they presented to the more moderate protagonists of Reformation.

Since the origins of Lollardy, the progress of Reforming beliefs had always been hampered by the suspicion that they might also involve anarchy or social revolution. Medieval and Tudor men were social pessimists with little trust in the resilience of human organisation. Especially since its alarming excesses under the mad John of Leyden at Münster in 1533–5, Anabaptism had confirmed the fear of many cautious people, especially those of the landed, *bourgeois* and clerical classes, that all changes in belief threatened the dislocation of ordered secular society. The English rebellions of the thirties and forties had owed nothing to extremist religions, yet they had heightened this general obsession with the problem of social order, and by 1549 it needed only Anabaptism to supply Catholics and uncommitted people with some formidable arguments against Protestantism in general. Faced by this menace even the gentle Cranmer was anxious to prove his respectability by denouncing Anabaptism more fiercely than he denounced Romanism. Today we find it logical that the moderate Protestants should have granted that same measure of toleration to the radical sects which they demanded for themselves. Yet with a few exceptions they lacked this logic, and they failed to discard the concept of punishable heresy. They also overestimated the strength of sectarianism and feared that by sparing it they would risk a repetition of the horrors which had attended the Kingdom of the Saints in Münster, when King John took sixteen wives and beheaded one of them in the presence of the others for saucily criticising his rule.[11]

In May–June 1535 some twenty-five Dutch Anabaptists were tried at St. Paul's and fourteen of them burned in London and other towns. The King excepted such foreign offenders from his general pardons and a few more went to the stake in 1538 and 1540. In the early stages these heretics seem all, or almost all, to have been Netherlandish or German immigrants, keeping in close touch with their continental brethren. By the reign of Edward VI a number of native converts were joining their ranks in Kent and Essex. In June 1549 Hooper writes to Bullinger that the Anabaptists are flocking to his London lectures, 'and give me much trouble with their opinions respecting the Incarnation of our Lord; for they deny altogether that Christ was born of the Virgin Mary according to the flesh. They contend that a man who is reconciled to God is without sin, and free from all stain of concupiscence, and that nothing of the old Adam remains in his nature; and a man, they say, who is thus regenerate cannot sin.' After retailing further heresies he concludes that, what with these people and the 'great proportion of the kingdom' which 'adheres to the popish faction', he greatly fears rebellion and civil discord. In the course of that year Hooper even wrote a treatise to disprove Anabaptist doctrines of the Incarnation,[12] while with similar objects works by Calvin and Bullinger were published in English translation.[13] In the April of that year Joan Bocher, alias Joan of Kent, underwent condemnation for denying that Christ was incarnate of the Virgin Mary. This remarkable woman was perhaps the wife of the London butcher Thombe, who abjured the same Melchiorite Anabaptist heresy.[14] A former seller of Tyndale's Testament, Joan had also known and venerated the martyr Anne Askew, who was not an Anabaptist. While her associates recanted, she remained defiant and after many delays suffered burning in May 1550. The story that Cranmer persuaded the distressed young King to sign her death-warrant is untrue: he made great efforts to save her, as he had saved Thombe, but was overruled by the Council. The only other extremist to suffer death was the Dutch surgeon George van Parris, a Unitarian who was tried before Cranmer (with Coverdale assisting as judge and interpreter) for denying the divinity of Christ.[15]

The more permissive attitudes taken by the Edwardian government toward public discussion became evident in the press, the list of religious books now printed showing a sharp increase over that for the last five years of Henry VIII. Some of these publications are distinctly radical in tone, as with *The harvest is at hand wherein the tares shall be bound and brent* (1548), by John Champneys, a Melchiorite Anabaptist who recanted his heresies at St. Pauls in 1549. He argues, for example, that the vernacular Bible now meets all a Christian's religious needs, and that the layman, reading it in a reverent spirit, would be more hindered than helped by the traditionalist clergy, who depend instead upon 'man's imaginings'.[16] A similar biblicist attitude appears in *A godly newe short treatyse instructyng every person, howe they shulde trade theyr lyves*, by the Kentish sectary Henry Hart, who also published *A consultarie for all Christians* and became the acknowledged leader of the so-called Freewillers.[17] This group, which showed critical interest in a variety of doctrines, acquired its name in later years, after the debate between Hart and the orthodox Protestant cleric John Bradford, both being then confined by Queen Mary's government to the King's Bench prison.

Over two dozen members of the same society had been arrested by Edward's Privy Council, when about sixty from both Essex and Kent had gathered at Christmas 1550 in the Essex village of Barking. They had met to hold what one of them described as 'argument of things of the Scriptures, specially wheather it were necessarie to stand or kneele, barhedde or covered, at prayer, which at length was concluded in ceremonie not to be materiall, but the hartes before God was it that imported [mattered] and no thing else.'[18] Depositions concerning other meetings quote members as declaring variously that learned men were the cause of all errors, that children were not born in original sin, that no man was irrevocably damned or saved, that gambling was wicked, that sinners and men unknown to the group should be shunned. These statements are so phrased as to suggest that they had been put forward in an animated debate.[19] All such manifestations of doctrinal radicalism the government viewed seriously, since issues of this type were being discussed in radical circles throughout much of Europe, and 'Anabaptists' of various sorts seemed to be threatening all organised religion, together with the entire social order. Champneys having been forced to recant, a high-level royal commission was appointed to deal with sectarians in Essex and Kent. Tracts by Bullinger and Calvin against the continental Anabaptists were published, armed with prefaces pointing the lesson for England, while in 1552 Archbishop Cranmer was asked by the Privy Council—almost certainly with the Freewillers in mind—to enquire into a 'sect newly sprung in Kent'.[20]

Since 1986, when Dr. J. W. Martin published the first thorough investigation of the available evidence,[21] the Freewillers have emerged as a group of unusual interest and apparent modernity. Here we are far from dependent upon the hostile evidence of legal records, or that of Catholics and 'orthodox' Protestants. The numerous writings by the sect's own propagandists Henry Hart, Thomas Cole[22] and John Ledley,[23] are informative; so are the surviving particulars of the encounters between Freewillers and their more moderate critics such as John Bradford. The membership included men of erudition and open-mindedness. Judging from Dr. Martin's notes upon the forty-seven known members, a good many of them are likely to have been literate clothiers and artisans, men better educated than the rank-and-file Lollards whom we have encountered in earlier records. Certain of them such as John Trew seem to have interpreted the Scriptures in pedestrian terms not dissimilar from those of the old style scripture-men. Nevertheless internal debate was lively and seems to have ranged over religious and ethical themes in a relatively broad and liberal fashion. Though on different occasions both Hart and Trew drafted articles of belief with a view to their general acceptance, this event did not occur. The shifting membership united to select themes of common interest, not to impose particular beliefs as a condition of entry. The extant sources suggest that the Freewillers lacked interest in some of the more fashionable disputes of the day, such as transubstantiation and the alternative eucharistic theologies. With the Family of Love, which we shall shortly examine, they shared somewhat meagre common interests. They doubted whether children were born in original sin, and rejected the membership of manifest sinners or unknown people. Yet both these principles were then common to numerous radical bodies. Unlike the Family of Love, the Freewillers display only slight relationships with those many continental sects which contempories lumped together as 'Anabaptists'. All in all, they give the impression of a discussion-group rather than that of an integrated sect under imperious or charismatic leadership. An essentially lay-minded association, they expressed vociferous doubts regarding the usefulness of ordained clergy, whom they had reason to regard as either conservative or self-seeking or both.

Whatever their disagreements, the Freewillers were theological opponents of Luther and even more obviously of Calvin. Their chief doctrinal interest lay in Predestination, which they specifically reject as 'meter for diviles then for Christian men'.[24] However commendable to modern eyes as 'liberal', a group so lacking in unanimity, decision and even charisma stood little chance of longevity amid the forces of Tudor religion and society. In the event the Freewillers fell into disarray before the death of Edward VI and as an organisation had ostensibly vanished by that of Queen Mary. Thomas Avington, Nicholas Shetterton and Humphrey Middleton went to the stake in June and July 1555. Meanwhile John Trew escaped by breaking parole with his jailor, and Henry Hart was recorded as dead in 1557, presumably from natural causes. Having had their brief fling, the more moderate members had long since made their peace with the Church of England. Robert Cole of Faversham, a priest whom John Bradford regarded as more or less orthodox, assisted Thomas Bentham to sustain the underground Protestants of London during the Marian persecution and survived to hold London benefices in Elizabeth's reign. Others had repented earlier still, notably the learned schoolmaster of Maidstone, Thomas Cole. Jailed as a Freewiller in 1550, he preached before Cranmer in 1552, denouncing a variety of sectarian heresies. On the accession of Mary he fled to Frankfurt, returning to become Archdeacon of Essex (1561) and to deliver a sermon before Queen Elizabeth herself in 1563.[25]

Not without reason John Strype called the Freewillers 'the first that made separation from the Reformed Church of England', though direct connections between this short-lived experiment and Elizabethan separatism would be hard to trace. Perhaps more meaningfully we might characterize them as early 'seekers' who wanted to define the parameters of the Christian faith by godly debate, as opposed to accepting the fiats of Popes, kings, bishops, ecclesiastical traditions and dogmatic Protestants. They constitute a somewhat fleeting portent. Dr. Martin justifiably bids us look forward and compare their activities with those later godly conferences: the Prophesyings of Elizabeth's early years, which Archbishop Grindal so bravely refused to extirpate. We know too little of their debates to locate their continental affinities with any sort of precision. Doubts concerning infant baptism, original sin and predestination to heaven and hell had become widespread throughout Europe. In 1524 Erasmus had attacked Luther's rigorous predestinarian dogma. Hans Denck (1495–1527) in the late twenties and Sebastian Franck (1499–1542–3) in the thirties had gone still further.[26] We now label radicals of this type as 'Spiritualists'. Deriving somewhat from the medieval mystics, they reject Luther's concept of a merely imputed righteousness and aim to achieve a degree of actual sanctification and sinlessness through the co-operation of the 'free' human will with the divine will. In their view salvation should derive from effort, not from passivity or mere reliance on the 'dead letter' of the Bible, which Denck calls the 'external word'. Even more momentous is the 'internal word' or 'inner light' of the spirit, which grows in authenticity and power as a man succeeds in subordinating his life to the will of God. In *The Sealed Book* (1539) Franck's humanism goes so far as to proclaim Plato and Plotinus as furnishing a better background to Christianity than Moses. He takes a certain divine element within the soul as the mark of man's dignity and the starting-point of his spiritual advance. Both these continental radicals hence accused Luther of forging new chains as intolerable as those of the Catholic Church. This range of ideas we shall however find far more clearly articulated by the sect known as the Family of Love, which began its migration into England even as the Freewillers disintegrated.

Though it caused no public uproar until the later seventies, the English Family of Love had its origins more than twenty years earlier and came to be the most important direct offshoot of Anabaptism in England.[27] Its charismatic founder Hendrik Niclaes (c.1502–c.1580) is said to have visited this country in 1552 or 1553, while his chief agent Christopher Vitel was gaining converts in Colchester and Cambridgeshire during the mid-fifties.[28] By this time a prosperous mercer, Niclaes could already look back upon an eventful past. As a Catholic child at Münster in Westphalia he had 'seen' strong visions and shown a precocious absorption with the doctrines of sin and salvation. About 1530, being in trouble for heresy, he fled to Amsterdam and some years later claimed to have received a divine command to found a new religious community. Rejecting Luther's doctrine of a merely imputed or forensic righteousness, he sought to create an association of actually 'sanctified' believers, people who had achieved a degree of spiritual regeneration beyond the power of sin. While he spoke of ceremonies as the mere husks of religion, he planned an elaborate hierarchy of elders, 'bishops' and priests. In the Netherlands the movement attracted eminent scholars like Abraham Ortelius and Justus Lipsius, while no less a printer than the famous Christopher Plantin of Antwerp produced the numerous tracts written by Niclaes. Their author was given as 'H. N.', standing not only for Hendrik Niclaes but also for *homo novus*! His 'bishop' in England, Christopher Vitel, is mentioned as a joiner and lay-preacher at Delft, but he was regarded as an Englishman and should probably be identified with a merchant of that name, active (1568) in the Netherlands trade. Like many of such origins, Vitel surmounted the barrier of languages. He translated some fifteen of H. N.'s tracts into tolerable English from 'base Almayne', i.e. Low German or Dutch.[29]

None of these English versions was in print before 1570, by which time numerous converts—probably for the most part artisans—had been made throughout East Anglia, Cambridgeshire, Surrey, Sussex and neighbouring counties, where mainstream Protestantism had long since taken root.[30] Judging from the 'H.N.' publications and from those of their enraged English attackers in 1578–9,[31] the Family of Love had some special points of appeal to naturally religious and aspiring minds: an aura of spiritual perfection and the amenities of a secret society of men and women bound by ties of Christian love and personal affection. Niclaes and Vitels also gained both rapt attention and notoriety by coining incantatory phrases, bidding their followers to become 'godded with God'[32] and to dwell in 'the spiritual land of peace'.

The ideology itself clearly relates to that of Niclaes's friend David Joris[33] and other notorious practitioners of 'spiritualist' Anabaptism. All the same, the English Familists tried to avoid creating alarm and acted *suaviter in modo*. It became widely known that, like continental Anabaptists, they attached no reality to original sin or infant baptism, limiting that sacrament to adult believers. On the other hand they did not obstruct public worship and they personally attended the established churches, both Catholic and Protestant. When revealed, however, these evasive tactics could in themselves arouse further suspicion, the more so, since individual members recanted without hesitation when in danger of punishment for heresy. Nevertheless the writers who in 1578–9 were to denounce the 'horrible sect' and its 'monstrous and horrible heresies' offered no tangible proofs of iniquity. From them we gather that the English Familists were mostly unlearned, except for reading English; that they made 'bishops' and elders, who distributed funds left voluntarily by members under a hat upon a table; they met in private houses, the hosts supplying refreshments. They were also alleged to hold goods in common, to greet new members with a kiss, and to call one another 'brothers and sisters in Christ'. At their meetings they ventured to expound the Scriptures 'according to their own minds, comparing one place with another'. When attending Anglican services they objected to being described in the Litany as 'miserable sinners', since they were convinced of their own regeneration. Though banned by royal proclamation in 1580, the Family somehow survived Puritan indignation and was still reprinting some of its old tracts during the Cromwellian Protectorate. Compared with many sects, it thus attained longevity, and when it evaporated in the last decade of the seventeenth century, its membership merged into the Society of Friends (Quakers) and other more or less congenial sects of that day.

That continental, Anabaptist-type sectarianism enjoyed only a limited success in mid-Tudor and Elizabethan England seems by no means surprising. Its sources were foreign and its early advance clearly indebted to the presence of numerous Netherlanders in the towns of East Anglia and the South-East. The tense spirituality and the linguistic excesses likewise showed signs of its tragic origins amid the mass-execution of Anabaptists by the Habsburg government of the Netherlands.[34] Except perhaps at the height of the Marian persecution, these aspects must have had restricted links with the popular mood in England. Moreover 'spiritualist' Anabaptism faced Protestant rivals just as hostile as the Catholic persecutors. With its trust in the 'inner light', it laid less emphasis on the plain, literal sense of the Scriptures than most English Lollards and Protestants had already come to expect. Meanwhile its doctrinal arch-enemy Calvinism grew menacingly alongside it in England, as in the Netherlands.

Despite all these limiting factors, the incursion of continental sectarianism held no little significance for the later history of religion in England. More ambitious and sophisticated than those of the native Lollardy, such high aspirations were to be transmitted to eighteenth-century nonconformism, in particular to the Quakers and the General Baptists. In Britain cognate ideas have continued to attract generations of people with more than average education and spirituality. When Niclaes claimed to represent the 'new man' he was talking within a notable historical context. Ernst Troeltsch (1865–1923), the first great sociologist of religion, realised that the sectarianism of the sixteenth century had fresh gifts to offer.[35] It started from, and then built upon, the experience of active believers, insisting upon a conscious conversion in any candidate for admission. Unlike the Roman and Protestant territorial Churches, the sects were wholly voluntary movements, entered upon not by proxy or tradition but by adult decision. Deliberately they organised themselves in smallish groups, rejecting as unspiritual that command over the individual believer claimed and exercised by the major churches. Similarly they made no effort to work in harness with secular government or to incorporate the ruling class within their structure. Withdrawing from prominent civic duties, legal proceedings and military service, they maintained an unpretentious life-style. They were in short 'people managing for themselves' without the need for exalted secular or sacerdotal hierarchies. They felt comfortable only under what they took to be the direct rule of Christ. The concept stood thus diametrically opposed to that of a mighty Church having its own corporate holiness, dispensing its grace to obedient subjects by means of the Word and the sacraments. We should not however assume that this spirit of freedom, this regard for the individual, made an immediate contribution to the cause of religious freedom. Small 'gathered churches' and confident prophets almost inevitably created a new elitism not dissimilar to that of the monastic orders centuries earlier. Some at least of the sects tended to consign the unenlightened remainder of the human race to perdition! Yet the 'new man' had come to stay. While in later times Troeltsch's stark antithesis between 'church type' and 'sect-type' religion may often have been blurred in practice, yet as a conceptual model it has become undeniably useful for an understanding of modern Christianity.

The impact of foreign scholars, refugees and sects upon the English Reformation cannot be assessed with much precision. Apart from the significant results of Bucer's association with Cranmer and the later stimulus exerted by Knox on the English Calvinists, their influence upon doctrinal and liturgical policy may not claim much importance. And while à Lasco exercised a firm hold upon John Hooper, the positions they adopted were too austere to command a large following in this country. Nevertheless the foreigners, so many of whom were not merely non-Lutherans but anti-Lutherans, helped to prevent Protestant thought from consolidating in its earlier forms. Especially did their presence generate new theological ideas in both universities. Cambridge in particular stood on the eve of its most dominant period in English intellectual life; Bucer and his associates undoubtedly furthered the process whereby the Cambridge of Robert Barnes grew up into that of William Perkins.[36]

As in that narrow world, so in the larger world of London, the foreigners enhanced the ferment of ideas. In à Lasco's congregation London saw for the first time a church of full-fledged Puritan type, one organised no longer upon episcopal or even sacerdotal principles but based upon a powerful group of ordained and elected 'elders' or 'presbyters'. Some of these supervised discipline; others (who were salaried) preached and taught. To produce an informed laity, there were two hours of expository sermons every Sunday and instructional classes called 'prophesyings' during the week. On the first Sunday of each month communions were celebrated, but they were preceded by compulsory services of preparation, in which the elders examined the lives of intending communicants and drew up lists of those fit to receive the sacrament. Foreign refugees did not automatically gain admittance to the church; if of mature age, they had to show knowledge of the Reformed faith and undertake to lead a Christian life. Excommunication was employed only when interviews and disputations with the offender had failed; moreover, it excluded only from the sacrament, not from attendance in church or from civil rights. Thus the laity were disciplined, yet for action, not for submission—disciplined in order to fit them to select ministers and to manage the Church in a fashion unknown since the early Christian era. The clergy themselves were closely regimented by their colleagues, while at a meeting held every three months complaints could be brought against them by any member of the congregation.[37] No wonder Bishop Ridley became uneasy when he saw these modes of church government licensed in his diocese. In the last two years of the reign three congregations, French, German and Italian, existed at the Austin Friars. They co-operated harmoniously in one church under a single constitution, and they afforded an exhibition of religious internationalism with some strange undertones for the founders of a national, State-controlled Church. During the Marian persecution, when the more radical English exiles on the continent were ostensibly imitating this former London model, the rival concepts of nationalist Anglicanism and internationalist Puritanism stood starkly opposed.

The extent to which these early contacts leavened the insular chauvinism of Tudor Englishmen remains a matter for debate. Medieval Londoners had been anything but internationalists, and those who—in the manner of their forefathers—ran amok against foreigners on Evil May Day 1517 had learned depressingly little on this practical matter from the Church Universal. But in 1553, when their sons discussed foreigners, they at least had the opportunity of setting the image of a Protestant refugee alongside that of a rascally foreign merchant. Very soon some influential Londoners would themselves be refugees, dependent on foreign goodwill. The pressures of the Reformation were internationalist as well as insular and we should treat with caution the reproach that it divided England from Europe. That this censure contains only a half-truth will become more apparent when we turn to the second phase of continental influence, that which developed through the Marian Exiles.

The Edwardian Bishops

After the change of government Cranmer's first ecclesiastical scheme was the completion and publication in March 1550 of the Ordinal, the alleged inperfections of which have since formed the main basis for rejection of Anglican orders by the Church of Rome.[38] This first Ordinal was a fairly conservative document, modelled on the Sarum Pontifical but restricting the orders to those of bishop, priest and deacon. It preserved the historic rites of prayer, the laying-on of hands and the delivery of 'instruments', including the paten and chalice given to priests and the pastoral staff to bishops. But in the case of priests Cranmer added a Bible, to indicate their preaching function. And whereas the priest had formerly been charged: 'Receive authority to offer sacrifice and celebrate mass both for the living and the dead', now the charge ran: 'Take thou authority to preach the word of God and to minister the holy sacraments in this congregation.' When a revised Ordinal came to be incorporated with the Prayer Book of 1552, Cranmer significantly made the Bible the only 'instrument' delivered to bishops and priests alike. In the case of deacons a New Testament figures as the 'instrument' in both versions, but this represented no real innovation, since a book of the Gospels had been handed to deacons in the medieval rite. Martin Bucer wrote his work *De Ordinatione Legitima* especially to guide Cranmer, and in numerous places the Primate's debt to the Strassburg Reformer patently appears. Even so, Cranmer's decisions often proved more conservative, and in both versions he displayed his customary skill in blending medieval with Reformation ideas. The new Ordinal was first used at St. Paul's in June 1550, when John Foxe appeared among those ordained deacon by Bishop Ridley.

Amongst the few who refused to subscribe to the Ordinal was Nicholas Heath, Bishop of Worcester, who went to the Fleet Prison and in October 1551 suffered deprivation. In June 1550 the government also decided to prosecute the imprisoned Gardiner under the Act of Uniformity, while during the subsequent months it began legal proceedings against Bishop George Day of Chichester and several other ecclesiastics of known conservative views. At this moment Somerset still lingered in the political arena, and he attempted to extricate Gardiner from the Tower on condition he should undertake to obey the Act of Uniformity. Yet this suggestion, made during Northumberland's absence in the North, was quashed on his return and in February 1551 Gardiner was duly deprived of the See of Winchester. Meanwhile during the summer of 1550 Cuthbert Tunstall, who had remained a consistent Henrician Catholic, had to face false charges of encouraging a conspiracy in the North and was placed under arrest in his own house in London. Defended against Northumberland by Cranmer, Tunstall was not brought to trial until October 1552, after which he suffered imprisonment and virtual deprivation of his See of Durham. In March 1553 an Act of Parliament divided this wealthy bishopric into two portions under two salaried bishops, one of whom would have been Ridley had not the government collapsed that summer.[39] These were far from being the only significant changes on the bench. In April 1550, six months after Bonner's deprivation, Ridley was nominated to London, into which Henry VIII's new See of Westminster was incorporated. John Ponet succeeded Ridley at Rochester and then in March 1551 progressed to Winchester. John Scory, the one-time Dominican who had become Cranmer's chaplain, replaced Ponet at Rochester but in May 1552 was nominated to succeed Day at Chichester. A further complicated manoeuvre affected the See of Gloucester, which until 1541 had been part of Worcester diocese and to which in July 1550 Hooper was nominated. When however, Worcester fell vacant by Heath's deprivation, Hooper resigned Gloucester in order to be named (May 1552) as bishop of both sees, which were now amalgamated. By all these measures the government secured an episcopate of strongly Protestant flavour; moreover, it took such opportunities to diminish the wealth of various bishoprics by 'exchanges' even less equitable than those made by Henry VIII.

Amid these developments the quarrel surrounding Hooper's accession foreshadowed the great rift within the Elizabethan Church.[40] His earlier life abroad had placed the new bishop far nearer to the foreign visitors than to those of his fellow-countrymen who had contrived to live alongside Henry VIII. Beginning his career as a Cistercian of Cleeve in Somerset he had fallen under the spells of Zwingli and of Bullinger. Having fled to Strassburg in order to avoid prosecution under the Six Articles, he there met and married a Flemish noblewoman. Subsequently he lived at Zürich with Bullinger (who baptised his daughter Rachel) and was deeply affected by the advanced views of John à Lasco. His belated return in 1549 brought a dynamic figure into English Protestant circles. Hooper's single-minded zeal became apparent to friends and enemies alike; even Dr. Richard Smith, who in earlier days had helped to drive him out of Oxford, admitted that 'he was so admired by the people that they held him for a prophet; nay, they looked upon him as some deity'. Becoming Somerset's chaplain he took a prominent part in the deprivation of Bonner and was offered the Gloucester bishopric as early as April 1550. Then difficulties began to arise, for Hooper had lost what little he ever possessed of the English capacity for compromise. He believed that if the Bible should be taken as final on any issue, it should be so taken on all issues. Consequently he could accept no ceremonial as lawful unless it were enjoined in the Scriptures. Moreover, the demands now made upon him seemed in themselves intolerable and he refused the proffered bishopric on two grounds. The oath of Supremacy had still to be sworn by God, the saints and holy evangelists, while the vestments seemed 'Aaronic' in that they conveyed the idea of a sacrificing priest. Northumberland stood prepared to oblige him. The letters patent nominating Hooper to the See of Gloucester are dated 3 July 1550 and on 5 August the Council issued a dispensation to empower the Archbishop to consecrate Hooper without the obnoxious vestments. But Cranmer and Ridley, braving the Duke's wrath, refused to consecrate Hooper on his own terms; this line they took not so much because they felt any enthusiasm for the oath or the vestments but rather because they did not desire to see so stiff-necked a radical upon the bench. In October Hooper presented a series of Latin 'notes' to the Council on his position and to these Ridley replied point by point in English. At last, after the saints had been removed from the oath and after his truculence had earned him a short spell of imprisonment, Hooper agreed in March 1551 to undergo consecration in vestments. Nevertheless, he gave no undertaking to wear them regularly, except 'that sometimes he should in his sermon show himself apparelled as the other bishops were'. By any standards his position was that of an extremist, since none of the foreign divines in England, apart from John à Lasco, is known to have pronounced vestments positively sinful.

Intelligibly enough, one so fanatical as John Hooper has found little favour in the eyes of English ecclesiastical historians, yet recent research upon his short but intensive career as a diocesan bishop has tended to enlarge his stature.[41] Finding his clergy and officials lethargic and ineffective, Hooper went to work amongst them with almost superhuman energy. He presided in person over his diocesan court and made frequent tours of the diocese on the spur of the moment. His charity and concern for the poor were daily manifest and he made it clear that his social sympathies lay not with the landlords but with the unprivileged; his views squared in fact with those of the 'Commonwealth Party'. Basing the picture not upon Foxe but upon the court records of Gloucester, Mr. Price has written that 'the personal touch of the bishop regularly shines through the dull formal records of the diocesan administration, bringing together unhappy husbands and wives, restoring concord among families divided against themselves over disputed wills, pointing out their follies to gossiping and quarrelling women, and giving good advice to all and sundry.[42] Without fear or favour toward the eminent he continued to impose penances upon offenders, yet in place of the old ritual actions he substituted definite statements of the offences committed and straightforward appeals for forgiveness.

Hooper's most difficult problem lay, however, in the ignorance and individualism of his clergy. In turn these faults sprang from the fact that pluralism and poor endowments encouraged only men of mediocre quality to seek livings in the diocese. In 1551 he found that, of the 311 clergy he examined, 168 could not repeat the Ten Commandments, thirty-nine did not know where the Lord's Prayer appeared in the Bible, while thirty-four could not say who was its author. He also lacked knowledgeable senior clerics to act as rural deans and hold other responsible offices. On the other hand, like so many dedicated Reformers, he was full of enthusiasm for the potentialities of the common people and felt himself to be teaching the Christian religion anew to those who had hitherto lacked opportunity to hear its claims. In a letter to William Cecil he writes, 'You and I, if we should kneel all the days of our life, could not give condign thanks to God for that he hath mercifully inclined the hearts of the people to wish and hunger for the word of God as they do. Doubtless it is a great flock that Christ will save in England ... there lacketh nothing among the people but sober, learned and wise men.'[43] If he did not transform his clergy this was chiefly because good ordinands proved hard to find in the brief time as his disposal. Hooper's struggle was not waged against Catholic resistance, for such little resistance as may be observed in the Gloucester diocese sprang from the immobility of custom rather than from an informed Catholicism. Rather did he need to fight the evils which sprang from the long spoliation of livings, that neglect of churches and congregations, for which so many agencies stood responsible—the Crown, the religious houses, the colleges and cathedral chapters, the lay patrons and speculators, even the parish clergy themselves. Hooper might do his utmost to play the part of a primitive apostolic bishop, but without tangible support from the government and from society at large he could scarcely hope to rebuild the material foundations of a teaching Church.

In his doctrinal beliefs, in the decisive character of his continental influences, even in his attempt to discipline clergy and laity, Hooper was a true forerunner of that large body of Elizabethan Puritans who remained despite misgivings within the fold of the national Church. Some of the other Edwardian bishops showed themselves as forerunners of a strongly Protestant, yet nevertheless more central Anglican position. A fair example appears in Robert Holgate, sometime Gilbertine prior and master of Sempringham, who became Bishop of Llandaff in 1537, Lord President of the Council in the North in 1538 and finally Archbishop of York in 1545.[44] In many respects he followed the old traditions of the prelatical civil-servant and educational benefactor, yet within his limits Holgate also showed himself a sincere Reformer. The year following his accession to the See of York he founded by letters patent three grammar schools, respectively at York, at Old Malton (where he had been prior) and at his birthplace, Hemsworth. For these he drew up detailed and thoughtful statutes, while showing his zeal for education by protecting and helping other northern schools during this difficult period. By his will, made after he had been deprived by Mary and was living quietly in London, he founded an almshouse at Hemsworth. This and two of his schools are still in existence.

Robert Holgate's ideals as a Protestant bishop may best be studied in the thirty injunctions which he issued in August 1552 for York Minster,[45] yet here again his chief emphasis lay on education, especially on that of the vicars choral and other junior members. They must, he orders, attend regular lectures in divinity, undergo a monthly examination, memorise weekly a chapter of St. Paul's Epistles in the Latin translation of Erasmus, possess a New Testament, reading a chapter after dinner and another after supper. In the Minster the tabernacles over the high altar must be replaced by sentences of Scripture. The Minster Library must be modernised to include the Fathers up to 600 years after the Ascension, and also scriptural commentaries by Erasmus, by the Lutherans Musculus and Brenz, and by Calvin and Bullinger. While Holgate's views on the nature of the eucharist were somewhat more conservative than those of Ridley and Cranmer, he saw at least as clearly as they that the future of reformed Christianity in England must depend upon an educational programme centred around the vernacular Scriptures. In such sober documents, just as surely as in Cranmer's Prayer Books, we see a truly creative stage in the evolution of Anglicanism. Such a programme typifies the best of the tradition which the Edwardian Anglicans handed on to their Elizabethan successors.

Clerical Marriage

Archbishop Holgate was one of those prelates who married in late middle age in order to demonstrate their Protestant principles. When taken to task for this offence under Mary, he claimed ungallantly that the step had been compelled by the Duke of Northumberland, who had taunted him with lingering papistry.[46] It so happened that his young wife Barbara Wentworth was a parishioner of our south Yorkshire commentator Robert Parkyn, who refers in deeply scandalised terms to the 'lewd example' set by his Archbishop. Parkyn's sense of justice was nevertheless to be gratified when presently the marriage turned to 'trouble and business'. Barbara was claimed as lawful wife by an impecunious local gentleman named Anthony Norman, to whom she had been contracted in church under the absurd system of child-marriages tolerated by ecclesiastical law. Both Norman and Barbara had since proved mutually unresponsive, and on reaching the age of consent—this was fourteen—had not cohabited as the law demanded for the completion of a binding marriage. But whereas in the end Holgate successfully resisted Norman's claim, his fellow-Reformer Bishop Ponet of Winchester had the misfortune to blunder into a genuinely illegal marriage. In July 1551 the London diarists noted with relish that Ponet had been divorced from the wife of a butcher of Nottingham 'with shame enough' and that henceforth he paid 'a certain money a year during his life' to her rightful spouse.[47]

Throughout the remainder of this reign, and much of the next, this matter of clerical marriage bulked large. Though bills to sanction it had passed Convocation and the Commons in 1547, they had failed to pass the Lords, and the clergy did not receive permission to marry until the enactment of a statute to that effect in February 1549.[48] Then despite a widespread popular taboo, many priests availed themselves of the new privilege during the four years which remained before the Marian reaction. Of the 319 priests beneficed in Essex about eighty-eight were to be deprived by Mary's government for marriage. In the diocese of Norwich about one in four was removed, while in London nearly a third underwent deprivation for marriage. The record for Lincolnshire remains less complete, but a very conservative estimate suggests over seventy deprivations in 616 parishes.[49] Even in the more conservative North the urge to matrimony proved far from rare, and in the York diocese about 100 incumbents (out of over 1,000) ventured upon this course.[50] These clerics were not necessarily keen Protestants. It has been shown that the Essex married clergy formed a very mixed group, learned and ignorant, godly and disreputable. Few of them left any clear evidence of special devotion to Protestant principles.[51] Though ardent Reformers attacked the celibate ideal as leading to vice and gloried in the estate of matrimony, many a mundane glebe-farmer in a country vicarage must have seen marriage in terms of worldly convenience and natural impulse. From the social and economic standpoints the change had much to commend it, especially in a rural background. If in his earlier years the married parson had many mouths to fill, later on he had hefty sons to till his glebe, besides a wife to order his household, tend his poultry and organise his relations with female parishioners. In the cases of incumbents who were small farmers, the transition to family life does not seem on balance to have produced impoverishment. A detailed comparison of probate inventories in the diocese of Lincoln has shown that there the rural clergy had bigger and far better-furnished houses at the end of the sixteenth century than on the eve of the Reformation. In comparison with tradesmen and other comparable laymen they also seem here to have progressed favourably.[52]

Despite such evidence, the broader question regarding clerical living standards has no simple answer; as with the gentry in the century 1540–1640, some clerics prospered while other battled hard with poverty. Rectors, including lay impropriators, enjoyed the great tithes and in a period of rising prices they had every chance to forge ahead. The income of vicarages, based on the small tithes, can be shown to have increased much less steeply than that of rectories, and many vicars can barely have maintained standards as the inflation advanced. Mere curates with fixed or but slightly increased stipends became even poorer than in the past. Even in 1650 some fifty-one Lancashire and Cheshire curates averaged less than £9 per annum, while twenty-three of them, with £5 or less, were worse off than many agricultural labourers.[53] In general, the processes which followed the Reformation, while diminishing the number of pluralists and very rich clergy, may have tended to increase inequalities among parish priests. And while it can be demonstrated that clerical households in 1600 were far more comfortable than those of 1500, this was also the case with all other classes of society above the pauper level. Taken as a whole the parish clergy may be thought to have obtained less than their fair share of the nation's increasing wealth, yet they were entering upon a new phase of social influence. As they enlarged their houses and bred their big families, they began to make a new contribution to English life. Their wives, sons and daughters extended the scope of the middle classes, subtly changed the ethos of organised religion and played a notable part in the historic achievements of Britain both at home and abroad. Nevertheless, the innovation of 1549 had to encounter many decades of opposition. While conservative old women in the North called the children of the vicarage 'priests' calves', Queen Elizabeth herself snubbed the wives of her bishops and would have had them expelled from the precincts of cathedrals. Her smart modernity had some limitations and it did not conceal the oddity of her complexes about marriage.

The Second Prayer Book

The Ordinal represented but the first stage of a movement far more decisive than that hitherto undertaken by Somerset. In May 1550, less than a month after his installation as Bishop of London, Ridley officially enjoined his clergy and churchwardens to turn from 'the old superstitious opinions' by removing altars and replacing them with 'the Lord's board after the form of an honest table decently covered in such place of the choir or chancel as shall be thought most meet by their discretion and agreement'. He also forbade celebrants to counterfeit the mass by kissing the board, elevating the sacrament or by other traditional gestures. Elsewhere Ridley expressed the view of the Reformers on this matter with blunt simplicity. 'Now, when we come unto the Lord's board, what do we come for? To sacrifice Christ again, and to crucify him again, or to feed upon him that was once only crucified and offered up for us? If we come to feed upon him, spiritually to eat his body, and spiritually to drink his blood (which is the true use of the Lord's Supper) then no man can deny but the form of a table is more meet for the Lord's board, than the form of an altar.' Accordingly, in June 1550 he made this change in St. Paul's and the London parish churches. In November the Council ordered all the bishops to follow his example. As they complied, further arguments arose concerning the position of the table in the chancel and the direction in which it should face. Ridley and others then took steps to prevent the attendance of people who did not intend to communicate, since they felt it necessary to discountenance the old notion of the mass as a good work in itself.[54] As usual, Hooper would have gone still further. In a Lent sermon of 1550 he had expressed the wish that the government would put preacher, minister and people together in one part of the church and close off the chancel, 'that separateth the congregation of Christ one from the other'. By this change all would understand what was read, while the communicant would hear and see plainly what was done, 'as it was used in the primitive Church'. Cranmer and Ridley nevertheless continued to resist Hooper and à Lasco in refusing either to abolish vestments or to seal off the chancels of churches. And much as they wished to see moderate advances upon the conservative Prayer Book of 1549, they now realised the danger of reopening the doors to this radical pressure. As they hesitated, Northumberland decided the matter by urging them to proceed.[55]

Concerning the genesis of the Second Prayer Book[56] we know little, apart from the fact that a draft was being discussed by the bishops as early as January 1551. The Book of 1549 had previously been submitted to Bucer, whose *Censura*, a critical appraisal in twenty-eight chapters, exercised marked effects upon the thinking of Cranmer and his fellow-revisers. The new Prayer Book acknowledged about two-thirds of the objections raised by Bucer against the old one, though it did not always meet them in quite the manner advocated by the Strassburg theologian. It made few changes in matins or evensong but significantly modified the structure of the mass, the very title of which now disappeared. To banish the suggestion of a solemn sacrificial approach, the Canon was split into three separated portions. The prayers relating to the communion of the people now came before the consecration of the elements, thus implying that consecration took place for the purpose of a congregational communion. The medieval vestments were expressly forbidden and only the use of the surplice required. The communion table was now specifically placed with its ends east and west instead of altarwise, the priest standing on the north side. No longer did it remain possible for the most determined traditionalist to counterfeit the spectacle of the mass. The words of administration were changed from the form of 1549—'The Body of our Lord Jesus Christ which was given for thee preserve thy body and soul unto everlasting life'—to a form with which Zwingli himself could scarcely have quarrelled—'Take and eat this in remembrance that Christ died for thee, and feed on him in thy heart by faith with thanksgiving.'

This second Prayer Book cannot rightly be judged by the normal criterion of liturgists, that of fidelity to old models.[57] Particularly in its communion service, the Book makes some deliberate breaks with the past. It is based on the notion that everything without scriptural warrant should be omitted and a form of worship evolved which the Apostles themselves could have sanctioned. Today this objective is no longer regarded by scholars as literally attainable, yet we should misunderstand the intention if we thought it any less ambitious. In this aim the communion service is doubtless an attempt at the impossible, but it is a gallant and a skilful attempt. While its literary excellence derives from Cranmer's Book of 1549, it may liturgically speaking be regarded as an original rather than an imitative work, and one which displays logical principles within its restricted terms of reference. Of the eucharistic doctrine alleged or implied, it has been said that the service primarily sought to express the command, 'Do this in remembrance of me.' The words of administration could indeed be taken to imply no more than a commemorative rite, and a receptionist view of the Presence. On the other hand, they do not directly contradict Ridley's 'Ratramnian' view, which Cranmer had accepted in 1546 and later claimed never to have discarded. In general, it seems certain that Cranmer and his associates were not aiming to write a Zwinglian or a Calvinist Prayer Book. Had they so intended, they would have paid some regard to the services devised by à Lasco for use at the Austin Friars and by Valérand Poullain for his refugee congregation. Demonstrably the Book of 1552 follows neither of these, both being far more revolutionary in their departure from the original shape of the mass.[58]

On Cranmer's own intentions and on the degree of his personal responsibility for the more 'advanced' features of the Book, leading scholars have differed, and the paucity of direct evidence does not encourage dogmatism. Certainly the Archbishop lay under heavy pressure from the Hooper-Knox-à Lasco group at the time of the Book's completion. It is also certain that this group had the ear of the Privy Council. The new liturgy was due to come into use on 1 November 1552, but in September Knox protested in a sermon before the King against the rubric directing that the people should communicate in a kneeling posture. When pressed by the Council to modify this rubric, Cranmer refused. Even though copies were already in the press, the Council then inserted (apparently on its own authority) the so-called 'Black Rubric', denying any intention to adore the elements by kneeling, or any presence of Christ's natural body therein. The evidence arising from this quarrel throws little fresh light on Cranmer's doctrinal position in the year 1552. And whether or not he remained dissatisfied on points of detail, he had incurred official responsibility for the Prayer Book which, despite the important amendments of 1559, forms substantially the present Prayer Book of the Church of England.

The Parliament which assembled the day after Somerset's execution passed in April 1552 the second Act of Uniformity, but not without protests from three lay peers and from the conservative bishops Thirlby of Norwich and Aldrich of Carlisle. This Act states that 'a great number of people in divers parts of this realm, following their own sensuality, and living either without knowledge or due fear of God, do wilfully and damnably ... abstain and refuse to come to their parish churches.' It then exhorts the bishops to use ecclesiastical censures to remedy this situation. Commanding that the new Book be used from 1 November next, it reasserts the authority of the former Act of Uniformity and in addition threatens those attending any other form of worship with six months' imprisonment for the first offence, a year for the second and life imprisonment for the third.[59] During the short period of their operation these penalties did not need significantly to be evoked. Once again, even the conservative element among the parish clergy operated the new services without overt signs of disapproval. They were organised neither outwardly nor inwardly to resist, but one cannot doubt that they made even stronger mental reservations than those they had entertained in 1549.

The Canon Law and the Articles of Religion

Alongside the Second Prayer Book Cranmer optimistically undertook two other great schemes—to reform the canon law and to codify the beliefs of his Church in a document widely acceptable among Protestants. It is hard to say which of these was the more arduous task. No aspect of ecclesiastical affairs stood in greater need of revision than the law administered in the church courts. In particular the field of matrimony afforded a confused prospect of irrational and sub-Christian principles. Here as usual, the government of Somerset had shown itself full of good intentions. By virtue of an Act of 1549 a reform-commission of eight had been appointed, but when this Act expired neither Northumberland nor his successors caused it to be renewed. Indeed, until the passage of the canons of 1603–4, there was a notable lack of practical enthusiasm.[60] The canon law had many foes, especially among the common lawyers and the civilians, who had no wish to reinvigorate their rival by means of reforms. Again, an interesting passage in the *Journal* of Edward VI seems to reflect the view instilled into the boy by his mentor Northumberland. It is to the simple effect that the execution of discipline could not be entrusted to the bishops, some of whom were papists, some ignorant, some aged, some of bad repute.

In the last resort the laymen deserve the main blame for this lost opportunity, and a nation which would neither abolish nor reform the jurisdiction of the Church ended by obtaining its just deserts. That the study of ecclesiastical law survived the threats of the Reformation was largely due to the college called Doctors' Commons, which had been formed in 1511 for advocates practising in the church courts, and which survived until 1857. Usually trained at the university in the civil law, these advocates received their canon law education both by working in the church courts and by studying in the great library built up by the gifts of bishops at Doctors' Commons. English ecclesiastical law therefore became even more strongly influenced by the civil law. As for the courts, they survived the Reformation almost intact, and the enormous deposit of Tudor books and papers in our diocesan registries affords an uncanny sense of continuity across the period of cataclysm. Through the reign of Elizabeth and far beyond, the church courts continued to grind through their cumbrous and irritating routines, attracting the abuse of the Puritans and the dislike of the laity, still undertaking the tutelage of the nation, yet remote from the spiritual aspirations and sensitive consciences of the age.

Of this missed opportunity Cranmer's *Reformatio Legum Ecclesiasticarum* forms a striking memorial, though it remained unpublished until Foxe undertook the task in 1571. While deriving all ecclesiastical jurisdiction from the Crown, it proposed to retain the traditional control of the church courts over marriage, tithes, testaments, perjury, slander and benefices. Again, had this code been adopted, the church would have continued to try heresy and to hand defiant offenders, 'all other remedies having been exhausted', to the secular arm for punishment. On the other hand, the *Reformatio* proposed some 'advanced' reforms of the divorce-law, recognising adultery, desertion and ill-treatment as sufficient reasons for the divorce of either partner. Equally forward-looking was its plan for annual diocesan conferences attended by laymen as well as by clergy. Had this one provision been enacted, an immense amount of tension between the two classes might have been saved in years to come. If the bishops had been compelled to consult regularly with their parish priests and with representatives of the laity, they might well have been spared some of the appalling attacks made upon them by the malcontent outsiders of subsequent generations. Despite the curtailment of episcopal estates, it may reasonably be argued that the Reformation failed to break with the feudal character of the bishop or to bring him out of his isolation into regular exchanges with his flock. It may well be the case that the best chance to accomplish such a reform without sacrificing the proper dignity of the office was missed at this early stage of Anglican history.

The parallel task met with more success. Cranmer had long ago been concerned with the compilation of articles of religion. In 1538 he and some of his colleagues had agreed with a group of Lutheran divines upon a series of thirteen articles based upon the Confession of Augsburg, and these he certainly had in mind when he reverted to the task under Edward VI. As early as 1549 he drew up a code to be signed by clerics desiring a licence to preach. From May 1552 some version of these articles came under discussion by the bishops; in the October it was referred by order of the Council to a committee of six, including John Knox. Discussions seem to have continued in a desultory fashion until at last a final series of articles, now numbering forty-two, received the royal assent on 12 June 1553.[61] The King had then less than a month to live, and consequently the importance of these articles lies in the fact that they were destined to become, after several excisions and additions, the familiar Thirty-nine Articles of Elizabeth. In both these recensions they form a decisively Protestant interpretation of the Faith. The saying that the Church of England has Calvinist Articles alongside a Catholic liturgy simplifies the facts, yet it has a rough and ready justice in relation to articles xii (xiii in the Thirty-nine), xvii and xviii. Here we are assured (xii) that good works done without the inspiration of Christ are not pleasant to God and 'have the nature of sin'. In case we are in any doubt about the unpleasant prospects of Socrates in the next world, article xviii denies that a man could be saved by diligently following any other law save that of Christ. And while this article was perhaps no more than an incautious attack upon the Anabaptists, article xvii cannot be glossed over by the phrase 'moderately Calvinistic'.[62] The text of 1553 says that 'predestination to life is the everlasting purpose of God, whereby (before the foundations of the world were laid) he hath constantly decreed by his own judgement secret to us, to deliver from curse and damnation those whom he hath chosen out of mankind, and to bring them to everlasting salvation by Christ, as vessels made to honour.' This is not the position of the moderate or 'sublapsarian' Calvinists, who at least conceded that the Fall was not predestined and that the election of the redeemed took place only thereafter. Article xvii still appears to contain the most rigorous 'supralapsarian' position—that the salvation of some men and (by implication) the damnation of others was from the first built into the very order of the universe. True, the phraseology is urbane, perhaps not wishing to invite comparisons with articles ii and xxx (xxxi in the 1571 version of the Thirty-nine), which imply that Christ died for all men, not merely for the elect. But the purely verbal nature of this restraint is stressed rather than concealed by the fact that article xvii hastens on to rather irrelevant considerations on the subject of human despair.

While Anglican writers have been reluctant to take this immoderate Calvinism at its face-value, they have seldom acknowledged an even more striking characteristic of the Articles—that they are in a very large part directed against the Anabaptists, the fashionable menace of 1552. Over a century ago this fact was nevertheless remarked in detail by Archdeacon Charles Hardwick, who was far from inclined to minimise the general validity of the Articles but who rightly showed that the attack on Anabaptism can be traced in no fewer than eighteen of them (ii–iv, viii–x, xv, xviii, xix, xxiv and xxxvi–xlii).[63] Some of these, one must hasten to add, could also stand in their own right as statements of central Christian traditions. On the other hand, by no means all of those with a more ephemeral interest were omitted when the Thirty-nine Articles came to be compiled. In these and in some of the anti-Roman Catholic articles the Anglican Church has thus been left with a rather heavy clutter of anachronisms. Like the Calvinist article xvii, these outmoded items have been retained in recent times because of the internal disharmonies which might follow any attempt to modernise the Articles. There also remains a lingering, superstitious reverence, from which a frank recognition of the historical and impermanent factors of 1552 might well help to wean the Church of England four centuries later. At least we are no longer terrified by Anabaptism!

The Forty-two Articles leave no doubt as to the medial position of the 'new' Church, yet it is chiefly medial between Rome and the Anabaptists, rather than between Rome and the Calvinists or between Rome and the Lutherans. As we have already seen, there are adiaphorist elements which recall Melanchthon and his English followers of the thirties. Several articles are directly borrowed from, or are very close to the Augsburg Confession, for example article xi, asserting justification 'by only faith in Jesus Christ'. Purgatory and the cults were denounced in a crushing article (xxiii, becoming xxii in the Thirty-nine) which has ever since been solidly maintained by the Church of England: 'The doctrine of School authors concerning purgatory, pardons, worshipping and adoration, as well of images as of relics, and also invocation of saints, is a fond thing vainly feigned, and grounded upon no warrant of Scripture, but rather repugnant to the word of God.'

Many of the remaining items, and portions of some already mentioned, are directed against medieval Catholicism: the Roman primacy and the infallibility of General Councils (xx, xxii, becoming xix, xxi); the scholastic accretions of recent centuries (xii, xiii, xxii); the doctrine of transubstantiation (xxix, becoming xxviii), and the concept of the mass as a sacrifice (xxx). As for the actual teaching on the eucharist in article xxix (much modified as xxviii of the Thirty-nine), its lack of precision must be accepted as deliberate. Its first clause suggests receptionism, limiting effective communion to worthy receivers; its second regards transubstantiation as 'repugnant to the plain words of Scripture'; its third (omitted from the Thirty-nine) echoes the Lollard and Zwinglian argument that the faithful should not believe in 'the real and bodily presence', on the ground that Christ's body cannot be present in many places at once; its fourth declares that the sacrament was not commanded by Christ to be 'kept, carried about, lifted up, nor worshipped'. The total effect of this article has been most variously regarded by theologians.[64] Few cautious readers would agree with Hardwick, that it repudiates the errors of the Zwinglians, or the precisely contrary view of Dix, that it forms 'the perfect summary of the Zwinglian belief in the Real Absence'. It savours more of compromise between Cranmer and his committee-rivals that of a real consensus of minds. It cannot be taken to prove that Cranmer had whole-heartedly embraced Zwinglianism, yet in both its omissions and its inclusions it could well indicate heavy pressure by the Hooper-Knox group upon the Primate. On the other hand, we have no direct evidence that Cranmer disagreed with the Articles, and in 1555 he appears to have accepted a general responsibility for them. He did, however, immediately reject the Privy Council's unscrupulous claim that they had been agreed on by Convocation. This claim was certainly untrue, but his protest was brushed aside by the astonishing reply 'that the Book was so entitled because it was set forth in the time of Convocation'.

So much must be said, yet the present writer must confess whenever he re-reads the Articles, he finds admiration becoming preponderant over other emotions. This, no doubt, is in part a literary admiration, yet it has some more solid ingredients. However strongly one may reject the Articles as a statement of twentieth-century thinking in the Anglican Church, one must admit that they wore remarkably well until the later nineteenth. However much they may now savour of long-dead ecclesiastical politics, they remain among the most striking formularies of an age when theology still lacked most of the weapons of textual criticism. They still deserve serious study as a historical monument, and even as a point of departure for any new codes which may be attempted. Despite the bargaining which seems to underlie them, the Articles cannot justly be dismissed as mere timid compromise; their flexibility represents at least the dawning of the notion that honest doubt, alternative solutions and agreements to differ have their places in the doctrinal sphere. In very large part they represent what was most sensible and maturely-considered in the Reforming thought of the mid-century, and their authors cannot be blamed if in later times misguided people took them as something which Protestantism of its very nature cannot and must not suppose itself capable—an immutable, obligatory and comprehensive code of beliefs. The most important function of the Articles was a pragmatic one. They were in due course to bring a much-needed element of stability to the intellectual and social scene. In their conscious attempt at a shrewd balance between the extremes of an unbalanced age, they are intensely English, and a student of English history unfamiliar with their text suffers from a grievous gap in his documentary knowledge.

The Fall of Northumberland

Also among the last acts of Northumberland's régime was the confiscation of plate, vestments and other valuables regarded by the government as unnecessary for the revised form of divine service. A Council order as early as 3 March 1551 frankly states 'that for as much as the King's Majesty had need presently of a mass of money, therefore commissions should be addressed unto all shires of England to take into the King's hands such church plate as remaineth, to be employed unto his Highness' use.'[65] Various inventories were ordered both before and after this decision, but the final seizure came in consequence of a new commission directed in January 1553 to Sir Richard Cotton, comptroller of the Household, and others.[66] This body was subsequently assisted by separate commissions for each shire. Having delivered a chalice to the incumbent (two chalices, if necessary, in cathedrals and large churches) and left a sufficient stock of surplices, the commissioners handed over the rest of the goods to the master of the Jewel House. Even ready money could be taken, if any were found, and handed to the treasurer of the Mint. This process was still in full swing at the accession of Queen Mary, who restored what little plate remained intact but kept plate already melted down and the money raised from sales.

While the second Act of Uniformity had rendered most of these objects liturgically inappropriate or superfluous,[67] the action remains difficult to defend even on these grounds. It did not, for example, take into account the need for new and larger cups demanded by a congregational communion in both kinds. To many contemporaries it seemed the most sordid of all governmental appropriations. Christopher Trychay, vicar of Morebath in Devon from 1520 to 1574, wrote in his parish book that the sale of church goods had been proceeding unofficially since 1545 'and no gifts were given to the Church, but all from the Church ... by the time of King Edward VI the Church ever decayed.'[68] Seeing everything threatened, and their incomes gravely diminished, some clerics and chapters joined in the scramble. In February 1533 the dean and two canons of Chester were imprisoned in the Fleet for stripping the cathedral of its lead.[69] Reckless in their financial desperation the politicians did not pause to reflect on the alarming degree to which they were fostering corruption and discouraging the interest of the people in their parish churches. And some degree of responsibility must also fall upon enthusiasts like Hooper, who would make no concessions toward gradualism and who seemed to suppose that the new forms of devotion could be implanted overnight in the minds of simple people. Yet in attempting to assess the state of opinion during these disillusioning years we should probably be mistaken on a point of fact if we supposed that the rapacious politicians and the tactless Puritans were driving many of the English people back into the Catholic fold. Such evidence as we can adduce suggests that Protestantism continued steadily to expand amongst the upper and middle orders, while able preachers could still make many converts among the working people of the towns. The Spanish resident Guaras thought that Somerset and Northumberland backed Protestantism 'both because they were themselves of this opinion and from seeing the people inclined to it',[70] while in 1551 the Venetian ambassador Barbaro reported that 'the detestation of the Pope was now so confirmed that no one, either of the old or new religion, can bear to hear him mentioned'.[71]

These judgements may be based on no evidence outside the London area. There are also hints of a popular mood little related to either creed—cautious, unspiritual, perhaps a little stunned by the events of the last twenty years. The failings of the party in power did not necessarily involve any sort of religious response. In 1553 the greater part of the nation was neither ardently Protestant nor ardently Catholic. Lord Paget had recently written to Somerset that both religions were sadly wanting in England. 'I fear at home is neither. The use of the old religion is forbidden, the use of the new is not yet printed in the stomachs of eleven of twelve parts of the realm.'[72] A related and no doubt common viewpoint is represented by Capper, one of the speakers in the *Discourse of the Common Weal*; he roundly denounces all the theologians for bringing strife and division among the people and thinks that education should be limited to useful modern languages and to literacy in English, so that 'we might read the holy Scriptures in our mother tongue'.[73] This indeterminacy is of the utmost importance in relation to the origins and the results of the Marian reaction. Mary was soon to be wafted in by the wind of legitimism, but not by the gale of a Catholic revival. If she wanted such a revival, she would have to foster it herself, and her opportunity was now at hand.

Northumberland's policy had one clear objective—the maintenance of his personal ascendancy, with which was bound up his personal survival.[74] On this second issue he can have had few illusions by the early months of 1553, when his general unpopularity was accompanied by a mounting spirit of distrust even among his Protestant adherents. Latimer, Knox and Bartholomew Traheron (the Calvinist layman who briefly held the deanery of Chichester) spoke pointedly of covetousness and pride in high places. For his part Northumberland threatened punishment to preachers guilty of attacks upon his friends, and he became extremely brusque in the House of Lords when Cranmer continued mildly to press for the reform of the canon law. Amongst the 'new' laymen like Paget and William Cecil he had contrived to give almost as much offence as among the established nobles like the Earls of Arundel and Westmorland. His most faithful supporters were notorious adventurers like Sir Thomas Palmer and Sir John Gates. Among the magnates he could boast only one devoted adherent, Henry Grey, Marquis of Dorset, whom he had created Duke of Suffolk after the death in 1551 of Charles Brandon's sons. This unintelligent nobleman had married King Henry's niece Frances Brandon and his main political asset was hence his daughter, Lady Jane Grey. When on 21 May 1553 Jane married Northumberland's son Guildford Dudley, the attempt to bring the crown itself into the Duke's family became completely transparent.

Already in August 1551 the Duke had brought the young King to sit in person on the Council and since then he had redoubled his efforts to maintain a complete control over his puppet. The task would have become increasingly difficult had the boy survived, since already he gave ample indications of unusual intelligence. On Edward's death observers of various shades of opinion suspected that Northumberland had poisoned the King in order to promote a less independent figure to the throne. Yet no real evidence supports this improbable notion. Desperately indeed should Northumberland have prayed for Edward's recovery from the decline which beset him early in the year 1553. The figure of the Princess Mary loomed ever larger as the months passed. She had gallantly maintained her personal right to practise the Catholic religion and no one felt any doubt regarding the results of her succession to the throne. Faced by this menace Northumberland naturally worked upon the pious Edward with the plea that only a change in the succession could ensure the survival of Protestantism. The King consequently agreed to a 'devise' whereby the princesses Mary and Elizabeth should both be excluded in favour of the children of Frances Brandon. The further intrigues and self-contradictory arguments whereby the Duke tried to consummate this design have little direct connection with our present subject. The squalid affair is relieved only by the noble spirit of Jane, who was still in her mid-teens when she won her small but secure place in the story of the Reformation. She won it not through the futile usurpation into which she was led but through those personal virtues which exemplified the educative power of Protestant humanism. Had such influences been widely brought to bear on pupils less exalted, the history of English spirituality might have been directed into serener courses than those which lay ahead.

When Edward died on 6 July, Northumberland made a surprising mistake—he failed to get Mary under lock and key. Unhindered she escaped from Hunsdon into East Anglia, where the gentry and people, though more inclined to Protestantism than those of most regions, embraced her cause with a singular unanimity. Their action showed that Tudor Englishmen placed peace, unity and lawful succession to the throne before any of the religious causes for which enthusiasts would have had them wage civil wars. Amongst Mary's earliest backers was the Protestant Sir Nicholas Throckmorton, whose contemporary biographer makes him say:[75]

> *And though I liked not the religion*
> *Which all her life Queen Mary had professed,*
> *Yet in my mind that wicked notion*
> *Right heirs for to displace, I did detest.*

Northumberland's appeal to the fear of Spanish domination fell on deaf ears. Though here he spoke truth, his notorious self-seeking and the rumour that he had poisoned Edward caused his outcry to seem merely that of a criminal at bay. He then made his second obvious error by leaving his fellow magnates behind and setting off in person to stifle the revolt against his authority. Swift intrigues developed both upon the Council and among the gentry of the southern counties. Even Protestant London was shocked when Ridley with wild courage declared both Mary and Elizabeth bastard children of Henry VIII and as such incapable of the succession. The hopelessness of the plan to enthrone Jane became most apparent to the Secretary of State, Sir

William Cecil, who had been the fly-wheel of Northumberland's daily administration and who was a Protestant and a trusted friend of Cranmer. Cecil joined the rush of councillors to meet Mary at Ipswich, and if self-preservation was his chief motive it is likely enough to have been accompanied by more patriotic considerations. By 19 July Jane's father Suffolk had abandoned the game. All the church bells were ringing for the lawful Queen; a *Te Deum* was sung in St. Paul's and the night blazed with bonfires. Meanwhile Northumberland received no ostensible aid as a result of the devout prayers submitted on his behalf by the trembling Protestant dons of Cambridge. On 20 July he pathetically threw up his own cap for Queen Mary, and four days later he was brought up Bishopsgate to the Tower of London, 'all the streets as he passed by standing with men in harness afore every man's door till he came to Tower Wharf, all the streets full of people, which cursed him, and calling him traitor without measure'.[76] And as the gates of the fortress closed behind him, the most dubious episode in the political control of the English Reformation came to an end.

12 Queen Mary's Contribution

The Reaction and Public Opinion

On Mary's arrival in the capital the population of the prisons rapidly changed. As Suffolk, Jane and the Dudleys left the scene, there reappeared the old Duke of Norfolk and Bishops Gardiner, Bonner, Tunstall, Heath and Day. And as Northumberland had injured the cause of the Reformation by his policies, so at his execution he continued the work by recanting and by exhorting the spectators to eschew all heresy. In the words of an eye-witness, 'He edified the people more than if all the Catholics in the land had preached for ten years.' Those who knew him were equally confident that he apostatised in the hope of a last-minute reprieve.[1] His sons, together with Jane and Cranmer, were duly convicted of treason but for the time being left in prison. Latimer, Ridley, Hooper, Coverdale, Becon, Rogers and other Protestant divines soon found themselves in captivity, though in their cases treason did not figure alongside heresy. The married, ex-monastic bishops, Ferrar of St. David's, Bird of Chester, Bush of Bristol and Holgate of York, were also deprived of their sees, though of these four Ferrar alone continued in his resistance and perished at the stake. Ochino, Martyr, à Lasco and Poullain, together with numerous other foreigners, received permission to leave for the continent; indeed during the first months of the reign, the less notorious of the English Protestants also found little difficulty in escaping abroad, and hundreds wisely availed themselves of the chance.

To the Catholics who had comforted her in adversity and led the East Anglian movement—Sir Robert Rochester, Sir Francis Englefield, Sir Henry Jerningham, Sir Edward Waldegrave—Mary added *politiques* like Paget, Arundel, Pembroke and Petre, thus constructing a Council of great numbers and apparent disunity. Historians may well have exaggerated the short-comings of Mary's Council, yet the outcome of its work suggests that its bulk was enlivened by little wisdom; it lacked antennae, breadth of view, and authority to enjoin prudence upon the Queen. A striking example of its impotence appears in its failure to get rid of the large non-Catholic group in the Commons, even though circular letters to this effect were despatched before every election to the sheriffs. Mary's parliaments varied in their degrees of compliance with her wishes but they all included a considerable group of members whose Protestant leanings were scarcely veiled by a show of conformity.[2] Both these men and their secular-minded colleagues stood prepared as typical Tudor parliamentarians to march with the government of the day, but they had every intention of preventing the route from becoming too arduous. In the Parliament of the autumn they consented, after 'marvellous dispute', to repeal the Acts of Uniformity and the other ecclesiastical legislation of Edward VI. A large minority of the Commons— the two estimates vary from a quarter to a third—had the courage to vote against this repeal. And once the first rejoicings had subsided, Mary began to receive some sharp reminders from this sober political world. Parliament would accept a return to the last years of Henry VIII but not a return to the Middle Ages. It refused to rescind the Royal Supremacy, and the scrupulous Queen often placed a non-committal '&c' after her secular titles. Likewise, the problems of papal power were left for future debate, no punishments attached to absence from the mass and heavy hints dropped that any attempt to restore ecclesiastical lands would be resisted. More pointedly still, when the Commons heard that Mary proposed to negotiate a marriage with her cousin Philip of Spain, they sent a deputation begging her to marry an Englishman, but in vain.

The Marian Parliaments showed distinct signs of restiveness. In October 1553 sixty members are listed as 'they which stood for the true religion'— meaning Protestantism—while in January 1555 106 members incurred legal proceedings as absentees. Later that year no less than 260 members out of a total of 392 are recorded as opposed to governmental policy, and in particular as resisting its attempt to penalise the religious exiles.[3] Even so, in their desire to detect the earliest origins of seventeenth-century resistance to the Crown, historians have made too much of such episodes. In 1986 Dr. Jennifer Loach in her scholarly work *Parliament and the Crown in the Reign of Mary Tudor* showed by a close examination of many individual members that there existed no parliamentary opposition party in our modern sense, organised for business, consistent in its objectives and responsive to a distinguishable leadership. As we shall observe, this sort of an opposition cannot be substantiated even during the earlier decades of Elizabeth's reign. Nevertheless, in regard not merely to the House of Commons but to the whole nation, revisionist scholars seem nowadays somewhat too anxious to present Mary and Philip as popular, almost 'successful' rulers. To go so far would be to ignore some massive and varied evidence indicating the contrary. Indeed much of the opposition must have lain concealed, since even humble people had a vast amount to lose by pertinacious defiance of the Crown, even life itself, should their opposition become overtly religious.

Early in the reign there arose a popular agitation in Kent and Essex for the restoration of Protestant worship,[4] while it was not long before iconoclasm and insults to Catholic clergy began to occur in London. Yet the dangerous factor lay less in religion than in the growing fear of foreign domination. Quite apart from the touchy nationalism which always marked Tudor public opinion, certain changing patterns had begun to work against Mary's plans for a close alliance with the Habsburgs. As native manufactures had developed, England had become less dependent upon the traditional ties with the rulers of the Netherlands, while the collapse of the Antwerp market in 1550 encouraged the search for new markets. Especially since Henry VIII had defied the Emperor, patriotic Englishmen had felt little attraction toward the Habsburgs or Spain, while Philip, though conscious of the need for caution, did nothing to revive in English minds the historic Anglo-Burgundian ties to which he was the lineal but not the spiritual heir. To suppose however that the English disliked Philip merely as a Spaniard would probably be mistaken. Any foreign prince who became King of England by marrying an English Queen would have become unpopular. Mary's subjects knew less about Spaniards than about their nearer European neighbours, while the epic struggle with Spain had not yet developed either in the Netherlands or on the high seas. All the same, in her pitiful honesty Mary took no pains to hide the loyalties derived from her Spanish forebears and from her violent partisanship of her mother. No doubt the very ease of her initial success helped to blind her to the constant necessity for wooing English opinion. The causes of her failure lay less in her religious intolerance than in her inability to be, like her successor on the throne, 'mere English'. Even the Emperor urged her to be *une bonne Anglaise*, but she lacked the temperamental and histrionic gifts demanded by the rôle. The Venetian ambassador Girolamo Soranzo wrote that she scorned to be English and boasted her descent from Spain.[5]

There can be no question regarding the intense unpopularity of the royal marriage arranged in January 1554 and celebrated in the subsequent July. Granted Mary's desperate need for an heir to prevent the accession of Elizabeth, who lay under constant suspicion of heresy, this still remained an imprudent means and one which she adopted not only against the will of Parliament but against the advice of Gardiner and at least a third of her Privy Council. Recent research has modified the view that the mood of the nation was merely one of sullen acquiescence. Active unrest proved as characteristic of this reign as of its predecessor; the Marian state papers are saturated with reports of sedition and discontent. Mary had been on the throne but a few months when a fourfold series of risings occurred. Sir Peter Carew, backed by the Earl of Devon, tried to raise Devonshire. Sir James Croft worked similarly in Wales and the Marches, while the Duke of Suffolk, along with his brothers Lords John and Thomas Grey, attempted with great ineptitude to stir the Midlands. The collapse of these three movements owed more to poor leadership, to respect for legitimate government and to the discouraging memory of recent fiascos than to the Queen's popularity, which had already entered upon a steep decline.[6] More important, can Wyatt's dangerous rising in Kent at the end of January 1554 be reasonably regarded as to some extent a Protestant crusade?

Sir Thomas Wyatt,[7] son of one celebrated poet, had also been a drinking-companion of another, the unfortunate Earl of Surrey. He could not pose convincingly as a Protestant zealot. For the benefit of the pious he talked about the restoration of God's Word, while Bishop Ponet, who had escaped abroad, ventured back to participate in his rebellion. While hatred for the idea of a foreign king can still be claimed as the most powerful factor in Wyatt's rising, we may no longer dismiss Protestant belief as a minor ingredient. Professor Thorp[8] has recently examined in detail the opinions and careers of fourteen of its best-known lay leaders. Of these none showed Catholic sympathies, while eight were certainly Protestant and three others almost certainly so. On the remaining three, evidence is lacking. Again, of nine clergy known to have participated, all were distinct Protestants. Moreover every contemporary, Catholic or Protestant, who left an analysis of the causes, believed that the religious element played a significant part. It is also true that the heresies of Kent were both widespread and complicated and that the county was soon to provide fifty-eight Protestant martyrs. Whatever the outlook of the rebels, 4,000 men marched on London with Wyatt, and when the London militia in their white coats confronted him at Strood on 29 January, they too shouted, 'We are all Englishmen' and spontaneously deserted to the rebel forces. It was a moment of dire peril, since Wyatt, unlike the rebels of earlier years, had struck at the heart of the State from very close quarters. Impeded by stupid counsellors and commanders Mary was saved by her personal courage and by the fortunate but rather unpredictable support of magnates like William Herbert, Earl of Pembroke, and John Russell, Earl of Bedford, who not many months earlier had sat on Northumberland's Council. Again, Wyatt's friends in London did not succeed in overcoming the caution of the city magistrates, to whom his name meant very little. The gamble ended as he rode up to Temple Bar, shouting 'I have kept touch',[9] only to be greeted by an ominous silence.

The retribution was handled without much acumen or equity. As he well deserved by contemporary standards, Suffolk was brought from the Tower and executed for his earlier treason; yet the beheading of his daughter has rightly clouded the Queen's reputation. Aged only sixteen, Jane was a paragon of piety and learning, and had reluctantly accepted the throne in obedience to her ambitious father. At the block she calmly and steadfastly asserted her Protestant faith in one of the noblest gestures of the English Reformation. Overcome by her fine bearing historians have often forgotten to add that this execution was an offence against decency, fit to be placed alongside the worst of those perpetrated by Henry VIII. A month later the already popular Princess Elizabeth was also sent to the Tower, and the Habsburg agent Simon Renard persistently intrigued to bring about her execution, in order to enhance Philip's prospects of succession to the English throne. On the scaffold Wyatt exonerated Elizabeth of any share in his revolt and no convincing evidence could be discovered against her. Despite a vehement desire to ensure a successor likely to preserve Catholicism, Mary shrank from a crime of this magnitude, and she presently placed her sister under the surveillance of Sir Henry Bedingfield at Woodstock. As shown by Bedingfield's report[10] on the slow journey through Buckinghamshire and the middle Thames valley, the Princess already enjoyed great popularity among the common people, who assembled to greet her at each village, offering cakes and other humble tokens of esteem.

Numerically speaking, Wyatt's followers did not suffer a harsh fate, and of the 480 convicted only about ninety suffered death. These were almost all poor people. The wealthier and more responsible offenders escaped with fines assessed not in accordance with their guilt but with the influence of their friends on the Council. In later years it became easy to misrepresent the obscure victims as martyrs for religion. Nevertheless, the Spanish match continued to diminish Mary's popularity even before she began seriously to persecute for religion. Quite apart from its intrinsic shortcomings, Marian Catholicism was stifled in its infancy through becoming linked in the minds of Englishmen with the idea of Spanish overlordship. Confirmed in later years by Alva's ferocity in the Netherlands and by Elizabeth's long struggle with Spain, this impression weakened the chances of any Catholic revival in England. Spain was long to remain the liability as well as the mainstay of the Counter-Reformation, and scarcely did she cease to menace the northern peoples when her spiritual heir, Louis XIV, rebuilt her image—for Englishmen an image which came to associate autocracy, aggression and persecuting Catholicism. And meanwhile *émigré* Catholicism inevitably developed its own blend of foreign idioms. But of all these later handicaps imposed upon the old Faith, the profoundest and the most avoidable was that imposed by Mary Tudor's nexus with Spain.

After Wyatt's failure Mary's second Parliament (April-May 1554) inevitably consented to the Spanish marriage, while circumscribing Philip's powers with every possible paper-safeguard. When Gardiner suggested that Mary should be permitted to disinherit Elizabeth and bequeath the crown by will, the ugly prospect of a foreign King immediately prevented either house from giving the plan serious consideration. By a strange irony the marriage thus helped to bring about the succession of Elizabeth and the consequent overthrow of Catholicism. This Parliament also saw the defeat of various ecclesiastical laws introduced by Gardiner, including measures to revive the anti-Lollard statutes and the Act of Six Articles. This result sprang, however, not from crypto-Protestant oppposition in the Commons but from the bitter quarrel between the lay peers, headed by Lord Paget, and the bishops, headed by Gardiner. These two factions on Mary's Council did not merely revive the old Henrician quarrel between Catholic erastians and Catholic clericals; they even transferred it to the public forum of Parliament in a manner quite alien to the spirit of Tudor conciliar government. While the clericals were soon to get their way over the heresy laws, Paget's faction duly defeated their attempts to recover the lands lost to the Church. This matter involved something more than the possible confiscation of property purchased by laymen. The idea of wholesale monastic revival was also anathema to the lay peers, because it might have entailed the revival of a clerical majority in the House of Lords. A true disciple of Henry VIII, Paget had no intention of allowing his master's work to be undone. Rather than see this he would have allied with the Protestants; given his way on this point he was prepared to let the clericals have their persecution.

The reunion with Rome aroused less contentious issues than the Spanish match or the former church lands. When Henry VIII abolished the Roman jurisdiction there had been few enthusiasts for papalism in England, and since then twenty years of savage anti-papal propaganda had taken effect, even among those who leaned to the old religion. The foreign residents in England, for what their views are worth, agree that no Catholic revival was taking place about this time. Soranzo thought in 1554 that a majority of the population felt dissatisfied with the restoration of Catholicism.[11] His successor Michiele believed in 1557 that the restoration of Catholicism was being accomplished out of fear, or by people wishing to ingratiate themselves with the Queen, while everyone, except a few pious Catholics over the age of thirty-five, wanted to return to an unrestricted life by abandoning the Faith.[12] A third Venetian, Suriano, observed that the people 'appeared to be Christians [i.e. Catholics] from fear rather than from will'.[13] Simon Renard took the view that the realm was only pretending to be converted and stood prepared to deny Catholicism if the Princess Elizabeth should succeed.[14] While, however, there is little reason to suppose that Englishmen were being converted to a more favourable view of the Papacy, the majority may not have been stirred by passionate feelings in either direction when, in November 1554, they at last witnessed the arrival of Reginald Pole as Papal Legate. By this time few Englishmen could argue from personal experience concerning the advantages and disadvantages of papal jurisdiction in their country, for if the Roman yoke had pressed but lightly in the reign of Henry VII, it had scarcely existed in England since the time of Wolsey's greatness. By now the issue belonged in large part to the field of ideas, and in London it paled into insignificance beside the presence of Philip and his tactless retinue.

A few days after Pole's arrival both houses of Parliament petitioned for reunion with Rome, and after formal intercession by Philip and Mary the Legate absolved the realm from schism. It remains notable that this third Parliament, the most compliant of the reign, had only consented to the admission of Pole on the clear understanding that no restoration of the monastic lands was being contemplated.[15] Thus satisfied on the crucial point Parliament repealed all statutes passed against papal authority since 1529; it even agreed to revive the anti-Lollard laws, though few of its members can have foreseen the scale upon which the Queen was soon to employ them. Mary's fourth Parliament (October–December 1555) gave more overt signs of disapproval, with which members as cautious as Sir William Cecil probably concurred. Yet Sir Anthony Kingston, revealed as an exceptionally violent person on other occasions, can hardly have typified the attitude of the Commons, when he forcibly prevented members leaving the chamber until they had voted down a government bill seeking to confiscate the revenues of Protestants who had fled abroad.[16] No doubt many members had friends among the exiles; all tended to bristle, for obvious reasons, when they saw religious policy tampering with the property of laymen, heretical or orthodox.

The Martyrs

The burnings for heresy began on 4 February 1555 with that of the biblical translator John Rogers. Within a week there followed him to the stake Bishop Hooper, the prominent London cleric Laurence Saunders, and the patriarchal rector of Hadleigh, Dr. Rowland Taylor. The persecution which followed has been blamed upon many individuals.[17] Foxe suggests that it was initiated by Gardiner and soon passed on to Bonner for execution. Yet here his familiar prejudices seem to distort and over-simplify the facts. With the arrival of Pole, and before the lighting of fires at Smithfield, Gardiner had lost most of his influence over policy. He died in November 1555, his appearances at heresy-trials being limited to the commission (on which he sat as Lord Chancellor) which condemned Hooper, Rogers and others in the previous January. Bonner was far more deeply and personally involved, yet as Bishop of London he was bound to examine a large proportion of the accused, many of whom were sent on to him by the Privy Council, by other bishops, by justices of the peace and commissioners appointed by the State. Short of resigning, Bonner could scarcely refuse to try, or abstain from condemning, a heretic who pertinaciously opposed transubstantiation. This situation he himself outlined in conversation with the martyr Archdeacon John Philpot, and he ended by regretting that in London he was under the eyes of the Court and could not evade the task of persecution. His zestful, coarse-grained personality and bullying demeanour did much to earn his unenviable reputation, but the actions presented by Foxe as sadistic could, even if accurately reported, be interpreted as rough but well-meaning attempts to frighten the less resolute offenders and so to save them from the flames. Sir John Harrington records an anecdote to the effect that, when someone reproached Bonner for allowing an elderly man to be whipped, he replied, 'If thou hadst been in his case, thou wouldst have thought it a good commutation of penance to have thy bum beaten to save thy body from burning.'[18]

The sources give me a distinct impression that the urge to severity came from the Queen herself. There are many official minutes and letters showing how constantly she incited both civil and ecclesiastical authorities to greater zeal in their unwelcome tasks. Even Bonner received an official reproof for his slackness in allowing heretics to go unpunished. She was neurotic, increasingly assailed by illness, and in the later stages embittered both by Philip's neglect and by the wounding attacks of Knox, Goodman, Ponet and other Reforming writers. The personal influences which lay behind her religious ardour remain a matter for argument. It has recently been claimed that Mary's ultimate aim was to revitalise a traditional English Catholicism: she evidently felt that her own ancient and hitherto orthodox kingdom of England should not strive desperately to impress the Pope by a grovelling obedience to Roman commands.[19] Yet was not her coolness toward the Papacy influenced less by religious 'patriotism' than by her husband's major problem: the ever more appalling political quarrel between the Spanish crown and the Neapolitan Pope? These aspects demand further investigation, though it would seem unlikely that future historians will ever manage to obliterate that haunting image of the 'Spanish Mary', to which we have alluded.

Even when due allowance has been made for our tendency to blame foreigners for what now seems the least English episode in our history, it remains more than probable that Mary received active encouragement from her Spanish confessors, some of whom were distinguished Dominicans closely involved with the work of the Inquisition. Bartolomé Carranza certainly took part in dealing with several heretics, including Cranmer himself, and subsequently boasted with a fine scorn for statistics that while in England he had caused 30,000 heretics to submit, be burned or go into exile.[20] Two other chaplains, Juan de Villagarcia and Pedro de Soto, had much to do with Cranmer's recantations. But the chief Spanish agent is likely to have been the Observant Alonso à Castro, who before coming over with Philip in 1554 had written two methodical books concerning the theory and practice of persecuting heretics. Both these he republished in 1556, with a preface urging Philip to continue the good work in England. For two years Alfonso belonged to the inner circle of Mary's court. Though in February 1555 he engaged in disputation with the imprisoned John Bradford, he avoided notoriety, and on one occasion he preached against haste and severity, urging that heretics should live and be converted. Here only a simpleton could avoid suspecting a device to divert English attention from the Spanish share in the persecution. Philip's own caution in England should not be allowed to obscure his later addiction to *autos-da-fé* or the fact that his own historians were to claim for him the glory for the English persecution. Yet while in England, the Spaniards had every reason to conceal their influence.[21]

As for Reginald Pole, he stood far closer to Mary than any other adviser during the period in question, and he is not known to have attempted any mitigation of her policy. When in a lengthy sermon[22] he urged severity upon the magistrates of London, he was certainly speaking to these suspected heretics according to his conscience, yet clearly underestimating the time and the repressive powers needed to restore England to the Catholic obedience. Opinions concerning Pole differed even among the Protestants themselves. Foxe described him as 'a papiste but no bloudy papiste', while less charitably Archbishop Parker (who lived through the Marian persecution in England) refers to him as *carnifex et flagellum Ecclesiae Anglicanae*.[23] Whatever the truth, it would seem naïve to judge Pole and the other Catholic prelates according to those modern humanitarian principles, which the sensitive Foxe approached far more closely than did the great majority of Tudor people. In his diocese of Canterbury Archdeacon Harpsfield and Pole's other deputies were exceptionally zealous in burning and imprisoning heretics, while the Cardinal's own communications with the fallen Cranmer never departed from that cold, official ferocity which he had long used against his enemies. Whatever the truth regarding Pole's active participation, he must bear much of the moral responsibility. From a merely pragmatic viewpoint it was unfortunate, both for herself and for her victims, that Mary chose as her *alter ego* a man who had abandoned his former conciliatory ideals, a rhetorical humanist deficient in that sort of humanity which raises a statesman to the first rank of his calling. Concerning the immensity of his problems—and in particular his acute lack of money to spend on the restitution of the old Faith—Dr. Pogson has recently written with both objective scholarship and legitimate sympathy.[24]

The best contemporary list of burnings, found among Cecil's papers and printed by Strype,[25] includes 282 persons. Of these Foxe records 275, and in addition there were a few other victims included in neither list. The executions were heavily concentrated in south-eastern England, a feature which—as will shortly appear—roughly reflects the actual distribution of Protestantism, though it could well be accentuated by the closer control exercised by the government over reluctant officialdom in areas near the capital. In London sixty-seven were burned, in Middlesex eleven and in Essex thirty-nine. The Kent victims number no less than fifty-eight, all except six of them executed at Canterbury. The other larger county totals are Sussex with twenty-three, Suffolk with eighteen and Norfolk with fourteen. Apart from Gloucestershire with its ten martyrs, very few offenders paid the ultimate penalty in western England and Wales. While a number of northerners suffered in the South, only one burning actually took place in the whole of the northern counties. Throughout England at least forty Protestants are known to have died in prison during the Marian reaction.

In our next chapter we shall survey not merely the victims, but the much larger body of 3,000 known and named Protestants occurring between 1525 and 1558, and recently collected from the surviving records by Dr. John Fines. We shall explain why these must constitute only the tiny visible tip of the Protestant iceberg: indeed in the great majority of cases these people were the activists and the risk-takers who got themselves into the pages of Foxe or into the official records, now so incomplete, of the Henrician and Marian persecutions. In due course we shall also point out some factors which apply particularly to the martyrs, for example, the roles of women and of very young persons. Another feature common to the martyrs, and to the Protestant body as a whole, is the immensely important contribution of artisans and skilled workers, the largest occupational group within Dr. Fines's 3,000 names, and also among the *c.*290 martyrs. Regarding the Protestant clerical leaders, one may credit them with no little constancy. Few who were caught tried to escape by denying their allegiance, though naturally many fled abroad or lay low in England. Five bishops and sixteen priests went to the stake during the Marian persecution. We are compelled to discuss in a later section the problems concerning the 800 or more people who fled abroad in order to avoid the supreme challenge. For the most part these 'Marian exiles' came from the gentry, the priesthood, the clerical students, the professional and the merchant classes. A few of them look far more like political than religious opponents of the government, most notably those who settled in pleasure-loving Venice in preference to the godly cities of Switzerland and Germany.

For what creed did the martyrs die a painful death? A learned Anglican historian held the view that 'at least two-thirds of the martyrs who were burnt by Queen Mary would almost undoubtedly, had Edward VI survived, have been burnt in the normal course by the Church of England'.[26]The remark has been duly adopted by certain apologists for Mary Tudor, yet it would seem invalid. After all, the Edwardian government in fact burned only two heretics, both extremists, during more than six years. Again, the evidence for Anabaptist heresies among the working-class martyrs is far too limited to warrant this conclusion. It cannot be denied that the body of Protestantism was widely permeated by a radical spirit derived from a variety of sources—neo-Lollard, Zwinglian, Calvinist, Anabaptist and others. Within the new national Church sectarian trends can already be perceived, and in this developing situation all its members could not possibly have maintained a precise harmony with the beliefs of Archbishop Cranmer or of whatever figure we may care to select as indicating a hypothetical Anglican norm. Though in general an honest partisan, Foxe toned down the most radical elements, some of which we have already noticed with the 'Free Willers' and the Family of Love. Men and women who went to the stake must obviously have been strong Protestants, yet there is no evidence inside or outside the pages of Foxe to indicate that the vast majority of them worshipped otherwise than from the Prayer Book of 1552, that they were classed by anyone as Anabaptists or even that their eucharistic beliefs stood to the left of Cranmer's or Hooper's. All save a handful can still be claimed as Anglican martyrs provided we admit that the infant Church of England already exhibited a fairly wide spectrum of emphases and bore singularly little resemblance to the Church as later envisaged by 'High' churchmen of the nineteenth and twentieth centuries.

To assess the immediate effects of these martyrdoms upon English public opinion is not a simple task. Very few people of that period denied in principle the justice of capital punishment for religious opinions; of the Marian martyrs Philpot, Rogers and others had specifically permitted the burning of Anabaptists, while several of the latter persuasion were again to be executed during the reign of Elizabeth. The mode of punishment itself remained in the normal repertoire of secular justice, especially for women convicted of capital crimes, until the later eighteenth century. Moreover, by current continental standards, the Marian burnings formed no great holocaust.[27] These facts agreed, the adverse and lasting effects upon the public mind should not be underestimated. By 1554 few Englishmen regarded a heretic with the horrified eyes of the thirteenth century, while when men judged the process quantitatively they are more likely to have judged it by the precedents of their own national history, which had seen no combustion on this scale. There is no reason to suppose that the majority of English Catholics relished the spectacle of a persecution along these lines. Some of the recorded instances of distaste and distress derive from people who did not share the religious views of the victims, while ample evidence remains that sheriffs, justices and gentry were reluctant to carry out these acts or grace them with their presence. Though even in the south-eastern and East Anglian counties many magistrates held Catholic views, those like

Edmund Tyrrel, who hunted down so many heretics in Essex, appear to have been exceptional and unpopular figures. In the later stages demonstrations of sympathy by the crowds toward the sufferers became so frequent that a proclamation forbade them under pain of death. Its ineffectiveness in one instance appears in a letter from Thomas Bentham, minister to the secret Anglican congregation in London and in Elizabethan times Bishop of Lichfield. He describes the scene at a burning of seven heretics caught at a prayer-meeting in a field near London. As the people crowded round the stake with consoling expressions, Bentham himself cried out, 'We know that they are the people of God, and therefore we cannot but wish well to them and say, God strengthen them. God Almighty, for Christ's sake strengthen them.' The crowd shouted in reply, 'Amen, Amen', and amid the confusion Bentham was able to withdraw unmolested.[28]

Mary lacked the ingredients for a popular and successful policy of repression—a general mood of orthodox religious exaltation or a sense of national peril. The Tudor public felt more pity for a politically inoffensive neighbour than, say, for a foreign-trained seminary priest thirty years later, since the latter could easily be depicted by authority as a murderous traitor in the pay of Spain and the Pope. A burning could be a very horrific affair, and in the wet English climate it was apt to be inordinately prolonged. It was often accompanied by touching family circumstances likely to excite pity even in that inscrutable creature, the Tudor bystander. Moreover, the great majority of the executions took place in those areas of England where positive sympathisers were most numerous. In London, Essex and Kent—crucial areas for any Tudor government—the persecution must have seemed more dramatic and more severe than the national total of victims might suggest to a modern observer. All in all, we cannot reasonably doubt that the response to Mary's policy in south-eastern England was both hostile and immediate. Foxe did not create anti-Marian sentiment, even if he did much to perpetuate it as anti-Catholic sentiment. In this longer perspective, there can be no question of Mary's folly in relation to her own aims and ideals. She did more than anyone, more even than Foxe himself, to create that unreasoning Protestant bigotry which for a century and a half after her death was to prove England's most evil inheritance from the Reformation. As usual, one extremism enhanced its opposite extremism; the noisome smoke inevitably followed the horrors of the fire.

While the great majority of the martyrs were obscure men and women, a number of Reformers eminent by reputation and character also summoned the fortitude to suffer for their beliefs. The leading clerical martyrs, Latimer, Ridley, Hooper, Ferrar, Philpot and Bradford, had hitherto been compromised by the self-seeking of their political associates; the fact that they showed themselves able to die with such aplomb changed at a stroke the moral status of Protestantism, the future of which depended in large degree upon its capacity to inspire a few Englishmen of prominent position and cast in a heroic mould. This was a period when opinion judged a man's spiritual situation by his conduct in the face of impending death, and when the example of a great spirit could prove immensely contagious. The course embarked upon by the government may largely be explained by its anticipation of weakness in its leading opponents. 'Thou wilt not burn in this gear, when it cometh to the purpose', said Sir Richard Southwell to the proto-martyr John Rogers.[29] At the outset there was indeed little reason to suppose that the new doctrines had attracted heroes.

The story of the Oxford martyrs, so ably retold by David Loades,[30] requires no detailed repetition. Equally impressive is that of Dr. Rowland Taylor, rector of Hadleigh in Suffolk, who may be taken as most character-istic of the new type of national hero.[31] Gigantic in physical stature, learned in the laws, unsparing in his zeal to bring Gospel Christianity to all sorts and conditions of men, endlessly active in practical charities to the poor, forward-looking in his valuation of marriage and family life, Taylor had also the obverse characteristics of the fighter. He could see nothing in the viewpoint of an opponent. A hard controversialist, he wounded without hesitation and stood always eager to exchange stroke for stroke in the cause. In earlier years Hadleigh had responded to the teaching of Bilney, and under Taylor it became famous throughout that region. According to Foxe a great number of its parishioners 'became exceedingly well learned in the holy Scriptures, as well women as men, so that a man might have found among them many that had often read the whole Bible through, and that could have said a great sort of St. Paul's epistles by heart, and very well and readily have given a godly learned sentence in any matter of controversy. Their children and servants were also brought up and trained so diligently in the right knowledge of God's word, that the whole town seemed rather a university of the learned, than a town of cloth-making or labouring people.'[32] Allowing for the enthusiasm of the martyrologist there can be no reasonable doubt that communities with something of this flavour had come into existence by the middle of the century. Being near the base of the social pyramid they represented one of the most solid achievements of the English Reformation and stood among the guarantees of its survival.

When the persecution set in, Taylor's fame and defiance placed him among the first of those to be prosecuted and condemned. In February 1555, a day or two before the burning, Bonner came to degrade him and by custom should have struck him on the breast with a crozier. Faced by Taylor's bulk and formidable demeanour the frightened chaplain of the bishop cried, 'My lord, strike him not, for he will sure strike again.' 'Yea, by St. Peter will I', replied Taylor, 'the cause is Christ's, and I were no good Christian, if I would not fight in my Master's quarrel.' So Bonner omitted this feature of the grim ceremonial, and once back in his cell with John Bradford, Taylor mirthfully recounted the story to his companion. 'And by my troth,' said he, rubbing his hands, 'I made him believe I would do so indeed!' To traverse the last intimate scenes with his wife, his children and his disciples might well seem to savour of Protestant propaganda. Yet they should be read by anyone genuinely interested to understand the spiritual dynamic now being achieved by the English Reformation. This was the choice of a man who had not, like Prior Houghton or Edmund Campion, taken his leave of mere human affections. While no more nobly met than theirs, the fate of a family man who had rubbed shoulders with all and sundry must have had a more obvious appeal to ordinary men and women in the world.

Very different from this, different from the equally unswerving witness of Ridley, Latimer and Hooper, was the conduct of Mary's most famous victim. Thomas Cranmer lacked the massive simplicity of his friend Taylor. Nature had scarcely fashioned him for a heroic rôle, and in the strictest sense he cannot be claimed as a martyr.[33] Though in terms of spiritual agony he may have suffered more than his colleagues, his courage failed him more than once throughout the prolonged processes. His defiance at the stake, magnificent though it was, came only after he realised that his former recantations had failed to save his body from the flames. Yet as so often, he managed to outwit more consistent adversaries, and the last surprising scene not only recalls its counterpart in *Samson Agonistes* but bears a curious harmony with a life which had always drawn strength from seeming weakness. Shortly before the execution the government decided to make capital out of Cranmer's recantations by printing them, together with the final one which he was due to pronounce at the stake. But this he failed to deliver. Instead, he managed before he was pulled down to repudiate all his recantations, to denounce the Pope as Antichrist and to repeat his Protestant doctrine of the eucharist. Then, as the faggots blazed around him, he received some extraordinary access of strength and held his guilty right hand in the fire, once withdrawing it to wipe his face, but only to replace it until the end came. Hundreds of people saw these events, and within a few days the government admitted them in terms which led people to doubt even the authenticity of the actual recantations. Hence, with their usual blend of bad luck and blundering, the Marians had failed to exploit the supreme opportunity they had so assiduously sought. To gain Cranmer's discrediting surrender rather than risk this appalling rebuff it would have been a thousand times preferable to have spared his life.

The madness of a system which would burn a virtuous human being for his inability to accept a metaphysical theory of the eucharist must stagger even a generation well accustomed to institutional and doctrinaire crimes. Moreover, many a modern observer would hesitate to attribute mental balance to a man who suffered himself to be burned over such an uncertainty. Yet the Marian reaction did at least reveal a wealth of human fortitude, of 'civil courage', of adherence to mere principle which the English have seldom in their history found a comparable chance to display. For both good and ill it became an integral part of the memory of a people; it took its place alongside King Alfred, the Black Prince and Agincourt as a factor in the evolution of our national self-consciousness. By every right it was a story which belonged to the common man, and slowly, indirectly, deviously, it helped to supply some of the elements of constitutional and social libertarianism. Though the contestants of the seventeenth century understood the nature of liberty better than those of the sixteenth, the later stage could scarcely have arrived save on the basis of the former. Though the memory of the Marian martyrs provoked Protestant bigotry, it also helped to provoke more worthy and creative attitudes—an independence of out-look, a confidence that the future belongs to God, a contempt for fashions and establishments; all those attitudes we find fully developed amid the contemporaries of Oliver Cromwell, John Milton and John Bunyan.

Amid the rise of interest in the history of women, new studies are being devoted to their role in the Reformation, and most recently to the female martyrs of the mid-Tudor period.[34] Concerning this last theme, nearly all our information derives from John Foxe, whose painstaking interest deserves credit, despite his patronising reference to these 'womanyshe and wyvishe' hearts, which by the special grace of God could become 'bold and manly' in the cause! With very few exceptions these martyrdoms were achieved by working-class housewives, widows and servants of all ages. Though some died at the stake alongside their husbands, they were not merely passive victims, guided only by human affection or despair. Rather do they appear as free agents who had trained themselves for the task, embracing the ideas of a biblical Christianity and a 'true' church. Their inspiration arose from hearing sermons, from witnessing other martyrdoms, above all from reading—or hearing read—the Bible, and becoming con-vinced that their salvation depended on their adherence to the cause. Many are shown as activist members of Protestant groups or congregations. Some deprived themselves of food in order to train for the conditions they would meet in prison. Others left their husbands and children, finding employment in strange places or hiding from persecution in 'bushes, groves and fields'. In their resolute, independent spirit, their rejection of women's conventional submissiveness, they seem a new race of beings in English history. Agreed, they have their contemporary counterparts in France and Germany, and possibly their temperamental forerunners among the 'eccentric' devotees of earlier centuries, such as Margery Kempe of Lynn (c.1373–after 1439). The latter had indeed been accused of Lollardy. If we follow their Puritan and sectarian successors into the reign of Elizabeth and the seventeeth century, we see the Reformation as a major episode in the spiritual history of women. Nevertheless one should compare those later cases of Margaret Clitheroe and other female sufferers for the Catholic cause, which suggest that the new spirit arose not simply from Protestantism but from the earnest temper of the religious struggle and from the growing literacy which offered women a new sense of equality with men.

In our reaction against Protestant bigotry we have tended overmuch to neglect the martyrs and to forget that aspect of their message which is still relevant to our need. It is the reverse of our craving for security. It is the simple and perennial message of unconquerable spirit, bereft of material weapons, yet prepared to take its stand in passive opposition to the might of principalities, powers and mob-instinct.

Therefore [wrote Latimer to Ridley], there is no remedy (namely now, when they have the master-bowl in their hand, and rule the roast) but patience. Better it is to suffer what cruelly they will put upon us, than to incur God's high indignation. Wherefore, good my lord, be of good cheer in the Lord, with due consideration what he requireth of you, and what he doth promise you. Our common enemy shall do no more than God will permit him. God is faithful, which will not suffer us to be tempted above our strength. Be at a point what ye will stand unto; stick unto that, and let them both say and do what they list. They can but kill the body, which otherwise is of itself mortal. ... The number of criers under the altar must needs be fulfilled: if we be segregated thereunto, happy be we.[35]

The Protestant Underground

During the Marian persecution a few well-known Protestants managed to live in obscurity without being compelled either to recant or to emigrate. The most notable among them was Matthew Parker, whom we last saw preaching to the Norfolk rebels in 1549. The future Primate was deeply compromised on the accession of Mary. An old patron of the White Horse, a friend of Bilney and Latimer, he had also been chaplain to Anne Boleyn, who confided to him the care of her daughter Elizabeth. Having tutored this very rewarding pupil, Parker had become master of Corpus Christi College, Cambridge, and latterly dean of Lincoln. Fortunate to avoid a charge of treason for his interest in the claims of Lady Jane Grey, he lost all his preferments and went to live in the house of a friend near Norwich. A great collector of manuscripts, an assiduous antiquary and editor of medieval chronicles, he rejoiced in his new leisure for study, even though it had to be passed in poor circumstances and in hourly fear of arrest. He also writes with great affection concerning his partners in poverty: 'my godly and most chaste wife, with my two most dear little sons'.[36] Here was a new type of ecclesiastic evolved by the Reformation.

The Protestant content of the many movements of sedition and protest during the later stages of the reign is not easy to unravel from the surrounding political and economic turmoil. The London printers were widely involved in both political and religious pamphleteering, and several of them, including John Day and Hugh Singleton, had to flee abroad.[37] Likewise the justices were ordered in 1557 to prohibit all stage plays, many having attacked the government.[38] In London the molestation of Catholic clergy involved at least two cases of attempted murder, while even the venerable Observants of Greenwich, Elstow and Peto, were stoned as they re-entered their old house.[39] During the spring and summer of 1555 there were disturbances in Sussex, one of the leaders being Thomas Reed, later burned for heresy at Lewes.[40] The following year a Suffolk schoolmaster named Cleobury and a local parish priest concerted a plot to proclaim the death of Mary and the accession of Elizabeth.[41] Suffolk in general and Ipswich in particular became notorious for their conspiracies, which were certainly Protestant-inspired.[42] Essex and East Anglia saw the labours of the wandering preacher George Eagles *alias* Trudgeover, whom Foxe depicts as a romantic innocent living close to nature in the woods and hedgerows. On the other hand, the Privy Council Register shows that he was pursued from July 1556 as an agent of sedition and was hanged for treason a year later.[43] This same official source proves beyond doubt the extreme restiveness of south-eastern England in Mary's later years. Even in quiet Lincolnshire agitators were in July 1558 attempting to create a rebellion.[44] When Paget thought optimistically of Mary's prospects, Cecil replied with reason, 'My Lord, you are therein so far deceived, that I fear rather an inundation of the contrary part, so universal a boiling and a bubbling I see.'[45]

Concerning the underground Protestant congregations, we know by far the most about that in London, which was formed early in the reign and had an attendance fluctuating between 40 and 200.[46] It boasted a brave and distinguished succession of ministers: Edmund Scambler, later Bishop of Norwich; Thomas Fowle, fellow of St. John's, Cambridge; John Rough, the old associate of Knox, who returned from abroad and suffered martyrdom; Augustine Bernher, Latimer's Swiss follower; and Thomas Bentham, the deprived fellow of Magdalen, who led the bold demonstration at the stake. The last-named, who relinquished his comfortable exile to face these perils, did even more than Matthew Parker to earn his Elizabethan bishopric. The London church maintained close contact with the Reformed churches and English Protestant exiles; like the latter it seems to have used the recent model of the Foreigners' church at the Austin Friars when planning its organisation. It had deacons who kept membership lists, collected and distributed large relief funds and succoured prisoners for religion. One of these deacons, the martyr Cuthbert Simpson, was described by an informer as 'paymaster to the prisoners in the Marshalsea, Ludgate, Lollards' Tower and other places of prison as the Compter, etc., and executor to the prisoners that die, and collector of the assembly when the reading is done'. Occasionally the minister excommunicated members, as in the case of Margaret Mearing, whom John Rough so punished for bringing strangers into the meeting and for talking too openly. When, however, he was thrown into prison, this valiant woman took him clean linen, courted arrest and ended by burning at the stake alongside him.[47]

Despite its congregational form there can be no doubt that the London church was an Anglican body and used the Prayer Book services. The informer Roger Sergeant reported: 'Commonly the usage is to have all the English service without any diminishing, wholly as it was in the time of King Edward the Sixth.' With these leaders it is most unlikely to have shown any leanings toward Anabaptism; one of the members was in fact accused of reading an anti-Anabaptist book,[48] very possibly William Turner's *Preservative against the Poison of Pelagius*. The meetings of the congregation took place at seven, eight or nine in the mornings, 'and then, soon after, they dine and tarry till two of the clock, and amongst other things they talk and make officers'. Spies and renegades called for elaborate security measures. We hear of meetings at an astonishing number of places, mostly along the Thames, which afforded special opportunities for escape. They met 'at one Church's house, hard by the water-side'; at the King's Head, Ratcliff, where the widow Alice Warner was hostess; at the Swan at Limehouse; at St. Katherine's (east of the Tower) in the house of a Dutch shoemaker named Frogg; 'at Horsleydown (in Bermondsey) beyond Battle Bridge, at a dyer's house betwixt two butchers there'; 'about Aldgate'; at Blackfriars, 'where they should have resorted to Sir Thomas Carden's house'; 'at the Saracen's Head at Islington ... under colour of hearing a play'; 'between Ratcliff and Rotherhithe in a ship called Jesus Ship'; 'in a cooper's house in Pudding Lane'. Once a party was besieged by government agents while in a house on Thames Street, but a resourceful seaman among them swam out from the back of the house, got a boat and using his shoes for oars painfully rowed his friends out of peril.

The London Protestants apparently managed to hold large meetings without being detected. An example appears in the almost novelish memoirs (1562) of Edward Underhill,[49] one of Queen Mary's bodyguard of gentlemen pensioners, who joined in protecting her during Wyatt's rebellion. He had nevertheless already been imprisoned for a month as a 'hot gospeller' and as author of a ballad, thought by members of the Council to be seditious or possibly heretical. In fact Underhill had long been a zealous Protestant. He associated with 'old Henry Daunce', the preaching bricklayer of Whitechapel, who 'in Mary's time used to preach the Gospel in his garden every holiday, where I have seen a thousand people'. When Underhill became worried lest his own collection of heretical books might be discovered, Daunce came to enclose it in a brick wall beside the chimney in Underhill's house. Soon afterwards, he thought it wise to remove to Coventry, but he returned soon after the advent of Queen Elizabeth and recovered his library intact.

Foxe speaks of John Rough as 'chief pastor of the congregation' but his evidence does not entirely prove Strype's statement that there were several organised subsidiary congregations.[50] Certainly a number of other clergy were active in London, one being Thomas Rose, the deprived vicar of West Ham, who escaped martyrdom by making a partial recantation, obtained permission to visit friends and so fled abroad.[51] The London priest and informer Stephen Morris mentions 'three preachers of King Edward's days', who 'lived mostly at the King's Head at Colchester', but when in London could be traced through the ale-house in Cornhill, 'for there is much resort [i.e. of Protestants] to that house'.[52] These three clerics obviously formed the connecting link between the London Protestants and the congregation in Colchester. One was John Pulleyne, a Yorkshireman and Oxford graduate, who had forfeited the rectory of St. Peter's Cornhill. He subsequently celebrated communion 'at two Eastertides' (1555–6) at his own house in the parish of St. Michael's Cornhill.[53] Among those associated with him was Christopher Goodman, Lady Margaret professor of divinity at Oxford, and an important political theorist. In Colchester Pulleyne 'preached privately to the brethren' and he may already have been (as he certainly later became) a disseminator of anti-Marian pamphlets. He was not denounced to Bonner until 1557, when he fled to Geneva and contributed to the Genevan versification of the Psalms. He is said, however, to have made previous secret journeys overseas to contact his patroness, the exiled Dowager Duchess of Suffolk. Another of the Colchester-London clerics was 'William, a Scot' so far unidentified; the third was Simon Harlestone, brother of Matthew Parker's wife. Foxe claims that Harlestone had been driven with his family from his home at Mendlesham in Suffolk and, according to Stephen Morris, he lived not only at Colchester but at Dedham nearby, being 'a great persuader of the people, and they do mightily build upon his doctrine'.

This Colchester congregation appears to have centred around twenty-two Protestants who went up to London, submitted, and then renewed their activities on returning home.[54] Thomas Tye, a priest of the town, complained that some were 'mocking also those that frequent the church, and calling them church-owls, and blasphemously calling the blessed sacrament of the altar a blind god'. In a subsequent report to Bonner placed by Foxe in 1557, Tye wrote that the heretics 'assemble upon the Sabbath Day in the time of divine service, sometimes in one house, sometimes in another, and keep their privy conventicles and schools of heresy'. The local officials, including Bonner's, had refused to take further action against them. Meanwhile Catholic priests were 'hemmed at in the open streets and called knaves', the sacrament of the altar was blasphemed and railed upon in every house and tavern in Colchester, prayer and fasting were disregarded and seditious talk had become rife. The outcome showed that this report did not lack substance. Prominent among the group were William Mount of Much Bentley, his wife Alice and her daughter Rose Allin, who were all burned, along with seven others, in April 1557 at Colchester. Some of the offenders seemed to bear a charmed life; along with the Mounts the priest mentions John Love of Colchester Heath, 'a perverse place', who had been twice convicted of heresy but had somehow managed to return home in triumph. It is evident that a persistent and oganised underground congregation existed in Colchester. These were the 'brethren' to whom John Pulleyne preached and who were visited by other clerics intermittently concealing themselves in London.

Other groups can scarcely be called congregations, since they do not seem to have enjoyed the regular ministrations of Protestant clergy. One of these was at Stoke by Nayland in Suffolk,[55] where even in 1558 many parishioners, 'especially the women', continued to absent themselves from the Catholic services. At Easter 1558 the authorities, reluctant to arrest so large a number, gave them a final respite of sixteen days in which to receive the sacrament. The group met and made a solemn compact with one another not to receive. They then approached their parish priest, one Cotes, with the suggestion that the communion should be ministered 'according to King Edward's Book'; it seems evident that they already knew he was secretly inclined to Protestantism, otherwise such a request would have been absurd. If Foxe is accurate, Cotes made the significant reply that 'to such as he favoured ... he would give it after the right sort; the rest should have it after the papistical fashion'. He was presumably not deceiving them, since they remained unmolested a further six months and then avoided the apparitors of the Bishop of Norwich by a temporary disappearance. Having been duly excommunicated some of them left the town, but by this time the reign had drawn to its close. This and others of Foxe's anecdotes concerning Stoke illustrate the important part played by women (now Protestant but later Catholic) in resisting the religious policies of Tudor governments.

Particulars concerning an Anglican congregation in Lancashire also came to the ears of Foxe, who reports them with a convincing wealth of circumstance, though with the one or two minor errors one would expect in the case of a district so unfamiliar to him.[56] At Shakerley near Bolton lived a nailmaker named Jeffrey Hurst, who married a sister of the martyr George Marsh. The latter, whose birthplace at Dean was also close by, taught Hurst a good deal of the doctrine which he himself had acquired at Cambridge and as curate to Laurence Saunders. Having absented himself from mass since Mary's accession Hurst had to flee into Yorkshire, where he was not known, but from time to time he returned by night to visit his family, 'bringing with him some preacher or other, who used to preach to them so long as the time would serve'. Foxe names four of these clerics, and says that whenever one of them came to Shakerley there asembled 'about twenty or twenty-four sometimes, but sixteen at least, who had there also sometimes communion'.

Elsewhere, both in Foxe and in diocesan records of heresy, it is indicated that Protestant meetings and resistance groups were by no means uncommon during these years. The Lincoln records afford several examples. In St. Martin's parish, Leicester, twenty-eight persons were indicted for displaying scorn towards the sacrament of the altar, while at Gaddesby in the same county the parishioners were charged with refusal to attend mass and to rebuild the altars.[57] At Ipswich in 1556 a large number of people went into hiding or fled to avoid participation in Catholic rites.[58] There may indeed have existed unrecorded congregations, but in most parts of England they cannot have been easy to organise, since the parish clergy were in general conservatives, or else unadventurous men, unwilling to become involved in such dangerous activities.

The existence of active Protestant clerics in Marian England was precarious and those who survived had to keep moving. John Pulleyne, for example, managed to administer the sacrament secretly in London at two successive Easters, but more of his time appears to have been spent in the strongly Protestant area of Colchester. The main London congregation had at least five successive ministers in the course of Mary's reign.[59] Lay leadership was another condition of Protestant worship. From prison Bishop Hooper wrote to 'lovers of the truth' on how to behave 'in this troublesome time'. He told them it was important 'many times to have assemblies together of such men and women as be of our religion in Christ, and there talk and renew among yourselves the truth of your religion ... make prayers together, confer with one another.'[60] As if in response to such advice, laymen came forward in various parts of England to maintain Protestant worship by reading together the Edwardian Prayer Book and expounding the Bible.

One striking case arose at Hadleigh, soon after Rowland Taylor's arrest. When the aged parish curate proved incapable of carrying on, a young artisan called John Alcocke, alleged to be 'singularly learned in holy Scripture', read to the parishioners regularly from the Prayer Book and 'gave them godly lessons and exhortations on the chapter that he read to them'. When arrested, he continued to write to members of the congregation from prison until his death.[61] Similarly in the Essex village of Great Bentley the lay martyr Ralph Allerton at first sought to keep the Protestant group alive by reading chapters of the New Testament. Later on he took to preaching, and with the help of William Mount, his wife and stepdaughter, he organized an underground congregation. At Allerton's trial in 1557, when he proclaimed his adherence to the Edwardian Church, the local priest complained that so many went to hear Allerton that few attended services in the parish church.[62] Another lay-conducted congregation included the forty or so men and women whom Foxe describes as engaged in prayer and 'the meditation of God's holy word' in a field near Islington. In May 1558 they were arrested by the local constable and taken off to prison. Of the twenty-two tried, thirteen were burned at the stake.[63] Yet another underground congregation came to light at Brighton early in Mary's reign, when twelve persons were arrested while 'saying the service in English set forth in the time of King Edward the Sixth'.[64]

All these congregations clearly regarded themselves as 'orthodox' Protestants, even though, lacking ordained clerics, they could not receive the sacraments as required by the Edwardian Prayer Book. Sometimes their forms of service may superficially have resembled those of radical groups which the Edwardian Church officialdom had regarded as heretical. Indeed, avowed groups of sectarians did also continue to meet, one of them being reported by the Catholic writer Miles Hogarde as denouncing with equal fervour both the established Churches, Protestant-Edwardian and Catholic-Marian. Yet the lay-run Anglican congregations may well have been more numerous than either the sectarian groups or those within which ordained Protestant clergy officiated.[65] The ostensibly isolated congregation at Shakerley in Lancashire could not have benefited from the ministrations of visiting Protestant clergy without the organising talent of the layman Jeffrey Hurst. One of the most striking aspects of the Marian period is the leadership suddenly developed by these laymen, who testify to the strength of early Protestantism at its roots.

As the Catholics were to discover in the next reign, the problem of concealing a priest in the normal English rural background afforded great difficulties, except through the efforts of a network of favourable squires. Had the Marian reaction lasted much longer, the Protestant exiles on the continent would almost certainly have conducted their English underground on lines not dissimilar to those followed by the Seminarists and Jesuits thirty years later. Over and above their personal fears and internal disputes the exiles had a clear common ambition—the preservation of Protestantism in England, and even within their brief period on the continent they were training over a hundred young men for the ministry. The most significant advances in the organisation of English Protestantism were in fact now being made, not by secret congregations and conventicles in England but by English Protestants in Frankfurt, Zürich, Geneva and other centres of exile activity.

The Marian North

Those few men and women who climbed the higher peaks of fortitude show us only one aspect of this strange but important episode of the English Reformation. They have tended to focus our attention too narrowly upon the dramatic events of south-eastern England, and as we now learn more of the situation in the quieter regions, the shortcomings of the reaction continue to emerge with at least equal clarity. What was happening in these parts of Marian England? In reading, for example, the manuscript act books of the diocese of York, we sense the colourless character of the régime in relation to a conservative society wherein a lively Catholicism might in time have been re-engendered. The North cannot be described as ardently Catholic but it still stood at the parting of the ways. It also displayed its share of cautious secularism, its own marked relics of the old proletarian heresy, together with a considerable dissemination of the new teachings among the gentry, the clothiers and the town populations. Cases of contempt shown toward Catholic clergy and the restored Catholic ritual were far less common in Yorkshire than in London, yet several clear examples have recently been discovered. In 1554 offences against the reserved sacrament were committed at Halifax and Hull, two places later celebrated for their solid Protestantism as well as for their summary methods of punishing criminals. At Beverley another group of oppositionists were found in possession of books by such notorious Protestant authors as Thomas Becon, Roger Hutchinson and Ridley's chaplain, Nicholas Grimald.[66] At this stage, as we shall observe, even these modest signs of Protestant advance were by no means matched in north-western England. As Dr. Haigh's researches on Lancashire have ably demonstrated, that county, apart from the Manchester area, lay virtually untouched, either by the Reformation or by post-medieval Catholic influences, until the later decades of Elizabeth.

In reply to the offenders, the Marian authorities had neither a programme for reconversion nor even up-to-date ideas on persecution. Heresy cases in the church courts were conducted not only in medieval forms but in a leisurely, archaic spirit before Dr. Rokeby, vicar-general of the diocese, and Dr. Dakyn, archdeacon of the East Riding. These elderly ecclesiastics represented Nicholas Heath, the newly-appointed yet merciful Archbishop of York, and they typify the agents upon whom Mary had to rely in the provinces.[67] Dakyn was a Henrician Catholic who had lacked enthusiasm for Rome, yet embraced the cause of Mary to the extent of composing Catholic school-statutes and sending a heretic to be burned at Richmond.

His colleague Rokeby was an eminent canonist and civil servant, always at the disposal of the government in power. From 1548 to 1573 he dutifully served every régime as a leading member of the Council in the North. While men of this stamp lacked the ardour of Archdeacon Harpsfield at Canterbury, their heretical opponents showed few traces of courage. Compared with the lurid scenes in south-eastern England, the picture in the North—and in general throughout the remoter provinces—is painted in pastel shades. Yet here, where the government had genuine conservative traditions upon which to build, it did not even begin to lay its foundations. Mary's experiences in East Anglia had not greatly interested her in the provinces, and the tether binding her to London was no longer than that which bound the rest of her family. Elizabeth also showed little curiosity concerning the more distant parts of her realm, but in her case it mattered less, since her popularity was far more firmly grounded in the dominant South-east.

In a multitude of ways the unusually informative records at York serve to stress the arid character of the Marian years. Apart from cases of heresy they are dominated by numerous processes brought against the married clergy.[68] As elsewhere, the Marian deprivations resulted from the fact of marriage, not from heretical doctrine, not even from ordination under the Edwardian rite. As we have seen, marriage was a poor index to Protestant convictions. The married clergy soon showed themselves anxious to please authority and so to recover their positions in clerical life. Their individual trials often lasted intermittently over several weeks. The Archbishop's Court of Audience, having established the fact of matrimony, first ordered the offender to abstain from sacerdotal functions. Later on he suffered formal deprivation of his benefice—a severer punishment than clerics had hitherto suffered for adultery—even though marriage had recently been legalised by statute law and by Convocation. The secular priests then undertook to live chastely apart from their 'pretensed' wives, and several introduced the latter into court, in order that they too should register express consent to the separation. Often the guilty pair were ordered to refrain from meeting, except in church or market, and to avoid referring to each other as husband and wife. The court, of course, took no further interest in the plight of the women and their children. In the cases of ex-monks a formal sentence of divorce was read, accompanied by even more solemn adjurations against renewed contacts. This stage concluded, the cleric performed in his church an act of penance similar to that associated with ordinary sexual lapses. When its completion had been duly certified, he was restored to sacerdotal functions and hence made free to seek a benefice, so long as it was not the one he had recently lost. Foxe sardonically writes that such submissive clerics had in fact found marriage less agreeable than they had anticipated, and were 'contented, of their own unconstant accord, to be separated from their wives'.[69] Nevertheless, a few of them were later in trouble for revisiting their spouses, while a good many are known to have re-established their family lives under Elizabeth. As already noticed, the Marian courts also punished certain former nuns who had committed matrimony under Edward VI. These were formally divorced and put to penance, in some cases being ordered to resume monastic apparel but licensed to live elsewhere than in the now disused buildings of their former houses. The whole trivial business remained irrelevant to the real needs of the Marian reaction.

Beyond all this arid legalism the Marian government accomplished singularly little in the North. The gentry showed not the slightest inclination to countenance the restoration of religious houses, and so far as we know betrayed no hint of superstitious misgivings about their ownership of monastic lands. Mary's own restorations in the North were necessarily few. She gave several manors back to Archbishop Heath and reinstated Manchester College and the chapter at Southwell Minster. At the request of the Earl of Shrewsbury she intervened at Sheffield to return to the burgesses the lands of the parish church, which by a flagrant abuse of the Chantries Act had been deemed appropriated to superstitious uses. But even the Edwardian politicians had made similar small-scale restitutions, and the little Mary could afford to restore cannot have reconverted many waverers to the Catholic Faith.[70] In these distant provinces, which did not directly feel the weight of the persecutions, all too little is known concerning the reactions of the man in the street when he heard of the martyrdoms. Yet in that world of localised sympathies and slow communications the wave of hatred which radiated from Smithfield is unlikely to have been impressive by the time it reached the North. That Yorkshire had not become actively disloyal is indicated by the complete failure of Thomas Stafford to find a following, when in April 1557 he invaded by sea and seized Scarborough. Even this minor and short-lived exploit was due to the staggering incompetence of the Privy Council, which had been forewarned in detail.[71]

Failure and End of the Reaction

If Mary had little trouble with the North and the West, there is no evidence that she began to inspire them with any positive Catholic enthusiasm. And if she failed here, she could scarcely succeed elsewhere. In the last resort, the chief weakness of her rule lay mainly in the fact that it lacked a real missionary-organisation. Such an organisation the English Catholics only achieved in the mid-Elizabethan period, when in the face of governmental repression it came too late to achieve more than a very limited success. Reginald Pole in exile had failed to anticipate the great work of William Allen, and Mary had no band of seminary priests to do her work. As the mediocrity of the parish clergy had hampered Cranmer, so now it hampered Mary, for they were the same clergy; most were in essence late-medieval clergy, little touched by the new spirit of reform, Catholic or Protestant.

Mary's restoration of certain religious houses also links with the medieval past rather than with the seminarist future. The Catholic cause needed training colleges, not retreats from the world. It is, of course, imaginable that in time the Benedictines at Westminster, the Carthusians at Sheen, the

Bridgettines at Syon and the three other smaller restored houses might have become power-houses of an English Counter-Reformation, yet their membership and short history under Mary gives little reason for such a belief. Though some estimable characters emerged from the past to resume their places in the cloister, the number of surviving monks with strong vocation and professional competence had become very small. By 1557 the six restored houses contained just over 100 religious persons out of some 1,500 still alive.[72] Certainly the monastic movement needed to be fostered for many years in a favourable setting, if it were to generate energy and begin to feed it back into the spiritual life of England. Even had Mary lived longer, she could have enjoyed little success as a result of these methods. The parlous situation of English Catholicism demanded measures more direct, more didactic, more swift in operation among the people. Axiomatically, a religious *policy* was concerned with the minds of men outside the cloister. In January 1555 St. Ignatius Loyola invited Pole to send young men from England to the Roman and German colleges for training as Jesuits. Characteristically Pole's reply covers Loyola's other points but maintains a frigid silence concerning this ardently-phrased offer, which was repeated in vain by Loyola during the subsequent July.

By and large Marian printed propaganda appears unimpressive, and during these years the opinions of convinced Catholics do not figure very prominently in surviving literary works. Those of Miles Hogarde are among the ablest and most widely representative.[74] A London hosier resident in Pudding Lane, he was inevitably subjected to some ridicule by better-educated authors, though his work remains vigorous and intelligible. Staunchly defending the right of laymen to express their views on the religious crisis, Hogarde published nine treatises between 1544 and 1557, four of them direct assaults upon Protestant belief and practice, the rest mainly on devotional themes. He presented two of his works, written out by professional scribes, to his heroine Queen Mary, whose 'servant' he claims to be on four of his title pages. Almost ignoring papacy, hierarchy and priesthood, he attributes the restoration of Catholicism to the Queen herself. Hogarde detests the Protestant preachers and ridicules the inconstancy of the heretics in such matters as the position in church of the communion-table. He also deplores the conduct of apprentices and 'other servants', who study the Bible with the express purpose of mocking priests: they scorn the passers-by 'or with their testaments utter some wise thrust of their owne devise'. Like the Yorkshire priest Robert Parkyn, Hogarde heaps contumely upon those clergymen who had married under Edward VI. As one would anticipate, he ventures little into theological argument. Though warmly insisting upon devout belief in the doctrine of transubstantiation, he deprecates curiosity concerning the nature of the miracle. Indeed, he has surprisingly little to say about the clearer points at issue: purgatory, saint-worship, monasticism and the papal supremacy. He nevertheless displays a deep sense of the Roman Church's authority and mission: it represents 'one faith, one spirite and one judgement, not lacerated, divided or torne, but whole and intier'. For the medieval past he has a romantic regard. It was 'the happy tyme' of traditional ceremonies, when English people 'lived in mervylous love and amitie, in true dealing and honest simplicitie'. Above all, it was the time when children were taught to pray morning and evening, to be reverent in church, to make the sign of the cross and to doff their hats on meeting 'men of ancient yeres'. Like Bishop Christopherson, Hogarde thus associated Catholic doctrine with social order and with respect for age and status. Like some of his Protestant adversaries, he bade the rulers restore a 'commonwealth' in which 'the old yeomanry' of England would increase and where farmers would till the land instead of grazing it; above all a commonwealth where nobles, merchants and yeomen would stick to their allotted functions. It would seem probable enough that many Catholic laymen shared with Latimer and his friends the ideal of an essentially traditional society, and that neither party in the religious dispute was abandoning what it believed to be 'old English' social values in favour of internationalist ideals, whether those of Rome or those of Geneva.

It should have been engraven on Mary's heart, not that she lost Calais but that she failed to discover the Counter-Reformation. Her government was haunted by the ghost of her father; intent upon the legal undoing of his legalism it forgot that in the last resort religious teaching mattered infinitely more than ecclesiastical legislation. The apparent religious and cultural sterility of these years has often been observed. For creative instruction the ceaseless processions made by government order round the streets and churches of London provided a poor substitute. The man who raised a laugh by handing a pudding to one of the peripatetic prebendaries[75] was no doubt a ribald Protestant, but his action might have been still more fitting had it come from a percipient Catholic. Nevertheless the time may possibly come when we shall need to qualify such criticisms. After all the Catholic spirituality of the Marian years has not yet been fully and sympathetically explored. The theme should not be monopolised by Pole and his circle, or by the Spanish visiting ecclesiastics. Whatever the case, such aspirations have been masked by the brevity of the period during which they could be manifested.

Marian printed propaganda failed to compensate in volume for its relative lack of force and cogency. Acording to Dr. Edward Baskerville's arduous analysis of the partisan books and pamphlets issued during Mary's reign,[76] the English Protestants, working from numerous Continental presses, managed to publish 114 items, as opposed to 93 by the Catholics working in England. Yet the literary predominance of the former appears to have been far greater than these figures would suggest. Many of the Catholic publications are devotional works or sermons with little combative force, whereas those of their adversaries are mostly aimed with skill at the literate public. As in the days of Tyndale, the books from overseas penetrated the feeble security-screen. The authors in exile could muster a formidable army of talent. Led by such writers as Bale, Goodman, Ponet and Knox, they also edited and reprinted Cranmer, Ridley, and Latimer, besides translating Protestant classics by Luther, Melanchthon and Calvin. In 1557 Whittingham and his assistants even produced a fresh version of the New Testament in

English, which formed the first instalment of the *Geneva Bible*. On the Catholic side, the potential leader Stephen Gardiner had his hands full as Lord Chancellor. Indeed, with a stroke of genius the Protestants republished his own book *De Vera Obedientia* (1535) thus making him reappear not as a loyal papalist but in his former guise as the antipapal backer of Henry VIII! Otherwise, with the exception of Bishop John Christopherson and possibly Hogarde, the Catholic controversialists appear at best as a group of devoted mediocrities. The Marian government itself, having effectively published Northumberland's confession of guilt, made little use of its victory over Wyatt, or of Cranmer's initial wavering, or even of the grovelling recantation of the famous humanist Sir John Cheke, kidnapped abroad by Marian agents for that express purpose.

The devotion of Mary and Pole to Rome and to Spain received some strange rewards when Paul IV, a Neapolitan who detested Spanish rule over his country, proceeded to extremities against Philip. In 1557 Mary found herself without financial resources but committed to war with France; Pole found his legatine commission revoked and himself summoned to Rome to be tried for heresy. Philip's neglect of English interests now justified everything which had been said against the Spanish marriage. Even Mary's ministers took little pains to hide their hatred, yet they could not justly blame him for their own surpassing blunders in relation to the defence of Calais. After 211 years in English hands the town fell in January 1558, and the Spanish ambassador wrote, 'I am told that, since the loss of Calais, not a third of the people who usually go to church are now attending'.[77] No doubt adolescent chauvinism and doctrinal uncertainties often went together, and this terrible affront to national pride cannot have been without its effect on religious opinion at this moment of climax.

The last months of the ill-starred reign were marked by a season of exceptional storms and floods and by fevers with a heavy mortality. Men drew the same conclusion as they had drawn five years earlier at the expense of Northumberland. 'God did so punish the realm with quartan agues', wrote Sir Thomas Smith, 'and with other long and new sicknesses, that in the last two years of the reign of Queen Mary, so many of her subjects was made away, what with the execution of sword and fire, what by sickness, that the third part of the men of England were consumed.'[78] About the time of Mary's departure her personal physicians Hughes and Owen both died, together with many leading ecclesiastics like William Peto, whom the Pope had wanted to set in Pole's place, and William Peryn, the Dominican devotional writer, one of the few of Mary's subjects conversant with the new Jesuit techniques of meditation. Yet of far greater historical significance were the deaths in 1557–8 of twelve out of the twenty-two diocesan bishops. Nature seemed determined to complete at least one side of Mary's work by removing what remained of the original cast from the drama of the English Reformation.

The Queen's last official acts continued in keeping with her previous policy. She transferred an extraordinary number of Crown livings to the bishops, appointed more Catholics to judicial and administrative offices; she even began to fill the vacant sees. For her failure to complete this important undertaking the Spanish ambassador blamed 'that accursed cardinal', Pole. At her death there were five vacant sees, a figure which had increased to ten by the end of the year. Hence when Elizabeth undertook the reversal of her religious policy, only a steadfast but depleted group of Catholic bishops stood in the way. Mary died on 17 November, Reginald Pole a few hours later, both displaying to the end of their sufferings an admirable piety and an unflinching sense of rectitude. Faithful to duty as they saw it, they had undergone great trials in the defence of an idea they were not conspicuously qualified to defend. Both displayed the tragedy of the doctrinaire called to practical leadership, yet lacking that instinct towards human beings, that sense of the possible in a real world, which have always proved more useful in English affairs than high principles and strict logic based on narrow premises. But shortcomings of this sort could never be alleged against the young Queen in whose honour the relieved Londoners feasted in the streets and lit bonfires on the night of Mary's death.

Unlike some of his younger contemporaries, the present writer still regards the reign of Mary Tudor as a failure, whether judged by her own objectives or by the interests of the nation. Agreed, she suffered persistent ill-luck. After the first few months of popularity she found herself beset by a host of thorny and intractable problems. At home her subjects predictably detested the presence of a foreign king. Even though his powers were officially circumscribed, Philip's heirs would be kings of England, yet bound by several continental ties and loyalties. Again, Mary's financial reforms never remedied a governmental shortage of funds, while the purchasers of ecclesiastical properties maintained their defensive suspicions. Abroad she encountered not only an enterprising King of France, intent to take Calais and expunge from his country the last traces of English occupation, but also the most intransigent of popes, who finally rendered her Spanish alliance and her marriage incompatible with her restoration of papalism in England. So troublous a situation demanded an astute politician with an exceptional flair for judging English opinion and assessing priorities. Mary herself was no sort of a politician and she failed moreover to appoint a chief minister endowed with such qualities. She was the prisoner of a sorrowful past which induced a neurotic admiration for her mother's country and kinsfolk. She knew all too well that while on her father's side she came of the great houses of Lancaster and York, her maternal grandparents were far greater monarchs: the 'Catholic Kings', Ferdinand and Isabella. In fairness it may be added that in choosing to marry her cousin she had also in mind his apparent ability to maintain her position as against France. Yet even in this respect he was to fail her.[79] After her brief months of happiness with the indifferent and unfaithful Philip, she found a congenial adviser in Reginald Pole, whose ardent aspirations did not make him the right man to guide her through the real world, least of all through the secular politics of that English world from which he had been exiled since the year 1532. So far we have tended to see Pole against the background of the persecution, yet in other respects it now seems clear enough that his attempt to reorganise the English Church encountered not only a lukewarm clergy but ecclesiastical funds so depleted as to have daunted the ablest administrator.[80] Thus in different senses both Mary and Pole remained mental exiles, stumbling along together in the light of memories and dogmas which failed to accommodate the hard facts of their situation in England. Yet no misjudgment was more fatal than their belief—shared in later years by that abler exile, Cardinal Allen—that the English heresy consisted in the main of a few pockets of small tradesmen, readily disposable by a judicious mixture of tuition and combustion.

Queen Mary still has her apologists who remain unsatisfied with our compassion, and desperately want to make her régime at least potentially successful. Some of them claim that the notorious enmity on the Privy Council between Gardiner and Paget was 'a creative rivalry' and that she and Pole, anticipating the most far-seeing decrees of Trent, 'appear to have produced a clergy distinguished for its integrity and level of education'. Surely they did not 'produce' a clergy at all! Though Catholic spirituality was not yet dead in England, the great majority of these men had recently been conducting the Edwardian services and were shortly to settle down as Elizabethan Protestants. It is also difficult to see how Mary and Pole 'educated' them, or indeed could have done so within four years. We are even told that 'the strength of the Catholic revival can be seen ... in the united front presented by the Marian bishops, in 1559'.[81] Yet how can the tiny, isolated group of Marian bishops, courageous as they proved in 1558–9, testify to a general Catholic revival among the parish clergy as a whole? More moderately, other admirers have claimed that Mary's real obstacle was shortage of time, that given a longer life she would in all likelihood have revived English Catholicism and restored its sway as the national religion. Hilaire Belloc, an enchanting writer but a most tendentious historian, wrote that her survival would have made the English Reformation 'an abortive and forgotten episode'.[82] Such guessing-games cannot be settled even by the most elaborate computers, but so far as actual facts can inspire reasonable conjectures, I can see few if any which support this optimistic prophecy. The fires of Smithfield cannot be squared with the ideas of reconciliation and healing. Mary never displayed the least flexibility of spirit or method, even when her most valued advisers, Charles V, Philip and their envoy Renard, enjoined a cautious and gradualist approach to the problem of English heresy. Even had she lived into old age, she could never have become a liberal Roman Catholic, eventually granting freedom of worship at least to the more moderate of her Protestant subjects. After 1553 nothing less than this could have produced peace and secular unity. In due course we shall examine the strong reasons for supposing that by this date Protestantism had become widespread and tenacious in London, East Anglia, Essex, Kent, East Sussex and the Thames Valley. Throughout much of this crucial area dissatisfaction and conspiracy became rife by 1554,[83] while even in 1558 the stream of martyrs and risk-takers showed not the slightest sign of running dry. If we try to invent a realistic scenario for the Queen's longer survival, it must surely contain ever more burnings, more exiles and plots, in all likelihood a descent into internal warfare, as in France, the Netherlands,

Bohemia and other countries divided by such politico-religious passions. There remain the strongest indications that the great majority of Englishmen—whatever their religious leanings—remained unfanatical and indisposed to see this violent outcome, or for that matter a Habsburg hegemony and a Spanish-type Inquisition erected in their country. On the other hand after Philip's advent—or even earlier—Mary became associated closely with several Spanish practitioners and theorists on the eradication of heresy, notably with à Castro, the publicist, and with Carranza, who ensured the execution of Cranmer, even after his recantation.[84] Amid all this gloomy polarisation, did Mary's ecclesiastical solution really stand a good chance of becoming a broadly acceptable English Catholicism?

This last issue turns less on the niceties of theological debate than upon those aspects of national consciousness and emotion which were beginning to create a gulf between Spanish and English life-styles. The deep 'natural' humanity of the Spanish nation, though preserved by her great poets and novelists, had been suffused by a type of ardour very different from those of the northern peoples, and deriving from a long medieval crusade for reunion against the Islamic 'infidel' inside the frontiers of Spain. Neither Queen Mary's subjects nor their ancestors had undergone this tempering of the spirit: to an overwhelming extent English Catholic opinion was still traditionalist rather than progressive or adventurous. Since England was neither Aragon nor Castile, no wise Tudor monarch should for a moment have contemplated such a spiritual emigration. Should the reader doubt the applicability of this diagnosis to the mid-sixteenth century, let him at least read the related history of the Netherlands, where a closely similar but more terrible confrontation of ideals was to occupy the subsequent half-century.

13 Three Retrospective Enquiries

Anticlericalism, Catholic and Protestant

At least one prominent historian of the English Reformation has sought to remove anticlerical emotions and controversies from the significant causes of the movement, and even to claim that the influence of anticlericalism is a 'fiction' invented by modern historians.[1] In truth the word covers a number of differing yet closely related phenomena. Though so complex in the outer world, anticlericalism was equally complex in the mind of the individual. Here it was compounded of more or less rational criticism and some longstanding but by no means altogether rationalised grudges and jealousies. It was all the more real and powerful because of these latter. Its many-sidedness and sheer breadth of appeal among laymen were the very factors which made it formidable. We should be ill-advised if we tried to dismiss the term anticlericalism from our vocabulary, just because it cannot be adequately paraphrased in a simple sentence. During the later Middle Ages harsh criticisms of the clergy became ever more prominent and more debilitating within the Catholic Church, not least because so much of it came from reformist clergymen. Stimulated not only by local factors but also by the highly controversial situations in which the late medieval papacy found itself, anticlericalism in its various forms became endemic throughout Europe. So far as we can measure its effects, it appears most virulent in Germany, where the prince bishops and other aristocratic churchmen were even more powerful and privileged than most of the English prelates.

In England the critical attitudes could only be dismissed as unimportant by glossing over the voluminous evidence of the fourteenth and fifteenth centuries, and then by starting the story in 1512—as so many historians of Tudor England have mistakenly done—with the case of Richard Hunne. Given this amputation, such a thesis might well end by returning to the idyll beloved by Victorian socialists, Catholics and 'High' Anglicans; the idyll of a harmonious medieval society, within which 'satisfied' peasants and crafts-men loved their devoted priests and desired no changes in the Church. Indeed, little separates these images from the simplistic belief that the

Reformation, directed by erastian rulers and Protestant ideologues, rent asunder a tranquil, balanced and supranational culture. Conducted on this rarified level, the Reformation debate is apt to lead both radical Protestants and militant Catholics into mutual incomprehension and unhealthily selective attitudes towards the sources. Yet it is hard to see how the vast body of evidence for anticlerical forces within English public opinion can be explained away, or even limited to the writers and lawyers. These forces quite certainly existed on a large scale both before and throughout the Reformation-process, though there will doubtless remain legitimate differences of opinion regarding their precise responsibility for the outcome. In truth, to attribute the Reformation wholly or even mainly to anticlericalism would be as irresponsible as to question the latter's substantial existence.

Like most European countries, England both manufactured and imported a variety of hostile attitudes toward the clergy during the fourteenth and fifteenth centuries. How could it have been otherwise? Collectively rich and politically influential, the priesthood claimed to be divinely endowed with vast powers over the lives and the salvation of all men. Moreover through their punitive jurisdiction in the ecclesiastical courts and their controls through the confessional, they still assiduously exercised these powers. Throughout the later Middle Ages, the involvement of the higher clergy in power-politics tended always to increase. Popes found secular allies and waged war on emperors, while bishops held great offices of state and—for example in the English Wars of the Roses—bore allegiances to political factions. Yet psychologically the situation began to change long before the Reformation and it changed most noticeably among laymen. Led moreover by Marsiglio's *Defensor Pacis*, John of Paris, Pierre Dubois, William of Occam, John Wycliffe and other learned schoolmen of the fourteenth century produced several works of Erastian theory which, in print two hundred years later, became familiar among educated Tudor Englishmen. The two works most read over this long period were the *Defensor* and the more popular *Disputacio inter clericum et militem*, probably written by Dubois in support of Philip IV of France, that scourge of the Papacy. In 1533–4 William Marshall's translation of the *Defensor* into English was financed by his patron Thomas Cromwell. It boldly claimed that the secular state could supply all the demands of earthly life, and that the activities of the clergy should be confined to the spiritual sphere. As for the *Disputacio*, it was translated by John de Trevisa about 1400 and later in more modern English. Appearing in print as early as 1473, it still attracted many English readers around 1540, perhaps through the influence of Cromwell. Such literature inspired even those episcopal supporters of Henry VIII's Reformation, Edward Fox and Stephen Gardiner.

Thus in England as elsewhere the later medieval centuries saw a slow but steady growth in urban life, in lay sophistication, educational expansion and professional *esprit de corps*. Most notably, the common lawyers, instruments of an effective state, were also an independent lay corporation with an obvious inducement to restrict the jurisdiction of ecclesiastical courts and lawyers, which often overlapped and competed with their own legal business. Likewise the most purposeful elements in local government, the urban oligarchies, consisted of wealthy merchants already intent to assume where possible the business administration of the churches and clergy within their walls. Even in the days of Henry II there had been critics of the clergy such as Walter Map; but by the accession of Henry VIII, the internal dynamics of the kingdom had changed beyond recognition and never in favour of the ecclesiastical power.

The critical spirit reached its first climax with the three greatest English writers of the late fourteenth century: Langland, Wycliffe and Chaucer. Despite a wealth of imaginative allegory, Langland built his great poem around the glaring contrast between his hero Piers Plowman, who kept the community alive, and on the other side those uncharitable prelates and corrupt priests who did nothing except for money. In the poet's view, even the friars had abandoned their mission to the poor in order to cultivate rich patrons and build expensive churches. With a crude prescience Langland announced that a king would arise to purge the English church.[2] His *Vision of Piers Plowman* has too often been presented as a medieval work with little relevance to later ages. On the contrary, it would seem that the early and middle Tudor period was the one in which the *Vision* attained its highest influence. Between 1520 and 1550 a series of imitative works in this tradition, mostly with the name of Piers in their titles, issued from the presses.[3] Finally in 1550 Robert Crowley published most of Langland's own text.[4] Its supposed relevance to mid-Tudor problems is signalised by various editorial changes, intended to link it with the 'social gospel' fashionable in the reign of Edward VI. Crowley also omitted some specifically Catholic elements of Langland's thought. This version passed through three quarto editions in 1550 and was to be reprinted in 1561.

Langland had been by no means the only writer of his day to stimulate anticlerical forces and eventually to impress Tudor readers and publicists. During the forties and fifties of the sixteenth century Crowley and other radical Protestants, highly conscious of Wyclife's importance as a prophet of clerical doom, published Lollard texts, such as the notorious *Wicket*.[5] Meanwhile Chaucer's *Canterbury Tales* attained five printed editions between 1478 and 1526, achieving through print a towering status in English literary culture.[6] His depictions of clergymen and church-officials seem to us good-humoured, yet in that context they became far from innocuous. In the *Prologue*, four of his five clerics are rogues and hypocrites, while the fifth, the virtuous and dutiful country parson, is not only contrasted with his grasping colleagues but linked with the Langland tradition by having as his brother the equally practical and charitable Ploughman. In the late development of these fourteenth-century traditions, Tudor publishing became both crucial and creative. Never did the writers of that earlier century gain so large a share of the nation's attention as in the days of Henry VIII and Edward VI. From this point we shall need to mention—though from a new angle—some evidence on the clergy already noticed during our earlier description of the English Church.

During the intervening fifteenth century critical attitudes toward churchmen had been widely displayed in both sermons[7] and popular poetry,[8] yet they were by no means limited to these forms. They found some major exponents among the leading clergy, at first in marked contrast with the political bishops, but later in equally marked accord with that humanist piety which began to appear during the reign of Henry VII. Of the first stage Thomas Gascoigne forms the exemplar; in the later stage we find figures already familiar, particularly Dean Colet and his friend William Melton, Chancellor of York. As Chancellor of the University of Oxford, Gascoigne belonged to the clerical establishment. Yet in his diffuse *Liber Veritatum*, written around the middle of the fifteenth century, he assures his readers—giving some concrete examples—that the people hated the bishops of that day, this not merely because they were politicians and courtiers, but also on account of their lordly establishments and their failure to preach the gospel.[9] In his *Sermon on the Seven Streams of Babylon* Gascoigne protests with vigour against the ordination of unworthy clerics, absenteeism and pluralism, the appropriation of churches and tithes to men without the cure of souls, the abuse of indulgences, dispensations and licences.[10] In regard to the keeping of concubines by priests, Gascoigne relates how a bishop of St. David's refused to allow some conscience-stricken priests to discard their illicit partners, explaining amicably that he, the bishop, would by agreeing lose 400 marks a year, hitherto paid him for granting them quasi-marital privileges.[11] We have already cited Chancellor Melton to the effect that the moral failings of the bucolic parish clergy were largely due to their lack of education.[12] Likewise in that notorious Convocation sermon of 1512, his friend Colet reverted to the greed of the priesthood, which had aroused disaffection and heresy among the people. The Dean of St. Paul's did not leave his distinguished audience with any illusion that such faults lay only with obscure country parsons. He refers also to the 'greediness and appetite of honour and dignity' which together with the 'heaping of benefices upon benefices' marked the careerist senior clergy. He also pointed to the need for a clerical education, not in unhelpful scholastic learning but in the Scriptures.[13] Meanwhile clerical satirists like Alexander Barclay[14] and John Skelton[15] scourged bishops and priests even more vigorously than they scourged the laity. Though sometimes mistakenly presented as a mere enemy of Wolsey, Skelton does in fact include in his strictures the whole of the clerical order; yet he is no forerunner of Protestant religion but a devotee of the Virgin, a harsh critic of Lutheranism in general and of its recent Cambridge adherents in particular.[16]

Modern research such as that by Margaret Bowker[17] and Peter Heath[18] has rightly argued that both contemporary and modern assailants generalised too severely about the learning and morals of the lower clergy. Nevertheless these same scholars are far from accepting the Victorian idyll. They criticise unselective recruitment and cite official documents showing that actual moral lapses were by no means rare. Even so, our present enquiry is little concerned with the accuracy of such charges, but with the widespread hostility apparent in the surviving evidence. Whole-hearted defenders of the clergy are conspicuously lacking. In those trenchant passages of Thomas

More already quoted,[19] he does not, as we might anticipate, defend the English clergy through thick and thin: rather is he concerned to exalt the sacred calling of a priest and to demand reforms of the current system which would help the unworthy men to match the higher Catholic ideals. One need scarcely add that most of the mid-Tudor Protestant critics are even less generous than their Catholic predecessors. In particular the vitriolic John Bale and the scurrilous but eloquent Simon Fish magnify that suspicion of sexual vices so inevitably directed against a celibate order by its enemies.[20] On seeking to re-examine both these and the more Protestant critics of the conservative clergy, I began by listing from memory seventeen familiar names,[21] plus a number of anonymous pamphlets of similar origins mostly appearing between 1530 and 1553. Soon afterwards I encountered the substantial work by John N. King, *English Reformation Literature: The Tudor Origins of the Protestant Tradition*, which added a list of minor pamphleteers, satirists and playwrights of the same period and with similar critical opinions.[22] Certainly these groups could not be claimed as remote intellectuals: their members were mostly literate laymen of obscure origins who wrote to attract working people at least as much as their social superiors. All in all, it would seem absurd to argue that this large and miscellaneous body of anticlerical writers bore no close relationship with the opinions of shopkeepers, craftsmen, small traders, even perhaps with those of peasant-farmers, the direct descendants of Piers Plowman himself! This point allowed, it still remains possible to exaggerate the number and continuity of documented quarrels at parish-level between priesthood and laity, although we do continue to unearth numerous tithe-suits, some between priests and people, others involving lay tithe-farmers.

Tithes generated infinite discord, especially in London, but were by no means the sole source of troubles in the parishes.[23] A more complex and typical image of parochial tensions was provided by my own examination of certain visitation books of the diocese of Peterborough, mainly compiled in 1546–8 and now available in the Northamptonshire Record Office at Delapre Abbey.[24] Fairly numerous clerical offences and shortcomings emerged: they are seldom exactly dated, but certainly belong to the late forties. The area itself, comprising Northamptonshire and Rutland, already contained some Protestant groups, as at Northampton, Oakham, Oundle, Lowick, Geddington and other places, yet this changing doctrinal scene makes far less impact than the old problems of clerical discipline and the maintenance of church fabrics. The data relevant to our present enquiry must here by summarised briefly. The vicar of St. Giles, Northampton, a former monk and a strong religious conservative, was charged with assaulting his sexton and polluting the church with the latter's blood. At Wardley a layman called Alyn Batt had 'violently, shamfully and cowardly stryken his curate, the parson of the same towne, on the heid with an hatchett, without any occasion showyd or given by the said parson unto the said Alyn Batt'. Two men blasphemed in the church at Rothwell and used the curate 'uncharitably'. Numerous incumbents were accused by their churchwardens with illegally refusing to repair the chancels of their churches, to subscribe to the cost of installing bibles, or with failure to show hospitality or give alms. At Great Billing the parson had the enviable income of £21 a year, but gave nothing away. The curate at Sulgrave had offended people by wearing modish lay costume. At Kislingbury the priest was said to be 'a common haunter of alehouses, givinge him selfe to drynkyng, ryotinge and playinge at unlawful games'. These accusations he denied, but was further accused of being 'a brawler and slanderer, a chider and a scolder'. At Culworth four parishioners testified 'that we have an unquyet vicar, and that he will not folowe the Kinges injunctions by the wrytinge of the boke of regester'.

Earlier in the reign a very few Northamptonshire clergy had shown themselves as by no means natural celibates. A middle-aged rector of Great Addington, no unlettered yokel but a bachelor of law, had two children by his cook Mrs. Byrde, a married woman who had duly done a spell in the village stocks. In 1526 this rector had become so unpopular that he discarded priestly attire and intimidated his critics by perambulating the village clad in chain mail.[25] In our visitation records of 1546 there appear scarcely any indications of concubinage, though the churchwardens of Pilton alleged that on 3 March 1545, at 11 p.m. they had taken their parson 'starke naked' in the house of a parishioner, along with the latter's wife. The four witnesses were not alone but *cum multis aliis*, having apparently organised a mass-spectatorship appropriate to this rare event in the ecclesiastical history of Pilton. It is nevertheless noteworthy that the victim remained rector there until his death in 1558!

The rest of the complaints against the clergy also illustrate the atmosphere but in themselves amount to little. A chantry priest retained and refused to deliver money left by a lady to found an obit. Moreover this same humble denizen of the hierarchy did not posess a surplice but sat in the choir without one, 'more lyke a servynge man than a prest, to evell ensample of other'. The Protestant legislation of 1547 was already proving distasteful to conservative clerics, for example to the master of the almshouse or hospital at Oakham. He was presented in November 1548 because he had not preached since the Royal Visitation, but had haunted taverns and unlawful games. Furthermore, he had 'enticed or lured' people from the parish church to his private Latin services and had distributed holy bread and holy water, 'forsakynge the herynge of Goddes worde and followyng his traditions'. Yet in general most of these charges are rather trivial, suggesting poor relationships and lack of co-operation between parsons and wardens, rather than serious offences on either side. Perhaps some other untoward events had been concealed, yet it should not be overlooked that in theory about 300 parishes were due to be visited during these years and that, for all we know, many of those missing from this record may have been models of Christian concord. The charges we describe should clearly be viewed in this wider perspective. Inasmuch as this rather conservative, unsensational area must typify much of late Henrician England, it suggests that the daily relations between laity and parish clergy were better than the rancorous hotbed, though falling distinctly short of the idyll. This mediocre situation accords in general with the standard recent works on English parish life of that period, and it broadly harmonises with my own impressions of Henrician Yorkshire and other familiar areas.

London appears distinctly more anticlerical than Northamptonshire from the 1540s, when the records of the Court of Aldermen begin to detail a series of assaults upon priests by young hooligans,[26] some fresh from a game of football. Already a chequered picture emerges from the act book of the Vicars General of the diocese of London extending over the period 1520 to 1538.[27] It includes a number of cases involving physical assaults and dire threats against incumbents and diocesan officials,[28] together with some thirty-four charges of sexual misconduct and about 90 charges of indiscipline brought against both regular and secular clerics. How should such a document be interpreted? On the one hand many more such acts were doubtless committed in turbulent London without ever being recorded, much less preserved in our extant sources. Again, the populations within which they occurred were very small in comparison with their equivalents in later centuries. On the other hand the period covered by the London book is quite long, so that by Tudor standards these figures should not be regarded as sensational. All in all, it seems clear enough that we must neither idealise the relations between clerics and laymen nor compare them favourably with those of later times. Senior ecclesiastics no longer acquire much wealth; clerical prosecutors do not probe into our private lives, but conversely we hardly ever stage murderous attacks on ministers of religion! In early Tudor England personal violence flared all too readily; it should be considered alongside Gascoigne's similar complaints a century earlier. Moreover these personal clashes are by no means the only aspects of anticlericalism to be studied in English local history. Where the Protestant Reformation first prospered, the preceding anticlerical forces seem to have been most intense. As Dr. Peter Clark has shown, [29] there occurred serious conflicts in almost every town in Kent between churchmen and the lay community. Here there had been some aggressive parish priests, yet a more crucial issue was the claim of religious houses to exercise extensive civil jurisdiction within the towns. Such situations should be sought elsewhere and may prove to have interesting social implications. In all likelihood this sort of maladjustment no longer sprang merely from ancient concentrations of urban ecclesiastical property, but also to some extent from the severe economic depression which faced so many towns during the early decades of the sixteenth century. Amid their local crises did townspeople consciously harbour the notion that the 'superfluous' wealth of the Church should be diverted to rescue civic finances? And though the local popularity of some religious houses survived until their dissolution, did their eventual disappearance from the urban scene help to diminish the stock of anticlerical feeling? At present such questions cannot be answered with much confidence.

If these varying situations to any degree typify English parish life preceding and accompanying the early stages of the Reformation, we can supply a feasible context to some sensational encounters, such as the quarrels of 1512 at Bowers Gifford, Essex, related by Peter Heath,[30] and the complex exchanges arising from the tithe dispute of 1530 at Hayes, Middlesex, which form a riotous chapter in Sir Geoffrey Elton's *Star Chamber Stories*.[31] In a sense such cases are exceptional, yet they belong to, and arise from, that oft-pious, oft-rancorous background of parish life, which we have sought to exemplify from London, Northamptonshire and Kent. Even the notorious cases are but peaks in that distinctly rugged landscape of church life which characterised the fifteenth century and at least the first half of the sixteenth. If the laymen seem ambivalent, so do the parish clergy. Even in the more conservative regions of England some very diverse clerical images must have been contending in the popular mind. Only a few incumbents were able (or licensed) to preach, and thoughtful parishioners can seldom have revered them as actual teachers of Christian belief. Truly, until Protestantism reinterpreted the Mass, even unlearned priests did attract reverence on account of their role in the daily miracle of transubstantiation, yet in villages and small towns laymen not infrequently encountered their priests as zealous enforcers of clerical perquisites or as all-too-human drinking-companions in the alehouses.[32]

Finally, amid the ostensible causes of popular anticlericalism, how much stress should we place upon ecclesiastical jurisdiction over the laity? The question does not admit of a simple answer: we cannot argue without serious reservations from that alleged outburst of hatred against the church courts which occurred in 1532.[33] These courts were then tendentiously depicted as a hateful burden upon the nation, but such a protest made by lawyers and parliamentarians proves little about Tudor public opinion in general. There are even signs that some litigants in civil cases found ecclesiastical jurisdiction convenient. It invaded what would now be reckoned important secular fields of law, and might well have involved lower costs and shorter delays than proceedings under the Common Law.[34] On the other hand, in London and Canterbury a decline in the volume of litigation in the church courts is thought to have begun as early as 1500.[35] Again, however useful the Church's handling of suits between party and party, a far less attractive spectacle appeared with the quasi-criminal jurisdiction exercised by the archdeacons' courts in regard to the common sexual offences. Privileged people, whose own sins were seldom exposed to public censure and ridicule, doubtless applauded such disciplining of the lower classes. Yet terms of derision and resentment were applied by working people to the archdeacons' 'bawdy court'.[36] Though generally accepted as age-old practice, and substantially surviving long after the advent of the Anglican Church, these juridical relations cannot at any stage have augmented the popularity and prestige of the clergy. Indeed, their control in both court and confessional over the sexuality of the people may well have provided a major cause of anticlericalism. In the last resort it remains one of those many factors hard either to verify or to dismiss by means of adequate documentary evidence.

How then should we summarise the contributions of anticlericalism to the development of the Reformation in England? That it had a long history and took many forms, that it was most clearly expressed by exceptional but doctrinally orthodox priests, we have already shown by reference to many examples. Nevertheless at the outset of the Henrician Reformation, popular opinion obviously contained some powerful antitheses. As we have insisted, Catholic modes of piety still in the 1530s commanded a widespread respect—though most markedly among the older generation—throughout the regions of England. Likewise the functions of the priest at the altar preserved much of his traditional status. On the other hand the sources we have cited make it probable that reverence toward clerical authority, never universal even in medieval times, had undergone a gradual decline ever since the fourteenth century. Slow in northern and western country areas but everywhere stronger in towns as opposed to rural parishes, this process may well have helped to predispose many people to accept the idea of reform, and possibly the Henrician revolution itself. Beyond this point even conservative opinion was divided. In 1528, while repudiating Lutheran theology, Thomas More demanded changes in the old system of clerical recruitment; but younger and less intellectual people cannot have found it so easy to determine where reforms of organisation ended and where the perils of doctrinal innovation began. Meanwhile elderly clerics like John Fisher bewailed even the former as indicating an actual loss of Christian faith by the laity.[37] In 1529, when Fisher spoke thus, few of the reformist parliamentarians whom he blamed were propounding actual heresy, since the grip of Lutheran doctrines remained as yet weak among them and within the nation at large. Thus far the growing demand for administrative and disciplinary changes amounted to little more than a revival of long-familiar complaints, though it was obviously amplified by the rapid expansion of printing and publishing. During the years of Wolsey's greatness popular satire and higher expectations of clerical performance went hand in hand, their most notable exponent being the anti-Lutheran publicist John Skelton. Yet here and at other periods of our history notable changes in religious outlook have occurred independently of any dominant ideology or technological advance. In any western country the mental atmosphere can be changed by an international, almost unchartable multitude of influences. Processes some-what comparable were to arise in England around the Restoration of Charles II and again during the last years of Queen Victoria. In each case age-gaps opened up and new generations of opinion rejected or modified older codes, taboos and interpretations.

Such changes of the *Zeitgeist* can begin in advance of the thinkers to whom they are later attributed. Indeed one might reasonably argue that Luther and Zwingli did not initiate the public demand for church reform any more than Marx and Engels created socialism. In addition we may well conclude that demand for change can be aroused by provocative conservatism. In Henrician England the clergy maintained a strong *esprit de corps* which ignored even the thoughtful criticisms by their own intellectuals, and came near to equating churchly customs, endowments and privileges with the recorded teachings of Christ. Of course such ultra-conservatism proved highly vulnerable when the vernacular Scriptures, in due course exposed to public examination, showed so plainly that this clerical equation could not be rationally maintained. Long since prophesied by Wycliffe and Langland, the monarchical purging of the Church took political and economic rather than disciplinary forms under Henry VIII. Likewise, even in conservative Northern England, the resistance proved as much politico-economic as religious. National opinion still showed many divisions, yet after the major crisis of 1536–7 it became on balance decisively loyal to the Crown. Both as cause and as effect, public opinion had strong links with state actions. Amongst those links was the established phenomenon of anticlericalism. The antitheses 'reformation from above' versus 'reformation from below' will not carry us far toward a true understanding of the English Reformation.

The Distribution and Growth of Protestantism to 1558

In which parts of England and Wales was Protestantism most heavily located during its first three decades?[38] Where on the other hand did it fail to make much impact among the people until late in the century? Again, what proportion of the total population is likely to have been affected previous to the accession of Elizabeth? The first two of these questions can be roughly answered. The third does not admit even of rough calculation: the sources available make it an unanswerable or even a nonsensical question. At the outset it must be made clear that we possess during this period no contemporary censuses of Protestants or of Catholics. As so often, the problems of mass-psychology must needs be approached by impressions, not in terms of genuine statistics: thus we can at best propound solutions claiming a strong probability. We are nevertheless fortunate in possessing a useful modern list, though one necessarily based upon the incomplete body of surviving evidence. This is the *Biographical Register of Early English Protestants c.1525–1558* compiled by Dr. John Fines after an exhaustive search of the printed sources, and of some others still in manuscript.[39] It contains the relevant facts concerning about 3,000 persons, most of them now obscure and some difficult to place into local contexts. The information is chiefly, though by no means wholly, drawn from Foxe and from the official records of Church and State. In the future fresh names will be added, perhaps mostly emerging from those many thousands of Tudor wills now in print or still in manuscript.

Conservatively-minded testators begin by bequeathing their souls to the Virgin and the company of the saints, while apparent converts to Protestantism, rejecting this unacceptable saint-worship, simply leave their souls to God or to Christ. A minority of Protestants reinforce their convictions by further evangelical sentences, often recording their trust to be redeemed solely by the merits of Christ on the cross. True, a will may in some cases reflect merely the custom of local scriveners or the counsel of a priest, rather than the personal beliefs of the testator. For this reason, if in future we want to add only certain (as distinct from probable) Protestants to the Fines *Register*, it would be prudent to select those testators who explicitly confirm their Protestant inclinations. Nevertheless, for mass-statistical purposes the deliberate omission of the saints should be allowed significance. It seems generally agreed that, used thus in large numbers, wills should indicate the broad trends of religious opinion in their several places and areas of origin.

Whatever the case, the Fines *Register* has many obvious and valuable uses for the social historian, always provided the user realises that it must not be taken as a contemporary census. No such censuses, efficient or otherwise, were compiled during this period. It is a list of *surviving* names and references in a field where these 'survivors' must be hugely outnumbered by the wholly unrecorded Protestants. Broadly speaking it is valuable as revealing the leaders, the bold risk-takers: those who were caught and charged with heresy, and for that very reason got their names into the extant act books of the church courts and other official records, or else into the voluminous *Acts and Monuments* of John Foxe. Though the *Register* thus represents only the visible tip of the Protestant iceberg, it should very roughly indicate the geographical distribution of the new religion. So used, it tends to confirm the statement of Foxe that the great majority of mid-Tudor Protestants lived in south-eastern England. Of the 3,000 names more than 2,000 can be exactly located, and over 70 per cent of these came from one of the following counties: London with Middlesex, Kent, Essex, Suffolk, Norfolk, East Sussex and—less intensively—parts of Oxfordshire, Berkshire and Buckinghamshire. It need scarcely be added that this great crescent of coastal counties, along with its westward extension up the Thames, is vastly more important than the formula 'London and Kent' sometimes perfunctorily given by historians inclined to minimise the early English Reformation. This large 'heartland' constituted the wealthiest, most populated and best educated region of England, the region most closely in touch with the exiled propagandists led by Tyndale, and also with the continental world of Erasmus.

Another approach to the question of regional distribution could involve a study of the distribution of martyrdoms during the Marian persecution of 1554–8. Of about 290 Marian martyrdoms, at least 277 can be exactly located, and of these no less than 230 (83 per cent) occurred in the same large south-eastern region.[40] This high percentage gives no occasion for surprise, when we reflect that the pressure for severity came largely from the Court, indeed from Queen Mary in person, from her more extreme councillors and from the enthusiasts whom they appointed as special commissioners. Yet she presumably attacked those same areas not just because they were accessible, but because they presented the most flagrant threat to her authority. Within the great crescent, London, Kent and Essex were by any criteria foremost in the movement.[41] Between them they furnished Dr. Fines with about half of his located names, while no less than 142 of the 290 Marian martyrdoms occurred at only three centres: London, Canterbury and Colchester.

Outside the south-east there developed certain secondary areas and towns, where Protestantism attracted a lesser yet fairly numerous follow-ing, for example Gloucestershire, with its many small but wealthy clothing-towns and its great port at Bristol.[42] While the new beliefs also attracted the similar towns and villages in Berkshire and Wiltshire,[43] a very few larger centres developed in the west Midlands, especially in the once great but now declining industrial city of Coventry and in the small cathedral city of Lichfield. These last places were situated near districts in Warwickshire and Staffordshire in which some activist squires and country people associated around the martyrs Joyce Lewis and Robert Glover. Yet still further westward along the Welsh Marches, even cities like Hereford and Shrewsbury resisted the preachers and remained predominantly conservative well into the reign of Elizabeth.[44]

North-western England had been scarcely touched by 1558, apart from a limited area of south-eastern Lancashire, where the missionaries John Bradford and George Marsh (both subsequently martyred) conducted preaching tours.[45] The situation differed in Yorkshire, the North being much less homogeneous in its conservatism than is commonly supposed. Yorkshire had direct access to the Lutheran ports of Germany and, traversed by the main road to the Scottish Borders, maintained relatively solid contacts with London and the South. Here the most obvious early Protestant centres were the port of Hull, its close neighbour Beverley and, across in the West Riding, the growing industrial centre of Leeds and the many weaving communities within the huge parish of Halifax.[46] The city of York also contained some Protestants, but its ethos remained distinctly conservative, as befitted an ancient ecclesiastical capital with a great metropolitan cathedral, forty parish churches, some hundreds of clergymen and, up to the Dissolution, several religious houses. The marked contrast between York and mercantile Hull—half its size and only forty miles distant—is instructive. At the latter the mere handful of clerics in the two churches was closely controlled by the merchant oligarchy. Further north the evangelizing of Durham, Newcastle and Northumberland remained in its infancy at the mid-century, but the Scottish war and the historic problems of the Marches induced Protector Somerset to back Protestant missionaries after his victory at Pinkie.[47]

Returning southward, we find the East Midlands a 'quiet' region but with a number of Protestant nuclei in towns like Northampton, Leicester, Oundle and Oakham, together with groups in several smaller places.[48] Despite the propinquity of Cambridge and the conversion of some gentry families, the northern deaneries of the vast diocese of Lincoln show far less activity than did neighbouring East Anglia. Yet even here the Henrician martyr Anne Askew had numerous admirers, while the widowed Duchess of Suffolk, a future exile, vigorously propaganded from her castle at Grimsthorpe.

Another broadly conservative region was the south-west, as already indicated in our description of the 1549 rebellion in Cornwall and Devon. This rising was partially directed against the new English prayer book. Nevertheless recent re-examinations of the sources have steadily tended to display the south-west as also manifesting powerful economic grievances and as divided by secular factions and feuds.[49] The local factor contributing most to the collapse of this revolt was the action of the Exeter city council. It contained both Catholic and Protestant councillors, but the two groups joined immediately in order to protect their city against the rebels, and thus successfully resisted a long siege. Meanwhile the local gentry and the seafaring communities tended to embrace Protestantism, perhaps influenced in some measure by their hatred of Spain and Portugal, already their trading rivals.[50] Some of the towns and ports contained internal religious divisions. Even those militant factions among the boys of Bodmin[51] could hardly have arisen had there been no Protestants in the town! Not far away in Wales, another complex of secular and religious factors needs to be distinguished: a Celtic language resistant to English; an old oral and manuscript culture hitherto patronised by the monasteries; an extreme paucity of printed books, with scarcely any in Welsh; poor communications and a clergy for the most part out of touch with biblical humanism and hostile toward the small group of Protestant bishops in Wales. Some educated Welshmen such as Sir John Price and William Salesbury keenly admired Erasmus, worked toward a Welsh Bible, yet won few followers until the Elizabethan period, when modern educated Welsh Catholicism also came to life.[52]

These glimpses of geographical distribution also prompt us to ask which types of communities most readily produced and harboured the early Protestant groups. Here the answer would seem relatively straightforward. At first sight one is impressed by the special rôle played in the movement by the largest towns, mainly in south-eastern England.[53] Norwich, Bristol, Coventry, Canterbury, Colchester and Ipswich contained major groups. Cities of this size, however small compared with London, offered a measure of concealment well beyond that attainable in villages. Contemporary reports suggest that in Colchester the large protestant group could even organise itself around a network of public houses.[54] Nevertheless another *locus classicus* was the small cloth-town, often compounded of textile operatives, farm workers and shop-owners. Of these we have already cited Foxe's famous picture of Hadleigh, the godly, bible-reading community said to resemble a university rather than a town of cloth-workers.[55] Within Kent, Essex and Suffolk the present writer has listed some twenty-four industrial places of this size and type, where mid-Tudor Protestants are distinctly recorded. Outside the south-east, such groups were perhaps most common in Gloucestershire. Many southern centres of Protestantism had contained Lollard conventicles in earlier years as with Amersham in Buckinghamshire. Here, despite his Scottish accent, John Knox preached with great success in 1553.

A third, and at least equally important background to the movement was presented by the very numerous port-towns of the east and south coasts of England. From Hull down to Dover and from Dover westward to the Devonshire Harbours, I observe no port of consequence which did not contain a larger or smaller group of Protestants. The riverside parishes of the city of London and the seagoing, ship-building places eastward along both banks of the Thames had a special prominence. Full of elusive foreigners and sailors, these were communities wherein gentry and priests had little authority, and where the detection of heretics was unlikely to be aided by local innkeepers and tradesmen. Likewise Foxe and other writers have much to say concerning the import of bibles and works of propaganda from Tyndale and his exiled confederates, which came across to English ports, usually concealed in barrels. Already we have observed Bishop Nix of Norwich as early as 1530 bemoaning the fact that heresy was increasing, not among the gentry and the commons but among the merchants and 'such that hath their abiding not far from the sea'.[56]

If from this welter of local evidence there emerges a broad conclusion, it must begin by stressing the wide variety of situations around the mid-century, and the inadequacy of sweeping formulae purporting to cover the nation as a whole. It is nevertheless clear that by the death of Edward VI Protestantism had not merely become a statutory obligation: it had now established a tenacious hold upon society in those restless, dynamic regions which the government could least afford to disregard. Opinions differ on the liveliness or otherwise of traditional Catholicism between Elizabeth's accession and the coming of the seminary priests and Jesuits two or three decades later. While in these years the old religion showed signs of decline, its very survival indicates a certain basic strength. It had after all undergone prolonged attacks, not merely by Lollardy, anticlericalism and Lutheran biblicism, but also by the prevalent chauvinist attitudes toward papal Rome and Habsburg Spain. Yet again, the climates of both educated and popular religion had been since the early years of the century somewhat radically modified through the attacks made by Erasmus and many other hard-line critics upon saint-worship, monasticism, indulgences and that ignorance of the Scriptures which still characterised many of the parish clergy. The recovery of English Catholicism needed (and eventually received) stronger spiritual forces than those ostensibly generated by the Marian campaign. As for the Marian policing and burning, these looked further than ever from eradicating Protestantism by the time Mary died. In 1553 the imperilled Protestant cause needed one thing more than any other: a dramatic but not too efficient persecution, and this it duly received. Conversely the last thing needed by English Catholicism was a persecution under unpopular foreign auspices.[57]

By what stages had the Protestant cause obtained its grip upon the south-east and certain other areas? Faced by this question, we must revert to the subject of research upon wills, which a number of scholars have pursued during recent years in regard to several counties and cities of varying religious complexions.[58] Still further researches of this kind are required and may conceivably produce surprises, yet already something like a common graph of the movement seems to be emerging. Protestant wills begin with small minorities of testators around 1530, move slowly upward for more than a decade, and more rapidly during the last year or two of Henry VIII. Then they bound upward at a steep angle during the freedom of the Edwardian years, only to be restrained, but not very drastically reduced, by the Marian persecution. Finally they surge higher than ever during the first years of Elizabeth. The graphs of both swiftly-moving and relatively slow-moving areas seem as yet to show corresponding trends on their respective levels. Of course, there remained northern and western districts with totals of Protestant-type wills too small to be significant. As Dr. Haigh and others have indicated, these particular situations did not radically change until the later decades of Elizabeth's reign. On the other hand all figures derived from wills are bound to minimise the actual volume of Protestantism, because virtually all Tudor wills were made by elderly and middle-aged people, whereas the new beliefs had found a large part of their support arising from the younger generation. That this last feature is no mere conjecture we shall shortly indicate.[59]

Concerning the overall strength of the new beliefs we can deduce little or nothing from merely negative evidence, for example, by crudely comparing the Fines total of 3,000 recorded and named Protestants with a national adult population of, say, two millions. Our sources being what they are, the 3,000 must remain only the 'visible tip' of mid-Tudor Protestant society. This we have already claimed, but without fully explaining the many reasons for deducing an enormous numerical difference between the number of actual Protestants and that of Protestants observable in our surviving records. In this regard the following factors must also be taken into account:

1. Faced by the threat of a painful death, a high proportion even of convinced Protestants concealed their allegiance by frequenting Catholic services. Here again is no common-sense guess: we have it from the bitter evidence of activists such as the martyrs Ralph Allerton and John Bradford, who denounced as 'neuters' and 'mongrels' those many of their followers who, against the dictates of conscience, continued to attend the Catholic Mass.[60]

2. Any attempt at a mathematical balance must be gravely threatened by the fact that English society contained many secular-minded people without strong confessional allegiances. The moralists from John Fisher to Thomas Cranmer fulminated against the parishioners who 'roistered' in the ale-houses during service times. Doubtless some of the countryfolk felt less interest in Christianity than in the popular 'religion' of spells and folk-medicine, though such attitudes were by no means incompatible with regular church-attendance. Likewise among the ambivalent population we might number not merely frightened Protestants but also many church-attenders with a formal piety, who painlessly followed the commands of successive governments. All in all it would seem somewhat absurd to regard every non-Protestant as in any meaningful sense a Catholic.

3. Our knowledge of the Protestants must be appreciably reduced by the grievous loss of ecclesiastical documents, especially of the court-books recording cases of heresy. This loss has left wide gaps even in the more fortunate archives, such as those of Lincoln, York and Norwich.[61] Until quite recent times, many registries lacked adequate staff to catalogue or conserve their early documents.

4. Nowhere was a full-scale census of Protestants ever attempted. In several dioceses our knowledge is again curtailed by the fact that no rigorous persecution ever occurred there. This may owe much to the doubts of Catholic bishops and other officials who, even on Foxe's partisan showing, did not always suppress their natural humanity.

5. Of the local groups or congregations of Protestants under persecution, we know of several only through a solitary mention in a personal letter or through some other fleeting and isolated document.[62] Since by far the greater part of such potential sources disappeared long ago, it can be reasonably inferred that many unrecorded groups existed under Mary but then merged into Elizabethan Anglicanism without leaving traces. Indeed it is likely that, under persecution, many groups were wise enough to avoid keeping any records whatsoever.

We have repeatedly mentioned the mass-study of wills, and again this remains perhaps the only method whereby we may come to a somewhat fuller knowledge of the comparative strength of the parties. So far as such investigations have gone, they wholly discourage the revisionist notion that, even in its 'heartland', pre-Elizabethan Protestantism consisted only of small minorities. During the reign of Edward VI as well as during the first years of Elizabeth, in several of the few areas as yet covered by this research, Protestant-type wills actually come to outnumber the conservative wills. This appears to be the case in Kent, Warwickshire, the city of Norwich and some parts even of conservative Yorkshire. At these stages of the Reformation it could well be that, throughout the 'heartland', convinced Protestants had in fact become more numerous than convinced Catholics. Nevertheless it looks most unlikely that the case will ever be proved or disproved beyond all doubt. While we must reject the obviously minimising estimates of early Protestantism, we should be ill-advised to stage a maximising campaign!

More work should be done before a definitive and full-scale social analysis of the early English Protestant body is attempted. Meanwhile we shall add here no more than a brief note concerning the prominent occupational groups represented in the Fines *Register*.[63] These groups seem to possess historical interest, not least because the *Register* tells us much about the minor activists in addition to the martyrs and the intellectuals. At present we know for certain the occupations of about 1320 people, constituting nearly half of the known Protestants between 1525 and 1558. Of these 1320, by far the largest group, 370 in number, are skilled craftsmen, 93 of them textile workers, 48 tailors and 34 printers. Not far distant in social status are the 16 shopkeepers, to whom we might add the 18 publicans and brewers, together with 15 drapers. Outside all these occupations we find only 41 husbandmen and unskilled workers. Yet before canonizing these statistics we should not fail to take note of the obscure 'remainder' of more than 1600 persons, unassigned by our records to any occupation. Since this 'remainder' contains very few gentry, clergy, and professional men—most of whom we could readily identify as such—it must contain a very high proportion of manual workers, skilled or unskilled. Thus if taken by itself and ignoring this 1600-strong 'remainder', the list of 1320 people who *are* assigned occupations must convey a large underestimate of the true working-class percentage.

What do we learn about the upper and middle orders in the list of 1320 persons? Among these we find no less than 453 clerics, who can be divided into three main groups: 106 former members of the religious orders; 89

'scholars' or students, enrolled as such with the Marian exiles and intended to spearhead future Protestant missions to England; 258 miscellaneous clerics, mainly parish priests but headed by the Edwardian bishops and higher clergy. The ex-monastic Protestants come from almost every male order which had survived in England until the Henrician dissolutions. The highest totals are those of the 21 Augustinian canons and the 45 friars, the latter including 17 Dominicans and 14 Franciscans. These numbers will surprise only those burdened by the stereotype of a passive, soporific monk, since in fact the monastic orders contained a good many intelligent and well-educated men, perfectly capable of campaigning, when once set free, for one side or the other. The significant fact remains that these two large groups, the friars and the Augustinian canons, were precisely those with members hitherto commonly working outside the cloister, and by no means lacking earlier opportunities to consider doctrinal problems in the social as well as in the theological dimension.

The number of named gentlemen and ladies, amounting in all to 150, would seem in no sense remarkably large, when one realises that it has been swollen by the exceptionally well-recorded body of Marian exiles. The 46 lawyers will again astonish nobody who has read the earlier chapters of this book. Long notorious for their anticlerical and Erastian opinions, the common lawyers promoted the movement without providing many of its religious activists. The same can be said of the 75 merchants in our list. Without much fuss or heroism these belonged to a group which had rendered important services to Protestantism, while their apparent geographical mobility may be somewhat illusory, since not many can have been in a position to emigrate and continue their businesses on the Continent. Taken as a whole these various figures, based upon a relatively small and perhaps somewhat unrepresentative sample of the Protestant body, remain unsensational: they correspond to a large extent with the social situation among the actual martyrs, but less necessarily with that of the whole Protestant body. They do modify the common notion that almost all the lower clergy and ex-religious remained faithful Catholics. And if anyone still regards the English Reformation as a sordid monument of middle-class self-interest these figures should help to dispose of that myth.

State policy and religious conversion both arose upon an anticlericalism no longer sterile, but enlivened, even made creative, both by intellectual priests and by simple Lollards. This is by no means the only general conclusion reached by the present writer after a recent examination of the evidence. In addition, the whole historic process, the timing and periodising of the English Reformation, now seem appreciably clearer than they did two or three decades ago. Obviously the state intervened and influenced the shape of the Reformation, yet we cannot measure the people's acceptance by the fluctuations of the mid-Tudor statute book or the minutes of the Privy Council. Even in less confused periods popular obedience has seldom proved instant and automatic in England. During the later years of Henry VIII a considerable part of his subjects genuinely disliked and opposed ecclesiastical change, even though their religious conservatism was diluted and distracted by political and economic grievances. Conversely during the reign of Mary there were in all probability numerous sincere Catholics and loyalists who deplored her marriage and doubted the wisdom of her doctrinal persecution. In view of the strong class-interests and regional differences of viewpoint which characterised the whole mid-Tudor period, no one set of attitudes can be accepted to represent national opinion. Even the broad conservatism which we attribute to the North and the West should be regarded as a rather crude approximation needing local refinements. To suggest that the Reformation 'failed to capture the people' until the 1580s is doubtless true in varying measures of certain regions, notably of the north-western counties. Throughout much of England Protestantism did indeed confront huge obstacles of mental immobility, as well as much active fidelity to the Catholic Faith. Yet to impose a 'late Reformation' scheme upon the great majority of the Tudor population does not fit the evidence as a whole. The very nature of public opinion, compounded as it is of multiple influences, moods, inner doubts and debates, should restrain the urge of modern historians to find simplistic, secular formulae. In addition, the limited coverage of public opinion by our records surviving from this period should restrain sweeping theories based solely upon a few anecdotes about individual persons and small groups.

The process of protestantising, insofar as we yet understand it, may be summarised as follows. Outside the south-eastern 'heartland', religious opinion remained in general static rather than mobile until the last years of Henry VIII, though one finds no evidence of popular enthusiasm for a specifically 'Roman' obedience. Then a clear access of Protestant strength developed in many parts of the realm throughout the reign of Edward VI, when there may have occurred one of the most rapid and far-reaching shifts of public opinion in our long national history. A couple of years after Edward's death the Marian ordeal by fire began to dignify and so consolidate these Protestant gains, this apparently even amongst the uninspired and mundane majority of the population. That martyrdoms proved a clinching and long-term argument and that the Marian experience forms the true climax of the historical drama—these beliefs would seem as clearly justified as ever. Both phases, the Edwardian and the Marian, appear as essential preludes to the Elizabethan settlement of 1559, which astute improvisation evinced from the first a surprising degree of viability, once given the exhaustion and dispersal of the hostile Marian forces. In England there followed a quiescent decade, climaxed by the extremely narrow mental and geographical limits of the revolt led by the Northern Earls in 1569. Here occurred nothing approaching a re-enactment of the Pilgrimage of Grace.

Like any important revolution, the rise of Protestantism had already released forces greater and more divisive than either its sponsors or its opponents could have foreseen. It thereafter entered a second phase, one in which the stakes and the contenders had noticeably altered. In England Roman Catholicism survived upon a much reduced but still significant scale, in view of its accessibility to nourishment from abroad. To anxious Elizabethans it appeared more formidable than it proved in fact, at all events so long as the political and dynastic complications dissuaded Spain from sending it military aid. Of those complications the one which bulked largest was the candidature for the English throne of Mary Stuart, a former Queen of France as well as a great-granddaughter of Henry VII. Not until her execution in 1587 could it pay Philip to place the crown of England on her head. Thus during this long impasse the continuance of the Reformation-contest mainly involved the character of the new Anglican Church, its doctrines and administrative structures, its relations with Crown and Parliament, its social and cultural ethos, its capacity for tolerating religious diversity, even its chances of retaining or recapturing some of the old Catholic values. Few Elizabethans can have felt sure that the definitive Protestant victory had already occurred in 1558–9: indeed there still lay ahead tasks of the utmost importance. In 1559, even in 1569, it seemed to many observers by no means certain that a 'Church of the Reformation' had been successfully founded, since by continental standards doctrinal 'purity' had not yet been achieved. A battle appeared to be won, yet nobody knew for certain what species of Protestantism would enjoy the fruits of victory.

The English Reformation as a Youth Movement

Looking at the whole period 1520–1558, can we see the growth of Protestantism as predominantly a movement *among the young*? Of this there is little doubt, at any rate in regard to south-eastern England. The Venetian ambassador Giovanni Michiel reported in 1557 that the Marian restoration of Catholicism was being accomplished out of fear, or by people wanting to ingratiate themselves with the Queen, while everyone, except a few pious Catholics over the age of thirty-five, wanted to return to an unrestricted life by abandoning the Faith.[64] Of course these are the impressions of an Italian in London; but a mass of London and south-eastern evidence does support the emphasis on youth, and much of it has been admirably set forth by Dr. Susan Brigden.[65] From 1543 we encounter Protestant anticlerical louts mocking and even assaulting priests in the streets of London: on one such occasion in 1543 they are meaningfully described as 'prenteses and mennes servantes which had played at fute ball'.[66] In 1554 Mary's former confessor Bishop John Christopherson denounced (in his *An exhortation to all menne to take hede of rebellion*) the 'Lutheran' children who mock their Catholic parents and say 'my father is an old doting fool and will fast upon the Friday; and my mother goeth always mumbling on her beads. But you shall see me of another sort, I warrant you'.[67] Amongst the English Protestant martyrs, both Henrician and Marian, I see ages at death given in only forty-eight cases, of whom just over half were aged thirty or less, about a third under twenty-five, and seven twenty or less. Looking more broadly at Dr. Fines's list of 3,000 known early Protestants, I have observed only 82 who were assigned precise ages, though a great many others were certainly young or very young. If one graphed the ages of these 82, the peak would come around the mid-twenties. Behind these rudimentary figures it would be easy to supply a mass of relevant anecdotal material about the young, and even about children, drawn both from Foxe and from other sources. We read also about the young provincial craftsmen who come up to London to serve apprenticeships, fall in with Protestant teachers and literature, defy Bishop Bonner and finish up in prison or at the stake. Such a one was John Tudson from Ipswich, aged eighteen and apprenticed in the city parish of St. Mary Botolph: from his burning, says the London diarist Machyn, the authorities banned all other young people, thus paying tribute to the youth movement, and to the dangerous power of example.[68] Another was Andrew Hewet of Faversham, apprentice to a tailor of Watling Street.[69] Jailed through the actions of an *agent provocateur*, he escaped with the aid of a file secreted by a fellow-prisoner, was recaptured and put on trial. Here Hewet announced that he would stand by the opinions of his mentor, the important controversialist John Frith, along with whom he was in fact burned early in the persecution. A third example was William Hunter, nineteen years of age, an apprentice silk-weaver from Brentwood, Essex, and Coleman Street parish.[70] Though Bishop Bonner is alleged to have left Hunter in irons for nine months, he nevertheless made real efforts to reconvert the youth. In the end Hunter was sent back for execution to Brentwood, where many old friends supported him to the finish, his own brother and the sheriff's son walking arm-in-arm with him to the stake. Here, according to Foxe, who seldom misses the chance of a dramatic touch, the sun suddenly came out and shone upon the victim at the last moment, when he threw his book of psalms to his brother, calling out 'I am not afraid'. A fourth prominent apprentice, bound to a London tallowchandler, was John Leaf from Kirby Moorside in the Vale of Pickering.[71] In the capital Leaf fell in with Tyndale's former assistant John Rogers, destined to become the first of all the Marian martyrs. He later admitted to being the 'scholar' of Rogers. At his burning in July 1555, Leaf's companion proved to be no less a man than John Bradford, the learned prebendary of St. Paul's, who might more appropriately be called a disciple of Zwingli rather than a Lutheran. It was thus to young Leaf from Yorkshire that Bradford spoke his famous valediction, 'Be of good comfort, brother, for we shall have a merry supper with the Lord this night'.

Such cases exemplify the mobility of young craftsmen, others of whom on their return home to conservative areas took back advanced religious views. Of such I found a superb example in the York diocesan records with the case of William Bull of Dewsbury, a clothworker who served in the early forties as an apprentice in Suffolk, and then in 1543 revisited his parents at Dewsbury, only to get into serious and prolonged trouble for retailing Protestant and anticlerical views in pungent proletarian language.[72] But to return momentarily to John Leaf, his case also illustrates the merging of diverse social and educational groups under the harrow of persecution. Especially in the underground Protestant congregations in Marian London could an intelligent but perhaps barely literate young man acquire quite a detailed grasp of current doctrinal controversy. This class-merging is equally exemplified in the Protestant circles of Paris during the 1550s. Of course, in whatever milieu we encounter early Protestants, we also encounter books, pamphlets, printers and readers as well as preachers and talkers. On the other hand, the incidence of literacy is somewhat fortuitous and by no means closely predictable through either social class or religious convictions. We are told that John Leaf, though apparently articulate in argument, could neither read nor write. Given the choice between signing a confession or a recantation, he condemned himself by making the confession, but being unable to use a pen, took a pin, pricked his hand and sent the document back to Bonner marked in his blood. On the other hand, yet another apprentice-martyr, Robert Purchase, a fuller of Barking and gaoled at Colchester, is specifically described as a literate man. Several of the stories of young sufferers for religion occur in manuscript testimonies sent to Foxe and, though not used in his book, are now in the Harleian Manuscripts. One of these, written by Archdeacon Louth, recounts the examination of Tom Drowrie, a blind boy of Gloucester, by John Williams, Chancellor of the cathedral there.[73] In this dialogue Drowrie neatly accuses Chancellor Williams of teaching him heresy, since it was notorious that under Edward VI, Williams had temporarily gone over to Protestantism. In the end, the Chancellor is said to have read the sentence 'with an unhappy tongue and more unhappy conscience', and in May 1556 Drowrie was burned at Gloucester along with a local bricklayer. Another of these items is a brief autobiography by John Davis, who dwelt in the late Henrician years with his uncle at Worcester and struck up a close friendship with the uncle's apprentice Peter Goffe. The latter then obtained an English bible and other 'godly books' which they secretly read together.[74] In due course these activities were discovered by the aunt of John Davis, called here 'an obstinate papist', whose likeminded friends got him arrested and, though only twelve years of age, put in irons for a long period, until the accession of Edward VI brought a happy end to his sufferings.

A still more graphic example of the youth-versus-age theme occurs in the narrative submitted to Foxe by William Maldon of Chelmsford.[75] This man relates how back in 1538 'poor men' of that town availed themselves of the recent permission to purchase bibles, and how on Sundays they sat reading aloud in the nave of the church, while others flocked in to listen. However, Maldon's conservative father pulled him forcibly out of this company and so aroused in the obstinate boy an immense desire to learn to read English on his own account. Soon afterwards William and his father's apprentice Thomas Jeffrey 'layed our money together and bought the Newe Testament in English, and hydde it in our bed strawe and so exercised it at convenient times. Then shortly after, my father set me to the kepyng of a shop of haberdashery and grosary wares, beyng a bowe shott from his howsse, and there I plyed my boke'. In actual fact his books included one regarded by most contemporaries as extremist: John Frith's work on the sacrament, the theology of which was Zwinglian. Not long afterwards Maldon had a conversation with his mother, during which he denounced as idolatry the veneration of the crucifix. She retorted with a true maternal irrelevance, 'Wilt thou not worshippe the crosse? And it was about thee when thou weart cristened, and must be layed on thee when thou art deade'. Informed by her, William's father came up to the bedroom with a large rod, pulled his son out of bed by the hair and beat him heavily, demanding to know who had been his teachers to heresy. Failing to extract a tear, the enraged father went away and returned with a halter, put it on William's neck and dragged him out again around the back of the apprentice, as William's mother and also his brother (the latter also apparently in the same bed) rent the air with their cries. Though Maldon senior stopped short of murder, William recorded that his neck gave him pain for six days afterwards.

Such coruscating family scenes may have happened frequently enough, since parents were obviously moved not by Catholic devotion alone, but also by their children's genuine peril, and by the fear of the social scandal which charges of heresy entailed. These clashes could happen also on the higher social levels, including that of Oxford academic life. Dr. John London, Warden of New College, is said to have combined several sexual lapses with the dissolving of monasteries for Cromwell and the persecution of Protestants for Gardiner. He had in his charge his undergraduate nephew Edward London, who ventured to write an anti-papal pamphlet in 1534, soon after the Henrician government had abolished papal jurisdiction.[76] Despite this latter event, the Warden (whose religious views were basically conservative) interviewed Edward in his garden at New College continuously from five o'clock until ten o'clock in the morning. The young man was warned that he would lose all his friends and make his poor mother 'never eate more brede that schall dow her good'. Their whole family had been free of heresy 'these many hundreyth yeres': indeed all heretics came to a bad end. As for the King, the Warden ventured to say that he had merely 'concevyed a lytyll malyce aganst the bysshope off Rome by cawse he wulde not aggre unto this maryage: yet I trust that the blyssyd kynge wyll were harnes on hys owne bake to feyghte agenste suych heretykes as thow arte'. In conclusion Dr. London came to the point and threatened that unless Edward revoked his beliefs, he would suffer expulsion and the world should know about it. Such events should make us recall Archdeacon Harpsfield's far more elevated story conerning the 'proud' Lutheran heresy of William Roper, the son-in-law of Sir Thomas More, who by prayer rescued him from this spiritual plight.[77] Such tensions between the generations were doubtless especially apt to occur in families whose sons went off to the universities or to London, places where religion was furiously debated and conversions to Protestantism became common. Over the years young Nicholas Ridley's expenses at Cambridge, Paris and Louvain were paid not by his father, a Northumbrian squire, but by his uncle Robert, a Cambridge D.D. well-beneficed in London and a staunch opponent of the Reformation. It would seem significant that Nicholas, though attracted years earlier by the new doctrines, refrained from open adherence until after his benefactor's death in 1536. His future friend and fellow-martyr John Hooper became involved in a more dramatic confrontation. Having graduated at Oxford in

1519, Hooper lived until the Dissolution as a Cistercian monk at Cleeve Abbey in Gloucestershire. Then, moving on to London, he embraced Zwinglian doctrines, fled abroad, married a Flemish lady of good family and became a disciple of Bullinger, Zwingli's famous successor at Zürich. Writing to Bullinger in 1546 from Strassburg, he bewails his ill-luck, 'for my father, of whom I am the only son and heir, is so opposed to me on account of Christ's religion, that should I refuse to act according to his wishes, I shall be sure to find him for the future, not a father, but a cruel tyrant'. He had now resolved to go home and try with the assistance of friends 'to obtain at least some portion of what I am entitled to, wherewith I may be able to subsist upon my slender means among you at Zürich'.[78]

Even schoolboys could acquire a very early awareness of the religious struggle. We have already observed the contention between the Old Religion and the New waged by the boys of Bodmin School in 1549. Similarly in March 1554, soon after the collapse of Wyatt's revolt, 300 London school-boys fought a dangerous battle on Finsbury Fields outside the northern wall of the city, having divided into two troops, one led by 'Prince Philip of Spain', the other by 'Master Wyatt'. The boy who impersonated the Prince came near to being lynched by his adversaries, and the Court of Aldermen, anxious to prove the city's loyalty to Queen Mary, imprisoned and thrashed the ringleaders.[79] Again, if young people were sometimes forbidden to attend executions, this was hardly on humane grounds, and there can be little doubt that they were commonly present. At the burning of the former Dominican friar John Lawrence in March 1555, the victim sat in the midst of the fire while children surrounded it, praying he should be given strength to bear the ordeal.[80] One can only hope that Foxe overdid this horrible scene. On the other hand, when it was clear that London opinion detested the Marian burnings, the authorities, including Bonner, tried hard to avoid condemning very young persons. The youngest victim had in fact died at Smithfield, not in Mary's reign but in July 1541 under the Six Articles Act. He was Richard Mekins, a London orphan said to be under 15, and the commissioners under Bonner had great difficulty in finding a jury prepared to convict him. In the event—as reported not merely by Foxe but by the London diarist Wriothesley—the unfortunate boy recanted at the stake, withdrew his denial of transubstantiation and so suffered hanging, not burning.[81]. These stories of rebellious youth have hitherto received less attention than they deserve. They illustrate the vitality of the early Reformation with greater force than does that more familiar image of elderly bishops witnessing to their faith at the stake in Oxford and elsewhere.

14 The Foundations of Elizabethan England

The Exiles

While the martyrs helped to ensure a reversal of Mary's policy, the eventual dynamic of that reversal may largely be ascribed to that other group of the Queen's opponents, the so-called Marian exiles.[1] In these people abroad we see a microcosm of mid-century English Protestant opinion, free for once from the inhibiting influences of an English government. Foxe states that some 800 English men and women fled abroad, and modern research has located at least 788 specific persons.[2] Though it cannot be assumed that the surviving records mention all the obscurer people, the movement certainly consisted in large part of noble, gentle, moneyed and clerical refugees. Of 472 men whose status is known, 166 were gentry, sixty-seven clergy, forty merchants and 119 young men classed as students and mainly intended for the ministry. The known working-class element consists only of thirty-two artisans and thirteen servants. The lawyers and physicians are not heavily represented among these names, but there appear at least seven printers, who helped to send back a steady stream of anti-Marian propaganda and who exemplified the tendency of English printers to embrace the Reformation as eagerly as continental printers had embraced humanism.

More important, the exiled clergy, so far from being ordinary parish priests, included the leading figures among the Protestant scholars of both universities, many of whom were to achieve bishoprics and other high offices in the Elizabethan Church. From Oxford came King Edward's tutor, Dr. Richard Cox,[3] dean of Christ Church and vice-chancellor of the University from 1547 to 1552. A man of strong, not to say overbearing personality, he had also been a prominent member of both Prayer Book commissions, while his zeal for uprooting 'Romish' practices at Oxford had caused him to be known there as 'the Cancellor'. Other notable exiles from Oxford were Laurence Humphrey and Thomas Bentham of Magdalen, William Cole of Corpus, the Lady Margaret professor, Christopher Goodman, and William Whittingham of Christ Church, who had studied abroad for three years, but had not yet been ordained at the time of his exploits in Frankfurt. From Cambridge came an equally varied group—Thomas Lever, master of St. John's, James Pilkington, a later master and ultimately Bishop of Durham, and young Perceval Wiburn, then already a fellow of the same college but destined to a stormy career as an Anglo-Genevan Puritan extending into the seventeenth century. Edwin Sandys, one of Queen Elizabeth's Archbishops of York, was vice-chancellor of Cambridge at Mary's accession and as one of those implicated in Northumberland's conspiracy he was well advised to leave for the continent.

One of the sadder stories is that of Sir John Cheke, provost of King's College, whose influence over Edward VI we have already observed. As a close associate of Cranmer he was in 1556 kidnapped in violation of a safe-conduct, sent back to England and placed in the Tower. After a long resistance he accepted a humiliating recantation and soon afterwards died broken-hearted at the age of forty-three. Yet another of Edward's tutors had gone abroad with Cheke—Sir Anthony Cooke, whose four intellectual daughters married those eminent Elizabethans, Sir William Cecil, Sir Nicholas Bacon, Sir Thomas Hoby and Sir Henry Killigrew, the last two of whom were also exiles. Another destined for an important rôle was Sir Francis Knollys, whose wife was first cousin to the Princess Elizabeth and whose mysterious first journey to the continent in 1553 may have been a mission from the Protestant opposition to Calvin. Alongside these men went a host of well-known preachers, pamphleteers and writers like John Knox, Anthony Gilby, Bishop Ponet and John Jewel. The last, since famous as a defender of the Elizabethan Settlement, had been a close friend of Peter Martyr at Oxford and had acted as notary to Cranmer and Ridley at their trials. He had then been forced to abjure before contriving to flee to Frankfurt. Altogether, it would be hard to find in European history such a concentration of intellectual and social distinction within an emigrant body of such modest numbers. And the great volume of clandestine support enjoyed by these people illustrates in itself the hold now gained by Protestantism upon the leadership of England.

It has been suggested that the exile was in the main a voluntary movement, not so much enforced as astutely planned in order to ensure a future religious revolution.[4] Able Protestants like Cecil came to regard it in this light, while others looked well to the future by educating young English clerics abroad, far from the lures of Papistry. Again, the stream began long before the persecution directly threatened ordinary Protestants. London businessmen helped to promote and finance it; advance agents went ahead to some of the centres of settlement, while strenuous efforts were made to organise and link the various communities abroad. On the other hand, much of the evidence does not square with this picture of an easy, orderly, confident emigration. The ideas of Cecil and his like scarcely disturb the fact that many of the refugees fled because of justified fear, and many others after the persecution had set in. And one proves nothing about the majority by recalling the exceptional case of Katherine, Dowager Duchess of Suffolk, who departed in great state, accompanied by her major-domo, gentle-women, joiner, brewer, kitchen-maid, laundress and fool, 'a Greek rider of horses' and her own recently-acquired little husband, Mr. Richard Bertie.[5]

Most of the emigrants went under very different circumstances. Their uncertain movements, their acute divergences of view and purpose, their open quarrels, afford anything but the impression of a co-ordinated political manœuvre directed by a group of master-minds, dreaming of the spacious Elizabethan days ahead. If many had access to large sums, others soon depended on charity, though perhaps their main hardship arose from the overcrowding of the walled cities of Germany and Switzerland. There they lived five families to a house, insecure, restive and intermittently troubled by the plague. The truth doubtless lies somewhere between the excessive optimism of the modern picture, and the old legend of hapless fugitives, weeping by the waters of Babylon. Wherever educated Englishmen were involved, no movement could be wholly unplanned or without a shrewd eye to the future. However intolerant and irascible, they had a flair for organisation unsurpassed in the world of their day and their situation obviously demanded political foresight. A cancellation of Mary's religious policy could not be brought about save by her death or by political revolution, yet in 1554–5 neither of these eventualities could be expected at any near date. The organisation of Protestant communities with long-term plans was hence bound to become the major aim of the clerical leadership and of their more responsible lay colleagues.

Men of this outlook normally passed into Germany and Switzerland, since neither the Netherlands government of Philip nor France under the orthodox Henry II welcomed Protestants. Nevertheless, a number of politically-minded gentry lingered in France, where the government also had ample reason to encourage anti-Spanish plotters and would-be invaders of England. In this category were Henry Dudley, Thomas Stafford, Bryan Fitzwilliam and Wyatt's fellow-conspirator Sir Peter Carew, though the last two later made their peace with Mary. The most colourful of all the romantics was Peter Killigrew of Arwennack in Cornwall, who lived in luxury on the proceeds of piracy against both Spanish and English shipping in the Channel. Such figures among the exiles foreshadowed certain aspects of Elizabethan character and enterprise, but it was not given to them to lay the solid foundations of the Elizabethan Settlement in Church and State. At this moment ideas mattered far more than muscles and the ideas were primarily theological even if at one remove they tended to become political.

During the years of exile eight English congregations were established in the continent. The original five were Emden, Wesel, Frankfurt, Strassburg, and Zürich, while Basel, Geneva and Aarau were their subsequent offshoots. Despite the pleas of Melanchthon the Lutheran states proved most inhospitable, partly because they believed English Protestants held the wrong sacramental beliefs, partly because they feared political complications. In 1547 the Lutheran princes and cities had been defeated and temporarily overrun by the forces of the Catholic Emperor Charles V. Whatever the justification for their subsequent caution, it killed any remaining possibility that the English Church might gravitate into a Lutheran orbit. At Wesel

Melanchthon's recommendation carried weight with the city authorities, but in 1556 the latter managed to rid themselves of their visitors. Shepherded, like Puritan emigrants of the next century, by their pastor (Thomas Lever), the whole congregation migrated thence to the pleasant town of Aarau, west of Zürich.[6]

Each of these communities developed its distinctive character. Emden, where some of John à Lasco's London congregation were worshipping by May 1554, became the chief centre of propaganda—it already had presses and was a port in easy contact with England. Hence flowed many of the pamphlets which drove Queen Mary to distraction and which came from the pens of John Knox, William Turner and John Scory. The last-named, having been deprived of his bishopric of Chichester, had at first recanted, but then taken his opportunity to escape to Emden, where he became minister to the congregation.[7] At Zürich, where both Peter Martyr and Heinrich Bullinger exercised much influence over the Englishmen, the latter nevertheless remained a distinctively Anglican body under their leaders Jewel, Parkhurst and Pilkington. This happy setting they had good reason to recall even in more prosperous times. 'O Zürich,' wrote Jewel after his return, 'how much oftener do I now think of thee than ever I thought of England when I was at Zürich.'[8] When Whittingham left Frankfurt under the dramatic circumstances we shall describe, John Foxe accompanied him, but instead of following most of Whittingham's group to Geneva he was attracted to Basel, perhaps on account of its pre-eminence in the world of printing and publishing. Here he soon set to work on his martyrological collections, and he found a helper in the future Primate Edmund Grindal, who not only polished Foxe's Latin but supplied much material for the lives of Cranmer and Bradford. At Basel Foxe joined a growing community of English students, who lived *in collegio* at the buildings of the former Clarakloster. Among his fellow-exiles there were two men due to attain fame in Elizabethan public life. Sir Francis Knollys was already forty years of age and a Protestant of many years standing, while Francis Walsingham was still a student fresh from Cambridge and Gray's Inn.

At Strassburg Peter Martyr prepared the way for the establishment of another peaceful and moderate community, basing its worship upon the Prayer Book. Here John Ponet the Edwardian bishop of Winchester wrote his *Short Treatise of Politic Power* which, published in 1556, was the first book by an English Reformer embracing the doctrine of tyrannicide.[9] It is based on the contention that God has conferred authority upon the community, which may establish any form of government it thinks best. No wise community would establish autocratic kingship—a man's allegiance is due first to God, then to his country, and only last to the king. Commonwealths can exist without kings, who are often in fact tyrants and brigands. It is merely a law of nature that bad kings should be deposed and tyrants punished with death. Under certain circumstances (which Ponet does not clearly define) even the killing of a tyrant by some private individual might be justified. While some parallels can be detected in medieval political thought, Ponet's treatise comes first in a new wave of anti-monarchical writings. It was written, strangely enough, by an anti-Calvinist Anglican, the highest-ranking ecclesiastic among the exiles. It has never been assessed at its true importance, for it antedates by several years those more brilliantly expressed but less radical Huguenot writings which have usually been taken to represent the tyrannicide-theories of the Reformation. Significantly again, Ponet's work was to be republished in 1639 and in 1642; it was still being studied on the eve of that new conflict to which its message seemed equally applicable. In view of the slightly later tyrannicide theories of Goodman and Knox, together with the later publications of the Huguenot theorists, it used to be supposed that Ponet derived his position from Calvin, who in fact equivocates on this issue. It now appears that Ponet derived much more from Melanchthon's Latin tract *On the Office of Princes*, published in 1539 when Philip of Hesse and other Protestant German rulers were already preparing for the war against their Catholic Emperor.[10]

Just as Ponet went further than his master Melanchthon, so the exiled Calvinist writers abandoned the circumspect attitudes of Calvin. In 1558 there appeared at Geneva Christopher Goodman's *How Superior Powers ought to be obeyed of their Subjects* and John Knox's *Appellation*.[11] These are closely related and say almost the same thing—that rebellion against ungodly and idolatrous sovereigns is a duty. They both go so far as to impose this duty not merely upon the nobles and the higher magistrates of a kingdom but upon the common people themselves. Such works show a striking abandonment of the godly prince and of that hatred for rebellion which had marked English Protestant thought during the previous reign. As usual, political thinking had adapted itself to the hard facts of the situation. There can be little doubt that these intellectuals stood prepared to applaud the assassination of Mary Tudor, while by 1558 Knox also felt the time ripe for an appeal to the nobility and estates of Scotland in order to overthrow the Catholic Regent, Mary of Guise.

The Geneva community was founded in October 1555 by forty-eight of the followers of Knox and Whittingham, after these leaders had left Frankfurt. At one time or another thereafter, over 200 Englishmen became members,[12] yet the common statement that only a quarter of the exiles were exposed to Genevan influence has no great significance. To be influenced, one was not compelled to visit Geneva any more than a good Marxist must necessarily visit Moscow or the British Library. The original ministers at Geneva were Goodman and Anthony Gilby; they were soon reinforced by other ecclesiastics of remarkable character, among them Scory, Bentham, Thomas Cole and Perceval Wiburn. Such men found a congenial home in the city of Calvin and if, when they became Elizabethan dignitaries, they could not seek to reproduce it, they nevertheless like Knox regarded it in retrospect as the model of a perfected Christian community. Already in 1555 many of them had become highly impatient with the non-biblical elements remaining in the Prayer Book of 1552. They resolved forthwith to lay the foundation of a truly scriptural religion, not only by improving on Cranmer's work but by re-translating the Bible itself and presenting it in a Reformed edition.

The first-fruits of this movement appeared in June 1557, when William Whittingham published a version of the New Testament with a prefatory epistle by Calvin and containing many revisions based on the work of Beza. Meanwhile, headed by Whittingham and Gilby and with some assistance from the veteran Coverdale, the exiles produced the Geneva Bible, often called the 'Breeches Bible' from its odd translation of *Genesis*, iii, 7. It was ultimately published there in April 1560 by the English printer Rowland Hall.[13] This Bible possessed many technical advantages over its predecessors. It had a convenient quarto format, and following Whittingham's Testament of 1557 it abandoned the old black-letter type for clear Italian characters. It also divided the chapters into numbered verses. The text was more revolutionary than any since Tyndale and many of its innovations were to be followed by the Authorised Version of 1611. The critical notes, though embodying the best Reformed scholarship of the day, bore in some cases a bitter partisan flavour. Under Elizabeth this Geneva Bible was to find no close rival. Some sixty editions appeared before the publication of the Authorised Version, whereas its competitor the Bishops' Bible (produced in 1568 to counteract its Puritan tendencies) attained only a quarter of that number. Even the Authorised Version did not immediately oust the Geneva Bible, since between 1611 and 1640 ten more editions of the latter came from the press. The exiles thus produced the version on which Shakespeare and the great majority of our Elizabethans and Jacobeans were reared, and it takes its place among the factors which explain the Calvinist flavour of Elizabethan Anglicanism.

At Geneva also, Whittingham, William Kethe and others began to compile a new edition of the Psalms in English verse.[14] Beginning with only fifty-one Psalms in 1556, the Anglo-Genevan Psalter underwent—like the Sternhold version to which it was partly indebted—a gradual expansion throughout successive editions. It was Kethe who wrote that spirited version of the hundredth Psalm so familiar in English hymn-books, and at Geneva in all likelihood it was first sung to the Old Hundredth, then a new tune. Like the Geneva Bible this compilation achieved great popularity in Elizabethan England; it also became parent to the *Scots Psalter* of 1564 and so attained a special influence among the Covenanters. All in all, had there been no exile-community save that in Geneva, the emigration must still have exerted conspicuous effects upon British history.

The Troubles at Frankfurt

The most controversial and best-documented of the settlements abroad we have left to the last. The *Brief Discourse of the Troubles Begun at Frankfurt*, first published by a group of English Puritans in 1574–5, was traditionally ascribed to William Whittingham in person, but is now thought to have been compiled by his inseparable companion Thomas Wood.[15] The story which it tells in such vivid detail has been so often retold as to leave an over-powering (though in fact untypical) impression of Protestant life in exile. At first blush these endless quarrels seem to form one of the more arid and even ridiculous episodes in Tudor history. Yet on closer examination the troubles are seen to involve broad and vital issues, for Frankfurt became the battleground of those controversies left unsolved by the reign of Edward VI, and soon to be revived under Elizabeth. The little group of English refugees amid the seething population of the great free city on the Main may have mystified their kindly and tolerant hosts, but to historians they display a preview of the tensions and divisions which have ever since that day beset Protestant society in the English-speaking world.

When in June 1554 Whittingham and a few of his friends arrived in Frankfurt, they were welcomed by the pastor of the French church, Valérand Poullain, formerly so prominent among the foreign Protestants in England. On his suggestion that the newcomers should join his own congregation, the city authorities permitted both to share the church of the White Ladies, but the English soon gained virtual freedom to order their own devotional lives. Whittingham, who knew Geneva well before he came to Frankfurt, then remodelled the Prayer Book of 1552 along Calvinist lines, abolishing vestments, the Litany, the oral responses and other features which savoured of the unreformed religion. The congregation made no strong objection and by the end of July had become an independent Church with elected ministers and deacons. Yet instead of working out their own experiment the Frankfurt leaders soon issued letters to the English in Strassburg and Zürich, inviting them to come and join in their enlightened proceedings at Frankfurt. The response from these more conservative groups lacked warmth. The men at Zürich replied politely but evasively, while those at Strassburg hinted that things had gone too far; indeed, they urged their compatriots at Frankfurt to appoint more competent ministers, suggesting the names of Cox, Ponet, Bale and Scory. So far from accepting this gratuitous advice, the Frankfurt congregation summoned John Knox from Geneva, allowed him to become their real leader and to oppose an iron front against any restoration of Cranmer's Prayer Book. Meanwhile, however, a group of Prayer Book adherents, led by Lever, began to emerge in Frankfurt, and in order to silence them Knox and Whittingham resolved upon a personal appeal to Calvin. They therefore drew up a Latin synopsis of the Prayer Book, apologising 'with a certain kind of pity' for short-comings, inevitable at the time of its composition.[16] This they submitted to Calvin, who replied in urbane and moderate terms. In his view the Book contained ineptitudes tolerable for a time but now due to be replaced by 'something more filed from rust, and purer'. He also counselled Knox and Whittingham not to be too fierce with those 'whose infirmity will not suffer them to ascend a higher step'.[17] On this wise sentence the recipients are not likely to have dwelt for long. We do not know the precise terms of the agreement which they made with their opponents in February 1555, but it seems to have represented their almost complete victory and to have allowed most of the Calvinist forms adopted by Whittingham.

Scarcely had a return to brotherly concord been celebrated when on 13 March 1555 the new and formidable figure of Dr. Richard Cox erupted upon the Frankfurt scene. Soon after Mary's accession the former 'Cancellor' had been imprisoned in the Marshalsea on a charge of treason and then placed under house-arrest. In May 1554 he had escaped to Antwerp. Since then he had consulted with various English groups on the continent, though it is uncertain whether he now came to Frankfurt as a commissioned agent of the Prayer Book parties at Strassburg and elsewhere. At all events, he came with John Jewel and other followers, and as befitted a former Prayer Book commissioner he had but one thought—to smash the Knox-Whittingham ascendancy at Frankfurt. At the first Sunday service after his arrival Cox created a disturbance by interjecting responses to the officiating minister. When the elders remonstrated, he and his followers made their Anglican and patriotic position very clear, saying that 'they would do as they had done in England, and that they would have the face of an English Church'. Knox replied, 'The Lord grant it to have the face of Christ's Church', but he now found himself in a difficult situation; he wanted to appeal to English nationalism against Spanish Mary and yet to convert Englishmen to an international creed.[18]

On the second Sunday Cox put one of his backers into the pulpit to read the Litany, while he and his faction made the responses from the body of the church. Tempers rose to a point not far short of physical violence. Knox denounced the Prayer Book of 1552 as superstitious, impure and imperfect. Amid recriminations and fiery debates the Frankfurt congregation divided itself into 'Coxians' and 'Knoxians'. All this had happened, however, before the newcomers had obtained formal admission to the congregation, and the Knoxians confidently expected that their opponents would henceforth be excluded, so long as they refused to subscribe to the recent agreement. Then, with a moderation unexplained by our sources and utterly out of keeping with his normal fanaticism, Knox himself surprised everyone by urging their admission. Yet so far from being mollified by this strange generosity, Cox redoubled his efforts to undermine the position of his chief antagonist. During the first days of doctrinal debating he failed, and even agreed to abandon private baptism, confirmation, saints' days, kneeling at communion, surplices, crosses and other features which he admitted to be 'not papistical, but by their nature indifferent'. Unsatisfied the Knoxians demanded also the abolition of the Litany, the responses, the *Te Deum* and other parts of the Prayer Book. At this point Cox refused further concessions, and Whittingham, who had the ear of the Frankfurt magistrates, now induced them to threaten the Coxians with expulsion if they would not conform. When Cox had already begun to acknowledge defeat, one of his party, Edward Isaac of Patrixbourne in Kent, also devised a political weapon. It was an unclean one, even though it was used against a man whose own methods lacked delicacy. Isaac observed that Knox in his *Faithful Admonition* had heavily libelled Mary, Philip and the Emperor Charles. He had called Mary 'false, dissembling, inconstant, proud and a breaker of promises', averring that 'if she had been sent to hell before these days, her cruelty would not have so manifestly appeared to the world'. Her father-in-law Charles he had called 'no less an enemy to Christ than was Nero', while Philip he regarded as fully implicated in the deeds of both. When Isaac, abetted by Henry Parry, later chancellor of Salisbury Cathedral, reported these opinions of Knox to the Frankfurt authorities, they could not turn the blind eye. They were most anxious not to offend the Emperor, who had recently held their city in his power and had treated it with clemency. They therefore decided to expel Knox, who on 26 March duly left for Geneva. Thanks to this stratagem Cox had thus been carried to outright victory inside a fortnight. For a time he strove to avoid the secession of Knox's followers, but in the summer Whittingham, Gilby, Goodman, Kethe, Foxe, Sir Francis Knollys and others, having failed in renewed attempts to enlist the support of the magistrates of Frankfurt, also left the city. Most of them migrated to Geneva with the interesting results we have already described.

The triumph of Cox contributed much to the survival of Cranmer's Prayer Book, but many of his own ideas on doctrine and church government would seem to modern eyes nearer to Geneva than to Canterbury. During the struggle he too had appealed to Calvin,[19] while the new *Book of Discipline* resulting from his success derived more from the Swiss Reformers and from the foreign refugees in Edwardian London than from anything which could be discovered in the previous practice of the English Church. It envisaged not only a pastor but a powerful group of elders, who acted as censors of manners, and a number of deacons responsible for assisting the poor and visiting the sick. The conflict at Frankfurt was not a conflict between erastian prelatists and Calvinists, but between Prayer Book Puritans and Genevan Puritans. Yet in this it did but foreshadow the dichotomy within the Anglican Church during the coming half-century.

Having made plans for an English university to promote the study of theology, Cox departed for Zürich, feeling that his great work had been accompished. Many of his supporters returned to Strassburg or Zürich, whence they had recently come to his aid. Yet Frankfurt had still to witness a second round of the contest not unrelated to the first. As soon as Cox had gone, an anti-sacerdotal party raised its head and, under circumstances somewhat obscure, forced the resignation of David Whitehead, the pastor left by Cox. In March 1556 they elected Robert Horne, the former dean of Durham, but he too became embroiled with the laymen, who were now led by John Hales, the civil servant and member of Parliament who had been so important in the party of social reform during Edward's reign. On the other side, among Horne's supporters was the rich merchant Richard Chambers, who had supported poor refugees from his own pocket and from a stream of secret subscriptions obtained from his business friends in London. Now he came under fire for his handling of the funds. But apart from such side issues the chief dispute raged over the pastor's authority over his congregation, and by February 1557 it resulted in the complete collapse of Horne's position and in the formulation of a fresh *Book of Discipline* by a committee.[20] This involved some startling principles. It made the Frankfurt congregation 'a particular visible Church',[21] in fact a self-governing body politic, owning no allegiance to monarchs or bishops and fully subordinating the authority of the minister to that of the congregation, the sole source of law. And as if to add the democratic to the congregational principle, certain of the humbler laymen, including two of Hales's servants, were now permitted to vote upon the adoption of the *Book of Discipline*.[22] With some reason it has been contended that the history of English Congregationalism and Independency begins here, rather than with Browne and Barrow. Though few of the group can have expected to impose such ideas at home, in this free context they emerged naturally enough.[23] As we have seen, they were also emerging in the surreptitious Protestant congregations at home. At Frankfurt they even scored an initial success. Having for some time waged a running battle with his critics Horne at last withdrew to the calmer atmosphere of Strassburg, while at Frankfurt a period of relative quiet occupied the remaining months to the death of Mary.

The full importance of these events was soon to become manifest in England. Radical groups had come to birth, this time not among poor Anabaptists or neo-Lollards but among educated and opinionated men of good social standing. They had become well versed in the arts of politico-religious intrigue; they stood prepared to entertain new modes of church government and to propound relationships between Church and State inconceivable to the subjects of Henry VIII. Weaned of uncritical royalism by the actions of Queen Mary, they had begun to derive nourishment both from Presbyterian and congregationalist principles. The political thinking of men like Ponet, Knox, Goodman and Hales showed a new attitude of irreverence toward monarchy in general. The spirit we have seen in the martyrs becomes even more explicit and conscious in the exiles; it is the spirit of the self-reliant oppositionist, the man with the hard core to his mind, the man with 'civil courage', proof against even the claims of the Tudor dynasty. Though these men could not foresee the day when their descendants would crush the monarchy itself, they were determined to win every possible concession to their own viewpoint as soon as Mary should pass from the scene. Even the more conservative of the exiles looked with respect to Genevan and other Reformed ideals; for them also there could be no return at Mary's death to the world of Henry VIII, or even to that of Protector Somerset.

In stressing the immense and often neglected importance of these exiles in the history of the English Reformation we should not fail to conclude on a note of caution. While on the continent, the exiles never became a single and united party, and some Anglican historians have too neatly labelled them as a Calvinist faction. Since 1540 English Protestantism had admittedly made a massive shift from its original Lutheran inspiration, yet while the pundit of Geneva may be regarded as the strongest single influence at work in the English exile-communities, he still represented only one influence among several.[24] The appeal of the Coxians to Calvin's authority did not mean that they had enrolled in his Church. Pilkington and Nowell, who were in charge of the Frankfurt congregation just before the return from the exile, rejected a proposal made by Knox, Whittingham and others at Geneva that the Prayer Book should be Calvinised and a Genevan order established as soon as possible in England. At Strassburg Grindal and Horne made a similar reply; so did Jewel and Peter Martyr at Zürich, where Martyr, the foreigner most trusted by the English, had joined forces with Bullinger. These moderates were at no stage submerged by Genevan influences. Their theology, it is true, differed little from that of Calvin. Nevertheless, they shrank from the full rigours of Genevan church government and social organisation. They were prepared to accept not only episcopacy but a considerable measure of state-control. They were loyal to Cranmer's memory and did not want a Prayer Book much more Protestant than that of 1552; indeed, they were soon to accept, provisionally at least, one less Protestant. In the last resort the importance of the Marian exiles lies in the fact that most of them were patriots who preserved Anglicanism rather than in the fact that some of them experimented with foreign and more radical ideas. When the exiles returned in 1558–9, a crucial stage in the combat had still to be fought, but neither the Catholic nor the pure Calvinist was a contender deserving to attract heavy wagers. Indeed it would now seem that the early Elizabethan changes in religion were far less dominated by the returning exiles than we used to believe only a few years ago.

The Revolution of 1559

As the daughter of Anne Boleyn, as a child of the Protestant humanism which had nourished Edward and Lady Jane, above all as the idol of the anti-Marian Londoners, the new Queen was deeply committed to reverse the religious settlement of her predecessor. At the moment of her accession the domestic situation was largely favourable to such a design. The Catholic bishops formed a depleted group; their strongest character, Bonner, had attracted general execration, while their moderates, like Heath and Tunstall, felt personally amicable toward Elizabeth and far from anxious to disrupt the kingdom. In the country the Catholic faction had no obvious nucleus; even in the North there existed as yet no camarilla of Catholic neo-feudalists prepared for a resort to arms. Philip's ambassador Feria estimated that the Catholic party was 'two-thirds larger than the other'.[25] Such estimates—and many were to be attempted by wishful thinkers—can only be regarded as impressionist guesses, and they presupposed in the individual a degree of clarity most untypical of this period. Elizabethan writers are for ever alleging that a high proportion of their compatriots lacked any keen sense of religion. Whatever the accuracy of Feria's conjecture, the majority of the people can hardly have been ardent or even convinced Catholics. Few religious revolutions have been more dramatic and momentous than that of 1558–9, yet none has encountered more feeble opposition.

The foreign situation seemed at first to demand a most cautious approach to religion. The financial and military weaknesses of the country were notorious, yet it was still at war with France and dependent upon the

Spanish alliance. For some months Philip toyed with the idea of holding England by marrying Elizabeth, and it seemed most unwise to disillusion him too rapidly by taking irrevocable steps toward Protestantism. Likewise, to attract outright denunciation by Rome might attract disaffection at home and abroad. The Pope soon hinted at Elizabeth's illegitimate origins and the French pressed him in this direction, since in the Dauphine Mary Stuart they controlled a rival candidate to the English throne. Again, the Lutheran states still appeared potential allies; their political and theological beliefs attracted Elizabeth and they would only be repelled by the Swiss-type Reformation advocated by the exiles now returning to England. For such reasons, secular wisdom suggested the avoidance of radical religious changes during the early months of the reign. Of the several extant papers of advice submitted to Elizabeth all save one agree on this principle of caution.[26] Sir Nicholas Throckmorton, a keen Reformer who had helped John Jewel to escape from England, urged the Queen to 'have a good eye that there be no innovations'. The prominent lawyer and official Richard Goodrich likewise hated Rome, but showed himself prepared to retain awhile the Papal Supremacy and a Catholic order of service. He and others urged that no important changes should be undertaken during the first Parliament. The exceptional paper, the *Device for the Alteration of Religion*, was written by an unknown Protestant enthusiast. It advocates the immediate establishment of a national Church with a Protestant liturgy and, since this in fact occurred, the *Device* was formerly accepted by historians as a governmental programme. We cannot however assume that in the first months of the reign the Queen and her Council had reached unanimity regarding the speed of the impending operation.

That the character and personal views of the new monarch exerted a restraining force cannot be doubted. Elizabeth was an admirer but not a mental replica of her father. Theological tastes and learning were not hereditary in the family, and her education had been chiefly linguistic. Though she admired 'advanced' intellectuals like Ochino and Jacobus Acontius,[27] and though she lacked religious fervour, we have no reason to credit those who depicted her as an Italianate atheist. Such unbelievers were then very rare, even in Italy. Yet a cool humanism matched her cool temperament, and she had already seen enough of the opposing fanaticisms to inspire her with distaste for both. Though an Edwardian Protestant, she leaned strongly toward external seemliness in church, liked vestments and hankered ineffectively after a celibate priesthood. She appears to have believed in a real presence in the sacrament. She cannot be credited either with the invention of Anglo-Catholicism or with a prophetic latitudinarian policy which foresaw the rich diversity of Anglicanism. Her preferences of 1558–9 nevertheless make this diversity possible; perhaps no young woman of twenty-five has ever taken personal decisions having consequences so momentous. While intelligent and cautious to the point of indecision, she exuded an air of authority. 'She seems to me', wrote Feria, 'incomparably more feared than her sister, and gives her orders and has her way absolutely, as her father did.'[28] Her religion was deeply permeated by a secular idealism which related to her office, to England, to the well-being of the subjects committed to her charge by a very English Deity. She was a consummate actress who looked convincing, even to zealots, when she kissed the Bible in public. She had the inestimable advantage of understanding Englishmen far better than Calvin, or Philip, or Mary Stuart; more clearly than the other Tudors she perceived their hunger for romance without expense.

This range of ideas had nothing in common with the internationalism of Geneva. Its religious content related to the kingdom of England, to some sort of Royal Supremacy and to the accepted medieval and Renaissance concepts of a society based, like the world of Nature itself, on order, degree and hierarchy. The old clerical pyramid extending from archbishops down to deacons and parish clerks may seem to modern observers little more than a mirrored image of feudal society, but to a national ruler of Elizabeth's day it continued to correspond in considerable measure with the facts of life and the needs of monarchy. Elizabeth was called to rule not a city-state, but a still half-feudal and largely rural nation. To preserve sovereignty and the chain of command it was safer to retain the clerical hierarchy and somehow to reconcile it with the aspirations of the squires and merchants, who had grown rich and numerous within the secular hierarchy and had substituted themselves for its former baronial pillars.

Inevitably, after the disorders and humiliations of the last decade, the figure of Henry VIII looked more commanding than any other which sprang to Elizabeth's imagination. The fact that she 'gloried' in her father might form a more valuable clue to her psychology than has yet been realised. But when she suggested to Feria that she would restore the religious position of Henry VIII,[29] she must have been impressing him with her conservatism rather than announcing a serious intention. At this stage one could not plan to deprive the Marian bishops and yet go back to the Six Articles. Even the most conservative of her immediate plans involved communion for the laity in both kinds, and other proposals which Henry had never sanctioned. When, however, she praised to Feria the Confession of Augsburg and professed her belief in a real presence, she probably voiced her actual opinions. Other evidence suggests that she may at first have considered taking the conservative Prayer Book of 1549 as a basis of reconciliation between those two important groups,[30] the Prayer Book Protestants and the many Catholics who lacked much enthusiasm for papalism. But even the former, the Coxians, would not have accepted this starting-point—no group of the returning exiles wanted a basis more conservative than that contained in the Book of 1552. 'Now is the time for the walls of Jerusalem to be built again in that kingdom, that the blood of so many martyrs, so largely shed, may not be in vain.' Men who had just been writing in this strain had no intention of returning either to the Augsburg Confession or to a Prayer Book almost accepted by the late Bishop Gardiner. During the early weeks of the reign Elizabeth does not appear to have been under heavy pressure from her Privy Council; like herself they were cautious people, waiting for a wind. As yet they included no divines in a position to carry weight. She excluded fifteen of Mary's Council while keeping eleven of the more pliant characters.[31] The seven newcomers were lay politicians inclined to a moderate Protestantism, chief among them Sir William Cecil, whom she immediately summoned to the office of Secretary and so to that wonderful partnership of forty years. Nevertheless, the settlement agreed upon by Parliament did not spring solely from the brains of Elizabeth and Cecil; it acknowledged the growing strength of Protestant opinion, though at this stage the latter's political strength was limited, since the exiles returned slowly, thus retarding the development of radical pressure inside and outside Parliament. In no sense did the settlement arise from a compromise between Elizabethan Protestants and Marian Catholics. By a whole series of actions before Parliament met, Elizabeth showed her personal and independent desire for a non-Catholic settlement. Pending parliamentary recognition she kept open her claim to the Royal Supremacy by adding '&c' after her royal titles. She chose William Bill, a noted Protestant, to be the first preacher at Paul's Cross, and she imprisoned a Catholic who answered him too fiercely. On the Christmas Sunday she commanded Bishop Oglethorpe to omit the elevation of the host at mass, and on his refusal she withdrew before it occurred. On 15 January 1559 at the coronation service, no elevation was permitted.[32] Ten days later, at the state opening of Parliament, she rudely ordered the abbot and monks of Westminster to extinguish their ceremonial tapers. 'Away with those torches, we can see well enough!' On the first day of its meeting the chosen preacher was none other than Dr. Richard Cox, who thundered at quite inordinate length. Already on 31 January Feria was writing to Philip that 'the Catholics are very fearful of the measures to be taken in this Parliament'.[33] All these hints were deliberately given by Elizabeth before she began to encounter any parliamentary pressure. However remote from Geneva, she intended from the first to figure in the character of a Protestant monarch. Whatever her pretences, one finds it almost impossible to believe that at any stage she seriously contemplated a concordat with Rome or even a return to her father's brand of conservative orthodoxy.

That the Parliament which began on 25 January 1559 was not packed, C. G. Bayne proved many years ago,[34] and the fact is now accepted by all serious students of parliamentary history. The elections were not even preceded by circular letters attempting to influence the composition of the Commons, about a third of whom had sat in Mary's last Parliament. No Catholic group emerged to oppose the Protestant activists, yet in the House of Lords a very different situation obtained. The lay peers included very few enthusiastic Protestants, yet the whole body was small, most of the peers being office-holders or otherwise closely connected with the court, men traditionally reluctant to stand in opposition to the monarchy. Only one lay peer, Lord Montague, steadily voted along Romanist lines. In contrast, the Marian bishops voted consistently against all Reforming legislation. Some of them attended very seldom, but all behaved with dignity and courage, knowing they would be overwhelmed, uncertain that they would be handled with mercy. They also desired to be patriotic Englishmen; they were concerned to obey their consciences rather than to provoke unrest. When

Bishop Scott of Chester, one of the most convinced papalists, opposed the new Act of Supremacy, he confessed he felt restrained from forceful speaking through respect to the Queen, 'unto whom I do acknowledge that I owe obedience, not only for wrath and displeasure's sake, but for conscience sake, and that by the Scriptures of God'.[35] The real problems concerning the revolution hence relate to events in the Commons, the records of which are regrettably laconic and sometimes difficult to harmonise.

From this point it must be observed that of late the events of 1559 have become subject to major differences of interpretation. Previous to the publication in 1953 of J. E. Neale's *Elizabeth I and her Parliaments* historians had agreed upon the image of a new Protestant Queen, backed by a loyal House of Commons, overriding the Catholic bishops and peers, and keenly restoring (with brief if significant modifications) both the Royal Supremacy and an Act of Uniformity based upon the Second Prayer Book of Edward VI. This scenario held the field from John Foxe to A. F. Pollard. Yet Neale, the justly renowned historian of the Elizabethan Parliaments, ventured a bold revision based upon close analysis and ingenious speculation.[36]. He saw the House of Lords as a side-show, unable to co-ordinate its own resistance, let alone to arouse the conservative forces still alive among the English people. He transferred to the Commons what he regarded as the significant tension of the period: the tension between a slow-moving, ultra-cautious monarchy and a far more Protestant House of Commons led by a dynamic cabal of Marian exiles and other continentally inspired Reformers. Though moderated by loyalty and patriotism and ending in compromise, this clash between royal conservatism and activism in the Commons seemed to Neale the dominant feature of Elizabeth's first parliament. He tended to read back from that more organised and better-documented Puritan opposition which marked the Parliaments from 1571 onwards. Could one not see this situation already existent in 1559 and 1563, when already some of the most loyal Protestants did in fact show impatience and regarded the English Church as 'but halfly reformed'?

Broadly speaking Neale's interpretation carried conviction until 1980–82, when two scholars, each working independently but along parallel lines, counter-revised Neale's revision, returning to a scheme not unlike the traditional interpretation. The more comprehensive and hard-hitting of these two books is that by Norman L. Jones,[37] the more elegant that of Winthrop S. Hudson.[38] To the main theme Hudson added a related topic: the part played by William Cecil's friends and associates, who formed so crucial a linkage between the government and the more activist Protestants. This so-called 'Cambridge Connection'—in fact a loose, informal network—had arisen from the fraternity of classical humanists headed by Sir John Cheke and known as 'the Athenians'. Though aspects of the new theory continue to be disputed, it does seem to accommodate more of the doubtful clues than does the Neale theory. Above all it demonstrates the slightness of any hard evidence for supposing that in 1559 Elizabeth marched out of step with those who were planning a fully Protestant Settlement. It gains support from the contemporary analysis of the membership of the 1559 House of

Commons to be found in the three Elizabethan volumes of the official *History of Parliament*. Insofar as these data refer to the Marian exiles they are summarised by K. R. Bartlett in an Appendix. Here we learn that only nineteen exiles sat in the Commons of 1559, increasing to twenty-six in 1563 and thereafter declining.[39] Even had they all been genuine Protestant activists they could scarcely have driven the 400 members into opposition against the government, but in fact their religious zeal must have varied widely. The largest group had returned neither from Frankfurt, nor from Geneva and the other godly cities of the Swiss Confederation, but from Venice, where an aristocrat-led faction, political rather than religious in its hatred of Mary, had assembled in her last years. This apparent paucity of zealous exiles should hardly surprise us, since extremely few, wherever they resided, can have heard the news of Mary's death, settled their continental affairs, travelled the long road to England and secured nomination or election by early January 1559. This is especially notable in the case of the 212 British exiles hitherto registered at Geneva, only one of whom was certainly returned as a member to the first two Elizabethan Parliaments.[40] It has long been known that this faction took no direct part in framing the Elizabethan Settlement, but we must now accustom ourselves to the thought that no group of exiles was in a position to bully either the Queen or the House. From such data and from the scrappy record of the activities of a few individuals, we can no longer discern in the Commons of 1559 a large pressure-group, hardened by common experience abroad and armed with ultra-protestant views well to the left of the Queen. On the other side Neale and others have almost certainly exaggerated the Queen's conservatism, which involved superficial seemliness rather than the essentials of Catholic doctrine. In 1559 or even in 1563 those who wanted a Protestant Settlement could not have afforded to offend the Queen.[41] In these Parliaments we now tend to see co-operation rather than disputation between government and Commons. It was only in 1571 that the significant battle-lines began to be drawn by political puritans, yet even recognizing this point of division, we should be incautious if we imagined to discover a clear prototype of the eventual rupture between Parliament and monarchy in the seventeenth century.

In 1559 the important opposition arose not in the Commons but in the House of Lords, where it was strongly led by the surviving Catholic bishops but rather weakly supported by a few Catholic peers, mostly courtiers with slight loyalties toward Rome and even slighter intentions to suffer for the old Faith. Before noticing this aspect we need first to examine the legislative activities of 1559, which have so deeply influenced the history of the Church of England and with it that of the nation. On 9 February the government introduced into the Commons 'a bill to restore the supremacy of the Church of England to the Crown of the realm'. It has been argued strongly (but not beyond all question) that at this point the government already envisaged a leisurely programme, which would have involved the postponement of a definitive Act of Uniformity to a future Parliament. Certainly the Protestant clergy, and probably many leading laymen, feared that the whole Settlement might thus be all too slowly and painfully enacted. These mildly impatient observers were not at this time led by the most rigidly Protestant ideologues. John Knox, who had so deeply offended the Queen by his writings, was not permitted to re-enter England. Christopher Goodman, who had given almost equal offence, speedily went to Scotland and did not see England again until 1565. Coverdale returned in the autumn of 1559 and Whittingham only in the summer of the following year. On the other hand the Coxian or Prayer Book exiles were vigorously if not numerously represented in the Commons. In the House their chief leaders were men we have already encountered in exile: Sir Anthony Cooke and Sir Francis Knollys, both of them having highly influential connections. Knollys in particular was to figure for many years among the most ardent Puritan laymen of the reign. These members and their like-minded associates had around them their spiritual directors, Cox, Jewel, Sandys, Grindal, Scory and others, who are likely to have been in London throughout the sessions. In addition the House itself contained very many of the crypto-Protestant and Henrician-minded members of Mary's Parliaments of 1553 and 1555.[42] Unopposed by any comparable number of active Catholics, undisturbed by doctrinaire Genevans, the Protestant element could be relied upon to keep abreast of, if not to outrun, any programme of Reformation proposed by the government. Yet these Coxians realised more clearly than anyone their dependence on the Queen, while on the other side several of her most trusted counsellors, such as Cecil, Bacon, Parry and the Earl of Bedford shared their religious views. Indeed Feria reported that Cecil was constantly abetting the Protestant activists,[43] a probable enough deduction, even though Cecil was as yet wise to avoid flamboyant gestures of support.

Led by Cooke the Commons seized upon the government's Supremacy bill, and when by 21 February it emerged from the committee stage, it was found to have been drastically re-written. It had been greatly extended to cover a Protestant form of service, becoming in effect a measure both of Supremacy and of Uniformity. The actual text of this amendment has not been preserved, but it appears to have revived Edward's second Act of Uniformity, the Prayer Book of 1552 and the Act permitting the marriage of the clergy. It also aimed to stiffen the penalties for refusing the oath of Supremacy. Having sent up the transformed bill to the Lords, the Commons on 27 February embarked on a new scheme—the revival of Cranmer's old committee to reform the canon law. Here they may well have designed to give authority to the abortive *Reformatio Legum*, the document which had seemed too radical even for the late Duke of Northumberland. The Queen regarded such notions with distaste, and this bill cannot have been conceived by the government.

When, between 13–18 March, the Supremacy bill was debated by the Lords, a committee of that House restored it to its previous tepid form, in which it received support by all save the bishops and a couple of Catholic peers. To this damping manoeuvre the reaction of the Commons proved vigorous. Without waiting for the emasculated bill to return to them they swiftly produced a counter-measure to legalise immediate Protestant worship: 'that no persons shall be punished for using the religion used in King Edward's last year'. This they cannot seriously have expected to impose upon the Lords, and their intention must rather have been to assure the Court of their determination. They remained nevertheless astute enough to avoid running risks and giving open offence by voting down the Lords' Supremacy bill; when it returned, they let it through, and by 22 March it awaited the royal assent. Pending its publication, the Queen issued on that day a proclamation allowing communion in both kinds, and she was still preparing to dissolve or prorogue Parliament before Easter. Perhaps she intended to summon another Parliament to continue the work in the autumn, when the balance of public opinion and of the political forces at home and abroad might be better assessed. During the interval, armed with the Supremacy, she would no doubt have sanctioned on her own initiative some form of English service, since she attended an English communion in her own chapel at Easter. Whatever the case, between 23 and 24 March— literally overnight— she altered her mind and instead of dissolving Parliament merely adjourned it to 3 April. The actual arguments which prompted this sudden change of front are not recorded, and Neale attributed it to the improvement of the foreign situation with the conclusion of the Peace of Cateau Cambrésis. One can however suggest a far more compelling reason. The plain fact remains that the government had not yet gained solid legislative results from this Parliament;[44] and it is indeed hard to see any political case for a dissolution at this time. The government was not being stampeded by the more radical enthusiasts in the Commons and had no apparent reason to suppose that an autumn Parliament would present a situation more easily manageable.

Moreover it had become highly urgent to dispel doubts by depriving the Catholic opposition of its remaining powers, and by now everyone must have known that the Marian prelates would refuse compromise and co-operation. The shrewder observers might also have expected that their removal would leave the whole parish clergy a compliant, lukewarm and leaderless body, an army of private soldiers incapable of arousing much sympathy or attention either at home or abroad. This proved in fact the case. After all, had not the majority of them already served under Edward VI as well as under Mary? On 20 March the Queen agreed to a conference or disputation between representative Catholic and Protestant divines, and she chose all except one of the latter from the available circle of the former exiles.[45] These men, Scory, Cox, Sandys, Grindal, Horne, Aylmer, Jewel and Whitehead, were soon, with the single exception of the last, to be her new bishops. The eighth disputant was Edmund Guest, who had emulated Matthew Parker by lying low in England during Mary's reign.[46] The Queen and her advisers did not love exiles as such; the fact remained that these men had become indispensable because of their exceptional opportunities to acquire a viable Protestant theology and because their active Protestant seniors had perished in the Marian persecution.

The actual conference, held in the choir of Westminster Abbey on 31 March and 3 April, proved a fiasco. It was not intended to afford the

Catholics a fair opportunity to put their case before the nation, but simply to deprive them of the plea that they had been suppressed without a hearing. The Protestants drew up the articles for debate, and these were listed by Jewel in a letter:

> Our first proposition is, that it is contrary to the word of God, and the practice of the primitive church, to use in the public prayers and administration of the sacraments any other language than what is understood by the people. The second is, that every provincial church, even without the bidding of a general council, has power either to establish, or change, or abrogate ceremonies and ecclesiastical rites, wherever it may seem to make for edification. The third is, that the propitiatory sacrifice, which the papists pretend to be in the mass, cannot be proved by the holy Scriptures.[47]

These points do not lack a general significance as bases of the Anglican position, but the second was also designed to force the Catholics into the open. They could not accept it without renouncing Rome, yet if they opposed it they would risk becoming involved in treason. It is hence not surprising that they created procedural difficulties and brought the conference to an abortive end on its second day. Here, however, they may have served their cause less effectively than by explicit disputation, since their refusal enabled the government to depict them as contumacious or incompetent to defend their own standpoint. In any case, two of their abler spokesmen, Bishops White of Winchester and Watson of Lincoln, soon found themselves in the Tower.

On reassembling after the adjournment the Commons again showed their spirit when they tried to restore the clergy dispossessed by Mary. Though the Lords rejected this bill, the Commons then drafted another to abolish the restored monasteries, their explicitly anti-Catholic language contrasting with the restraint of government-sponsored legislation. Meanwhile the government was introducing into the Lords a measure of its own, enabling the Crown during vacancies of episcopal sees to subtract estates from them, and to assign them, in exchange, tenths, tithes and impropriated benefices of equal value—equal as estimated by royal commissioners. For obvious reasons, a large element among the laity was still prepared to allow further grasping exploits against the bishops. In Cecil's case something more than a financial motive was involved, for this worthy successor of Thomas Cromwell once said that the way to reduce the political power of the Church was to diminish its wealth. Nevertheless, many zealous Protestants no longer shared this view, and the 90 members who opposed the bill appear to have represented that Reformed element which protested throughout the reign against impoverishing the Church. And once they were appointed, the new Protestant bishops also protested, though in vain.[48]

The remaining important events of the session after Easter 1559 revolved around the two central measures of Supremacy and Uniformity. In the matter of the Supremacy, Elizabeth had again changed her mind and had decided—it was said on the representations of Thomas Lever[49]—to drop the title of Supreme Head and accept that of Supreme Governor. The former seemed inappropriate to an age better attuned to the anti-feminist views of St. Paul than to the advantages of female sovereigns. A third Supremacy bill embodying this change was drafted, and after some minor conservative amendments in the Lords and some Protestant ones in the Commons it duly passed before the end of April.

This prophetic measure[50] repealed the Marian Statutes which had re-instated Roman jurisdiction and the heresy laws. It revived ten statutes of Henry VIII, including those of Annates and Appeals; by consequence it restored the Henrician mode of electing bishops by *congé d'élire*, and not the Edwardian method of appointment by letters patent. It abolished all 'usurped and foreign' jurisdictions; it authorised the Queen to visit and correct the Church through her commissioners. This last section formed the basis of Elizabeth's various ecclesiastical commissions, especially the High Commission and its now better-documented equivalent for the Province of York. The Act showed its lay origins by the careful limitations which it placed upon the powers of such ecclesiastical commissioners. They were to adjudge no matter to be heresy except upon the authority of the canonical Scriptures, of the first four General Councils of the Church or of the English High Court of Parliament, with the assent of the clergy in Convocation. The Act imposed an oath of Supremacy upon all ecclesiastical persons and upon all judges, justices, mayors and other officers of the State. Loss of benefice or office would follow refusal. The oath was also to be tendered to those about to enter into office, and even to men taking holy orders or university degrees. Again, persons maintaining any foreign authority would lose all their properties or benefices for a first offence. For a second they would fall under the penalties of *Praemunire*. For a third the penalties of high treason would follow.

What sort of Supremacy emerged from this Act? The Queen later took pains to depict it as identical with that wielded by her father, but under James I the great jurist John Selden rightly thought otherwise. 'There's a great difference between head of the Church and supreme governor, as our canons call the King. Conceive it thus: there is in the Kingdom of England a college of physicians: the King is supreme governor of those, but not head of them, nor president of the college, nor the best physician.'[51] If this description fitted Elizabeth and James, it would not have fitted Henry VIII, who saw himself as the functioning head of his Church and chief physician to the souls of his subjects. Over matters of dogma and ritual Elizabeth did not exercise this same personal and quasi-papal control. Moreover she had a partner. Parliament, having enhanced its status during the minority of her brother, was becoming a co-ordinate power rather than a mere agent. Parliament now defined certain aspects of the Queen's legal authority over the Church. In effect, it told her to act through ecclesiastical commissioners and it defined rather narrowly their powers. Never again could England see a vicegerent like Thomas Cromwell, a personal deputy of the King, lording it over the episcopate in Convocation. And while Elizabeth took no small part in controlling the policies of the Anglican Church, she exercised her influence indirectly, often covertly and with an infuriating reluctance to appear responsible for contentious rulings. No longer was the throne occupied by a crowned theologian, confounding Parliaments and bishops with God's learning; its occupant was an adroit and devious politician, operating through the interstices of Statute Law.

Meanwhile, as the government reviewed the vital matter of public worship, it became ever more obvious that only the Prayer Book of 1552 could form the basis for negotiation with the Protestant divines, who were all serious Reformers, as deeply committed by their past conduct as the Marian bishops themselves. Admittedly the Queen had bishoprics to offer them, but they would have faced ignominy among their friends as well as pangs of conscience had they agreed even to discuss the conservative Prayer Book of 1549. Almost nothing is known about the deliberations of the committee which took instead the Book of 1552 and agreed to certain changes in its text. These changes were few in number but considerable in significance; they were all designed to meet the Queen's political needs and her relatively conservative tastes. Offensive references to the Pope disappeared. A certain latitude of eucharistic belief was allowed by prefixing the 1549 words of administration: 'The body of our Lord Jesus Christ, which was given for thee ...', to the words of 1552: 'Take and eat this in remembrance ...'. Likewise the new Book omitted the Knoxian 'Black Rubric', which had explained away the practice of kneeling at the reception of communion. These provisions retained commemorative phraseology, yet reopened the way for belief in a real presence falling short of transubstantiation. Thanks in part to a shift of interest among Protestants this bold solution was to raise surprisingly little contention in Elizabethan times.

A very different future awaited the other important change made in the Book of 1552—the notorious Ornaments Rubric inserted before Morning and Evening Prayer. Instead of preserving the Rubric of 1552 (that the minister should never wear alb, vestment or cope) it ordered that the ornaments of the church and the ministers should be those in use 'by authority of Parliament, in the second year of the reign of King Edward VI'. Here was an odd inaccuracy, since the Book of 1549 had been authorised in the third year of King Edward. Moreover, the Act of Uniformity which accompanied Elizabeth's new Book added that these ornaments should continue in use 'until other order shall be therein taken by the authority of the Queen's Majesty, with the advice of her commissioners ... for causes ecclesiastical, or of the Metropolitan of this realm'. The Reformers leapt to the mistaken conclusion that the Queen did not intend to press upon them the obnoxious vestments of 1549. 'Our gloss upon this text', wrote Edwin Sandys, 'is that we shall not be forced to use them.'[52] On the contrary, the Queen, perhaps nettled by their thrustful tactics, proceeded to hold them to their bargain. This misunderstanding soon led to a renewal of the hostilities first provoked by the scruples of John Hooper. Cox, Sandys and Jewel were also to quarrel with the Queen over the ornaments of her chapel, the last two almost to the point of losing their bishoprics. The Vestiarian Controversy formed merely the first of a series of intermittent clashes over vestments lasting until our own times. Blundering attempts to obtain a legal decision succeeded only in creating more complex and irrational situations, while in recent times uniformity would have involved violence toward one or more of the major schools of thought within the Anglican communion.

The penalties under the Act of Uniformity were graduated similarly to those of the Edwardian Acts, but made in some particulars rather more severe. Forms of service other than those in the new Prayer Book were forbidden and clerics attempting to use them became liable to deprivation of all benefices for a year and to imprisonment for six months. For a second offence the penalties were permanent deprivation and a year's imprisonment; for a third, life imprisonment. Those openly attacking the Book were liable to fines of 100 marks (£66. 13s. 4d.) in the first instance, 400 marks in the second, total forfeiture of goods and life imprisonment in the third. Absentees from church must now forfeit the sum of one shilling per Sunday, to be levied by the churchwardens and used to help the poor. The Act also empowered the judges of assize and municipal officers to seek out and punish all these offences. The bishops were authorised to co-operate with the justices, while retaining in addition their ecclesiastical jurisdiction.[53]

Despite the opposition of the Marian bishops, this Act of Uniformity enjoyed as rapid a passage through the Lords as through the Commons. Nine lay peers voted against it; with one or two exceptions they were not Romanists but conservatives who possibly thought to please the Queen by demonstrating against a measure appearing to emanate less from her than from Protestant enthusiasts inside and outside the Commons. Whether or not this view contains a measure of truth, she had little to regret in the course of events since her accession. By 8 May when Parliament was at last dissolved she had gained very nearly all the essential bases befitting her title of Supreme Governor. In the former editions of this present book the writer regarded the Elizabethan Settlement as most obviously 'a compromise between the Queen's prejudices, and those of Dr. Richard Cox and his ebullient friends in the House of Commons'. He no longer believes this statement to be accurate and now supposes that her position throughout all these negotiations stood very near to that of the Coxians. Her potential critics, the former Genevans, had not been able to transfer their pressures to Westminster, and for them at least the legislation of 1559 marked a decided repulse. Their day was yet to come. Calvinist Puritanism was to enjoy a long period of steady advance, though fortunately for Elizabeth and for the nation its persuasive powers were demonstrated in the field of theological studies rather than in that of church government.

The four years following the parliamentary decision saw the Queen still to a certain degree under the diplomatic protection of Philip II, yet carefully completing the foundations of the Elizabethan Church. As her first Primate she could have made no cleverer choice than her former tutor Matthew Parker, modest and retiring in his reluctance to assume office, judicious and tolerant in its exercise: as a non-exile he had avoided rigid continental allegiances, as a historian and antiquarian he had not become overmuch entangled in bitter doctrinal controversy. His chief colleague John Jewel proved not only a model bishop of Salisbury but a most able defender of the national Church in his *Apologia Ecclesiae Anglicanae* (1562). There followed a literary event of still more momentous consequences: the publication in 1563 of the first English edition of John Foxe's *Acts and Monuments*, which was to lie for many generations alongside the Bible and the Prayer Book in countless gentle, clerical and middle-class houses, even in those where other books seldom intruded. In the same year the Edwardian Forty-two Articles of Religion were revised and reissued as the Thirty-nine, though without modification of their essentials. Yet only one early Elizabethan event can compare in broad historical importance with the parliamentary actions of 1559. This event was Elizabeth's well-timed intervention in Scotland. In July 1560 her expedition culminated in the Treaty of Edinburgh, driving French influence from the northern kingdom and placing control in the hands of John Knox, William Maitland of Lethington and the Protestant Lords of the Congregation. Thereafter Queen Mary Stuart failed to prevent the steady convergence of the two countries, which continued its triumphal course through history, past the milestones of 1603, 1643 and 1707. The master-stroke of 1560 opened the way for Knox's second and more profound contribution to the English Reformation, since the influences which there-after flowed between the two kingdoms were by no means altogether one-sided. Moreover, this convergence meant that the overseas western world would at last be pervaded by a British Protestantism more broadly based, and more securely linked to Reformed beliefs, than the original Anglican Settlement of Elizabeth. In defending the latter politically, the Queen had changed its future religious environment and alliances more radically than she or any Elizabethan could have realised.

Over and beyond these changes of interpretation, the sources have demanded a closer biographical analysis of the Marian exiles and their attitudes toward the Elizabethan Settlement. Such an analysis has recently been published by Professor N. M. Sutherland.[54] Here it is shown that the exiles who arrived in time to enter or influence the Parliament of 1559 can no longer be regarded as radical or rebellious exponents of Puritanism. However dramatic their postures on the Continent, once returned to England they became anxious to dissociate themselves from the revolu-tionary treatises of Goodman and Knox. Indeed, no integrated Puritan faction opposing Elizabeth's government can be discerned much before the 1570s. While at one time or another former exiles are to be found occupying no less than seventeen English bishoprics, they and their lay associates emerge as moderate 'establishment men' who loyally supported the govern-ment in 1559 and thereafter aided it to complete and maintain the Settlement propounded in that crucial year. To all the eight Parliaments held from 1559 to 1593 only forty-two former exiles were elected and at no stage did they form a powerful, cohesive party in the House of Commons.

15 The Residual Problems

The Anglican Church

The Elizabethan settlement was less a pacification than a compromise between contending forces which Elizabeth and her Stuart successors failed to reconcile. The gradual consolidation of an Anglican Church must nevertheless be numbered among the achievements of this versatile age. As a Christian body it was neither created nor re-created by the Statutes of Supremacy and Uniformity, and even when the Queen died its full potential was still hard to discern. By then Richard Hooker's *Laws of Ecclesiastical Polity*[1] had gone far to accomplish such a feat of prophecy, but the Church had not yet achieved that poise between Protestant and Catholic ideals which Hooker desired to see. In its spiritual realities it had hitherto been not merely a Protestant, but in remarkable degree a Puritan Church. And scarcely had it begun to understand Hooker's dream when the miscalculations of its ill-chosen leaders involved it in well-nigh fatal disaster.

Between the accession of Elizabeth and the Civil Wars the Church of England became in many respects well adapted to its place and period. It proved less socially and intellectually oppressive than most churches of that day. By the limited standards of the period it allowed very considerable freedom for experiment and speculation. Born in years of internal tension, growing to maturity amid cultural ferment and alongside a great national literature, it had little chance to relapse into the dull pietism which beset some state-churches. While gratifying the general demand for a centralised Church coterminous with the nation, it also left room for some real divergences of outlook. It could produce a few saints; it could not merely tolerate but foster a number of geniuses. It could find work for individualists more easily than either Rome or Geneva; even among its clergy it could admit John Donne and Robert Herrick as well as Nicholas Ferrar and George Herbert. Since the days of Edward VI its devotional appeal had never been limited to the educated classes and, though it was slow to convert certain remote areas of the kingdom, its hold upon the people steadily strengthened and its Prayer Book became widely loved. Alongside its disappointing failures it inevitably made some progress in the tasks of practical reform, for both in Catholic and in Protestant countries organised religion now manifested a growing spirit of integrity, consistency, devotion and discipline. In England, if reforms owed much to Puritan idealism and agitation, some of them must also be credited to the bishops and their officials, whose assiduity becomes more apparent as we familiarise ourselves with hitherto unknown archives in the diocesan registries. Here we see officialdom striving to ensure regular services, audible reading and at least quarterly sermons, to provide complete church furniture, to enforce peaceable and reverent behaviour by the laity, to remove superstitious objects and customs.

The chief problem before the Elizabethan bishops was the education of the clergy, and several set a praiseworthy example by the examinations and other modes of pressure which they applied.[2] Their efforts, together with the growing influx of graduates, the rise of public literacy, the increasing plenitude of books on all subjects, had made a real impact on the clergy by the middle of the reign. The bishops continued to complain about their poor latinity, but the book-lists of many country parsons suggest that both general and scriptural knowledge were expanding in consonance with the growing opportunities of the period. The proportion of graduates varied greatly from one area to another, but everywhere it grew. In the diocese of Worcester it was nineteen per cent in 1560, twenty-three per cent in 1580, fifty-two per cent in 1620 and eighty-four per cent in 1640. This seems to represent a more typical growth than that in the favoured diocese of Oxford, where in the same period the figures increase from thirty-eight per cent in 1560 to ninety-six per cent in 1640.[3] From the outset of the Reformation—and this would also have happened had England remained Catholic—the old fringe of disreputable and criminous clerks had been gradually falling away. Elizabethan England at least attained Sir Thomas More's modest ambition—a less numerous but more respectable clergy.

Concerning the Elizabethan bishops, we generalise and moralise at our peril.[4] They ranged from near-saints to worldly courtiers. Most had middle-class origins and, in an age of climbers, few wholly freed themselves from the habits of social ambition. Several were nepotists, who strained the resources of their sees in order to establish their children in the charmed circle of county families. A few obtained preferment by methods little short of simony. Yet alongside such behaviour, even the less admirable contrived to appear devout and to achieve a minimum respectability. While the bishops remained dutiful servants of the monarchy, they resided in their dioceses to a greater extent than did their medieval predecessors. Few held high office under the Crown, and their secular duties resembled those of justices of the peace rather than those of ambassadors or officers of state. Amid many enemies and still more dangerous friends they did their duty by Church and country. It would be pleasant to record that their ability and wisdom improved along with those of their clergy, but in fact the team which served Charles I was weaker than that which served Elizabeth at any part of her reign.

The darkest aspects of the Anglican Church resulted from its failure to solve the financial problems which so gravely impaired its efficiency and its morale. These material cares, depicted with fine scholarship by Christopher Hill,[5] deserve a more detailed treatment that we can here attempt, for they had hitherto been underweighted by less realistic historians. They sprang from a fundamental inconsistency in the outlook of the official and moneyed classes. The new religious emphases lay heavily upon preaching. This fact and the rising standards of public education demanded a more learned ministry, which demanded in turn a larger, more buoyant financial provision in order to attract the ablest men and to maintain their standards in an age of steady inflation. This need obtained widespread recognition, but it disposed few laymen to make financial sacrifices. Their knowledge that the Church had already sustained great material losses did not cure their itch to exploit its resources. Like her brother and her father Elizabeth often granted long and favourable leases of episcopal land to officials and courtiers. The bishops were constrained to accept these unfavourable bargains through their own need for royal favours and for popularity among influential laymen. Again, an ill-considered parliamentary Act of 1549[6] had exempted various classes of former tithe-payers, and had made tithes more difficult to collect. In any case, while they could be assessed on agricultural produce, no one could seriously pretend to estimate the 'new' wealth born of rising trade and industry; hence in the cities the continued payment of personal tithe depended upon the elastic consciences of the payers. To this problem the common law courts now proceeded to contribute; having asserted their right to a share in the tithe-cases, these courts refused to enforce clerical claims except where formal contracts could be produced.

Meanwhile, the gentry who had succeeded the monks as holders of impropriated benefices continued to allow vicars only the small tithes, or in unendowed vicarages, to pay them meagre stipends. The stingy squire who paid and treated his vicar as a superior servant and neglected his share in the church repairs was far from universal, yet he was not uncommon. The Reformation brought into the landed classes many small men, who could not begin to emulate the old barons and bishops as patrons. A process which was otherwise politically and even socially beneficial did not thereby help to repair the endowment of the Church. Sometimes the impropriator had little to spare and saw no reason to be generous over what was in essence a business deal, for impropriated livings continued to be freely bought and sold by laymen. In 1603 these benefices were estimated by the bishops to number 3,849 out of a total of about 9,284.[7] As we have seen, the economic experiences of the parish clergy varied most widely. There nevertheless remained too many livings incapable of supporting men dedicated to study and preaching rather than to farming or some other remunerative sideline. Again, as the bishops never tired of saying, poverty diminished the standing of the Church in a materialist world. It was not so much absolute indigence as failure to keep pace with rising lay standards which prejudiced careers in the Church. In several of the richer and more Puritan towns preachers were independently maintained by the corporations at high salaries. On the other hand it was not unknown for prosperous laymen to make hypocritical reference to the spiritual benefits of clerical austerity, while both White Kennett and Sir Thomas Wilson wondered whether Elizabeth deliberately kept the clergy poor in order to preserve their utter dependence on the Crown.[8] She was not in fact wholly oblivious to the political importance of a preaching clergy, and in 1599 she endowed four stipendiary preachers with annual incomes of £50 each in order to maintain the Settlement in semi-Catholic Lancashire. But this gesture strained her limited generosity, and it was not followed up in other unreliable areas. While James I realised more clearly the common interest which should have bound together Church and Crown, by this time it had become almost impossible to dip into the pockets of ungenerous and impecunious laymen. In due course Archbishop Laud made vigorous efforts to recover impropriations and force the citizens of London to pay tithe,[9] but he had gathered little beyond some additional hatred by the time his rule collapsed. Even after the Restoration no radical reform was forthcoming, and the crisis of endowments lingered on to be partially solved by piecemeal augmentations and by Queen Anne's Bounty. That there remained poor incumbents, and gross inequities as between one incumbent and another, should not be blamed purely upon our medieval and Tudor ancestors, since under more favourable circumstances later generations have continued to tolerate so much of the muddle and injustice bequeathed to the national Church by the past. This sombre story serves as one of the many reminders that the Reformation had very real limits upon its power to reform, yet we should view with scepticism those theories which blame a supposed Protestant deprecation of good works. Protestantism even at its most uncompromising never disbelieved in good works; it merely disbelieved that they availed to justify or save the doer. If our Elizabethans lacked generosity toward the Church, in the field of secular charity—including education—good works continued to abound. Moreover, those who truly believed in Protestant religion were loudest in their condemnation of covetous impropriators and exploiting courtiers. Elizabethan and Jacobean Puritans understood well enough that the further spoliation of the Church must end by injuring religion itself. Whereas at least some of the financial scandals of the medieval Church had arisen from actual abuses of Catholic doctrine, those of the Anglican Church cannot accurately be dignified by theological explanations, for they were the patent offspring of Mammon.

The Catholics

Of the external threats presented to the Settlement that of Catholicism remained insignificant for a decade. It then assumed menacing proportions between 1569 and 1588, yet was largely contained by the end of the reign.[10]

When in the summer of 1559 Elizabeth's commissioners toured the provinces, they found an insignificant number of Catholic clergy venturing to refuse the oath of Supremacy.[11] Men as conservative as Robert Parkyn continued in their benefices till death removed them. During the first years some of the more nominal conformists may have been saying masses in secret to groups of Catholics, yet little open defiance appeared. Ironically enough, the early years of the reign, when the government did not persecute Catholics, was probably the period when the Catholic Church lost most of its remaining hold upon the English people.[12] When at last in 1569 a Catholic-feudal rebellion arose, it completely failed to engage more than a small section of northern England and did not even come near to capturing York. Until the papal bull of 1570 excommunicated Elizabeth and urged her subjects to depose her, Catholic recusancy occurred upon a very small scale. Though the steadfastness of a few priests and a good many laymen prepared the ground during the early Elizabethan years, English Catholicism was qualitatively preserved during the last three decades of the reign by the adventurous labours of the Seminarists and Jesuits. Their work was rendered vastly more difficult by the violence of the bull which the Pope issued in direct contravention of Philip's cautious advice. In 1585 the Seminarists were declared traitors by English law, and when one of them was captured, the magistrates commonly asked him: 'If the Pope and the King of Spain landed in England, for whom would you fight?' Even the most resolute found the question difficult, for how many Englishmen would accept conversion at the point of the Spanish pike or risk seeing in their own country the horrors of the French Wars of Religion? Seen as individuals, these missionaries are true heroes and martyrs, yet the fact remains that they were sent by superiors and rulers with every intention of arousing civil war and of using their work as a basis for the forcible imposition of a foreign Catholic monarch upon England. The practical difficulty before the government was to distinguish between the small minority of Catholics which concerted murder-plots against the Queen, and the great majority which wanted somehow to combine the two loyalties and which duly demonstrated its political allegiance to Elizabeth during the Armada year. Caught between the millstones of State and Papacy a steady stream of priests suffered with admirable fortitude the atrocious deaths of traitors.

During the eighties and nineties under missionary influence the number of recusants grew apace in certain areas of England; they were devoted people prepared to risk imprisonment and the theoretically overwhelming but slackly enforced fines imposed by the Statute of 1581.[13] Except in Lancashire,[14] these open Catholics constituted a very small part of the population. Fortunately, at this late stage we begin to encounter documents which appear to afford approximate statistics, an amenity hitherto lacking in regard to both Catholics and Protestants. For Yorkshire we happen to possess a census of recusants compiled in 1604, district by district, with exceptional thoroughness and care.[15] Their numbers had of late shown a sudden increase, because of their hopes that the new King would inaugurate a policy of toleration. In this large area, which contained several of the major

Catholic districts in England, the discoverable recusants achieved a total of less than 3,500 in a population of more than 300,000. Even this small figure contained several hundred people who attended the Anglican matins and evensong but who refused to communicate. In most parts of England there must also have existed a fringe of sympathisers, deterred from open defiance by the fear of fines; yet since Tudor officialdom did not compile psychological surveys, no one can pretend to estimate their number. There seems, however, no reason to suppose that these so-called church-papists remained very numerous toward the end of the reign. The new English Catholicism developed a certain aristocratic distinction and background. The priests, its chief creators, sprang from gentle families which sent their sons abroad to be trained in Cardinal Allen's colleges or by the Jesuits. Returning on the perilous 'English Mission' they passed in disguise from one country house to another, these being the chief places of concealment in a countryside where all newcomers were conspicuous.[16] Accordingly, a large part of their converts came from the families, servants and tenants of Catholic squires.

The greater dangers presented by the Counter-Reformation did not, however, lie in recusancy but in the assassination-plots directed against the Queen and in the threat of a foreign invasion which would tempt English Catholics to desert their national allegiance. Cardinal Allen and his most successful emissary Father Robert Parsons firmly believed in the Pope's right to depose heretical monarchs and intervened accordingly in the world of politics.[17] For many years one of Cecil's recurring nightmares might appropriately have appeared in diagrammatic form—a map of western Europe, with one arrow stretching from Spain to Ireland, a second from Ireland to Lancashire and a third from Lancashire to London.[18] Yet thanks in part to the immense preoccupations and the naval problems of Spain this diagram never developed into military fact. English Catholicism looked, in short, more politically formidable than it was, and its adherents suffered accordingly. Already identified in patriotic Elizabethan minds with foreign powers, it had to attempt the reconversion of England from bases in enemy territory and in league with conspiracy against the only possible English government. The devotion of its laity and the heroism of its priesthood, great as they were, could not accomplish an impossible task. That Catholicism survived in England as a minority-religion has nevertheless proved in the long run a religious and cultural enrichment of the first order.

Puritanism: A Brief Anatomy

Whereas the Catholics were dangerous to Elizabeth through external forces, the Puritan problem remained internal, not only to English society but to the English Church itself.[19] And that Puritanism contained heavier explosive charges than Catholicism, the history of the seventeenth century was to demonstrate. Since its inception the term has been used in various senses.

If we narrow it to Separatism and Presbyterianism, it lacks any formidable content until after 1640. The earlier Separatists like Robert Harrison, Robert Browne and John Penry represented, together with the congregations in London and Norwich, a minute element in the religious life of their own day. Cartwright's Presbyterianism and the Marprelate Tracts occupied only one short period of Elizabeth's reign, and the former attained no serious renewal until the era of the Civil Wars. Most modern historians have recognised the essential unity of a greater phenomenon by giving the term Puritanism a far wider scope. This was, wrote Trevelyan, 'the religion of all those who wished either to purify the usage of the established Church from the taint of popery, or to worship separately by forms so purified'. At least since the eighteenth century, such wide definitions have been common because they are useful and significant. When Daniel Neal and Benjamin Brook compiled their immense biographical collections of the great Puritans, they were very largely writing about Calvinistic clergymen of the Anglican Church.[20]

If we so define the phenomenon, it seems most inaccurate to see in the reign of Elizabeth a conflict between 'Anglicanism' and 'Puritanism'. Parker and Jewel were in very real senses forerunners of the 'balanced' Anglicanism of Hooker, yet even so the vast majority of Elizabethan Englishmen who cared deeply about religion were either Roman Catholics of Anglican Puritans. Until 1600 or later that spirituality within the Anglican Church which could reasonably be described as non-Puritan remained rather exiguous. Even Archbishop Whitgift, who so fiercely disciplined Puritan mislikers of the surplice, did not differ from them upon the essential points of theology. He was a strict Calvinist, who upbraided Cartwright himself for venturing to say that the doctrine of free will was 'not repugnant to salvation'.[21] In 1595–6 Peter Baro, the French Lady Margaret professor at Cambridge, taught that Christ died for all men and that human free will had a rôle to play in salvation. Further attacks on Calvin had already been made by Baro's pupil William Barrett.[22] The outraged authorities of Calvinist Cambridge fell with wrath upon these anticipators of Arminius, and if Whitgift prevented their entire humiliation, he also made it clear at this time that he too disagreed with their liberalism. His Lambeth Articles of 1595 do very little to temper the most rigorous predestinatory doctrine. The change of front in the leadership of the Church scarcely began until 1599, when Whitgift, aged and incapable, virtually assigned the Primate's functions to Richard Bancroft, Bishop of London. The latter now demonstrated his broader sympathies by ordering the London clergy to march in Peter Baro's funeral procession. At the Hampton Court Conference in 1604 it was Bancroft who successfully opposed Puritan efforts to attach Whitgift's Lambeth Articles to the Thirty-nine Articles as part of the official summary of belief. These events, following upon the reception of Hooker's great work, mark the undermining of the Anglo-Puritan dominance and the recovery of a medial tradition, which eschewed the rigours of orthodox Calvinism, deprecated bibliolatry, stressed the rôle of reason in interpreting the Christian Faith and resisted the demands for changes in liturgy,

church-government and the Articles. It should be stressed that this movement was not simply based upon the new liberal tendencies in continental
Protestant theology. To a certain extent it may also be regarded as a
restatement of our own *via media*, adumbrated long ago by the Henrician
and Edwardian moderates and always recoverable from Cranmer's Prayer
Book, especially as modified by Elizabeth in 1559.

In itself the retention of Bishops in no way impugned the Puritan
character of the Elizabethan Church. Despite Martin Marprelate neither
Calvin nor Knox had denounced the episcopal office, while on the other side
Hooker supported it with no trace of fanaticism. He even denied the
necessity of episcopal ordination. Matthew Parker apart, all the important
earlier Elizabethan bishops had been Marian exiles, having strong ties with
Geneva, Zürich and Strassburg. It was the Genevan spirit which dominated
Cambridge and fired the minds of the young clergymen poured out by that
university into the parishes during Elizabeth's reign. The real Protestantising
of the clergy did not take place in 1559, or by subsequent resignations or
deprivation. It took the form of a steady influx of Puritan recruits, apparently
speeded by the high average age of the beneficed clergy in 1559. This
factor had been produced in its turn by the surplus of unemployed clerics
and the consequently small number of ordinations during the crisis of the
Reformation.

Throughout Elizabethan England Puritan preachers dominated the pulpits,
even though many of them were intermittently engaged in disputes with
their bishops. As their sermons show, their preaching ability and their
numbers had no equivalent in pre-Reformation or mid-Tudor England. In
London were Edward Dering and Henry Smith, at Norwich John More, in
Suffolk John Knewstub, in Essex Richard Rogers, in Kent Dudley Fenner,
in Sussex Thomas Underdown, in Leicestershire Anthony Gilby and Arthur
Hildersham, in north Oxfordshire John Dod, in Yorkshire Giles Wigginton,
Edmund Bunney, John Favour and several others. And in Cambridge itself
the young men could model their styles on the great master, William
Perkins.[23] These are merely a small selection from the more obvious names.
The same outlook can be traced in the wills of many obscure clerics who did
not preserve or publish their sermons. Many held for a time the well-paid
office of lecturer or town-preacher in one or other of the little Genevas
created by Puritan magistrates. Though, as we have seen, new forces took
shape among the Jacobean and Caroline divines, this sober Puritan tradition
continued strong inside the Church and not a few of its traits can be
observed even in men whose theological principles would entitle them to be
called Arminians. It became a most pervasive spirit, and even at the height of
Laud's career the Church of England did not begin to look like a Church of
the Counter-Reformation. Puritanism in our sense was never limited to
Nonconformists; it was a powerful element in the origins of the Anglican
Church and it was first through that Church that it won its abiding rôle in
the life and outlook of the nation. To the present writer, as to most
Anglicans, it would seem clear that Archbishops Laud and Neile brought
some valid if not very profound criticisms against their Puritan adversaries.

Armed with more statesmanship they might have manoeuvred the Church without disaster into a more latitudinarian position, one with scope and tolerance for all except extremists. Yet it remains a gross misuse of terminology to call their party Anglican and to begrudge that label to their opponents, or to their Puritan predecessors, Archbishops Grindal and Hutton. Puritanism belonged to the mainstream of the Reformation. From the outset the national Church took its stand upon the principles of the Reformation, and among its early members the Puritans bulk very large indeed.

In more recent times the distinction and the peculiar Englishness of the Anglican Church has arisen, not from the claim of any one of its groups to special insight but from its success as an experiment in practical toleration and co-operation between varying schools of thought. In the very occasional need to enforce this experiment has lain the chief justification for a measure of state-control. Charles I understood this ideal as dimly as most of his subjects. He also failed to grasp the already historic function of Puritanism within the English Church, and in his reign the monarchy declined into an instrument of the Laudian minority-group. Today English Christians are still seeking to mitigate the more untoward effects of that chain-reaction which, after a series of bitter blows and counter-blows, culminated in the Clarendon Code and a more decisive cleavage between Anglicans and Nonconformists.

To assess the true character of the Puritan movement inside and outside the Church we must free our minds from the present popular use of the term, deriving in large part from satire directed against Victorian religious hypocrisy. That by any modern standards the actual movement had some critical weaknesses would hardly be denied, yet it has often suffered unduly at the hands of doctrinaire critics who have fixed their gaze upon some unrepresentative aspect of a large and complicated phenomenon. The characteristics of Puritanism which I now attempt to summarise are based to a minimal extent upon my private judgement, but rather upon detailed and documented surveys by Patrick Collinson, M. M. Knappen and other scholars profoundly acquainted with Puritan sermons, pamphlets, social treatises and devotional works.

This has been called a clerical movement, yet its clergy were far more closely controlled by laymen than were those of the Middle Ages. It aspired to bring lay and clerical society closer together and to abolish the dual standard sanctioned by the medieval Church. In England it always enjoyed heavy support among the gentry and substantial merchants. Even the venturesome Presbyterian classis-movement of 1582–9 was heavily backed by lay congregations which encouraged their incumbents to set aside the Prayer Book.[24] To the end of Elizabeth's reign it can be said to have commanded a majority in the House of Commons. Its active lay leaders stood among the most influential men in the land—Sir Francis Knollys, Sir Walter Mildmay, Ambrose Dudley, Earl of Warwick, Sir Francis Walsingham and Robert Beale. The Queen's devout cousin, Henry Hastings, Earl of Huntingdon, Lord President of the Council in the North, stood at the centre of the great web of Puritanism in the Midlands and the northern counties. Puritans were patronised by individualist politicians from the Earl of Leicester downwards. Cecil, it is true, seems accounted a lost leader by the godly; his attitude to religious zeal became ever more suspicious and coloured by erastianism, yet even Cecil protected several important Puritans and was very far from wanting to see Whitgift domineering over scrupulous ministers.

During the present century the rôle of Puritanism among the laity has been given a fresh interpretation by Max Weber and Tawney. At all events when read incautiously, the latter's *Religion and the Rise of Capitalism* has tended to disseminate the image of the Puritan as a ruthless man of business, justifying the profit-motive by his 'doctrine of stewardship' and regarding even economic opportunity as a trust or stewardship reposed by God in the elect. The present writer is one of those who find it impossible to accept this image as characteristic of the movement. Comparatively late in its history Puritanism did indeed help to produce a few writers capable of thinking in some such terms. Yet even if the business world, where Puritanism made so many converts, sometimes rationalised itself religiously in this way, we need not for a moment ascribe the development of its economic practices and principles to Puritanism.

As Tawney himself reminded us, Catholic bankers were the leading figures in the sixteenth-century world of business, while the creative centres of modern big-scale finance—Antwerp, Lyons, Augsburg, Genoa and Venice—were all in Catholic countries. And centuries earlier, while Dante had put the Cahorsine money-lenders in hell, Pope Innocent IV, with far greater prescience, had called them *Romanae ecclesiae filii speciales*.[25] It might also be pleaded that even the doctrine of stewardship looks less repulsive in the context of seventeenth-century pioneering expansion than it is apt to look in modern eyes. Yet the fact remains that such ideas are utterly unrepresentative of classical Puritanism and even of Puritan economic theory. Looking at the whole movement we see an essentially other-worldly religion, dominated not only by an almost morbid moral sensitivity but by a real distrust of 'modern' capitalist tendencies. In his detailed survey of Tudor Puritanism, Knappen proved this point beyond much doubt, while subsequently the learned survey of English Protestant thought between 1570 and 1640 by C. H. and K. George concluded that such thought stood utterly opposed to the whole spirit of capitalist enterprise.[26] During this period the Puritans showed themselves to have inherited the tradition of Latimer and Hales; they were more outspoken than any group in their denunciation of usury, economic greed and social injustice. With these sins they classed the covetous behaviour of the laymen responsible for the economic and social servitude of the clergy. Puritan theory derives chiefly from clerical writers with small reason to feel complacent over modern tendencies. Again, the whole puritan century ending at the Restoration can boast a good record of generosity, beneficence and public spirit. Professor Jordan's researches[27] purported to justify Arthur Hildersham's claim (*c.* 1635) that more money had been put into English hospitals, charities, colleges and schools during the last sixty years than in any previous century. These gifts were admittedly made in an inflated currency, and the London merchants, by far the biggest Puritan givers, may possibly have been sacrificing less than their generous Catholic grandfathers. Yet broadly considered, the Reformation appears to have made men neither more nor less generous; it simply deflected gifts from the Church to other charitable objects. The image conjured up by too narrow a concentration upon economic theorists may best be redefined by studying a wide selection of real Puritans. Among the host of such corrective figures one might begin with the dedicated organiser of the Presbyterian underground John Field[28]; with the severe but generous Huntingdon; with Sir Walter Mildmay, founder of the Puritan seminary Emmanuel College; with Richard Greenham, the charitable, unworldly rector of Dry Drayton; or with the diarist Lady Margaret Hoby, immersed in prayer, beneficence and morose self-examination at Hackness.[29]

If 'progressive' economic theory cannot be accepted as a norm of Puritanism, neither can particular theories of government or of church-government.[30] There were Episcopalian, Presbyterian and Congregationalist Puritans. Some showed themselves political opportunists, ready to clutch for the support of any powerful man, whatever his ulterior motives. If certain Puritans made heroic colonists or successfully resisted autocratic government, this may have been due less to Puritan political theory than to their religiously disciplined personalities, to their training in ecclesiastical and social cohesion and in the last resort to the fact that their antagonists forced such rôles upon them. Throughout the world of that day local circumstances so often inspired the political thought and action of churchmen. It remains highly improbable that a political movement remotely like the one headed by Pym and Hampden could ever have developed in a Catholic society. Milton could not have put forth his magnificent plea for freedom of thought and publication except at the culmination of a long Puritan attack upon royal and prelatical authority. Yet without minimising the religious elements of the so-called Puritan Revolution, we should all nowadays acknowledge the immense weight of its secular causes.

How much positive generalisation dare we then apply to the social and political effects of English Puritanism? We might reasonably claim that it flourished most as a social religion among townsmen, that it required a modicum of education, thoughtfulness and independence of spirit, again that in time it helped to produce minds passionately addicted to certain limited yet important notions of civic and personal freedom. It taught a man to stand on his own feet and put a useful stock of biblical texts in his head. Despite some exceptions like the Levellers, Puritans seldom accepted democratic egalitarianism in lay life. But however they defined the Church they accorded it an authority of its own, and their clerics at least were anti-erastian. For them the Church had its own social rules, and they believed that within it a man's standing should depend less upon worldly rank than upon spiritual gifts and moral repute.

Today many historians would consider the political achievement of Puritanism in terms far more concrete than these, in terms almost expressible by statistics and maps. Puritanism took an important share in bringing into line those areas of western England, Wales and the North which had been slowest to accept the implications of Tudor government and Protestant religion.[31] Contemporaries felt no doubt that in these 'dark corners of the land' the religious and political tasks were closely interrelated. 'Where preaching wanteth, obedience failed', wrote Archbishop Grindal to Elizabeth, and he went on to instance the parish of Halifax, which 'by continual preaching had been better instructed than the rest' and hence in 1569 stood 'ready to bring 3 or 4,000 men into the field to serve you against the said rebels.[32] Like John Wesley in later times, the Puritans saw that the diffusion of ideas could not be left to supine and conservative incumbents but depended in no small part on a supply of trained preachers, in many cases itinerant. Upon a truly astonishing scale, successful London merchants provided preachers, schools and charities in their provincial birthplaces, especially in Lancashire, Yorkshire and the Marches of Wales.[33] Even while Puritanism seemed to be creating division, in another and deeper sense it was uniting the kingdom.

When we have finished our efforts to modernise and secularise Puritanism, it remains an obstinately religious phenomenon, and its common characteristics must be sought in its religious teachings. It had no system of mysticism. In so far as it placed any emphasis upon religious 'experiences', these were simple and communicable; they gave no reason for founding esoteric communities or for solitary withdrawal. Worldly problems it tended to reduce to moral problems; to goodness it subordinated aesthetic and intellectual values. While it taught strict sobriety and moderation in all things, it did not, as popularly imagined, devote special attention to sexual morality. As for the deliberate mortification of the flesh, this savoured of Rome and was usually taken by Puritan writers to be the outcome and the source of spiritual pride.[34] The basis of moral life, like that of religious belief, was to be sought in the Bible, which Puritans exalted not merely above the Church in general but above all contemporary Protestant churches. Puritan theologians insisted not only that General Councils could err but that even the pronouncements of Luther and Calvin could not be taken as final. To this limited degree they were exponents of a belief in the progressive self-revelation of God to man. Their over-emphasis upon the Old Testament has been commonly exaggerated, and they were not guilty of fundamentalism in the sense of attaching equal authority to all parts of the Bible. They saw that even the New Testament contained disharmonies and that certain of its passages must be controlled by others more important. In general they took those passages as normative which described and regulated the life of the young Christian churches.[35]

Puritanism may have seemed 'non-Anglican' to patriots (as well as to verbalists) because it continued to entertain a close regard for foreign Reformation movements, because its theologians so frequently cited 'the best Reformed churches' in support of ideas disapproved by the monarch and by insular conservatives. Nevertheless, its internationalism did not entail a wholesale acceptance of the new non-religious currents of knowledge.

Many, though not all, of its champions tended to distrust abstract learning and scientific curiosity.[36] All the same, the Puritan outlook contributed to the atmosphere which fostered the growth of the natural sciences. Demanding an orderly universe which reflected the Divine purpose, it denounced superstitious beliefs, and even the hallowing of material objects, thus tending to reduce the empires of popular magic and religious ritual. Its enthusiasm for education remained immense, however restricted in purpose. It aspired to create Bible-reading laymen and women; equally, it aimed to produce a highly educated clergy, to achieve a new situation where even obscure ministers could preach effectively and act as genuine spiritual pastors to the most intelligent of their flocks. Preaching had above all to be 'plain'; it had to deliver the message with an absence of rhetorical and literary flourishes. Puritans thought that the future of the Church lay with a clergy distinguished not by miraculous sacramental functions but by a new fervour, a superior intellectual equipment, a power to communicate. This ambition did not however, presuppose a return to the old, narrow, clerical *esprit de corps*. The main purpose of the new cleric was to impart zeal to laymen, making them able to join in selecting their own ministers, to examine their own spiritual lives, to lead family prayers, to read godly books and take part in ecclesiastical administration. On all sides 'zeal' became the watchword.[37]

In the last resort Puritans were denoted and united less by theological dogma than by attitudes of mind and by a way of life. Like the Lollards and other sectaries who formed a restricted part of their historical ancestry, they were characterised as much by domestic withdrawal as by doctrinal expansion. They met in private houses to study the Scriptures, walked around together singing psalms, made excursions to hear their favourite 'godly' preachers. So far as they bred fanatics, even these tended to be disciplined rather than demonstrative. In Elizabethan England Puritan enthusiasts commonly flourished under the protection of sympathetic noblemen and Justices of the Peace. They did not want to leave the Church of England but to reform it from within; in fact until the Laudian years they represented an elite establishment rather than a rebellious minority. Few can be fairly described as fanatics and many were disposed to compromise, except upon the few issues they regarded as basic essentials of the Christian faith. In the mid-seventeenth century John Geree, himself a Puritan divine in trouble with an Arminian bishop, wrote *The Character of an old English Puritane or Nonconformist* (1646) and there depicted an essentially moderate devotee. Thus seen from within the movement, the old-time Puritan wanted a seemly order in church, but rejected 'superstitious' rites. 'He reverences authority within its sphere', but not if it constrained him to 'worship God after the traditions of men'. With a strong appetite for sermons and constantly applying himself to prayer, he believed in varying prayers to fit present wants and occasions, yet he did not reject the set forms of the Prayer Book. While he would have scandalous people excluded from communion, he was no fussy perfectionist in the management of churches. He obeyed 'just' commands, and when he disobeyed 'unjust' ones, 'his refusal was modest and with submission to penalties, unless he could procure indulgences from authority'.[38] Since that time Puritanism has become an ever more flexible term, allowing for many definitions and images. If however we must choose among the contemporary writers, it would seem certain that this retrospect from 1646 is far more historically informative than Shakespeare's Malvolio, who has already almost become Molière's Tartuffe!

It remains to mention certain cultural effects of Puritanism which emerged in the later decades of Elizabeth and which have been recently discussed by Professor Collinson.[39] In some degree these effects mark a withdrawal from the popular protest of the pre-Elizabethan Reformation. Unlike their predecessors, the Puritans appeared as elderly disapprovers, not as young protesters. Whereas, for example, Marian Protestants could meet in public houses and take beer before a sermon, the godly people later in the century disparaged this convivial setting and thought it improper to be 'talking of Scripture on the ale bench'. Again, whereas the early Protestants freely used the popular stage to propagandise by means of scriptural plays, Puritan opinion, as represented by the formidable Philip Stubbes,[40] hated the theatre and denounced such plays as sacrilegious. The merits of Christ's passion were no longer to be 'derided and jested at, as they be, in these filthie playes and interludes'. Scurrility and divinity must not be mixed.

Similar defensive attitudes appear in regard to the old broadside ballads and their musical settings. To the Puritan mind popular rhymes and tunes were forms too darkly tarnished by the secular world to become vehicles of religion. The Psalms, formerly adapted to tunes of secular origin, were now equipped with their own sacred music. To the exclusion of other texts, they were to be sung by men's and women's voices in unison. On this unique role of the Psalms Calvin himself had issued decisive commands. Indeed, all this supposed purification of the approaches to religion reflects the ever-extending prestige of Geneva. Calvin also refused to distinguish between idols and images, and Puritanism again followed his lead in establishing the strictest control over religious art, already denigrated by its semi-pagan character in Renaissance Italy. In 1627 the Puritan ascetic John Carter published an official homily, announcing that 'the seeking out of images is the beginning of whoredom'. These joyless prohibitions seem at least consistent in their aims if not in their results. They were all intended to reduce the presentation of Christianity to the plain Word, so ending the trivialisation apparent in saint-cults, legends and superstitions, above all exalting the majesty and the mystery of God. Whether in the somewhat longer run these aims were substantially attained will always present a subject for debate. Nevertheless, that in some branches of provincial Nonconformity both the spirit and the letter of Puritanism survived into the twentieth century, the present writer can testify from personal knowledge. On the other hand we have good reason to suppose that the Puritan outlook, with its rejection of vulgar 'magical' superstitions and its acclamation of a universe regulated by divine laws, did something to further the early development of modern science.[41]

We have hitherto concentrated chiefly upon the creative aspects of the

Puritan movement. These were unduly stifled by Elizabeth; she erected her barriers at the wrong points and by excessive suspicion failed to elicit for her national Church many of the gifts which a controlled Puritanism might have bestowed. Yet she did right to prevent the monopolising of that Church by the Puritan spirit, just as Charles I did wrong in allowing its Laudian enemies to attempt a counter-monopoly. The complete triumph of Puritanism would have submerged other religious values developing within Anglicanism. It would also have imposed an undue strain upon that large proportion of the English people who were willing to worship in church but not to embrace so intense and so disciplined a religious life. A national church cannot become a club for religious athletes. And while Puritanism promoted some forms of freedom, it unquestionably limited others. At all events until the period of the Civil Wars, very few of its adherents approached a broad conception of religious toleration. Though they accorded liberty of conscience and worship to other 'moderate' Protestants, their attitude toward their Roman Catholic adversaries remained implacable, even when less desperate political circumstances should have suggested a more humane and more Christian approach. In becoming the heirs of Calvin they had dropped the gentler tradition of Melanchthon.

Over the social failings of Puritanism modern observers agree more readily than over its religious limitations. Many would criticise its excessive contempt for the medieval past, its insensitivity toward sacramental values, its inordinate concern with predestinarian dogma and with supposed assurances of personal salvation, its fussy rejection of externals so modest as the surplice, the marriage-ring, the sign of the cross in baptism. It was indeed a most arbitrary assumption that ritual and fine music, so far from stimulating devotion, must necessarily divert the worshipper's attention from the major Christian truths. For the present writer such criticisms, however valid, are somewhat overshadowed by a profounder though more debatable matter. Colet, Luther, Calvin and the English Puritans display in turn that growing tendency among the critics of Catholicism—the tendency to turn from the veneration of many saints to the veneration of the great Saint. Some ignorant things have been said against Pauline Christianity, and it might be presumptuous for any Christian to attack the Reformers on account of the intensity with which they studied St. Paul. It nevertheless remains possible, and most tempting for intelligent and systematic minds, to dwell too exclusively upon Paul's wonderful presentation of the Gospel, to hang too devoutly upon his lightest word. A wholly unsuperstitious Christianity must centre its gaze not upon a man, not even upon this supremely dedicated man, but upon the Son of Man chiefly revealed in the Four Gospels. To this rotund proposition the Reformers would no doubt have added a fervent Amen; and they would have contended that this was precisely the aim of their Reformation. Yet it might not be impertinent to ask them, and in particular the English Puritans, whether their practical emphases were so Christocentric as their basic principles demanded. Attempting to summarise the approach of the large body of Elizabethan Puritan writers, Knappen[42] has written that they show 'a surprising lack of

Christological thought ... it is true, the Four Gospels do not appear to have attracted them particularly ... certainly the person of Christ figures very little in their literature'. These are the hard misgivings which every reader of Puritan literature must sometimes have felt, but the final word should perhaps await a still further investigation of the theological content of Puritan writings. If it be true that the Puritan ideal was less involved with the person of Christ than it should have been, this does not of course mean that it had failed to differentiate itself from the popular cults of earlier centuries. If it taught men to see Christ through the eyes of St. Paul instead of through a cloud of minor saints, gilded legends and plain myths, this surely marked a growth in the fullness of knowledge. Then as now, Christians gave but limited time and mental energy to their religion and, if their minds were for ever clouded by the swarms of sparrows, they were unlikely to soar with the eagles. And let us frankly add that the Puritan Reformers of Tudor and Stuart England were not the only intelligent Christians who have found it more congenial to weave philosophical theology around the Epistles than to follow Paul himself and be drawn into the spirit of Jesus. As in our century, so in theis, how many could truly say, or even in the secret places of the heart aspired to say, 'I live, yet not I, but Christ liveth in me'?

16 An Epilogue

The Origins of Religious Toleration

The effects of the English Reformation upon the growth of religious toleration and the ideal of religious liberty were discussed over fifty years ago by Professor J. W. Allen and, in much greater detail, by Professor W. K. Jordan. To their admirable work some additions of substance have since been made, and here we propose to expand slightly upon a few of the issues raised by their researches.[1] We have already witnessed the intolerance of 'moderate' Reformers toward Anabaptist beliefs. Amid a movement initially based upon the claims of the individual conscience, such attitudes look to us as obnoxious as their converse—mass hysteria against the Catholic religion amongst Englishmen over-excited by the menace of political Catholicism. The least critical admirer of the Reformation could not ignore the magnitude of these divergences from modern Christian and indeed from modern western norms, and he could only palliate them by reference to that genuine fear of spiritual, social and political chaos which best our Tudor and Stuart ancestors. Such emotions had not a little in common with those felt in earlier years by pious Catholics in the face of heresy, yet among Protestants they can hardly claim the same degree of rational consistency. The interest of the subject does not, however, cease at this point. From the first there had also existed in Protestant thought—in Zwingli, Melanchthon and Bucer, as well as among the Anabaptists—a more liberal tradition, which John Frith was perhaps the first to echo in England. When Frith claimed that no one interpretation of the presence in the eucharist should be made obligatory, when Starkey acknowledged that some current beliefs and observances should be regarded as *adiaphora*, then at least the seeds of a doctrine of toleration had already begun to grow in English minds.

Amid English Reformation writings we can trace one series of toleration-manifestoes related to Zwingli and to Anabaptism. *The Sum of Scripture*, condemned by Archbishop Warham in 1530, asserts that true Christianity has nothing to do with persecution, that 'the secular sword belongeth not to Christ's Kingdom'. In 1547 *A Brief and Plain Declaration* disclaims Anabaptism yet declares that the doctrine of Jesus was peace and that Christians seeking to establish the Kingdom of God on earth must only employ the weapons of the Spirit. A lost Anabaptist work, which happens to be described in detail by John Knox, dismissed the whole concept of persecution as belonging to the Old Testament and being utterly foreign to the nature of Christianity.[2] Similar notions began also to dawn upon thinkers otherwise violently opposed to Anabaptism. George Joye cited history to show the powerlessness of persecution to resist the truth. Thomas Starkey deprecated the excessive reliance placed by Church and State upon law and legal coercion. We cannot, he says in effect, make virtuous men by these mechanisms. Anticlericals like St. German countenanced the preservation of religious order by the temporal power but they also attacked the whole basis of ecclesiastical persecution. One of them, the ex-friar and London mercer Henry Brinklow, went still further and claimed that since faith is a gift of God, no man should be put to death for lack of it. True Christians cannot, in his view, desire to persecute for heresy; even the temporal power should, as in Germany, banish heretics rather than burn them. This same moderation of the traditional penalty was proposed some years later (*A New Dialogue*; 1548, *A Preservative*, 1551) by William Turner, whom we have already encountered as a 'commonwealth man', physician to Protector Somerset and later dean of Wells. This able Puritan individualist describes heresy as 'no material thing that we must fight withall, but ghostly'. It is therefore 'most meet that we should fight with the sword of God's word and with a spiritual fire against them, else we are like to profit but little in our business'.[3] John Foxe also stood staunchly among those who bade the Church rely upon its spiritual weapons. Under Elizabeth he strove hard to save Anabaptists from the fire, and he enunciated a sweeping doctrine of tolerance, even toward Catholics, many of whose doctrines he detested with every fibre of his being.[4] Thomas Cranmer would not go so far, yet he was reluctant to persecute even Anabaptists, used Catholics with gentleness and showed unexampled latitude in allowing liberty of worship to foreign Protestants.

When considering ideas of toleration amid the first generation of English Reformers it would be anachronistic to envisage a kindly Renaissance humanism fighting against an obscurantist Protestant biblicism. During this part of the story the chief hero is not Erasmus of Rotterdam but the New Testament itself. After all, the notion was bound to occur at least to some of these diligent Bible-readers that Christ and his Apostles nowhere envisaged or advocated the winning of human hearts through juridical persecution and physical duress. Many must indeed have noted this fact, but all too few drew the practical conclusions which seem to us so obvious.

A good many Elizabethan writers and parliamentary speakers[5] advocated religious toleration and its corollary, the simplification of doctrine. Of the theorists the most distinguished were laymen, like the engineer and prospector Jacobus Acontius, the jurist Alberico Gentilis, and Edwin Sandys, a son of the Archbishop and a pupil of Hooker.[6] Acontius, the most far-sighted of all, even contrived to remain *persona grata* with the Queen while publishing views on religious liberty which flouted the standards of Catholic and Protestant states alike. He regarded all forms of persecution as springing from the sin of personal arrogance, and in his bold relativism he denied that absolute truth could be ensured by any doctrinal system or any Church. And though as a Protestant he looked upon the Bible as the one certain guide to faith, Acontius rejected as näive the prevalent notion that free minds would come to interpret it uniformly. His outlook, obviously deriving something from Renaissance scepticism, remained alive in Elizabethan England and can thenceforth be claimed as one of the many pillars of tolerationist theory. In the complex minds of the Queen and her great minister it found answering chords.

Neither Elizabeth nor Burghley wanted to wage a religious persecution, and it remains broadly true that they avoided anything resembling one for over a decade, in fact until openly subversive political Catholicism forced their hands. In the world of these *politiques* some hard practical considerations had replaced the old Augustinian-Thomist concept of heresy as a sin worthy of capital punishment. From the time when the European states took responsibility for religious order from the hands of the Church Universal, the ancient sanctions were doomed. Hooker had to defend the Elizabethan Settlement on religious grounds, but even he was bound to regard the Anglican Church as merely one of those which together comprised the Catholic Church, and he freely admitted that men could attain salvation under the tutelage of Rome. In 1601 Bancroft made real efforts to arrange a compromise whereby Catholics would obtain a large measure of toleration in return for their rejection of the Papal claim to depose princes. Again, when we are tempted to view Arminianism as prone to renew religious persecution, we should recall that this movement arose as a protest against Calvinist intolerance and that its later persecuting tendency displayed its weak dependence on the State and involved it in ruin. While the Reformation was slow to produce genuine tolerance among its devotees, it soon destroyed the more solid psychological bases for religious persecution. Once Catholic Christendom had been succeeded by a multiplicity of national churches and dissenting groups, persecution also began to occasion practical disadvantages which could be seen, intermittently at least, to outweigh the advantages of uniformity. Such situations inevitably led to practical experiments in toleration, and where it was proved that such toleration could subsist without disaster, the more positive ideals of religious liberty were bound sooner or later to make their appeal. At varying rates most of the peoples bought their freedom. The price in terms of spiritual confusion often proved high, for history is usually a hard bargainer with men.

The Complexity of the English Reformation

In the foregoing account we have sought to understand the English Reformation as an integral part of the European Reformation, and also to see the whole movement as more profound, more radical than any mere attack upon the disciplinary shortcomings of the late medieval Church. Not altogether without reason, the Reformers believed that the Church had long since tended to drift away from Christ's teaching and from Apostolic principles as recorded in the New Testament. They fought not against the Renaissance Papacy alone, but against what they regarded as a thousand years of hierarchical misunderstanding and popular superstition. Likewise Luther and his followers did not simply combat Pope Leo's indulgence-selling; they rejected the whole doctrine of Purgatory, upon which that campaign depended. Despite the widespread existence of anticlericalism in its various forms, the most powerful forces within the Reformation—those most able to arouse ordinary lay people—derived largely from biblical preaching and printing, from the weight of the New Testament texts as opposed to mere churchly tradition. These last had indeed proved a far from unmixed blessing. 'Unwritten verities' could be ambivalent, and even in the simpler cases could form a clog upon any advances of spiritual and theological understanding. All too readily did medieval churchmen assume that every papal decree, and the conclusions of every Council held by their predecessors, had been instantly and forever ratified in Heaven. In England as elsewhere, the lasting appeal of Protestantism lay in its effort to relieve Church and society from over-imaginative, man-made inventions, now exposed by biblical scholars as alien to the foundation-documents of the Faith. Yet passing to the particular case of England, we have discovered many special complications and problems, some religious, others secular and even insular in character. We have had to display the English Reformation as multi-dimensional and complex in its causes, its progress, its consequences. The subject is seldom easy to handle and whichever side one supports one should remain conscious that the other side can also offer a formidable case!

We have observed conflicts between King and Pope, Church and State, common lawyers and canon lawyers, laymen and clerics, ecclesiastical and lay landowners, citizens and bishops. We have witnessed many ideological clashes on church government and finance, clerical privilege, Church–State relations, the rôle of ecclesiastical law, the definition of heresy, the theologies of the eucharist, justification and grace. But above all we have learned to view the movement as most essentially a process of Protestantisation among the English people, a process not always favoured by the State, a process exerting a mass of direct and indirect influences not only upon English history but upon much of western civilisation. For the present writer the unifying theme lies in a change of viewpoint concerning the documents, nature and functions of religion, both in the individual and in society. Yet athwart the Reformation struggles, and greatly complicating their outcome, ran a series of cross-currents—the old agrarian and social discontents of the peasantry, the threat of a Spanish hegemony over Europe, the secularisation of culture, the impact of the printing press, the rise of prices which dislocated State finance and all sorts of customary payments and relationships between men. Above all, in England as in the Netherlands, Protestantism became at last inextricably involved with the national self-assertion of a people fighting for its religious independence and its due place in a new European and extra-European order.

We have dealt with worldly forces and spiritual forces; most commonly have we been dealing with mixtures of the two and with the rationalisation of self-interest. We have seen that the Reformation left unaffected few aspects of our national life, whether religious, intellectual, social, economic or political. It ended by producing not one English religion but a series of English religions, all of them claiming a primeval authenticity. But from the outset it completely transcended the bounds of ecclesiastical history. So ubiquitous were its influences that we cannot begin intelligently to speculate on the courses which our history would have taken in its absence. The English Reformation ranks as one of those many causal phenomena beginning relatively far back in our national history and destroying in advance all attempts to 'explain' the present by mere reference to recent history.

Those factors which made possible and effective the revolutionary behaviour of Henry VIII might in themselves form the subject of a major work of scholarship. Even had he not quarrelled over his divorce with the Habsburg-controlled Papacy, he could scarcely have avoided a whole series of politico-religious conflicts. The advance of humanist bible-studies, recognised even in conservative Spain, could not be indefinitely ignored by the English Church and the English monarchy. Again, for many years genuine abuses had sprung from the outworn administrative and disciplinary systems of the Church. They had been magnified not only by the conduct of avaricious and uncultivated clerics but also by lay jealousy and malice. The Crown did not need to whip up anticlerical feeling; its task was to canalise, even to restrain such feeling. Anticlericalism probably owed less to the actual faults of the clergy than to a gradual shift in the attitude of lay society and to the growth of its literacy and intellectual resilience, its wealth, its political power. Lay resentment against tithes and against the moral jurisdiction and the heavy probate fees of the church courts, the rise of lay education, the import of bibles in English, the declining reputation of the Roman Curia, the survival of Lollardy and neo-Lollard anti-church opinion, the inveterate hostility of the common lawyers, the long-remembered scandal of Richard Hunne, the colourful but disastrous experiment with Thomas Wolsey; all these influences and many more had created before the meeting of the Reformation Parliament a sharply critical atmosphere, particularly in London. They did not in themselves entail a Protestant Reformation, but they could hardly have resulted in less than a series of readjustments between England and Rome, still more between Church and State, most markedly of all between the clerical order and lay society. Henry VIII became involved in these matters without wanting a doctrinal Reformation and without at first realising either the dangers presented by regional conservatism or the enormous powers which the anticlericalism of his subjects and their lack of positive affection for Rome had placed in his hands. His intervention nevertheless ended by producing religious change, because it pushed England out of step with the continental Reformation movements, began new sequences of insular events and so helped to confer a unique character upon the English Reformation.

In the field of religion many weaknesses of the Church were plainly apparent to intelligent but orthodox contemporaries. Though we should beware of exaggerating their importance in ordinary custom-ridden minds, we find heavy support from the sources when we refuse to see them through the pre-Raphaelite spectacles of our grandfathers. Scholastic religion, having overestimated its powers, had ended in disharmony, irrelevance and discredit. Beliefs of marginal authenticity, especially those relating to purgatory and saint-worship, had been suffered in everyday practice to occupy central places in the Christian life. The professional education of parish priests was criticised as quite inadequate by numerous writers of unquestioned Catholic orthodoxy, and its character was reflected in the paucity of direct religious teaching outside the larger towns. With certain notable exceptions monasticism was uninspired; it shed little spiritual light into the world outside the cloister and its amassing of appropriated benefices hampered the didactic functions of the Church. Again, when ordination was so little selective, and clerical marriage banned, a small fringe of disreputable clerics was bound to accumulate and to taint the moral reputation of the priesthood. The authority of the latter had come to depend in too great a degree upon its sacramental functions, too little upon the moral and intellectual preeminence of clergymen in society. The finest aspects of late medieval religious life, mysticism and the related *devotio moderna*, tended to be too demanding and esoteric for ordinary people, whereas the popular cult-religion—John Myrc's world of flying demons and saintly thaumaturges—seemed to the sophisticated both childish and unduly directed to the raising of money.

At least by the year 1500 the fostering of a sound middle way of devotion between these extremes should have become the chief aim of the Church, yet in England more than in most countries such a development was inhibited by the old anti-Lollard suspicions against religious literature in the vernacular and especially against biblical translation. Our bishops, in these matters among the most cautious and unimaginative in Europe, had in so many cases been servants of the Crown, often educated in the Roman law and always busied by secular duties; they tended to think of the Church in terms of jurisdiction rather than in terms of religious education. Even the more intelligent and spiritually-minded, like John Fisher, failed to perceive that a shifting lay outlook demanded new methods, and they tended merely to be shocked when, to put the matter crudely in our modern terms, they found the gentry, lawyers and merchants of the Renaissance age less docile than the illiterate barons and villeins of a former world.

In the atmosphere of the sixteenth century it had become more difficult to soothe lay curiosity by an ecclesiastically-processed version of the Faith. Nevertheless, in the first instance it was a group of intellectual clerics, some of them friars, who discovered Luther and introduced his concepts into both English universities. This movement soon found lay supporters, both in the international world of the merchants and among members of the former

Lollard groups of London and south-eastern England. A new and incomparably powerful weapon came to hand in Tyndale's New Testament, itself made possible through the protection afforded to Tyndale (and to subsequent translators) by an astute confederacy of businessmen in London and Antwerp. The force of this new appeal to the laity resided less in Luther's doctrine of the priesthood of all believers than in the fact that the new Protestant churches first encouraged in no small part by Erasmus and then, enormously aided by the printers, had placed the primary evidences of the Christian faith in the hands of laymen, and in vernacular translations. The gulf so revealed between the Church of St. Paul and that of Cardinal Wolsey supplied the clinching argument for revisions both of theology and of institutions. Neither in England nor elsewhere was the existing establishment organised to guide, control and survive a general study of the Apostolic Church. By the same token many who felt called to study it were unqualified to do so intelligently. There followed an unpleasant clash between the Reformers, too often arrogant in their new-found knowledge, and the bishops, who showed too little enthusiasm for common-sense reforms but placed only a half-hearted reliance on the stake and the dungeon. The State was left as *deus ex machina*.

To critical people in search of positive beliefs Lutheranism offered a seductive solution. It streamlined the teaching of the New Testament around the doctrine of Justification by Faith Alone, a belief which abruptly demolished the need for the cult-religion and for a whole mass of hoary observances. Anglican and Catholic writers have seldom given full weight to the intrinsic attractiveness of these reformist ideas to many minds of that century: however much repetition and overstatement may since have staled them, they lacked nothing in freshness and vitality for many of our best Tudor minds. Whatever its merits and demerits, the rise of Protestantism was based upon a positive evangel; we deceive ourselves if we describe the process in terms of drab negation or attribute its success merely to the shortcomings of contemporary Catholicism or to political chicanery.

Meanwhile, Henry VIII carried the great conservative bulk of the nation with him in his dual action—the severance of England from the Roman jurisdiction and the curtailment of the wealth and privileges enjoyed by the English Church. Having initiated these processes he found himself confronted by the unwelcome demand for a third revolution, embracing Lutheran doctrine and based upon the presentation of the Bible in Protestant dress by Tyndale and Tyndale's followers. Despite his imperious vanity and doctrinal conservatism Henry opposed these developments neither so passionately nor so consistently as historians have often supposed. His new Archbishop had strong sympathies with the Lutherans. In Thomas Cromwell the King found an administrative virtuoso capable of executing the immense technical tasks involved in the subjugation of the Church, yet he also allowed Cromwell scope to develop ideas more radical than his own. The minister organised the first great barrage of press-propaganda in English history, and his publicists not only defended the royal policy but anticipated several of the basic concepts of the Anglican *via media*. Still more important,

Cromwell took the lead in making the English Bible public property in further revisions by Coverdale and other English Protestants. The sale of bibles, and free access to them in the churches, proved an event of primary importance in the history of the Reformation; it was just as irreversible as the dispersal of the monastic lands, and in the long run more revolutionary in its implications.

If Henry had foreseen the ultimate political dangers of Calvinist Protestantism, he might have been prompted to thrust aside his scruples and adopt as his State-religion a fully-fledged Lutheranism, with its veneration for the godly prince. Yet whether this step would have exorcised more radical creeds or merely paved the way for their advent, we can only conjecture. In the event, he attempted from 1539 to re-assert Catholic doctrine, but his efforts were spasmodic and ineffective. That the Reformation had already become far more than any mere act of state can be seen from that most crucial episode in the social history of the English Reformation—the conversion of an ever-growing minority among the people of south-eastern England to Protestant opinions, even while those opinions were still discouraged by the King. Judging by scattered evidence, including the religious phraseology in wills, this process had begun to acquire momentum before 1540 and was not arrested by the Six Articles persecution. Moreover, it had certainly gained a strong if cautious following within the Court. The future Duke of Somerset exemplified this process, while the King himself ran counter to the spirit of his own statutes in allowing his young heir to be educated by men of the new religious outlook. These quiet advances of Protestantism during Henry's last years account for the ease with which Somerset established it as the official religion from the beginning of the new reign. His championship, followed by that of Northumberland, gave it an invaluable breathing-space of more than six years, during which it spread and consolidated itself beyond the likelihood of extinction by any machinery available to Tudor governments. By the end of Edward's reign it had taken full advantage of the old basis of proletarian heresy and had penetrated deeply into the working classes of south-eastern England, which supplied the great majority of the Protestant martyrs under Mary.

The Edwardian years display a rough poetic justice. The seizure of chantries and church goods marred the public image of the Reformation in the eyes of many people. The fund of social idealism amongst the Reformers, deeply impressive on paper and in the pulpit, availed little at this stage to check the profiteering which it so vociferously denounced. On the other side, Cranmer's accomplished liturgical work survived persecution to afford a solid basis for Elizabeth's resumption of the Edwardian experiment. More than any other factor this work gave a distinctive and unique flavour to the national Church. Cranmer bequeathed to the latter a liturgy too politically and devotionally attractive to be displaced by Calvinist or other continental models; he also preserved some Catholic elements, which half a century later attained a new importance when Anglicanism sought to broaden its scope, and again in the nineteenth century with the Tractarian movement.

While Cranmer and Ridley showed that Englishmen could read the Bible and the Fathers and then do some theological thinking on their own account, Hooper used his longer continental associations to help found a Puritan tradition with its roots in Zürich and Geneva. So far as foreign influences are concerned—and the most patriotic English churchman could not deny their immense importance—the reign of Edward VI saw a major reorientation. Before its close the direct influence of Wittenberg had decisively waned and in the main the foreign pressures were coming from Swiss sources and increasingly from Calvin's Geneva. In the event they came in two waves. Protestant scholars and refugees from the severities of Charles V—who at this point made his second great contribution to the English Reformation—flooded into Edwardian England. Some were welcomed to key-positions in the universities, while others provided a public exhibition of Reformed religion in and around London. Amongst these men the close disciples of Luther formed a minor element. The second wave arrived a decade later with the gradual return to England of the Marian exiles, who had been repulsed by Lutheran Germany but welcomed at Geneva, Zürich, Strassburg, Frankfurt and other centres where consubstantiation and prince-worship were not regarded as passports to respectability. In these foreign backgrounds Ponet, Knox, Goodman and others evolved anti-monarchical theories of politics more advanced than those about to emanate from the Huguenots. The immensely important change from prince-worship to 'civil courage', the change which made the Puritan attitude to authority so very different from that of Henry VIII's subjects, had begun both among the martyrs at home and among the English exiles on the continent.

Even while Mary was burning Englishmen for rejecting transubstantiation, Protestant theology began to lose interest in this old bone of contention and transferred its attention to the more modish disputes over grace and predestination arising from the favourite themes of Calvin. Another sign of change in late Edwardian and Marian England was the rise of surreptitious sects organised on a congregational basis. Apart from the licensed model of the Foreigners' Church at the Austin Friars, the first examples came from the Anabaptists, who began to attract a following of native converts in London, East Anglia and Kent. The supposition that the Marian martyrs contained more than a handful of such sectaries we have seen to be based on no solid grounds. Indeed the Marian authorities, quite intelligibly, hunted Anglicans with more zeal than they hunted sectarians, while the latter seldom embraced martyrdom in the manner of the Netherlandish Anabaptists. Yet even Anglicans, both in their secret church in Marian London and at their various centres abroad, gained some interesting experience of congregational organisation and hence of self-reliance during the Marian persecution. Here again we observe an interesting tributary to the stream of Elizabethan Puritanism.

Its reputation badly compromised by Northumberland, the Reformation derived unexpected support from the blunders of Queen Mary. At first she incurred hatred through her Spanish marriage, but in the end the fires of Smithfield did not fail to damn her cause, at all events in London and the south-east, where for the most part the drama was enacted and where public opinion had to be respected by any successful English government. Equally important, the conduct of the eminent clerical martyrs raised the sagging moral status of the Protestant cause. Public opinion cannot, however, be regarded as homogeneous throughout mid-Tudor England, and we should be wise to abandon simplifying statements as to what 'the Englishman' thought concerning all these vicissitudes. During this long crisis there were slow-moving areas and swift-moving areas, yet whereas Protestantism appealed to the latter, Mary failed to enlist the positive enthusiasm of the former. Our new knowledge of the Marian North gives no hint that she aroused its still conservative society from the torpor into which the failure of its previous reactions and its lack of spiritual leaders had plunged it. And even in several parts of Yorkshire there is clear evidence both of an advancing Protestantism and of a proletarian heresy still owing something to the old Lollard tradition. On the other hand throughout most of Lancashire and the Border counties Protestant beliefs scarcely preponderated until the last decades of Elizabeth's reign, or even later still.

If the Reformation were ever to be checked, a Catholic riposte was now due or overdue, yet it did not substantially materialise in Marian England. The type of spirituality we associate with the Counter-Reformation remained conspicuously absent. Though Loyola was an older man than Calvin, and his contemporary in the University of Paris, his movement struck England with the seminary priests a quarter of a century after the initial impact of Calvinism. In view of the shortages of time and money it would be ungenerous to ascribe this failure to Reginald Pole. Yet he showed no grasp of missionary methods, while his general mismanagement of the reaction illustrates both his personal lack of 'instinct' and the stultifying effect of long exile upon its victims. By contrast, English Protestantism could count itself fortunate to avoid the latter fate, for Mary's early death meant that most of the 800 Protestant exiles spent four years or less abroad—a period long enough to broaden and sharpen their minds, yet not so long as to deprive them of a sense of the realities at home. Even the intrigues and brawls between Coxians and Knoxians at Frankfurt did something to fit them for the work ahead and to keep alive the Anglican tradition.

Even so, the critical events which followed Elizabeth's accession owed less than we once supposed to the acumen and devotion of these returning exiles. Nowadays it might be wiser to attribute the relative success of early Elizabethan Anglicanism in large part to the weakness of the opposing forces and to the Queen's need for a settlement which should be neither Catholic nor Calvinist. While at this time Protestantism inspired only a minority of the nation, so did Catholicism. A fair amount of evidence shows the existence of a third factor comprised of secularism, relative indifference to religion, weariness of doctrinal contentions, obsession with peace and security. It is hard to resist the impression that this third force exerted at least as much weight as all the religious impulses in sanctioning the Elizabethan Settlement and in guaranteeing its stability against pressures from enthusiasts on the left and on the right. This mundane phenomenon should not be too roughly criticised by historians of religion. To some extent it represented the nation's instinct for material self-preservation, yet it was not wholly a negative reaction against the perils of religious fanaticism. Something more creative than mere disillusion or self-interest was also coming to birth in English society. The later acts of the drama we have described were enacted upon a shifting platform of European and of national culture.[7] The Copernican enlargement of the universe, the transoceanic discovery of non-Christian civilisations, the increasing dominance of society by its former middle orders, with the resultant substitution of the family-man for chivalric and monastic models, these and many other forces were now swiftly reshaping the mental contours of educated society throughout the West.

The belief that English humanism declined after the execution of Thomas More was long since revealed as fictitious by scholars like Bush and Caspari.[8] But the label 'humanism' with its classical, Italian and Erasmian connotations seems quite inadequate to express the whole of this tidal movement, the direction and depth of which can best be ascertained by examining the intellectual interests, not of great or even eminent minds, but of ordinary readers and writers in Tudor England. Provincial surveys undertaken by the present author and others suggest a striking mental development among such people around the mid-century.[9] Before about 1550–1560 the interests of these literate provincial Englishmen relate over-whelmingly to religion and to the Church; lay writers remain relatively few and the whole scene is still dominated by the professional interests of clergymen. Thereafter a dramatic broadening and diversification becomes apparent. Both laymen and clerics are now concerned with science, medicine, natural history, poetry, genealogy, history, the law, social and economic problems. Religious writing and publication do not necessarily decline in bulk, but they occupy a far smaller share of an enormously swelling output. In England as elsewhere, this powerful upgrowth of lay interests and lay writers occurred for reasons largely independent of the Reformation. Puritan zeal failed to retard it and it developed apace around and even within the Puritan mind. While it cooled the atmosphere, it also complicated the intellectual and spiritual situation of the educated man. In Sir Thomas Browne's famous metaphor he had now become an Amphibian, able to swim in more than one distinct element. This new situation may well be regarded as marking the end of the Middle Ages, yet in time it also caused the teachings of Luther and even Calvin to seem less than complete answers to the questioning of humanity.

While the *dénouement* of the Reformation under Elizabeth and the early Stuarts cannot properly be understood without reference to this mighty underlying change, the first stages of the Anglican Settlement were shaped by narrower and more immediate influences. Those exiles most under Genevan influence did not return in time to dominate the political bargaining of 1559, the parties to which were the Queen herself and the Prayer Book exiles. Many of the latter stood as far to the left as users of the Prayer Book could possibly stand; they too respected Calvin and had shown themselves prepared to revise the 1552 Book in a Protestant sense. In the event Elizabeth compelled them to revise it in a somewhat conservative direction. Ere long Genevan and other forms of radicalism attempted to pull the Anglican Church in their direction, yet their efforts were inhibited not merely by the conservative tastes of the Queen but by erastianism and secularism, above all by the fear of disunity in the face of Spain and political Catholicism. As the insensitivity of the Spanish Tudor had made the Elizabethan Settlement possible, so the fear of Philip ended by consolidating that Settlement and by checking for several decades the fissiparous tendencies within English Protestantism.

Nevertheless, the Puritan movement maintained its integrity and critical spirit, even when it was directing from within the otherwise rather meagre spiritual life of the Elizabethan Church. Though Separatist and Presbyterian tendencies never gained many followers under Elizabeth, Puritanism had only to be mishandled in the succeeding period of relative international tranquillity, in order to be driven anew into restless tendencies and to be turned at last against the monarchy itself. I have been concerned somewhat to defend Puritanism against its detractors. Britons who respect their own historic achievements can scarcely do otherwise, for Puritanism entered our bone and sinew; it gave an immense access of strength and discipline to our nation in the days of its grandeur. I should nevertheless regard it as a force more suited to pervade than to dominate the English spirit, for the latter was proceeding toward types of creativity and freedom incompatible with full-fledged Genevan patterns of intellectual and social discipline. Within the narrower field of theology the hitherto Anglo-Puritan Church began before 1600 to produce non-Puritan ways of thought.[10] The reconciliation of these so-called Arminian ideas with the dominant Puritan tenor of English life demanded a degree of statesmanship greater than that possessed by the Stuart kings and a more genuinely latitudinarian temper than that of William Laud and his associates.

The material results of the English Reformation will certainly form the subject of further local and regional researches, pending which most generalisation should be regarded as tentative. In the present state of knowledge we can scarcely assign to these material results a commanding place in the economic and social history of Tudor England. The rapid dispersal of monastic lands amongst a host of purchasers helped to endow younger sons who might otherwise have remained landless, and it contributed beyond doubt to that remarkable increase in the number of landed families observable throughout England from the mid-century. There seems every reason to distrust the once popular image of easy-going monkish landlords undergoing replacement by rack-renting squires. We have seen that strong forces operated against the prevalence of either of these stylised characters. Rising rents and fines must be seen against a background of population-pressure and monetary inflation, concerning which contemporary analysis was often mistaken or insensitive. While aggrieved tenants did not lack legal remedies, they should in general have been well able to absorb these additional costs, since as producers and sellers of foodstuffs they were among the biggest beneficiaries from the inflationary process. Here further research should proceed with an open mind and in the full realisation that the economic impacts of the Reformation will prove almost impossible to disentangle from a host of independent factors—debasement, inflation, enclosure and the pressure of rising population upon relatively static production.

We have also attempted by concrete examples to display the decreasing appreciation and care which early sixteenth century parishioners showed for the chantries and other institutions added by late medieval piety to the endowment of parish life in England. Here there lay an important field for reform and even for reconversion to changed uses, yet mere legal confiscation could not be justified by pleas of superstitious usage. The Edwardian government of self-styled Protestants, over-hasty, morally degenerating and financially bankrupt, was in no posture to rehabilitate parochial ministration, charity and education. In particular, the debt of English education to Henry VIII proved more substantial than its debt to the government of his son whose name was undeservedly attached to the grammar schools he refounded. Nevertheless, it now seems unlikely that substantial damage accrued to English schools, while the spate of new schools and of charitable benefactions in general effectively delivers Tudor and Stuart Protestantism from sweeping charges of neglect towards the young and the poor. If from the early years of the century good works were channelled to a decreasing extent through the Church,[11] the change was inevitable in an age when laymen had come to abound in disposable wealth and administrative experience. This tendency we may already have exaggerated, since the Anglican Church, and later the other denominations, continued to play a very considerable rôle in education and charitable endeavour. A change more certainly apparent during the century which followed the reign of Henry VIII lies in the exiguous part of the national wealth now expended upon ecclesiastical buildings, or upon the plastic arts in the service of the Church.

Ironically enough, the Crown might be regarded as—next to the Church— the greatest material loser by the processes of dissolution. Henry VIII and his son's ministers undertook these steps during a period of heavily mounting costs and inflexible taxation. The consequent sale and dispersal of ecclesiastical lands ensured the economic demotion of the Church, while the Crown merely surmounted a dangerous crisis without achieving economic stability. The kings of Spain, who continued exploiting the taxable capacity of a swollen Church benefited more than the kings of England, who seized a great share of ecclesiastical wealth only to lose most of it within a few decades.[12] This loss gradually brought the Crown into competition with its accomplice in secularisation and successor in ownership—a class far more numerous, more critical, more wealthy, more indestructible than the neo-feudalists of the fifteenth century. In contrast with this depressive affect on government, the change brought stimulus to the national economy. Whereas in seventeenth-century Spain, economists constantly regretted their lack of a middle class with creative habits of investment, in England the gradual growth of a more fluid and productive economy was apparently promoted by these alterations in land-ownership and class-structure. A free market in land, exploitation of the land, rising manufactures, expanding internal and overseas trade, increasing population, these are interrelated developments which displaced the domestic balance of power and enhanced the rôle of England in that enormous world now being revealed to European enterprise. The contributions of the Reformation to this complex will never be assessed with any sort of precision, yet one finds it impossible to doubt that the laicising of landed capital was a vastly more potent factor for change than any support which late Protestant economic theory may have given to an already long-established capitalist ethic. In sum, it is probably safe to suppose that throughout the economic field the English Reformation did little more than accentuate trends of theory and practice already operative at its outset and by no means dependent upon its support.

Confusion has usually resulted from attempts to denounce or to justify essentially religious movements by reference to the non-religious phenomena accompanying them. When the Reformation is being debated in terms of religious and ethical values, its political, economic and social background, which sprang in large part from a pre-existent order, should be introduced into the debate with restraint and discrimination. When, for example, French historians deplore the supposed impoverishment inflicted by the English Reformation upon the peasantry, it is legitimate to ask them whether the lot of the French peasantry was more equitable under Louis XIV than that of its English counterpart under Queen Anne. The worlds of religion and economics were never closely geared together. It is certain that Catholic principles did not prevent the subjects of Henry VIII from buying monastic lands, and it is questionable whether at any stage the practices or codes of Protestant landlords and businessmen can be distinguished ethically from those of their Catholic counterparts. After all, since the time of the ancient Greeks, the Mediterranean world has never lacked 'business enterprise'. Again, it would be less than rational to impugn the religious opinions of Cranmer or Hooper because they failed to control the desperate financial policies of Northumberland. With an equal lack of good sense one might blame the horrors of the Fourth Crusade upon Innocent III or condemn the Counter-Reformation by reference to the cruel persecutions of Louis XIV. In short, the Reformation has been too often distorted, its worldly effects misrepresented, by all sorts of doctrinaires, anachronists and wishful thinkers, both sacred and profane by inspiration. But perhaps we are all nowadays learning to move more cautiously within these difficult borderlands between religious and secular history. If not, it seems high time we began!

Toward a Longer Perspective

Looking back on the foregoing narrative with such impartiality as I can command, my first reflection concerns its incompleteness. My examination of the Elizabethan *dénouement* has been all too brief; at the tragic yet strangely fruitful divisions of the seventeenth century I have given no more than a few glances, though they stand among the more direct results of the English Reformation. The growth of Presbyterianism and of the Congregationalist, Baptist, Quaker and other denominations during the central decades of that century could well be regarded as a second English Reformation—and the advent of Methodism in the eighteenth century as a third. This explosion of the Puritan movement passed outside the religious field and shattered beyond repair the dream of an authoritarian orthodoxy in Church and State which had in no small measure survived into the Protestant world. The vital Revolution of 1688 occurred in large part through the gross misjudgement of James II, who deliberately ran his head into the durable wall built by the English Reformation. The fact that changes of this type tended to occur first in Protestant countries suggests that the Reformation of the sixteenth century was an early if involuntary stage in the rise of societies which permit a multiplicity of religions, liberty of choice to the individual and freedom of worship even to minor and unpopular sects. To us this outcome looks far more inevitable than it did even to the most far seeing and liberal of the original Reformers. But in the longer run, even those countries where the Counter-Reformation succeeded could not for-ever resist the tide of toleration; having suffered much for their hesitancy they at last followed suit. And it might have been predicted that Spain, then the grand eccentric of the European family, would offer the most formidable resistance, at all events among the nations of western Europe. Elsewhere the spirits of the dead Anabaptists could look down upon a nineteenth-century world where their demand for freedom had at last been largely met.

Could we embark in detail upon the English aspects of this second Reformation, there would be no final resting-place in 1662 or in 1688, for long afterwards, even down to our own day, further sequels continue to illuminate the nature and the immense potentialities of the events we have described. The pietist, humanist and scientific trends of the eighteenth century all made their impacts upon the Protestant mind and, especially in Britain, kept it lively. What do they know of the Reformation who have not met John Wesley and his friends or who have not sensed the devout and eventually beneficent forces at work in late Georgian England? On the one hand, the Methodist and Evangelical movements sprang almost directly from spiritual impulses initiated by the Reformers; on the other, Protestant beliefs made interesting combinations with the secular thought of the Age of Reason. This latter phase has been harshly regarded by modern Protestant theologians; like most attempts to integrate revealed Christianity and 'modern' discovery, it had its blind alleys and its sub-Christian implications. Yet it had this saving grace—that it was not a new orthodoxy imposed by churches and states as binding upon their members. It might indeed have been disastrous had English Christians failed to take seriously Newton's universe and the philosophical thinking in which it became clothed. They could no more ignore these developments than their predecessors could have ignored scholasticism or humanism. If the Protestant churches in England paid a price for joining the hurly-burly of a new free world of thought, they also gained immeasurable benefits; in the long run they acquired new vistas, more humility, more self-knowledge from these astringent experiences.

Another sequel to the rise of English Protestantism was its capacity for expansion, both in territories mainly populated by Britons and to no small extent among hitherto non-Christian peoples. The English and Scottish Reformations came to resemble an intense source of light projected across time and falling upon great screens of space. From one viewpoint this process can be regarded as an ideological function of imperialism, yet it could also display in abundance the finest Christian missionary qualities, however unfashionable these may have become in recent years.

British Protestantism, it is true, also fell for a time into selfish and hypocritical company, which stifled its social liberalism, made it dissociate spiritual from physical well-being and greatly diminished its influence throughout the urban working classes. If it proved slow to denounce slavery, it took even longer to denounce child-labour and sub-human industrial conditions at home. Like the rest of Christianity, it did not until our own day develop much sensibility toward the living world, for example in regard to our kinship with the higher animals, upon which mankind has hitherto inflicted so enormous a volume of unnecessary pain. Despite such failures Anglicanism and the major Nonconformist churches assumed the status of world-religions. For better or worse, British Protestantism placed its ineradicable stamp upon the image of Britain throughout the world. Most strikingly it showed its capacity to give birth to self-governing churches, even as secular imperialism created self-governing dominions. Today, as the ties of Empire and Commonwealth loosen, men of many nations continue to use Thomas Cranmer's Prayer Book—or adaptations of it—and to owe deep if unconscious debts to a host of Tudor and Stuart Englishmen. Yet while religion became a major factor in our transoceanic enterprises, it failed to fulfil its initial promise to draw us more closely to the continent of Europe. Whatever view may be taken of the solidity of the bridges built by medieval churchmen across the narrow seas, it is certainly true that until quite recent days Protestant churchmen did far too little to promote understanding between the nations of Europe.

Upon North America, however, our Reformation made a reverberating impact, and for the twentieth century its chief living significance might well be thought to lie in the United States. There many churches, both British and continental, have together created a profoundly Protestant culture far overflowing the bounds of religious life, a culture which has demonstrated more successfully than its European equivalents that even an exaggerated concern for material production and consumption need not destroy church-going, manifest devotion and social generosity. Within this culture the churches originating in England and Scotland have played the predominant part, thanks largely to the former intellectual ascendancy and westward expansion of New England. In world history the New England colonies take a most prominent place among those many social and political experiments heavily coloured by the Reformation. It has become a commonplace among

American sociologists that this Puritan heritage, held steady by the churches which derive directly from its tradition, continues to play a striking rôle in the moral and didactic attitudes of the American people. That often fruitful, often dangerous idealism which sees persons, peoples and governments in stark antitheses of good and evil has been widely attributed to this persistent tradition. Certainly, it is far from fanciful to see here the re-entry of Puritanism, diluted and half-secularised, upon a new and enormous plane of world affairs. Within the same gigantic society, still in process of self-creation, the tradition of the English Reformation has merged most fruit-fully with the Lutheran and Calvinist revivals which had their origins in nineteenth-century Europe. Perhaps in North America and Australasia rather than in Europe will a re-grouping of the split forces of the Reformation come to shape the future of Christianity and even to embark upon the long task of reconciliation with the Catholic world. Whatever the event, if we seek the relevance of the English Reformation to the problems of our own century, we should be wise to let our thoughts flow freely outside the British Isles.

In our own age common prudence suggests that the rivalries of Christian churches should be limited to friendly debate. With most of the world still awaiting conversion and with anti-Christian forces growing ever stronger, we can no longer afford to waste our energies in recriminations, in winning converts from one another or even in duplication of effort. One purpose of historiography is to free men from the dead hand of history. If he entertains any practical objectives in the study of the Reformation, the Christian historian may legitimately hope to close at least some of the old rifts by explaining them with a due blend of sympathy and of hard-headed realism. In so doing, he can also underline the obvious truth that none of the parties to the original dispute had anything like a monopoly of virtue, of good sense, of charity, of understanding in the Faith. In the English-speaking world, a better comprehension of doctrine and of history has enormously narrowed the gap between the Anglican-Episcopalian churches and those of the other leading Protestant denominations. Had it been consummated, the attempted reunion of Anglicans and Methodists in Britain would have represented an even greater triumph for maturity than the creation in 1925 of the United Church of Canada by the former Congregational, Methodist and Presbyterian churches of that country. Despite the failures, attractive vistas of reunion, close collaboration and common worship are still widely, perhaps prematurely, entertained.

In its most 'political' forms, the Roman-Anglican ecumenical movement has sometimes threatened to involve the vulgar trading of one disputed dogma against another, and the cynical (or naïve) adoption of ambiguous terms, differently interpreted as between the negotiating parties. Forced developments of any sort will inevitably postpone true progress. The present writer can only hope that future negotiators will in the course of time modify the false ideals of the past and remove their resplendent, armour-plated theocracies in favour of some less rigid, less exclusive, less vain-glorious apparel. For example, should it not become normal for Christians with distinct differences of opinion and doctrine to worship frequently together? And in this movement should not the Church of England seek a creative role, at ease with its own internal differences, as an intellectually adult society should be toward the end of the twentieth century? Such a process would presumably entail the abandonment of obsequious adherence to every ecclesiastical precedent, and in particular of that widespread identification of the ideas 'Catholic' and 'medieval'. After all, to cite only one of the more obvious aberrations, did not the medieval Church devoutly advocate the burning alive of 'heretics', even of those who merely could not accept the doctrine of transubstantiation? And what of those whose treason-laws automatically assigned death to Catholic missionary priests, even when no specific treason had been proved? Truly, our reverence for 'historic Christianity' needs to be discriminating.

Even between Protestants and Catholics a host of sensible experiments in co-operation need not await doctrinal *rapprochement*. In this ninth decade of our century one would need to be blind not to observe here a new spirit at work on both sides. As never before, the Catholic world is making efforts to understand the development of non-Catholic Christianity, while throughout the Protestant world there is growing an appreciation not merely for Catholic virtues as seen in individuals but for that magnificent capacity to produce holiness shown by Catholicism throughout the ages. In his own small academic sphere the writer (who has constant occasion to work with Catholic historians) can testify to the surprising growth of charity and understanding which has developed during the last thirty years. Convinced Christians are willy-nilly in some degree denominational partisans, yet today we are all becoming less guilty of conscious and half-conscious attempts to strain or to expurgate the facts of the great controversial age of the Reformation. Very few among us believe that unity of beliefs can be attained through gladiatorial debates in the style of the medieval schoolmen, let alone by prelatical legislation. There appears at least a striking tendency among professional historians and serious students to respect and accommodate historical facts, however unpalatable to their various confessional outlooks. This in itself is a remarkable advance for the cause of Truth. In time even the writers of cheap proselytising literature will find it possible— indeed more effective—to follow the trend.

This much said, it would be idle to deny that some of the barriers between Protestants and Catholics remain formidable, and only facile optimism would forecast any dramatic approaches toward full doctrinal agreement or institutional integration. When we have finished bewailing the greed, folly and fanaticism of the sixteenth century, the Reformation still stands in mountainous bulk across the landscapes of western Christianity. It concerned significant issues which still live to perplex and divide us. Even today some of the principles which it sought to establish could neither be conscientiously abandoned by the Protestant Churches nor be conceded by the Roman Catholic Church without an utter abnegation of its historic claims. The later liberalising, the variety and contradictions of Protestant thought have in some senses led the two still further apart. This situation applies also to the Church of England, the orders of which have been declared invalid by the Papacy, despite the strong Anglican aspiration to be 'catholic' as well as 'reformed'. For all their impressive façades of bishops, convocations, moderators, assemblies, boards and synods, the Protestant Churches have become different in kind from the Church of Rome. Despite the growing urge to unity, only a dwindling fragment of their members desire to see anything approaching uniformity of belief and practice. The weight of their own ecclesiastical traditions presses lightly upon most intelligent Protestants, and few are disposed to grovel before the Thirty-nine Articles or the Westminster Confession, remarkable as these may have been in their day and generation. To many even the venerable early creeds may no longer seem adequate summaries of basic Christian belief. Some, like the present writer, find one of the more fruitful concepts of the Reformation in the doctrine of *adiaphora*, or 'things indifferent'. Extending this they would maintain that all the Christian churches have shipped more ballast than the New Testament sources will justify, that the quality of a man's faith does not depend upon the number of propositions he can swallow, that philosophic and imaginative theology (Thomist, Calvinist, modern teutonic or any other) should never again be allowed to leave its proper plane of hypothesis and make itself binding or even officially recommended.

It might well be contended that the Reformers themselves erred through their inability to throw off the vainglorious scholastic spirit, to avoid rebuilding, all too high above the documents, the exciting but insecure towers of ratiocination. If in this dark life we need credal formularies, let them at least be clear, short and simple; let them try to be truly representative of the teaching and living of Jesus; above all, let them impose as little as possible of any man's corrupt and arrogant imagination. Imperfectly as the Reformers executed their task, too swiftly as they froze the living things in their minds, this desire to free man's image of God from anthropomorphism and marginal cults, to envisage the magnitude and the uniqueness of Christ's sacrifice, to cast aside misleading unessentials and accretions, to bring men nearer in love to the real person of the Founder, this type of aspiration lies at the heart of their message for our own century. As the best of them sought in humility to recover the ever-living Word made Flesh, so we and our successors can continue the search in still greater humility, without any illusion that our own attempts will be specially privileged or successful. When they talk of God, or of the Son of God, fallen creatures and visible churches should at least be tentative. It needed Christ himself to interpret the world of the Spirit in the lame words of men.

References

Where essential, references are made to primary sources, but it would have been inappropiate (and prodigal of space) to attempt reference to such sources for the more routine passages and the 'accepted' facts. Hence I have often cited secondary authorities where these provide useful ranges of reference to the primary sources. Apart from indicating my chief authorities, the notes are also designed to provide modern bibliographical guidance on many topics. Unless otherwise stated, Arabic numerals refer to pages and Roman numerals to volumes. Places of publication are given only when they may prove vital: e.g. for very recent, rare, old or foreign publications.

Common Abbreviations

A. P. C.	*Acts of the Privy Council*, ed. J. R. Dasent
B. I. H. R.	*Bulletin of the Institute of Historical Research*
B. L.	British Library
Dixon	R. W. Dixon, *History of the Church of England*
D. N. B.	*Dictionary of National Biography*
Dugmore	C. W. Dugmore, *The Mass and the English Reformers*
E. E. T. S.	*Early English Text Society*
E. H. R.	*English Historical Review*
Foxe	J. Foxe, *Acts and Monuments*, ed. Cattley and Townsend
Garrett	C. H. Garrett, *The Marian Exiles*
Gee and Hardy	H. Gee and W. J. Hardy, *Documents Illustrative of English Church History*
Hughes	P. Hughes, *The Reformation in England*
J. E. H.	*Journal of Ecclesiastical History*
Knappen	M. M. Knappen, *Tudor Puritanism*

L. & P.	*Letters and Papers of Henry VIII*, ed. Brewer, Gairdner and Brodie
Lollards and Protestants	A. G. Dickens, *Lollards and Protestants in the Diocese of York*
O. D. C. C.	*Oxford Dictionary of the Christian Church*, ed. F. L. Cross, 2 edn.
Pol. Hist. Eng.	*Political History of England*, ed. W. Hunt and R. L. Poole [most references are to vol. vi, by A. F. Pollard]
Reformation Studies	A. G. Dickens, *Reformation Studies*
Ridley	J. Ridley, *Thomas Cranmer*
Span. Cal.	*Calendar of State Papers, Spanish*
S. T. C.	*Short Title Catalogue ... 1475–1640*, ed. A. W. Pollard and G. R. Redgrave
Strype, *Eccles.Mem.*	J. Strype, *Ecclesiastical Memorials*
T. R. H. S.	*Transactions of the Royal Historical Society*
Tudor Bibliog.	*Bibliography of British History, Tudor Period*, ed. C. Read (1959)
V. C. H.	*Victoria County History*
Ven. Cal.	*Calendar of State Papers, Venetian*

Chapter 1, pages 13–24

1. Daniel, xi. Note also the chaining of Satan for a thousand years, prophesied in Revelation, xx. Some controversialists identified the 'beast' with the Papacy, which had indeed become more powerful since about AD 1000. On these ideas in England, see F. J. Levy, *Tudor Historical Thought* (San Marino, 1967), ch. 3

2. *De quatuor summis imperiis lib. iii* (Strasbourg, 1556); *J. Sleidani de statu religionis et reipublicae Carolo Quinto Caesare commentarii* (Strasbourg, 1555). On Sleidan and his writings see A. G. Dickens in R. B. Knox (ed.), *Reformation, Conformity and Dissent* (1977); D. R. Kelley in *Jnl. of Modern History*, lii. On the extensive surrounding literature, see Ingeborg B. Vogelstein, *Johann Sleidan's Commentaries* (New York, 1986)

3. A. G. Dickens and J. M. Tonkin, *The Reformation in Historical Thought* (Cambridge, Mass. and London, 1985), 7–9, 41–2, 46–7, 63–4

4. On Dietrich of Niem, who anticipated Luther in distinguishing between the 'true' Catholic Church and the 'false' Papal Church, see E. F. Jacob, *Essays in the Conciliar Epoch* (1943) 24–43. The main references for Ebendorfer are in *New Catholic Encyclopedia*, v, 27

5. H. Chadwick, *The Early Church* (*Pelican History of the Church*, 1967), 122–7. Readers wishing to sample recent thought on the social and mental history of early Christianity might also begin with the following:

H. Chadwick, *History and Thought of the Early Church* (1982; T. D. Barnes, *Early Christianity and the Roman Empire* (1984); W. H. C. Frend, *Religion Popular and Unpopular in the Earlier Christian Centuries* (1976) and ibid., *Town and Country in the Earlier Christian Centuries* (1980)

6. J. G. Davies, *The Early Christian Church* (1965), 119ff, 163ff, 170ff; H. Chadwick, *The Early Church*, 125–30

7. Ibid., 71

8. Ibid., 152

9. On the origins of saint-worship, ibid., 215–6, 271

10. *Leviathan*, pt. iv, ch. 47

11. Cf. R. I. Moore, *The Formation of a Persecuting Society: power and deviance in Western Europe, 950–1250* (1987). The 'hardening' process may have owed something to the spirit of Augustine: compare, e.g., his horrific passages on damnation, noting G. Bonner on H. Chadwick's *Augustine* (1986), *J. E. H.*, xxxviii, 627–8

12. On the development of Reformation ideas from medieval theory and from the break-up of scholasticism, see especially A. McGrath, *The Intellectual Origins of the European Reformation* (1987) ch. 1; G. Leff, *Heresy in the Later Middle Ages* (2 vols., 1967), *passim*; H. A. Oberman, *Masters of the Reformation* (1981), chs. 3, 6. For an outline of one important theme, see 'Theology, Influence of Greek Philosophy on', *New Catholic Encyclopedia*, xiv, 58–61; note also the pre-scholastic and early scholastic authors listed in 'Scholasticism', ibid., xxi, 1154

13. K. Thomas, *Religion and the Decline of Magic* (1971). For other relevant works see Dickens and Tonkin, op. cit., 413–4, and nn. 102–19

14. On the 'blurring' see K. Thomas, op. cit., esp. 32–6, 46, 51–6. The impact of Protestantism against both sorts of 'magic' is then discussed, 58–88

15. ibid., 301–2

16. Gee and Hardy, 271

17. 2 Macc., xii, 33–45; Matt., xii, 31ff; 1 Cor. iii, 11–15

18. See esp. the famous passage in the *Paraclesis* (1516), translated by J. C. Olin, *Christian Humanism and the Reformation* (Harper Torchbook, New York, 1965), 96–7

19. A. G. Dickens, 'Luther and the Humanists', in P. Mack and M. C. Jacob (eds.), *Politics and Culture in Early Modern Europe: Essays in Honour of H. G. Koenigsberger* (1987), 209, cites relevant passages

20. Despite the declaration of J. R. Green that 'England became the people of a book', a full-scale work on popular enthusiasm for the Bible has not yet come to my notice. Meanwhile the brief work by D. Wilson, *The People and the Book* (1970) has made a start. Note also Marvin W. Anderson, ch. 7, n. 41 below

21. On these unpopular features of Lutheranism see G. Strauss, *Luther's House of Learning* (Baltimore and London, 1978), esp. the final three chapters

399

Chapter 2, pages 25–45

1. Durham University Library, Cosin MS v.v. 19
2. B. L. Sloane MS 1584
3. A sympathetic sketch of the popular religion is in H. Maynard Smith, *Pre-Reformation England* (1938), ch. iii, iv. On the cults: Helen C. White, *Tudor Books of Saints and Martyrs* (Madison, Wisc., 1963)
4. *The Pilgrimage of Robert Langton*, ed. E. M. Blackie (Cambridge, Mass., 1924)
5. *Visitations of the Diocese of Norwich*, ed. A. Jessopp (*Camden Soc.*, 2 ser., xliii), 320; C. E. Woodruff in *Archaeologia Cantiana*, xliv, 13–32
6. Sir T. More, *English Works* (1557), 337–8
7. For the Parkyn MSS and my commentaries, see *Tudor Treatises* (*Yorks. Archaeol. Soc., Record Ser.*, cxxv), 18ff; *Reformation Studies*, 247–83
8. Printed, *Tudor Treatises*, 67–88
9. Printed, *E. H. R.*, lxii, 58–83
10. Letters in *Transactions, Hunter Archaeol. Soc.*, vi, pt. 6, 280–4
11. Bodleian MS Eng. Poet. e. 59; compare the present writer in *Bodleian Library Record*, iv, no. 2, 67ff
12. P. Janelle, *L'Angleterre Catholique à la Veille du Schisme* (Paris, 1935), 13ff
13. *Dialogue concerning Heresyes* (1528) in *Works* (1557), 233–4, but compare 186; P. Janelle, op. cit., 17
14. References in E. F. Jacob, *The Fifteenth Century* (*Oxford History of England*, 1961), 663ff, and J. W. Adamson in *The Library*, 4 ser., x, 163ff
15. J. J. Scarisbrick, *The Reformation and the English People* (1984), ch. 2; H. F. Westlake, *Parish Guilds of Medieval England* (1919); D. M. Owen, *Church and Society in Medieval Lincolnshire* (1971); C. M. Barron, 'The Parish Fraternities of Medieval London', in C. M. Barron and C. Harper-Bill (eds.), *The Church in Medieval Society* (1985)
16. *The First Churchwardens' Book of Louth*, ed. R. C. Dudding, 181. Compare *V. C. H., London*, i, 238
17. *York Plays*, ed. L. Toulmin Smith (1885), *Introduction*; A. C. Cawley, *The Wakefield Pageants in the Towneley Cycle* (1958); T. Wright, *Chester Plays* (*Shakespeare Soc.*, 1843). Other refs. in H. Maynard Smith, op. cit., 141–9
18. *Lollards and Protestants*, 232; J. Strype, *Eccles. Mem.*, iii(2)), 390–2
19. See on these rewards the instructions for a parish priest in B. L. Harleian MS 4172, fos. 8v–9. This and other authorities are cited by E. G. Ashby, *Some Aspects of Parish Life in the City of London from 1429 to 1529* (London M.A. thesis, 1951), 315ff. Further discussion in *Journal of Theological Studies*, new ser., xiv, 229
20. H. Maynard Smith, op. cit., ch. i, describes Henry's will and obsequies
21. C. C. Butterworth, *The English Primers, 1529–1545* (1953), ch. i, gives detail on earlier versions
22. *A Relation of the Island of England* (*Camden Soc.*, 1 ser., xxxvii), 23

23. Select bibliography on mysticism in *O. D. C. C.*, 952; on the *devotio moderna*, ibid. 398

24. On the English mystics see D. Knowles, *The English Mystical Tradition* (1964); on Hilton: Helen Gardner in *Essays and Studies, English Association*, xxii, 103ff

25. *Clifford Letters of the Sixteenth Century*, ed. A. G. Dickens (*Surtees Soc.*, clxxii), 68–9

26. Trinity College, Cambridge, MS 1160. Fr. Andrew Gray kindly informed me that the official Carthusian *cartae* give 1528 as his terminal date

27. Pembroke College, Cambridge, MS 221

28. *To Hew Heremyte* (P.R.O., SP 1/239, fos. 266–7v) is printed in E. M. Nugent, *The Thought and Culture of the English Renaissance*, (1956) 388ff

29. Lincoln Cathedral Library, MS A. 6, 8

30. M. Chauncy, *Historia Aliquot Martyrum* (Mainz, 1550) was translated anonymously as *The History of the Sufferings of Eighteen Carthusians* (1890)

31. D. Knowles, *The Religious Orders in England* (1948–59), iii, 368–9

32. *The Spiritual Exercises of a Dominican Friar*, ed. C. Kirchberger (1929)

33. G. Sitwell in *The Month*, April 1959, 218ff; O. de Veghel, *Benoit de Canfield* (Rome, 1949); H. Bremond, *A Literary History of Religious Thought in France* (1928–36); ii, 111–26

34. D. Knowles, *The English Mystical Tradition*, ch. 9

Chapter 3, pages 46–60

1. For recent Wycliffe studies see A. Kenny (ed.), *Wyclif in his Times* (1986), especially the items by Hudson, Keen and Leff. For Wycliffe's career, see A. B. Emden, *Biographical Register of the University of Oxford to 1500*, iii, 2103–6. K. B. McFarlane, *John Wycliffe and the Beginnings of English Nonconformity* (1952) is important but unsympathetic to Wycliffe as a man of religion.

2. On Wycliffe and Hussitism: M. Wilks, 'Reformatio Regni', *Studies in Church History* ix; F. Smahel, 'Wyclif's Fortune in Hussite Bohemia', *B.I.H.R.*, xliii; A. Kenny, op. cit.

3. On earlier Lollardy see e.g. H. S. Cronin, 'The Twelve Conclusions of the Lollards', *E.H.R.*, xxii; V. H. H. Green, *Bishop Reginald Pecock* (1945); A. Hudson (ed.), *English Wycliffite Writings* (1978)

4. On the connections between Lollardy and the Reformation, the present writer's article (1964) reprinted in *Reformation Studies*, 363–82, largely anticipated this present chapter; the best general account is J. A. F. Thomson, *The Later Lollards 1414–1520* (1965). See also M. Aston, *Lollards and Reformers* (1984); A. Hudson, *Lollards and their Books* (1985) esp. ch. 15; A. Hope, 'Lollardy: the Stone that the Builders

Rejected', in P. Lake and M. Dowling (eds.), *Protestantism and the National Church in 16th Century England* (1987)

5. J. F. Mozley, *John Foxe and his Book* (1940) defends Foxe against his Victorian critics
6. *Lollards and Protestants*, gives references for this and the subsequent passages on the York diocese
7. Registers cited in *Reformation Studies*, 367–9
8. M. Bowker, *The Henrician Reformation. The Diocese of Lincoln under John Longland* (1981). The major episode of 1521 by no means concluded Longland's anti-Lollard activities
9. *V.C.H. London*, i, 234–8; *L. & P.*, iv (2), nos. 4029–30; J. Strype, *Eccles. Mem.*, i(1), 113–34; (2), 50–62; E. G. Ashby, op. cit., ch. 9
10. Warham's Register, Lambeth Palace Library, MS 1108, fos. 164–81; *British Magazine*, xxiii–xxv *passim*. On Kent see P. Clark, *English Provincial Society ... Religion, Politics and Society in Kent*, 34–107. Foxe's main passages on Kent: iv, 181–2, 722–3; v, 647–54
11. Foxe, iv, 213; *V.C.H. Berkshire*, ii, 21
12. Foxe, iv, 557–8
13. J. Fines, 'Heresy Trials in the Diocese of Coventry and Lichfield', *J.E.H.*, xiv
14. E. E. Reynolds, *St John Fisher* (1955), 120
15. Foxe iv, 208–14
16. Strype, op. cit., i(2), 54–5
17. Foxe, iv, 584
18. *Lollards and Protestants*, 24–7
19. *Original Letters*, i (Parker Soc., 1846), 221
20. C. Sturge, *Cuthbert Tunstal* (1938), 362–3
21. *Erasmi Epistolae*, ed. P. S. Allen, 11 vols. (1906–58), v, 292
22. D. Wilkins, *Concilia* (1737), iii, 804–7
23. E.g., *S.T.C.*, 15225, 20036, 24045, 25588, 25590–91; see M. Aston, op. cit., ch. 7 and A. Hudson, op. cit., ch. 15. The former (ch.8) has also a related theme, 'John Wycliffe's Reformation Reputation'

Chapter 4, pages 61–81

1. *The Register or Chronicle of Butley Priory*, ed. A. G. Dickens (1951), 58–9
2. J. A. Guy, *The Cardinal's Court: the Impact of Thomas Wolsey in Star Chamber* (1977)
3. A. F. Pollard, *Wolsey* (1929), 308–12
4. M. Kelly, *Canterbury Jurisdiction and Influence during the Episcopate of William Warham, 1503–1532* (Cambridge Ph.D. thesis, 1963)
5. E. Cavendish, *The Life and Death of Cardinal Wolsey*, ed. R. S. Sylvester (E.E.T.S., no. 243) 90, 116

6. *A Sermon of Cuthbert Byshop of Duresme* (1539); C. Sturge, *Cuthbert Tunstal*, 193. For an anti-papal sermon of 1516, *L. & P.*, ii, no. 2692
7. E. Hall, *Henry VIII*, ed. C. Whibley (1904), ii, 95
8. J. J. Scarisbrick, 'Clerical Taxation in England, 1485–1547', *J.E.H.*, xi, 41–54
9. *Letters of Richard Fox, 1486–1527* (1929), ed. P. S. and H. M. Allen, 93, 97
10. On these bishops: S. Lander, 'The Diocese of Chichester 1508–58' (Cambridge Ph. D. thesis, 1978) and the same author's essay in R. O'Day and F. Heal (eds), *Continuity and Change* (1976); F. Heal, 'The Bishops of Ely and their Diocese during the Reformation Period' (Cambridge Ph.D. thesis, 1972); M. Bowker, *The Henrician Reformation* (above, ch. 3, n. 8)
11. For a case where a cathedral maintained its prescriptive rights, J. A. F. Thomson, 'Two Exeter Decanal Elections, 1509', *Southern History*, viii
12. On the education and background of the bishops: L. B. Smith, *Tudor Prelates and Politics* (1953); J. J. Scarisbrick, 'The Conservative Episcopate in England' (Cambridge Ph.D. thesis, 1955); C. Harper-Bill, 'Dean Colet's Convocation Sermon and the Pre-Reformation Church in England', *History*, lxxiii (1988), 198–201
13. *Clifford Letters of the Sixteenth Century* (*Surtees Soc.*, clxxii), 42–4 gives refs.
14. Cited with other relevant More passages, Hughes, i, 86ff
15. *L'Angleterre Catholique à la Veille du Schisme* (Paris, 1965), 33–6
16. *Sermo Exhortatorius Cancelarii Eboracensis* (W. de Worde, *c.* 1510)
17. York figures from J. H. Moran, 'Clerical Recruitment in the Diocese of York, 1340–1530', *J.E.H.*., xxxiv. Lincoln figures from M. Bowker, *Secular Clergy in the Diocese of Lincoln 1495–1520* (1968), 38, 70
18. P. Heath, *English Parish Clergy on the Eve of the Reformation* (1969), ch. 5 is a widely documented account of selection and educational standards. M. Bowker, *Secular clergy* (above, n. 17) has much on these problems in the Lincoln diocese: see below, ch. 13, nn. 17–18
19. G. R. Elton, *Star Chamber Stories* (1958), ch. 6
20. A. Hamilton Thompson, *The English Clergy* (1947), 115–16
21. Refs. in H. Maynard Smith, *Pre-Reformation England*, 34–5
22. Latimer says this (*Sermons, Everyman* edn., 85) of vicars with 12–14 marks a year. On the wealth (or rather poverty) of the parish clergy, P. Heath, op. cit., ch. 8; M. L. Zell, 'Economic Problems of the Parochial Clergy', R. O'Day and F. Heal (eds.), *Princes and Paupers in the English Church* (1981); J. Pound, 'Clerical Poverty ... some East Anglian Evidence', *J.E.H.*, xxxvii
23. H. Ellis, *Original Letters*, 3 ser., ii, 338; 'exile': meagre, poor
24. Borthwick Institute, York, Diocesan Records, R. VII.G.600
25. A. G. Dickens in *Proceedings, Cambridge Antiquarian Soc.*, xlii, 21–9
26. J. Bale, *Yet a Course at the Romyshe Fox* (1543), 364
27. D. Knowles and R. N. Hadcock, *Medieval Religious Houses* (1953), 364
28. The figures in Hughes, i, 40 involve an average of four inhabitants, but

they seem based on the unreliable calculations of F. A. Gasquet, *Henry VIII and the English Monasteries* (1888), ii, 23–4, 237, 322–3

29. *Register of Butley Priory* (n. 1 above), app.i
30. Hughes, i, 44: on the poverty of most nunneries, ibid., i, 71
31. A. Savine, *English Monasteries on the Eve of the Dissolution* (1909), 287
32. *Visitations of the Diocese of Lincoln*, ed. A. Hamilton Thompson (*Lincoln Record Soc.*, xxxiii–v–vii)
33. Below, ch. 5, n. 2
34. *Collectanea Anglo-Premonstratensia*, ed. F. A. Gasquet (*Camden Soc.*, 3 ser., vi, x, xii)
35. *Yorks. Archaeol. Journal*, xvi, 446–7
36. For a little-known example of a 'bad' house, Marton Priory, Yorks., see J. S. Purvis, ibid., xxxv, 393–403
37. A. G. Little, *The Greyfriars in Oxford* (*Oxford Hist. Soc.*, xx), 54
38. D. Knowles, *The Religious Orders in England*, (1948–59) remains the standard work both on the state of the Tudor monasteries and on the process of their dissolution. On William More, ibid., ch. 9
39. I. S. Leadam in *T.R.H.S.*, 2 ser., vi, vii, viii, xiv, and in *The Domesday of Enclosures* (2 vols., 1897), especially i, 48–9. Compare the cases of depopulation by monasteries cited by M. Beresford, *The Lost Villages of England* (1954) index, under 'monasteries as depopulators'
40. *Utopia* (*Everyman* edn.), 24
41. Called *Rede me and be not wrothe* by some literary histories, and attributed to William Roy. See the passage printed by R. H. Tawney and E. Power, *Tudor Economic Documents* (1924), iii, 20–21
42. *Select Cases ... in the Star Chamber*, ii (*Selden Soc.*, xxv), pp. xciiff
43. *Register of Butley Priory* (n.1 above), 16, 50
44. E.g. *L. & P.*, x, nos. 716, 858, 916; xiii (2), no. 306
45. A. Savine, op.cit., 238
46. D. Knowles, op. cit., iii, 212ff
47. Above, ch. 2, n. 30

Chapter 5, pages 82–105

1. A. E. McGrath analyses Luther's central doctrines with clinical precision in *The Intellectual Origins of the European Reformation* (1987), a field rendered easier for non-theologians by his book *Reformation Thought. An Inroduction* (1988). Of the many older studies see esp. E. G. Rupp, *The Righteousness of God* (1953)
2. For the human implications of Luther's justificatory teaching, see J. S. Whale, *The Protestant Tradition* (1955), pt. i; on its impact upon English Reformers: E. G. Rupp, *Studies in the Making of the English Protestant Tradition* (1947), ch. 8
3. On the two planes or 'kingdoms' see W. D. J. Cargill Thompson,

Studies in the Reformation (1980), ch. 2; for Luther's moral standpoint, see E. G. Rupp and B. Drewery (eds.), *Martin Luther* (1970), 50–4, esp. 53

4. Excellent on his thought: W. P. Stevens, *The Theology of Huldrych Zwingli* (1986), See also the refs. in W. K. Jordan, *The Development of Religious Toleration in England*, i, 327–8. Best biography in English: G. R. Potter, *Zwingli* (1976)

5. McGrath (above n. 1) is again valuable on 'the multiplicity of faiths' presented by late scholasticism. For other views compare J. Mackinnon, *The Origins of the Reformation*, 348ff, and E. G. Rupp, *The Righteousness of God*, 88ff

6. J. Colet, *Exposition of St Paul's Epistle to the Romans*, trans. J. H. Lupton (1873), has useful introduction. E. W. Hunt, *Dean Colet and his Theology* (1956) amplifies this. Lupton's *Life of John Colet* (1887) is still of value, but for modern approaches: P. I. Kaufman in *Church History*, xlvi, and in *Jnl. of British Studies*, xxii; W. A. Clebsch in *Anglican Theological Review*, xxxvii; L. Miles, *John Colet and the Platonic Tradition* (1962); C. Harper-Bill, 'Dean Colet's Convocation Sermon', *History*,lxxiii (1988)

7. H. A. Enno van Gelder, *The Two Reformations of the 16th Century*, trans. J. F. Finlay (The Hague, 1961). On the immense influence of Erasmus upon most branches of the Protestant Reformation: McGrath, n. 1 above; G. H. Williams, *The Radical Reformation* (1962)

8. Foxe, v, 415–16. For refs. to the dates which follow, see C. S. Meyer, *J.E.H.*, ix, 173–87

9. J. A. Muller, *Stephen Gardiner, and the Tudor Reaction* (1926), 14, 342, n. 6

10. On Barnes: E. G. Rupp, *The English Protestant Tradition*, 31–46

11. *L. & P.*, iv(1), no. 1962; *Greyfriars Chron. (Camden Soc.*, 1 ser., liii), 33

12. *L. & P.*, iv(3), no. 6385; the same letter in which he denounces Gonville Hall as a centre of heresy.

13. W. A. Clebsch, *England's Earliest Protestants 1520–1535* (New Haven and London, 1964), esp. chs. 6–11, has valuable surveys of the theology of Tyndale, Frith and other leaders. J. F. Mozley, *William Tyndale* (1937), is scholarly but rather uncritical. A good interpretative study is C. H. Williams, *William Tyndale* (1969). Of the numerous articles, note esp. the following: L. J. Trinterud, 'A Reappraisal of William Tyndale's Debt to Martin Luther', *Church History*, xxxi; M. McGiffert, 'William Tyndale's Conception of Covenant', *J.E.H.*, xxxii; J. G. Moller, 'The Beginnings of Puritan Covenant Theology', *J.E.H.*, xiv; M. W. Anderson, 'William Tyndale: a Martyr for all Seasons', *Sixteenth Century Jnl.*, xvii. On the shifting theological background: B. Hall, 'The Early Rise and Gradual Decline of Lutheranism in England', *Studies in Church History*, *Subsidia* 2 (1979). On Tyndale's political thought see Q. Skinner, *The Foundations of Modern Political Thought*, ii, *The Reformation*, 66–73. For Tyndale's main works see *Tudor Bibliog.*, pp. 118–19, 169, 172, and *S.T.C.* under 'Tyndale'

14. R. Pineas, 'William Tyndale's Use of History as a Weapon of Religious Controversy', *Harvard Theological Review*, lv
15. *Lollards and Protestants*, 131–7
16. Dixon, i, 413–14, from Alesius and Foxe
17. W. Tyndale, *Obedience of a Christian Man* in *Doctrinal Treatises (Parker Soc.*, 1848), 255. Reprints of Tyndale's chief works are in this and the other two volumes published by the Parker Society in 1849 and 1850 respectively
18. The subsequent paragraph is largely indebted to E. N. Chuilleanáin, 'The Debate between Thomas More and William Tyndale, 1528–33: Ideas on Literature and Religion', *J. E. H.*, xxix, which also contains numerous important references
19. On Roy and Jerome Barlow: E. G. Rupp, op. cit., 52ff, and above, ch. 4, n. 41
20. C. C. Butterworth and A. G. Chester, *George Joye, 1495?–1553* (Philadelphia and Oxford, 1962); also J. F. Mozley, *Coverdale and his Bibles*, (1953), 42ff. The latter remains standard for Coverdale himself. On *The Supper of the Lord*: W. D. J. Cargill Thompson, *Studies in the Reformation*, ed. C. W. Dugmore (1980), 83–93
21. Foxe, v, 421ff and app. 6
22. Foxe, v, 1–16. Foxe edited *The Whole Works of W. Tyndall, John Frith and Doctor Barnes* (1572). Clebsch, op. cit., chs. 6–8 covers Frith's life and theology
23. On adiaphorism in Melanchthon and in the English writers, W. G. Zeeveld, *Foundations of Tudor Policy*, esp. 137ff, corrected by Q. Skinner, op. cit., 103–4. It appears also in Barnes and Frith: Clebsch, op. cit., 64, 105–7, 120–6, 131
24. Foxe, iv, 619–56; T. F. Tout in *D.N.B.*; Rupp, op. cit., 22–31; C. Sturge, *Cuthbert Tunstal*, 137–9
25. On Stafford: C. H. and T. Cooper, *Athenae Cantabrigienses* (1858–61), i, 39; H. Maynard Smith, *Henry VIII and the Reformation* (1948), 259–60; H. C. Porter, *Reformation and Reaction in Tudor Cambridge* (1958), 42
26. *Span. Cal.*, iv (1), 349–50

Chapter 6, pages 106–129

1. Erastianism: the ascendancy of State over Church in ecclesiastical affairs, so-called after the Swiss theologian Thomas Erastus (1524–83)
2. Brief bibliography in *O.D.C.C.*, 878; best edn. of *Defensor Pacis*, ed. C. W. Previté-Orton (1928); summaries in G. H. Sabine, *Hist. of Political Theory* (1951), ch. 15, and in E. Armstrong, *Italian Studies*, 59–72. See also commentary by C. W. Previté-Orton, *Proc. British Academy*, xxi, 137–84

3. G. Barraclough, *Papal Provisions* (1935); W. T. Waugh, *E.H.R.*, xxxvii, 173ff, and *History*, viii, 289; further refs by G. L. Harriss, *Past & Present*, xxv, 15ff

4. Refs. in *O.D.C.C.*, 1213; I. D. Thornley in *Tudor Studies presented to A. F. Pollard* (1924), 182–207

5. Ed. D. M. Brodie (1948)

6. D. Wilkins, *Concilia*, iii, 651; J. H. Lupton, *Life of John Colet* (1887), 293ff; M. Kelly, *Canterbury Jurisdiction and Influence* (above, ch. 4, n. 4) 110ff

7. A. F. Pollard, *Wolsey*, 31ff, helped by E. Jeffries Davis, *E.H.R.*, xxx, 477ff, gave the first useful account. A Ogle, *The Tragedy of the Lollards' Tower* (1949) largely replaced earlier surveys, though it needs corrections from S. F. C. Milsom, *E.H.R.*, lxxvi, 80–2, and from the editors of Thomas More's *Dialogue Concerning Heresies* in *Complete Works of St Thomas More* (Yale edn.), vol. 6. Note also R. Marius, *Thomas More* (1985), ch. 8

8. *History of the English Church in the Sixteenth Century*, ch. 3

9. *V.C.H., London*, i, 236ff; on tithe suits, see below, ch. 13, n. 23

10. *E.H.R.*, xxx, 481

11. Chapuys, 13 Dec. 1529 in *Span. Cal.*, iv(1), 367; E. Hall, *Henry VIII*, ed. C. Whibley, ii, 163ff

12. Ibid., ii, 225ff

13. F. Le Van Baumer, *The Early Tudor Theory of Kingship* (New Haven, 1940), ch. iii, and the same author in *American Hist. Rev.*, xlii, 631ff. On St German: J. B. Trapp, *The Complete Works of St Thomas More*, (Yale edn.) vol. 9, xli–liv; J. Guy, 'Thomas More and Christopher St German' in A. Fox and J. Guy (eds.), *Reassessing the Henrician Age* (1986) ch. 5

14. Fish, cited by Foxe, iv, 659ff; modern edn. by J. M. Cowper, *E.E.T.S.*, extra ser., xiii

15. The writs themselves mention church-reform (Rymer, *Foedera*, xiv, 302). For some of the points which follow, see G. W. O. Woodward, *Schweitzer Beiträge zur Allgemeinen Geschichte*, Band 16 (1958), 56ff. On all stages of this parliament see S. E. Lehmberg, *The Reformation Parliament 1529–1536* (1970)

16. Detail in A. F. Pollard, *Wolsey*, ch. 6. The lead taken by More in his astonishingly violent attack on Wolsey cannot be doubted: see ibid., 256, n. 3; R. W. Chambers, *Thomas More* (edn. 1963), 230–1; R. Marius, op. cit., 365–7, examines More's motives

17. I owe this point to G. W. O. Woodward

18. J. J. Scarisbrick, *Henry VIII* (1968), 273ff

19. *The Letters of Stephen Gardiner* ed. J. A. Muller (1933), 392

20. Cf. J. A. Guy, *E.H.R.*, xcvii, and G. W. Bernard, *J.E.H.*, xxxvii

21. The large literature on the Divorce is best approached through Scarisbrick, op. cit., ch. 7, 8, which has the best account of the canon law aspects.

22. *L. & P.*, v, no. 45

23. J. J. Scarisbrick, 'Henry VIII and the Vatican Library', *Bibliothèque d'Humanisme et Renaissance*, xxiv, 211–16

Chapter 7, pages 130–166

1. Brief biography: A. G. Dickens, *Thomas Cromwell and the English Reformation* (1959): see 185ff for select bibliog. to 1957, noting esp. the contributions by G. R. Elton
2. On these writers and their relations with Cromwell's policy: W. G. Zeeveld, *Foundations of Tudor Policy* (Cambridge, Mass., 1948); F. Le Van Baumer, *The Early Tudor Theory of Kingship* (New Haven, 1940); Baumer also on Starkey and Marsiglio, *Politica*, ii, 188–205; G. R. Elton, 'Reform by Statute: Thomas Starkey's Dialogue and Thomas Cromwell's Policy', *Proc. of the British Academy*, liv (1968); J. A. Guy, 'Thomas Cromwell and the Intellectual Origins of the Henrician Revolution', A. Fox and J. A. Guy, op. cit., ch. 6, n. 13. The strongly Erasmian flavour of Cromwell's circle is stressed by J. K. McConica. *English Humanists and Reformation Politics* (1965), ch. 6. See also n. 10 below
3. *D.N.B.*, Marshall, William; *L. & P.*, vii, no. 423
4. The familiar statutes which follow are discussed in several standard constitutional histories. The chief relevant passages are reprinted in Gee and Hardy; J. R. Tanner, *Tudor Constitutional Documents* (1930); G. R. Elton, *The Tudor Constitution* (1960)
5. Detail in G. R. Elton, *The Tudor Revolution in Government* (1953), 76ff
6. On this theme: S. E. Lehmberg, 'The Religious Beliefs of Thomas Cromwell', in R. L. DeMolen (ed.), *Leaders of the Reformation* (1984), ch. 5; G. R. Elton, *Reform and Reformation: England 1509–1558* (1977), 171–3; 'Thomas Cromwell's Decline and Fall', in Elton's *Studies in Tudor and Stuart Politics and Government* (1974), i, 220–6; A. G. Dickens, op. cit., 178–85
7. Foxe, v, 363
8. Ibid., v, 236
9. Lehmberg, op. cit., 148
10. W. G. Zeeveld, op. cit., ch. 6; Lehmberg, op. cit., 143–8; A. G. Dickens and J. M. Tonkin, *The Reformation in Historical Thought* (above, ch. 1 n. 3), ch. 3
11. Summarised in Dixon, ii, 233–4 from the Latin version in *Journals of the House of Lords*, i, 129
12. Edward Hall, *The Union of the Two Noble Families*, etc. (1550), fos. cclx–lxxii
13. Note Sir Nicholas Bacon's motto *mediocria firma* on his portrait (National Portrait Gallery) reproduced in J. E. Neale, *Elizabeth I and her Parliaments 1559–1581* (1953), i, 42. His opening speech to the 1559 Parliament echoed the spirit of Cromwell's and Henry's speeches (ibid., 42–3)
14. On this theme I am greatly indebted to an exhaustive analysis of the fall of Anne Boleyn lent me in typescript by Dr. G. W. Bernard. For the opposite view, that she was essentially the victim of a court-conspiracy, see E. W. Ives, *Anne Boleyn* (1984), ch. 4
15. This evidence is ably assembled by M. Dowling, 'Anne Boleyn and Reform', *J.E.H.*, xxxv

16. *Span. Cal.*, V(2), p. 85
17. Compare G. R. Elton in *E.H.R.*, lxvi, and J. P. Cooper in ibid., lxxii
18. Printed, Gee and Hardy, 145–53
19. D. Wilkins, *Concilia*, iii, 746
20. On this and sequel: M. Kelly in *T.R.H.S.*, 5 ser., xv, 97ff
21. Printed, Gee and Hardy, 154–76
22. E. Hall, *Henry VIII*, ed. Whibley, ii, 209–12
23. G. R. Elton in *E.H.R.*, lxvi; R. Koebner in *B.I.H.R.*, xxvi; G. L. Harriss in *Past & Present*, xxv
24. F. D. Logan, 'Thomas Cromwell and the Vicegerency in Spirituals,' *E.H.R.*, ciii
25. Dickens, op. cit., 142ff summarises S.T.C., no. 292
26. G. W. O. Woodward; see n. 15 to ch. 6 above
27. Other examples in Woodward, op. cit., 65
28. Ed. J. Caley and J. Hunter (1810–34); chief commentary: A. Savine, *English Monasteries on the Eve of the Dissolution* (1909)
29. F. C. Dietz, *English Government Finance, 1485–1558 (Univ. of Illinois Studies in the Social Sciences*, ix (1920), 80–2, 138
30. I. D. Thornley in *E.H.R.*, xxxii, 556ff; G. R. Elton, *The Tudor Constitution*, 59ff
31. A section on Thomas More concludes this present chapter
32. *Span. Cal.*, iv(2) nos. 1130 (p. 813), 1133 (p. 821). Chapuys should always be regarded with great caution, but he had no obvious motive for fabricating these communications
33. On the neo-feudal conspiracy, see refs. in G. Mattingly, *Catherine of Aragon* (1950), 328 and on the court-conspiracy, G. R. Elton, 'Politics and the Pilgrimage of Grace' in his *Studies in Tudor and Stuart Politics and Government*, iii, (1983), 183–215
34. The work of M. H. and R. Dodds, *The Pilgrimage of Grace and the Exeter Conspiracy* (2 vols., 1915), now requires some additions and corrections, but has remained the basis of all more recent work on the vast body of surviving evidence. M. E. James has made many important contributions to the northern background, including 'Obedience and Dissent in Henrician England: the Lincolnshire Rebellion 1536', *Past & Present*, xlviii, and *Change and Continuity in the Tudor North (Borthwick Papers*, no. 27, 1965): see also ibid., no. 30, 1966, and *Northern History*, i. Also important are: R. B. Smith, *Land and Politics in the England of Henry VIII: the West Riding of Yorkshire*, (1970) ch. 5; M. Bowker, 'Lincolnshire 1536: heresy, schism or religious discontent?', *Studies in Church History*, ix; C. Haigh, *The Last Days of the Lancashire Monasteries and the Pilgrimage of Grace (Chetham Soc.*, 3 ser., 17); S. M. Harrison, *The Pilgrimage of Grace in the Lake Counties (Royal Historical Society Studies in History*, no. 27, 1981). The strongly social-economic interpretation began with R. R. Reid, *The King's Council in the North* (1921) esp. 121–44. A. G. Dickens, 'Secular and Religious Motivation in the Pilgrimage of Grace', *Reformation Studies*, has been taken to minimize the religious motivation as a whole, but was intended

rather to show that such ardour was of short duration and that social-economic grievances were always explicit. On such issues see also the criticism by C. S. L. Davies, 'The Pilgrimage of Grace Reconsidered', *Past & Present*, xli. Robert Aske's social 'case' for the monasteries should now be read alongside C. Cross, 'Monasticism and Society in the Diocese of York, 1520–1540', *T.R.H.S.*, 5 ser., xxxviii

35. M. H. and R. Dodds, op. cit., i, 139
36. *E.H.R.*, v, 335–6
37. M. H. and R. Dodds, op. cit., i, 347–8, 383, discusses this and other divisions of opinion.
38. *Lollards and Protestants*, 126–31
39. Zeeveld, op. cit., 232–3
40. J. C. Cox, *The Parish Registers of England* (1910) especially 1–4, 236–8
41. On the subsequent passages see J. F. Mozley, *Coverdale and his Bibles* (above, ch. 5, n. 20); A. W. Pollard, *Records of the English Bible* (1911); J. Isaacs in *The Bible in its Ancient and English Versions*, ed. H. W. Robinson, (1940), 146–95. Among the recent works on Tudor bibles note Marvin W. Anderson, *The Battle for the Gospel* (Lexington, Mass., 1987)
42. *L. & P.*, v, no. 221
43. In 1583 by Dr William Fulke, who may have received it from Coverdale: see J. F. Mozley, op. cit., 112–13
44. On Rogers see Foxe, vi, 596
45. *L. & P.*, xiv(2, no. 214
46. Castillon's report on a conversation with Cromwell, printed in A. W. Pollard, op. cit., 249–51; compare *L. & P.*, xiii(2), no. 1163
47. J. F. Mozley, op. cit., 214ff
48. *L. & P.*, xiv(2), no. 1086, printed in A. W. Pollard, op. cit., 236–7
49. *State Papers of Henry VIII*, i, 589–90
50. *D.N.B.*, Taverner, Richard; on his Bible see J. F. Mozley, op. cit., 347–8
51. On Gardiner's plea for latinisation see ibid., 273–6, and A. W. Pollard, op. cit., 272–5
52. I cite the 'Great Bible' as reprinted in *The English Hexapla* (1841)
53. R. W. Chambers, *Thomas More* (1937)
54. William Roper, *The Lyfe of Sir Thomas Moore Knighte*, ed. E. V. Hitchcock, *E.E.T.S.*, no. 197 (1935)
55. N. Harpsfield, *The Life and Death of Sir Thomas More Knight*, ed. E. V. Hitchcock, *E.E.T.S.*, no. 186 (1932)
56. T. Stapleton, *The Life and Illustrious Martyrdom of Sir Thomas More*, trans. P. E. Hallet (1928)
57. See esp. G. R. Elton's two articles, 'Thomas More, Councillor' and 'The Real Thomas More', reprinted respectively in vols. i and iii of his *Studies in Tudor and Stuart Politics and Government* (1974, 1983). His *Policy and Police* (1972), 400–25 has a valuable discussion on More's opposition to the Crown and the responsibilities for his condemnation
58. J. A. Guy, *The Public Career of Sir Thomas More* (1980) also illuminates the English political context during his middle and later life

59. R. Marius, *Thomas More* (New York, 1984; London, 1985)

60. A. Fox, *Thomas More: History and Providence* (Oxford, 1982). In addition, most aspects of his career are discussed in R. S. Sylvester and G. P. Marc'hadour (eds.), *Essential Articles for the Study of Thomas More* (Hamden, Conn., 1977) and of course in R. Marius, op. cit.

61. B. I. Bradshaw, 'The Controversial Thomas More', *J.E.H.*, xxxvi

62. Cf. R. Mansfield, *Phoenix of his Age* (Toronto, 1979), ch. 2

63. J. C. Olin (ed.), *Desiderius Erasmus: Christian Humanism and the Reformation* (New York, 1965), 146–9; A. Fox, chs. 1–3 in A. Fox and J. Guy (eds.), op. cit. above, ch. 6 n. 13

64. Craig Thompson (ed.), *Inquisitio de Fide, Yale Studies in Religion*, xv (New Haven, 1950)

65. P. Smith, *Erasmus* (New York, 1923, 1962) Index s.v. Melanchthon: R. Bainton, *Erasmus of Christendom* (New York, 1969), 175, 263. Conversely, on Luther as Christian humanist, see A. G. Dickens, 'Luther and the Humanists', Phyllis Mack and Margaret C. Jacob (eds.), *Politics and Culture in Early Modern Europe* (Cambridge, 1987). For Erasmus on his own *via media*, see the letter in *Opus Epistolarum*, ed. P. S. Allen, 1906–58, v, no. 1356; trans. Bainton, op. cit., 175–6. Further observations on the More-Erasmus relationship are in J. K. McConica, op. cit., Appendix II

66. Reproduced, e.g. in A. G. Dickens, *Reformation and Society* (1966), 86

67. G. H. Williams, *The Radical Reformation* (1962), Index, p. 880, cites 29 passages on this theme, some lengthy. See also *Mennonite Encyclopedia* (4 vols., Scotsdale, Penna., 1955), ii, 239–40. See below, ch. 11, n. 26 and note also the immense influence of Erasmus upon Zwingli

68. R. Bainton, op. cit., 182–92 summarizes the situation; so does P. Smith, op. cit., ch. 12

69. Roper, op. cit. 6, was told by More that 'he gave himself to devotion and prayer ... religiously living there without vow for about four years', until he started visiting the Colt family, eventually marrying Jane. Did Roper get this right? It seems unlikely that a Carthusian house would have had a lay 'boarder' for such a period, though More doubtless attended their services meticulously and had such personal contacts as the rule allowed

70. On the issue of marriage, sexuality and vocation, Marius, op. cit., xxii–iii, 14–15, 34–43; Fox, op. cit., esp. ch. 1

71. *The Complete Works of St. Thomas More*, Yale edn., vi 346. The *Dialogue Concerning Heresies*, bk iv, chs. 1–8 consists largely of attacks upon Luther. On More as controversialist, J. B. Trapp, op. cit., ch. 6, n. 13 above, pp. xviiff; R. Pineas, *Thomas More and Tudor Polemics* (Bloomington and London, 1968)

72. Compare Roper, op. cit., 67–8, where More is alleged to have told the King that he had overstressed papal authority in the *Assertio septem sacramentorum*. Contrast Roper's account (92–4) of More's trial-declaration. I have not yet seen B. Cogan, *The Common Corps of Christendom* (Leiden, 1982) which concerns More's writings. Thomas

Starkey retained an interest in Conciliar theory, see also T. F. Mayer, *Jnl. of the Hist. of Ideas*, xlix (1988)

73. L. Miles, 'Persecution and the *Dialogue of Comfort*', *Jnl. of British Studies*, v, p. 28, n. 48

74. L. Miles, op. cit., and note the same author on More's last saintly months: 'The Dialogue of Comfort and More's Execution', *Modern Language Review*, lxii (1966)

75. *Dialogue Concerning Heresies*, bk iv, ch. 13–18. On More's campaign against the heretics, see also Marius, op. cit., ch. 25; Clebsch, op. cit., 278–83. J. B. Trapp, op. cit., pp. xxxff points out that More's victims would have been more numerous had they not promptly fled abroad

76. Refs in Q. Skinner, *The Foundations of Modern Political Thought*, ii, *The Age of Reformation* (1978), 70

77. L. Miles, 'Persecution' (n. 73 above), 20–9, gives detail on these cases

78. Ibid., 20–4

79. Marius, op. cit., 152–82 has a useful discussion. On Utopian religion, ibid., 17–83, 280–1, 353. The standard edition of *Utopia* is edited by E. Surtz and J. H. Hexter, *Complete Works*, iv

80. Hughes, i, 86–8 quotes at length the relevant passages from *A Dialogue of Sir Thomas More Knight* (1528)

81. For More's views on Hunne, Marius, op. cit., 123–4, 129, 135–41, 339, 350; J. D. M. Derrett, *The Apology, Complete Works*, ix, 215–46

82. Marius, op. cit., ch. 16

83. J. C. Olin (n. 63 above), 92–106 translates the *Paraclesis*: for the passage on popular bible-reading, 96–8

84. On More's attitudes to the English Bible, Marius, op. cit., 347–9, 427–8. For him the Bible was essentially a gift of the Church, and only to be studied under its auspices and guidance

85. Ibid., 12, 165–6, 224–5, 233–4

86. Ibid., 419, 478–9

87. W. Roper, op. cit., 21

Chapter 8, pages 167–191

1. *Register of Butley Priory* (above, ch. 4, n. 1), 67

2. *L. & P.*, vii, no. 1355. Already in 1532, Henry had dissolved Christchurch, Aldgate, without papal authorisation; E. Jeffries Davis, *T.R.H.S.*, 4 ser., viii, 127–50

3. R. B. Merriman, *Life and Letters of Thomas Cromwell* (1902), ii, 265

4. R. Ehrenberg, *Capital and Finance in the Age of the Renaissance* (1928), 108

5. D. Knowles, *The Religious Orders in England*, iii, pt. 3; G. W. O. Woodward, *The Dissolution of the Monasteries* (1966); J. Youings, *The Dissolution of the Monasteries* (1971, also prints many documents)

6. *Sermons* (*Parker Soc.*, 1844), 123
7. Spelman's *History and Fate of Sacrilege* was written *c.*1633, published 1698
8. E. Hall, *Henry VIII*, ed. C. Whibley, ii, 268
9. G. W. O. Woodward, *E.H.R.*, lxxvi, 385–401
10. G. A. J. Hodgett, *J.E.H.*, xiii, 195–202
11. Full account in W. C. Richardson, *History of the Court of Augmentations* (Baton Rouge, 1961)
12. On pensions, A. G. Dickens, *E.H.R.*, lv, 384–418, and G. A. J. Hodgett, *Lincoln Record Society*, liii, pp. xvii–xix. G. Baskerville, *English Monks and the Dissolution of the Monasteries* (1937) has valuable information but in general conveys an over-optimistic view. His best work is in the detailed articles, e.g. *Surrey Archaeological Collections*, xlvii, 12–28; *Essays in History presented to R. L. Poole* (1927), 436–65
13. Refs. to York diocesan records in A. G. Dickens, 'The Marian Reaction in the Diocese of York', in *Reformation Studies*, 144–5
14. Ibid., 145–6
15. *Yorks. Archaeol. Journal*, xix, 100–4
16. Baskerville, op. cit., 242–3, but see G. A. J. Hodgett, *J.E.H.*, xiii, 201
17. Described in detail by the present writer; above n. 12
18. J. Hunter, *South Yorkshire* (1828–31), ii, 274–6
19. At least 110 religious persons, distributed across all the Orders in England, appear in J. Fines, *Biographical Register of Early English Protestants*. Doubtless many others were insufficiently prominent to get into the (now very incomplete) records of the period 1525–58
20. A. Savine, *English Monasteries on the Eve of the Dissolution* (1909), 100
21. N. R. Ker, *Medieval Libraries of Great Britain*, pp. xiff; N. R. Ker, *The Library*, 4 ser., xxiii, 7ff
22. M. Aston, 'English Ruins and English History' in her *Lollards and Reformers* (1984), ch. 10
23. E. Jeffries Davis, 'The Transformation of London', *Tudor Studies presented to A. F. Pollard* (1924), 287–314
24. For Henry VIII's schemes, *L. & P.*, xiv(1), nos. 868, 1189–90; xiv(2), nos. 429–30; Dixon, ii, 221–6; *King Henry the Eighth's Scheme of Bishopricks*, ed. H. Cole (1838)
25. D. Knowles, op. cit., iii, 389–92
26. A. F. Leach, *The Schools of Medieval England* (1915), 311ff
27. *Complaynt of Roderyck Mors*, *E.E.T.S.*, extra ser., pp. 9, 33
28. Ed. E. Lamond (3 edn 1954), 85
29. *Sermons* (*parker Soc.*, 1844), 63–5, 247–9, etc.
30. M. Beresford, *The Lost Villages of England*, 166
31. *Discourse of the Common Weal* (above, n. 26), 19
32. H. R. Trevor-Roper, 'The Gentry, 1540–1640' (*Econ. Hist. Rev. Suppl.* i)
33. E. Kerridge in *Econ. Hist. Rev.*, 2 ser., vi, 16–34
34. M. E. Finch, *The Wealth of Five Northamptonshire Families* (*Northants. Record Soc.*, xix), 165–9

35. A. Simpson, *The Wealth of the Gentry, 1540–1660* (1961)
36. E.g. *York Civic Records*, vi (*Yorks. Archaeol. Soc. Record Ser.*, cxii), 17; present writer in *V.C.H., City of York*, 132–3
37. Tabulated in H. A. L. Fisher, *Pol. Hist. Eng.*, v, app. ii
38. On the subsequent passages see especially H. J. Habakkuk, 'The Market for Monastic Property', *Econ. Hist. Rev.*, 2 ser., x, 362–80
39. S. B. Liljegren, *The Fall of the Monasteries* (Lund, 1924), 85
40. R. B. Smith, *Land and Politics in the England of Henry VIII. The West Riding of Yorkshire 1530–1546* (1970)
41. J. Thirsk, *Fenland Farming in the Sixteenth Century* (1953)
42. W. G. Hoskins, *The Midland Peasant* (1957), 141
43. G. A. J. Hodgett, *The Dissolution of the Monasteries in Lincolnshire* (London M.A. thesis, 1947)
44. J. Youings, *Devon Monastic Lands: Calendar of Particulars for Grants* (*Devon and Cornwall Record Soc.*, new ser., i)
45. S. T. Bindoff, *Tudor England* (1950), 124–7
46. R. B. Smith, op. cit., ch. 6
47. On this theme see C. J. Kitching, 'The Disposal of Monastic and Chantry Lands', in F. Heal and R. O'Day (eds.), *Church and Society in England: Henry VIII to James I* (1977), ch. 6; J. Youings, *The Dissolution of the Monasteries*, 117–31
48. A. L. Rowse, *Tudor Cornwall* (1941), 222
49. *D.N.B.*, York, Sir John; *Select Cases in the Court of Requests* (*Selden Soc.*, xii), 198ff, 201ff
50. F. G. Emmison, *Tudor Secretary* (1961), ch. 14, especially 269–70
51. Ed. A. G. Dickens in *Bedfordshire Hist. Record Soc.*, xxxvi, 38ff
52. On Harrington see not only R. H. Tawney in *Proc. British Academy*, xxvii, 199ff, but the criticism by C. B. Macpherson in *Past & Present*, xvii
53. Based mainly on *The Visitation of Yorkshire … 1584–5 … 1612*, ed. J. Foster (1875)
54. *Harleian Soc.*, xii
55. Ibid., xliii
56. Ibid., l, li, lii, lv
57. Ibid., xiii, xiv
58. Ibid., lxvi
59. A. L. Rowse, op. cit., 212; 'spry' is a form of 'spray', i.e. branch

Chapter 9, pages 192–221

1. Refs. to authorities for Cranmer's career are in J. Ridley, *Thomas Cranmer* (1962). Other biographies are those by G. W. Bromiley (1956) and F. E. Hutchinson (1951). On his theological and liturgical work, see below nn. 21, 26. An independent assessment, justifiably more favourable

than that of Ridley, arises from P. N. Brooks, *Cranmer in Context* (1989), which presents an illuminating selection from Cranmer's writings

2. Ridley, 148–51
3. R. B. Merriman, *Life and Letters of Thomas Cromwell* (1902), ii, 128–31
4. Modern lives by Honor McCusker (Bryn Mawr, 1942) and Jesse W. Harris (Urbana, 1949)
5. Listed by W. T. Davies, *A Bibliography of John Bale* (1940)
6. *Illustrium Majoris Britanniae Scriptorum*, &c. (1548–9; 1557–9); also *Index Britanniae Scriptorum*, ed. Poole and Bateson (1902)
7. *Summary Catalogue of Western MSS in the Bodleian Library*, nos. 3429, 3460, 27635–6
8. In Bale's *Select Works (Parker Soc.*, 1849), 1ff, 136ff
9. *L. & P.*, xiv(1), no. 47
10. *Kynge Johan (Camden Soc.*, 1 ser., ii). Nicholas Udall, the 'Father of English Comedy', was also a notable Protestant publicist. On the early Protestant theatre see E. K. Chambers, *The Medieval Stage* (1903), ii, 216–26; I. Lancashire, *Dramatic Texts and Records of Britain* (1984, nos. 320–9, 1087–1110
11. On Starkey and Morison see W. G. Zeeveld, *Foundations of Tudor Policy; Early Eng. Text Soc.*, extra ser., xii and xxxii; F. Le Van Baumer, *The Early Tudor Theory of Kingship* (New Haven, 1940). On Taverner see *D.N.B.*: J. F. Mozley, *Coverdale and his Bibles*, 347–8
12. On Lambert see Foxe, v, 181ff; comment in Ridley, 94–5, 174–6; Dugmore, 177–81
13. P. Janelle, *Obedience in Church and State* (1930); my summary is also based on that in Hughes, i, 337–41
14. On Cromwell's foreign policy see R. B. Merriman, op. cit., i, 213–41
15. Compare G. Constant, *The Reformation in England* (1934), i, 404ff; text in C. Hardwick, *History of the Articles of Religion* (1890), 237–58
16. Text in C. Lloyd, *Formularies of Faith* (1825), 21–212
17. Detail in Dixon, ii, 251ff. On the later career of Barnes, see *D.N.B.*; E. G. Rupp, *The English Protestant Tradition*, chs. 2, 6; J. A. Muller, *Stephen Gardiner*, ch. 13; Clebsch, op. cit., chs. 4, 5
18. Summarised in Dixon, ii, 233–4; G. Burnet, *History of the Reformation*, ed. N. Pocock (1865), i, 438
19. W. G. Zeeveld, op. cit., 152–6
20. Gee and Hardy, 269–81
21. C. H. Smyth, *Cranmer and the Reformation under Edward VI* (1926), ch. 10: his dating is accepted by E. C. Ratcliff, 'The liturgical work of Archbishop Cranmer', *J.E.H.*, vii, 194. A study of the manuscript evidence is J. Wickham Legg, *Cranmer's Liturgical Projects* (1915)
22. Refs. to the primers in H. Maynard Smith, *Henry VIII and the Reformation*, 394–9
23. Details in Dixon, ii, 328–33
24. On these attacks see Ridley, 186 and ch. 15: the chief source is Morice's *Anecdotes*, printed in *Narratives of . . . the Reformation (Camden Soc.*, 1 ser., lxxvii): see 215–9

25. *The King's Book*, as reprinted by the Church Historical Society in 1932, amounts to little more than the text in C. Lloyd, op. cit., 213ff. On the doctrine of the Church see 69ff as well as 31–7; on the mass see 163–5 as well as 50–57. On the circumstances see D. Wilkins, *Concilia*, iii, 868; J. A. Muller, *The Letters of Stephen Gardiner*, (1933), 259

26. On the doctrinal issues see esp. P. N. Brooks, *Thomas Cranmer's Doctrine of the Eucharist* (1965). On Cranmer's development see also C. H. Smyth, op. cit., 48–66, and Dugmore, ch. v–viii; note criticisms by T. M. Parker in *Journal of Theological Studies*, new ser., xii, 132–46, and Dugmore's rejoinder in ibid, xiv, 227–34. Further refs. in Ridley, 168–70, 252–4, 280–3. Smyth's term 'Suvermerianism' has not proved acceptable to theologians. On Cranmer's adaptation of Justus Jonas, see F. A. Gasquet and E. Bishop, *Edward VI and the Book of Common Prayer* (1890), 129–31. On Gardiner's view, mentioned below, see Dugmore, ch. viii, and on Tunstall's, ibid., 152–4

27. Ed. C. S. Cobb in *Alcuin Club Collections*, xviii

28. H. Maynard Smith, op. cit., 403–4

29. They were published 1547. A reprint was ed. by J. Griffiths (1859)

30. J. F. Mozley, op. cit., ch. 13 gives further detail

31. *Narratives of . . . the Reformation* (n. 24 above), 349–51

32. Mozley, op. cit., 284

33. See Mozley, op. cit., 265–9, for an attempt to reconcile Foxe's details with those given in 1547 by William Palmer

34. Fuller account in *Lollards and Protestants*, 171–2, 215–18. The enquiry on the evidence of wills is geographically extended in ch. 13 below

35. *Lollards and Protestants*, 172

36. Ibid., 149–50

37. Ibid., 114–31

38. E. Hall, *Henry VIII*, ed. C. Whibley, ii, 285–6

39. *Ricart's Kalendar* (*Camden Soc.*, 2 ser., v), 55; *L. & P.*, xiv(1), no. 184. On Bristol in 1533 see *L. & P.*, vi, nos. 796, 799, 873

40. Beginning in 1519 editions of works by Erasmus appeared in England: they became numerous from the later 1530s *S.T.C.*, 10437–10510; E. J. Devereux, *Renaissance English Translations of Erasmus: a Bibliography to 1700* (Toronto, 1983)

41. I lean to Elton's view (*Reform and Reformation*, 328–9) that in his last years the king's mental energies declined

42. Cf. Patrick C. Swenson, 'Patronage from the Privy Chamber. Sir Anthony Denny and Religious Reform', *Jnl. of British Studies*, xxvii; background: D. R. Starkey, *The King's Privy Chamber, 1485–1547* (Ph.D. thesis, Cambridge, 1973): pending fuller publication, see Starkey, *The Reign of Henry VIII. Personalities and Politics* (1985), chs. 7, 8. On Denny, ibid., 133–6; biography in S. T. Bindoff, ed., *History of Parliament. The Commons 1509–1558*, ii, 27–9; M. Dowling, *Humanism in the Age of Henry VIII* (1986), 62–3 and her essay 'The Gospel and the Court', in P. Lake and M. Dowling, (eds.), *Protestantism and the National Church in Sixteenth Century England* (1987)

43. Foxe, v, 605
44. Compare his protection of Katherine Parr, when she was under attack (ibid., v. 553, 557–61); cf. M. Dowling, *Humanism* (n. 42 above), 67–8
45. *D.N.B.*, Butts; M. Dowling, 'The Gospel and the Court', 39–40, 47, 49–53, 64–71, and ibid., 'Anne Boleyn and Reform', *J.E.H.*, xxxv, 35, 38–9, 42
46. Ibid., 66. Elizabeth appears to have been taught by William Grindal and Katherine Ashley from 1544, apparently after Lady Champernoun's widowhood and retirement
47. E. Casady, *Henry Howard, Earl of Surrey* (New York, 1938) is still essential
48. For refs. to the evangelical aspects of Surrey's poems, see W. A. Sessions, *Henry Howard Earl of Surrey* (Boston, Mass., 1987), 100–2, 104–7, 109, 112, 121
49. M. Dowling, *Humanism*, 235–7
50. On Edward VI and his circle see esp. J. G. Nichols, *Literary Remains of King Edward VI*, 2 vols., *Roxburghe Club* (1851; W. K. Jordan, *The Chronicle and Political Papers of King Edward VI* (1966)
51. On these cases see E. Trollope in *Assoc. Archit. Soc. Rep.*, vi, 117ff; *Lollards and Protestants*, 33–4
52. Above, n. 8
53. For Surrey's fall, see E. Casady, op. cit., ch. 9

Chapter 10, pages 222–255

1. Short Calvin bibliographies in *O.D.C.D.*, 222–4 and in B. Hall, *John Calvin* (*Historical Association*, G. 33), 38–9
2. On the early influence of Calvin, see C. D. Cremeans, *The Reception of Calvinist Thought in England* (Urbana, 1949), 29–40
3. These events are summarised by A. F. Pollard, *Pol. Hist. Eng.*, vi, ch. 1; also in *D.N.B.*, 'Seymour, Edward'; but see below, n. 7
4. Ridley, 262–3
5. Ibid., 265ff; Dixon, ii, 423ff
6. *Pol. Hist. Eng.*, vi, 16
7. A. F. Pollard, loc. cit., but on the political issues, this and his *England under Protector Somerset* (1900) are now largely superseded by M. L. Bush, *The Government Policy of Protector Somerset* (1975)
8. 1 Edward VI cap. 14 in Gee and Hardy, 328–57; note comments in *Pol. Hist. Eng.*, vi, 18–20
9. 37 Henry VIII cap. 4
10. *A.P.C.*, *1550–1552*, 74; an example of a free chapel in *Suffolk Institute of Archaeology, Proc.*, xii, 33; Dixon, ii, 381–2, lists colleges
11. For a list (incomplete) of printed chantry surveys see *Tudor Bibliog.*, 180; additions in *E.H.R.*, lv, 413, n. 3; and in *Texts and Calendars*, ed. E. L. C. Mullins (*Royal Hist. Soc.*), 561, s.v. chantry certificates

12. Printed in *Surtees Soc.*, xci, xcii
13. W. Camden, *Britannia* (edn. 1753), i, p. ccxxx
14. A. Kreider, *English Chantries. The Road to Dissolution* (Cambridge, Mass., 1975), 75–9
15. M. Bowker, *The Henrician Reformation* (above, ch. 3, n. 8), 101
16. *Suffolk Institute of Archaeology, Proc.*, xii, 30–71, *passim*
17. *Somerset Record Soc.*, ii; index gives refs. to these places
18. Details in *Lollards and Protestants*, 207
19. *Transactions, Bristol and Gloucester Arch. Soc.*, viii, 253
20. *A.P.C., 1547–1550*, 193, 195
21. A. G. Dickens, 'A Municipal Dissolution of Chantries at York, 1536' *Reformation Studies*, ch. 4
22. *Oxfordshire Record Soc.*, i, 3, 5
23. Ibid. i, 42
24. Figures based on the histories of hospitals in *V.C.H., Yorks.*, iii
25. *Surtees Soc.*, xci, 175
26. Ibid., xvii, 400
27. *V.C.H., Cumberland*, ii, 55
28. *Surtees Soc.*, xci, 61
29. *Oxfordshire Record Soc.*, i, 14–16
30. *Shropshire Arch. and Nat. Hist. Soc.*, 3 ser., x, 269–392; *Surtees Soc.*, xci, xcii
31. Joan Simon, *British Jnl. of Educational Studies*, iii, no. 2, 127ff; iv, no. 1, 32ff
32. Based on P. J. Wallis and W. E. Tate. *A Register of Old Yorks. Grammar Schools, Univ. of Leeds Inst. of Education, Researches and Studies*, no. 13
33. J. H. Moran, *The Growth of English Schooling* 1340–1348 (Princeton, N.J., 1986); see also her article 'Literacy and Education in Northern England', *Northern History*, xvii. See ibid., 303–4 for the main works of N. Orme on medieval schools
34. Cited by N. Wood, *The Reformation and English Education* (1931), 181–2
35. C. Haigh, *Reformation and Resistance in Tudor Lancashire* (1975), 48–51
36. *Surtees Soc.*, xci, 192
37. *Oxfordshire Record Soc.*, i, 23
38. Ibid., i, xvi–xvii
39. C. Kitching, 'Church and Chapelry in 16th Century England', *Studies in Church History*, xvi
40. They often sold off the plate, leaving little for the commissioners who in 1552 came to confiscate church goods. Cf. Haigh, op. cit., 148–50
41. A. G. Dickens in *Yorks. Arch. Jnl.*, xxxiv, 151ff
42. *Yorks Star Chamber Proceedings*, ii (*Yorks. Arch. Record Soc.*, xlv), 13–36
43. *York Civic Records*, v (ibid., cx), *passim*
44. *Oxfordshire Record Soc.*, i, 44; the communicants were earlier (probably in error) numbered 460 (ibid., 22)

45. Ibid. 19–20; *Shropshire Arch. and Nat. Hist. Soc.*, 3 ser., x, 327–8; *Surtees Soc.*, xci, p. xiv; cxii, p. vii

46. Refs. in Dixon, ii, 381–2

47. Following analysis based on A. Hamilton Thompson, *The English Clergy* (1974), 78ff

48. C. Kitching, op. cit., above, ch. 8, n. 47

49. B. L. Add. MS 5813, ed. A. G. Dickens in *Tudor Treatises* (*Yorks. Arch. Record Soc.*, cxxv)

50. Ibid., 126–7

51. Ed. A. G. Dickens, *Yorks. Arch. Jnl.*, xxxvii

52. G. Burnet, *History of the Reformation*, ed. N. Pocock, (1865), v. 197–217, prints the bishops' replies

53. Dugmore, 124–5

54. The literature on the Prayer Book is extensive: see *Tudor Bibliog.*, 165–81. F. Procter and H. W. Frere, *A New Hist. of the Book of Common Prayer* (1914) is a serviceable general account. See also F. E. Brightman, *The English Rite*; E. C. Ratcliff, *The Booke of Common Prayer, Alcuin Club*, 1949; ibid., in *J.E.H.*, vii, 189–203; Dugmore, chs. vi, vii; T. M. Parker, *The English Reformation* (1950), chs. vii, viii; the chapters (ii and iii) respectively by Dugmore and Parker, in *The English Prayer Books 1549–1662* (S.P.C.K. for Alcuin Club, 1963). For the Edwardian Acts of Uniformity, see Gee and Hardy, 358ff, 369ff

55. Procter and Frere, op. cit., 50–2

56. Dugmore, 130

57. F. Rose-Troup, *The Western Rebellion of 1549* (1913); A. L. Rowse, *Tudor Cornwall*, 262ff

58. F. W. Russell, *Kett's Rebellion in Norfolk* (1859) is still indispensable; good modern analysis in S. T. Bindoff, *Ket's Rebellion* (*Historical Association*, G. 12)

59. See n. 41 above

60. *John Bon and Mast Person*, reprinted in *Tudor Tracts*, ed. A. F. Pollard (1903), 159–99

61. On this Ipswich group se A. G. Dickens in *Notes and Queries*, Dec. 1934, 513; *S.T.C.*, nos. 18055–6, 20661–3; Foxe, v. 254; viii. 223–5; 598–600

62. Sig. Aiii, Bi

63. Summarised by Dugmore, 120–3; compare *S.T.C.*, nos. 24162–6

64. Several obscure pamphlets are summarised but in some cases misdated by an anonymous writer in *Church Quarterly Review*, xxxv (1892–3); for examples of 'liberalism' see 44–5, 59

65. *S.T.C.*, nos. 2419–2700

66. The standard monograph is W. R. D. Jones, *The Tudor Commonwealth 1529–1559* (1970); see also C. S. L. Davies, *Peace, Print and Protestantism* (1976), 272ff, and summary by G. R. Elton, 'Reform and the "Commonwealth-Men" of Edward VI's Reign', in P. Clark, A. G. R. Smith and N. Tyacke (eds.), *The English Commonwealth 1547–1640, Essays ... presented to Joel Hurstfield* (1979), 23–38

67. W. R. D. Jones, *William Turner, Tudor Naturalist, Physician and Divine* (1988) supplants most earlier publications
68. On Crowley's activites see J. W. Martin, 'The Publishing Career of Robert Crowley: a Sidelight on the Tudor Book Trade', *Publishing History*, xiv, 58–98; ibid., 'Robert Crowley in Two Protestant Churches', in his *Religious Radicals in Tudor England* (1989), ch. 8. On Crowley's edn. of *Piers Plowman* see J. N. King in *Modern Philology*, lxxiii
69. *D.N.B.*; M. L. Bush, (op. cit., above, n.7) 40–3
70. M. Dewar, 'The Authorship of the Discourse of the Commonwealth, *Econ. Hist. Rev.*, 2 ser., xix, 388–400; M. Dewar also edited the *Discourse* (1969) and Smith's later work *De Republica Anglorum* (written 1565, first published 1583). This latter, as Jones (op. cit., 218) remarks, is lacking in 'the note of idealist criticism which had been so characteristic of mid-century Commonwealth thought.' Note also Dewar's biography, *Sir Thomas Smith. A Tudor Intellectual in Office* (1964)
71. The less prominent figures and forerunners are also discussed by Jones, op. cit., ch. 3. On Scory see ibid., 165; on Cheke, ibid., index. On Cromwell's own relevance, see e.g. G. R. Elton, 'The Political Creed of Thomas Cromwell', *T.R.H.S.*, 5th ser., vi, 69–92, esp. 88
72. See e.g. Cromwell's letter of January 1534 in R. B. Merriman, *Life and Letters of Thomas Cromwell* i, 373 and the Injunctions in Gee and Hardy, 269ff
73. D. S. Bailey, *Thomas Becon and the Reformation of the Church in England* (1952); on what follows see esp. 81–2, 97, 120
74. E.g. *Greyfriars' Chronicle* (*Camden Soc.*, 1 ser., liii), 55, 57, 63
75. B. L. Harleian MS 425, fo. 124ff, printed in *Narratives of ... the Reformation* (*Camden Soc.*, 1 ser., lxxvii), 71–84
76. Ridley, 298–9
77. Ibid., 302–3
78. *Pol. Hist. Eng.*, vi, 45–6

Chapter 11, pages 256–286

1. *Pol. Hist. Eng.*., vi, ch. iii; G. Scott Thomson, *Lords Lieutenants in the Sixteenth Century*, 24ff; W. C. Richardson, *History of the Court of Augmentations*, (above, ch. 8, n. 11) ch. 6
2. Compare D. Hoak, 'Rehabilitating the Duke of Northumberland', J. Loach and R. Tittler (eds.), *The Mid-Tudor Polity* (1980)
3. Ridley, 327–30. On foreign refugees, see *Tudor Bibliog.*, nos. 163–5; A. Pettegree, *Foreign Protestant Communities in Sixteenth-century London* (1986)
4. *Cal. Pat. Edw. VI*, iii, 317
5. C. Hopf, *Martin Bucer and the English Reformation*; H. Eells, *Martin Bucer* (New Haven, 1931); *Tudor Bibliog.*, nos. 2124, 2127

6. Cited by E. G. Rupp in *New Cambridge Modern History*, ii, 111
7. *D.N.B.*, Utenhove, John. On Glastonbury, see Dixon, iii, 236, 427
8. Modern sketch and select bibliog. of Knox in J. D. Mackie, *John Knox* (*Historical Association*, G.20)
9. On Bradford and Marsh: C. Haigh, op. cit., Index; *V.C.H. Lancashire*, ii, 48; on the schemes for itinerant preachers, see J. E. C. Hill in *T.R.H.S.*, 5 ser., xiii, 79ff
10. G. H. Williams, *The Radical Reformation* (1962); E. Payne, *New Cambridge Modern History*, ii, 119–33; On the English radicals and their Anabaptist antecedents: I. B. Horst, *The Radical Brethren*, (Nieuwkoop, 1972). The most important later research is in J. W. Martin, *Religious Radicals in Tudor England* (1989). Note also J. F. Davis, *Heresy and Reformation in the South-East of England* (*Royal Hist. Soc.*, 1983), chs. 5, 6
11. G. H. Williams, op. cit., ch. xiii
12. *Original Letters* (*Parker Soc.* 1846–7), 65–6; *A Lesson of the Incarnation of Christ* in *Later Writings of John Hooper* (*Parker Soc.*, 1825), 1–18
13. G. H. Williams op. cit., 780, gives titles
14. D. Wilkins, *Concilia*, iv, 42–3. Michael Thombe presumably had Netherlandish or German antecedents. A John Thombe, previously a subject of the Emperor, was naturalised in June 1549 (*Huguenot Soc.*, viii, 232): see also Horst op. cit., 111–12
15. D. Wilkins, op. cit., iv, 44–5. Note also the Unitarian priest John Ashton in ibid., 41. On Joan Bocher see esp. Horst, op. cit., 109–11, noting his points on Cranmer
16. *The harvest is at hand*, *S.T.C.*, 4956, sigs. B4v, D4, E2, E6v, D8. On Champneys: I. B. Horst, op. cit., 112–5; J. Fines, *Biographical Register of Early English Protestants* (1981–5)
17. Respectively *S.T.C.*, 12887 (1548), with two later editions, perhaps within the same year; *S.T.C.*, 12564, published by John Oswen in 1549 at Worcester. On Hart see J. W. Martin, *Religious Radicals*, ch. 4
18. *A.P.C.*, *1550–1552*, pp. 198–9
19. Printed in Champlin Burrage, *The Early English Dissenters* (1912), ii, 1–4
20. J. Strype, *Cranmer* (1840), 254–7; *Eccles. Mem.*, ii(1), 385; *A.P.C.*, *1562–4*, 131, where on 27 September 1552 Cranmer is sent 'a boke of examinations' regarding 'the sect newly sprung in Kent'
21. J. W. Martin, 'The First that made Separation from the Reformed Church of England', *Religious Radicals*, ch. 3
22. Ibid., 65. The clerical schoolmaster Thomas Cole of Maidstone is distinct from the other clerical member, Robert Cole of Faversham (ibid., 64–5)
23. John Ledley of Ashford (ibid., 67–8) was an active agent who also contributed prayers to a collection printed in the early fifties (*S.T.C.*, 17776)
24. J. W. Martin, op. cit., 50
25. Referenced biographies of all these men appear in ibid., 64–70

26. G. H. Williams, *The Radical Reformation* is informative on Denck and Franck. For further literature in English, see e.g. R. H. Bainton and E. W. Gritsch, *Bibliography of the Continental Reformation* (Hamden, Conn., 1972) 141–2, 156. These and other spiritualists are biographed in the *Allgemeine Deutsche Biographie*. Following various continental scholars, G. H. Williams often stresses the links between Erasmus and the spiritualists; compare ch. 7, n. 67 above. In this field Rufus M. Jones, *Spiritual Reformers in the 16th and 17th Centuries* (1914), chs. 2–5 is still useful. He also discusses English Anabaptism and the Family of Love in his *Studies in Mystical Religion* (1909), chs. 17–18

27. Chief monographs; A. Hamilton, *The Family of Love* (1981) and Jean D. Moss, '*Godded with God*'. *Hendrik Niclaes and the Family of Love* (*American Philosophical Society*, Philadelphia, 1981). See also Horst, op. cit., esp. 152–4. G. H. Williams, *The Radical Reformation* remains indispensable on the European background, but less impressive (788–90) on England. The vast complexity of Anabaptism is also illustrated by H. J. Hillerbrand, *A Bibliog. of Anabaptism 1520–1630* (Elkhart, Indiana, 1962). This work has a sequel covering publications 1962–74 (St Louis, 1975)

28. For the basic refs. to Niclaes and Vitel in England see C. Fell Smith in *D.N.B.*, xiv, 427–31 and xx, 375–6. On the doctrines of Niclaes, see A. Hamilton, op. cit.,34–43. On Vitel see J. W. Martin, 'Christopher Vitel: an Elizabethen Mechanick Preacher,' *Religious Radicals*, ch. 11. On other aspects of Familism and the sects, ibid., chs. 10, 12. D. M. Loades, 'Anabaptism and English Sectarianism'. *Studies in Church History, Subsidia 2* (1979). On the broader picture, see B. R. White, *The English Separatist Tradition* (1971) and M. R. Watts, *The Dissenters* (1978). It seems likely enough that Niclaes revisited England in later years: n. 30 below

29. *S.T.C.*, 18549–18563, inclusive

30. For Surrey, less heavily Protestanised in pre-Elizabethan times than Kent, Essex and East Anglia, see J. W. Martin, 'Elizabethan Familists and Other Separatists in the Guildford area', *B.I.H.R.*, li, which gives refs. to the important Familist depositions of 1561 before Sir William More of Loseley, now among the Loseley MSS at the Folger Library. In 1561 the Surrey Familists spoke of Niclaes as 'Henryke, a Dutchman, the hede of all the Congregacion; he is permanent in no place, but still wandreth to vysyte his flock'. On the movement in Cambridgeshire, see F. Heal in *Studies in Church History*, ix, and M. Spufford, *Contrasting Communities* (1974), index, 'Family of Love'

31. The main attackers were: J. Rogers, *The Displaying of an Horrible Sect* (1578–9), *S.T.C.*, 21181, 21182; W. Wilkinson, *A Confutation of certaine articles delivered unto the Family of Love* (1579), *S.T.C.*, 25665; J. Knewstub, *A Confutation of monstrous and horrible heresies taught by H.N.* (1579), *S.T.C.*, 15040; S. Bateman, *The Golden Book of the Leaden Goddes* (1577), *S.T.C.*, 1583

32. The notion that God descended into man in the figure of Christ and

thereby 'deified' man derives from the *Theologia Germanica* and other medieval German mystical works: this term *Vergottung* was not, of course, used with blasphemous intent (A. Hamilton, op. cit., 8). In the early experiences of Niclaes it assumed an element of pantheism, as with his vision of being incorporated into a mountain (ibid., 25)

33. On David Joris, see initially R. H. Bainton, *The Travail of Religious Liberty* (1953), 121–44; then compare the further secondary authorities cited in ibid. 257

34. Bainton emphasises this aspect in his account of Joris: see previous note

35. Especially in *Die Soziallehren der christichen Kirchen und Gruppen* (1912); English translation by O. Wyon: *The Social Teaching of the Christian Churches* (1931)

36. On Bucer in Cambridge see H. C. Porter, *Reformation and Reaction in Tudor Cambridge*, 51–67

37. Knappen, 91–5, from à Lasco's *Forma ac Ratio*

38. On the Ordinal: Ridley, 307–8; E. C. Ratcliff in *J.E.H.*, vii, 201

39. C. Sturge, *Cuthbert Tunstal*, 281–96

40. C. Hopf in *Jnl. of Theological Studies*, xliv, 194–9; *Writings of John Bradford, Letters, Treatises,* (Parker Soc., 1853), 373–93; Ridley, 308–10, 313–15; Knappen, 82–9

41. F. D. Price, 'Gloucester Diocese under Bishop Hooper' in *Trans. Bristol and Gloucester Arch. Soc.*, lx, 51–151; J. Gairdner in *E.H.R.*, xix, 98–121; on Hooper's social liberalism see Knappen, 406–8

42. F. D. Price, op. cit., 82–3

43. *Hist. MSS Comm., Cecil*, i, 107, dated 2 Feb. 1553

44. A. G. Dickens, 'Robert Holgate', *Reformation Studies*, ch. 15

45. Printed in *Alcuin Club Collections*, xv, 310ff

46. A. G. Dickens, op. cit. 24–5, and in *E.H.R.*, lii, 428ff; lvi, 450ff

47. H. Machyn, *Diary* (Camden Soc., 1 ser., xlii), 8; *Greyfriars' Chronicle* (ibid., liii), 70

48. 2 & 3 Edw. VI cap. 21; *Lords' Journals*, i, 343

49. Hilda Grieve in *T.R.H.S.*, 4 ser., xxii, 142–3; G. Baskerville in *E.H.R.*, xlviii, 44; E. L. C. Mullins, *The Effects of the Marian and Elizabethan Religious Settlements upon the Clergy of London* (London M.A. thesis, 1948), 122; R. B. Walker, *A History of the Reformation in the Archdeaconries of Lincoln and Stow* (Liverpool Ph.D. thesis, 1959), 217–19

50. A. G. Dickens, 'The Marian Reaction in the Diocese of York', *Reformation Studies*, 104–5

51. H. Grieve, op. cit., 150, 159

52. F. W. Brooks in *Jnl. of the British Arch. Assn.*, 3 ser., x, 23–37

53. J. E. C. Hill, *Economic Problems of the Church* (1956), 108–13; A. Tindal Hart, *The Country Priest in English History*, (1959), ch. 7

54. Refs. in Dugmore, 150–56

55. Ibid., 158–9

56. On the Second Prayer Book, see refs., in ch. 10, n. 52 above

57. Ratcliff, op. cit., 200–1

58. Dugmore, 163–72
59. Gee and Hardy, 369–72
60. On these events and on the *Reformatio Legum* below, see L. T. Dibdin and C. E. Chadwyck-Healey, *English Church Law and Divorce* (1912) and related refs. in *Tudor Bibliog.*, 211–12. A convenient edn. is *The Reformation of the Ecclesiastical Laws*, ed. E. Cardwell (1850). On the revival see J. E. Neale, *Elizabeth I and her Parliaments*, i, 194ff. On the heresy clauses, see Ridley, 333–4
61. The Forty-two Articles are discussed in all standard commentaries on the Thirty-nine; see *Tudor Bibliog.*, nos. 1922–3, 1936 and bibliog. in *O.D.C.C.*, 524–5, 1368
62. Compare W. R. Matthews, *The Thirty-Nine Articles* (1961)
63. C. Hardwick, *A History of the Articles of Religion* (1851), *passim*
64. Dugmore, 172–3; T. M. Parker in *Jnl. of Theological Studies*, new ser., xii, 136
65. *A.P.C., 1550–1552*, 228
66. Printed in *Surtees Soc.*, xcvii, 4ff
67. For typical surveys in print, see *Surtees Soc.*, xcvii; *Alcuin Club Collections*, vi, vii, ix, xx, xxiii; H. B. Walters, *London Churches at the Reformation* (1939)
68. *Somerset Record Soc.*, iv, 218
69. *A.P.C., 1552–1554*, 218
70. Antonio Guaras, *The Accession of Queen Mary*, ed. R. Garnett (1892). 81
71. *Ven. Cal.*, v, 346
72. Cited by J. A. Froude, *History of England* (1870), iv, 362, citing 'State Papers Domestic'
73. *Discourse of the Common Weal*, ed. E. Lamond, 21–2
74. For Northumberland's conspiracy see *Pol. Hist. Eng.*, vi, ch. 5
75. 'The Life and Death of Sir Nicholas Throckmorton', a verse-biography in B. L.Add. MS 58541: the passage is on fo. 137v (old ref., p. 272). Throckmorton,later implicated in Wyatt's revolt, escaped through the unusual independence of a jury
76. C. Wriothesley, *Chronicle*, ii *(Camden Soc.*, 2 ser., xx), 90–1

Chapter 12, pages 287–315

1. *Pol. Hist. Eng.*, vi, 97–8
2. On the Marian Council a more favourable view is suggested by A. Weikel in J. Loach and R. Tittler (eds.), *The Mid-Tudor Polity*. On the 'atmosphere' of Mary's government, E. H. Harbison, *Rival Ambassadors at the Court of Queen Mary* (Princeton, 1940) is revealing
3. *History of Parliament. The Commons 1509–1558*, i (1982) Apps. xi, xii, xiii (pp. 16–23). On this and related themes the best survey is that by

J. Loach, *Parliament and the Crown in the Reign of Mary Tudor* (1986): it also has (ch. 1) a good account of Mary's accession. In general modern histories of the mid-Tudor period have concentrated far too exclusively upon the role of the Commons as distinct from that of the Lords. This situation has been rectified by M. R. Graves, *The House of Lords in the Parliaments of Edward VI and Mary* (1981)

4. E.g. *A.P.C.*, *1552–1554*, 373, 375, 387, 389, 391, 395, 426, etc. On sedition and rebellion, I used D. M. Loades, *Popular Subversion and Government Security in England during the Reign of Mary I* (Cambridge Ph.D. thesis, 1961). Most of this is now in his *Two Tudor Conspiracies* (1965) and *The Reign of Mary Tudor* (1979)

5. *Ven. Cal.*, v, 560

6. D. M. Loades, *Popular Subversion*, ch. vii

7. Revolt and resultant punishment treated by ibid., chs. viii–x. Most informative contemporary narrative: John Proctor's, reprinted in *Tudor Tracts*, ed. A. F. Pollard (1903), 199–257

8. M. R. Thorp, 'Religion and the Wyatt Rebellion of 1554', (*Church History*, xlvii)

9. *Greyfriars of London Chronicle* (*Camden Soc.*, 1 ser. liii), 87

10. B. L. Add. MS. 34563, ed. C. R. Manning, *Norfolk Archaeology*, iv (1855), 133–231

11. *Ven. Cal.*, v, 556

12. Ibid., vi, 1074–5

13. Ibid., vi, 1018

14. *Papiers d'État du Cardinal de Granvelle*, ed. C. Weiss (*Documents inédits sur l'histoire de France*, Paris, 1841–52), iv, 432–3

15. *Pol. Hist. Eng.*, vi, 130

16. On Cecil's position: C. Read, *Mr Secretary Cecil and Queen Elizabeth* (1955) 108ff; on both Cecil and Kingston at this juncture: J. Loach, op. cit., 149–55

17. On responsibility for the persecution, and its statistics, see J. H. Blunt, *The Reformation of the Church of England* (1878–92) ii, 220ff. See also H. E. Malden, *T.R.H.S.*, 2 ser., ii, 61–76; *Pol. Hist. Eng*, vi, 133–4, 153–7; J. W. Martin, *B.I.H.R.*, lviii; and n. 84 below

18. Cited by J. H. Blunt, op. cit., ii, 245n. The remarks to Philpot are in Foxe, vii, 645, 647. For a cautious defence of Bonner see G. Alexander, *History*, lx

19. E. Russell, 'Marian Oxford and the Counter Reformation', in C. M. Barron and C. Harper-Bill (eds.), *The Church and Pre-Formation Society* (1985), 221–13

20. H. C. Lea, *History of the Inquisition of Spain* (1888), ii, 49–50

21. J. H. Blunt, op. cit., 245ff, possibly exaggerates Spanish influence. Dixon, iv, 339–43, tries unconvincingly to exculpate the Spaniards

22. J. Strype, *Eccles. Mem.*, iii(2, 482–510)

23. Cited by J. A. Froude, *History of England*, vi, 99

24. R. H. Pogson, articles cited below, n. 80

25. J. Strype, op. cit., iii(2), 554–6, gives places and numbers, but not names;

J. W. Martin, 'Sidelights on Foxe's Account of the Marian Martyrs', *Religious Radicals*, ch. 9; the article by P. Collinson cited below, ch. 16, n. 4

26. C. H. Smyth, *Cranmer and the Reformation under Edward VI* (1926), 3
27. *Pol. Hist. Eng.*, vi, 157
28. Strype, op. cit., iii(2), 133–5; on Bentham see also Garrett, 86–7. Compare Renard's report that 'plusieurs ... se sont voulu voluntairement mettre au feug sur le bûche à costé de ceulz que l'on brusloit' (*Papiers d'État du Cardinal de Granvelle*, iv, 404). For other examples of public sympathy see D. M. Loades, *The Reign of Mary Tudor*, 334; P. Collinson, *The Religion of Protestants* (1982), 189–90
29. Foxe, vi, 596
30. D. M. Loades, *The Oxford Martyrs* (1970)
31. W. J. Brown, *Life of Rowland Taylor* (1959)
32. Fox, vi, 676–8. On Hadleigh (where Bilney had introduced the new doctrines), see D. MacCulloch, *Suffolk and the Tudors* (1986), 163–5, 170–2
33. Ridley, ch. xxv, discusses and documents the final episode.
34. The topic was largely introduced by R. H. Bainton, *Women of the Reformation in France and England* (Boston, Mass., 1973). My present passage derives much from E. Macek, 'The Emergence of a Feminine Spirituality in the *Book of Martyrs*', *Sixteenth Century Journal*, xix (1988). She cites e.g. R. W. Warnicke, *Women of the English Renaissance and Reformation* (Westport, Conn., 1983), and N. Z. Davis, *Society and Culture in Early Modern France* (Stanford, 1975). Patrick Collinson's essay on Anne Locke, repr. in *Godly People*, ch. 10, exemplifies the growing interest in the Puritan women of Elizabethan and Jacobean England. Ample material exists for parallel studies on the Catholic side.
35. Foxe, vii, 423
36. J. Strype, *Matthew Parker* (1821), i. 65–6
37. Garrett, 142–3, 288–9
38. *A.P.C., 1556–1558*, 119; compare ibid., 102, 148, 169; J. Strype, *Eccles. Mem.*, iii (2), 413–14
39. *A.P.C., 1554–1556*, 169
40. Ibid., 115–59 *passim*; Foxe, viii, 151
41. Described in D. M. Loades, *The Reign of Mary Tudor*, 281–2
42. Ibid., 280–3, 290. At Ipswich the pamphleteers Peter Moone and John Ramsey were involved, ibid., 167, 181; A. G. Dickens, *Notes and Queries* (1954), 513. *D.N.B.*, Ramsay, John (d.1551) confuses this cleric with the Ipswich man. Note the important role of the printer John Oswen at Ipswich (1548) and later at Worcester
43. Fox, viii, 393–7; *A.P.C., 1554–1556*, 310, 312, 318; *1556–1558*, 18, 129–30, 142, 215
44. Ibid., 336
45. H. N. Birt, *The Elizabethan Settlement* (1907), 510 cites B. L. Harleian MS 4992, fo. 7

46. On the London congregation see Fox, viii, 384, 414–61, 558–60; J. Strype, op. cit., iii(2), 132–5; Knappen, 159–62
47. Foxe, viii, 450–1
48. Foxe, viii, 384. Here we cannot necessarily equate Cuthbert Simpson with 'one Simson' (Dixon, iii, 209), associated with the Freewillers of Bocking. The latter may, e.g., have been the John Simson in Foxe, vii, 330. The charges against Cuthbert Simpson indicate nothing beyond Anglicanism, and the surname was common enough. On problems of identity see J. Fines, *Biographical Register of Early English Protestants* (above, ch. 11 n. 16), Introduction
49. B. L. Harleian MS 425, printed in A. F. Pollard, *Tudor Tracts* (above, ch. 10, n. 60)
50. J. Strype, op. cit., iii(2), 132
51. Foxe, viii, 584–90
52. Foxe, viii, 384; Garrett, 176, 262
53. Foxe, vii, 738
54. On Colchester see Foxe, viii, 383–93
55. Foxe, viii, 556–7. The names and other references to heresy there show that this Stoke was involved, not Stoke-by-Clare. Compare Foxe, vii, 382; viii, 389
56. Foxe, viii, 562–6; on Marsh see ibid., vii, 39–68
57. Lincoln Diocesan Records, Vj.13, fos. 158b, 162b
58. Foxe, viii, 598–600
59. Foxe, vii, 738; viii, 384, 558–9, 562
60. Ibid., vi, 662–4. See also vii, 688 for a similar recommendation by John Philpot. On the general issue see J. W. Martin, 'The Protestant Underground Congregations of Mary's Reign', *Religious Radicals*, ch. 7
61. Foxe, vi, 676–81; viii, 731–6
62. Ibid., viii, 391–3, 405, 409–12
63. Ibid., viii, 468–82
64. Ibid., vii, 321–7
65. Miles Hogarde, *The displaying of the Protestants* (1556), fo. 124
66. *Lollards and Protestants*, 223–35
67. Detail in A. G. Dickens, 'The Marian Reaction in the Diocese of York', *Reformation Studies*, 98–100
68. Ibid., 99–111
69. Foxe, vi, 439
70. Dickens, op. cit., ii, 23–9
71. Refs. in *Lollards and Protestants*, 213–14
72. An account of the restorations is in D. Knowles, *The Religious Orders in England*, iii, ch. 34
73. The relevant passages are printed and discussed by J. H. Crehan, 'St. Ignatius and Cardinal Pole', *Archivum Historicum Societatis Iesu*, xxv, 72–98. Loyola, who showed great insight into the priorities, died in 1556, and his successor Lainez was less pressing. It remains very possible that Pole foresaw the hostility which the mass-introduction of a 'Spanish' Order might provoke in England

74. Here I follow J. W. Martin, 'Miles Hogarde', *Religious Radicals*, ch. 5
75. *Greyfriars' Chronicle*, 95; on processions see also ibid., 94, 97
76. E. J. Baskerville, *Chronological Bibliography of Propaganda and Polemic Published in English* [1553–1558], (Philadelphia, 1979), esp. pp. 6–9
77. Cited in *Pol. Hist. Eng.*, vi, 172, n. 3
78. Cited by J. A. Froude, op. cit., vi, 84
79. Note her speech of 16 November 1553 in Robert Wingfield's *Vita Mariae Reginae* (*Camden 4 ser.*, xxix, 229)
80. R. H. Pogson, 'Revival and Reform in Mary Tudor's Church. A Question of Money', *J.E.H.*, xxv, 249–65; ibid., 'Reginald Pole and the Priorities of Government in Mary Tudor's Church', *Hist. Jnl.*, xviii, 3–21; ibid., 'The legacy of the Schism: Confusion, Continuity and Change in the Marian Clergy', in J. Loach and R. Tittler (eds.), *The Mid-Tudor Polity c. 1540–1560* (1980), 116–36
81. Ibid., 4–7. Yet one perceptive move was the purge of Protestant masters from several important schools and their replacement by Catholics: see N. Orme, *English Schools in the Middle Ages* (1973), 285–7
82. H. Belloc, *Preface* to G. Constant, *The Reformation in England. I. The English Schism* (1939), p. ix
83. This conclusion is based not merely on Wyatt's revolt and on several reports by the Imperial and Venetian ambassadors in England, but still more on innumerable passages in the *A.P.C.* themselves from early 1554 until the end of the reign. For Protestantism's strength in south-eastern England, see below, ch. 13
84. On Bartolomé Carranza, Juan de Villagarcia, Pedro de Soto and Alonso à Castro, see J. H. Blunt, *The Reformation of the Church of England*, ii, 249–58 and D. M. Loades, *The Reign of Mary Tudor*, Index s.v. Spain. On the subsequent rise of anti-Spanish feeling: W. S. Maltby, *The Black Legend in England* (Durham, N.C., 1971)

Chapter 13, pages 316–338

1. C. Haigh, 'Anticlericalism and the English Reformation' in *History*, lxviii, 391–406; cf. A. G. Dickens, 'The Shape of Anticlericalism and the English Reformation' in E. I. Kouri and T. Scott (eds.), *Politics and Society in Reformation Europe* (1987). In Germany anticlericalism was more intensive: cf. R. W. Scribner, *Popular Culture and Popular Movements in Reformation Germany* (1987), ch. 11
2. The main anticlerical passages appear in the translation into modern English by J. F. Goodridge, *Langland, Piers the Plowman* (Penguin Classics, 1966), 63, 91, 101, 107, 114–21, 126, 130–5, 149, 181–8
3. *S.T.C.*, 5069; 19903-4-5-8; 20086. Compare other folk-champions, some (like Robin Hood) from earlier times, others like Colin Clout (Skelton) and Roderyck Mors (Brinkelow) invented by recent authors,

but all co-existing as critics of feudalism and of the Church during the Tudor period. Yet another such hero is Jack up Land (*S.T.C.*, 5098)

4. *S.T.C.*, 19906-8. Cf. J. N. King, 'Robert Crowley's edition of Piers Plowman', *Modern Philology*, lxiii, 342-52
5. *S.T.C.*, 25590-91-91A
6. *S.T.C.*, 5083-4-5-6
7. G. R. Owst, *Preaching in Medieval England* (1926); see Index, s.v. Vices, clerical, for numerous examples
8. V. J. Scattergood, *Politics and Poetry in the Fifteenth Century* (1971), ch. 7
9. J. E. T. Rogers (ed.), *Loci e Libro Veritatum* (1881), 41-2
10. Ibid., 53-9
11. Ibid., 35-6
12. *S.T.C.*, 17806; A. G. Dickens, 'The Writers of Tudor Yorkshire', *Reformation Studies*, ch. 7. For Chancellor Melton's sermon see above, ch. 4, n. 15; P. Heath, *English Parish Clergy on the Eve of the Reformation* (1969), 15-16, 70-2, 76-7, 92, 187, 191
13. *S.T.C.*, 5545. The English version (*S.T.C.*, 5550) is repr. in J. H. Lupton, *Life of John Colet* (1887), 293-304. Note also P. I. Kaufman, 'John Colet's *Opus de Sacramentis* and Clerical Anticlericalism', *Jnl. of British Studies*, xxii, 1-22
14. *S.T.C.*, 3545-6-7-7A; *Cambridge History of English Literature*, iii, 56-7
15. Ibid., iii. 67-79; M. Pollet, *John Skelton. Poet of Tudor England* (1971)
16. Ibid., ch. 9; *S.T.C.*, 22609: *A replycacion agaynst certayne yong scolers* (*c.* 1528)
17. These themes have occurred above, ch. 4. In addition to the evidence, critical passages occur in both works of Dr. Bowker on the diocese of Lincoln (above, ch. 3, 8 and ch. 4, n. 17). For incontinent and unruly clerics see her *Secular Clergy*, 117-22, 172-86, and for anticlericalism, her *Henrician Reformation*, 7, 38, 47
18. P. Heath, op. cit., anticlericalism, 10, 192-6; education and ignorance, 73-5, 91, 188-9; incontinence of clergy, 104-18 *passim*; neglect of services and buildings, 109-11; clergy as landowners and traders in litigation with laity, 162, 191
19. Above, ch. 2, n. 6
20. Above, ch. 6, n. 14; ch. 9, nn. 4-10
21. W. Tyndale, E. Hall, J. Frith, Sir F. Bigod, W. Holme, R. Morison, W. Turner, S. Fish, H. Brinklow, J. Barlow, R. Crowley, J. Knox, P. Moore, J. Ramsey, T. Lever, J. Foxe
22. E.g., W. Baldwin, L. Shepherd, W. Samuel, F. Seager, W. Lynne, W. Punt, R. Hurlestone, W. Kethe
23. On quarrels over tithes: P. Clark, *English Provincial Society ... Religion, Politics and Society in Kent* (1977), Index, s.v. Tithes; P. Heath, op. cit. Index, s.v. Tithes; J. S. Purvis, *Tudor Parish Documents in the Diocese of York* (1948), 180. Main articles: Helen Miller, *B.I.H.R.*, xxxv; Susan Brigden, *J.E.H.*, xxii; J. A. F. Thomson, *E.H.R.*, lxxviii; see also below, n. 34, refs. to Houlbrooke and Wunderli

24. A. G. Dickens, 'Early Protestantism and the Church in Northamptonshire', *Northamptonshire Past and Present*, viii (1983–4), 30–2 gives refs. for the subsequent detail

25. M. Bowker, *The Secular Clergy*, 118–19 from Lincoln Register 23, fo. 216

26. S. Brigden, 'Youth and the English Reformation', *Past & Present*, xcv

27. Greater London Record Office, DL/C/300 ('Foxford'), *passim*: several cases 1525–9 (fos. 100, 137, 175v) illustrate personal hatreds against the Bishop's officers for their repression of bible-reading

28. On the manuscript and the cases stated below see C. A. McLaren, 'An Early 16th Century Act Book of the Diocese of London', *Jnl. of the Society of Archivists*, iii, 336–41

29. P. Clark, op. cit., chs. 1, 2, esp. 12–14, 28–9, 36–8

30. P. Heath, op. cit., 10–12

31. G. R. Elton, *Star Chamber Stories*, 174–220

32. P. Clark, *The English Alehouse* (1983), 74, 124; A. G. Dickens, 'Early Protestantism' (n. 24 above), 35–6. Heavy drinking and alehouse-keeping in vicarages occurred even in the Elizabethan period: e.g. J. S. Purvis, *Tudor Parish Documents* (n. 23 above), 3, 17, 159, 196

33. On the Commons Supplication against the Ordinaries, see above, ch. 7. Somewhat different views on its origins and character have been expressed by G. R. Elton, J. P. Cooper and J. A. Guy; cf. C. Haigh (n. 1 above), 397. Obviously the Supplication cannot be accepted as a consensus of public opinion on the ecclesiastical courts. Rather did it reflect the fears of more important people, now that heresy-charges were more likely to be pressed by the Church. On this last issue see M. Bowker, 'Some Archdeacons' Court Books and the Commons' Supplication' in D. A. Bullough and R. L. Storey (eds.), *The Study of Medieval Records* (1971), 311–13, and compare M. Kelly, 'The Submission of the Clergy', *T.R.H.S.*, 5 ser., xv, 106

34. R. A. Houlbrooke, *Church Courts and the People during the English Reformation* (1979), 116, 149, 271–2; R. M. Wunderli, *London Church Courts and Society on the Eve of the Reformation* (Cambridge, Mass., 1984), esp. ch. 4; S. Lander, 'Church Courts and the Reformation in the Diocese of Chichester' in R. O'Day and F. Heal (eds.), *Continuity and Change. Personnel and Administration of the Church of England 1500–1642* (1976); B. Woodcock, *Medieval Ecclesiastical Courts in the Diocese of Canterbury* (1952)

35. B. Woodcock, op. cit., 109–10, 125. Cf. S. Lander, op. cit., 228; P. Clark, *English Provincial Society* (n. 23 above), 28

36. Cf. F. G. Emmison, *Elizabethan Life*, ii, *Morals and the Church Courts* (1973), 66–7, 310, 313

37. Above, ch. 6

38. This section is based on my more detailed and referenced article 'The Early Expansion of Protestantism in England 1520–1558', *Archive for Reformation History*, xxviii (1987)

39. Note the bibliography of sources in his initial volume (Sutton Courtenay

Press, 1981). Useful summaries of the grass-roots advance of Protestantism in England are those by R. B. Manning in *Sixteenth Century Essays and Studies*, i (1970), and inevitably somewhat dated by subsequent research); D. M. Palliser in F. Heal and R. O'Day (eds.), *Church and Society in England: Henry VIII to James I* (1977)

40. For the number and places of the Marian martyrdoms see J. H. Blunt, *The Reformation of the Church of England*, ii, 220–4

41. A good account of the early Reformation in Kent is in P. Clark, *English Provincial Society* (n. 23 above), chs. 2, 3, 5. On Essex J. E. Oxley, *The Reformation in Essex* (1965), chs. 8–10 is useful, but too brief on the early Protestants and the persecution, upon which in Essex Foxe is esp. informative. On the primacy of Kent, Essex and London for radical sectarianism, see e.g. J. W. Martin, 'The First that made Separation from the Reformed Church of England', *Religious Radicals*, ch. 3; J. H. Blunt, op. cit., ii, 225–6. On this and many other aspects of the region, original contributions were made by J. F. Davis, *Heresy and Reformation in the South-East of England*, above ch. 11, n. 10. On the Thames Valley see Sir H. Bedingfield's reports (May, 1554) in *Norfolk Archaeology*, iv (1855), 133–231; on Sussex: M. J. Kitch, 'The Reformation in Sussex', *Studies in Sussex Church History*, ed. M. J. Kitch (1981), 77–98; G. J. Mayhew, below, n. 58. Interesting aspects of the early Reformation in Hampshire are revealed by R. Fritze in P. Lake and M. Dowling (eds.), *Protestantism and the National Church* (1987), ch. 6. A useful county-survey of the Reformation period is in *V.C.H., Hertfordshire*, iv, 307–33, but this county seems less affected than its neighbour Buckinghamshire, which also had a much stronger Lollard tradition. A valuable recent contribution on an important Protestant county is in D. Mac-Culloch, *Suffolk and the Tudors* (1986), ch. 5

42. On Gloucestershire see the three able essays by K. G. Powell, *Bristol and Gloucestershire Archaeological Society*, xc, 141–57; ibid., xcii, 96–120; *The Marian Martyrs and the Reformation in Bristol* (*Historical Association*, Bristol, 1972)

43. I. T. Shield, *The Reformation in the Diocese of Salisbury* (Oxford B. Litt. thesis, 1960), *passim*

44. For the West Midlands, Foxe, viii, 247–56, 384–405, and on Coventry, *V.C.H., Warwickshire*, ii, 33–8

45. C. Haigh, *Reformation and Resistance in Tudor Lancashire* (1975) ably covers the social and religious aspects of a very conservative county

46. For early Yorkshire Protestantism, *Lollards and Protestants*, esp. Index, s.v. Halifax, Hull, Leeds, Beverley; D. M. Palliser, *The Reformation in York* (*Borthwick Papers*, 40, 1971); M. C. Cross, 'The Development of Protestantism in Leeds and Hull', *Northern History*, xviii, 230–8, and the same author's 'Parochial Structure and the Dissemination of Protestantism ... A Tale of Two Cities', *Studies in Church History*, xvi, and her *Urban Magistrates and Ministers: Religion in Hull and Leeds from the Reformation to the Civil War* (*Borthwick Papers*, 67, 1985)

47. R. Howell, *Newcastle upon Tyne and the Puritan Revolution* (1967), 63–82

48. On Protestantism in the diocese of Lincoln, see e.g. *L. & P.*, xiv(2), no. 214; Lincoln Archives Office Vj. 13, fos. 1586, 1626; Foxe, viii, 242; G. E. Corrie (ed.), *Sermons by Hugh Latimer (Parker Soc.*, 1844), 282, 326, 447; *A.P.C.*, ii, 140–1; J. Strype, *Eccles. Mem.*, iii(2), 392; R. B. Walker, 'Reformation and Reaction in the County of Lincoln', *Lincs. Architectural and Archaeological Soc., Reports and Papers*, new series, ix, 49–62; M. Bowker, *Henrician Reformation*, chs. 2, 4; A. G. Dickens, 'Early Protestantism and the Church in Northamptonshire', n. 24 above. D. Wilson, *A Tudor Tapestry* gives leads on the involved relationships of Anne Askew. The noble families also need more investigation. The Duke of Suffolk was cautious, but the Duchess propaganded at Grimsthorpe until her flight abroad (S. J. Gunn, *Charles Brandon, Duke of Suffolk* (1988), 103–7, 159–64, 198–203, 209). In 1553 the fall of the Greys at Bradgate (where John Aylmer was chaplain and tutor) must have injured Protestantism in Leicestershire and nearby areas.

49. J. Youings, 'The South-Western Rebellion of 1549', *Southern History*, i, 99–122 For further background, R. Whiting, *The Reformation in the South-West of England (Exeter Ph.D. thesis*, 1977), esp. 293–8

50. A. L. Rowse, *Tudor Cornwall* (1941), chs. 12, 15

51. F. E. Halliday (ed.), *Richard Carew of Anthony. The Survey of Cornwall* (1953), 196–7

52. Glanmor Williams, *Religion and Welsh Literature in the Age of the Reformation. Proceedings of the British Academy*, lxix, 371–408, and the same author's *Welsh Reformation Essays* (1987), *passim*

53. Even the largest English provincial cities (Norwich, Bristol, Coventry, Newcastle and York) had total populations of 10–12,000, whereas mid-Tudor London may have had 70,000 or more.

54. On Colchester public houses and Protestants, William Wilkinson, *A Confutation of Certaine Articles* (1579: *S.T.C.*, 25665). On the inns of London, above, ch. 12, and compare Foxe, viii, 382–93

55. Above, ch. 12

56. *L. & P..*, iv(3), no. 6385

57. Often the Imperial ambassador and the successive Venetian envoys testified strongly to the Londoners' hatred of Mary's marriage and persecution (*Span. Cal.*, xiii, 139–40; *Ven. Cal.*, v, 346, 356; vi(1), 94; vi(2), 1018, 1074). Here foreigners had long been numerous but unpopular, as witnessed by the 'Evil May Day' riots of 1517; see on this theme the refs. in ch. 11, n. 3

58. For statistics from wills, see e.g. P. Clark (n. 23 above), 41, 58–60, 76–7, 100, 102, 152, 420; G. J. Mayhew on East Sussex, *Southern History*, v (1963), 38–67; *Lollards and Protestants*, 171–2, 215–8, 220–1; Elaine Sheppard on Norwich, *Norfolk Archaeology*, xxxviii (1983), 44–58; W. J. Sheils, *The Puritans in the Diocese of Peterborough (Northamptonshire Record Soc.*, xxx, 15–18; D. M. Palliser, *The Reformation in York* (above, n. 46), 32; M. C. Cross: articles listed above, n. 46

59. I refer here to the subsequent section

60. Foxe, viii. 407; A. Townsend (ed.), *Writings of John Bradford (Parker Soc.*, 1848), 390

61. M. Bowker, *Henrician Reformation*, 181; R. A. Houlbrooke, 'Persecution of Heresy and Protestantism in the Diocese of Norwich under Henry VIII', *Norfolk Archaeol.*, xxxv, 311. Our knowledge of early Protestantism in Northamptonshire depends in very large degree on the two 'stray' act books at Delapre Abbey: N.R.O., Arch III and Inst. I

62. See e.g. J. Strype, op. cit., iii(2), 434 (Surrey); Foxe, vi. 26–8 (Portsmouth); J. Hutchins, *History and Antiquities ... of Dorset* (1863), ii, 46 (Lyme Regis); P. Collinson, *The Elizabethan Puritan Movement* (1967), 21 (South Moulton); J. G. Nichols (ed.), *Narratives ... of the Reformation (Camden Soc.*, 1st ser., lxxvii (1837), 71–84 (Poole and Southampton)

63. The following figures are based on notes supplied by Dr Fines; some may need to be modified as research proceeds

64. Michiele's lengthy report at the end of his mission (13 May 1557) is translated in *Ven. Cal., vi*, no. 884, pp. 1074–5

65. S. Brigden, 'Youth and the English Reformation' (n. 26 above)

66. Ibid., 57

67. *S.T.C.*, 5027, sig. Tijv

68. Foxe, vii, 717, 747

69. Ibid., v, 16–18

70. Ibid., vi, 704, 722–9, 740

71. Ibid., vii, 192–3

72. *Lollards and Protestants*, 48ff

73. Foxe, vi, 654; vii, 144–5; Gloucester Diocesan Records, II, 207

74. *Narratives of ... the Reformation*, 60–8

75. Ibid., 348–51: Foxe viii, 638–9

76. P. Janelle, *L'Angleterre Catholique à la Veille du Schisme* (Paris, 1955), 339–45; cf. *L. & P.*, vii, no. 146

77. N. Harpsfield, *The Life and Death of Sir Thomas More*, ed. E. V. Hitchcock, *E.E.T.S.*, no. 186 (1932), 84–6

78. In both cases *D.N.B.* has the main references; for Hooper's letter see *Original Letters Relative to the English Reformation*, ed. H. Robinson *(Parker Soc.*, 1846), 34

79. The present writer hopes shortly to publish a full account. Main references: *Ambassades de Messieurs de Noailles en Angleterre*, ed. A. Vertot (Leyden, 1753), ii, 128–9; Corporation of London Record Office, Court of Aldermen, Repertory 13, fos. 131, 132b

80. Foxe, vi, 704, 737–40; cf. Brigden, op. cit., 65–6

81. Foxe, v, 441–2; vi, 711; C. Wriothesley, *Chron. of England*, ed. W. D. Hamilton *(Camden Soc.*, 2 ser., xi), i, 126

Chapter 14, pages 339–361

1. C. H. Garrett, *The Marian Exiles* (1938) is indispensable for the biographies of the exiles, but she seems curiously hostile toward them,

and has some debatable general conclusions. Knappen, ch. 6, has a good short account of Frankfurt. Other works listed in *Tudor Bibliog.*, 182–3. Of these A. B. Hinds, *The Making of the England of Elizabeth* (1895) is a pioneering essay, still useful

2. Statistics in Garrett, 40–2
3. The names which follow are all in *D.N.B.*, supplemented by Garrett
4. Garret, 1–29, 58–9
5. Ibid., 11
6. Ibid., 50–2
7. Ibid., 49–50
8. Hinds, op. cit., 44. cites Lever and Sandys to similar effect
9. Fuller summary in J. W. Allen, *History of Political Thought in the Sixteenth Century* (1928), 118ff
10. Cf. Q. Skinner, *The Foundations of Modern Political Thought* (1978), ii, 189: on Goodman and Knox, ibid., ii, 221–6
11. Several other English publicists, not all exiles, held similar views. Cf. G. Bowler, 'Marian Protestants and the Idea of Violent Resistance to Tyranny' in P. Lake and M. Dowling (eds.), *Protestantism and the National Church* (1988)
12. Knappen, 142
13. On the Geneva version see *The Bible in its Ancient and English Versions*, ed. H. W. Robinson, 181–9
14. See above, ch. 10, n. 65; also 'Metrical Psalters' in *O.D.C.C.*, 911 and refs.
15. P. Collinson in *J.E.H.*, ix, replaces previous investigations of the authorship. The convenient modern edition of *A Brief Discourse* was ed. by E. Arber (1908)
16. Ibid., 44–9
17. Ibid., 50–1
18. See Knappen, 117, 127–8
19. *A Brief Discourse*, 76–80, gives the letter and Calvin's reply
20. Knappen, 154ff; A. B. Hinds, op. cit., 47–65
21. *A Brief Discourse*, 150
22. Garrett, 22
23. On the rise of congregational principles, see Knappen, ch. 8
24. Ibid., 137; W. M. Southgate, 'The Marian Exiles and the Influence of John Calvin', *History*, xxvii, 148–52
25. *Span. Cal., Elizabeth I* (1558–67), p. 39
26. Cf. J. E. Neale, *Elizabeth I and her Parliaments* (1953–7), i, 35ff
27. *Pol. Hist. Eng.*, vi, 179
28. *Span. Cal., Eliz., I* (1558–67), p. 7
29. Ibid., p. 37
30. Dugmore, 213–14
31. *Pol. Hist. Eng.*, vi, 182ff gives details
32. The three accounts of the coronation differ. C. G. Bayne, 'The Coronation of Queen Elizabeth', *E.H.R.*, xxii, 650–73, argues (661–2) that she withdrew into a 'traverse', but H. A. Wilson doubts this: *E.H.R.*, xxiii, 89–90

33. *Span. Cal., Eliz., I* (1558–67), p. 25
34. C. G. Bayne, 'The first House of Commons of Queen Elizabeth', *E.H.R.*, xxiii, 455ff, 643ff
35. J. Strype, *Annals of the Reformation* (1820–40), i(2), 408
36. Neale, op. cit., 33–84 *passim*
37. N. L. Jones, *Faith by Statute. Parliament and the Settlement of Religion* (*Royal Historical Society*, 1982)
38. W. S. Hudson, *The Cambridge Connection and the Elizabethan Settlement of 1559* (Durham, North Carolina, 1980)
39. *The House of Commons, 1558–1603*, ed. P. W. Hasler, i, App. xi, 102–10. They attained the total of 20 in 1572: three survived in the Parliament of 1593
40. H. J. Cowell, 'Sixteenth-Century English-speaking Refugee Churches at Geneva and Frankfurt', *Huguenot Society, Proceedings*, xvi (1937–41), 211–12
41. On the decline of her relations with Protestant clergy see W. S. Hudson, op. cit., ch. 9; P. Collinson, *The Elizabethan Puritan Movement* (1967), 45–83, *passim*
42. For the list of MPs who voted for the retention of the Royal Supremacy in 1555, see *The House of Commons, 1509–1558*, ed. S. T. Bindoff, i, App. xxiii. The list of those who in September 1555 'stood for the true religion' is in ibid., App. xi
43. Neale, op. cit., 57–8
44. On this issue see N. L. Jones, op. cit., 114–27
45. A factual account of the conference is in Dixon, v, 74–85
46. *D.N.B*, Guest, Edmund; on his later role see Dugmore, 213–4, 223–5
47. *Zürich Letters (Parker Soc., 1842)*, 11
48. Neale, op. cit., 74–5; cf. 1 Eliz. cap. 19
49. *Correspondence of Matthew Parker (Parker Soc., 1853)*, 66
50. Gee and Hardy, 442–57
51. G. W. Prothero, *Select Statutes and other Constitutional Documents* (edn. 1913), 412
52. *Correspondence of Matthew Parker*, 65
53. Gee and Hardy, 458–66
54. N. M. Sutherland, 'The Marian Exiles and the Establishment of the Elizabethan Régime', *Archive for Reformation History*, lxxvii (1987)

Chapter 15, pages 362–377

1. Books i–iv, 1594; Book v, 1597
2. Good examples in *Lincoln Episcopal Records* (*Lincoln Record Soc.*, ii, p. xii) and in *The State of the Church* (ibid., xxiii; see pp. xviiiff). For general accounts of the Elizabethan Church see e.g. W. P. Haugaard, *Elizabeth and the English Reformation* (1968) and M. C. Cross, *The Royal Supremacy in the Elizabethan Church* (1969)

3. Miss D. M. Barratt's figures, cited by Hill (n. 4 below), 207
4. Broad picture in A. L. Rowse, *The England of Elizabeth* (1950, 407ff, and in J. E. C. Hill, *Economic Problems of the Church* 1956), chs. i, ii. Works on individual prelates: V. J. K. Brook, *A Life of Archbishop Parker* (1962) and *Whitgift and the English Church* (1957); W. M. Southgate, *John Jewel and the Problem of Doctrinal Authority* (Cambridge, Mass., 1962); S. B. Babbage, *Puritanism and Richard Bancroft* (1962); J. E. Booty, *John Jewel as Apologist of the Church of England* (1963); P. Collinson, *Archbishop Grindal, 1519–1583. The Struggle for a Reformed Church* (1979)
5. The rest of this section is largely based on J. E. C. Hill, op. cit.
6. Ibid., 91
7. Ibid., 144–5
8. Ibid., 215. Compare Sandys on the lack of preachers, especially in the North, J. Strype, *Annals of the Reformation* (1820–40), iii(2), 69–70
9. Hill, op. cit., ch. 12
10. For the large literature on English Catholicism under Elizabeth, see *Tudor Bibliog.*, 189ff. In addition, note Hughes, iii, 239ff; numerous articles in *Recusant History* and *The Month*; and many volumes of the *Catholic Record Society*. There are also several important theses, some of them cited below, n. 13. A notably original survey is that by J. Bossy, *The English Catholic Community 1570–1850* (1975); see also P. McGrath, *Papists and Puritans under Elizabeth I* (1967) and A. C. F. Beales, *Education under Penalty* (1963), which ranges widely and has a good bibliography
11. Probably about 200 were deprived. Birt and Pollen have argued for a larger figure, and have supposed unexplained disappearances of clerics during the subsequent years to have been the results of resignation by Catholics (refs. in J. B. Black, *The Reign of Elizabeth* (1936), 17, note). In some cases this may be true, but we should beware of straining this negative evidence, especially when it contradicts the submissive character of the Tudor parish clergy, even of those who remained at heart Catholics
12. The argument for a vigorous continuity of English Catholicism, 1558–1580, is put by C. Haigh in *Past & Present*, xciii, and by J. J. Scarisbrick, *The Reformation and the English People* (1984), ch. 7. Rather different lines are taken by J. Bossy in *Past & Present*, xxi; by J. C. H. Aveling, *The Handle and the Axe* (1976) and by A. Pritchard, *Catholic Loyalism in Elizabethan England* (Chapel Hill, N.C., 1979)
13. On the slack enforcement of the £20 per month fee, see F. X. Walker, *The Implementation of the Elizabethan Statutes against Recusants* (London Ph.D. thesis, 1961); M. O'Dwyer, *Catholic Recusants in Essex* (London M.A. thesis, 1960), ch. 7; J. E. Paul, *The Hampshire Recusants in the Reign of Elizabeth* (Southampton Ph.D. thesis, 1959). ch. xi. See also M. O'Dwyer in *The Month*, July 1958, 28ff
14. On Lancashire recusancy, see J. S. Leatherbarrow, *The Lancashire Elizabethan Recusants* (*Chetham Soc.*, cx), and comment by A. L. Rowse, op. cit., 440ff

15. On Yorkshire recusancy see A. G. Dickens, *Reformation Studies*, chs. 8, 9 and (in collaboration with J. A. Newton) ibid., ch. 10; J. C. H. Aveling, *Post-Reformation Catholicism in East Yorkshire (East Yorks. Local Hist. Soc.*, (1960) and his *Northern Catholics* (1966); A. C. Southern in *Biographical Studies*, ii (1953), 135ff

16. Many of the best examples are in H. Foley, *Records of the English Province of the Society of Jesus* (7 vols., 1877–84)

17. On their theory see A. Pritchard, op. cit., ch. 2

18. Compare 'Lord Burghley's Map of Lancashire, 1590' in *Catholic Record Society, Miscellanea*, iv, 162–222

19. For the best short summary and select bibliography see P. Collinson, *English Puritanism (Historical Association*, G. 106, 1983). His four volumes embrace the best recent scholarship: *The Elizabethan Puritan Movement* (1967); *Godly People: Essays on English Protestantism and Puritanism* (1983); *The Religion of Protestants* (1982); *The Birthpangs of Protestant England* (1988). The following remain standard works: M. M. Knappen, *Tudor Puritanism* (Chicago, 1939); J. E. C. Hill, *Society and Puritanism in Pre-Revolutionary England* (1964); A. F. Scott Pearson, *Thomas Cartwright and Elizabethan Puritanism* (1925, repr. Gloucester, Mass., 1966; H. C. Porter, *Reformation and Reaction in Tudor Cambridge* (1958); C. H. and K. George, *The Protestant Mind of the English Reformation* (Princeton, 1961). Of the several recent works, P. Lake, *Moderate Puritans in the Elizabethan Church* (1982) is important. For regional studies, see Collinson's bibliography in *English Puritanism*, 46, adding D.MacCulloch, *Suffolk and the Tudors* (1986)

20. D. Neal, *The History of the Puritans* (1732–8); B. Brook, *The Lives of the Puritans* (1813)

21. C. H. and K. George, op. cit., 66

22. On Arminianism and its effects upon Anglicans, Puritans and politics see esp. N. Tyacke, *Anti-Calvinists. The Rise of English Arminianism* (1987) and compare the debate 'Arminianism Reconsidered' between N. Tyacke and P. White, *Past & Present*, cxv. Note also H. C. Porter, op. cit., chs. 15–17 and P. Lake, *Anglicans and Puritans?* (1988)

23. These names are largely drawn from Knappen 387 ff; H. C. Porter, op. cit., ch. 12; R. A. Marchant, *The Puritans and the Church Courts in The Diocese of York* (1960), 222–318

24. P. Collinson, *The Elizabethan Puritan Movement*, pts. 3, 4, 7 passim

25. R. H. Tawney, *Religion and the Rise of Capitalism* (Pelican, 1938), 43, 260 On the broad economic issues, see M. J. Kitch, *Capitalism and the Reformation* (1967)

26. C. H. and K. George, op. cit., 66

27. W. K. Jordan, *Philanthropy in England* (1959), esp. ch. 6; *The Charities of London* (1960); *The Charities of Rural England* (1961); L. Stone in *E.H.R.*, lxxvii, 327–9; the article by Bittle and Lane cited below, ch. 16, n. 11

28. On John Field see P. Collinson, *Godly People*, ch. 13

29. On Mildmay, M. M. Knappen, 469 ff; on Greenham, ibid., 382ff; on

Huntingdon, M. C. Cross, *The Puritan Earl* (1966); on Lady Hoby, *Diary of Lady Margaret Hoby*, ed. D. M. Meads (1930). On the role of women, see P. Collinson, *Godly People*, 273–87

30. Knappen, 333ff
31. On this theme: J. E. C. Hill, 'Puritans and the Dark Corners of the Land', *T.R.H.S.*, 5 Ser., xiii; and compare C. Haigh, 'Puritan Evangelism in the Reign of Elizabeth I', *E.H.R.*, xcii
32. J. Strype, *Edmund Grindal* (1821), 562
33. This emerges from Jordan's work, n. 27 above; compare Hill, op. cit., n. 31 above, 94ff
34. Knappen, ch. xxiii corrects popular misconceptions on asceticism in Puritan thought. On Puritan religious and social regimentation see P. Collinson, *The Elizabethan Puritan Movement*, Index, s.v. Discipline
35. Knappen, 355–60
36. Ibid., ch. xxvi; See below, n. 39
37. ibid., 348ff
38. This passage is cited and discussed by M. R. Watts, *The Dissenters* (1978), 15–16
39. P. Collinson, *From Iconoclasm to Iconophobia* (Stenton Lecture, University of Reading, 1986). My two succeeding paragraphs are largely based on this work
40. P. Stubbes, *The Anatomie of Abuses* (1583), which attained four edns. by 1595. During this period violent controversies raged between his supporters and his enemies
41. J. E. C. Hill, *The Intellectual Origins of the English Revolution* (1965); C. Webster, *The Great Instauration: Science, Medicine and Reform 1626–1660* (1975); J. Dillenberger, *Protestant Thought and Natural Science* (1960); K. V. Thomas, *Religion and the Decline of Magic* (1971), Index, s.v. 'Protestantism' and 'Puritanism'. Note also the works cited below, ch. 16, n.7
42. Knappen, 376

Chapter 16, pages 378–396

1. J. W. Allen, *A History of Political Thought in the Sixteenth Century* (1928), pt. ii, ch. ix, and compare pt. i, ch. v; W. K. Jordan, *The Development of Religious Toleration in England*, i (1932). Q. Skinner, *The Foundations of Modern Political Thought* (1978), ii, 241–54, mainly discusses the parallel issues in France; A. G. Dickens and J. M. Tonkin, *The Reformation in Historical Thought*, Index, s.v. 'Toleration'. For other Tudor tolerationists, not discussed below, see A. G. Dickens, 'Religious Toleration and Liberalism in Tudor England,' *Reformation Studies*, ch. 20
2. For these three works, Jordan, op. cit., 57ff, 66ff, 74ff. Note also the

passages on Barnes, 64–6 and on Starkey, 60–1. On Frith: W. A. Clebsch, *England's Earliest Protestants*, (above, ch. 5, n. 13), chs. 6–8 and Dickens, op. cit., 430–1

3. On Brinklow, ibid., 61ff and on Turner, ibid. 72ff

4. The recent bibliography on Foxe has become extensive: a large part occurs in P. Collinson's notes to his article 'Truth and Legend: the Veracity of John Foxe's Book of Martyrs', in A. C. Duke and C. A. Tamse (eds.), *Clio's Mirror: Historiography in Britain and the Netherlands* (Zutphen, 1985). On Foxe's views, J. F. Mozley, *John Foxe and his Book* (1940) remains useful

5. Examples of tolerationist speeches in Parliament: Allen, op. cit., 231, 237–8

6. On Acontius and Gentilis, Jordan, op. cit., 303ff. On Sandys, ibid. 367ff and Allen, op. cit., 241ff

7. Several American scholars took the lead here: e.g. P. H. Kocher, *Science and Religion in Elizabethan England* (San Marino, 1953); F. R. Johnson, *Astronomical Thought in Renaissance England* (Baltimore, 1937); L. B. Wright, *Middle Class Culture in Elizabethan England* (Chapel Hill, 1935). See above, ch. 15, n. 41

8. J. K. McConica, *English Humanists and Reformation Politics under Henry VIII and Edward VI* (1965); D. Bush, *The Renaissance and English Humanism* (Toronto, 1939), 73–9; F. Caspari, *Humanism and the Social Order in Tudor England* (Chicago, 1954), 133; A. Fox, chs. 1–3 in A. Fox and J. A. Guy, *Reassessing the Henrician Age* (1986)

9. A. G. Dickens, 'The Writers of Tudor Yorkshire', *Reformation Studies* ch. 11; I. Luxton, 'The Reformation and Popular Culture', *Church and Society in England* (above, ch. 8, n. 47)

10. On this major them, N. Tyacke, above, ch. 15, n. 22

11. See W. G. Bittle and R. T. Lane, 'Inflation and Philanthropy in England: A Reassessment of W. K. Jordan's Data', *Econ. Hist. Rev.*, 2 ser., xxix. Note esp. the table (p. 209) correcting Jordan's figures (*Philanthropy in England*, 369–73) to allow for inflation, when comparing secular donations with religious donations over the period 1480–1660

12. J. H. Elliott, 'The Decline of Spain', *Past & Present*, xx

Index

Grindal, Edmund, Archbishop of
Canterbury, 265, 342, 349, 355–6, 370,
373
Grove, Thomas, 53
Guaras, Antonio, 283
Guest, Edmund, Bishop of Salisbury,
356
Guildford, Sir Henry, 117
Guilds, parish, 33, 230–1, 233, 238, 240,
242
Guisborough, 217
Guise, Mary of, 343
Guy, John, 125, 160
Gysborn, John, 27–30

Habakkuk, H.J., 182
Hacker, John, 52, 55–6
Hackness, 372
Haddington, 260
Hadleigh, Suffolk, 293, 298, 306, 328
Haigh, Dr., 307, 330
Hailes, Gloucestershire, 158
Hales, John, 186, 250, 254, 347–8, 371
Halifax, 56, 58, 215, 307, 327, 373
Hall, Edward, 95, 117, 124, 170;
Rowland, 344
Hamerton, John, 241
Hampden, John, 372
Hampole, 72
Hampshire, 252, 261
Hampton Court Conference, 368
Hancocke, Thomas, 252–3
Hardwick, Charles, 281
Hardwick Hall, 189
Harlestone, Simon, 304
Harpsfield, John, 212; Nicholas, 160,
294, 308, 337
Harrington, James, 189; Sir John, 293
Harrison, Robert, 368; S.M., 147
Hart, Henry, 263–5
Hartlepool, 26
Harvey, William, 90
Hastings, Henry, Earl of Huntingdon,
370–2
Hatfield, Hertfordshire, 226
Hayes, 70, 322
Heath, Nicholas, Archbishop of York,
207, 243, 270–1, 287, 307, 309, 349;
Peter, 69, 319, 322
Heidelberg, 259
Hemsworth, 273

Henbury, Gloucester, 233
Henley-on-Thames, 56
Henneage, Sir Thomas, 183
Henry II of France, 341
Henry II, 162, 318; Henry III, 109;
Henry IV, 149; Henry VII, 25, 36, 51,
62, 110–11, 171, 292, 319, 334
Henry VIII, 21–2, 24–5, 28, 31–2, 36,
42–4, 47–8, 50, 53–6, 58, 60, 63–5,
67–8, 73, 79–80, 90, 97–8, 104–5, 109,
111, 131, 166, 168, 180, 187, 191, 239,
241–2, 246, 248, 261, 263, 271, 288–92,
312, 317–18, 324–5, 329, 348, 350–1,
358, 369, 386, 390–1; his character and
views, 106, 108, 112, 115–18, 120,
122–3, 125–8, 135–42, 145, 147, 149,
152, 172, 176–9, 181–2, 184–5,
196–202, 204–20, 226, 332–3, 382,
384–5; his *Assertio Septem
Sacramentorum*, 116; divorce, 61, 68,
123–9, 139–42, 146, 148, 168, 192–3,
382, foundations, 175, 230–1, 239;
claim to Empire, 140; death, 185, 206,
212, 218, 221–2, 227, 230; *see* Statutes;
Supremacy
Herbert, George, 362; William, Earl of
Pembroke, 218, 287, 290; family, 180
Hereford, 192, 243, 327
Hereford, Nicholas, 47
Heresy, heretics, 16–17, 32, 36, 47, 59,
85–7, 92, 95, 99, 102–4, 107–8, 111,
114–16, 118–19, 121–2, 135, 137, 142,
146, 148–50, 153, 155, 161, 163–5, 187,
193, 195, 197, 202–3, 207, 213–14, 216,
218–20, 246, 252, 262–3, 266–7, 287,
289–97, 301, 304–5, 307–8, 310, 312,
314–15, 319, 324, 329–30, 336, 358,
367, 378–9, 385, 387; *see* Anabaptists;
Lollards, etc.
Herrick, Robert, 362
Hesse, Landgrave of, 199; Philip of, 343
Hessle, 237
Hewet, Andrew, 335
Hildersham, Arthur, 369, 371
Hill, J.E.C., 367
Hilles, Richard, 58
Hilsey, John, Bishop of Rochester, 158,
205
Hilton, Walter, 32, 39–42, 44, 79
Hinksey, 100
Hoby, Lady Margaret, 372; Sir Thomas,
340